Gender and Rights

The International Library of Essays on Rights
Series Editor: Tom Campbell

Titles in the Series:

Disability Rights
Peter Blanck

Indigenous Rights
Anthony Connolly

Children's Rights, Volumes I and II
Michael D.A. Freeman

Language and Cultural Rights
Leslie Green

Consumer Rights
Geraint Howells and Iain Ramsay

Group Rights
Peter Jones

Genocide and Human Rights
Mark Lattimer

Theories of Rights
Ten Chin Liew

Social Rights
Lord Raymond Plant and Selina Chen

Gender and Rights
Deborah L. Rhode and Carol Sanger

Bills of Rights
Mark Tushnet

Gender and Rights

Edited by

Deborah L. Rhode and Carol Sanger

Stanford Law School, USA and Columbia University School of Law, USA

Routledge
Taylor & Francis Group
LONDON AND NEW YORK

First published 2005 by Ashgate Publishing

Reissued 2018 by Routledge
2 Park Square, Milton Park, Abingdon, Oxon, OX14 4RN
711 Third Avenue, New York, NY 10017, USA

Routledge is an imprint of the Taylor & Francis Group, an informa business

A Library of Congress record exists under LC control number: 2004056755

ISBN 13: 978-0-815-38915-6 (hbk)
ISBN 13: 978-1-351-15772-8 (ebk)

Contents

Acknowledgements ix
Series Preface xiii
Introduction: Asserting Rights in the Twenty-first Century Carol Sanger xv

PART I GENDER AND RIGHTS

1 Carol Smart (1989), 'The Problem of Rights', in Carol Smart, *Feminism and the Power of Law*, London/New York: Taylor & Francis, pp. 138–59, 159a. 3
2 Elizabeth Kiss (1995), 'Alchemy or Fool's Gold? Assessing Feminist Doubts About Rights', *Dissent*, pp. 342–47. 27
3 Jeremy Waldron (1988), 'When Justice Replaces Affection: The Need for Rights', *Harvard Journal of Law and Public Policy*, **11**, pp. 625–47. 33
4 Kristin Bumiller (1987), 'Victims in the Shadow of the Law: A Critique of the Model of Legal Protection', *Signs: Journal of Women in Culture and Society*, **12**, pp. 421–39. 57
5 Carlos A. Ball (2002), 'That We Are Human, We Have Rights', *Gay and Lesbian Review*, **9**, pp. 31–32. 77

PART II SOURCES OF WELL-BEING AND HARM

6 Amartya Sen (1990), 'More than 100 Million Women are Missing', *New York Review of Books*, **37**, 20 December, pp. 61–66. 81
7 Martha Nussbaum (1999), 'Women and Cultural Universals', in *Sex and Social Justice*, Oxford: Oxford University Press, pp. 29–54, 377–84. 85
8 Bina Agarwal (1995), 'Gender, Property, and Land Rights: Bridging a Critical Gap in Economic Analysis and Policy', in Edith Kuiper and Jolande Sap with Susan Feiner, Notburga Ott and Zafiris Tzannatos (eds), *Out of the Margins: Feminist Perspectives on Economics*, London/New York: Routledge, pp. 264–94. 119
9 Catharine A. MacKinnon (1994), 'Reflections on Law in the Everyday Life of Women', in Austin Sarat and Thomas R. Kearns (eds), *Law in Everyday Life*, Ann Arbor: University of Michigan Press, pp. 109–22. 151
10 Deborah L. Rhode (1997), 'The "No Problem" Problem', in *Speaking of Sex*, Cambridge, MA: Harvard University Press, pp. 1–20, 253–60. 165
11 Robin West (2002), 'The Right to Care', in Eva Feder Kittay and Ellen Feder (eds), *The Subject of Care: Feminist Perspectives on Dependency*, Lanham/Boulder/New York/Oxford: Rowman & Littlefield, pp. 88–114. 193

PART III FAMILY

12 Martha Minow and Mary Lyndon Shanley (1996), 'Relational Rights and Responsibilities: Revisioning the Family in Liberal Political Theory and Law', *Hypatia*, **11**, pp. 4–29. 223
13 Ayelet Shachar (1998), 'Group Identity and Women's Rights in Family Law: The Perils of Multicultural Accommodation', *Journal of Political Philosophy*, **6**, pp. 285–305. 249
14 Susan Moller Okin (1989), 'Vulnerability by Marriage', in Susan Moller Okin, *Justice, Gender and the Family*, New York: Basic Books, pp. 134–69, 201–209. 271
15 William N. Eskridge, Jr (2000), 'Comparative Law and the Same-Sex Marriage Debate: A Step-by-Step Approach Toward State Recognition', *McGeorge Law Review*, **31**, pp. 641–72. 317

PART IV VIOLENCE

16 Radhika Coomaraswamy (2002), 'Identity Within: Cultural Relativism, Minority Rights and the Empowerment of Women', *George Washington International Law Review*, **34**, pp. 483–513. 351
17 Renée Römkens (2001), 'Law as a Trojan Horse: Unintended Consequences of Rights-Based Interventions to Support Battered Women', *Yale Journal of Law and Feminism*, **13**, pp. 265–90. 383
18 Leti Volpp (1994), '(Mis)Identifying Culture: Asian Women and the "Cultural Defense"', *Harvard Women's Law Journal*, **57**, pp. 113–31. 409
19 Suzanne B. Goldberg (1993), 'Give Me Liberty or Give Me Death: Political Asylum and the Global Persecution of Lesbians and Gay Men', *Cornell International Law Journal*, **26**, pp. 605–23. 429

PART V WORK

20 Martha C. Nussbaum (1998), '"Whether from Reason or Prejudice": Taking Money for Bodily Services', *Journal of Legal Studies*, **27**, pp. 693–724. 451
21 Susanne Baer (2003), '*Dignity or Equality*? Responses to Workplace Harassment in European, German, and U.S. Law', in C. MacKinnon and R. Siegel (eds), *Directions in Sexual Harassment Law*, New Haven, CT: Yale University Press, pp. 582–601. 483
22 Kamala Kempadoo and Ranya Ghuma (1999), 'For the Children: Trends in International Policies and Law on Sex Tourism', in Kamala Kempadoo (ed.), *Sun, Sex, and Gold: Tourism and Sex Work in the Caribbean*, Lanham/Boulder/New York/Oxford: Rowman & Littlefield, pp. 291–308, 308a–308c. 503
23 Deborah L. Rhode (1996), 'The Myths of Meritocracy', *Fordham Law Review*, **65**, pp. 585–94. 525

PART VI POLITICAL PROCESS AND PARTICIPATION

24 Noga Morag-Levine (1999), 'Imported Problem Definitions, Legal Culture and the Local Dynamics of Israeli Abortion Politics', *Israel Affairs*, **5**, pp. 226–45. 537

25 Judy Fudge (1989), 'The Effect of Entrenching a Bill of Rights upon Political Discourse: Feminist Demands and Sexual Violence in Canada', *International Journal of the Sociology of Law*, **17**, pp. 445–63. 557

26 Susan Gal (1997), 'Gender in the Post-Socialist Transition: The Abortion Debate in Hungary', in Roger N. Lancaster and Micaela di Leonardo (eds), *The Gender Sexuality Reader*, London/New York: Routledge, pp. 122–33. 577

27 Karen Bird (2003), 'Who are the Women? Where are the Women? And What Difference Can They Make? Effects of Gender Parity in French Municipal Elections', *French Politics*, **1**, pp. 5–38. 589

28 Sally J. Kenney (2002), 'Breaking the Silence: Gender Mainstreaming and the Composition of the European Court of Justice', *Feminist Legal Studies*, **10**, pp. 257–70, 270a–270c. 623

Name Index 641

Acknowledgements

In selecting and organizing the articles and essays in this collection we have benefited tremendously from discussions with Anita Allen, Susan Brison, Katherine Franke, Barbara Herman, Nicola Lacey, Larry Helfer, Martha Minow, Kim Scheppele, Molly Shanley, Seana Shiffrin, Jeremy Waldron and Robin West.

We are also grateful for the excellent research assistance of Andra Nahal Behrouz (Columbia Law School, 2004), Erin Dougherty (Columbia Law School, 2005) and Avlana Eisenberg (Stanford Law School, 2004).

The editors and publishers wish to thank the following for permission to use copyright material.

Blackwell Publishing Limited for the essay: Ayelet Shachar (1998), 'Group Identity and Women's Rights in Family Law: The Perils of Multicultural Accommodation', *Journal of Political Philosophy*, **6**, pp. 285–305. Copyright © 1998 Blackwell Publishing.

Elsevier for the essay: Judy Fudge (1989), 'The Effect of Entrenching a Bill of Rights upon Political Discourse: Feminist Demands and Sexual Violence in Canada', *International Journal of the Sociology of Law*, **17**, pp. 445–63. Copyright © 1989 Academic Press Ltd.

Gay and Lesbian Review for the essay: Carlos A. Ball (2002), 'That We Are Human, We Have Rights', *Gay and Lesbian Review*, **9**, pp. 31–32.

Foundation for the Study of Independent Social Ideas for the essay: Elizabeth Kiss (1995), 'Alchemy or Fool's Gold? Assessing Feminist Doubts About Rights', *Dissent*, pp. 342–47.

George Washington International Law Review for the essay: Radhika Coomaraswamy (2002), 'Identity Within: Cultural Relativism, Minority Rights and the Empowerment of Women', *George Washington International Law Review*, **34**, pp. 483–513.

Harvard Law School Publication Center for the essay: Leti Volpp (1994), '(Mis)Identifying Culture: Asian Women and the "Cultural Defense"', *Harvard Women's Law Journal*, **57**, pp. 113–31. Copyright © 1994 President and Fellows of Harvard College.

Harvard University Press for the essay: Deborah L. Rhode (1997), 'The "No Problem" Problem', in *Speaking of Sex*, Cambridge, MA: Harvard University Press, pp. 1–20, 253–60. Copyright © 1997 Deborah L. Rhode.

Indiana University Press for the essay: Martha Minow and Mary Lyndon Shanley (1996), 'Relational Rights and Responsibilities: Revisioning the Family in Liberal Political Theory and Law', *Hypatia*, **11**, pp. 4–29. Copyright © 1996 Martha Minow and Mary Lyndon Shanley.

New York Review of Books for the essay: Amartya Sen (1990), 'More than 100 Million Women are Missing', *New York Review of Books*, **37**, 20 December, pp. 61–66. Copyright © 1990 NYREV, Inc.

Perseus Books Group for the essay: Susan Moller Okin (1989), 'Vulnerability by Marriage', in Susan Moller Okin, *Justice, Gender and the Family*, New York: Basic Books, pp. 134–69, 201–209. Copyright © 1989 Basic Books, Inc.

Deborah L. Rhode (1996), 'The Myths of Meritocracy', *Fordham Law Review*, **65**, pp. 585–94. Copyright © 1996 Fordham Law Review and Deborah L. Rhode.

Rowman and Littlefield Publishers, Inc. for the essays: Robin West (2002), 'The Right to Care', in Eva Feder Kittay and Ellen Feder (eds), *The Subject of Care: Feminist Perspectives on Dependency*, Lanham/Boulder/New York/Oxford: Rowman & Littlefield, pp. 88–114; Kamala Kempadoo and Ranya Ghuma (1999), 'For the Children: Trends in International Policies and Law on Sex Tourism', in Kamala Kempadoo (ed.), *Sun, Sex, and Gold: Tourism and Sex Work in the Caribbean*, Lanham/Boulder/New York/Oxford: Rowman & Littlefield, pp. 291–308, 308a–308c.

Taylor and Francis for the essays: Carol Smart (1989), 'The Problem of Rights', in Carol Smart, *Feminism and the Power of Law*, London/New York: Taylor & Francis, pp. 138–59, 159a; Bina Agarwal (1995), 'Gender, Property, and Land Rights: Bridging a Critical Gap in Economic Analysis and Policy', in Edith Kuiper and Jolande Sap with Susan Feiner, Notburga Ott and Zafiris Tzannatos (eds), *Out of the Margins: Feminist Perspectives on Economics*, London/New York: Routledge, pp. 264–94; Noga Morag-Levine (1999), 'Imported Problem Definitions, Legal Culture and the Local Dynamics of Israeli Abortion Politics', *Israel Affairs*, **5**, pp. 226–45; Susan Gal (1997), 'Gender in the Post-Socialist Transition: The Abortion Debate in Hungary', in Roger N. Lancaster and Micaela di Leonardo (eds), *The Gender Sexuality Reader*, London/New York: Routledge, pp. 122–33; Sally J. Kenney (2002), 'Breaking the Silence: Gender Mainstreaming and the Composition of the European Court of Justice', *Feminist Legal Studies*, **10**, pp. 257–70, 270a–270c.

University of Chicago for the essay: Martha C. Nussbaum (1998), '"Whether from Reason or Prejudice": Taking Money for Bodily Services', *Journal of Legal Studies*, **27**, pp. 693–724. Copyright © 1998 University of Chicago.

University of Chicago Press for the essay: Kristin Bumiller (1987), 'Victims in the Shadow of the Law: A Critique of the Model of Legal Protection', *Signs: Journal of Women in Culture and Society*, **12**, pp. 421–39.

Yale Journal of Law and Feminism for the essay: Renée Römkens (2001), 'Law as a Trojan Horse: Unintended Consequences of Rights-Based Interventions to Support Battered Women', *Yale Journal of Law and Feminism*, **13**, pp. 265–90.

Yale University Press for the essay: Susanne Baer (2003), '*Dignity or Equality*? Responses to Workplace Harassment in European, German, and U.S. Law', in C. MacKinnon and R. Siegel (eds), *Directions in Sexual Harassment Law*, New Haven, CT: Yale University Press, pp. 582–601.

Every effort has been made to trace all the copyright holders, but if any have been inadvertently overlooked the publishers will be pleased to make the necessary arrangement at the first opportunity.

Series Preface

Much of contemporary moral, political and legal discourse is conducted in terms of rights and increasingly in terms of human rights. Yet there is considerable disagreement about the nature of rights, their foundations and their practical implications and more concrete controversies as to the content, scope and force and particular rights. Consequently the discourse of rights calls for extensive analysis in its general meaning and significance, particularly in relation to the nature, location of content of the duties and responsibilities that correlate with rights. Equally important is the determination of the forms of argument that are appropriate to establish whether or not someone or some group has or has not a particular right, and what that might entail in practice.

This series brings together essays that exhibit careful analysis of the concept of rights and detailed knowledge of specific rights and the variety of systems of rights articulation, interpretation, protection and enforcement. Volumes deal with general philosophical and practical issues about different sorts of rights, taking account of international human rights, regional rights conventions and regimes, and domestic bills of rights, as well as the moral and political literature concerning the articulation and implementation of rights.

The volumes are intended to assist those engaged in scholarly research by making available the most important and enduring essays on particular topics. Essays are reproduced in full with the original pagination for ease of reference and citation.

The editors are selected for their eminence in the study of law, politics and philosophy. Each volume represents the editor's selection of the most seminal recent essays in English on an aspect of rights or on rights in a particular field. An introduction presents an overview of the issues in that particular area of rights together with comments on the background and significance of the selected essays.

TOM CAMPBELL
Series Editor
Professorial Fellow, The Centre for Applied Philosophy and Public Ethics (CAPPE),
Charles Sturt University, Canberra

Introduction: Asserting Rights in the Twenty-first Century

Gender and Rights

The relationship between women and rights has never been easy to define. Over the last several hundred years it has been argued that women don't want rights, don't need rights (or don't need them anymore), aren't temperamentally suited for rights and wouldn't benefit from them even if they were to get some. Those who advocate rights for women – as well as those who have attempted to exercise them – have been subject to ridicule and to intellectual, reputational and sometimes even physical attack. Rights are, after all, the medium by which people stand up for themselves and demand recognition and respect, and not everyone is comfortable conjoining femininity with this form of assertiveness. Heralded by some after publishing *A Vindication of the Rights of Women* in 1792, Mary Wollstonecraft was also condemned as a harridan, a virago and 'an assertrix of female rights'. But Wollstonecraft's vilification resulted not only from claiming rights for women, but also from practising them. Her sexual cohabitation and out-of-wedlock child were taken less as applications of her political theory than as notorious violations of social rules and, once revealed, a century-long 'fog of censure descended on her reputation' (see Taylor, 2003).

Concerns that rights are the wrong approach to justice and equality have often come from political theorists (historically male) and others who stood to lose status, power and property if women's rights took a hold.[1] In recent years, however, categorical views of women's rights have been replaced by more subtle accounts that explore the complicated significance of rights for women and other subordinated groups. Newer critics (now often female) are concerned with 'the [morally] undesirable vision of self and society' that rights-talk implies – a world organized around duties but not care, around entitlements but not cooperation (Kiss, 1997).[2]

In this volume, we proceed from the premise that rights are problematic but not that they are problematic 'all the way down'. We start with the assumption that rights are a useful means of achieving gender equality. To be sure, the essays included here present an array of arguments and examples across countries and legal systems of how rights sometimes fail, fall short or even make things demonstrably worse. Nonetheless, we stick by the view that rights are only problematic *almost* all the way down. These essays also examine the promise and the achievement of rights: how they can work – sometimes in conjunction with other strategies and theories of justice – to improve the lives of those for whom gender has been a source of disadvantage and deprivation. As Deborah Rhode has observed, 'the central problem with a rights-based framework is not that [rights] are inherently limiting but that they have operated within a limited institutional and imaginative universe (Rhode, 1990, p. 635). Rights may not deliver a knock-out punch to every structural or individual injustice, but they serve a mediating function and offer 'a new place from which to negotiate power, domination, and hierarchy with new tools' (Franke, 2002, p. 310). They provide both a theory of justice and a mechanism for achieving it (Sen, 1995).

In using the term 'rights', we don't mean just the abstract principles of natural rights theory; we also mean the formal entitlements secured for individuals by legal conventions, constitutions and statutes (such as the US Civil Rights Act), by the fundamental laws of nations, and by regional and international charters and covenants. But rights are not just positive law. They also involve the practices of arguing in and about these various formulations, breathing new life into old ones, expanding and applying existing ones, and calling for new and unprecedented rights. Our consideration of rights therefore includes the arguments and critiques, legal strategies and political efforts necessary to establish categories and regimes of gender rights.

Although the discussion so far has focused on *women* and rights, the title of this volume speaks not of women but of *gender*. As historian Joan Scott observed in her influential work, *Gender and the Politics of History*, the term 'gender' has at times been used as a strategic synonym for women: it not only sounded more hip but, back in the days of women's liberation, the more neutral-sounding term 'posed no critical threat' (Scott, 1988, p. 31). Abandoning this earlier lure, we do not regard women and gender as equivalents and locate the essays presented here firmly within the conceptual framework of gender. We accept a now-familiar definition: gender as the social construction and significance of biological difference. What has any particular culture and its institutions – political, familial, economic, religious and so on – come to understand sex to mean or to require? While the answers differ somewhat, it is safe (if discouraging) to say that, at least as a starting point, gender distinctions typically embody the unequal distribution of power, resources and status across human endeavours. Gender is, in Scott's phrase, 'a primary way of signifying relationships of power' (Scott, 1988, p. 42).

Of course, gender is only *one* of the signifiers of power. It regularly combines with and intensifies other factors and forces – race, ethnicity, colonialism, sexual orientation, urbanization, age and so on – to differing effect. Men, as well as women, can suffer the disadvantages of gendered status. In South Africa, for example, the masculinity of black men was constructed against a kaleidoscope of political, economic and social oppression, a system in which adult men could be addressed as 'Boy' to take but one small but telling manifestation (see Morrell, 1998). Gender is commonly deployed in post-colonial and other moments of political transition to establish or reassert traditional power relationships: the use of women and homosexuals in current political campaigns is discussed below in connection with gender and political processes. The concept of gender captures how sex, and it all stands for, is used to categorize and constitute individuals. In ways that 'sex' does not, gender also accommodates the claims and concerns of gays, lesbians, transsexual and transgendered people who claim no exclusive sexual affiliation but whose treatment at work, in families, in prisons and on the street is regularly marked by discrimination and violence.

To be sure, there have been recent calls to abandon the concept of gender and move on; Toril Moi (1999) and Iris Marion Young (2003), among others, suggest that gender might usefully be replaced by category of the 'lived body' – the 'unified idea of a physical body acting and experiencing in a specific sociocultural context' (Young, 2003). But although gender theorists, activists and advocates will continue to refine and rethink the classifications of people in relation to their bodies and self-presentations, 'gender', even as conventionally formulated, continues to prove a challenging framework of analysis. Courts in the United States have puzzled over how to fit gender into existing legal categories. Does the harassment of an employee by a supervisor of the same sex constitute sex discrimination under current employment law, as Katherine Franke (1995) argues? What about sex stereotyping on the job when the employee is not an unfeminine woman but an effeminate man (see Case, 1995)? Current debates in family law engage and challenge the role of gender within the institutions of marriage and parenting (see Bagnall *et al.*, 1984; Polikoff, 2000). The criminal law similarly confronts the significance of gender in its prohibitions against sexual practices such as sodomy when engaged in by same-sex couples.[3]

Gender categories are important not only as a matter of conceptual and descriptive integrity but also as a strategic tool in legal reform and litigation. Considerations of gender influence advocacy choices regarding parties, fora, legal theories and remedies. For example, the development of sex discrimination jurisprudence in the United States during the 1970s was carefully designed to feature cases in which men were on the losing end of statutory classifications (Ginsburg and Flagg, 1989). Statutes preventing *husbands*, but not wives, from receiving alimony or spousal employment benefits were targeted, challenged and overturned. Once established, doctrines of sex equality were then deployed to redress discrimination against women. More recently, gays, lesbians and other sexual minorities have also invoked existing legal doctrine to advance their claims for equal participation in employment, intimate relationships, education and politics.

Depending on the nature of a particular claim and the available doctrine, claimants are likely to proceed pragmatically with regard to fora as well. Attentive to the receptivity of a particular law-making body to persuasion and argumentation, they may look to international law and tribunals or to national and regional legal systems. For example, Robert Wintemute explains that, in Europe and the United Kingdom, lesbian, gay, bisexual and transgendered individuals have become 'adept practitioners' of human rights. This is because, although small in numbers, these politically unpopular groups are nonetheless threatening to the majority populations and are unlikely to find redress through electoral processes (Wintemute, 2005). As this example suggests, different kinds of rights – human rights, statutory rights, constitutional rights – have different sources and different constituencies. This jurisdictional dynamic is part of the complex process of asserting and establishing gender-based claims.

About this Volume

We have organized the 28 essays presented here into six substantive categories: Gender and Rights, Sources of Well-being and Harm, Family, Violence, Work, and Political Process and Participation. These six categories are familiar sites of gendered activity and gender inequities and provide a useful structure for thinking about the development of rights in context. The categories also encompass, sometimes *sub silentio*, such abstract themes as autonomy, subordination, equality and essentialism that so often lurk below the surface of most analysis of gender and law. Although several of the essays consider the social and familial conditions that prompt rights claims or create rights impediments, the volume focuses primarily on rights through the lens of law and legal theory. In addition, the essays are presented in their entirety rather than in snippets. This permits the reader to evaluate the complete argument and to cite pages in the original volumes.

It is worth noting at the outset that there is nothing inevitable or fixed about the assignment of one or another essay to a particular category. The essays could well be shuffled and dealt out anew to form different, but equally coherent, combinations. This categorical flexibility makes sense: the processes and phenomena that produce gender inequities – the policies and practices of markets, politics and families – exist across the formal boundaries of an anthology. So, for example, because violence and fear of violence are pervasive, ongoing aspects of women's lives in almost every society, violence is presented as a distinct category. Yet the topic could well be considered under any of the other categories: as an artifact of culture and thus an ongoing source of harm; as a regular feature of family life; a subtle if not uncommon workplace practice; and a strategic political tactic, as when mass rape is used to demoralize or annihilate an entire community.

Culture – the dense intertwined structure of the physical, moral, and economic conditions of life – similarly operates across categories and that is how we present it here. Essays in every category address the role of culture in relation to background conditions, rights claims, and enforcement. Remedies, for example, may require the invocation of official enforcement mechanisms, such as the criminal justice system or international refugee law. At the same time, legal recourse is often complicated by such cultural forces as religious traditions that preserve the authority of husbands and fathers in family relationships. Such traditions may operate as informal practices but also at more formal levels, such as state reservations to the UN Convention on the Elimination of Discrimination Against Women by several Muslim countries (see Brandt and Kaplan, 1995–96). In thinking about cultural practices, we note that designating a practice as cultural (as opposed to normal or 'how *we* do it') is often a matter of perspective. When the observed practice is one's own, its cultural location may become relatively invisible. For example, as Uma Narayan has usefully observed, Western fascination (often on the part of feminists) with dowry deaths in India obscures the cultural phenomenon of wife murders in the United States (Narayan, 1997).

Although we have organized this collection around six categories of activity, we also propose an alternative structure for thinking about gender and rights – one that proceeds not area by substantive area but instead progresses along a 'rights chronology'. Rights, especially when connected to gender, tend not to arrive like Venus emerging full-blown, but evolve over time. They are something like a work in progress, where the work is gender justice. From this perspective, rights could be analysed as a five-stage progression: the initial articulation of the right; its theoretical justification or argumentation; advocacy on its behalf; recognition or enactment; and, finally, enforcement and effect. We therefore complement the substantive categories with this chronological framework and approach the essays from two perspectives: their contribution to particular areas of rights and their position within a rights progression. This combination of rights substance and rights evolution more clearly illuminates the challenges, vicissitudes and successes of rights claims.

A timeline that begins with the articulation of a right presupposes two conditions. The first is that the conduct or circumstance that the right seeks to remedy has already been identified as wrongful. Ordinary or traditional practices such as the unequal distribution of food or harassment at work or honour killings must no longer be regarded as acceptable on the grounds that they are natural, divine or biological. Instead, they must register as harm or injustice. In socio-legal terms the recognition of harm by the injured person has been called 'naming' or 'saying to oneself that a particular experience has been injurious' (Felsteiner *et al.*, 1980, p. 634).

The second condition involves some degree of legal consciousness on the part of the individual. To think even tentatively in the vocabulary of rights, people must recognize or be able to imagine that they can turn to the formal structure of law for protection or remedy. This belief goes beyond naming the objectionable conduct or condition as a harm. It embodies the more dynamic view that something can be done about it. The individual grasps a connection between the harm experienced and the fact that a principle already governs the situation and is standing by, ready to be applied. An excellent example of the complex, always contextual, development of legal consciousness is found in historian Hendrik Hartog's (1993) account of Abigail Bailey, an eighteenth-century colonial wife who slowly came to believe that her husband's ongoing molestation of their daughter was not part of God's scheme and that she could indeed invoke law to separate from her husband without violating her wifely or spiritual obligations. To borrow again from socio-legal vocabulary, this step has been called 'claiming' or the view that something must be done in response to the injury (Felsteiner *et al.*, 1980).

In Abigail Bailey's case, laws protecting her right to separate from her husband were already in place; she needed only to accept their applicability to her situation and act. In other cases, the right may not yet have been recognized or even formulated. Sometimes the articulation of a right may be a simple matter of extending an existing entitlement to a group to which it has been denied, such as women's twentieth-century claims to vote or to serve on juries (Kerber, 1998). Other gender-based rights are brand-new – their articulation the result of imaginative (and empirically informed) reassessment of some social fact, a political goal or a legal doctrine. A good example is the work of Catherine MacKinnon (1979) and others in transforming unwanted sexual advances at work from a problematic, but ordinary, part of a working girl's day to behaviour cognizable as the right to work unhampered by sexual harassment.[4] Another example of rights is the relatively new category of 'reproductive rights'. This term has generally referred to women's control over their fertility, whether by contraception, abortion or by protection against unwanted sexual intercourse. Of course, the scope of any particular right – who it protects and from what – may develop over time as the initial formation takes hold (or fails to take hold) and is tested, challenged and refined. Thus, the term 'reproductive rights' now encompasses claims to reproductive health and fertility treatment and is also used by men who seek control over the use of frozen sperm or frozen embryos. Like its definition, the sources of a right's authority may also expand. Reproductive rights are now also included within the purview of human rights (Yamin and Maine, 1999). These examples illustrate how rights migrate and splinter. There are now express claims to recognize 'sexual rights' – claims to sexual identity, activity and enjoyment that are distinct and disconnected from concerns over reproduction (Miller, 2000).

In this way, a newly articulated right can be innovative even while it is incomplete. One critique of sexual harassment law in the United States has been that it fails on its own terms to protect workers against harassment that is *not* sexual in nature, such as violence, bullying and other methods of undermining women's competency at work (Schultz, 1998). By contrast, as Susanne Baer's comparison study (Chapter 21) makes clear, German harassment law is based on protecting the dignitary interests of all workers (see also Franke, 1997). The example shows how the core justification of the right – the ecology of the argumentative environment – may determine its scope.

The final stage in the rights chronology concerns the enforcement and practical effect of rights. The happiest examples are ones in which good-faith implementation of well-designed remedies successfully redresses the particular injustice. The Nineteenth Amendment to the US Constitution giving women the vote would seem a straightforward example. But even this accomplishment had its limits: after its enactment, black women (and black men) still could not vote in the southern states under a separate set of prohibitions. In addition, not all claims for rights complete the course just sketched. Some, like the doomed Equal Rights Amendment to the US Constitution, stall and fail (see Mansbridge, 1986; Mackinnon, 1989). Other rights may come into existence, yet not securely so, so that they remain subject to political shifts. In Germany and Eastern Europe, for example, changes in governmental structure wrought by reunification and democratization have altered the scope of abortion rights once considered secure (Gal, 1997; Funk and Mueller, 1993). Similarly, judicially created rights, like abortion in the United States, remain dependent on the views of elected or politically appointed judges. Finally, rights consciousness can encourage an overly formalistic confidence in the fact of an entitlement. Enactment can be taken as proof that, because something has been done, the case for gender complaining is closed. In thinking about the efficacy and durability of rights, claimants and their advocates must keep these vagaries and impediments in mind, as opponents of gender rights surely do.

Gender and Rights

The essays in Part I of this volume offer a general overview and critique of rights and rights strategies as they relate to gender. We begin with Carol Smart's concern that rights may have already done their best work. Certainly, rights have been an attractive and profitable strategy for women historically. The early twentieth-century women's movement was founded on the idea of equality, a goal typically formulated and achieved through legal rights. Rights and 'rights talk' have ongoing symbolic appeal and efficacy. As Smart notes, framing an issue in terms of rights means that it can 'be brought under the umbrella of trade union debates, parliamentary consideration, media reportage, and so on' (p. 8). The language itself makes the claim accessible.

Yet despite such conceptual and practical advantages, Smart insists that rights remain problematic. Rights are an aggressive and querulous idiom. They make the claimant look unappealingly selfish, self-interested, and demanding. Moreover, rights are not the exclusive property of the disadvantaged. Husbands and foetuses may assert claims adverse to those of women, as in contests over custody or abortion. Rights also need tending. Once enacted, they must be enforced and sustained. This often requires assertive and skilled action under adverse social or legal circumstances that may in the end prevent much actual advantage to the rights-holder. Finally, the formal acquisition of rights is often taken to mean that everything is now fixed. This can result in a premature sense of accomplishment, particularly in societies like the United States where a substantial premium is placed on 'closure'. Each of these problems – rights talk as shrill, the personal and political costs of realizing and sustaining a right, the potential use of rights against claimants and a mistaken celebration of gender equity – is further developed in later essays.

In Chapter 2 Elizabeth Kiss takes up Smart's challenge and bluntly asks whether feminist criticism of rights might in fact be right. Is the moral vision associated with rights necessarily one of nasty individualism, an unencumbered self who helps out only if she wants to? Does a rights-focus diminish other values, such as the ethic of care? Do rights accomplish much or is their achievement more symbolic than real? Kiss specially notes two additional rights deficiencies: rights defined so that they don't accomplish very much – the argument sometimes made with regard to formal equality – and rights used for disturbingly non-feminist ends. Here Kiss provides the example of breast implants ('It's my body and I'll do what I like!') although one might also consider the troubling and increasingly common practice of sex-selective abortion, now made cheaper and easier by technology. In the end, however, Kiss urges feminists not to throw rights out with the bath water but rather to recognize their lure *and* their limitations, their constraints *and* their centrality to the feminist project.

A different defence of rights is offered by Jeremy Waldron in Chapter 3. Using marriage as his example, Waldron presents the idea of rights as safety net, valuable not as the primary basis of obligation between intimates but as a fall-back regime when lovers' affection for one another fades. Thinking about formal rights as a fall-back mechanism when love and its sidekick, altruism, subside highlights a rights-related phenomenon common to family law. People in intimate relationships often fail to protect themselves legally in the event that things go wrong precisely because things are going so well. When informal arrangements are agreeable, cohabitants do not marry, fathers do not legitimize biological children and stepparents do not adopt their stepchildren. Consequently, when marital status or paternity later becomes legally significant – for the purposes of property division or custody, for example – the *de facto* spouse or parent has been lulled by earlier affection into fatal inaction. This leads to a second problem. Rights can operate as fall-backs only if they are in place from the start. Rights over children illustrate the point. When divorcing parents cannot agree who should raise the children, courts decide for them under established rules of custody. But consider the problem faced by unmarried parents who are unable to agree about custody *and* unable to fall back on a set of legal rules. The ex-same-sex partner of a child's biological mother, for example, does not have the same custody or visitation rights as an ex-husband simply because she is not an ex-spouse and cannot be. If the once happy partnership of a lesbian couple later dissolves, in most jurisdictions the non-biological mother is unable to make any legal claim to the child who she has helped to raise.[5]

Waldron makes a second important claim for a formal structure of rights – one that arises not from tension *within* the relationship but from tensions between the couple and the communities to which they belong. Enter Romeo and Juliet. Their calamity was not wholly a matter of crossed stars and coordination failures, argues Waldron, but rather their inability to act outside the exclusive structures provided by their warring clans. A structure of rights that stands apart from communal or affective attachments offers an independent and perhaps more enduring basis for action. This interrogation of the relationship between rights, the individual and the community continues throughout this volume.

Even when rights are in place, their realization may be thwarted if the mechanisms of enforcement extract too high a cost from the intended beneficiary. In Chapter 4 Kristin Bumiller analyses why victims of civil rights violations have not more regularly turned to existing laws for redress. Her conclusions introduce the complex psychological and social costs *to the victim* of vindicating her rights through legal process. Some adopt an 'ethic of survival' to avoid public self-characterization as a victim. The formal elimination of legal barriers may mean little when the personal price of enforcement makes the beneficiary worse off. The existence of the law, used or unused, may therefore offer only the illusion of progress (see generally Fineman, 1991). In addition, as other essays clarify, rights enforcement often brings new players into the script – prosecutors, police, bureaucrats – with distinct professional practices, priorities and values that may only partly intersect with those of rights claimants. The participation of these third parties can significantly influence remedial outcomes and must be kept in mind at the stage when the definition of rights and the mechanisms for enforcement are crafted.

Bumiller's essay underscores the importance of an ongoing division of labour with regard to rights in practice. Each stage of the rights progression calls upon a special set of skills, energy, and insights: theorizing, politicking and so on. A similar division of labour attaches to rights scholarship. That task includes not only foundational theorizing and practical advocacy but sometimes the more tedious work of monitoring the implementation of rights and drawing attention to failures, paradoxes and emerging contradictions. This is often the least glamorous part of rights work – the interviewing, witnessing and measuring that provide a factual basis for evaluating rights.[6] The work is crucial, however, for making sure that rights do not end up merely as abstract entitlements but instead serve the causes and concerns that inspired them in the first place.

The final essay in Part I reminds us that rights attach to women and men not because they are *gendered* beings but because they are *human* beings. This is the essence of the case put forth by Carlos Ball in Chapter 5: that gay men and lesbians are, and must be regarded as, human. As Ball notes, not all people at all times have been included within that category. Women, when thought to be without the faculty of rational thought, were considered something less than human; African-Americans, when held to be the property of others, were something less than human. Only when the full humanity of women and African-Americans was accepted did they begin to acquire the rights necessary for full participation in civic, familial and political endeavours. Ball applies this analysis to the case of love. Because the capacity to love others is a fundamental part of what makes us human, only when lesbians and gay men are viewed as fully human will they be able to 'participate in institutions such as marriage and parenting that are meant to account and provide for the basic capacities of human beings in the areas of physical and emotional intimacy' (p. 78).

Sources of Well-being and Harm

Part II provides an analytical background for thinking about some of the structural forces that underlie gender inequities. Culture plays a constant role in setting and sustaining the conditions of gendered life. It is therefore a source of well-being *and* a continual source of harm. To show just how high and unmistakeable the stakes of unequal treatment on the basis of gender are, we begin with Amartya Sen's stark demographic account of male-female population ratios (Chapter 6). Although women are biologically hardier than men and, all things being equal, live longer, women do *not* live longer than men in many regions of the world. Sen shows that, in certain parts of the world, hundreds of millions of women are missing – their lives ended by infanticide or shortened by inadequate provision of food, care and medicine. When things are not equal, women die.

Following Sen, Martha Nussbaum rejects the use of culture to justify the often dismal state of gender affairs (see Sen, 1995). She notes that the club of culture is often raised to knock down suggested reforms on the ground that they are insufficiently attentive to such concerns as contextualized lives, women's agency and anti-essentialist values. In her essay on 'Women and Cultural Universals' (Chapter 7), Nussbaum develops an approach to equality that replaces cultural distinctiveness with a universalist position focusing on human capabilities. This approach dwells not on rights or traditions, but rather on a list of specific human capabilities that make up the ingredients for an active, flourishing human life. These range from the physical (a life of normal length, bodily health and integrity) to the intellectual (thought and practical reason) to the social (affiliation, play and civic participation). Nussbaum argues that women's defensive endorsement of cultural norms ought not be credited until women have first developed their own capacities for security, thought and affiliation. Policy goals should therefore be aimed at whatever it takes to permit all individuals to develop the capacities necessary to live a good life. Education provides a solid example; it is a means to develop the capability to think, earn, provide and participate in civic, commercial and domestic life (Nussbaum, 2003).

The capabilities approach is, at least in conception, 'rights-free'. Nussbaum explains that this has certain advantages. Because capabilities, unlike rights, are not linked to any particular cultural, legal or historical tradition, an analysis focusing on capabilities proceeds (somewhat) freed from the risks or accusations about privileging Western perspectives (Nussbaum, 1999, pp. 96–101). (Of course, the identification of capabilities remains open to challenge as being itself culturally biased.) Nevertheless, Nussbaum acknowledges that rights still have value in public discourse. The 'rhetorically direct' language of rights gives issues something of a reputational bump. Presenting a claim as a right 'tells people right away that we are dealing with an especially urgent set of functions, backed up by a sense of the justified claim that all human beings have to have such things, by virtue of being human' (ibid., p. 100). In the strongest sense, rights signal the insistent universalism of the capabilities approach. There are also substantive links between capabilities and rights. Rights language underscores the ethical justification behind the specification of any particular capability so that one can draw 'strong normative conclusions from the fact of the basic capabilities' (ibid.). Rights therefore help frame even those approaches to gender equality that are not explicitly so founded. Talk of equality often begs the question: equality of what? Should we be equalizing money, resources, lifetimes, power or happiness? The capabilities approach takes this question seriously from the outset by indicating explicitly, or at least by opening an explicit debate about, the aspects in which people's lives should be made equal.

Bina Agarwal's essay (Chapter 8) identifies a specific source of harm to women: the gender gap in ownership and control of property. This, for Agarwal, is the single most critical cause of women's economic and social disadvantage, particularly in South Asia. While others have addressed the spiritual need for a *room* of one's own, Agarwal holds out for a 'field of one's own' (Agarwal, 1944). As things stand, the current allocation of food, care and support for rural women is mediated through husbands and in-laws who often provide little more than subsistence. Independent rights to arable land – an economically viable plot – are therefore necessary for physical well-being. Giving women title to land also strengthens their bargaining power within their families and within local political and economic communities. Agarwal acknowledges the mighty obstacles to such property reform. These include the complex relationships between inheritance law and dowry practices and the tradition of daughters giving up claims to parental lands in favour of brothers who may, at some later time, provide support for their unmarried or widowed sisters. The social practice of female seclusion further compromises the ability of women to bring legal claims. Although Agarwal locates her argument in the economy and culture of South Asia, the crucial relationship between women's property rights and marriage also exists in more developed countries, as Susan Okin's essay in Part III makes clear.

Catherine MacKinnon's 'Reflections on Law in the Everyday Life of Women' (Chapter 9) identifies a different source of pervasive harm. She offers a bleak introductory description of women's daily lives: 'men are served, children are cared for, home is made, work is done, the sun goes down' (p. 151). That is the cheerful part. MacKinnon then surveys the subordinated state of women across all areas of life and concludes that the absence of law in women's lives is a principal cause of their subordination. Law has comprehensively failed to provide equality in the workplace, in the criminal justice system and in the bedroom. The law that is missing on MacKinnon's account is *official* law; the *informal* rules that actually govern women's lives 'go under the heading of socialization, pressure, religion, popular culture, masculinity and femininity, everyday life' (p. 154). Although MacKinnon challenges law to move from a source of harm to a mechanism for well-being, she sceptically suspects that women's use of law may itself 'delegitimatize law' so that male supremacy will have to find 'other guises for the dominance it currently exercises through law' (p. 164). On this account, critiques of rights on the grounds that they are too 'legalistic' are beside the point. Women need the use and protection of *more* effective law, not less.

Deborah Rhode (Chapter 10) adds a fourth and subtle source of harm: the widespread denial or dismissal of the fact of gender inequality. She offers three sources for what she calls the '"no problem" problem' (pp. 165–66). The first is the position that things may not be as bad as some people say. This view is held not only by men, who don't want to think of themselves as oppressors, but also by women, who don't want to think of themselves as victims. Minimizing one's subordinated status is a good way of keeping the peace at home, keeping one's position at work or just staying sane. Things are therefore fine – or fine enough. A second component of denial acknowledges gender disparities but insists that they do not reflect injustice. *Au contraire*! Any disadvantages are the result of women's own personal choices or limited capabilities. A familiar example is the charge against battered women who do not leave their batterers and who therefore ought not complain: their misery is of their own making (Schneider, 2000). Finally, Rhode describes a round-robin of denial regarding responsibility. Citing the failure in the United States to guarantee paid parental leave following childbirth or adoption, she explains that '[m]ale government leaders look to employers, employers look to government, and both look to families' (p. 181). If no policy-maker or employer or individual is responsible, then the problem is no-one's to solve. In consequence, women (in most cases, *poor* women) continue to care for children without sufficient financial support or job protection.

Part II concludes by considering a potential source of well-being: the recognition of caregiving as the basis for a claim for support against the state. In Chapter 11 Robin West engages in the first stages of a rights chronology: the articulation and justification of a new entitlement. She argues that caregiving for the young or for the elderly not only creates enormous economic vulnerability for caregivers but disables them from participating in political and cultural life on equal terms with other citizens. Yet despite the crucial role of care in producing the autonomous individuals whom liberalism seeks to serve, West notes that there has never been a right to material support for those who do this work. To be sure, throughout the last century, many Western European countries enacted maternalist policies encouraging, rewarding and compensating mothers (see Koven and Michel, 1993). On occasion even the United States has provided stipends for mothers, or at least for morally worthy and white mothers, as during the Progressive Era in the early twentieth century. However, West chooses not to rely on the availability of statutory provision in favour of a more fundamental claim. She argues that caregivers' position as an historically subordinated group, the dysfunction of political processes in providing support for them and 'our self-understanding that caregiving is indispensable to a liberal state' all 'point in the direction of . . . rights' (p. 203). Her claim becomes the more persuasive as privatization, discussed below, increasingly relieves the state from responsibility for services like caregiving which are once again lodged within the family.

In developing her argument, West explores a constitutional line of cases that includes parenting as an aspect of liberty and might, by extension, treat caregiving as a parent-like activity. Recognizing that the right to care is new and unfamiliar, she is willing to take the long view. The incorporation of a new right – a new moral claim – into how we think and talk about obligation and duty, may take time. Indeed, not all women will support a right that makes caretaking more comfortable out of concern that this will serve policy goals seeking once again to tether all women to the home. From a rights perspective, however, West's claim has the status of a moral right even though she confines it to the realm of private moral life. It is a claim about the directions in which our legal (and constitutional) rights should develop.

Family

Arguments favouring a rights-free approach to justice have often arisen in the family – a site long considered inappropriate for the invocation or application of formal entitlements. The family was thought to be *above* rights. On this account, the allocation of resources and obligation was based not on fairness or equality but on nobler values such as love and altruism (see Okin, 1987). To insist on rights would demean and diminish the enterprise, tainting the harmonious private sphere with the self-interested fractiousness of the public sphere. If women started to think in terms of rights, they would 'lose touch with an essential theme in a female orientation and thereby jeopardize the depth of the contribution women can make to a masculine culture' (Hardwig, 1984, p. 450).[7] This analysis resulted in a perverse irony: the attributes thought to ennoble women in the home – plenty of heart but not much reason – were often thought to disable them as participating, rights-bearing members of the polity (see Rhode, 1989).

The interrelation between rights and power within the family and outside of it are the subject of Susan Okin's important essay on marriage (Chapter 14). The essay makes clear that rights are not always – or not always in the first instance – legal in conception. Her critique of the gendered family begins with economist Albert O. Hirschman's correlation between an individual's influence within an organization and the ability to leave it: the easier the possibility of exit, the greater the ability to influence (Hirschmann, 1970). Okin applies this insight to traditional heterosexual marriage, an institution whose arrangements decrease the labour force marketability of wives. This makes them less able to leave the marriage, which in turn makes them less powerful within the marriage. Okin argues that this reinforcing loop of disadvantage occurs before, during and after the knot is tied. Because women plan to marry, they have traditionally sought and received less education. While married, they do most of the household work and therefore fall behind in employable skills. Finally, upon divorce, they typically own less property and have less earning capacity. In short, marriage from beginning to end increases women's vulnerability within the home and outside of it. To fix this gendered imbalance, Okin suggests a variety of reforms – alternative property regimes, paid household labour and restructured workplace norms. She also questions whether same-sex relationships, in which the power allocation is not prefigured by a gender regime, might offer a different, less oppressive model.

Traditional family structures highlight the tensions between a liberal conception of rights and a communitarian structure of obligation. Martha Minow and Mary Shanley (Chapter 12) approach the problem by asking what people owe one another as family members and what theories of obligation best satisfy modern domestic arrangements. They review the logic and the limitations of three models: contract-based theories premised on consent; community-based theories in which civil society and social norms prevail; and rights-based theories in which family members have rights against one another and the family as a whole has rights against the state. Finding each model lacking, the authors propose an alternative framework: a theory of *relational* rights and responsibilities that aims to take account of two paradoxical features of family life. The first is that family members are simultaneously singular individuals *and* persons defined by relationships of dependence with others. The second paradox is that family relationships simultaneously exist outside of the political order yet are also shaped by it. The theory of relational rights and responsibilities provides a framework for thinking through the complexities of modern family life – such issues as same-sex marriage, the acquisition of children and the allocation of decisional authority – more expansively than the rigid theories of contract, community or rights that have until now structured, but not sufficiently advanced, the discussion.

In Chapter 13 Ayelet Shachar takes on the complexities of cultural preservation and the subordination of women in the family, the area where multicultural accommodation 'hits the hardest'. Shachar observes that women often (and quite reasonably) find value, meaning and status in the traditions of their communities. Loyalty to group norms may be especially fierce in minority cultures where solidarity in relation to the cultural majority may take on special meaning, even as the traditions themselves harm women. Two examples make Shachar's case. The first concerns the power to determine who officially belongs to the community and who does not. Because membership often hinges on birth lineage or on marriage, women often play a central role in this function. Yet women who marry *outside* their tribe or religion may be sanctioned within the group, even if their marriage is valid as a matter of state law. Their children, for example, may not be counted as full members and may therefore lose valuable property rights.[8]

Shachar's second example concerns the rules governing the dissolution of a marriage. Under Jewish religious law (Halakhah), a husband can prevent his wife from getting a proper religious divorce. In such a case the children born into the wife's second valid civil marriage are nonetheless considered illegitimate under Jewish law with various ill consequences. Another example is found in the US Indian Child Welfare Act (ICWA), which vests control over the custody of Native American children in the tribes and not in their parents. In such cases, where jurisdictional authority is located in the tribe or religion, cultural practices take on the force of legal rights often to the disadvantage of the group's less powerful members. Thus an Indian mother who has chosen to place her child for adoption with a non-Indian family loses that right under ICWA: the tribe decides the child's placement.[9] In thinking through the parameters of this kind of multicultural accommodation, Shachar urges that the interests of *three* parties should be included in the mix: the state, the group *and* the individual who is usually on the rights-deprived side of the equation.

The final essay in Part III on rights and the family considers current contestation over the extension of an existing right – marriage – to new beneficiaries. Is marriage a right that extends to all couples regardless of sex? In 2003 the Supreme Court of Massachusetts held that the state constitutional guarantee of equal protection of law required the extension of marriage to same-sex couples.[10] Canada and the Netherlands similarly authorize same-sex marriages. In contrast, most other countries and most US states have taken the position that marriage is a legal status available only to unions between one man and one woman. The right to the *benefits* of marriage may have traction – as with civil unions or registered partnerships or the French Civil Solidarity Pact (PACS) – but not the institution of marriage itself.

In his essay on comparative approaches to same-sex marriage in the United States and in Europe, William Eskridge (Chapter 15) explores how the scope of a right may influence not only its own political livelihood but the broader society. Eskridge describes a step-by-step approach, a kind of legal incrementalism, and suggests that claims for lesser forms of marriage, such as same-sex unions, may have distinct value. They not only provide the tangible benefits of marriage but may serve to move public opinion on the plurality of forms that families take. This in turn contributes to greater gay–straight interaction, which has gradually led to such other legal reforms such as the decriminalization of sodomy, non-discriminatory employment statutes, protective hate crime legislation and a broader menu of legal options for structuring families. Eskridge's comparative data on incremental approaches to same-sex marriage indicate that the enactment of marriage-like relationships such as civil unions has led, in some countries, to an increased social acceptability of gays and lesbians. This may bring about further legal reforms in such other areas as employment and criminal law, which in turn may further normalize the status of gays and lesbians. In this way, rights can bestow, recognize and prompt various forms of ordinary social interactions – in jobs and in neighbourhoods – that constitute secure, meaningful, and equal participation in all forms of public and private life.

Violence

Violence is a fact of life for those who disrupt traditional notions about what it means to look like, act like, or simply to be a man or a woman. Violating gender norms attracts violence. And violence is not simply *directed* at women and sexual minorities: these groups are distinctly accused of *causing* the very violence that they endure. Wives and girlfriends, for example, are often assaulted by partners on the grounds that they have been disobedient – a strange term to describe adult women, but one that stands for a kind of infidelity to gender roles such as meals not served on time or an attempt to leave home without permission (Mahoney, 1991). The treatment of sexually unfaithful wives, often understood as a matter of law to have acted wrongfully in relation to their husbands, is another example. Thus, husbands who kill adulterous wives may be charged with manslaughter – not murder – if the killing was in response to seeing (or, in some cases, hearing about) a wife's adultery (see Coker, 1992; Lee, 2003a). In such cases, the victim is understood to have provoked the attack psychologically so that the legal defence of provocation may be invoked. As Leti Volpp's essay (Chapter 18) clarifies, this aspect of culture – or imagined culture – has incorporated itself into the legal defence strategies of some batterers in the United States. Volpp analyses a criminal case in which a Chinese-American defendant had smashed in his wife's skull. Persuaded by testimony from an anthropologist that a Chinese husband would suffer particular shame or loss of face by virtue of his wife's infidelity, the judge held that the husband in this case had suffered enough and sentenced him to five years' probation but no jail time for the manslaughter conviction.

Men who disrupt or defy gender roles are also the common victims of crime (Lee, 2003a). On account of nothing more than their public existence gay men, or men who are only thought to be gay, disturb and unsettle gender boundaries and, on this ground alone, become targets of violence. Here, too, the victim is often said to have provoked the attack. 'Gay panic' or 'homosexual rage defense' has been incorporated into the US criminal justice rules under heat of passion or other defences. Courts have held that it is reasonable for a man to react violently if he thinks he is being sexually approached by another man, even when the alleged approach is only verbal (Lee, 2003b). Simply knowing that someone is gay can be taken as a form of provocation; hence the 'don't ask/don't tell' policy stance of the US army (Thomas, 1993).

One response to criminal acts motivated by the social identity of the victim has been the enactment of hate crime legislation – statutes that increase penalties if the offence is motivated by bias or hate (see generally Jacobs and Potter, 1998). Hate crime legislation is often marshalled on behalf of groups typically targeted for violence on account of race, nationality or sexual identity. Some argue that such legislation is necessary to signal the state's opposition to violence against minorities (Perry, 2001). Others contend that sexual minorities should *not* make special rights claims in the area of criminal law, since to do so only perpetuates inequality by classifying people into those who are thought especially worthy of protection (here, victims of hate crimes) and those who are not – for example, death-row inmates who 'get what they deserve' (Kohn, 2001–2002).

The use of rights in the area of criminal law is further complicated by the phenomenon of unintended and undesirable consequences. In Chapter 17 Renée Römkens offers two examples in her sophisticated analysis of rights-based interventions to support battered women in the United States and in the Netherlands. The first concerns the Family Violence Option, a statutory provision exempting battered women from the work requirement imposed by US welfare reforms of the 1990s.[11] As Römkens explains, this special rule for battered women was at odds with welfare reform's general emphasis on individual responsibility for improving one's condition; the title of the US legislation is the Personal Responsibility and Work Opportunity Reconciliation Act. Accordingly, those administering the Family Violence Option were reluctant to grant waivers to battered women who were further stigmatized for even requesting the work waiver. Other scholars have similarly described how welfare recipients may fare badly at the hands of social workers and other bureaucrats unmotivated by, or untrained for, their task (see White, 1990).

Problems of implementation result not only from institutional inadequacies and competing objectives, but also from the assignment of jurisdiction of recourse to one or another institution. In her essay Römkens analyses an innovative programme from the Netherlands designed to protect battered women through the provision of an electronic alarm system. As implemented by police and prosecutors, however, the goal of the programme migrated from protecting battered women to building a sound case for the prosecution in court. Evidence of battering considered less than ideal for trial purposes was also held inadequate for the purposes of securing an electronic alarm or protective order. As the law began to operate on its own terms with its own players and purposes, the original needs of battered women were gradually obscured. Others argue more forcefully that the very offices often responsible for the enforcement of gender rights, such as the police, are from the outset, 'the professional embodiment of masculinity and so unlikely to have much innate institutional understanding or sympathy regarding gendered violence' (Messerschmidt *from* Perry, 2001). For example, violence against gay men at the hands of the police is not an uncommon phenomenon, as the discussion of the Hernandez–Montiel asylum case below indicates.

The unintended consequences of protective legislation often emerges in the context of the criminal justice system, where the right to be safe in one's person is often and sensibly lodged (Schneider, 2000). Judith Greenberg's (2003) study of dowry deaths in India shows how criminalization in that context fell short because the statutory focus on dowry deaths served to obscure other more common forms of domestic violence. The tendency to hold wicked mothers-in-law individually responsible for the deaths of daughters-in-law obscured deeper and more structural causes of abuse.

Justifying a particular right – establishing its moral foundation – is intimately tied to the process of advocacy: the more persuasive or appealing the justification, the more likely that law-makers, whether legislative bodies, judges, or tribunals, will recognize the right. This necessary mix of theory and advocacy becomes more complicated when the wrongfulness of the practice is disputed by those who suffer from the conduct or custom at the same time that they defend or sustain it. This reprises the conundrum of accommodating cultural practices raised earlier by Shachar. Another vivid example is the practice of female genital mutilation or female genital *surgery* – the contrasting labels underscoring the nature of the dispute (see Gunning, 1991). If challenges to the practice are sometimes regarded as 'meddling' by colonizing Western feminists, is it then possible to intervene with any sense of integrity? Is it possible to intervene even against *violent* practices when the Convention for the Elimination of All Forms of Discrimination Against Women (CEDAW) provides for state reservations against at least some of its provisions?

In Chapter 16 Radhika Coomaraswamy answers these questions with a definite 'yes'. In her essay on cultural relativism, Coomaraswamy reviews three cultural practices common in various and sizeable parts of the world – honour killings of women thought to be unfaithful, Sati or widow-burning, and female genital mutilation (FGM). She observes that each practice serves a range of social functions, some that might be characterized as beneficial and others not. These purposes include rites of passage, identity formation, increasing female marriageability, and control of female sexuality. However, Coomaraswamy forcefully argues that honour killings, Sati and FMG have something else in common: each is a form of torture. Torture is defined under the UN Torture Convention as the infliction of severe pain or suffering for a purpose that includes punishment or discrimination carried out with the consent or acquiescence of a public official.[12] Without abandoning other sources of protection, such as CEDAW or various state gender discrimination laws, Coomaraswamy urges that we can at least begin to distinguish among cultural rituals and customs by identifying and opposing those that most resemble torture.

Violence and remedies against it are a matter not only of national practices and national protections, but also of international law. One important example is the international prosecution of gendered crimes such as rape and sexual slavery that occur during armed conflict or mass violence. Recent cases before the International Criminal Tribunals for Rwanda and for Yugoslavia have determined that these gendered acts of violence are actionable under various theories: as acts of genocide, as torture, and as crimes against humanity (see Askin, 2003).

Protections against various forms of sexual violence may also be remedied under the laws of refugee and asylum. The United Nations Convention Relating to the Status of Refugees defines a refugee as someone who has fled his country on account of a well-founded fear of persecution on account of race, religion, nationality, political opinion or membership of a particular social group.[13] What, then, is the status of a woman who flees her country because she speaks out against her government's policies on women? Or a woman who flees to avoid female genital surgery at the hand of her family or who refuses to wear a veil and is stoned in consequence? Is a man who is beaten by police for dressing like a woman being persecuted on the basis of membership in a social group? Since the early 1990s, aided by United Nations Guidelines, Canada and the United States have recognized that persecution can be both sexualized and sex-based and have granted asylum to women in each of the categories just mentioned (see Blum and Kelly, 2001). New Zealand and Australia have granted refugee status to women on the basis of domestic violence on the grounds that state inaction against battering husbands constitutes a form of persecution (Anker, 2002).

In the final essay in Part IV Suzanne Goldberg explores how 'gender asylum law' has been challenged to include not only women but sexual minorities such as lesbians, gays, and others. Goldberg develops the argument that violence against individuals on the basis of sexual orientation is indeed persecution of a social group. She argues that sexual identity, like sex, should be considered a fundamental aspect of human identity – one not subject to change – and that it therefore satisfies the requirement for 'social group' status under refugee law. Indeed, in 2000 the US Ninth Circuit Court of Appeals found that the sexual assaults by police upon a Mexican man who dressed like a woman were indeed persecution against a member of a social group and granted Mr Hernandez-Montiel's application for asylum.[14]

Work

Rights are implicated from top to bottom with regard to work. Paid employment is necessary not only for economic self-sufficiency but also as a meaningful component of self-esteem and full participation in society (see Schultz, 2001; Williams, 2002; Rhode, 2002; Ertman, 2002). It bears emphasis that much of the work that women already do is unpaid – shopping, cooking, cleaning, fetching, and caring generally for the young and the elderly as well as for many able-bodied men. The question then remains not whether women work but rather what jobs they hold, the conditions under which they perform them and the circumstances under which they are hired, fired, paid and promoted. Similar issues arise for some men. The deeply gendered nature of work has meant, for example, that in many countries gays and lesbians cannot teach in schools or serve in the armed forces (or can serve in the United States military but only if they do not reveal their sexual orientation) (Halley, 1999).

Rights in statutes, in treaties and in constitutions now attempt to regulate and remedy certain forms of gender discrimination at work. Statutory provision for affirmative action or pay equity are two examples. So are protections against sexual harassment, as described in Susanne Baer's essay (Chapter 21), which compares the Berman approach, taken in Germany and based on the dignitary interests of workers, with that of the United States which is premised instead on workplace equality. Baer offers an historical explanation for these different theoretical foundations. In Germany following the Second World War, the concept of dignity emerged as the universal standard signifying fundamental human worth. In the United States, in part as a result of the 1960s civil rights movement, equality became the core value. These distinctions are embedded in the respective national constitutions. Under the German Basic Law, dignity comes first; in contrast, the word is not found in the US Constitution. After reviewing the deficiencies of each approach in remedying sex discrimination at work, Baer develops a doctrinal hybrid: the concept of equal respect. Of course, sound doctrine does not always carry the day. As Deborah Rhode's essay on 'The Myths of Meritocracy' (Chapter 23) reveals, obstacles to equality at work often operate under the radar of statutory and other protections. These include unconscious gender biases, lack of mentoring, and the problem of the 'double shift' at home and at work. Too often, gender-based disparities are attributed to women's preferences rather than to the constraints which shape the preferences.

The other two essays in Part V explore rights in connection with prostitution, an activity that some argue is not properly classified as work on any fair description of work as consensual. Martha Nussbaum (Chapter 20) considers this point in her essay on the exchange of money for bodily services. She compares prostitution with other forms of work where money is paid for human labour, such as teaching, domestic service and factory work (see generally Ertman and Zelizer, 2004). She concludes that the stigma of prostitution, rather than the work itself, creates the dignitary harm. But stigma alone cannot explain why prostitution is criminalized and other forms of stigmatizing work are not. Nussbaum therefore explores other rationales for criminalizing payment for this particular bodily service, such as morality, coercion, health and the commodification of sex (see also Anderson, 1993; Pateman, 1988). Insisting that debates over criminalization miss the heart of the prostitution problem, Nussbaum urges scholars and policy-makers to worry less about prostitution (other than regulating its coercive and health dimensions) and concentrate instead on producing other avenues for income and education for women so that sex work is no longer the best available choice.

The essay by Kamala Kempadoo and Ranya Ghuma (Chapter 22) concerns the regulation of a specific form of prostitution in today's flourishing global market in sex trade and tourism: child prostitution. The authors focus on the particular problem of policy formation with regard to adult versus child prostitution, and their essay addresses a problem of central interest to feminist scholars: competing interests among rights-holders. A familiar example is the 'maternal-foetal conflict', often discussed in the context of drug use by pregnant women. Do pregnant women owe their foetus a healthy prenatal environment when that environment is the mother's own body (see Roberts, 1991)? The authors look at a different and more subtle example of competition between adults and children. In their study of sex tourism in the Caribbean, Kempadoo and Ghuma argue that the focus by international organizations, NGOs and national governments on *child* prostitution within the sex industry obscures the situation – and the rights – of adult prostitutes. Public concern over children is marshalled at the expense of the interests of adults. The authors contrast the politically appealing goal of eradicating prostitution to save vulnerable children with a different set of policies that accept adult prostitution as a form of work that should be regulated rather than abolished.

Political Process and Participation

The essays in Part VI highlight how rights are shaped by the broader political cultures in which they arise. The examples – from Israel, Canada, France, and Hungary – also show how cultural values intersect with, and influence, various stages in the rights progression – that is, the evolution of a right from articulation to enactment to enforcement.

In her study of competing conceptualizations of abortion in the United States and Israel, Noga Morag-Levine (Chapter 24) refines our thinking about the use of rights to frame an issue by asking why the legal language of rights, imported into the Israeli abortion debate largely by US immigrants, failed to take hold in Israel. She offers two explanations: the general deference in Israel to nationally defined collective values (in contrast to individual rights in the United States) and the perceived normality of state intervention into all aspects of personal life. These values do not mean that women in Israel never want or never get abortions: they do so regularly under a system of medical approval similar to that of Great Britain (Sheldon, 1998). The point is that reproduction control in Israel is not framed around rights but around other values and concerns, such as religion, the demographic needs of the state and the social welfare of poor women. Morag-Levine demonstrates that although rights rhetoric may travel from one country to another, the rights themselves may not take root when the indigenous political culture is resistant to rights as the means of framing and achieving a particular goal.

The reconstitution of post-socialist abortion law demonstrates how an issue connected to women's welfare is shaped in part by its orientation to rights. As Susan Gal explains in Chapter 26, abortion in Hungary was never viewed as an issue of US-style 'reproductive rights' but rather as an aspect of the welfare state's responsibility to women and children. As elsewhere in Eastern Europe, the once-lenient abortion laws of the Hungarian communist era were debated and revised during the political transition of the 1990s. Abortion became a focal point not because the populace was specially concerned with the practice *per se*, but because abortion provided the text on which other salient issues – anti-communism, Hungarian nationalism and moral leadership – could be played out. Women, hesitant to defend their need for abortion for fear of feeding accusations of selfishness, remained relatively silent. The usefulness of gender in moments of political reorganization is demonstrated in post-colonial as well as post-socialist transitions. Katherine Franke (2004) describes President Mugabe's deployment of sexual politics in Zimbabwe. His brutal and repressive campaign against homosexuals was used to 'reclaim' an authentic, pre-colonial nationhood in which homosexuality is a European abomination and Zimbabwe is healthily and nationalistically heterosexual. Franke observes that the assault on homosexuality serves 'as a principal entry point in the creation of a culture of intolerance' which then radiates out from gay men to all women and then to political opponents more generally.

A different aspect of rights creation emerges in Judy Fudge's essay on the entrenchment of equal rights in the 1982 Canadian Charter of Rights and Freedoms (Chapter 25). Fudge explains that the movement to include a constitutional sex equality provision – a claim for formal equality – had a powerful energizing effect on feminist organizations throughout Canada. Women united to ensure that a strong version of the sex equality provision – one not subject to legislative override – would be included. Once the Charter provision was enacted, however, its implementation left the political realm and entered the judicial. In that forum, Fudge argues, the abstract language of equality now provided opportunities for decisions inimical to women's welfare: for example, courts struck down a series of criminal laws designed to protect women on the ground that they failed to treat men the same as women. Fudge suggests that the battle for substantive equality was therefore fought and, to some extent, lost through litigation in the courts. Other scholars assess the Canadian Supreme Court's application of the

Charter quite differently. Catherine MacKinnon, for example, argues that the Canadian Court has impressively interpreted the Charter to 'effectuate its purpose' – that is, to promote sex equality – in ways unhampered by doctrinal limitations of US equality jurisprudence (MacKinnon, 1991; 2004).

A campaign for a different measure of equality in representation took place in France during the 1990s during the debate over *parité*, or equal access by women to candidacies for electoral office. In 1999 the French Constitution was amended to require that the political parties fill half of all candidacies for most public offices with women or else lose certain campaign funding. During the campaign over the amendment, *parité* was denounced as fundamentally undemocratic – a violation of the principle of universality set out in the French Declaration of the Rights of Man and Citizen of 1789 – and simultaneously heralded as the necessary step for bringing about actual gender equality in the governance of the state (see Sineau, 2003; Faure, 2003). In Chapter 27 Karen Bird examines both the political origins of *parité*, as well as the broader question of why women have been so significantly underrepresented in French political life. (The answer includes a century of maternalistic policies designed to keep women in the home.)

And what has been the impact of *parité* on the sex-based composition of elected bodies in France and on the content of enacted legislation? Bird offers two important preliminary conclusions. The first is that women elected to office under *parité* are as likely as elected men to come from local political elites, a finding that underscores concern over gender's ongoing intersection with class. Second, despite the socio-economic similarity with men, women elected since *parité* appear to hold a 'distinctive set of perspectives on politics' (p. 615), such as greater concern about issues of family responsibility. Because women tend to be elected to local councils, Bird suggests that they are likely to make a difference with respect to policy decisions on these more local issues. There is, of course, much more to learn about the impact of women's increased political participation on policy outcomes. Here again, scholars must take up the task of monitoring the implementation of *parité* to assess the impact of this form of gender equalization on substantive gender equality.

Finally, the relation between courts and gender equality is taken up from a different perspective in Sally Kenney's essay on gender mainstreaming and the composition of the judiciary (see Chapter 28). Her inquiry focuses on the dawdling pace at which women have been appointed to the European Court of Justice. While addressing the political, historical and structural causes of the absence of women on the Court, Kenney also provides theoretical and policy justifications for why women judges matter. She concludes that, as a matter of proper representation, sound deliberation and judicial legitimacy, the European Court – and, we might suppose, other courts as well – are better served by the inclusion of women judges.

Technology, Globalization, and Privatization

Three additional phenomena – technology, globalization, and privatization – complicate any thoughtful consideration of gender and rights in the twenty-first century. Although the full impact of these dynamic forces cannot be fully developed here, they must be accounted for, even if briefly. Each significantly shapes the structure of current politics, morality and markets and therefore has a corresponding impact on the acquisition and maintenance of rights.

Recent innovations in medical technology are a case in point. Technological advances in genetic testing and prenatal diagnostics now make it possible to detect a variety of foetal abnormalities (see Browner and Press, 1995). This enables pregnant women to make more informed decisions about various prenatal medical interventions or continuing a pregnancy (Mahowald, 1996). At the same time, however, amniocentesis and ultrasound now also make it possible to identify one particular and often objectionable gene – the XX chromosome of the female foetus. As a result, in certain communities and in certain parts of the world, female foetuses are regularly aborted, freeing the family to try anew for the desired boy. Sex-selective abortion raises the question of gender rights in its starkest form. From one cultural perspective, the practice is nothing more than sensible family planning now made easier by the high-tech diagnosis. From the perspective of medical ethics, the practice is morally problematic and, in some countries, has been condemned.[16] And from a rights perspective, the voluntary abortion of female foetuses forces us to consider how reproductive freedom can be reconciled with gender equality (see Cherry, 1995).

The Internet similarly complicates the relationship between technology and rights in that it provides an almost unlimited source of information regarding health and employment, as well as striking opportunities for unbounded social and political solidarity. The Internet can also remedy what Martha Nussbaum has called the 'worldwide crisis in female education' – the absence of basic primary and secondary education for girls and women (Nussbaum, 1999, pp. 325–55). Access to this technology is now a necessary component of women's welfare if they are to live up to their capabilities in the modern world (Meyer, 1999). Yet the Internet is not all progress and enlightenment. One of its most popular and persistent uses is for viewing and downloading cyberpornography (MacKinnon, 1995). To the extent that pornography harms women through direct participation and as a result of continued sexual objectification, the use and regulation of the Internet is as much a challenge as an opportunity.

Concerns about borderless communications lead to a second complicating development: globalization. The phrase often suggests the excitement and synergies of free trade in ideas, labour and capital. But, as the work of Saskia Sassen (2003) and others makes clear, the transnational movement of ideas, labour and capital also includes a vast system of illegal traffic in domestic and sex workers. Barbara Ehrenreich and Arlie Hochschild (2003) observe that this dimension of globalization – the importation of childcare, homemaking, and sexual services from poorer countries to richer ones – uncannily replicates the familiar gender dependencies of the traditional family. Richer nations, they suggest, act like the old-fashioned man of the house, dependent on a dutiful wife; poor countries now play the wifely role by providing workers who take on the labour she once performed (Ehrenreich and Hochschild, 2003). In this way, the traditional gendered division of labour has itself gone global.

Privatization is the third powerful influence on the contemporary role of rights. In the past, the term may have referred simply to the notion that the market is the best mechanism for resource allocation, but, as Judy Fudge and Brenda Cossman observe in their study of privatization in Canada, privatization now encompasses a broader restructuring of the relation between the polity and the state. In many nations, responsibility for individual welfare is becoming less a matter of public obligation and increasingly a matter of private concern (Fudge and Cossman, 2002, pp. 3–4). Decoupled from the state, welfare provision becomes more haphazard and more vulnerable to public mood and political pressure. This shift is accomplished through a variety of policies: deregulation, familization (the relocation of once public services into the realm of the family) and what Fudge and Cossman call depolitization or the removal of certain issues, goods, and services from political contestation (see, for example, Schmall, 2001, pp. 3–4). As caretaking duties are again delegated to families, women bear the burden of this assignment, even as they seek more active participation in the paid workforce. To the extent that privatization relieves the state from various support obligations, the role of rights is itself circumscribed. This is particularly problematic when privatization further reinforces the gendered division of labour.

Rights claims and strategies operate against this complex background of dynamic forces. Depending on a complex calculus of politics, culture, personalities and history, the twenty-first century finds different rights at different stages of development and implementation. Not all such developments are felicitous, as many of the essays here critically address. Yet the essays in this volume also accept and celebrate the promise of rights as a means towards gender justice across the board. Ideas about women's abilities, horizons and preferences may have changed from those laid out by that eighteenth-century troublemaker, Mary Wollstonecraft. Yet vindicating rights for women and gender rights more broadly remains a challenge. There is much to dispute around the edges (and sometimes at the core) of specific rights: their contours, justifications, practicalities, applications and costs. Yet, as this volume shows, thinking through such complications, if not resolving them in every instance, is always worth our collective energies and effort.

Notes

1 For a useful collection of feminist critiques of classic political theorists, see Shanley and Pateman (1991).
2 The influential work of developmental psychologist Carol Gilligan, for example, has suggested that women are less rights-oriented than men, not because their moral reasoning is less advanced but because their relationships to others are based on intimate forms of connection, not a hierarchy of rights. See Gilligan (1982).
3 *Lawrence* v. *Texas*, 539 US 558 (2003); *State* v. *Limon*, 83 P.3d 229 (Kan. App. 2004).
4 For an excellent collection of essays on sexual harassment 25 years later, see MacKinnon and Siegel (2004).
5 See, for example, *Alison D.* v. *Virginia M.*, 77 NY 2d 651 (1991).
6 For a fine example of painstaking monitoring, see Yamin and Maine (1999).
7 Hardwig argues that rights would incline women to 'atomistic, asocial, and primarily egotistic' behaviours (Hardwig, 1984, p. 449).
8 See *Santa Clara Pueblo* v. *Martinez*, 436 US 49 (1978).
9 See *Mississippi Band of Choctaw Indians* v. *Holyfield*, 490 US 30 (1989).
10 *Goodridge* v. *Department of Public Health*, 798 NE 2d 941 (Mass. 2003).
11 For another focused analysis of the programme, see Czapanskiy (2003).
12 Convention Against Torture and Other Cruel, Inhuman or Degrading Treatment or Punishment, 10 December 1984, art.1, para. 1, G.A, Res. 39/46, 39 UN GAOR, Supp. No. 51, UN Doc. A/RES/ 39/708 (1984).
13 Convention Relating to the Status of Refugees, 22 April 1954, art.1, para. a.
14 *Hernandez-Montiel* v. *INS*, 225 F.3d 1084 (9th Cir. 2000). Certainly, how a right is framed in one context may have troubling consequences is another. For example, Janet Halley (1994) has warned against the precedential risks of arguing for the immutability of gay identity.
15 The word *parité* is not actually in the amendment which refers instead to *égalité*.
16 See Society of Obstetricians and Gynecologists of Canada, Policy Statement on Gender Selection, available at http://www.csdms.com/pdf/05.pdf (last accessed on 21 July 2004).

References

Agarwal, Bina (1944), *A Field of One's Own: Gender and Land Rights in South Asia*, Cambridge: Cambridge University Press.

Anderson, Elizabeth (1993), *Value in Ethics and in Economics*, Cambridge, MA: Harvard University Press.

Anker, Deborah (2002), 'Refugee Law, Gender, and the Human Rights Paradigm', *Harvard Human Rights Journal*, **15**, pp. 133–54.

Askin, Kelly (2003), 'Prosecuting Wartime Rape and Other Gender-related Crimes Under International Law: Extraordinary Advances, Enduring Obstacles', *Berkeley Journal of International Law*, **21**, pp. 288–349.

Bagnall, Robert *et al.* (1984), 'Burdens on Gay Litigants and Bias in the Court System: Homosexual Panic, Child Custody, and Anonymous Parties', *Harvard Civil Rights–Civil Liberties Law Review*, **19**, pp. 497–559.

Blum, Carolyn and Kelly, Nancy (2001), 'The Protection of Women Refugees', in Kelly D. Askin and Dorean M. Koenig (eds), *Women and International Human Rights Law*, Vol. 3, New York: Transnational Publishers, pp. 197–239.

Brandt, Michele and Kaplan, Jeffrey A. (1995–96), 'The Tension Between Women's Rights and Religious Rights: Reservations to CEDAW by Egypt, Bangladesh and Tunisia', *Journal of Law and Religion*, **12**, pp. 105–42.

Browner, Carole H. and Press, Nancy Ann (1995), 'The Normalization of Prenatal Diagnostic Screening', in Faye D. Ginsburg and Rayna Rapp (eds), *Conceiving the New World Order: The Global Politics of Reproduction*, Berkeley: University of California Press, pp. 307–22.

Case, Mary Anne C. (1995), 'Disaggregating Gender from Sex and Sexual Orientation: The Effeminate Man in the Law and Feminist Jurisprudence', *Yale Law Journal*, **105**, pp. 1–105.

Cherry, April L. (1995), 'A Feminist Understanding of Sex-Selective Abortion: Solely a Matter of Choice?', *Wisconsin Women's Law Journal*, **10**, pp. 161–223.

Coker, Donna K. (1992), 'Heat of Passion and Wife Killing: Men Who Batter/Men Who Kill', *South California Review of Law and Women's Studies*, **2**, pp. 71–130.

Czapanskiy, Karen (2003), 'Domestic Violence and the Maryland Family Violence Option', *American University Journal of Gender, Social Policy and the Law*, **11**, pp. 447–64.

Ehrenreich, Barbara and Hochschild, Arlie (eds) (2003), *Global Woman: Nannies, Maids and Sex Workers in the New Economy*, New York: Metropolitan Books.

Ertman, Martha M. (2002), 'Love and Work: A Response to Vicki Schultz's Life's Work', *Columbia Law Review*, **102**, pp. 848–64.

Ertman, Martha M. and Zelizer, Viviana (2004), *Rethinking Commodification: Cases and Readings in Law and Culture*, New York: New York University Press.

Faure, Christine (2003), 'Women's History after *Parité*', in Roger Celestin, Eliane DalMolin and Isabelle De Courtivron (eds), *Beyond French Feminisms: Debates on Women, Politics and Culture in France, 1981–2001*, Austin: University of Texas Press, pp. 39–49.

Felsteiner, William, Abel, Richard and Sarat, Austin (1980), 'The Emergence and Transformation of Disputes: Naming, Blaming, Claiming . . .', *Law and Society Review*, **15**, pp. 631–54.

Fineman, Martha (1991), *The Illusion of Equality: The Rhetoric and Reality of Divorce Reform*, Chicago: University of Chicago Press.

Franke, Katherine M. (1995), 'The Central Mistake of Sex Discrimination Law: The Disaggregation of Sex from Gender', *University of Pennsylvania Law Review*, **144**, pp. 1–99.

Franke, Katherine M. (1997), 'What's Wrong With Sexual Harassment?', *Stanford Law Review*, **49**, pp. 691–772.

Franke, Katherine M. (2002), 'Women Imagining Justice', *Yale Journal of Law and Feminism*, **14**, pp. 307–12.

Franke, Katherine M. (2004), 'Sexual Tensions of Post-Empire', *Studies in Law, Politics and Society*, **33**, pp. 65–90.

Fudge, Judy and Cossman, Brenda (2002), 'Introduction', in Brenda Cossman and Judy Fudge (eds), *Privatization, Law, and the Challenge to Feminism*, Toronto: University of Toronto Press.

Funk, Nanette and Mueller, Magda (eds) (1993), *Gender Politics and Post-Communism: Reflections from Eastern Europe and the Former Soviet Union*, London: Routledge.
Gal, Susan (1997), 'Gender in the Post-Socialist Transition: The Abortion Debate in Hungary', in Roger N. Lancaster and Micaela di Leonardo (eds), *The Gender Sexuality Reader*, London: Routledge, pp. 122–33.
Gilligan, Carol (1982), *In a Different Voice: Psychological Theory and Women's Development*, Cambridge, MA: Harvard University Press.
Ginsburg, Ruth Bader and Flagg, Barbara (1989), 'Some Reflections on the Feminist Legal Thought of the 1970s', *University of Chicago Legal Forum*, pp. 9–22.
Greenberg, Judith G. (2003), 'Criminalizing Dowry Deaths: The Indian Experience', *American University Journal of Gender, Social Policy and Law*, **11**, pp. 801–46.
Gunning, Isabelle R. (1991), 'Arrogant Perceptions, World Traveling and Multicultural Feminism: The Case of Female Genital Surgeries', *Columbia Human Rights Law Review*, **23**, pp. 189–248.
Halley, Janet (1994), 'Sexual Orientation and the Politics of the Biology: A Critique of the Argument from Immutability', *Stanford Law Review*, **46**, pp. 503–68.
Halley, Janet (1999), *Don't: A Reader's Guide to the Military's Anti-Gay Policy*, Durham, NC: Duke University Press.
Hardwig, John (1984), 'Should Women Think in Terms of Rights?', *Ethics*, **94**, pp. 441–55.
Hartog, Hendrik (1993), 'Abigail Bailey's Coverture: Law in a Married Woman's Consciousness', in Austin Sarat and Thomas Kearns (eds), *Law and Everyday Life*, Ann Arbor: University of Michigan Press, pp. 63–108.
Hirschman, Albert O. (1970), *Exit, Voice, and Loyalty: Responses to Decline in Firms, Organizations, and States*, Cambridge, MA: Harvard University Press.
Jacobs, James and Potter, Kimberley (1998), *Hate Crimes: Criminal Law and Identity Politics*, Oxford: Oxford University Press, pp. 65–78.
Kerber, Linda (1998), *No Constitutional Right to Be Ladies: Women and the Obligations of Citizenship*, New York: Hill and Wang.
Kiss, Elizabeth (1997), 'Alchemy or Fool's Gold? Assessing Feminist Doubts About Rights', in Mary Shanley and Uma Narayan (eds), *Reconstructing Political Theory*, New York: Polity Press.
Kohn, Sally (2001–2002), 'Greasing the Wheel: How the Criminal Justice System Hurts Gay, Lesbian, Bisexual and Transgendered People and Why Hate Laws Won't Save Them', *New York University Review of Law and Social Change*, **27**, pp. 257–80.
Koven, Seth and Michel, Sonya (eds) (1993), *Mothers of a New World*, New York: Routledge.
Lee, Cynthia (2003a), 'Female Infidelity', in *Murder and the Reasonable Man*, New York: New York University Press, pp. 17–45.
Lee, Cynthia (2003b), 'Gay Panic', in *Murder and the Reasonable Man*, New York: New York University Press, pp. 67–95.
MacKinnon, Catharine A. (1979), *Sexual Harassment of Working Women*, New Haven, CT: Yale University Press.
MacKinnon, Catharine A. (1989), 'Unthinking ERA Thinking' (book review), *University of Chicago Law Review*, **54**, pp. 759–70.
MacKinnon, Catharine A. (1991), 'Reflections on Sex Equality Under Law', *Yale Law Journal*, **100**, pp. 1281–327.
MacKinnon, Catharine A. (1995), 'Vindication and Resistance: A Response to the Carnegie Mellon Study of Pornography in Cyberspace', *Georgia Law Journal*, **83**, pp. 1959–67.
MacKinnon, Catharine A. (2004), 'Toward a New Theory of Equality', in *Women's Lives, Men's Laws*, Cambridge, MA: Harvard University Press.
MacKinnon, Catharine A. and Siegel, Reva (eds) (2004), *Directions in Sexual Harassment Law*, New Haven, CT: Yale University Press, pp. 582–601.
Mahoney, Martha (1991), 'Legal Images of Battered Women: Redefining the Issue of Separation', *Michigan Law Review*, **90**, pp. 1–94.
Mahowald, Mary B. (1996), 'Genetic Technologies and Their Implications for Women', *University of Chicago Law School Roundtable*, **3**, pp. 439–63.
Mansbridge, Jane (1986), *Why We Lost the ERA*, Chicago: University of Chicago Press.

Meyer, Carlin (1995), 'Reclaiming Sex from the Pornographers: Cybersexual Possibilities', *Georgia Law Journal*, **83**, pp. 1969–2007.
Miller, Alice M. (2000), 'Sexual but Not Reproductive: Exploring the Junction and Disjunction of Sexual and Reproductive Rights', *Health and Human Rights*, **4**(2), pp. 69–109.
Moi, Toril (1999), 'What is a Woman?', in *What is a Woman? and Other Essays*, Oxford: Oxford University Press, pp. 3–120.
Morrell, Robert (1998), 'Of Boys and Men: Masculinity and Gender in Southern African Studies', *Journal of South African Studies*, **24**, pp. 605–30.
Narayan, Uma (1997), 'Cross-Cultural Connections, Border-Crossings, and "Death by Culture:" Thinking about Dowry Murders in India and Domestic-Violence Murders in the United States', in *Dislocating Cultures*, New York: Routledge, pp. 81–117.
Nussbaum, Martha (1999), *Women and Human Development*, Cambridge: Cambridge University Press.
Nussbaum, Martha (2003), 'Women's Education: A Global Challenge', *Signs: Journal of Women in Culture and Society*, **29**, pp. 325–55.
Okin, Susan (1987), 'Justice and Gender', *Philosophy and Public Affairs*, **16**, pp. 42–72.
Pateman, Carole (1988), 'What's Wrong with Prostitution?', in *The Sexual Contract*, New York: Polity Press, pp. 189–218.
Perry, Barbara (2001), *In the Name of Hate: Understanding Hate Crimes*, New York: Routledge.
Polikoff, Nancy (2000), 'Recognizing Partners But not Parents/Recognizing Parents But not Partners: Gay and Lesbian Families in Europe and the United States', *New York Law School Journal of Human Rights*, **17**, pp. 711–51.
Rhode, Deborah L. (1989), 'Natural Rights and Natural Roles', in *Justice and Gender: Sex Discrimination and the Law*, Cambridge, MA: Harvard University Press, pp. 9–28.
Rhode, Deborah L. (1990), 'Feminist Critical Theories', *Stanford Law Review*, **42**, pp. 617–38.
Rhode, Deborah L. (2002), 'Balanced Lives', *Columbia Law Review*, **102**, pp. 834–37.
Roberts, Dorothy (1991), 'Punishing Drug Addicts Who Have Babies: Women of Color, Equality, and the Right of Privacy', *Harvard Law Review*, **104**, pp. 1419–82.
Sassen, Saskia (2003), 'Global Cities and Survival Circuits', in Barbara Ehrenreich and Arlie Russell Hochschild (eds) (2003), *Global Woman, Nannies, Maids and Sex Workers in the New Economy*, New York: Metropolitan Books, pp. 254–74.
Schmall, Lorraine A. (2001), 'Transnational Issues of Women and Pension Security and Reform', *New York International Law Review*, **14**, pp. 87–126.
Schneider, Elizabeth (2000), *Battered Women and Feminist Law Making*, New Haven, CT: Yale University Press.
Schultz, Vicki (1998), 'Reconceptualizing Sexual Harassment', *Yale Law Journal*, **107**, pp. 1683–805.
Schultz, Vicki (2001), 'Life's Work', *Columbia Law Review*, **100**, pp. 1881–964.
Scott, Joan (1988), *Gender and the Politics of History*, New York: Columbia University Press.
Sen, Amartya (1995), 'Gender Inequality and Theories of Justice', in Martha C. Nussbaum and Jonathan Glover (eds), *Women, Culture and Development*, Oxford: Clarendon Press, pp. 259–73.
Shanley, Mary and Patemen, Carole (eds) (1991), *Feminist Interpretations and Political Theory*, New York: Polity Press.
Sheldon, Sally (1998), 'The Abortion Act: A Critical Perspective', in Ellie Lee (ed.), *Abortion Law and Politics Today*, New York: St Martin's Press, pp. 43–58.
Sineau, Mariette (2003), '*Parité* in Politics: From a Radical Idea to a Consensual Reform', in Roger Celestin, Eliane DalMolin and Isabelle De Courtivron (eds), *Beyond French Feminisms: Debates on Women, Politics and Culture in France, 1981–2001*, Austin: University of Texas Press, pp. 113–26.
Taylor, Barbara (2003), *Mary Wollstonecraft and the Feminist Imagination*, Cambridge: Cambridge University Press.
Thomas, Kendall (1993), 'Shower/Closet', *Assemblage: Critical Journal of Architecture and Design*, ed. Mark Wigley, no. 20, April, pp. 80–81.
White, Lucie E. (1990), 'Subordination, Rhetorical Survival Skills, and Sunday Shoes: Notes on the Hearing of Mrs. G.', *Buffalo Law Review*, **38**, pp. 1–58.
Williams, Joan (2002), '"It's Snowing Down South": How to Help Mothers and Avoid Recycling the Sameness/Difference Debate', *Columbia Law Review*, **102**, pp. 812–33.

Wintemute, Robert (2005), 'Sexual Orientation and Gender Identity', in Colin Harvey (ed.), *Human Rights in the Community: Rights as Agents for Change*, Oxford: Hart Publishing.
Yamin, Alicia Ely and Maine, Deborah P. (1999), 'Maternal Mortality as a Human Rights Issue: Measuring Compliance with International Treaty Obligations', *Human Rights Quarterly*, Issue 3, **21**, pp. 563–607.
Young, Iris Marion (2003), 'Lived Body Versus Gender: Reflections on Social Structure and Subjectivity', in Robin N. Fiore and Hilda Lindemann Nelson (eds), *Recognition, Responsibility, and Rights*, Lanham, MD: Rowman and Littlefield, pp. 3–18.

Part I
Gender and Rights

[1]
THE PROBLEM OF RIGHTS

Carol Smart

In this chapter I wish to raise a dilemma for feminism. I have outlined in previous chapters the limits of law reform, indeed, I have tried to go far beyond this formulation altogether. If we reject the idea of law as a simple tool of liberation or of oppression, and look at how it constitutes a kind of institutionalized and formalized site of power struggles — one that can provide resources for women, children, and men, albeit differentially — then it is possible to acknowledge that it remains an important strategic element in political confrontations. Yet it seems we cannot know in advance whether a recourse to law will empower women, children, or men, although there is a substantial and well-founded fear that legal power works better for (white, middle-class) men than for anyone else.

In resorting to law, especially law structured on patriarchal precedents, women risk invoking a power that will work against them rather than for them. We know, for example, that the Sex Discrimination Act 1975 and Race Relations Act 1976 in the UK have been largely unsuccessful in changing the discrimination against women and ethnic communities (Appleby and Ellis 1984; Gregory 1988). We also know that the more women and minority groups resort to law, the more hostility is generated. A backlash is created that may take the form of violence, or a counter-use of law to re-establish traditional rights which will nullify minority rights.

Using law is, therefore, hazardous. Yet, it would hardly be preferable to turn the clock back to a time when women had virtually no rights. So although second-wave feminists may be critical of first-wave liberal feminists for their emphasis on formal legal equality, and their apparent attempts to have women admitted to the male order, it is unlikely that we would willingly give up any of the legal reforms they achieved.

In a way this is an oversimplification of the value of legal rights. First-wave feminists used the concept of equal rights to fight against legally imposed impediments. They were not trying to use the concept of rights as a legal tool to remove discrimination in all aspects of life. As Sachs and Wilson (1978) have shown, legislation, legal regulations, and the interpretation of statutes denied women access to professional occupations and universities in the nineteenth and early twentieth centuries. The law was quite overt in its distribution of privileges and power to men, husbands and sons. It was important as a first step that these legal privileges were removed. It is, therefore, unjustified to visit a late twentieth-century disillusionment with legal rights, upon a nineteenth-century feminism which faced a very different set of circumstances. The campaign for the vote, for married women's property rights, for custody rights and so on, were politically important. The fact that history has shown that women's oppression is not simply a matter of equal rights under the law should not blind us to the importance of those early struggles.

It is increasingly clear that in the late twentieth-century law has ceased formally to allocate rights to men which it denies to women. Law may remain oppressive to women, but the form it takes is no longer the denial of formal rights which are preserved for men. Hence, while it might have been appropriate for early feminists to demand legal rights, the continuation of the same demand for legal rights is now problematic. I am suggesting that the rhetoric of rights has become exhausted, and may even be detrimental. This is especially the case where women are demanding rights which are not intended (in an abstract sense) to create equal rights with men, but where the demand is for a 'special' right (e.g. women's right to choose) for which there has been no masculine equivalent. I shall explore these ideas in relation to reproduction and abortion, and child custody. First, however, I shall examine why the rhetoric and strategy of rights remain so attractive to feminists.

THE ATTRACTION OF RIGHTS

Mitchell (1987) has argued that feminism's history corresponds with the history of the concept of equality. She traces the emergence of feminist thought in the eighteenth century and argues that in its earliest formulations it was heavily reliant upon the emergent notion of equality. However, she points out that equality, as envisaged by John Stuart Mill and the liberals of the nineteenth century, was an equality formulated within the order of capitalism. Hence it was always an equality of individuals *under the law*, in the context of structural inequalities based on class, race, and gender. It is, of course, not a new insight to point out that the liberal notion of equality is too limited to affect structural inequalities. However, it does need to be stressed that as liberalism gained ascendancy as a philosophy to guide legal and social policy (Clarke *et al.* 1987) the idea that equality (of opportunity) was desirable was inextricably bound up with the idea that it was achievable through the law. This view in turn is based upon a conceptualization of law as a (potentially) neutral arbiter and protector of the weak, rather than as implicated in the very oppression that it is hoped it will eradicate (Smart 1984).

The growth of modern feminism, therefore, corresponds both to notions of equality and the idea that equality of opportunity can be achieved through law in the form of legal rights. The very language of rights, which was so challenging to the conservative order, was both empowering in that they could be claimed by everyone no matter what class or gender, and limiting in that it constructed law as the centre of so many political campaigns. This was particularly true of feminist campaigns which sought to extend the philosophy of the 'rights of man' to encompass woman. Early feminists like Caroline Norton, Barbara Leigh Smith Bodichon, Frances Power Cobbe, and Anna Martin who campaigned at different times in the areas of child custody, matrimonial property, divorce, domestic violence, and maternity benefits, all drew upon the basic idea that women's vulnerability in marriage was the consequence of unequal legal rights which gave husbands undue power (see Dobash and Dobash 1980; Brophy and Smart 1985; Clarke *et al.* 1987). They all, in different ways, argued that the existing law denied women's citizenship or membership of a democratric order. Hence campaigners like Frances Power Cobbe drew analogies between the law's treatment of lunatics, criminals, children, and women (Cobbe 1869). In so doing she was trying to create a new legal subjectivity for women, based upon a recognition of law's power to create legal subjects with specific rights. This was not a power that Cobbe challenged, on the contrary she was content that children, criminals, and lunatics should continue to be 'disqualified'; rather she wished the privileges of 'qualification' to be extended to women.

Feminist discourse constructed women as citizens, as persons worthy of sharing the privileges of the newly emergent democratic order of the nineteenth century. It was part of the feminist strategy to celebrate the work that women did in the family, to draw attention to the responsibilities they held in the private sphere, in fact to argue that domestic work constituted responsible and necessary activity. Hence women's work in caring for children was highlighted, as was their crucial role in maintaining the home and domestic economy. The thrust of the argument was that women should be counted, not discounted. Part of the strategy deployed was to draw public attention to the abuses of power that the 'disqualification' of women had led to in the private sphere. Hence Cobbe published 'horror' stories of wife beating (Cobbe 1878), Norton published pamphlets describing her own motherly distress at being denied access to her children after separating from her husband (Norton 1982), Martin depicted women in 'mean streets' suffering from unnecessary hardships caused by the failure or inability of husbands to maintain them and their children (Martin 1911). The common philosophy that all of these arguments drew upon was the appeal to unfairness which was constructed from the notion that fairness and equity were basic human rights which should be afforded legal recognition or protection.

The appeal to law on the basis of basic rights was no less than an appeal to the state to re-order power relations. Even if the contemporary feminist movement tends to dismiss early feminism as liberal reformism, the anti-feminists of the nineteenth and twentieth centuries recognized that these appeals threatened the patriarchal order of the family. Take, for example, the following quotation made during the early nineteenth-century campaign to extend custody rights to mothers.

> It is notorious that one of the strongest hindrances in all cases . . . to prevent wives from lightly separating from their husbands is that knowledge that they will thereby lose their maternal rights. This at all times has been a safeguard to preserve the institution of marriage.
> (Jahled Brenton 1838, quoted in Pinchbeck and Hewitt 1973: 374)

Some ninety years later a similar view was voiced in the debate over whether wives should have equal rights to husbands in marriage.

> [T]he status of women has very much changed in the last twenty five years . . . [she] has almost the same status as a man. She has not altogether the same status because it is necessary to preserve the family as a unit and if you have a unit you must have a head.
> (Parliamentary Debates 1924: vol. 57, col. 191)

Yet as early as 1700 Mary Astell had queried this political stance.

> If Absolute Sovereignty be not necessary in a State how comes it to be so in a Family? or if in a Family why not in a State; since no reason can be alleg'd for the one that will not hold more strongly for the other.
> (quoted in Mitchell 1987: 31)

The point is that the English common law gave privileges to men which were enshrined in their legal rights. The early feminists wanted these rights diminished and used the same basic strategy and philosophy that had extended the franchise to all men and that ultimately challenged the legitimacy of slavery. It should be recognized, however, that such claims on the state could only arise as the state itself became more centralized and developed the relevant technologies to enforce its prescriptions. To put it simply, just as modern criminal law is dependent upon the existence of a police force, so developments in women's rights in marriage were dependent upon centralized information on marriage, births, divorce, and separation. To claim the protection of legal rights, women had to be subjected to more refined notions of qualification. For example, in cases of maintenance they must prove themselves legally married, or in cases of illegitimacy they must prove paternity, or in cases of child custody they must prove that they meet the best interests of children.

The claim of rights has therefore generated more centralized knowledge about sexual relationships, marriage relationships, child care organization, and so on. To be 'equitable' in the allocation of rights the law requires that certain obligations be met. In so doing it creates the possibility for greater and greater surveillance. Such developments could not have been easily foreseen by the early feminists, yet they constitute a new form of oppression for women (and others) (e.g. see Smart 1982; Bottomley 1985; Thèry 1986). It is only as feminist work has begun to recognize the limits of the claim to rights *and* the regulatory potential of claiming protection from the state, that the appeal to rights has become less attractive.

We are, therefore, faced with a dilemma. Historically rights have been almost an intrinsic part of feminist claims. Now rights constitute a political language through which certain interests can be advanced. To couch a claim in terms of rights is a major step towards a recognition of a social wrong. Hence, Catharine MacKinnon (1987) has argued that transposing the notion of sexual harassment into a matter of employment rights, and pornography into a matter of civil rights, has put these issues onto a visible public agenda. To claim that an issue is a matter of rights is to give the claim legitimacy.

It is also the case that to pose an issue in terms of rights is to make the claim 'popular'. This is not to say that everyone agrees, but it makes the claim accessible, it means that it can be brought under the umbrella of trade union debates, parliamentary consideration, media reportage, and so on. It enters into a linguistic currency to which everyone has access. Moreover, whilst the extension of rights is associated with the foundations of democracy and freedom, the claim to rights is always already loaded. It is almost as hard to be against rights as it is to be against virtue.

Rights also have another appeal. They are depicted as a protection of the weak against the strong, or the individual against the state. No matter how (in)effective they are in achieving such protections, there is little doubt that a reduction in rights is equated with a loss of power or protection. Hence the (now) regular challenge to women's abortion rights in the UK is regarded as an attempt to reduce women's autonomy and ability to determine their own reproductive careers. A change to the existing legislation which reduced women's access to abortion would be a real diminution of women's rights even in a context where we know that not all women have access to abortion or adequate contraceptive methods.

We cannot deny that rights do amount to legal and political power resources. However, the value of such resources seems to be ascertainable more in terms of losses if such rights diminish, than in terms of gains if such rights are sustained. This is not as paradoxical as it may seem. The denial of rights in a given area like abortion will have the definite consequence of forcing women to go through with pregnancies which are unwanted. The provision of abortion rights does not however, guarantee that any woman who wants an abortion can have one. The law may concede a right, but if the state refuses to fund abortions or abortion clinics, it is an empty right.

The dilemma that needs to be faced is whether to continue the feminist tradition of couching claims in terms of rights.

THE PROBLEM OF RIGHTS

There are several problems with using rights as part of a feminist strategy. The first is that rights oversimplify complex power relations. This means that the acquisition of rights in a given area may create the impression that a power difference has been 'resolved'.

Yet the exercise of power in, for example, the private sphere may have little to do with legal rights. That women have the right to apply to the courts for injunctions to remove a man who is violent from the family home has not stopped the problem of domestic violence. This is not because women are ignorant of the law (although they may be), nor is it because the law is defective (although it undoubtedly is, McCann 1985), rather it is because the legal right can treat the woman and man involved only as adversaries. Whilst this might be applicable in many circumstances, it overlays the existence of other elements to the relationship. For example, there may be an economic dependence which prevents the woman exercising her 'rights', or a concern for the welfare of the children might lead a mother to think that it is better to keep the father in the family (Pahl 1985). Exercising rights in this area always has some undesirable consequences. This is most obvious in cases of child sexual abuse, where the strategy of using law to prevent further abuse (i.e. the right of a child not to be sexually abused) often leads to consequences that children find worse than — or as bad as — the original abuse. In this sense the exercise of a right does not empower the weaker individual. It may simply draw the state's attention to a situation, and bring about consequences which are quite disastrous for the individuals involved. This is not, of course, an argument against rights. It is, however, meant to alert us to the fact that legal rights do not resolve problems. Rather they transpose the problem into one that is defined as having a legal solution. This may not be the problem identified by the individuals whose rights are being invoked, moreover the solution may itself do little to alter the power relations that remain intact. Hence with child sexual abuse, the state may punish a man by imprisoning him for a number of months or even years, but will not prevent him from returning to his family on release and starting to abuse his children again.

The second main problem with rights is related to this last issue. Whilst a child or a wife may have the right not to be molested, the husband also has rights that the law will uphold. For example, the right to live in 'his' home, the right to see 'his' children. Although these rights can be removed in extreme situations, there is a reluctance to do so and consequently the resort to rights can be effectively countered by the resort to competing rights. In cases of child sexual abuse it has become common to hear the argument that legal procedures cannot be modified to help children give evidence in court because, in spite of their right not to be abused, the accused has a prior right to a particular form of trial.

A third problem with rights is that they are often formulated to deal with a social wrong, yet they are always (in the UK at least) focused on the individual who must prove that her rights have been violated. Hence an act like the Sex Discrimination Act 1975 provides certain rights, yet for these to have any impact for women in general requires that vast numbers of individual women can prove that they have been denied their rights through a form of unlawful discrimination. So whilst a few women may have benefited from taking action under this legislation, the vast majority have not benefited from their gains.

The last major problem with rights is the way in which those rights formulated to protect the individual against the state, or the weak against the strong, may be appropriated by the more powerful. Hence the Sex Discrimination Act may be used as much by men as by women. Moreover, rights devised to give protection against the state may now be used by individuals against less powerful individuals. The chief example of this is the recourse to the European Convention on Human Rights which is now being used to extend the authority of unmarried men over their illegitimate children. This has been documented in relation to the Marckx case (de Hondt and Holtrust 1986). Without going into the complexities here, the development of using the Convention rests upon the 'right to a family life' which unmarried fathers have argued is denied to them by the laws on illegitimacy. Such fathers are attempting to claim rights over children which married fathers enjoy. Yet the 'right to a family life' was originally formulated with the problem of state measures like apartheid, forced mobility of labour, and immigration policies in mind. However, such rights have now become in effect 'usable' against individual unmarried mothers. There is no countervailing right not to have a family life in such circumstances.

The problem of the recourse to rights has, of course, been well documented and debated elsewhere (e.g. Hirst 1980, 1986). For feminism, however, it remains an unresolved debate if only because there is some common ground on the need to protect existing rights, even if there is disagreement over whether to pursue new rights claims. But we are also entering into a new era in which rights claims may be becoming less and less valuable. Indeed, it may be that rights claims are becoming counter-productive and associated with mere self-interest. Feminism as a whole is increasingly depicted as a self-interested lobby which seeks rights without responsibility, and is negligent as to the consequences for children and the family. It may be that the assumption that legal rights should be a basic element of democracy will be increasingly replaced by notions of the welfare of children, the needs of the family, and the desire for stability (Anderson and Dawson 1986).

RIGHTS AND REPRODUCTION

The juxtaposing of the concept of reproduction with the legal notion of rights produces a very powerful political effect. On one level it is still regarded as deeply shocking that what are regarded as natural, god-given biological functions can be conceptualized in terms which are legalistic and contingent. On the other hand, for women who have ever expressed a desire to control their reproductive capacities, the notion of rights gives a social legitimacy to this personal goal. Reproductive rights brings the private realm of anxiety over conception into the public sphere where women can discover what they have in common. This has been immensely important in the struggle to gain a greater acceptance of the idea that women should have as much control as possible, and has even had the pragmatic effect of creating improved provision for abortion and contraception.

When legal abortion was introduced into England and Wales in 1967 it was against a backcloth of the horror of backstreet abortions and in the context of social and legal policies which were severely detrimental to women (Ferris 1966). Women were depicted as victims of inadequate birth control, of severe illegitimacy laws, of unscrupulous backstreet abortionists, and of a stigma against one-parent families. Therapeutic abortion, which was to be regulated by a paternalistic medical profession, was seen as the enlightened answer to this problem. There was considerable opposition to the legislation of course and it did not become law without a struggle (Greenwood and Young 1976). Interestingly the role of the Women's Movement in relation to abortion became more and more clearly defined only as campaigns to amend and abolish the Act became more vociferous. It was during the campaigns against the anti-abortion Corrie Bill and White Bill[1] that slogans about 'A Woman's Right to Choose' became widespread.

The conflict between 'pro-choice' and 'pro-life' groups (the former being the women's movement and the pro-abortion lobby, the latter being the Society for the Protection of the Unborn Child and other anti-abortionists) was on several grounds. The one that has become the most significant, however, is the conflict of rights. This refers to the claim by women that they must have a right to determine the reproductive capacities of their own bodies, and the counter-claim that such a right must take second place to the right of the foetus (usually referred to as a child) to life. As Kingdom (1985a) has pointed out, there is no satisfactory resolution to such a conflict of rights claims. In fact she recommends that feminists should be wary of resorting to a rights claim at all. I shall discuss her argument below, but first I wish to explore why social and medical developments have created conditions which are increasingly detrimental to a 'woman's right to choose'.

In the 1960s the woman who resorted to abortion was regarded as the victim. Moreover, the fact that wealthy women could afford to buy safe abortions whilst poorer women had to risk dangerous practices and infections was treated as the grossest hypocrisy. By the 1980s the image of the woman seeking abortion had changed. It became common to hear the argument that because contraceptives are available from the National Health Service no woman should have an unwanted pregnancy. This assertion ignores the social conditions under which women become pregnant and, no less significant, the fact that many contraceptives are fallible and the 'safest' may have serious and unwelcome side effects. Notwithstanding this, the woman seeking an abortion is no longer seen in terms of a woman with restricted choices or the desperate victim of the 1960s but the careless young ne'er-do-well of the 1980s. The other dominant image became that of the 'women's libber' who thought she should have the freedom to have as many sexual experiences as she wanted, followed by abortion on demand. The idea grew that women were using abortion as a form of convenient late contraception, a practice which was seen as a sign of the callousness of the feminist movement.

So from being defined as victims, women seeking abortions became defined as immoral and self-interested. The extent of their guilt was then compounded by the growing recognition of the problem of infertility and the 'famine' in babies for adoption. The juxtaposition of images of women who long for children, but cannot have them, with (misconstrued) ideas of the woman who gets pregnant carelessly and then, apparently equally carelessly, terminates her pregnancy, creates an antipathy towards the latter. It seems that not only are these women selfish in relation to themselves and their unborn children, but also in relation to the growing numbers of infertile couples who want to adopt the unwanted child. The imagery divides women against women so that rather than the social conditions of fertility and infertility being treated as common cause, they become moments of antagonism. All public sympathy goes to the woman who is following the 'natural' course, who is trying to become a mother rather than rejecting motherhood.

This shifting image of the woman who wants an abortion makes the formulation of feminist claims in terms of rights increasingly unpopular. But there is another dimension to this 'unpopularity' which has taken shape in the 1980s. This results from developments in medical technology which can, in some cases, sustain the lives of prematurely born infants. It is now possible to preserve the life of a foetus of 24 weeks' gestation and it may be possible to lower this level in time. When this is combined with popular notions of *in vitro* fertilization (test-tube babies) medicine seems poised to be able to sustain foetal life from the moment of conception. Under such conditions (which may in fact never be realized) it is the mother who becomes the major threat to foetal life. The foetus can be identified as separate from the mother far earlier than imagined. Under these circumstances it appears that one branch of medicine has the capacity to 'save' foetal lives, whilst another branch, at the instigation of the mother, is terminating these lives. In such a scenario it could become a political imperative to use medicine to protect the foetus against the wishes of the mother, since technology may allow the foetus life independent of the mother. These possibilities change the parameters of the abortion debate, for feminists and others. When medical knowledge was at the stage when it could not preserve foetal life, the abortion of a foetus which could not survive outside the womb was accepted on the basis that the decision to abort really only concerned the mother's body and life. The possibility that the foetus could survive alters this balance and gives rise to the idea that life, rather than potential life, is being extinguished.

In the UK, the provisions of the Abortion Law (Amendment) Act of 1967 permit a legal abortion until the twenty-eighth week of pregnancy. It is difficult to unravel the origins of this time scale, however traditionally it would seem that a distinction has been made between different stages of pregnancy, and the foetus has been regarded differently at each stage. Hence, prior to the criminalization of all abortions in the 1861 Offences Against the Person Act, there were different attitudes towards abortions and miscarriages occurring before the foetus had 'quickened' (approximately half way through a full term pregnancy). Such attitudes may have been linked to the belief that the soul of a child did not enter it until part way through the pregnancy, or it might have reflected the stage at which the foetus began to kick and feel alive inside a woman's body. They might also have been linked to the varying degrees of physical trauma associated with a miscarriage/abortion which comes late in the pregnancy. Whatever the complex reasons, pregnancy has been viewed in terms of stages, with the different stages having different meanings — cultural and medical. Yet the development of medical technologies challenges this view of pregnancy because (in theory) a foetus can develop into personhood from any stage of development. This does not simply mean that the time limit for abortions might be moved — since it was never absolutely fixed and was always open to contestation by theoretical argument. What it ultimately means is that any abortion at all becomes problematic. It is not impossible to imagine foetuses being removed from women who do not want children, in order to be 'incubated' on behalf of infertile couples. In such a scenario the unwilling mother becomes a sort of surrogate mother. Such developments also give greater strength to the foetal rights movement because where rights are seen as naturally inherent in human life, the sooner in a preganancy that the foetus is seen as an independent life form, the sooner it should be accorded legal rights. We can envisage the mother becoming the person with the fewest rights as medics and moralists strive to preserve the foetus.

Indeed the introduction of the Abortion (Amendment) Bill in the UK in 1987 is a good example of this process (see Berer 1988). This Bill had the intention of reducing the time limit for legal abortions from 28 weeks to 18 weeks. Abortions could be carried out after this time only if the foetus was badly deformed or handicapped, if the life of the mother was threatened, or if the pregnancy arose from rape or incest. This Bill was an odd mixture of principles since it is hard to understand why a foetus conceived through rape should have less protection than any other foetus since the foetus is not responsible for its origins. This clause was, however, a partial recognition of women's feelings and in this sense significant. The main aim of the Bill, however, was to shift the balance between the rights of the foetus and the rights of the mother. Should legislation eventually follow this, or a similar Bill, it means that her rights will be curtailed earlier in the pregnancy. This fits with the growing idea that the foetus is capable of independent survival earlier in the pregnancy.

In the two decades in which Britain has had relatively liberal abortion laws there has been a major change in the moral calculus. The woman with an unwanted pregnancy is regarded in a revised light, whilst the foetus has become, with apparent medical justification, a baby with rights. It should be made clear that these medical claims are ones made by the anti-abortion campaigners rather than the medical profession as a whole, but they are none the less claims which can demonstrate a medical backing. Science it seems, can provide a moral basis for legal rights. At such a time, when women's rights are so contested, it may seem inappropriate to consider whether we should abandon a rights strategy. However, if rights claims are more likely to work against women's various interests than for them, it is important to consider the alternatives.

Kingdom (1985b, 1986) has argued against using rights in this area. Basically her argument is that rights simply produce counter claims to other rights and we have to recognize that foetal rights, children's rights, and men's rights may well have greater political purchase than women's rights in the 1980s. She argues,

THE PROBLEM OF RIGHTS

> If feminists claim that a woman has the right to reproduce, there is no obvious reason why that right should not be claimed for men too, and on traditional liberal ground of equality it would be difficult to oppose that claim.
>
> (1986: 61)

As discussed in Chapter One, men have indeed begun to make this claim in the form of individual attempts to restrict women's access to abortion. This is, in effect, claiming a right to reproduce, or at least claiming a right to decide whether a biological offspring is born. Similar counter-rights claims are being made in other areas where women are seen to have too much control over children, e.g. in the arenas of child custody and illegitimacy. I shall discuss these in detail below, but the trend towards counter-claims is unmistakable and poses a real problem for feminist strategy in the future.

The problem of rights claims producing counter-rights claims is not the only problem with formulating the issues in this way. Kingdom argues that the claim for 'a woman's right to choose' glosses over the reality of women's lives where choice is, in fact, very restricted. As Petchesky has argued,

> For a Native American woman on welfare, who every time she appears in the clinic for prenatal care is asked whether she would like an abortion, 'the right to choose an abortion' may appear dubious if not offensive.
>
> The 'right to choose' means little when women are powerless. In cultures where 'illegitimacy' is stigmatised or where female infants are devalued, women may resort to abortion or infanticide with impunity; but that option clearly grows out of female subordination.
>
> (1984: 8, 11)

The point that Petchesky and Kingdom both make is that individual choice is a problematic concept where the social relations of reproduction make choice an unrealistic option, and where abstract ideals of individual self-determination — based on individual rights — can fuel a *laissez-faire* policy which fails to protect women. Neither *laissez-faire* nor state regulation are automatically good or bad. State regulation may force women to have only one child, whilst *laissez-faire* may offer her expensive medical abortions or cheap and dangerous backstreet ones. In the former she appears to have no choice, in the latter she has Hobson's choice.

Kingdom argues that part of women's claim to abortion rights in the UK has included an implicit demand for safe abortions. It has been presumed that once a right is conceded that the state should facilitate the exercise of this right. Hence, in the UK the right to education has tended to mean the right to adequate state provided, free education. So the language of rights carries with it a presumed lever on the state. This is a lever that has worked to a greater or lesser extent since the turn of the century. However, this lever may no longer operate as political conditions change. Since 1979 rights have been increasingly transformed into individual rights. That is to say that the state feels little or no obligation to ensure that the collectivity can enjoy rights. So rights claims have a different purchase as political and economic climates change. Such considerations might lead us to consider whether victories in the field of rights claims are not rather hollow.

RIGHTS OR PLIGHTS

It is very difficult to formulate demands of the state which can command popular support and which are translatable into legislation and policy without drawing on the discourse of rights. Not only are rights part of the very history of modern social movements, they also give status to the groups or minorities who are making demands. The person demanding her rights is not a supplicant or a seeker of charity, but a person with dignity demanding a just outcome according to widely accepted criteria of fairness. Hence the transition from charity for the handicapped or medical treatment for homosexuals to rights for the disabled and gay rights reflects more than a change in terminology.

With reproductive rights, most especially abortion rights, the women's movement was instrumental in transforming the politics of abortion from a benevolent response to the 'plight' of unfortunate women, to a question of legitimate rights that should apply to all women. Although the 'plight' imagery has not faded completely, it has been a measure of political success that matters which were once the focus of charitable works are now questions of adequate provision to meet legitimate demand. The problem with abandoning the rights discourse is that the image of the desperate woman returns. She is already a major part of the debate on infertility treatment where women are not seen as having rights to treatment but are required to prove their motivation and need through a willingness to undergo immensely stressful treatment programmes. The fear is that women may have to sacrifice their dignity in the area of abortion if we abandon rights.

To some extent this fear is justified, but this is for very specific reasons. It is possible to go beyond rights claims, as I shall argue in the next section, however, with abortion and reproductive rights we have not reached a stage where these rights have become taken for granted. If there were adequate National Health Service abortion facilities in the UK and if access to such clinics was simplified, not requiring the 'approval' of two doctors before a woman could have a termination, then the focus on rights could give way to considerations about the relative usefulness of abortion facilities for ethnic minority women, or of linking a range of reproductive services for women. However, not only are facilities extremely patchy and inadequate, but campaigners have been unable to transcend the claim to rights because of regular attempts by the anti-abortion lobby to abolish or severely restrict access to abortions. Pro-choice campaigners are left with little option but to resort to right or plight claims. So while Kingdom and Petchesky are correct in drawing attention to the problems of individual rights in this area, it is extremely hard to see a way out of the dilemma.

CHILD CUSTODY AND RIGHTS

The field of child custody reveals a different history and different emphasis on rights to the field of abortion and reproduction. Certainly the issue of equal rights as between mothers and fathers has been central. As Brophy (1982) has shown, the absolute right of fathers to the legal custody of legitimate children was only very gradually influenced by mothers' claims for some rights (e.g. to access to their children) and eventually to equal rights. Women in the UK were only granted equal guardianship rights with their husbands over children in an ongoing marriage in 1973. Prior to this the husband was entitled to the last say in decisions concerning legitimate children. However, in cases of custody (and care and control) of children after divorce or separation, the absolute right of the father dwindled throughout the twentieth century as the courts became more concerned with the welfare of the child and began to recognize the work of mothers in rearing children.

So although mothers' and women's organizations argued for equal rights to guardianship during marriage and custody after divorce, the main shift in legal practice was based upon a recognition of who provided the daily care for children. Indeed, as Brophy (1985) has pointed out, the courts routinely ratify arrangements on custody which simply reflect the sexual division of childcare during mariage. Hence the award of custody to a mother after divorce is not based on a rights claims, but on the simple recognition that women, who have done the caring, will go on doing it.

The development of legal policy on custody has, therefore, not been based on competing rights so much as on the notion of the welfare of the child. This has prevented counter-rights claims to a large extent, and has brought some recognition of the work of women in caring for children. However, in the field of custody of legitimate children and the area of illegitimacy, rights claims, combined with a reinterpretation of the welfare principle, are coming to the fore once again. It is worth tracing some of the developments in these areas to clarify the issues. I shall start with illegitimacy.

Mothers of illegitimate children have automatic rights of guardianship and the right to sole custody. These rights can only be shared if the father of the child applies to a court under the 1987 Family Law Reform Act. However, the rights of the mother were only enshrined in legislation in 1975 (the Children Act) although in practice mothers were given full legal responsibility over their illegitimate children from 1841. These 'rights' were not regarded as rewards however. On the contrary, during the nineteenth century and most of the twentieth century the legal duties of unmarried mothers were very much a part of the punishment of illegitimacy. It was not until the second-wave feminist movement that some women began to realize that having children outside marriage brought certain benefits, for example legal autonomy from the putative father. The married mother is entitled to sole custody only if it has been awarded to her by a court, but the unmarried mother has it automatically. At the point at which (some) unmarried mothers began to recognize the advantages of their legal position (some) unmarried fathers began to identify their legal status as problematic. Whilst historically unmarried fathers seemed to welcome the fact that there were few legal ties between themselves and their illegitimate children, there developed a redefinition of this situation, most especially where putative fathers were paying money to children on affiliation orders, and yet had no say in the care or upbringing of the child. There grew a demand for equal rights for unmarried fathers, a demand which fell on sympathetic ears. As the Law Commission Working Paper on Illegitimacy stated, 'From a strictly legal point of view, the father of an illegitimate child is today probably at a greater disadvantage than the child itself' (1979: 14). It was increasingly argued that the 'modern' father was taking a major role in the upbringing of children, that children need fathers and that the law should do everything possible to retain fathering bonds, and that autonomous motherhood was bad for children (Green 1976; Wallerstein and Kelly 1980; Morgan 1986).

The same arguments became apparent in the area of custody after divorce. Basically there are two main elements to this. The first is a simple claim to equal rights. In fact married fathers do have equal rights, but it is argued that the courts have a preference for mothers in practice (Maidment 1981). This assumption, which is contested (Eekelaar and Clive 1977; Brophy 1989), forms the basis of an appeal for equal treatment on the level of legal custody, although it is not usually a request for the shared physical care of children. The other element of the argument is that the law should not sever the bonds between fathers and children by awarding sole custody to mothers. It is felt that marriage bonds and parenting bonds should be treated differently for the sake of the children whose development requires continued contact with fathers. The award of sole custody does not in fact sever bonds between fathers and children because the courts routinely award the non-custodial parent what is known as 'reasonable access'. However, the fathers' rights lobby has argued that this is not enough, and the symbolic statement of an order for joint custody is necessary — in the interests of children.

The fathers' rights movement (e.g. Families Need Fathers) is an example of the development of counter-rights claims. It has won the legitimacy that accompanies rights claims, but it has also occupied the terrain of children's welfare. It has argued that, in principle, to protect fathers' rights is also to protect children's welfare. This is, of course, debatable. Studies of fatherhood in the 1980s have not shown that men are taking a serious role in caring for children (Henwood *et al.* 1987; Lewis and O'Brien 1987), and some studies on children after divorce have argued that joint custody can create new opportunities for conflict and is therefore damaging to children (Goldstein *et al.* 1980). The problem is, however, that the opposing rights claims can only produce a contest in which more and more evidence is built up on each side, no resolution can be found.

The resolution of custody disputes over legitimate children at the moment is based upon a number of factors, including an assessment of who has been doing the caring, who can provide a better home, and the views of the child if she is old enough. One way out of the dilemma of the rights dispute that seems to be poised to overtake this area is the adoption of a primary carer principle. This principle would reflect the value of child care, and yet because it is not gender specific, it does not raise the problem of fathers' rights versus mothers' rights. Fathers who provide daily care for their children would then be in a strong position when it came to custody decisions. This has the benefit of not excluding men from engaging in more of the work of caring, but also reflects the reality of child care as it is presently organized. It would also meet the question of the welfare of children (cf. Smart and Sevenhuijsen 1989).

It is most important that feminist campaigns in this area avoid the trap of competing rights claims. The Rights of Women (ROW) response to the English Law Commission's (1986) working paper on custody succeeds in doing this by supporting the primary carer principle (Brophy 1987). What is important to recognize is that ROW's response acknowledges the need for legal intervention in custody decisions as a way of protecting women against husbands who seek to extend their authority over wives and children beyond divorce. It also stresses the need for law to recognize the provision of physical care, and to give greater weight to this than symbolic care or bonds. In other words this legal provision would be grounded in the reality of child care as it is currently organized, without creating obstacles to alternative forms of caring which might develop.

There is little doubt that a feminist approach which simply prioritized women's rights in this field would have little chance of influencing legal developments. Indeed, the success of the rights claim made by the fathers' rights movement is based on the fact that it is demanding an equalization of rights with mothers, not rights over children. Moreover they argue that these rights coincide with the welfare of children. In any case, the idea that parents should have rights over children is falling out of favour in the courts. Access is now regarded as a right of the child, not the parent (Re C (1985) FLR

804), whilst parental rights as a whole are now perceived as dwindling rights which diminish as children develop the capacity to make decisions for themselves (Gillick v West Norfolk and Wisbech Area Health Authority (1985) 1 All.E.R. 533). As women do not wish to formulate their demands in terms of rights *over* children, and as they cannot formulate them in terms of equal rights (it being assumed that they already have an undue level of rights), it might seem advisable to avoid the rights and counter-rights discourse which is being mounted by fathers' rights groups altogether, and to replace it with a claim based in the material reality of women's lives — namely the primary carer principle.

CONCLUDING REMARKS

In the area of child custody it would seem both possible and desirable to transcend the limitations of rights discourse. It is feasible to conceptualize a law reform which recognizes the position of the person who provides daily care for children, whilst allowing for progressive changes in childbearing patterns to develop in the future. Such a provision does not mean that there will be no conflicts over child custody, but it does provide a degree of security for the primary carer and it does not exclude fathers who might wish to share in the work of child care.

This raises the question of whether this, or a similar formulation, might get over the problem of rights in the area of abortion. A presumption that the person who will care for a child should have the greatest say in whether or not there should be a termination has some merit. However, formulated in this rather narrow way it would obviously have drawbacks. One could imagine third parties offering to care for a child resulting from an unwanted pregnancy, and thereby denying the carrying mother the choice of a termination. It therefore becomes imperative to extend the caring principle backwards into the period of the pregnancy. Himmelweit (1988) has argued that we need to reconceptualize pregnancy as a period when women are actually actively nurturing the foetus. This challenges the ideas that the foetus and the mother are simply separate entities which the rights argument does so much to sustain. If pregnancy is seen as a period of nurturing then the mother's active participation and willingness to provide care becomes central to any decisions which may have to be taken. As primary nurturers, women's material conditions would provide the basis for her being given priority in decision making. This avoids the possibility that decisions would be taken over women's heads to force them to go through with unwanted pregnancies. It does not eliminate the difficulty of such decisions, neither does it mean that women will have absolute 'choice', but it removes the risks associated with the escalation of rights claims which are operating to the detriment of women's position. As Himmelweit argues, 'While using individual rights to argue the case for abortion has proved successful in the past, we may not be reaching the limits of its usefulness, even as a defensive tactic' (Himmelweit 1988: 53). The primary carer/nurturer principle has the additional benefit of arising from the conditions of women's lives rather than from the abstract concept of rights which has been developed within the restrictive parameters of legal jurisprudence. It would seem to be a more sensitive course in that it acknowledges that, for many women, deciding to have a termination is not simply a matter of exercising their rights. It is an extremely difficult decision to make, and one which provokes hostility the more it is apparently reduced to a demand for rights which necessarily insist on taking priority over other rights.

I have tried to establish that the concept of rights has severe limitations, and may even be detrimental to the development of progressive policies supported by the Women's Movement. Yet in the area of abortion (and other reproductive concerns) the concept of rights may still have some purchase in terms of a consciousness-changing potential and in transforming women from supplicants into self-determining people. Yet if abortion rights were not subject to constant challenge by those who wish to abolish legal terminations altogether, no doubt the issue of rights could fade in significance to be overtaken by less narrow, liberal, individualist principles. The Women's Movement could then concentrate more on the provision of adequate services, swifter processing which would avoid late abortions, and more widespread information and well-women centres. The dilemma over rights is therefore a consequence of the political climate, it does not arise from a narrow interest in legal jurisprudence nor from an offensive strategy by the Women's Movement to extend rights over other persons. This position on rights is primarily a defensive one which has been forced upon the feminist movement. Under these circumstances it is difficult to abandon the

THE PROBLEM OF RIGHTS

rights discourse, yet its efficacy is undoubtedly waning and it is becoming all the more urgent to reformulate demands which are grounded in women's experiences, rather than in abstract notions like rights which are increasingly defined as unjustified and selfish prerogatives.

Bibliography

Anderson, D. and Dawson, G. (eds) (1986) *Family Portraits*, London: Social Affairs Unit.

Applebey, G. and Ellis, E. (1984) ' "Formal Investigations". The Commission for Racial Equality and the Equal Opportunities Commission as law enforcement agencies', *Public Law*, 1984: 236 – 76.

Berer, M. (1988) 'Whatever happened to "A Woman's Right to Choose"?', *Feminist Review*, 29: 24 – 37.

Bottomley, A. (1985) 'What is happening to family law? A feminist critique of conciliation', in J. Brophy and C. Smart (eds), *Women in Law*, London: Routledge & Kegan Paul.

Brophy, J. (1982) 'Parental rights and children's welfare: some problems of feminists' strategy in the 1920s', *International Journal of Sociology of Law*, 10 (2), 149 – 68.

(1985) 'Child care and the growth of power: the status of mothers in custody disputes', in J. Brophy and C. Smart (eds), *Women in Law*, London: Routledge & Kegan Paul.

(1987) '*Family law: review of child care law: custody — ROW's response*, London: Rights of Women.

(1989) 'Custody law, childcare and inequality in Britain', in C. Smart and S. Sevenhuijsen (eds), *Child Custody and the Politics of Gender*, London: Routledge.

Brophy, J. and Smart, C. (eds) (1985) *Women in Law*, London: Routledge & Kegan Paul.

Clarke, J., Cochrane, A. and Smart, C. (1987) *Ideologies of Welfare, Hutchinson:* London.

Cobbe, F. P. (1869) *Criminals, Idiots, Women, and Minors: Is the classification sound?* Manchester: A. Ireland & Co.

(1878) 'Wife torture in England', *Contemporary Review*, April: 55 – 87.

de Hondt, I. and Holtrust, N. (1986) 'The European Convention and the "Marckx Judgement" effect', *International Journal of the Sociology of Law*, 14 (3/4): 317 – 28.

Dobash, R. E. and Dobash, R. (1980) *Violence Against Wives*, Somerset: Open Books.

Eekelaar, J. and Clive, E. (1977) *Custody after Divorce*, Oxford: Centre for Socio-Legal Studies.

Ferris, P. (1966) *The Nameless*, London: Hutchinson.

Goldstein, J., Freud, A., and Solnit, A. J. (1980) *Beyond the Best Interests of the Child*, London: Burnett Books.

Green, M. (1976) *Goodbye Father*, London: Routledge & Kegan Paul.

Greenwood, V. and Young, J. (1976) *Abortion in Demand*, London: Pluto Press.

Gregory, J. (1988) *Sex, Race and the Law*, London: Sage.

Henwood, M., Rimmer, L. and Wicks, M. (1987) *Inside the Family*, London: Family Policy Studies Centre, Occasional Paper 6.

FEMINISM AND THE POWER OF LAW

Himmelweit, S. (1988) 'More than "A Woman's Right to Choose"?', *Feminist Review*, 29: 38 – 56.
Hirst, P. (1980) 'Law, socialism and rights', in P. Carlen and M. Collison (eds), *Radical Issues in Criminology*, Oxford: Martin Robertson.
(1986)'Law and sexual difference', *Oxford Literary Review*, 8 (1 and 2): 193 – 8.
Kingdom, E. (1985a) 'Legal Recognition of a Woman's Right to Choose', in J. Brophy and C. Smart (eds), *Women in Law*, London: Routledge & Kegan Paul.
(1985b) 'The sexual politics of sterilisation', *Journal of Law and Society,* 12 (1): 19 – 34.
(1986) 'The right to reproduce*', Medicine, Ethics and Law*, 32, 13th Annual Conference of Association for Legal and Social Philosophy, Leeds, 4 – 6 April.
Lewis, C. and O'Brien, M. (eds) (1987) *Reassessing Fatherhood*, London: Sage.
MacKinnon, C. (1982) 'Feminism, Marxism, method, and the state: an agenda for for theory', *Signs*, 7 (3): 515 – 44.
(1987) *Feminism Unmodified: Discourses on Life and Law*, London: Harvard University Press.
McCann, K. (1985) 'Battered women and the law: the limits of the legislation', in J. Brophy and C. Smart (eds), *Women in Law,* London: Routledge & Kegan Paul.
Maidment, S. (1981) *Child Custody: What Chance for Fathers?* Foreword from Finer Series no. 7, London: National Council for One Parent Families.
Martin, A. (1911) *Mothers in Mean Streets*, London: United Suffragists.
Mitchell, J. (1975) *Psychoanalysis and Feminism*, Harmondsworth: Penguin.
(1987) 'Women and equality', in A. Phillips (ed.), *Women and Equality*, Oxford: Blackwell.
Morgan, P. (1986) 'Feminist attempts to sack father: a case of unfair dismissal?', in D. Anderson and G. Dawson (eds), *Family Portraits*, London: Social Affairs Unit.
Norton, C. (1982) *Caroline Norton's Defence*, Chicago: Academy Chicago.
Pahl, J. (ed.) (1985) *Private Violence and Public Policy*, London: Routledge & Kegan Paul.
Petchesky, R. P. (1984) *Abortion and Woman's Choice*, London: Longman.
Pinchbeck, I. and Hewitt, M. (1973) *Children in English Society*, vol. II, London: Routledge & Kegan Paul.
Sachs, A. and Wilson, J. H. (1978) *Sexism and the Law: A Study of Male Beliefs and Judicial Bias*, Oxford: Martin Robertson.
Smart, C. (1982) 'Regulating families or legitimating patriarchy? Family Law in Britain', *International Journal of the Sociology of Law*, 10 (2): 129 – 47.
(1984) *The Ties That Bind*, London: Routledge & Kegan Paul.
Smart, C. and Sevenhuijsen, S. (eds) (1989) *Child Custody and the Politics of Gender*, London: Routledge.
Thèry, I. (1986) 'The interest of the child and the regulation of the post-divorce family', *International Journal of the Sociology of Law*, 14 (3/4): 341 – 58.
Wallerstein, J. S. and Kelly, J. B. (1980) *Surviving the Break Up*, New York: Basic Books.

[2]

ALCHEMY OR FOOL'S GOLD?

Assessing Feminist Doubts About Rights

Elizabeth Kiss

Should rights play an important role in feminist theory and practice? The answer to this question is not as simple as it first appears, for contemporary feminism has a profoundly ambiguous relationship to rights. On the one hand, so many feminist goals have been and continue to be expressed as demands for rights that their central role seems assured. Women claim rights, for example, to full participation in political, professional, and economic life; to control over their reproductive lives; and to gender equality within marriage. Rights have figured prominently in the rhetoric of the women's movement from the beginning, even if the line of descent has not been smooth: feminists have had to rebel against the Fathers of rights theory, who preached the equal dignity of all while systematically denying it to most. Nevertheless, struggles by women to vindicate rights have changed the social world, altering relationships, practices, and institutions, and affecting the way innumerable women perceive themselves. Small wonder, then, that some theorists have ascribed a transformative power to rights, a power Patricia Williams recently likened to alchemy.[1]

Contemporary Anglo-American feminist theory, on the other hand, paints a dramatically less positive picture, expressing misgivings about or even outright hostility to rights talk. I don't mean that feminist theorists deny the gains women have achieved in the last century through struggles for rights. But in looking to the future, many of them take a negative or skeptical attitude: the language of rights, they claim, cannot adequately represent women's experience; nor can it articulate the moral and political problems of greatest concern to feminists.

Indeed, the most striking aspect of feminist doubts about rights is that they come from so many otherwise disparate viewpoints. For feminism is not, of course, a unitary movement, but rather a diverse and contentious field of inquiry and action. Feminists agree on the salience of gender and on the need to overcome women's subordination. Beyond that, we disagree about almost everything—theories, histories, and strategies. Yet doubts about rights are widely shared. Feminists who embrace an "ethic of care" contrast their approach with a culturally masculine "ethic of rights." Proponents of a feminist politics of difference describe rights talk as overly abstract and impersonal. Other feminist scholars criticize rights for reflecting a selfish and atomistic view of human nature and an aggressive and conflictual view of social life; others still, for encouraging rigid, rule-bound approaches to moral and social life. Some feminist "post-structuralists" characterize rights language as inextricably bound up with hierarchies of gender and with the outdated and patriarchal fiction of a unitary self. To focus on rights, they all say, is to abandon an effective commitment to women's emancipation.

Are feminist critics of rights right? Or do they misjudge rights, or misunderstand their value for women? I will divide my response to these questions into three parts. The first two concern critiques of the concept of rights—of the images of self and society legitimated by rights and of the role of rights within political and moral argument. In the third part, I will turn to feminist concerns about their practical value.

Feminism and Rights

Connections and Boundaries

The most common feminist criticism of rights is the charge that they entail an undesirable vision of self and society. Rights talk, Nancy Hirschmann has argued in a recent example of this view, provides a language of "distrust and competition" rather than of "relationship." As rights-bearers "we are separated . . . from each other" so that "to respect a person's rights is to keep one's distance from her."[2] Rights define us as bounded selves requiring protection from the encroachments of others, who threaten our autonomy and integrity. The concept implies a moral absolutism in which the self is unencumbered by obligations to others; it legitimates aggressive selfishness and denies community. As Simone Weil complained half a century ago, rights produce a "shrill clamor of claims and counter-claims."[3]

Arguments like these lead some feminists to conclude that the moral vision of self and society associated with the concept of rights is characteristically masculine, morally unattractive, or both. Echoing Carol Gilligan's influential contrast between two moral voices, the first expressing an "ethic of care," the second an "ethic of rights," critics contrast a feminist (or feminine) self, connected to others, with a rights-bearing self, which is (or at least thinks it is) separate from others. It is no coincidence, they suggest, that Joel Feinberg, in his well-known essay "The Nature and Value of Rights," wrote that "Having rights enables us to 'stand up like men,' to look others in the eye, and to feel in some fundamental way the equal of anyone."[4] Women, these critics suggest, shouldn't strive to "stand up like men." In a few cases, feminist theorists portray the dangers of rights talk in more apocalyptic tones: the rights-bearing person is self- destructive and lives in a socially fragmented world that threatens to collapse into a "Kafkaesque nightmare of solitary individuals."[5]

This feminist critique equates the concept of a right with a claim to noninterference. In doing so it ignores the complexity and range of the idea. The guarantee to be left alone, free of interference from others, is certainly a central image of what it means to have a right. It is particularly associated with the classical liberal triad of life, liberty, and property. But it does not fit many traditional liberal rights such as rights to vote, to a fair trial, to marry or divorce, to form associations, or to enter contracts. These kinds of rights disappear from view in feminist critiques, which therefore ignore the ways in which rights express and institutionalize not only abstract and conflictual but also concrete and cooperative values. There is nothing isolating about a right to vote. Indeed, as Martha Minow has argued, the very act of ascribing rights to someone implies a moral connection to them. Rights define a community; inclusion in that community means that my interests, aspirations, and vulnerabilities matter.

The internal complexity of rights was perhaps best captured by Wesley Hohfeld in 1919 when he noted that rights can confer *liberties, immunities, claims, and powers*. The feminist view that rights separate and protect us from others conceives rights as liberties to do as we please and immunities from interference. It entirely ignores the ways in which rights give us claims on other people and powers to alter moral and legal relationships.

To be sure, the capacity of rights talk to demarcate boundaries and revoke access is not always put to morally attractive uses. Rights talk can be used to justify selfishness, privilege, and indifference in the face of human suffering. Rights have figured prominently in moral and political arguments that downplay the extent of human interdependence and that minimize the moral claims people can make on one another. Many feminists want to criticize such views and the laissez-faire arrangements they legitimate. But there is no necessary link between the concept of rights and a substantive political position like libertarianism. Moral vocabularies do not carry a no-risk guarantee; they can always be put to a range of uses.

The conceptual critique of rights is problematic even if we recast it as an explicit argument against the liberty and immunity rights celebrated by libertarians. It fails on logical grounds because liberties and immunities typically define, rather than deny, relationships. By specifying what people can do or expect from each other, such rights transform relationships, altering their internal distribution of power. Thus the claim that wives have a socially guaranteed immunity right against coerced marital sex profoundly alters marriage: it gives wives new power and transforms them into something more than performers of sexual duties. But this immunity does not deny or destroy the relationship of marriage; it redefines it.

The deeper problem with the conceptual critique is that it fails to recognize the specific importance of liberty and immunity rights to women. The boundary-marking characteristic of liberties and immunities is of critical importance to society's most vulnerable members. Many struggles central to the feminist movement, such as those to repeal the laws of coverture, to make marriage consensual, and to criminalize rape and sexual harassment are efforts by women to set their own boundaries. Marilyn Frye has argued that "total powerlessness is being unconditionally accessible . . . the slave who decides to exclude the master from her hut is declaring herself not a slave."[6] Feminists who issue sweeping denunciations of rights as too abstract, individualistic, and conflictual ignore the ways in which women need precisely these kinds of rights. Vulnerable and stigmatized groups have the most to gain from the protection that "abstract and impersonal" frameworks can provide. When a woman is still struggling for "'a room of her own,'" Frances Olsen has noted, "she is unlikely to complain that rights isolate her."

In a world in which many women are continually vulnerable to abuse, especially abuse by people claiming connection to them through bonds of love, family, religion, or culture, an uncritical celebration of "connection" at the expense of "demarcation" commits a utopian fallacy. In its strongest form—where it claims or implies that women should *abandon* the language of rights—this critique is undertaken from a politically naive perspective, distant from the lives of most women.

Reasons for Skepticism

Feminist attacks on rights because of the images of self they foster operate as surrogates for a substantive critique of unattractive political views. But why have so many feminists found this overstated critique so compelling? Why, in other words, might attention to women's lives encourage skepticism toward rights?

As many feminist theorists have pointed out, the injuries and deprivations women experience because of their gender have never been adequately captured by traditional conceptions of rights. On the contrary, these conceptions have served to obscure—even to legitimate— women's injuries. The classic example is the way relationships of inequality, abuse, and exploitation within marriage have been given moral protection by liberal conceptions of the private realm. Feminists have persuasively criticized traditional understandings of the public/private distinction, stressing how politics shapes these boundaries and how oppressive power relationships persist within them.

Yet the problem, as I've argued, is not with rights as such. Many protections critical to women are best understood as liberty or immunity rights guaranteed by the state. The problem with traditional liberal or libertarian views is their tendency to cast the state as the primary rights violator, ignoring the ways in which non-state actors (for instance, employers or spouses) can threaten freedom and well-being. So we should be skeptical about arguments that claim natural, self-evident, or in some other sense final validity for any particular version of rights theory. Rights have to be assessed by whether they actually make a difference in people's lives.

Beyond Rights: Care and Other Values

A second set of feminist doubts about rights arises from a conviction that we should pay more attention to other concepts and values. Contemporary moral and political thought, on this view, is excessively dominated by a legalist and rationalist model of moral life. It ignores or underplays the importance of activities, relationships, and attitudes that have traditionally been associated with women. Feminist writers aim to correct this one-sidedness by drawing on a critical but appreciative encounter with women's lives.

This shift in focus is best exemplified by work within the ethics of care, inspired in large part by Carol Gilligan. In her influential book *In a Different Voice*, Gilligan took issue with conventional models of moral development. She described a distinctive moral voice, which spoke of caring and relationship and which, she claimed, was more commonly employed by women. Gilligan's arguments have been taken up (as well as criticized) by feminist moral and political theorists. According to them, the mainstream of contemporary ethics has ignored or underplayed the relevance of intimate relationships in moral life in favor of a public, rational, legislative model. In the process, personal connections, and the attentiveness and responsibility that is the first virtue of human relationships like those between parents (especially, given traditional gender roles, mothers) and children, have not received the theoretical attention they deserve. In our relationships with partners, spouses, children, and friends, we tend to regard an attitude defined by and limited to a concern for the other person's rights as morally problematic: it constitutes a failure of intimacy.

Rights talk does not capture the whole of morality. This may seem an obvious point, but it is one thing to acknowledge it and quite another to develop a rich and persuasive account of other moral concepts and values. Theorists of care have begun to do this. Their writings also provide insight into the rights project, suggesting that achieving greater respect for others requires not so much a better capacity to discern universal principles as what Annette Baier has called "a progress of sentiments."[8]

Contrary to the claims of some feminist theorists, however, the ethics of care gives us no reason to abandon rights talk. We still need general principles that tell us who should receive care, why care is important, and what distinguishes its valuable from its ineffective or dangerous forms. Affirming the moral importance of personal relationships does not resolve the hard choices about caring for intimates, fellow citizens, and strangers that political communities must face. These choices require attention to the *distribution* of care and so raise questions of justice. Not surprisingly, the most promising attempts by feminist theorists to think about the policy implications of an ethic of care have paid explicit and unapologetic attention to rights. Theories of care that ignore the ways in which intimacy can be a site of inequality, exploitation, and abuse threaten to romanticize the very relationships (like marriage and family) that feminist proponents of rights sought to criticize in the first place.

Practical Questions

The feminist objection that poses the most direct challenge to rights-focused approaches to politics is also the most concrete and practical: it claims that a rights approach fails to enable women actually to change their lives. Rights will not achieve gender justice. They appear to grant a valuable moral victory but actually help to obscure women's continuing subordination. Feminists should not "abandon women to their rights." In stark contrast to Patricia Williams's argument that rights are talismans of empowerment with a transformative potential analogous to alchemy, this objection portrays rights as instruments of abandonment with the allure of fool's gold.

To abandon someone is to be indifferent to their fate, to fail to show concern for how they fare. How can a social policy based on a defense of rights constitute a failure of concern? The argument about abandonment is, I think, complex; there are a number of distinct issues at stake. I shall indicate three ways in which rights can fail us in practice: the problem may be *definitional, strategic,* or *substantive.* The first is when rights are defined in such a way that women are systematically left out of their enjoyment or exercise. The second refers to the tendency of rights advocates to be insensitive to strategic questions about how a given right can be effectively institutionalized. And the third is exemplified by situations in which people systematically do themselves harm by exercising a right. In practice, definitional, strategic, and substantive concerns are often intertwined. But it is helpful to distinguish them because they lead to different sorts of "abandonment" and pose different challenges to rights theory and policy.

(1) Focusing on rights can be unhelpful or harmful if they are defined in ways that systematically leave women out. This can happen explicitly or implicitly. The obvious example of explicit exclusion is slavery, in which some people are singled out as objects of the rights of others. In a slave system, rights are violated when a slave escapes. Other examples of exclusionary definitions are laws that once gave husbands automatic rights over their wives' property and prevented married women from owning property in their own right. Another example is the marital exception to rape laws, which makes it impossible for a husband to be charged with raping his wife.

In these cases it seems obvious that a (revisionist) concern with rights is precisely what is necessary: women must be legally recognized as having the right to own property and to consent (or not) to sexual intercourse. What is needed, in other words, is a redefinition of rights.

But the rights critique that I am exploring is formulated as an injunction against abandoning women *to* their rights. The problem is not that the women do not have the rights in question but that having them is unhelpful. This may be the case if a right is defined in a way that, despite apparent gender neutrality, excludes women—for example, a medical insurance plan that supposedly offers equal coverage for male and female workers but then excludes pregnancy-related expenses. Another example: self-defense laws that require a proportionality of force that is unrealistic in cases of unequal physical strength. Rights to equal opportunity may also be biased by gender neutral requirements that systematically exclude women, such as minimum height rules for certain jobs. Again, the challenge is to redefine rights and rules so that they are no longer exclusionary in their effects. The solution to these problems is more thinking about rights rather than less.

(2) Rights-based approaches can also abandon those they are supposed to help when they ignore crucial strategic issues about how rights can be made effective. There are at least three ways in which this can occur: first, formal equality of rights can obscure real inequalities that make it difficult or even impossible for those in less powerful positions to exercise their rights. This is the classic critique articulated with elegant irony by Anatole France: "The law, in its majesty, grants rich and poor alike an equal right to sleep under bridges." Women (like other disadvantaged groups) may have formally equal rights in the labor market but be doomed, through inequalities of wealth, education, and influence, and the invidious effects of prejudice and harassment, to lower status jobs. The gap between legal principle and practice can work the other way, too. As Kim Scheppele has argued, some West European legal systems appear to limit abortion severely, but in practice early abortions are easy to obtain. By contrast, the post-*Roe* United States affords constitutional protection for early abortions, but these have become increasingly difficult to obtain in many parts of the country.[9]

Second, a right may be vitiated or at least seriously weakened if the procedures or strategies associated with claiming it, and in particular for demanding redress when it has been violated, are themselves ineffective, intimidating, or degrading. Soviet-style legal systems provided extreme examples of this phenomenon, guaranteeing rights in the Constitution and then vitiating them through statutory clauses that required that they be exercised "in accordance with socialist values"—which, in effect, made illegal any exercise of a right in opposition to the ruling party. Less dramatic examples of this phenomenon are depressingly common. Legal and administrative procedures for claiming redress can be costly, can further victimize the victim, can enmesh victims in intimidating professional-client relationships. By focusing on individual litigation, they can also privatize and narrow claims of harm in ways that obscure the larger structural inequalities at the root of the problem. Formal procedures for dealing with rape, gender discrimination, and sexual harassment exhibit many of these features.

Third, rights strategies may concentrate on attaining ex post facto redress for violation or neglect of rights rather than on the forms of mobilization required to prevent the violation or neglect in the first place. This is also a form of abandonment, since the harm has already occurred by the time the rights strategy kicks in. Moreover, successful redress may be so indirect that it is not experienced as helpful by the person who was harmed.

Taken together, these three examples reveal how rights strategies can abandon those they are supposed to help by ignoring the social and political changes required to make rights effective. But they do not demonstrate the futility of rights as such. The lesson to be drawn from these examples is that we should conceive of rights not as commodities the law grants us, but as relationships to be established and secured.

(3) More complex problems about rights and abandonment are raised by what I have called substantive issues. Sometimes people harm themselves in exercising their rights. Of course, any moral system that values personal autonomy has to accept that people will make mistakes. A commitment to freedom means letting people make their *own* mistakes. But widespread harmful exer-

cises of a right may reflect deeper moral problems within a society.

A number of complex but important feminist issues fall into this category. For instance, women make uncoerced decisions in wealthy Western societies to starve themselves so as to attain a waif-like look. Their choices are heavily influenced, of course, by advertising and the media—but this doesn't alter the fact that they are choices. And yet the effects of these choices are clearly harmful and even, occasionally, deadly. Another example is the widespread voluntary use by women of implants for breast enlargement to "cure" the "problem" that plastic surgeons call "micromastia" (small breast size). Women who opt for breast implants are clearly exercising a right over their bodies. But the fact that an estimated 1.6 million women in the United States have chosen to enlarge their breasts for cosmetic reasons is troubling from a feminist perspective.

The issue is contextual. I can imagine a society with greater gender equality than ours in which men and women would change the shape of their body parts to please themselves and their loved ones, just as people change their hair styles. What is problematic about current practices of breast enlargement (beyond the health risks these procedures may entail) is what they reveal about women's judgments of their own worth and social value—and so about the gendered nature of self-respect in our society.

More urgent are those cases in which hierarchies and vulnerabilities of gender combine with those of class, culture, and race to constrain women's hopes and dreams in ways that are self-limiting and even self-destructive. Voluntary pregnancy by very young women who want to become mothers because they see this as the one positive accomplishment available to them (despite the fact that early parenthood is likely to limit their opportunities) provides a poignant example.

Addressing such issues requires continued efforts to widen women's private and public opportunities and rights. But there is another dimension to these cases that is not, I think, well captured by rights talk. The contemporary vernacular of rights combines a commitment to moral equality with a complex set of normative relationships—liberties, immunities, claims, and powers—designed to make that equality possible. But rights cannot, by themselves, answer the question of what equality means and requires. Rights don't provide us with the capacity to critically scrutinize our assumptions, or the ability to imagine and pursue better things. Feminists must also address substantive moral and cultural questions about women's (and men's) aspirations and desires, their sense of what is good and what can give meaning to their lives.

Feminism represents a profound cultural criticism and a radical dream, a dream of a world that has overcome women's social subordination. In their efforts to articulate this critique and to realize this dream, feminists need to confront issues that transcend the realm of rights. But it is misguided and dangerous for them to turn their back on rights in the process. □

Notes

[1] Patricia Williams, *The Alchemy of Race and Rights* (Harvard University Press, 1991).

[2] Nancy Hirschmann, *Rethinking Obligation* (Cornell University Press, 1992), pp. 232, 286.

[3] Simone Weil, *Selected Essays: 1934-1943*, ed. Richard Rees (Oxford University Press, 1962), p. 21.

[4] Joel Feinberg, "The Nature and Value of Rights," *Rights, Justice, and the Bounds of Liberty* (Princeton University Press, 1980), p. 151.

[5] Elizabeth Fox-Genovese, *Feminism Without Illusions* (University of North Carolina Press, 1991), p. 32.

[6] Marilyn Frye, *The Politics of Reality: Essays in Feminist Theory* (Freedom, California: The Crossing Press, 1983), pp. 103-4.

[7] Frances Olsen, "Statutory Rape: A Feminist Critique of Rights Analysis," *University of Texas Law Review* 387 (1984).

[8] Annette Baier, "Hume, the Women's Moral Theorist?" in Eva Kittay and Diana Meyers, eds., *Women and Moral Theory* (Rowman and Littlefield, 1987), p. 40.

[9] Kim Lane Scheppele, "Constitutionalizing Abortion," paper presented to the American Political Science Association, Chicago, September 1992, p. 3.

[3]

WHEN JUSTICE REPLACES AFFECTION: THE NEED FOR RIGHTS

JEREMY WALDRON*

I.

Why do individuals need rights? In a world crying out for a greater emphasis on fraternity and communal responsibility in social life, what is the point of an institution that legitimates the making of querulous and adversarial claims by individuals against their fellows? If human relations can be founded on affection, why is so much made in modern jurisprudence of formal and impersonal rights as a starting point for the evaluation of laws and institutions? In answering these questions, I take as my starting point a disagreement between the philosophers Kant and Hegel regarding the role of rights in marriage.

In his work on the philosophy of law, Immanuel Kant likened marriage to a contract between two people for "life-long reciprocal possession of their sexual faculties."[1] He was quick to add that, though it is a contract, it is "not on that account a matter of arbitrary will"; rather, it is a matter of necessity for anyone who wants to enjoy another person sexually. In sexual relations, Kant says, one party is used as an object by the other, and that *prima facie* is incompatible with the basic "Law of Humanity" prohibiting the use of any human agent as a mere means to the satisfaction of one's desires. That situation can be rectified "only . . . under the one condition that as the one Person is acquired by the other as a *res*, that same Person equally acquires the other reciprocally, and thus regains and re-establishes the rational Personality."[2] Kant went on to say that the reciprocity of rights that this solution presupposes leads to a requirement of monogamy, because in a polygamous regime, one of the partners may be giving more to the other than the

* Acting Professor of Law, University of California, Berkeley. B.A. Otago 1974, LL.B. Otago, 1978, D.Phil. Oxford 1986. An earlier version of this article was delivered as a public lecture at the University of Michigan in December 1986. I would like to thank Daniela Gabetti, Alan Gibbard, Don Herzog, John Kingdon, Larry Mohr, Peter Railton, Donald Regan, Jonathan Simon, and Kim Scheppele for their suggestions. I am also grateful to Kristin Luker, Philip Selznick, Judith Squires, and Susan Sterett, for conversations and comments on these issues.

1. I. KANT, THE PHILOSOPHY OF LAW: AN EXPOSITION OF THE FUNDAMENTAL PRINCIPLES OF JURISPRUDENCE AS THE SCIENCE OF RIGHT 110 (W. Hastie trans. 1887).
2. *Id.* at 110-11.

other is to her.[3] The contract has got to be a matter of *equal* right in order to satisfy the fundamental test of respect for persons.

Sometimes it seems that Kant was not content with this contractualist characterization of marriage. In one place, he went further and argued that the rights involved are like rights of property:

> The Personal Right thus acquired is at the same time, real in kind. This characteristic of it is established by the fact that if one of the married Persons run away or enter into the possession of another, the other is entitled, at any time, and incontestably, to bring such a one back to the former relation, as if that Person were a Thing.[4]

Many have thought that such ideas are perhaps better ignored in the overall assessment of Kant's philosophy of morals.

The Kantian view of marriage as a purely contractual arrangement was adamantly repudiated by Hegel—"shameful," he said, "is the only word for it."[5] Hegel conceded that marriage originates in a contract between two people and that therefore, in its dependence on their say-so to get it underway, it has some of the contingency and "arbitrariness" that are normally associated with contractual relations.[6] But, according to Hegel, rights and contract are far from telling us the complete story about the institution. For one thing, the public character of the marriage celebration (whether the ceremony is religious or civil)—the procedures of notification, licensing, witnessing, solemnization, registration, and so on—attest to a significance that goes far beyond a mere meeting of the wills or "the mutual caprice" of the prospective partners.[7] For another thing, the parties celebrate their marriage not merely as a *quid pro quo* but in order to attain a union of desire, affection, interest, and identity that goes far beyond anything that could possibly be specified in even the fine print of a contract. There is a world of difference, on this view, between the Kantian "contract for reciprocal use" and the "love, trust, and common sharing of their existence as individuals" which is what married partners com-

---

3. *Id.* at 111-12.
4. *Id.* at 111.
5. G.W.F. Hegel, Philosophy of Right 58, at ¶ 75 (T. Knox trans. 1967).
6. *Id.* at 111-12, at ¶ 162.
7. *Id.* at 113-14, at ¶ 164; *id.* at 262, at ¶ 161[A].

mit themselves to.[8] As Hegel puts it, if marriage begins in an agreement, "it is precisely a contract to transcend the standpoint of contract," that is, to transcend the standpoint of "individual self-subsistent units" making claims against one another, which is how contracting parties are normally understood.[9]

There are two distinct aspects to this critique. On the one hand, Hegel is attacking Kant's specific use of *contract* to characterize the marriage bond; the suggestion is that *this* legal concept is inappropriate in the particular context (though I imagine he would take even greater exception to Kant's use of the terminology of property!). On the other hand, he is also attacking the much broader target of Kant's pervasive legalism: the temptation, to which Kantians so often succumb, to reduce social institutions of all kinds to some formal array of legalistic rights and duties. Here it is not so much the idea of *contract*, but the more general idea of *a right*, that is out of place. This is the aspect of Hegel's critique that I will focus on, because I think it raises interesting and far-reaching issues about liberal rights-based approaches to social and communal relations.

Few of us would disagree with Hegel's basic point: Claims of right should have little part to play in the context of a normal loving marriage. If we hear one partner complaining to the other about a denial or withdrawal of conjugal *rights*, we know that something has already gone wrong with the interplay of desire and affection between the partners. The same would be true if people started talking about their *right* to a partner's fidelity, their *right* to be freed from child-care or domestic chores once in a while, their equal *right* to pursue a career, their *right* to draw equally on the family income, and so on. In each case, the substance of the claim may be indispensable for a happy and loving marriage in the modern world. But it is its presentation *as a claim*—that is, as an entitlement that one party presses peremptorily, querulously, and adversarially against the other—that would lead to our misgivings. We would certainly look for all these things in a marriage, but we would hope to see them upheld and conceded, not as matters of right, but as the natural outcome of the most intimate mutual concern and respect brought to bear by the partners on the common problems that they face. Even if rights like these were acknowledged as the

8. *Id.* at 112, at ¶ 163.
9. *Id.*

ground-rules of the relationship in some sort of formal agreement drawn up by the partners, there would still be something unpleasant about their *asserting* them as rights or, as the phrase goes, "*standing on their rights*" in the normal functioning of the relationship. Such behavior would be seen as a way of blocking and preventing warmth and intimacy, replacing relatively unbounded and immediate care and sensitivity with rigid and abstract formulas of justice.

The point can be generalized: To stand on one's rights is to distance oneself from those to whom the claim is made; it is to announce, so to speak, an opening of hostilities; and it is to acknowledge that other warmer bonds of kinship, affection, and intimacy can no longer hold. To do this in a context where adversarial hostility is inappropriate is a serious moral failing.[10] As Hegel put it in an Addition to the *Philosophy of Right*: "To have no interest except in one's formal right may be pure obstinacy, often a fitting accompaniment of a cold heart and restricted sympathies. It is uncultured people who insist most on their rights, while noble minds look on other aspects of the thing."[11]

II.

Is there not anything, then, to be said for the Kantian position? I think there is this. Though marriage is certainly more than a matter of rights and correlative duties, and though one will not expect to hear claims of right in a happily functioning marriage, nevertheless the strength and security of the marriage commitment in the modern world depends in part on there being an array of legalistic rights and duties that the partners know they can fall back on, if ever their mutual affection fades. That is the idea I will consider in this paper.

I want to explore this idea against the background of some criticisms that have been made of rights-based liberalism. In

10. *See, e.g.*, Young, *Dispensing with Moral Rights*, 6 POLITICAL THEORY 63, 68 (1978):

> [O]ften not only is such an appeal to rights otiose, but it is morally jarring (rather than dignified) to insist on one's due . . . . This means of protecting what are conceived to be legitimate interests is, even if understandable, not morally desirable since it does nothing to mend the ruptured relations.

See also Louden, *Rights Infatuation and the Impoverishment of Theory*, 17 J. VALUE INQUIRY 87, 99 (1983) ("In extreme cases [of rights infatuation], a severe form of moral inertia takes over, at which point it becomes difficult to get the rights infatuationist to do anything but claim his rights.").

11. Hegel, *supra* note 5, at 235, at ¶ 37[A].

recent years, liberal theories have come under attack from socialists and communitarians for their implausible suggestion that the bonds of social life should be thought of as constituted primarily by the rights and rights-based relations of initially atomistic individuals.[12] I will consider how much of that attack would be mitigated or refuted if liberals were to concede that the structure of rights is not constitutive of social life, but instead to be understood as a position of fall-back and security in case other constituent elements of social relations ever come apart. To go back to the marriage example, I will suggest that there is a need for an array of formal and legalistic rights and duties, not to constitute the affective bond, but to provide each person with secure knowledge of what she can count on in the unhappy event that there turns out to be no other basis for her dealings with her erstwhile partner in the relationship. The importance of rights ought to be much easier to defend from this somewhat less inflated position.

But the argument is not merely a strategic retreat for liberals. Liberals are entitled to ask their communitarian critics how this important function of security is to be performed in a community that repudiates rights and legalism, and under the auspices of a theory that gives individual rights no part to play at all. Is it to be supposed that the intimate and affective relations that characterize various forms of community will never come apart, that affections will never change, and that people will never feel the urge to exit from some relationships and initiate others? If so, communitarianism in the modern world presents itself as naive or desperately dangerous, and probably both. Or is it supposed that a society will be pervaded by such a strong background sense of affection and responsibility, that we will be able to afford to allow people to change their intimate relations as they please without any attempt to articulate formally the terms on which they are to do so? That, for example, in the marriage case, we can somehow count on goodwill to provide for the continued care of person's partner or children if they need it? Again, if this is the view that communitarians rely on, they are dangerously underestimating both the possibility for

12. *See, e.g.*, LIBERALISM AND ITS CRITICS (M. Sandel ed. 1984) (hereinafter LIBERALISM); M. SANDEL, LIBERALISM AND THE LIMITS OF JUSTICE (1982); A. MACINTYRE, AFTER VIRTUE: A STUDY IN MORAL THEORY (1981); Taylor, *Atomism*, in POWERS, POSSESSIONS AND FREEDOM: ESSAYS IN HONOUR OF C.B. MACPHERSON (A. Kontos ed. 1979); R. UNGER, KNOWLEDGE AND POLITICS (1976).

things to go wrong between human beings, and the human need for some sort of background guarantee, on which, in the last resort, one can rely in the face of that possibility.

Before continuing it may be worth saying a word or two about *communitarianism*. The new communitarianism is by no means a rigidly defined body of thought; the term refers rather to a trend in modern critiques of liberal political philosophy. In the work of writers like Roberto Unger, Michael Sandel, Alasdair Macintyre, and Charles Taylor, liberal theories of rights have been attacked for their individualism, for the way they parade the desires and interests of the human individual as the be-all and end-all of politics, at the expense of notions like community, fraternity and a shared social good.[13] It is not that liberals ignore those values altogether; but it is alleged that they give them only an instrumental significance or treat them merely as particular moral causes which individuals may or may not espouse. Partly it is a matter of perspective on society. For liberal theories of rights, the point of reference is the "unencumbered" individual, who is free to shrug off his communal and other allegiances whenever he chooses. The relatively unaffectionate and formalistic language of rights and contract theory is said to be an expression of his essential detachability from affective commitments; its formalism expresses the facts deemed most important about his moral status, without reference to any content or community. Communitarians, on the other hand, take as their point of reference the shared lives of people who regard themselves as, in Sandel's words, "defined to some extent by the community of which they are a part"[14]—people who cannot imagine a standpoint of political judgment over and above their particular communal identity.

It is important to stress that community here is not an *abstract* idea; one's communal identity depends on the particularity of one's past. As Macintyre puts it, "I am someone's son or daughter, someone else's cousin or uncle; I am a citizen of this or that city, a member of this or that guild or profession."[15] Apart from the particularity of these attachments, there is said to be no standpoint for abstract political thought, communal or

13. There is a good general discussion of the communitarian critique in Gutman, *Communitarian Critics of Liberalism*, 14 Phil. & Pub. Aff. 308 (1985).

14. *See* Sandel, *Introduction*, Liberalism, *supra* note 12, at 5.

15. A. Macintyre, *supra* note 12, 204-05. *See also* M. Sandel, *supra* note 12, at 179.

individual. The discourse of this communitarian politics, then, will be informal and engaged rather than impersonal and abstract. Political thought will be a matter of the discovery and recognition of the particular social selves we are, rather than the deliberate choice and articulation of abstract principles of right. There are also other strands in the communitarian literature—notably a strand of civic republicanism that is by no means so clearly incompatible with the traditional liberal point of view—but these are the ones I deal with in this article.[16]

III.

I chose marriage as my starting point because I wanted to illustrate two things. The first is the claim I have already outlined. The function of matrimonial law, with its contractual rules and formulas and rigid rights and duties, is not necessarily to constitute the marriage bond; its function is to provide a basis on which affective ties can be converted into legal responsibilities in the unhappy situation where affection can no longer be guaranteed.

But I also want to develop a second point. The structure of impersonal rules and rights not only provides a background guarantee; it also furnishes a basis on which people can act to initiate *new* relations with other people even from a position of alienation from the affective bonds of existing attachments and community. Impersonal rules and rights provide a basis for new beginnings and for moral initiatives which challenge existing affections, driving them in new directions or along lines that might seem uncomfortable or challenging to well-worn traditional folkways. Such initiatives may be valued on social as well as individual grounds: Not only do they make life bearable for alienated individuals by allowing them to start out in new directions, but they also provide a dynamic for social progress by challenging the existing types of relationships with new ones.[17] If we value these initiatives for either or both of these reasons, we have to ask: Under what conditions are they possible in human affairs? The traditional liberal reply is that people

16. For a discussion of civic republicanism, see H. Arendt, On Revolution (1973), B. Smith, Politics and Remembrance: Republican Themes in Machiavelli, Burke, and Tocqueville (1985), and *Civic Republicanism and its Critics*, 14 Political Theory 423 (1986) (symposium).

17. For the importance of new beginnings in human affairs, see H. Arendt, The Human Condition 177-78 (1958).

must be free from legal coercion and social pressure so they can try out new experiments in living.[18] But other conditions may be necessary besides negative freedom. Can people take new initiatives in a social vacuum? Once men and women repudiate the existing affections of their community, are they in a position to develop new types of relationship without any help from social structures at all? If the answer is no, then there is a reason to ensure that *some* social structures at least should be established on a basis which distances them somewhat from existing communal affections. That may be the job of legal rules and legal rights: to constitute a non-affective framework for actions which are novel from a communal point of view. Without some such impersonal framework, the creative human desire for new initiatives faces a terrifying vacuum: If it is not to be stifled by existing community, it must take its chances in a world beyond community. But that would be a world unstructured by *any* basis for security and expectation.

I want to illustrate this with an example. At a superficial level, Shakespeare's *Romeo and Juliet* is a noble and lamentable tragedy of star-crossed "death-marked" love:[19] The fates bring the lovers together and, at the end, it is the fates who cruelly divide them. But *Romeo and Juliet* can also be read as a deeper text about the dangers that beset a new and unforeseen social initiative—in this case a romantic initiative—in circumstances where the only available structures for social action are those embedded in the affections and disaffections of the existing community. The bonds which tie together the members of the respective clans of Capulet and Montague, and which divide the clans from one another, are such as to rule out of the question the union that the young lovers seek. Driven by their need for each other, Juliet and Romeo seek to create a marriage for themselves outside those inhibiting bonds.

The tragedy is that this cannot reliably be done in that social world, for there is no framework of public or impersonal law, standing apart from communal attachments, of which people can avail themselves in circumstances like these. Even the apparent voice of order in the play—Prince Escalus—is presented as head of a third clan and himself deeply implicated in the dis-

18. J.S. Mill, On Liberty (Indianapolis ed. 1955).

19. W. Shakespeare, *Prologue, Romeo and Juliet*, in The Complete Works 379 (S. Wells & G. Taylor eds. 1986).

affection between Capulet and Montague.[20] So the lovers have to take their chances in a world outside the public realm. The arrangements they make are of necessity covert and clandestine. There is no public and hence no visible and reliable way of co-ordinating actions and expectations. There is no way of counting on any but their own resources in a world where formally and publicly their relationship does not exist. Secret letters go astray. Another marriage is contracted for Juliet because it is thought this one did not exist.[21] Communications break down, actions are misread, and timing fails as the lovers try to act in concert in a world that provides no structure or landmarks for co-ordination. Their only hope of success is for Juliet to assume "the form of death" to the social world in which she was brought up, and to resurrect herself in the giddy space of a world beyond the city walls.[22]

On the superficial reading, the lovers are cursed by wretched bad luck in the final Act. If only Friar Lawrence's letter had got through, if only Balthazar had seen Friar Lawrence before riding to talk with Romeo, if only Juliet had awoken a minute or two before Romeo took the poison—the tragedy might have been averted, and everyone might have lived happily ever after. But on the deeper reading, misunderstanding, lack of co-ordination, failure in planning and communication, mistiming, and eventual catastrophe are more or less inevitable. For action, there is, as Romeo discovers, "no world without Verona walls."[23] There is nothing outside the structures of their warring clans that these two can rely on—no points of salience, no common framework of expectations, and no public knowledge—just their own meagre resources and those of their understandably pusillanimous allies. Man is a social animal; only a

20. *Id.* at 412 (Act V, Scene 3—Prince Escalus: "And I, for winking at your discords too / Have lost a brace of kinsmen. All are punished.").

21. *Id.*, 402-03 (Act III, Scene 5):

> NURSE: . . . Romeo
> Is banished, and all the world to nothing
> That he dares ne'er come back to challenge you.
> Or, if he do, it needs must be by stealth.
> . . . .
> Beshrew my very heart,
> I think you are happy in this second match,
> For it excels your first; or if it did not,
> Your first is dead, or 'twere as good he were
> As living hence and you no use of him.

22. *Id.* at 412 (Act V, Scene 3).

23. *Id.* at 398 (Act III, Scene 3).

god can live outside a state. We do not have the resources in ourselves to co-ordinate our activity without some social structures.[24]

There are two morals one can draw from this story. The first is cautionary: Don't fall in love with someone from a hostile clan, or in other words, "Don't ever try to act outside the structures of your community." But the second moral, and the one I want to draw upon, is addressed not to young lovers, but to those of our colleagues who call for a return to a particularist communitarian form of politics: "Don't urge us to identify the structures for social action too closely with the affections of existing communities. For in a human world, the limits of those affections may sometimes leave people with nowhere to go, and no reliable basis on which they can take new initiatives or constitute bearable lives for themselves."

What this implies is that it is important for there to be a structure of rights that people can count on for organizing their lives, a structure which stands somewhat apart from communal or affective attachments and which can be relied on to survive as a basis for action no matter what happens to those attachments. In this regard, we are not just talking about a structure of claim-rights, but also a structure of what Hohfeld called "powers," or what Hart called secondary rules of change: some basis on which individuals or groups can reconstitute their relations to take new initiatives in social life without having to count on the affective support of the communities to which they have hitherto belonged.[25] Of course, we need not parade this as the most desirable basis for social action. The Veronan equivalent of marriage by a judge in a civil ceremony, which ought to have been available to Romeo and Juliet when their families failed to provide the necessary support, would seem a cold and arid setting for a wedding, compared to the lavish ceremony which a loving community might have made available to them. That the liberal can concede. The point is that the civil ceremony would have been better than nothing—better, that is, than the lovers being driven by the disaffection of their families

24. *Cf.* Aristotle, *Politics*, in 2 THE COMPLETE WORKS OF ARISTOTLE (J. Barnes ed. 1984) (Book I, Chapter 2) ("[M]an is by nature a political animal. And he who by nature and not by mere accident is without a state, is either a bad man or above humanity . . . .").

25. *See* W. HOHFELD, FUNDAMENTAL LEGAL CONCEPTIONS AS APPLIED IN JUDICIAL REASONING (1923); H.L.A. HART, THE CONCEPT OF LAW 27 n. (1961).

to take their chances in an outside world devoid of public structures upon which they could finally and in the last resort rely.[26]

IV.

I have used the marriage example to illustrate these points, but I do not want to give the impression that marriage is my sole concern. There are other areas of law and politics that can be used to make related points about the indispensibility of individual rights.

One is the area of welfare rights. It is common to hear laments about the loss of face-to-face charity and caring, whether by individuals or in family groups, and its replacement in modern society by more impersonal systems of welfare agencies and formalized welfare entitlements. Certainly, there is a very important debate to be had about the nature and extent of our provision for need in society— one that I cannot go into here. But it may be worth pointing out why the replacement of face-to-face caring by more impersonal structures is not altogether the disaster that some people make it out to be.

Consider care for the elderly. Age brings with it a certain amount of dependence: As one gets older, one's capacity to secure an income diminishes while one's needs increase. There have been societies, perhaps ours in an earlier age, or China, both now and in the past, where the old have been able to count on the support of their adult children as their needs increase and their capacities diminish. That mode of caring strikes us as an attractive one, for it is based on ties of kinship, affection, and love, and it reciprocates in an almost symmetrical way the care that the parent once lavished on her children.

Moreover, it has the advantage of being personal: The care is between this particular old person and her children (who can be sensitive to the detail of her needs), rather than between old people and young people in general. Still, there are good reasons in the modern world why many old people feel less than confident about relying on their children's support. One problem is demographic: Even in kin-oriented societies such as China, there are proportionately fewer working adults to support an increasing population of the aged. But other problems

26. These reflections on *Romeo and Juliet* were first stimulated by Germaine Greer. *See* Greer, *Romeo and Juliet*, in 1 SHAKESPEARE IN PERSPECTIVE 22-23 (R. Sales ed. 1982).

go deeper into modern life. People's lives and careers are complex, shifting, and often risky and demanding. They cannot always guarantee a secure base for themselves, let alone provide an assurance of security for their parents. And people are torn by other motives in modern life which, though not intrinsically hostile to the provision of this care, make it somewhat less certain that this will be something they necessarily want to do.

To insist, then, in a communitarian spirit, that care for the aged should remain the responsibility of the family, we would have to accept either or maybe both of two costs. We would have to place limits on the *other* demands that adult children would be permitted to respond to, the risks they could run, and the mobility they could seek. (I suspect, by the way, that in the present state of things, this would involve limiting once again the capacity of *women* to move and flourish outside the home. A great many of the concerns about communitarianism articulated in this paper are above all *feminist* concerns.) Or, if we were not prepared to do that (and maybe even if we were), we would have to accept the cost of exposing the elderly to a certain amount of insecurity and uncertainty in addition to the other burdens of their age. Neither in this country nor in Europe have people been willing to accept those costs. Instead, we have opted for less personal, less affective modes of care. People are encouraged to purchase an income for their old age in the marketplace, so they can rely on a pension check from a finance house even if they cannot rely on the warm support of their children. And, as a fall-back position, the impersonal agencies of the state guarantee an income, either to all the elderly, or to those who have not made or have not been able to make impersonal provision for themselves. Thus, although we may not care for them on a face-to-face basis, we both provide impersonal structures to enable them to care for themselves, and respond collectively and impersonally as a society to the rights that they have to our support. Our choice of this impersonality is well described in an English context by Michael Ignatieff in his book, *The Needs of Strangers*:

> As we stand together in line at the post office, while they cash their pension cheques, some tiny portion of my income is transferred into their pockets through the numberless capillaries of the state. The mediated quality of our relationship seems necessary to both of us. They are dependent on the state, not upon me, and we are both glad of it. . . . My

> responsibilities towards them are mediated through a vast division of labour. In my name a social worker climbs the stairs to their rooms and makes sure they are as warm and as clean as they can be persuaded to be. When they get too old to go out, a volunteer will bring them a hot meal, make up their beds, and if the volunteer is a compassionate person, listen to their whispering streams of memory. When they can't go on, an ambulance will take them to the hospital, and when they die, a nurse will be there to listen to the ebbing of their breath. It is this solidarity among strangers, this transformation through the division of labour of needs into rights and rights into care that gives us whatever fragile basis we have for saying that we live in a moral community.[27]

It is not that a system of rights is the only imaginable way in which needs could be dealt with in a caring society. We could set things up in a way that encouraged old people to rely on the warm and loving support of their families. But even if we did that, I think we would still want to set up a system of rights as a fall-back—as a basis on which some *assurance* of support could be given, without risking the insecurity, resentment and indignity of leaving the elderly completely at "the uncertain mercy of their sons and daughters."[28]

V.

These points suggest some more general reflections about the distribution of resources and well-being. There is a passage in the work of Karl Marx, and a tradition of Marxist thought, which criticizes philosophers who emphasize justice and individual rights in their accounts of social distribution. In his *Critique of the Gotha Programm*, Marx heaped derision on even egalitarian theories as proposals for the distribution of social wealth. He regarded all such proposals as "obsolete verbal rubbish"[29] so far as the reform of capitalism was concerned, and as too utopian and naive for the early stages of socialist construction. He was, however, prepared to predict that a time would come when people would lose their concern for justice and rights altogether:

> In a higher phase of communist society . . . after labour has become not only a means of life but life's prime want; after

27. M. IGNATIEFF, THE NEEDS OF STRANGERS 9-10 (1984).
28. *Id.* at 17.
29. Marx, *Critique of the Gotha Programme*, in KARL MARX: SELECTED WRITINGS 569 (D. McLellan ed. 1977) (hereinafter MARX).

> the productive forces have also increased with the all-round development of the individual, and all the springs of co-operative wealth flow more abundantly—only then can the narrow horizon of bourgeois right be crossed in its entirety and society inscribe on its banners: From each according to his ability, to each according to his needs![30]

The suggestion here is precisely *not* that in a communist society people would have a *right* to the satisfaction of their needs. On the contrary, in a communist society we would be able to do away with rights as such altogether, and goods and services would be supplied naturally to needs and wants as they arose without the mediation of rigid individual entitlements. On the basis of this sort of talk, rights and rigid formulas of law have been regarded by many Marxists as essentially bourgeois forms destined to disappear with the rest of bourgeois society, including the restricted conditions of production which make that society possible. Bourgeois philosophers are therefore engaged, they say, in asking the wrong questions when they worry about what rights people would have in an ideal society.[31]

Some communitarians have echoed this theme. Sandel takes John Rawls to task for insisting on the primacy of distributive justice when Rawls himself acknowledges that justice makes sense only relative to circumstances in which resources are scarce and human sympathies limited. Sandel says it is easy to imagine small-scale communities in which neither of those conditions obtained: communities in which claims of justice and right would be replaced by spontaneous affection. In such a community, he says,

> Individual rights and fair decision procedures are seldom invoked, not because injustice is rampant but because their appeal is preempted by a spirit of generosity in which I am rarely inclined to *claim* my fair share. Nor does this generosity necessarily imply that I receive out of kindness a share that is equal to or greater than the share I would be entitled to under fair principles of justice. I may get less. The point is not that I get what I would otherwise get, only more spontaneously, but simply that questions of what I get and what I am due do not loom large in the context of this overall way

30. *Id.* at 568-69.

31. For a general discussion of the place of rights and justice in Marx's thought, see A. BUCHANAN, MARX AND JUSTICE: THE RADICAL CRITIQUE OF LIBERALISM (1982); MARX, JUSTICE, AND HISTORY (M. Cohen ed. 1980).

of life.[32]

I do not want to embark on a discussion of how far-fetched the Marxian idea of the "abolition of scarcity" is. We should note, however, that for the purposes of this argument, scarcity refers simply to the existence of opportunity costs in the use of resources, and that many economists would regard the idea of the "abolition" of opportunity costs as incoherent rather than merely improbable.[33] Nor do I want to make any comment on the changes in human sympathies that Sandel and Marx are relying on, except to say that as long as goods are scarce in the sense just outlined, anything other than a situation in which each person's altruistic affections and strategies overlap perfectly with those of everyone else is going to be a situation in which competition for resources and hence the circumstances of justice continue to prevail.

If anything, the competition may be more intense if we all become altruists. History indicates that passionate altruists tend to struggle much more ferociously for their ideals than those who are merely self-interested. And surely perfect uncompetitive altruism is unlikely (to say the least!) in a world in which, we are told, concern for others will be situated concretely in the particularity of each person's life rather than given abstractly as a general formula like the principle of utility.[34]

But even if we grant Sandel and Marx their assumptions, an unrepentant bourgeois philosopher might want to insist that there is *still* a place for rights in Marx's prosperous higher phase of communism and in Sandel's affectionate *gemeinschaft*. For it matters to people that they and their loved ones have enough to eat, it matters to them that they have access to at least some of the resources necessary for the pursuit of their own projects and aspirations, and it is likely to go on mattering sufficiently for them to want some greater *assurance* of that

32. M. SANDEL, *supra* note 12, at 33. *Cf.* J. RAWLS, A THEORY OF JUSTICE 126 n. (1971), and D. HUME, A TREATISE ON HUMAN NATURE 485 n. (L. Selby-Bigge ed. 1888).

33. *Cf.* A. NOVE, THE ECONOMICS OF FEASIBLE SOCIALISM 15-20 (1983). Marx's view was that the abolition of scarcity was a crucial prerequisite for socialism because without it and without what he called "a great increase in productive power . . . want is merely made general, and with destitution the struggle for necessities and all the old filthy business would necessarily be reproduced." Marx, *The German Ideology*, in MARX, *supra* note 29, at 171.

34. *See* citations *supra* note 15. For an explanation of how collective action problems may arise even among altruists, see D. PARFIT, REASONS AND PERSONS (1984).

other than merely the affections of their fellow citizens. Even if we concede that distribution can take place on the basis of spontaneous co-operation in circumstances of plenty, and even if we concede that it is desirable that it should take place on that basis, people will want some assurance that the circumstances that make this possible are going to continue. I cannot imagine that in any conceivable society on earth this is something they will be able to take for granted; everything we know warns us of the dangers of such trust and complacency, touching no doubt though it is. (Again the background question is: Are the socialists and communitarians asking us to think concretely or in terms of abstract possibilities?) So rights once again have at least a fall-back function to perform. People might want to have some sense of what they *could* claim as their due in the unhappy though no doubt unlikely case that goods become scarce, or affections turn out to be limited after all.[35]

VI.

Interestingly, it is not only welfare rights that perform this fall-back function. A similar analysis is possible in the area of market relations—the area that liberals and their critics see as the domain *par excellence* of individual rights—as Marx described it, "a very Eden of the innate rights of man . . . the exclusive realm of Freedom, Equality, Property and Bentham."[36] At first sight, it is tempting to say about markets, not what we have said so far about rights—that they involve fall-back positions for social relations constituted by affection or community—but rather that markets involve an area of social relations that *is* actually constituted by structures of contract and individual right, an area in which there is no prominent component of affection or community at all. We know, of course, that this is

35. This raises an interesting question. When a theorist of justice evaluates the distribution of wealth in society, should she be concerned with what people are entitled to, or with what they actually get? The idea of rights as fall-back guarantees suggests the former rather than the latter, because what people actually get may depend on an interplay of factors, including affective factors, which are independent of their rights. But still there are reasons to be cautious about concentrating too exclusively on formal entitlements. Such concentration can too easily lead us to look only at *legal* entitlements, ignoring the fact that certain non-legal structures in society may determine not only what people actually get but also what they can rely on *in extremis*. There may also be a lot of interplay between people's sense of their formal entitlements and their sense of what they actually receive. Expectations are not fixed, and what may originally have been given out of affection may come in time to be regarded as a guarantee.

36. 1 K. Marx, Capital 280 (E. Mandel ed. 1976).

sociologically naive: A market cannot exist without an ethic of fidelity and without some underpinning for its property entitlements.[37] But still, the ethics, the ideology, and the force that make markets possible are not much more than what is presupposed by the idea of rights anyway, and the point is that they do not necessarily include any of the more robust and substantial ideas and affections associated in the modern mind with the idea of community.

Certainly the higher levels of the capitalist market—secondary capital markets, commodity markets, international trade and so on—have this character of being mainly rights-constituted (though even there the network of individual rights is supplemented by more or less rigid codes of professional honor among those who trade in them). Similarly, in more mundane markets, we buy and sell in department stores with little more to bond us to our market partners than reciprocal self-interest and the laws of contract. In these contexts, then, it is true that rights do not *underwrite* affective arrangements; rather, they *make possible* an enormous variety of arms-length dealings between people who are in almost all other respects strangers to one another.

The point can be put in terms of an analogy with the *Romeo and Juliet* argument. If we were limited to the structures of *gemeinschaft*, if there were a sense that economic transactions and economic co-operation had always to be predicated upon substantial and affectionate solidarity, then the result would indeed be a warm and caring society, but also a desperately primitive and impoverished one. Human life would not be solitary, but many of the devices by which we have succeeded in mitigating its poverty, its nastiness, its brutishness, and its brevity would be limited or unavailable.[38] The division of labour, national and international trade, commercial research and development, and above all the co-ordination of the activity of millions of different centers of production, distribution, and exchange would be impossible. Those who wanted to take an initiative and deal with strangers, or strike bargains with those they neither cared for nor expected to care for them, would, like Shakespeare's lovers, have to step outside the world of social structures and rule-governed expectations altogether, and

37. *See* E. Durkheim, The Division of Labour in Society (1933).
38. *See* A. Nove, *supra* note 33, at 4-26.

take their chances in an environment where there was nothing to count on but the unstructured self-interest of others. They would be stuck, as it were, in a perpetual black market.[39] Ground rules of rights and contract, on the other hand, conceived independently of communal bonds, make it possible for us to initiate dealings every day, directly or indirectly, with thousands of people we barely know, and to take advantage of their situation and abilities as they take advantage of ours, with the confidence that there are rules available to facilitate, structure, and secure these dealings even when there is no affection to base them on.[40]

Having said all that, it should be noted that there are many transactions, which we would call market transactions, that are not solely or explicitly constituted by rights and contracts. Transactions in the local store, for example, may be governed by implicit friendship and goodwill as much as by self-interest and legal obligation. Someone may ask, "Why can't all economic transactions be like that?" I think I have already given an answer, but it is important to stress that, even if they were, there would *still* be a role for rights to play. My grocer can deal with me in an informal, friendly way, sometimes giving me credit when I need it, or ordering some trivial item that I want, and so on, only if he has confidence that in the last resort he would be able to recover the money I owe if I abused his friendship, and that no-one else can take unfair advantage of the "goodwill" he has accumulated. He may hope (just like the partners to a normal marriage) that he never has to invoke these formal guarantees, but that is quite compatible with the proposition that his assurance of their existence is one of the reasons he is able to act as informally as he does. Once again, we find that, far from destroying or replacing affective ties, fall-back rights may be their pre-condition, at least in an imperfect world.

39. In environments like this—black markets—there are no structures of rules, and hence no basis for security, expectations and co-ordination in contractual dealings. That would be the fate of *all* dealings between strangers, if we were to insist on legitimating only those economic transactions that were clothed in the substantial affections of the community.

40. For a similar perspective on markets and affection, see A. Smith, An Inquiry into the Nature and Causes of the Wealth of Nations 18 (E. Cannan ed. 1976) ("In civilized society, [man] stands in need of the cooperation and assistance of great multitudes, while his whole life is scarce sufficient to gain the friendship of a few persons.").

VII.

I want to conclude my analysis with a couple of more theoretical points about this particular approach to rights. The first is a modest disclaimer. This theory of rights as fallbacks is intended to explain some of the rights we rely on in social life, but it is not intended as a *comprehensive* theory of rights. There probably is something wrong with the idea that there has to be just *one* theory that generates and explains everything so far as rights are concerned. There may be several theories, and as a consequence, not all rights will necessarily have to have the same normative shape or moral importance.

In particular, the idea of rights as fall-backs should be distinguished from that of rights as setting minimum acceptable standards of behavior. The rights that one would have to fall back on when a marriage breaks up in bitterness may, for example, impose much higher standards of behavior than one might necessarily want to impose as *minima* for a happily functioning marriage. But I make this point mainly because I am not clear exactly how so-called "human" rights or constitutional guarantees would fit into my analysis. Consider, for example, Article Three of the European Convention on Human Rights: "No one shall be subjected to torture or to inhuman or degrading treatment or punishment."[41] Perhaps this could be squeezed into the framework of my analysis by saying that in ordinary political arrangements between state and citizen, the issue of torture simply does not arise; but that people need this as something to fall back on when normal politics collapse. Someone who wants to stress the affective side of political commitment—love for one's country, the patriotic cherishing of its constitution—would still have to leave room for that.

However, I think the "minimum standards" conception captures more accurately the sense of this provision. The claim is that the government in *all* its dealings with citizens, normal or abnormal, must never let its conduct descend to this level. Certainly citizens need to be able to rely on a *guarantee* that this will never happen; and there is that common element of guarantee in both conceptions. But the constitutional right is intended to operate as a *constant* constraint, not as something that can be

41. Art. 3, Convention for the Protection of Human Rights and Fundamental Freedoms, *reprinted in* A. ROBERTSON, HUMAN RIGHTS IN EUROPE 294-95 (1977).

relied on to come into the picture but only when other bases for political restraint have failed.

Either way, communitarians and other opponents of the rights tradition would do well to reflect on this need for articulated guarantees as part of the security that people require of their society. They are entitled to insist, of course, that liberals should think more seriously than many of them have about the communal structures that make rights possible as effective guarantees for all.[42] But that has not been the main point of this paper—the importance of community and communal bonds is conceded. The main point is that some rights, at least, would be necessary as fall-backs in many areas, even if on the whole we wanted to constitute normal social relations in those areas on a basis other than rights.

VIII.

My final point is about the individualism of this analysis. Someone might accept the need for formal legalistic structures as fall-backs to underpin social relations that are constituted on other terms. But they may still question why it is necessary for those *in extremis* arrangements to be presented as rights *of an individual.* Surely groups and communities as such need to have something they can fall back on as well.

The point is a good one as far as it goes. *Romeo and Juliet* is not so much about the need for *individual* rights (though it can be expressed in those terms) as about the needs of *a couple,* needs that would of course be unintelligible apart from their involvement with one another. Similarly a village or local community, an ethnic group, or a family, may need to know what they can count on, and how they can organize their relations with other groups, once their affectionate bonds to their neighbors or to the larger society have been broken. In these contexts, we may want to talk about the rights of groups, or we may think that other less individual-oriented legal terms are appropriate.[43] Moreover, in other contexts, one affectionate or communal bond may be backed up by another: When a marriage

42. *See generally* Taylor, *supra* note 12.
43. On group rights, see N. Glazer, *Individual Rights, Against Group Rights,* in HUMAN RIGHTS (E. Kamenka & A. Tay eds. 1978). *See also* Waldron, *Can Communal Goods Be Human Rights?*, 28 ARCH. EUR. SOC. 296 (1987). For an excellent discussion of individualism in this context, see J. RAZ, THE MORALITY OF FREEDOM 104-32 (1986).

fails and a woman is violently assaulted by her husband, she may find greater security in the communal atmosphere of a Woman's Refuge than in the austere individualism of the law courts.

Still there is some point to stressing that a set of legal rules conceived as fall-backs will have to include rights for individual men and women whatever else it includes. For any given social relation, there is always the possibility that it may disintegrate completely, leaving a naked individual bereft of any substantial bond to others, wanting to know where she stands. To recognize this possibility is not necessarily to embrace ontological individualism.[44] It may still be true that the individual is the creation of the social, not the other way round, and that man, as Marx put it, is "an animal which can develop into an individual only in society."[45] All one needs to accept is that, as it were, individual *fall-out* from social relations is possible. And, indeed, if it is the case that the precipitated individual is going to be an incomplete and alienated being, confused, frightened, and truncated as a result of the social rupture, then surely the case for her protection and security in these unhappy circumstances is if anything even more substantial.

Of course, modernists among us accept something much more positive than this: that though an individual standing apart from all social relations is unimaginable, nevertheless it is a good thing that modern men and women feel able to distance themselves from, reflect upon, and consciously embrace or repudiate any or all of the relations that constitute their history.[46] Though we live in and for communities of one sort or another most of the time, our communal attachments are never so remote from our capacities as conscious, articulate, thinking, choosing, creating beings that we cannot subject them to scrutiny and consideration. Rights as fall-backs give us the vantage point from which that can be done. The point is not simply the liberal one about the importance of individuals' autonomously shaping their lives. It is also that these processes of individual thought, reflection, and change are source of many of the new beginnings in the world, including new communal beginnings.

44. For a discussion of the different meanings of the word "individualism," see S. Lukes, Individualism (1973).

45. Marx, *Grundrisse*, in Marx, *supra* note 29, at 346.

46. *See* M. Berman, All that is Solid Melts into the Air: The Experiment of Modernity (1982); M. Ignatieff, *supra* note 27, at ch. 5.

We should be careful not to undermine the possibility of that.[47]

In recent communitarian literature, Sandel and others have condemned this image of the individual: They say it seems to "rule out in advance any end whose adoption or pursuit could engage or transform the identity of the self."[48] The modern liberal self is said to stand apart from its attachments, particularly those attachments which might involve "more or less expansive self-understandings" to take in one's connections with others as well.

> One consequence of this distance is to put the self beyond the reach of experience, to make it vulnerable, to fix its identity once and for all. No commitment could grip me so deeply that I could not understand myself without it. No transformation of life purposes and plans could be so unsettling as to disrupt the contours of my identity. No project could be so essential that turning away from it would call into question the person I am.[49]

Communal bonds, says Sandel, can never be *constitutive* of a liberal self, so long as it retains this facility for questioning them. He calls instead for a conception of the self that is at least capable of being identified completely and essentially with some communal history or commitment (taking for granted that we know what "completely" and "essentially" mean in this context).

The critique appears to be an attractive one, for it associates flexibility of attachments with shallowness. "To imagine a person incapable of constitutive attachments is . . . to imagine a person wholly without character, without depth."[50] The sense we get is that one who knows she can alter her attachments—the liberal individual—cannot possibly feel as intensely or wholehearted about them than one who knows she cannot. But that is a mistake, based at best on a simplistic view about the relation between the metaphysics of the self and the phenomenology of commitment, and at worst on the mere rhetorical power of ill-understood terms like "essence," "identity," and "constitutive." To retain the capacity to review our commitments, we do not always have to be *holding something back* from them. Having the capacity to reflect means *being able to make an*

47. *See* H. Arendt, *supra* note 17.
48. M. Sandel, *supra* note 12, at 64-65.
49. *Id.* at 62.
50. *Id.* at 179.

effort when one needs to, to wrench away and construct the necessary psychological distance. It does not require a continuous reserve of commitment and energy which *could* have been associated with one's attachment but is not, and it certainly does not mean sitting back all the time in the isolated citadel of self treating the attachment as a curious and contingent event in which one has no interest. In modern experience, intensity, whole-heartedness, and the sense of having identified comprehensively with a project or commitment, are as much features of the commitments that people *choose* and the ones they could give up *if* they wanted to, as of the commitments which people *discover* they have and find they cannot question—many moderns would say more so. To repeat a point I have made a number of times: Having something to fall back on if an attachment fails may be a *condition* of being able to identify intensely with one's attachments, rather than something which derogates from that intensity.

At any rate, these reflections at least make the nub of the controversy clear, between communitarians and their modernist opponents. The debate is not between those who see social life as constitutively communal and those who do not. Nor is it between community and the values of bare individualism. It is between those who, on the one hand, yearn for communal bonds so rigid that the question of what happens when they come apart will not arise or need to be faced, and, on the other hand, those who are, firstly, realistic enough to notice the tragedy of the broken bond and ask "What happens next?"; and, secondly, optimistic enough to embrace the possibility of the creative construction of new bonds and new connections, and ask "How is that possible?". Those are the battle-lines; in this article, I have tried to indicate the role that rights may play in that controversy.

[4]

VICTIMS IN THE SHADOW OF THE LAW: A CRITIQUE OF THE MODEL OF LEGAL PROTECTION

KRISTIN BUMILLER

The twentieth anniversary of the 1964 Civil Rights Act marked the end of an era of uncertain progress. Despite dramatic victories in constitutional litigation and the visibility of group-based struggles, civil rights strategies had limited success in initiating major economic and social change.[1] The limited progress has prompted a new sense of realism among groups who experience discrimination—a sense of how little the situation has changed even though overt prejudice may be less prevalent. The modest progress of the civil rights movement has not made "rights-focused" struggles unattractive, however; in fact, there is a proliferation of civil rights strategies

[1] For a longitudinal study of the effects of civil rights reforms on black and white incomes, see Donald J. McCrone and Richard J. Hardy, "Civil Rights and the Achievement of Racial Economic Equality, 1948–1975," *American Journal of Political Science* 22, no. 1 (February 1978): 1–17. These sentiments have been expressed by Coretta Scott King on the twentieth anniversary of the 1964 Civil Rights Act: "'Segregationist' politicians don't stand at the school house door anymore. But segregated housing patterns and more subtle forms of racism prevent equal access to a quality education. . . . All too often 'last hired, first fired' is still the rule for minorities. . . . Recent Supreme Court decisions have shown us how vulnerable affirmative action policies can be when the Court's longstanding commitment to equality is undermined. It also shows how susceptible the . . . [C]ourt is to the winds of political change" (Robert Peer, "Civil Rights Act Is Accessed as a Modest Step," *New York Times* [July 1, 1984]).

for reform. Organized groups are striving to extend the same legal protections won for blacks in order to prohibit discrimination on the basis of sex, age, and sexual preference and to control sexual harassment and pornography.[2] These groups see such legal guarantees as symbolic victories and as initial steps toward improved social status.

Contemporary antidiscrimination policies are based on a model of legal protection.[3] From this perspective, the law is a powerful and effective instrument. The law provides victims with a tool by which they can force perpetrators of unlawful conduct to comply with socially established norms. The model of legal protection assumes that those who have suffered harms will recognize their injuries and invoke the protective measures of law. Since most antidiscrimination laws rely primarily on victims to identify violations, report them to public authorities, and participate in enforcement proceedings, these laws tacitly assume that such behavior is reasonably unproblematic. In other words, because protective laws place responsibility on the victim to perceive and report violations, they assume that those in the protected class can and will accept these burdens.[4]

[2] For an example of how the antidiscrimination strategy is translated into legal protection for sexual harassment, see Catharine MacKinnon, *Sexual Harassment of Working Women* (New Haven, Conn.: Yale University Press, 1979).

[3] The constitutional revolution arising from the civil war established a method of federal intervention that forms the "seeds of failure" within present-day antidiscrimination strategies. See C. Vann Woodward, "Seeds of Failure in Radical Race Policy," in *New Frontiers of the American Reconstruction*, ed. Harold Hyman (Urbana: University of Illinois Press, 1966); Harold Hyman and William M. Wiecek, *Equal Justice under Law: Constitutional Development, 1835–1875* (New York: Harper & Row, 1982); Stanley Kutler, *Judicial Power and Reconstruction Politics* (Chicago: University of Chicago Press, 1968); Arthur Bestor, "The American Civil War as a Constitutional Crisis," *American Historical Review* 69 (1964): 327–52. As the grand design of reconstruction policies was met with increasing obstructions and violence, the protection of the black citizen was delegated to enforcement by the courts. This marked the end of the duty of reconstruction politicians to scrutinize civil rights' protection and the beginning of the reliance on legal procedures that were viewed as effective remedies. The moral purpose of the reconstruction was lost to faith in legal effectiveness. The black citizen, the "initial and primary beneficiary" of civil rights law "became all but invisible" (Hyman and Wiecek, 509).

[4] This is an idealization of the model of legal protection as it reflects the historical purposes of antidiscrimination policies. This model and its critique have been applied to other areas of law: Anthony Platt, *The Child Savers: The Invention of Delinquency* (Chicago: University of Chicago Press, 1977); Joseph Gusfield, *The Culture of Public Problems* (Chicago: University of Chicago Press, 1981); Martha Fineman, "Implementing Equality: Ideology, Contradiction, and Social Change," *Wisconsin Law Review*, no. 4 (1983), 789–886. Legal protection also reflects assumptions in dominant research paradigms in law and society. See, for proactive law, Donald Black, "The Mobilization of Law," *Journal of Legal Studies* 2 (1972): 125–49; dispute processing, e.g., Richard Abel, "A Comparative Theory of Dispute Institutions in Society," *Law and Society Review* 8 (Winter 1973): 217–315. It also has broader significance in legal theory, e.g., the work of the nineteenth-century German jurist Jhering, and instrumental strains of legal realism; see Jerome Frank, *Law and the Modern Mind* (New York: Brentano's, 1930).

Spring 1987 / SIGNS

Research on antidiscrimination policies has often relied on the model of legal protection, and, as a consequence, it has been uninformed by the social-situational viewpoint of women and men of color. Strategies of equal protection may inadequately address the burdens imposed on women and men of color because they accept the authoritative discourse of law rather than question the compatibility of legal rules with everyday life. From a feminist perspective, legal discourses are problem-solving approaches that reflect the ideology of the powerful and ignore the realities of the powerless.[5] The acceptance of a situation of sexual or racial discrimination as a legal problem (a bipolar, rights-oriented, isolated dispute) structures the interpretation for both the participants and outsiders. In such a system interaction with the law is alienating for social victims just as the language of legality is alienated from everyday discourse.

The voices of the excluded classes of blacks and women within Western cultures have been quieted in academic work influenced by doctrinal analysis and the methodological framework of the dispute processing paradigm.[6] This project takes on as its central focus the struggles of women, and in particular the life situations of women of color, because these struggles bear more relevance to the implementation of antidiscrimination policies than the abstract world of legal enactments. The image of the victim[7] portrayed by this study is a product of contemporary conditions of sexual and racial oppression: many respond in an ineffectual and defensive manner to a complex network of victimizations and a few (who are exceptionally prepared for struggle) stage dramatic battles against discrimination. The study examines the choices discrimination victims make in light of the perceived social constraints and the vision of protective law. Unlike conventional legal analysis that magnifies the authority of legal rules vis-à-vis other social constructions, these in-depth portrayals of responses to discrimination illustrate how the link between economic, social, psycho-

[5] For example, Carol Gilligan, *In a Different Voice: Psychological Theory and Women's Development* (Cambridge, Mass.: Harvard University Press, 1982).

[6] There are exceptions, including studies focusing on disputing outside of the contemporary American context; see, e.g., Boaventura de Sousa Santos, "The Law of the Oppressed: The Construction and Reproduction of Legality in Pasargada," *Law and Society Review* 12 (Fall 1977): 5–126. For a study within the U.S. context, see Sally Merry, "Going to Court: Strategies of Dispute Management in an Urban Neighborhood," *Law and Society Review* 13 (Summer 1979): 891–924. Both articles attempt to examine attitudes toward law without imposing the model of legal protection.

[7] "Victim" is used in this context to refer to the diminished role created and characterized by the law, government bureaucrats, and social services directed at serving the needs of the disadvantaged. The word "victim" is used with hesitation, since the word evokes and reinforces its own social reality. The portrayal of victims within the study attempts to appreciate their strength under extreme conditions of oppression. The powerful and the powerless cannot be talked about in isolation of each other: the political psychology of the victim is constituted from exchanges between victims and those who impose their authority.

logical, sexual, and legal roles creates an ethic of survival that precludes the protective role of law.

The research project

The initial source of data for this study was a household survey designed to measure the incidence of civil disputes. In the survey, conducted by the Civil Litigation Research Project (CLRP) in 1980, a sample of 560 discrimination claims was obtained from approximately 5,000 households. Respondents were asked if they had experienced "illegal or unfair treatment" because of their "race, age, sex, handicaps, union membership, or other things."[8] In this way, it was possible to obtain a sample of discrimination grievances that had not reached courts or public agencies. Preliminary analysis indicated that approximately half of the aggrieved individuals did not make a claim to the other party, nearly two-thirds did nothing further to rectify their perceived mistreatment, and only a very small percentage had achieved successful resolution of their claims.[9] Discrimination grievances had a significantly lower rate of escalation into court cases than civil matters such as contract disputes or landlord-tenant problems. The size of the gap is indicative of the more problematic relationship between victims and the law in discrimination cases compared to other civil cases. This study began with the anticipation that to bring the complaint into the realm of public action forced victims to encounter deeper and more encompassing conflicts of racial, gender, and social identity than complaints arising from relationships defined by legal roles (i.e., landlord/tenant). What accounts for the apparent acceptance of defeat among those who experience discriminatory treatment? Why is it unlikely that those who experience discrimination will take their claims to courts or other legal channels?

Although the survey probed for open-ended responses to the question

[8] The initial survey was conducted by the CLRP by telephone in five federal judicial districts: South Carolina, Eastern Pennsylvania, Eastern Wisconsin, New Mexico, and Central California. The districts were chosen to maximize geographical and demographic diversity. The respondents were asked whether anyone in their household had experienced one or more of a list of problems in the past three years. If the respondents indicated they experienced a discrimination problem they were administered an additional "problem" questionnaire with forty-four closed-ended and open-ended questions. The data reported in table 1 are derived from open-ended questions included in the survey that were previously uncoded. The methodology is described in Herbert M. Kritzer, "Studying Disputes: Learning from the CLRP Experience," *Law and Society Review* 15, no. 3/4 (1980–81): 503–24.

[9] Richard E. Miller and Austin Sarat, "Grievances, Claims, and Disputes: Assessing the Adversary Culture," *Law and Society Review* 15, no. 3/4 (1980–81): 525–66. The aggrieved party makes a "claim" when she communicates her entitlement to the party responsible for the perceived harm.

"Why didn't you complain?" it could not provide the depth necessary to present a view of discrimination from the victim's perspective. A subsample of eighteen persons in Milwaukee and Los Angeles-were selected for in-depth interviewing.[10] The format of the interviews was unstructured but directed at probing for interpretations of the discrimination incident, people's attitudes about themselves and their social status, and their justifications for their beliefs and actions.[11] The interviews were conducted from April to October 1982. Each face-to-face interview was two to four hours long. The participants in the interviews are representative of those affected by the social inequalities and the pattern of discrimination in American society: six black and Hispanic women, nine white women, and three black and American Indian men.[12]

The response to discrimination

In the civil litigation research project survey on incidence of civil disputes, each individual who perceived they experienced discrimination and made no protest was asked to explain their decision with the question "Why didn't you complain?" In response to this question, participants denied the worthiness of their own interests in comparison to their opponents' (table 1). Some respondents accounted for their inaction in terms of the harm their opponent could impose on them (e.g., responses 5, 8, and 9 in table 1). Others acknowledged they should have done something, yet either blamed themselves for not pursuing the dispute or accepted the inevitability of the situation (e.g., responses 1, 2, 3, 4, and 11 in table 1). The explanations focus on an interpretation of immediate circumstances rather than norms or rights; for example, the expense of legal action and the

[10] The intensive interviewing was conducted in two judicial districts: Eastern Wisconsin (Milwaukee metropolitan area) and Central California (Los Angeles County). Interviews were attempted with all respondents experiencing discrimination problems in the two districts. Cases were eliminated if an individual had refused to provide their name, address, and phone number and if their description of the problem was inappropriate.

[11] The prototype of this method of research in political science is Robert Lane, *Political Ideology* (New York: Free Press, 1962). A recent study of similar design is Jennifer Hochschild, *What's Fair? American Beliefs about Distributive Justice* (Cambridge, Mass.: Harvard University Press, 1981).

[12] The characteristics of the interviewees were as follows: race, nine white, five black, four Hispanic and American Indian; sex, fifteen women, three men; type of problem, eleven employment, two employment and housing, two housing, three other; type of discrimination, nine sex, seven race, one age. These characteristics correspond to the overall CLRP sample in which the responses were distributed as follows: type of problem, 56 percent employment, 12 percent education, 18 percent housing, 14 percent other; type of discrimination, 13 percent age, 22 percent sex, 31 percent race, and 34 percent other. There was a disproportionate number of women in the intensive interview sample because they had a higher response rate.

TABLE 1 **RESPONSES TO THE QUESTION: "WHY DIDN'T YOU COMPLAIN?"**

Coded Responses*	Responses	
1. It would do no good/end results the same/a way of life	35	(19.9)
2. Not worth it/not a major problem	18	(10.2)
3. Need to solve the problem immediately/situation easily replaceable	17	(9.7)
4. Gave up/I don't know why I didn't complain/I'm easy going	17	(9.7)
5. Fear of retaliation or being known as a troublemaker	16	(9.1)
6. Don't know who to complain to	14	(8.0)
7. Could not prove/no evidence	13	(7.4)
8. Avoid dealing with them in the future	12	(6.8)
9. Don't want to cause trouble	9	(5.1)
10. Excessive time or cost	9	(5.1)
11. Rules cannot be changed	8	(4.6)
12. Other	8	(4.6)

NOTE.—Numbers in parentheses are percentages.
*Open-ended responses were coded into these twelve categories.

inability to prove discriminatory motives (e.g., responses 6, 7, and 10 in table 1).[13]

The model of legal protection would suggest that the failure of persons to use the law stems from the victims' inability to serve their own needs: lack of information and knowledge about their rights and their limited resources for utilizing legal channels. These persons were not rejected by unresponsive agencies, deterred by the unavailability of lawyers, or barred from pursuing legal claims by technicalities. Although the anticipation of these factors played a role in their decision making, they did not take action primarily because they legitimized their own defeat. For the most part, the problem is never conceptualized in terms of public action. In this universe of discrimination problems far removed from legal fora, the labeling of acts as discriminatory and the eventual deflation of the conflict by apology or self-blame serve as coping mechanisms for suppressing burgeoning discontent.[14]

These data reveal a general pattern of response but provide limited insight into the social-psychological situation. More adequate explanations

[13] Attribution theory attempts to explain why individuals blame themselves for the dispute (i.e., the need to maintain perceived control); this provides a limited psychological explanation for behavior, but it does not raise questions about the consequences of self-defeat. See Dan Coates and Steven Penrod, "Social Psychology and the Emergence of Disputes," *Law and Society Review* 15, no. 3/4 (1980–81): 655–80. For an interpretation similar to my own, see Sally Merry and Susan S. Silbey, "What Do Plaintiffs Want? Re-examining the Concept of Dispute," *Justice System Journal* 9, no. 2 (1984): 151–78.

[14] Simone de Beauvoir has described this as a "rite of justice," which manifests society's respect for each citizen's individuality. When procedural justice does not allow for a meaningful expression of individual rights, this rite of justice becomes a ritual of degradation (Simone de Beauvoir, *The Ethics of Ambiguity* [Secaucus, N.J.: Citadel Press, 1980]). See also the framing of the problem as the stultification of individual action in Murray Edelman, "Art as Liberating Political Communication," *Institut für Höhere Studien Journal* 6 (1982): 1–15.

for legal action or inaction can be found in participants' responses examined within the context of their lives: the social exchange between authorities and those who experience discrimination, the social and psychological mechanisms that stifle conflict, and the role of legal ideology in influencing individual choice. In combination with the general survey data examined above, intensive interviews can elaborate the victim's view of social reality and their perception of alternative courses of action.[15]

Rather than treating participants' socially constructed viewpoints as mere reflections of elite ideology, the interpretations of the interviews in this study were focused on strategies taken by individuals engaged in legal conflict.[16] The specific objectives of interpretation were: (1) to develop a meaningful understanding of the conflict in the context of individual lives; (2) to analyze the structure of their rationalizations for action or inaction; (3) to discover when and how law enters personal spheres; and (4) to understand power at the extreme points of its exercise.[17]

[15] The interviews were guided by forty questions on the following topics: (1) the circumstances of the discrimination incident; (2) the relationship of the incident to other acts of discrimination or other forms of perceived mistreatment; (3) justifications for the respondents' actions in response to the incident; (4) their feelings about fairness, competition, merit, and status inequalities; (5) their attitudes about their own self-worth and competence; (6) their political mind: degree of trust in government, political alienation and cynicism, extent of political participation, and attitudes toward leaders and authority; (7) their knowledge of the political and legal process and their interpretation of antidiscrimination law; (8) the consequences of the actions they took in response to the discrimination problem and their evaluations, in retrospect, about how their strategies in the conflict situation were modified over time; (9) their beliefs about the effectiveness of political and legal action.

[16] This issue is especially problematic given that this study does not rely on an objective definition of discriminatory treatment. To what extent are these individuals' perceptions a reflection of ideology or "unmasked" personal knowledge? In terms of dispute processing methodology, see David M. Trubek, "The Construction and Deconstruction of a Disputes-focused Approach: An Afterword," *Law and Society Review* 15, no. 3/4 (1980–81): 738–40; also see Karl Mannheim, *Ideology and Utopia* (New York: Harcourt, Brace, Jovanovich, 1936); Georg Lukács, *History and Class Consciousness* (Cambridge, Mass.: MIT Press, 1968); Herbert Marcuse, *One-Dimensional Man* (Boston: Beacon Press, 1964). These issues have also been addressed within the dispute processing framework. See, e.g., William Felstiner et al., "The Emergence and Transformation of Disputes," *Law and Society Review* 15, no. 3/4 (1980–81): 631–54; and Lynn Mather and Barbara Yngvesson, "Language, Audience, and the Transformation of Disputes," *Law and Society Review* 15, no. 3/4 (1980–81): 773–821.

[17] This is a brief summary of the methodological framework for the interviews. These objectives draw eclectically from theoretical writings: Ralf Dahrendorf's concept of "life chances," *Life Chances* (Chicago: University of Chicago Press, 1979); Bruno Bettelheim's social-psychological understanding of the structure of rationalizations in "extreme situations," *Surviving* (New York: Vintage, 1980); Niklas Luhmann's analysis of law in interactional systems, "Communication about Law in Interactional Systems," in *Advances in Social Theory and Methodology*, ed. K. Knorr-Cetina and A. V. Cicourel (Boston: Routledge & Kegan Paul, 1981); and Michel Foucault's microphysics of power, *Power/Knowledge* (New York: Pantheon Books, 1980).

The creation of illegitimate bonds

Discrimination conflicts usually occur in situations where there are asymmetrical power relations. In most instances of discrimination the perpetrator acts in an authoritative role (employer, landlord, or teacher, e.g.). In these roles people wield power by virtue of their expertise, their ability to enforce orders, the permanence of their positions, or their mystique.[18]

The participants in this study who experienced discrimination often portrayed perpetrators as tyrants. Several individuals referred to the "regal" qualities of those who discriminate against them. Mrs. Perkins, when denied a job in a department store, reacted toward her employer in these words: "She is very attractive. She'd wear clothes like she stepped out of a spring garden. She'd walk like a model; she was something else. You'd have to see her. She had an office in the back of the store. She sits like she's the *Queen*, Queen Elizabeth. Like you'd have to bow down to her. That's the feeling I get when I see her." Mrs. Perkins was intimidated by the personnel officer's regal appearance. She was particularly sensitive to how the environment surrounding the woman was designed to impress her "subjects" and protect her authority. Mrs. Perkins was, in fact, afraid to begin a disagreement because she felt she lacked the language skills and the social presence to confront her opponent.

Carmen also described her supervisor on the job in regal terms: "He was a bit of a *tyrant*—screamed a lot and yelled a lot. The type of person who would make you cry, then apologize instantly. Like, heck, I am the boss and the ruler, and I do things my way, always." Carmen considered her employer's demand for total control immature, like the actions of a brutal ruler. Even though she responded more cynically to the regal manner than did Mrs. Perkins, she felt caught in an explosive and abusive exchange.

Other tyrant-like employers achieved total control through verbal abuse. Nora believes that she never received an explanation for her pay differential because "to be quite honest with you we were terrified with the owner of the company. He ran a very tight ship and if you disagreed with him you were sure to cause nothing but trouble." The tactic of a less effective tyrant (a military dictator), Virginia's supervisor, was to impose a chain of command that allowed the top ranks to reserve credit for accomplishments. To Virginia he was the "chicken colonel" (he was a former army colonel) because he could exercise authority only behind closed doors (but

[18] For a similar analysis, see Richard Sennett, *Authority* (New York: Vintage, 1980); for application to other forms of victimization see Bettelheim; Stanley Elkins, *Slavery* (Chicago: University of Chicago Press, 1959); Susan Griffin, *Woman and Nature* (New York: Harper & Row, 1978); Eugene Genovese, *Roll, Jordan, Roll* (New York: Vintage, 1976); Malcolm X, *The Autobiography of Malcolm X* (New York: Ballantine Books, 1965).

paper-thin walls); Virginia was his "secretary," and so he claimed credit for her work.

The authority figures described by these participants behave according to Machiavelli's instructions to *The Prince*: they control by fear and simplification of reality. As tyrants the perpetrators are brutal simplifiers of the situation through appearances that disguise realities. The effectiveness of their rule according to Machiavelli rests on the subject's willingness to be "always taken by what a thing seems to be and by what comes of it."[19] The employee believes "what seems to be"—that her supervisor exercises royal supremacy—and "what comes of it"—the finality of the authority's total control. All conflicting interests and demands are subdued by the employee's retraction in fear. The bonds of the tyrant image are powerful because the disrespect for royalty is self-deceptive; it allows the subjects to regard their superiors as immature and arrogant and yet justifies their own impotence. Tyrants are not legitimate rulers; yet within these demoralized bonds the illegitimacy of the rulers sustains rather than defeats them. The image of the tyrant transforms the exchange between the perpetrator and victim into a situation where the perpetrator controls and the victim transgresses.

The potential for explosion reinforces the inviolable bonds of the victim/oppressor relationship. Since the expression of anger is unacceptable in bureaucratic settings, there are no minor infractions within normal ranges of behavior: there is only rebellion and submission.[20] The victims of discrimination, therefore, perceive their own reactions to injustice as explosive and extreme. Most of the individuals admitted to extreme anger (often violent in intent), which persisted for long periods of time. A seventy-two-year-old woman involved in an age discrimination dispute said in reference to her employer: "I wanted to punch her. I was angry for a couple of weeks. I would like to take a good swing at her and teach her a couple of things. . . . I'd still [two years later] like to punch her." Another woman, after being fired, claimed: "I felt like bombing the place." John indicated that he was so angry that he could not deal with it verbally; if he expressed his rage, he would have to "take it out on the street." Debbie, in a sexual harassment dispute with a fellow employee, felt: "There are times I would love to punch him out—to get out the frustration." Patricia, after being fired from a newly acquired job because they were "looking for a white person" to fill the position, was angry for months. Two to three years afterward it would make her angry whenever she thought about it. In only

[19] Niccolo Machiavelli, *The Prince*, in *Masterworks of Government*, ed. L. D. Abbott (New York: McGraw-Hill Book Co., 1947), 162.

[20] See Genovese; and Franz Fanon, *The Wretched of the Earth* (New York: Grove Press, 1963).

one case did anger lead to physical violence: when a black woman slapped a white, fellow employee who had made a racist comment.

These people seem to respond to the violation of their dignity within these power relations with intense anger, expressed in the very terms that had been prohibited—immediate physical retaliation—but the result was that anger silenced the victims.[21] They were intimidated by the social unacceptability of their anger; therefore, they confronted their emotions by exercising control. As Patricia explains, she can only remain angry if it is "vital," otherwise if she let herself get angry, "then I'd be angry all the time." Others admit they "don't know how to fight," they "stay quiet," "calm down," or "absorb a lot of anger before [they] let go." These rationalizations about the desirability of control may stifle the expression of injustice in any form.

An ethic of survival

The attitude about their successes and failures of those individuals who confronted discrimination is best described in Virginia's words: "The main measurement of success [was] basically survival." The ethic of survival means different things to different people, depending on how they define their responsibilities and their bases for self-respect and how they view their struggles and needs.[22]

Carmen, for example, considers her encounter with discriminatory treatment an inevitable event in the life of a woman of color. Carmen, who worked as a clerk in a discount department store for almost ten years, discovered that after a promotion to a more responsible position as an area supervisor her salary was lower than those of men in the same position. Carmen chose not to make a formal complaint. She made this decision because of a complex set of constraints that reveals that her powerlessness in obtaining equal pay is linked to her powerlessness in other domains. She needs the job because she has responsibilities as a single parent for four children. She also recognizes that in any dispute it would be "me against a

[21] When victims, consumed by anger, avoid face-to-face confrontations, they lose the opportunity to exercise their authority. When Patricia returns to pick up her final paycheck, she finds her employer "embarrassed" like "someone who made a decision they are not proud of." Patricia felt that if she started a confrontation the employer "would get very upset." This confirmed Patricia's suspicions about the discriminatory nature of the firing, yet she did not pursue the matter with the employer. John describes a similar incident with his district supervisor: "All of a sudden he gets loud and tells me he is not prejudiced, I didn't ask for that. I just looked at him, walked out, and I let it go at that . . . that let the cat out of the bag."

[22] For an interesting analysis of how an individual's ethic of survival is defined in oppressive situations, see Barrington Moore, *Injustice* (New York: M. E. Sharpe, 1978); Robert Coles, *Children of Crisis* (Boston: Little, Brown & Co., 1964); and Robert Coles and Jane H. Coles, *Women of Crisis* (Boston: Little, Brown & Co., 1978).

large corporation," and then it becomes "your word against [a more powerful] somebody else's." There are risks involved in "not knowing what the outcome will be," and she has reason to suspect the chances for successful resolution are low, having seen "too many people let go for the things that make you wonder." Carmen justifies her acquiescence by explaining that she is like many people who, when something bad happens, "get it out of the way and don't make waves."

She avoids the full impact of accepting the definition of the problem as discrimination, and thus identifying herself as the victim, with careful distinctions about the nature of her mistreatment. Her employer may have discriminated against her "without even realizing it." It is only when she hears certain insinuations that women are incompetent at their jobs that it gains conscious importance. Carmen attempts to avoid the label of victim by denying her group origins. While it is impossible for her to deny her womanhood, she can disavow her ethnic identity because of her coloring and married name. Therefore, she is not vulnerable to others who would say, "She is Puerto Rican, so we treat her *this* way." Discrimination is to Carmen something "they are constantly *pushing at you*." Avoiding acts of discrimination given its ever-present nature is impossible; what is dreaded is the status of "being a victim of discrimination," a role that seizes and marks its possessor.

Despite her deliberate efforts to see her mistreatment as something other than discrimination, she confronts the reality of her circumstances, that she was doing a good job and yet not receiving just rewards. For her to acknowledge an undeniable injustice she must come first to believe that she has failed to live up to some preconceived standard of self-protection, that she was by her own estimation "not that brave of a person." Confronting discrimination under these circumstances is a no-win situation that "depends upon you as an individual and how much you can take" (whether you are enduring precomplaint unjust treatment or postcomplaint retaliation). When Carmen feels depressed about what has happened to her, she has to remind herself that she "has nothing to be ashamed of."

Ironically, at the heart of the trap of victimhood is the strong and positive dimension to Carmen's self-evaluation of her experiences. Carmen prides herself on her ability to downplay the problem and act realistically. She is proud of her independence and her success in the personal domain of her family life. The pride in her own strength is linked to her identity as a woman. For example, in reference to her accomplishment of maintaining a house on her own for five years she proclaims, "I keep it going myself, I did it myself, a *woman*." She finds it necessary to remind herself that a part of her identity, her womanhood, is capable of surviving. Thus Carmen draws strength from her ability to endure, yet her energies are drained into the act of survival.

John's ethic of survival is "making it through the rain." Like Carmen, his primary sense of responsibility is to his child, though one of his complaints about the ordeal of discrimination on the job is that it made him more irritable around his young daughter. John believes that each person has the responsibility to do the job their employers assign because "they are the ones that give me my paycheck, you should do them right." When the employer is discriminatory it does not change the basic requirements of the relationship: "What right does someone have to hassle me like that when I am doing my job? I took it from them, but I don't take it from very many individuals—they give me my paycheck; [with] individuals my boiling point is a little lower."

This sense of responsibility is revealed in the two ways in which he demonstrates his loyalty. First, despite opportunities to "steal from the company," John has "a little wishy-washy" code of honesty that prevents him. Second, he feels more loyalty to the employer than to the union, not because he believes the company serves his best interests but "because the union can only help so much." He expects that if he filed a complaint with the union the company would investigate him and they would find a reason to fire him whether they had grounds or not. Even though he does not expect fair treatment from his employer, he has even less faith in his co-workers' support.

His overall philosophy is "I don't need a lot." John does not attribute his ability to endure the strain of a discriminatory situation on the job to strength of character but, rather, to the ability to "weather the storm." By his own estimation, in his weakness he endures: "My personality is what kept my job, my color created the problem. If it came to a point where I felt less than a man for taking the abuse, I would have quit; [as things were] if I had quit I would have felt less of myself."

These two portrayals illustrate how victims of discrimination protect themselves from the hardships imposed by relying on an illusive and private honor. Their sense of honor or pride, seen in the context of how they create opportunities and constraints within an ethic of survival, is a justification to submit personal needs to the demands of powerful institutions. Thus the discrimination victim upholds the appearance of justice even within a system that denies her equality. The victim's ethics are maintained within an individual, self-defined realm. Institutional and bureaucratic grievance procedures invade this personal ethic and strengthen the illusion that institutions are fair and that discrimination is not prevalent as long as the victims of discrimination believe their individual misfortune stems from the acts of aberrant individuals and from business practices.[23] Honor subdues aggression—as in John's commitment to

[23] Lukács, speaking of the bureaucrat's conscientiousness, saw that it is "precisely his 'honor' and his 'sense of responsibility' that exact his total submission. . . . It points to the fact that the division of labor . . . invades the realm of ethics. . . . This strengthens the reified

Spring 1987 / SIGNS

honest dealings with a firm that institutes racially discriminatory business practices. Pride subdues powerlessness—as in Carmen's need to "like herself" when she is powerless to combat pay differentials she acknowledges as unfair. When neither institutional practices nor the law of equal opportunity affirm a moral commitment to standards, the victims of discrimination cannot find purpose beyond their individual fate.[24]

The discrimination victim's view of the law

Claiming discrimination

In order for an individual to press a claim that unfavorable treatment stems from discriminatory practices she must assume the role of the victim. This transforms a social conflict into a psychological contest to reconcile a positive self-image with the image of the victim as powerless and defeated. Deciding whether or not to make a public claim of discrimination thus becomes intertwined with the process of reconciling these self-images.[25]

In this study, those interviewed discussed the discrimination they experience in qualified terms. Some approached it by denying self-involvement: "Sometimes I don't even feel like I was personally being discriminated against, as if they did not know who I was or saw who I was." Another approach characterized acts of discrimination as the result of personal likes and dislikes: "You come across it so often it is really ridiculous."

To experience discrimination, by these accounts, is to sense one's own invisibility and to grasp the reality of differential treatment. The women perceived that neither the mistreatment nor their response to it focused on a deliberate attack against them, but injustices resulted from being discounted or ignored.[26]

The legal concept of discrimination has a historical and analytical basis in the identification with a group cause.[27] To put this concept into opera-

structure of consciousness . . . as long as the fate of the worker still appears to be an individual fate" ([n. 16 above], 99–100).

[24] Max Weber, *Economy and Society*, 2 vols., ed. Guenther Roth and Claus Wittich (Berkeley: University of California Press, 1968), 2:884–85.

[25] The law creates a juridical person in its image. See Joseph Vining, *Legal Identity* (New Haven, Conn.: Yale University Press, 1978); John Noonan, *Persons and Masks of the Law* (New York: Farrar, Strauss, & Giroux, 1976).

[26] Ralph Ellison, *Invisible Man* (New York: Vintage Books, 1957); Gordon Allport, *The Nature of Prejudice* (Boston: Beacon Press, 1954).

[27] Owen Fiss, "Groups and the Equal Protection Clause," in *Equality and Preferential Treatment*, ed. Marshall Cohen et al. (Princeton, N.J.: Princeton University Press, 1977), argues that the norms of the judicial craft accentuate antidiscrimination laws' narrow focus on objectivity and individualism. Fiss describes, on the doctrinal level, the highly individualistic

tion, so to speak, involves finding a basis for the claim in terms of the individual's group identity.[28] Yet, these respondents resist perceiving their situation as the result of their group identity. In some cases, they depersonalize their mistreatment rather than identify with the group fate: "[Discrimination] depends upon who you are working for, changes in supervisors [solve the problem]"; "[discrimination] occurred because he has a problem and I was sort of a scapegoat." Or "I expected [discrimination]; that's the way men treat women." These statements disassociate the experience of discrimination from group identity, causes, or concerns, either by emphasizing the idiosyncratic nature of the perpetrator's actions or by universalizing the presence of discrimination. Several respondents supported these rationalizations by pointing out that everyone is vulnerable to some type of discrimination. A black man explained: "I don't walk around with my head buried in the sand. People discriminate against anything and anybody." Two respondents referred to discrimination directed at their "fat relatives" as examples of the prevalence of discrimination. A few men even attempt to defend discrimination as unavoidable: "I even discriminate against Mexicans." In sum, the respondents felt that it was self-defeating to associate an illogical and irrational process of mistreatment with a real cause. When someone did state their claim in terms of group concerns, they met resistance: "Most of the people I talked to thought I overreacted [when I complained of discrimination] . . . [I think it was] because I was labeled a feminist."

Even though these individuals express ambivalence about claiming discrimination publicly, they believe they have been seriously harmed. Their ambivalence places them in a self-imposed trap. They struggle with an image of themselves and their actions that produces an uncomfortable sense of exceptionality.[29] While antidiscrimination law ostensibly promotes

---

nature of antidiscrimination law given the designers' deliberate protection of persons rather than classes and the court's rejection of natural classes. In the Supreme Court's interpretations, references to groups are continually scrutinized to assure they do not offend the value of individuality.

[28] Realizing discriminatory treatment is like recognizing a group-identified mask that partly reflects the identity of the wearer, racial or sexual stereotypes, and the image of the victim found in antidiscrimination doctrine. Sylvia, who encountered discrimination in school, felt that without discrimination "I would have thought more of me, myself." She was uncomfortable about being labeled as "Latin" or "Mexican" by other students. She explained, "Sometimes it would hurt, sometimes it would make me feel funny, *and well, I am Mexican.*" The all-inclusiveness of the label demeans her, and at the same time, the label deeply reflects her social and personal self. What seems alien at the same moment is essential to her being. See Franz Fanon, *Black Skin, White Masks* (New York: Grove Press, 1967).

[29] Hannah Arendt describes the need to escape from the group identity in her biography of Rachel Varnhagen (1771–1833), a woman caught in the dilemmas of a period of German-Jewish assimilation. Arendt assesses the mood: "A political struggle for equal rights might have taken the place of a personal struggle . . . [but] Jews did not even want to be emancipated

dignity and universal human rights, in practice individuals may prefer the dignity found in their anonymity to an attempt to exercise their rights under such law.[30]

The reluctance to move beyond the perception of discrimination to claim formally the protection of antidiscrimination law is partly due to a resistance to the negative image of the victim. Moreover, this ambivalence deflects potential conflict because they choose not to categorize their mistreatment within narrow boundaries of discriminatory activity, thereby accepting the power of the law but restricting its domain.[31] Their reluctance to cross the boundary between normalcy and victimhood forces them to justify the perpetrators' actions. Those who transgress the social boundaries of discrimination experience sanctions—the label of the victim (the powerless outsider) or the label of a group stereotype (the potential zealot).

The intruding presence in everyday life

Despite the fact that victims are reluctant to use the law, they cling to the belief that it benefits them. Mrs. Perkins, when asked to report her age on an employment application, explained, "I told her I thought you weren't asking that anymore." She also indicated that she was sure she could "report her . . . right then and there." She knew that "they weren't supposed to consider your religion, age, your color, or whatever the heck it was and she sure did." All the respondents, when asked if they felt the law was on their side in the dispute, suggested that, at least in principle, the law would have supported their position. For example, one respondent involved in a housing dispute explained: "I knew I had the right. It made me feel good, that I knew if I wanted to [I could make a claim]."

---

as a whole; all they wanted was to escape from Jewishness, as individuals if possible. Their urge was secretly and silently to settle what seemed to them a personal problem, a personal misfortune"(Hannah Arendt, *Rachel Varnhagen: The Life of a Jewish Woman* [New York: Harcourt, Brace, Jovanovich, 1974], 7).

30 Tocqueville warns that democratic freedom can silence the proclamation of right: "The body is left free and the soul is enslaved." The "master" says: "You are free to think differently from me, and to retain your life, your property, and all that you possess; but you are henceforth a stranger among your people. You will retain your civil rights, but they will be useless to you . . . for you will never be chosen by your fellow citizens. . . . You will remain among men, but you will be deprived of the rights of mankind." The claim of right, Tocqueville explains, brings with it the severest sanction in a democratic society (Alexis de Tocqueville, *Democracy in America*, ed. Richard D. Heffner [New York: Mentor, 1956], 118).

31 For example, their reluctance to pursue claims is fostered by the perception that in the legal realm their accounts are worthless without "objective proof." They believe the law will not recognize their claim because "everything is verbal," "there is no formal bookkeeping or job descriptions," and "everything went on behind closed doors, nobody heard what I asked him." These statements devalue their self-knowledge in relation to the opponents' administrative procedures and the legally imposed standards of burden of proof.

Their assumption that there are absolute guarantees in the law seems to contradict their attitudes toward the law once it is employed.[32] After they engaged the apparatus of law or even considered invoking it, the respondents saw legal resolution as a risky course of action. They feared legal intervention would worsen their situation.

The prospect of legal intervention heightened a sense of powerlessness and produced a fear of loss of control. Nora believed that the decision to go to court was like opening up a "Pandora's box." Delma described her feelings: "I might have taken it to court; I might have done that. I went to the [unemployment office], and she confronted me and I felt so helpless. It was just his word against mine, and I am dumb . . . and there is nothing I can do." The unemployment office was a preview of the confrontation in court, where she would feel exposed, forced to defend herself with nothing other than her own words and intelligence.

Victims of discrimination also fear that their powerlessness will be accentuated in the legal forum because the legal disposition will address only a part of the problem.[33] As one respondent reasoned, the law will "not represent personality: it is cut and dry—there [is] not room for emotion." Behavior and loyalties may change when allies are asked to participate in legal proceedings: "[Going to court] would mean that people would have to speak up. In the lounge they might say you are really getting screwed. To say that in a court of law is different. When your neck is on the chopping block, you ain't going to start talking."

Legal intervention also had the effect of restructuring conflict, according to respondents, by provoking extreme hostility.[34] The respondents claimed that they avoided legal action in order to maintain civilities or remain employed: "If I didn't want to work there anymore, then I think I

[32] Antidiscrimination law is potentially broad in its application. For example, in Title VII discrimination is defined broadly, including situations where employers fail to hire, to discharge, or otherwise discriminate with respect to compensation, terms, conditions, and privileges of employment and practices that "limit, segregate, or classify . . . in any way that would deprive or tend to otherwise adversely affect his [*sic*] status." The wording of the statute suggests the law was designed to prohibit subtle forms of discrimination. The statute, however, has been narrowly applied by the courts because the burden of proof rests with the plaintiff. A prima facie case is established when the plaintiff shows "(i) that he [*sic*] belongs to a racial minority; (ii) that he applied and was qualified for a job for which the employer was seeking applicants; (iii) that, despite his qualifications, he was rejected; and (iv) that, after his rejection, the position remained open and the employer continued to seek applicants from persons of complainant's qualifications" (McDonnell Douglas Corp. v. Green, 411 U.S. 792 [1973]). Factors that may invalidate a claim include failure to bring a claim within specified time limits, failure to pursue proper administrative channels, inability to prove discriminatory impact of tests or other procedures, and the employer's priority to maintain practices that are "business necessities."

[33] See W. Lance Bennett and Martha S. Feldman, *Restructuring Reality in the Courtroom* (New Brunswick, N.J.: Rutgers University Press, 1981).

[34] Luhmann (n. 17 above).

would take legal action." When law is effective, it is at best a stopgap measure, to use when defeat is already certain to salvage a situation after one is resigned to defeat. The respondents felt that the law can only delay what they perceive as the inevitable revenge.[35]

Several respondents revealed that when they were confronted with the prospect of initiating a legal action they worried about their own guilt, as if they were charged with criminal offenses. Delma, while considering whether to file a complaint, mused, "Maybe it is me, maybe I am doing something wrong." Another woman, one who precipitated an act of violence after which she lost her job, reflected, "What I had done was against the rules, but what she had done was also against the rules. I didn't take legal action against it because I knew I had done a wrong part, I didn't try to take away from what I had done." John also reveals his feeling of guilt once he discovers himself singled out for discriminatory treatment. He felt as if his whole life was on trial; he was always on the defensive and compelled to prove he was doing his best possible work.

More generally, these discrimination victims felt it was necessary to prevent law from aggravating their situations. Often this meant blocking the law from taking over the relative normalcy of day-to-day life.[36] As Carmen said, "What was important to me at the time was trying to erase the situation. I was split between the idea of pursuing it in court and just letting it die. I couldn't stand the stress." Another woman explained, "The situation is really blocked out, because I don't want them to take action against me."

Conclusion

These descriptions of the social reality of victims explain why only an exceptional few who perceive they have experienced discrimination

[35] Luhmann has developed a model of the communicative process that accounts for the transformation of a conflict once a legal theme has been introduced. Once a dispute has been thematized as a legal conflict, the participants require social support. In some cases, law can be advantageous to the weaker party because it removes law to a rule-oriented context. But Luhmann explains, "not all interaction systems can handle this kind of alienation" (244–45). The legal thematization may rudely displace the power relations and move the communication interaction into the sphere of the legal system that is incompatible with the subsystems of interaction (meaning everyday life).

[36] The view of the law held by victims of discrimination is in stark contrast to the anticipated response to protective law. The collection of statements by individuals who feel they have experienced discrimination creates a composite picture analogous to the themes about law presented in Kafka's *The Trial.* "If I had behaved sensibly, nothing further would have happened, all this would have been nipped in the bud. But one is so unprepared." The solution seems to be to reestablish boundaries that push legality away from the victim's life (Franz Kafka, *The Trial* [New York: Schocken Books, 1968], 20).

achieve successful resolution of their problems.[37] This study offers three explanations for victims' reluctance to assert the worthiness of their interests and their acceptance of defeat as inevitable. First, the bonds between the perpetrator and the discrimination victim drive the conflict to self-destructive or explosive reactions. Second, these individuals are guided by an ethic of survival that encourages self-sacrifice rather than action. And third, the potential for legal remedies is diminished by a view of the law that engenders fear of legal intervention. Injured persons reluctantly employ the label of discrimination because they shun the role of the victim, and they fear legal intervention will disrupt the delicate balance of power between themselves and their opponents.

The hostile image of the law held by respondents considering legal recourse is a harsh reality compared to the spirit of protective law that promises to give purpose and justice to its beneficiaries' lives. In contemporary American society it is typically assumed that the "rule of law" is strengthened by the increase in enforcement powers, the clarification of goals, or the removal of discretion, so that the right-bearer is protected. Yet when people contemplate invoking the right of "equal treatment under law," they find themselves in a position with only undesirable alternatives. The invocation of antidiscrimination law does not enable the victim to overcome power differentials in situations where she or he is pitted against the more powerful opponent. The bonds of victimhood are reinforced rather than broken by the intervention of legal discourse.

The civil rights movement has produced numerous lessons about the limits of the law. Evaluations of doctrinal development and policy implementation have demonstrated the limited role of courts in restructuring social and economic relations.[38] Champions of litigation may misrepresent the problem by ignoring the complexity of systematic processes of discrimination that operate throughout society and then misrepresent the solution by creating the impression that the elimination of legal barriers is sufficient to achieve racial equality. Litigation thus becomes the focal point of activism at the cost of possibly more dynamic attacks on the root causes of

[37] Other studies have attempted to account for unsuccessful resolution of claims when they are brought to legal agencies. See Leon Mayhew, *Law and Equal Opportunity* (Cambridge, Mass.: Harvard University Press, 1968); Patricia Ward Crowe, "Complainant Reactions to the Massachusetts Commission against Discrimination," *Law and Society Review* 12, no. 2 (Winter 1978): 217–36; Joel Handler, *Social Movements and the Legal System* (New York: Academic Press, 1978). These studies found that complaints were systematically "dismissed for lack of probable cause," there were frequent "double-victimizations" due to the degradation imposed by the hearing process, and many routine cases were abandoned due to a preference for class actions and agency co-optation.

[38] For example, see Stuart Scheingold, *The Politics of Rights* (New Haven, Conn.: Yale University Press, 1974); Charles A. Bullock and Charles M. Lamb, *The Implementation of Civil Rights Policy* (Monterey, Calif.: Brooks/Cole, 1984); Donald Horowitz, *The Courts and Social Policy* (Washington, D.C.: Brookings Institution, 1977).

racial and sexual subordination.[39] Moreover, legal ideologies can constrain the social vision of the victim and promote self-blame. The mythologies which perpetuate racism and sexism are reflected in both the benevolent policies of legal reformers and the self-image of those who experience discrimination.

The inaction of discrimination victims is problematic from the vantage point of the ideology of legal protection. From the social reality of the victim, however, we find that "survival is a form of resistance."[40] In this study, the majority of these individuals view protest as contrary to their well-being and livelihood. The situation creates a paradox of irrationality, in which people engaged in discrimination conflicts believe they are better off if they decide not to pursue their interests.[41] To act aggressively and battle for a principle requires "irrational" sacrifices and defeats the individual's ethic of survival.

Though antidiscrimination law may have produced positive social change, legal strategies put unacceptable burdens on disadvantaged groups with little promise of success. The gap between the symbolic life of the law and the ineffectiveness of the law in action imposes a cost borne by the intended beneficiaries of civil rights policies. The inability of civil rights strategies to fulfill their promise appears to have left many who experience discrimination on uncertain ground between public and private action where they are without faith in themselves or the law.

Department of Political Science
Johns Hopkins University

[39] Derrick Bell, "Foreword: The Civil Rights Chronicles," *Harvard Law Review* 99, no. 1 (November 1985): 4–83.

[40] For example, see the use of the phrase in Gerda Lerner, *Black Women in White America* (New York: Vintage, 1972), 287.

[41] The paradox of irrationality is employed in the study of police behavior to account for why rational negotiations are impossible with a suspect who has nothing to lose. See William Ker Muir, *Police: Street Corner Politicians* (Chicago: University of Chicago Press, 1977). For an analogy to criminal defendants, see Malcolm Feeley, *The Process Is the Punishment* (New York: Russell Sage, 1979). He observes that for defendants the cost of invoking one's rights frequently is greater than the loss of the rights themselves.

[5]

That We Are Human, We Have Rights

CARLOS A. BALL

ONE OF THE PERENNIAL disagreements in moral and political philosophy is whether it is possible to reach ethical and political judgments that have universal applicability—judgments that apply across all cultures and historical periods.

On one side are those who believe that all human beings share certain fundamental attributes—such as the ability to reason and to decide for oneself how to lead one's life—without which it would be impossible to lead fully human lives. Those attributes, in turn, impose moral and political obligations on both societies and individuals. If all human beings share a basic ability to make important decisions about their own lives, then that capacity should be respected by others. For many thinkers, therefore, rights to free speech and to the free exercise of religion, say, are rights that we enjoy as human beings regardless of where or when we happen to live.

On the other side are philosophers who question the idea that human beings share characteristics that cut across cultures and historical periods. Accordingly, the priorities and values of societies, rather then the attributes of human beings, are what determine what is right politically and morally. They would maintain that values like diversity or freedom of speech and religion in the West are nothing more than an artifact of Western societies' attachment to a cultural definition of the person that emphasizes individual autonomy over communal goals. But there is nothing intrinsic about human beings that requires a respect for freedom of speech or religion. In short, different societies have different understandings of the "truth," and the last thing one can do is to judge one such understanding to be better than another.

While this may seem an arcane debate among philosophers, it can have major ramifications for how we frame important moral and political issues. For example, the gay rights movement currently finds itself in a pitched battle with religious conservatives over many issues related to the meaning of marriage and family, and whether the cause of gay rights prevails could depend on how we present our case. To illustrate what's at stake, let me introduce briefly the ideas of two highly influential contemporary American philosophers, Richard Rorty and Martha Nussbaum. In brief, Rorty rejects the notion that human beings share certain attributes that make them human and endow them with rights, while Nussbaum embraces just this proposition. For reasons that will soon become clear, I think Nussbaum's argument provides a better framework for advancing the full social and legal equality of lesbians and gay men.

Carlos A. Ball teaches law at Penn State University. His book, The Morality of Gay Rights: An Exploration in Political Philosophy, *was published by Routledge.*

Among contemporary American philosophers, Richard Rorty is arguably the most influential proponent of the idea that we should base our moral and political arguments on the shared norms and values of our society rather than on distinctive human attributes. For example, he advises that we *not* rely on the idea of a "common humanity" when arguing on behalf of marginalized groups, whether members of racial minorities or women or gay people. Instead, we should refer to elements that are specific to American society, such as the fact that American citizens have shared understandings about the meaning and value of liberty and equality. If we focus on these local ideals rather than on universal human attributes or values, Rorty contends, we'll be in a better position to progress toward a more inclusive and tolerant society. In an example of what he has in mind, Rorty argues that the best way to end the "hopelessness and misery of the lives of [some] young blacks in American cities" is to "insist that it is outrageous that an American should live without hope." We should focus on what it means to be an American and on the values that we share as Americans, and forget about abstract discussions of what it means to be "human."

The trouble with Rorty's approach is that heterosexist societies such as ours not only deny lesbians and gay men their basic rights as citizens, but also their basic rights as human beings.

The trouble with Rorty's approach when applied to gay rights issues, it seems to me, is that heterosexist societies such as ours deny lesbians and gay men not only their basic rights as citizens, but also their basic rights as human beings. In the U.S., the very humanity of lesbians and gay men is questioned in two principal ways. First, GLBT people's sexuality is portrayed as perverse and depraved, and sometimes even compared to bestiality. To this day, many criminal statutes are on the books that equate sodomy with crimes against nature and bestiality, while conservative philosophers such as John Finnis contend that same-sex sex is, morally speaking, akin to the "[c]opulation of humans with animals." After Matthew Shepard was beaten to death in Laramie, Wyoming, a resident of that town told an interviewer that if asked by his children about the young man's death, he would tell them that "gay people do ... what animals do." Apparently, then, the sexual behavior of lesbians and gay men calls into question their very humanity.

The second way in which our society dehumanizes lesbians and gay men is by viewing them only through the prism of sex rather than as full human beings who share fundamental human needs and capacities associated with loving another person. Thus who they are in the eyes of society is being determined by one characteristic rather than by what Martin Luther King called "the content of their character." In the political arena, the struggle for equality has had to contend with the view that lesbians and gay men are obsessed with sex. This image of GLBT people, in turn, has been used to justify their exclusion from important rights, such as marital and parental ones, that others in our society enjoy. During the heated debates over the Defense of Marriage Act back in 1996, for example, Congressman Tom Coburn of Oklahoma explained on the House floor that the institution of marriage needed to be protected from homosexuality, which he argued was about nothing more than sexual lust.

Such statements, which are commonplace in our public discourse on gay rights, ignore the fact that lesbians and gay men enter into loving relationships just as heterosexuals do, and thus deny our common humanity. Others may recognize that such relationships exist but demean them as morally suspect or somehow inferior to heterosexual bonds, an argument that likewise attacks gay people's very humanity. Given the extent to which such arguments have been the accepted norm in our society, it is not particularly useful to argue, as philosophers like Rorty do, that we should base our claim to equality only on prevailing social values, or that it's a waste of time to argue that all human beings, including lesbians and gay men, share certain fundamental attributes that go beyond the standards of any particular society.

Let me further illustrate what I mean by this by contrasting Rorty's views with those of the philosopher Martha Nussbaum. While Rorty contends that we should not bother with arguments about what makes us human, Nussbaum believes that there are certain basic capabilities that are fundamental parts of our humanity, including the ability to think and reason, to love and take care of others, to control one's body and protect it against abuse by others, to engage in various forms of familial and social interactions, and to laugh, play, and enjoy recreational activities of our choosing. Human beings, regardless of when and where they live, share these basic capabilities. This is not to deny that some societies deprive their people of the right to exercise basic capacities to varying degrees. Whenever this occurs, individuals are prevented from living lives that are fully human. In Nussbaum's view, societies have a moral and political obligation to create the necessary structures and conditions that make it possible for all citizens to realize their full humanity.

The practical application of this can be illustrated as follows. In the late 1990's, three same-sex couples in Vermont went to their town clerk seeking a marriage license. The couples had been in committed relationships for periods ranging from four to twenty years. In addition, two of the couples had raised children together. After they were turned down by the clerks, they sued the state of Vermont. The state defended itself in the lawsuit by arguing that it was under no constitutional obligation to legally recognize same-gender relationships. The state Supreme Court in a case called *Baker v. State* rejected the state's argument and ordered it to provide lesbians and gay men with the same legal rights and benefits provided to heterosexual couples.

Some of the arguments that the court relied on in reaching its decision place gay rights issues in the broader context of what it means to be human. The court argued that marriage "is a singularly human relationship" and "the essential aspect of the [plaintiffs'] claim is simply and fundamentally for inclusion in the family of state-sanctioned human relations." The court then cited the U.S. Supreme Court's opinion in *Dred Scott v. Sandford*—the infamous 19th-century ruling that blacks were not citizens entitled to constitutional protections—to remind us that "[t]he past provides many instances where the law refused to see a human being when it should have." Vermont's refusal to recognize committed same-sex relationships was likewise a failure to acknowledge the plaintiffs' full humanity. The court could not approve of such a view because the Vermont constitution enshrined a principle of equality that required it to view lesbians and gay men as full human beings. As the court eloquently noted, "to acknowledge plaintiffs as Vermonters who seek nothing more, nor less, than legal protection and security for their avowed commitment to an intimate and lasting human relationship is simply, when all is said and done, a recognition of our common humanity."

Despite the victory in Vermont and incremental but steady gains in other states, many gay academics remain skeptical of grounding arguments about justice and equality on universal human attributes. They have some legitimate concerns, including the fact that to be "human" has been subject to varying interpretations, often equated (in our society) with being male, white, and heterosexual. For example, feminists have properly objected to the way in which the ability to reason, which has long been considered by philosophers to be a quintessential human attribute, has been viewed as a more "male" trait than a "female" one. If being human is equated with being rational, and if women are defined as less rational than men, then half of the population is being excluded from the realm of the fully human.

As history amply reveals, it is certainly possible to define what it means to be human in such a way as to support those in power while excluding, say, racial minorities, women, or gay people. However, the best way to address this problem, in my view, is *not* to give up altogether on the concept of the human being as a source of moral and political rights. Instead, the better choice is to articulate and defend a more convincing and nonoppressive conception of what it means to be human. As the late law professor Peter Cicchino eloquently put it, it is important to think about what it means to be human from within a "spirit of self-correction, of constant and careful attention to the rich texture and fine detail of human experience, and a profound sensibility to the marginalized and oppressed."

Philosophers will always disagree on which are the attributes that truly define our humanity. It is difficult to disagree with the proposition, however, that the capacity to love others is a fundamental part of what makes us human. Most gay rights issues implicate, in one form or another, the human capacity to love others. Whether we like it or not, therefore, we cannot avoid questions of what it means to be human in our debates over gay rights.

It was only when women were viewed as fully human (as having the capability to reason and to make intelligent decisions about their lives and their futures) that society granted them the right to vote as well as the opportunity to seek happiness and fulfillment outside as well as inside the home. It was only when African Americans were viewed as fully human that society granted them meaningful access to the most basic civil rights. Similarly, it is only when lesbians and gay men are finally viewed as fully human that they will be offered the opportunity to participate in institutions such as marriage and parenting that are meant to account and provide for the basic capacities of human beings in the areas of physical and emotional intimacy.

Part II
Sources of Well-being and Harm

[6]

More Than 100 Million Women Are Missing

Amartya Sen

It is often said that women make up a majority of the world's population. They do not. This mistaken belief is based on generalizing from the contemporary situation in Europe and North America, where the ratio of women to men is typically around 1.05 or 1.06, or higher. In South Asia, West Asia, and China, the ratio of women to men can be as low as 0.94, or even lower, and it varies widely elsewhere in Asia, in Africa, and in Latin America. How can we understand and explain these differences, and react to them?

1.

At birth, boys outnumber girls everywhere in the world, by much the same proportion—there are around 105 or 106 male children for every 100 female children. Just why the biology of reproduction leads to this result remains a subject of debate. But after conception, biology seems on the whole to favor women. Considerable research has shown that if men and women receive similar nutritional and medical attention and general health care, women tend to live noticeably longer than men. Women seem to be, on the whole, more resistant to disease and in general hardier than men, an advantage they enjoy not only after they are forty years old but also at the beginning of life, especially during the months immediately following birth, and even in the womb. When given the same care as males, females tend to have better survival rates than males.[1]

Women outnumber men substantially in Europe, the US, and Japan, where, despite the persistence of various types of bias against women (men having distinct advantages in higher education, job specialization, and promotion to senior executive positions, for example), women suffer little discrimination in basic nutrition and health care. The greater number of women in these countries is partly the result of social and environmental differences that increase mortality among men, such as a higher likelihood that men will die from violence, for example, and from diseases related to smoking. But even after these are taken into account, the longer lifetimes enjoyed by women given similar care appear to relate to the biological advantages that women have over men in resisting disease. Whether the higher frequency of male births over female births has evolutionary links to this potentially greater survival rate among women is a question of some interest in itself. Women seem to have lower death rates than men at most ages whenever they get roughly similar treatment in matters of life and death.

The fate of women is quite different in most of Asia and North Africa. In these places the failure to give women medical care similar to what men get and to provide them with comparable food and social services results in fewer women surviving than would be the case if they had equal care. In India, for example, except in the period immediately following birth, the death rate is higher for women than for men fairly consistently in all age groups until the late thirties. This relates to higher rates of disease from which women suffer, and ultimately to the relative neglect of females, especially in health care and medical attention.[2] Similar neglect of women vis-à-vis men can be seen also in many other parts of the world. The result is a lower proportion of women than would be the case if they had equal care—in most of Asia and North Africa, and to a lesser extent Latin America.

This pattern is not uniform in all parts of the third world, however. Sub-Saharan Africa, for example, ravaged as it is by extreme poverty, hunger, and famine, has a substantial excess rather than deficit of women, the ratio of women to men being around 1.02. The "third world" in this matter is not a useful category, because it is so diverse. Even within Asia, which has the lowest proportion of women in the world, Southeast Asia and East Asia (apart from China) have a ratio of women to men that is slightly higher than one to one (around 1.01). Indeed, sharp diversities also exist within particular regions—sometimes even within a particular country. For example, the ratio of women to men in the Indian states of Punjab and Haryana, which happen to be among the country's richest, is a remarkably low 0.86, while the state of Kerala in southwestern India has a ratio higher than 1.03, similar to that in Europe, North America, and Japan.

To get an idea of the numbers of people involved in the different ratios of women to men, we can estimate the number of "missing women" in a country, say, China or India, by calculating the number of extra women who would have been in China or India if these countries had the same ratio of women to men as obtain in areas of the world in which they receive similar care. If we could expect equal populations of the two sexes, the low ratio of 0.94 women to men in South Asia, West Asia, and China would indicate a 6 percent deficit of women; but since, in countries where men and women receive similar care, the ratio is about 1.05, the real shortfall is about 11 percent. In China alone this amounts to 50 million "missing women," taking 1.05 as the benchmark ratio When that number is added to those in South Asia, West Asia, and North Africa, a great many more than 100 million women are "missing." These numbers tell us, quietly, a terrible story of inequality and neglect leading to the excess mortality of women.

Photograph © Jacques Pavlovsky/Sygma

Women harvesting peanuts, Senegal, 1980

2.

To account for the neglect of women, two simplistic explanations have often been presented or, more often, implicitly assumed. One view emphasizes the cultural contrasts between East and West (or between the Occident and the Orient), claiming that Western civilization is less sexist than Eastern. That women outnumber men in Western countries may appear to lend support to this Kipling-like generalization. (Kipling himself was not, of course, much bothered by concerns about sexism, and even made "the twain" meet in romantically masculine circumstances: "But there is neither East nor West, Border, nor Breed, nor Birth, / When two strong men stand face to face, tho' they come from the ends of the earth!") The other simple argument looks instead at stages of economic development, seeing the unequal nutrition and health care provided for women as a feature of underdevelopment, a characteristic of poor economies awaiting economic advancement.

There may be elements of truth in each of these explanations, but neither is very convincing as a general thesis. To some extent, the two simple explanations, in terms of "economic development" and "East-West" divisions, also tend to undermine each other. A combined cultural and economic analysis would seem to be necessary, and, I will

---

[1] An assessment of the available evidence can be found in Ingrid Waldron's "The Role of Genetic and Biological Factors in Sex Differences in Mortality," in A. D. Lopez and L. T. Ruzicka, eds., *Sex Differences in Mortality* (Canberra: Department of Demography, Australian National University, 1983). On the pervasive cultural influences on mortality and the difficulties in forming a biological view of survival advantages, see Sheila Ryan Johansson, "Mortality, Welfare and Gender: Continuity and Change in Explanations for Male/Female Mortality Differences over Three Centuries," in *Continuity and Change*, forthcoming.

[2] These and related data are presented and assessed in my joint paper with Jocelyn Kynch, "Indian Women: Well-being and Survival," *Cambridge Journal of Economics*, Vol. 7 (1983), and in my *Commodities and Capabilities* (Amsterdam: North-Holland, 1985), Appendix B. See also Lincoln Chen et al., "Sex Bias in the Family Allocation of Food and Health Care in Rural Bangladesh," in *Population and Development Review*, Vol. 7 (1981); Barbara Miller, *The Endangered Sex: Neglect of Female Children in Rural North India* (Cornell University Press, 1981); Pranab Bardhan, *Land, Labor, and Rural Poverty* (Columbia University Press, 1984); Devaki Jain and Nirmala Banerji, eds., *Tyranny of the Household* (New Delhi: Vikas, 1985); Barbara Harriss and Elizabeth Watson, "The Sex Ratio in South Asia," in J. H. Momsen and J. G. Townsend, eds., *Geography of Gender in the Third World* (State University of New York Press, 1987); Monica Das Gupta, "Selective Discrimination against Female Children in Rural Punjab, India," in *Population and Development Review*, Vol. 13 (1987).

argue, it would have to take note of many other social conditions in addition to the features identified in the simple aggregative theses.

To take the cultural view first, the East-West explanation is obviously flawed because experiences within the East and West diverge so sharply. Japan, for example, unlike most of Asia, has a ratio of women to men that is not very different from that in Europe or North America. This might suggest, at least superficially, that real income and economic development do more to explain the bias against providing women with the conditions for survival than whether the society is Western or Oriental. In the censuses of 1899 and 1908 Japan had a clear and substantial deficit of women, but by 1940 the numbers of men and women were nearly equal, and in the postwar decades, as Japan became a rich and highly industrialized country, it moved firmly in the direction of a large surplus, rather than a deficit, of women. Some countries in East Asia and Southeast Asia also provide exceptions to the deficit of women; in Thailand and Indonesia, for example, women substantially outnumber men.

In its rudimentary, undiscriminating form, the East-West explanation also fails to take into account other characteristics of these societies. For example, the ratios of women to men in South Asia are among the lowest in the world (around 0.94 in India and Bangladesh, and 0.90 in Pakistan—the lowest ratio for any large country), but that region has been among the pioneers in electing women as top political leaders. Indeed, each of the four large South Asian countries—India, Pakistan, Bangladesh, and Sri Lanka—either has had a woman as the elected head of government (Sri Lanka, India, and Pakistan), or has had women leading the main opposition parties (as in Bangladesh).

It is, of course, true that these successes in South Asia have been achieved only by upper-class women, and that having a woman head of government has not, by itself, done much for women in general in these countries. However, the point here is only to question the tendency to see the contrast between East and West as simply based on more sexism or less. The large electoral successes of women in achieving high positions in government in South Asia indicate that the analysis has to be more complex.

It is, of course, also true that these women leaders reached their powerful positions with the help of dynastic connections—Indira Gandhi was the daughter of Jawaharlal Nehru, Benazir Bhutto the daughter of Zulfikar Bhutto, and so on. But it would be absurd to overlook—just on that ground—the significance of their rise to power through popular mandate. Dynastic connections are not new in politics and are pervasive features of political succession in many countries. That Indira Gandhi derived her political strength partly from her father's position is not in itself more significant than the fact that Rajiv Gandhi's political credibility derived largely from his mother's political eminence, or the fact (perhaps less well known) that Indira Gandhi's father—the great Jawaharlal Nehru—initially rose to prominence as the son of Motilal Nehru, who had been president of the Congress party. The dynastic aspects of South Asian politics have certainly helped women to come to power through electoral support, but it is still true that so far as winning elections is concerned, South Asia would seem to be some distance ahead of the United States and most European countries when it comes to discrimination according to gender.

In this context it is useful also to compare the ratios of women in American and Indian legislatures. In the US House of Representatives the proportion of women is 6.4 percent, while in the present and the last lower houses of the Indian Parliament, women's proportions have been respectively 5.3 and 7.9 percent. Only two of the 100 US Senators are women, and this 2 percent ratio contrasts with more than 9 and 10 percent women respectively in the last and present "upper house," Rajya Sabha, in India. (In a different, but not altogether unrelated, sphere, I had a much higher proportion of tenured women colleagues when I was teaching at Delhi University than I now have at Harvard.) The cultural climate in different societies must have a clear relevance to differences between men and women—both in survival and in other ways as well—but it would be hopeless to see the divergences simply as a contrast between the sexist East and the unbiased West.

How good is the other (i.e., the purely economic) explanation for women's inequality? Certainly all the countries with large deficits of women are more or less poor, if we measure poverty by real incomes, and no sizable country with a high gross national product per head has such a deficit. There are reasons to expect a reduction of differential female mortality with economic progress. For example, the rate of maternal mortality at childbirth can be expected to decrease both with better hospital facilities and the reduction in birth rate that usually accompanies economic development.

However, in this simple form, an economic analysis does not explain very much, since many poor countries do not, in fact, have deficits of women. As was noted earlier, sub-Saharan Africa, poor and underdeveloped as it is, has a substantial excess of women. Southeast and East Asia (but not China) also differ from many other relatively poor countries in this respect, although to a lesser degree. Within India, as was noted earlier, Punjab and Haryana—among the richest and most economically advanced Indian states—have very low ratios of women to men (around 0.86), in contrast to the much poorer state of Kerala, where the ratio is greater than 1.03.

Indeed, economic development is quite often accompanied by a relative worsening in the rate of survival of women (even as life expectancy improves in absolute terms for both men and women). For example, in India the gap between the life expectancy of men and women has narrowed recently, but only after many decades when women's relative position deteriorated. There has been a steady decline in the ratio of women to men in the population, from more than 97 women to 100 men at the turn of the century (in 1901), to 93 women in 1971, and the ratio is only a little higher now. The deterioration in women's position results largely from their unequal sharing in the advantages of medical and social progress. Economic development does not invariably reduce women's disadvantages in mortality.

A significant proportional decline in the population of women occurred in China after the economic and social reforms introduced there in 1979. The Chinese Statistical Yearbooks show a steady decline in the already very low ratio of women to men in the population, from 94.32 in 1979 to 93.42 in 1985 and 1986. (It has risen since then, to 93.98 in 1989—still lower than what it was in 1979). Life expectancy was significantly higher for females than for males until the economic reforms, but seems to have fallen behind since then.[3] Of course, the years following the reforms were also years of great economic growth and, in many ways, of social progress, yet women's relative prospects for survival deteriorated. These and other cases show that rapid economic development may go hand in hand with worsening relative mortality of women.

3.

Despite their superficial plausibility, neither the alleged contrast between "East" and "West," nor the simple hypothesis of female deprivation as a characteristic of economic "underdevelopment" gives us anything like an adequate understanding of the geography of female deprivation in social well-being and survival. We have to examine the complex ways in which economic, social, and cultural factors can influence the regional differences.

It is certainly true that, for example, the status and power of women in the family differ greatly from one region to another, and there are good reasons to expect that these social features would be related to the economic role and independence of women. For example, employment outside the home and owning assets can both be important for women's economic independence and power; and these factors may have far-reaching effects on the divisions of benefits and chores within the family and can greatly influence what are implicitly accepted as women's "entitlements."

Indeed, men and women have both interests in common and conflicting interests that affect family decisions; and it is possible to see decision making in the family taking the form of the pursuit of cooperation in which solutions for the conflicting aspects of family life are implicitly agreed on. Such "cooperative conflicts" are a general feature of many group relations, and an analysis of cooperative conflicts can provide a useful way of understanding the influences that affect the "deal" that women get in the division of benefits within the family. There are gains to be made by men and women through following implicitly agreed-on patterns of behavior; but there are many possible agreements—some more favorable to one party than others. The choice of one such cooperative arrangement from among the range of possibilities leads to a particular distribution of joint benefits. (Elsewhere, I have tried to analyze the general nature of "cooperative conflicts" and the application of the analysis of such conflicts to family economics.[4])

Conflicts in family life are typically resolved through implicitly agreed-on patterns of behavior that may or may not be particularly egalitarian. The very nature of family living—sharing a home and experiences—requires that the elements of conflict must not be explicitly emphasized (giving persistent attention to conflicts will usually be seen as aberrant behavior); and sometimes the deprived woman would not even have a clear idea of the extent of her relative deprivation. Similarly, the perception of who is doing "productive" work, who is "contributing" how much to the family's prosperity, can be very influential, even though the underlying principles regarding how "contributions" or "productivity" are to be assessed may be rarely discussed explicitly. These issues of social perception are, I believe, of pervasive importance in gender inequality, even in the richer countries, but they can have a particularly powerful influence in sustaining female deprivation in many of the poorer countries.[5]

The division of a family's joint benefits is likely to be less unfavorable to women if (1) they can earn an outside income; (2) their work is recognized as productive (this is easier to achieve with work done outside the home); (3) they own some economic resources and have some rights to fall back on; and (4) there is a clear-headed understanding of the ways in which women are deprived and a recognition of the possibilities of changing this situation. This last category can be much influenced by education for women and by participatory political action.

Considerable empirical evidence, mostly studies of particular localities, suggests that what is usually defined as "gainful" employment (i.e., working outside the home for a wage, or in such "productive" occupations as farming), as opposed to unpaid and unhonored housework—no matter how demanding—can substantially enhance the deal that women get.[6] Indeed, "gainful" employment of women can make the solution of "cooperative conflicts" less unfavorable to women in many ways. First, outside employment for wages can provide women with an income to which

[3]See the World Bank's *World Development Report 1990* (Oxford University Press, 1990), Table 32. See also Judith Banister, *China's Changing Population* (Stanford University Press, 1987), Chapter 4, though the change in life expectancy may not have been as large as these early estimates had suggested, as Banister herself has later noted.

[4]"Gender and Cooperative Conflicts," Working Paper of the World Institute of Development Economics Research (1986), in Irene Tinker, ed., *Persistent Inequalities: Women and World Development* (Oxford University Press, 1990). In the same volume see also the papers of Ester Boserup, Hanna Papanek, and Irene Tinker on closely related subjects.

[5]The recent literature on the modeling of family relations as "bargaining problems," despite being usefully suggestive and insightful, has suffered a little from giving an inadequate role to the importance of perceptions (as opposed to objectively identified interests) of the parties involved. On the relevance of perception, including perceptual distortions (a variant of what Marx had called "false perception"), in family relations, see my "Gender and Cooperative Conflicts." See also my *Resources, Values and Development* (Harvard University Press, 1984), Chapters 15 and 16; Gail Wilson, *Money in the Family* (Avebury/Gower, 1987).

[6]See the case studies and the literature cited in my "Gender and Cooperative Conflicts." A pioneering study of some of these issues was provided by Ester Boserup, *Women's Role in Economic Development* (St. Martin's, 1970). See also Bina Agarwal, "Social Security and the Family," in E. Ahmad, et al., *Social Security in Developing Countries*, to be published by Oxford University Press in 1991.

they have easier access, and it can also serve as a means of making a living on which women can rely, making them less vulnerable. Second, the social respect that is associated with being a "bread winner" (and a "productive" contributor to the family's joint prosperity) can improve women's status and standing in the family, and may influence the prevailing cultural traditions regarding who gets what in the division of joint benefits. Third, when outside employment takes the form of jobs with some security and legal protection, the corresponding rights that women get can make their economic position much less vulnerable and precarious. Fourth, working outside the home also provides experience of the outside world, and this can be socially important in improving women's position within the family. In this respect outside work may be "educational" as well.

These factors may not only improve the "deal" women get in the family, they can also counter the relative neglect of girls as they grow up. Boys are preferred in many countries because they are expected to provide more economic security for their parents in old age; but the force of this bias can be weakened if women as well as men can regularly work at paid jobs. Moreover, if the status of women does in general rise and women's contributions become more recognized, female children may receive more attention. Similarly, the exposure of women to the world through work outside the home can weaken, through its educational effect, the hold of traditional beliefs and behavior.

In comparing different regions of Asia and Africa, if we try to relate the relative survival prospects of women to the "gainful employment" of both sexes—i.e., work outside the home, possibly for a wage—we do find a strong association. If the different regions of Asia and Africa (with the exception of China) are ranked according to the proportion of women in so-called gainful employment relative to the proportion of men in such employment, we get the following ranking, in descending order:[7]

1. Sub-Saharan Africa
2. Southeast and Eastern Asia
3. Western Asia
4. Southern Asia
5. Northern Africa

Ranking the ratios of life expectancy of females to those of males produces a remarkably similar ordering:

1. Sub-Saharan Africa
2. Southeast and Eastern Asia
3. Western Asia
4. Northern Africa
5. Southern Asia

That the two rankings are much the same, except for a switch between the two lowest-ranking regions (lowest in terms of both indicators), suggests a link between employment and survival prospects. In addition to the overall correspondence between the two rankings, the particular contrasts between sub-Saharan Africa and North Africa, and that between Southern (and Western) Asia and Southeast (and Eastern) Asia are suggestive distinctions *within* Africa and Asia respectively, linking women's gainful employment and survival prospects.

It is, of course, possible that what we are seeing here is not a demonstration that gainful employment causes better survival prospects but the influence of some other factor correlated with each. In fact, on the basis of such broad relations, it is very hard to draw any firm conclusion; but evidence of similar relations can be found also in other comparisons.[8] For example, Punjab, the richest Indian state, has the lowest ratio of women to men (0.86) in India; it also has the lowest ratio of women in "gainful" employment compared to men. The influence of outside employment on women's well-being has also been documented in a number of studies of specific communities in different parts of the world.[9]

Photograph © K. Nichols/Magnum

Women harvesting potatoes in Rwanda

4.

The case of China deserves particular attention. It is a country with a traditional bias against women, but after the revolution the Chinese leaders did pay considerable attention to reducing inequality between men and women.[10] This was helped both by a general expansion of basic health and medical services accessible to all and by the increase in women's gainful employment, along with greater social recognition of the importance of women in the economy and the society.

There has been a remarkable general expansion of longevity, and despite the temporary setback during the terrible famines of 1958–1961 (following the disastrous failure of the so-called Great Leap Forward), the Chinese life expectancy at birth increased from the low forties around 1950 to the high sixties by the time the economic reforms were introduced in 1979. The sharp reduction in general mortality (including female mortality) is all the more remarkable in view of the fact that it took place despite deep economic problems in the form of widespread industrial inefficiency, a rather stagnant agriculture, and relatively little increase in output per head. Female death rates declined sharply—both as a part of a general mortality reduction and also relatively, vis-à-vis male mortality. Women's life expectancy at birth overtook that of men—itself much enhanced—and was significantly ahead at the time the economic and social reforms were introduced in 1979.

Those reforms immediately increased the rate of economic growth and broke the agricultural stagnation. The official figures suggest a doubling of agricultural output between 1979 and 1986—a remarkable achievement even if some elements of exaggeration are eliminated from these figures. But at the same time, the official figures also record an *increase* in the general mortality rates after the reforms, with a consistently higher death rate than what China had achieved by 1979. There seems to be also a worsening of the relative survival of women, including a decline, discussed earlier, of the ratio of women to men in the population, which went down from 94.3 in 1979 to 93.4 in 1985 and 1986. There are problems in interpreting the available data and difficulties in arriving at firm conclusions, but the view that women's life expectancy has again become lower than that of men has gained support. For example, the World Bank's most recent *World Development Report* suggests a life expectancy of sixty-nine years for men and sixty-six years for women (even though the confounded nature of the subject is well reflected by the fact that the same *Report* also suggests an average life expectancy of seventy years for men and women put together).[11]

Why have women's survival prospects in China deteriorated, especially in relative terms, since 1979? Several experts have noted that recently Chinese leaders have tended, on the whole, to reduce the emphasis on equality for women; it is no longer much discussed, and indeed, as the sociologist Margery Wolf puts it, it is a case of a "revolution postponed."[12] But this fact, while important, does not explain why the relative survival prospects of women would have so deteriorated during the early years of the reforms, just at the time when there was a rapid expansion of overall economic prosperity.

The compulsory measures to control the size of families which were introduced in 1979 may have been an important factor. In some parts of the country the authorities insisted on the "one-child family." This restriction, given the strong preference for boys in China, led to a neglect of girls that was often severe. Some evidence exists of female infanticide. In the early years after the reforms, infant mortality for girls appeared to increase considerably. Some estimates had suggested that the rate of female infant mortality rose from 37.7 per thousand in 1978 to 67.2 per thousand in 1984.[13] Even if this seems exaggerated in the light of later data, the survival prospects of female children clearly have been unfavorably affected by restrictions on the size of the family. Later legal concessions (including the permission to have a second child if the first one is a girl) reflect some official recognition of these problems.

A second factor relevant to the survival problems of Chinese women is the general crisis in health services since the economic reforms. As the agricultural production brigades and collectives, which had traditionally provided much of the funding for China's extensive rural health programs, were dismantled, they were replaced by the so-called "responsibility system," in which agriculture was centered in the family. Agricultural production improved, but cutbacks in communal facilities placed severe financial restrictions on China's extensive rural medical services. Communal agriculture may not have done much for agricultural production as such, but it had been a main source of support for China's innovative and extensive rural medical services. So far as gender is concerned, the effects of the reduced scope of these services are officially neutral, but in view of the pro-male bias in Chinese rural society, the cutback in medical services would have had a particularly severe impact on women and female children. (It is also the pro-male bias in the general culture that made the one-child policy, which too is neutral in form, unfavorable to female children in terms of its actual impact.)

Third, the "responsibility system" arguably has reduced women's involvement in recognized gainful employment in agriculture. In the new system's more traditional arrangement of work responsibilities, women's work in the household economy may again suffer from the lack of recognition that typically affects household work throughout the world.[14] The impact of this change on the status of women within the household may be negative, for the reasons previously described. Expanded employment opportunities for women outside agriculture in some regions may at least partially balance this effect. But the weakening of social security arrangements since the reforms would also have made old age more precarious, and since such insecurity is one of the persistent motives for families' preferring boys over girls, this change too can be contributing to the worsening of care for female children.[15]

[7]Details can be found in my "Gender and Cooperative Conflicts."

[8]For example, see Pranab Bardhan, *Land, Labor, and Rural Poverty* on different states in India and the literature cited there.

[9]See the literature cited in my "Gender and Cooperative Conflicts."

[10]See Elisabeth Croll, *Chinese Women Since Mao* (M. E. Sharpe, 1984).

[11]See *World Development Report 1990*, Tables 1 and 32. See also Banister, *China's Changing Population*, Chapter 4, and Athar Hussain and Nicholas Stern, *On the recent increase in death rate in China*, China Paper #8 (London: STICERD/London School of Economics, 1990).

[12]See Margery Wolf, *Revolution Postponed: Women in Contemporary China* (Stanford University Press, 1984).

[13]See Banister, *China's Changing Population*, Table 4.12.

[14]On this and related matters, see Nahid Aslanbeigui and Gale Summerfield, "The Impact of the Responsibility System on Women in Rural China: A Theoretical Application of Sen's Theory of Entitlement," in *World Development*, Vol. 17 (1989).

[15]These and other aspects of the problem are discussed more extensively in my joint book with Jean Drèze, *Hunger and Public Action* (Oxford University Press, 1989).

5.

Analyses based on simple conflicts between East and West or on "under-development" clearly do not take us very far. The variables that appear important—for example, female employment or female literacy—combine both economic and cultural effects. To ascribe importance to the influence of gainful employment on women's prospects for survival may superficially look like another attempt at a simple economic explanation, but it would be a mistake to see it this way. The deeper question is why such outside employment is more prevalent in, say, sub-Saharan Africa than in North Africa, or in Southeast and Eastern Asia than in Western and Southern Asia. Here the cultural, including religious, backgrounds of the respective regions are surely important. Economic causes for women's deprivation have to be integrated with other—social and cultural—factors to give depth to the explanation.

Of course, gainful employment is not the only factor affecting women's chances of survival. Women's education and their economic rights—including property rights—may be crucial variables as well.[16] Consider the state of Kerala in India, which I mentioned earlier. It does not have a deficit of women—its ratio of women to men of more than 1.03 is closer to that of Europe (1.05) than those of China, West Asia, and India as a whole (0.94). The life expectancy of women at birth in Kerala, which had already reached sixty-eight years by the time of the last census in 1981 (and is estimated to be seventy-two years now), is considerably higher than men's sixty-four years at that time (and sixty-seven now). While women are generally able to find "gainful employment" in Kerala—certainly much more so than in Punjab—the state is not exceptional in this regard. What is exceptional is Kerala's remarkably high literacy rate; not only is it much higher than elsewhere in India, it is also substantially higher than in China, especially for women.

Kerala's experience of state-funded expansion of basic education, which has been consolidated by left-wing state governments in recent decades, began, in fact, nearly two centuries ago, led by the rulers of the kingdoms of Travancore and Cochin. (These two native states were not part of British India; they were joined together with a small part of the old Madras presidency to form the new state of Kerala after independence.) Indeed, as early as 1817, Rani Gouri Parvathi Bai, the young queen of Travancore, issued clear instructions for public support of education:

> The state should defray the entire cost of education of its people in order that there might be no backwardness in the spread of enlightenment among them, that by diffusion of education they might be better subjects and public servants and that the reputation of the State might be advanced thereby.[17]

Moreover, in parts of Kerala, property is usually inherited through the family's female line. These factors, as well as the generally high level of communal medicine, help to explain why women in Kerala do not suffer disadvantages in obtaining the means for survival. While it would be difficult to "split up" the respective contributions made by each of these different influences, it would be a mistake not to include all these factors among the potentially interesting variables that deserve examination.

In view of the enormity of the problems of women's survival in large parts of Asia and Africa, it is surprising that these disadvantages have received such inadequate attention. The numbers of "missing women" in relation to the numbers that could be expected if men and women received similar care in health, medicine, and nutrition, are remarkably large. A great many more than a hundred million women are simply not there because women are neglected compared with men. If this situation is to be corrected by political action and public policy, the reasons why there are so many "missing" women must first be better understood. We confront here what is clearly one of the more momentous, and neglected, problems facing the world today. □

[16] For interesting investigations of the role of education, broadly defined, in influencing women's well-being in Bangladesh and India, see Martha Chen, *A Quiet Revolution: Women in Transition in Rural Bangladesh* (Schenkman Books, 1983); and Alaka Basu, *Culture, the Status of Women and Demographic Behavior* (New Delhi: National Council of Applied Economic Research, 1988).

[17] Kerala has also had considerable missionary activity in schooling (a fifth of the population is, in fact, Christian), has had international trading and political contacts (both with east and west Asia) for a very long time, and it was from Kerala that the great Hindu philosopher and educator Śankarācārya, who lived during AD 788–820, had launched his big movement of setting up centers of study and worship across India.

[7]

WOMEN AND CULTURAL UNIVERSALS

Martha Nussbaum

We shall only solve our problems if we see them as human problems arising out of a special situation; and we shall not solve them if we see them as African problems, generated by our being somehow unlike others.

—Kwame Anthony Appiah, *Africa in the Philosophy of Cultures*

Being a woman is not yet a way of being a human being.

—Catharine MacKinnon

I. A Matter of Survival

"I may die, but still I cannot go out. If there's something in the house, we eat. Otherwise, we go to sleep." So Metha Bai, a young widow in Rajasthan, India, with two young children, described her plight as a member of a caste whose women are traditionally prohibited from working outside the home—even when, as here, survival itself is at issue. If she stays at home, she and her children may shortly die. If she attempts to go out, her in-laws will beat her and abuse her children. For now, Metha Bai's father travels from 100 miles away to plow her small plot of land. But he is aging, and Metha Bai fears that she and her children will shortly die with him.[1]

In this case, as in many others throughout the world, cultural traditions pose obstacles to women's health and flourishing. Depressingly, many traditions portray women as less important than men, less deserving of basic life support or of fundamental rights that are strongly correlated with quality of life, such as the right to work and the right to political participation. Sometimes, as in the case of Metha Bai, the women themselves resist these traditions. Sometimes, on the other hand, the traditions have become so deeply internalized that they seem to record what is "right" and "natural," and women themselves endorse their own second-class status.

Such cases are hardly confined to non-Western or developing countries. As recently as 1873, the U.S. Supreme Court upheld a law that forbade women to practice law in the state of Illinois, on the grounds that "[t]he constitution of the family organization, which is founded in the divine ordinance, as well as in the nature of things, indicates the domestic sphere as that which properly belongs to the domain and functions of womanhood."[2] And in 1993, a woman who was threatened and grossly harassed by her male coworkers, after becoming the first woman to work in the heavy metal shop in the General Motors plant in Indiana, was described by a federal district judge as having provoked the men's conduct by her "unladylike" behavior—behavior that consisted in using a four-letter word a few times in a five-year period.[3] Clearly our own society still appeals to tradition in its own way to justify women's unequal treatment.

What should people concerned with justice say about this? And should they say anything at all? On the one hand, it seems impossible to deny that traditions, both Western and non-Western, perpetrate injustice against women in many fundamental ways, touching on some of the most central elements of a human being's quality of life—health, education, political liberty and participation, employment, self-respect, and life itself. On the other hand, hasty judgments that a tradition in some distant part of the world is morally retrograde are familiar legacies of colonialism and imperialism and are correctly regarded with suspicion by sensitive thinkers in the contemporary world. To say that a practice endorsed by tradition is bad is to risk erring by imposing one's own way on others, who surely have their own ideas of what is right and good. To say that a practice is all right whenever local tradition endorses it as right and good is to risk erring by withholding critical judgment where real evil and oppression are surely present. To avoid the whole issue because the matter of proper judgment is so fiendishly difficult is tempting but perhaps the worst option of all. It suggests the sort of moral collapse depicted by Dante when he describes the crowd of souls who mill around in the vestibule of hell, dragging their banner now one way, now another, never willing to set it down and take a definite stand on any moral or political question. Such people, he implies, are the most despicable of all. They cannot even get into hell because they have not been willing to stand for anything in life, one way or another. To express the spirit of this chapter very succinctly, it is better to risk being consigned by critics to the "hell" reserved for alleged Westernizers and imperialists—however unjustified such criticism would in fact be—than to stand around in the vestibule waiting for a time when everyone will like what we are going to say. And what we are going to say is: that there are universal obligations to protect human functioning and its dignity, and that the dignity of women is equal to that of men. If that involves assault on many local traditions, both Western and non-Western, so much the better, because any tradition that denies these things is unjust. Or, as a young Bangladeshi wife said when local religious leaders threatened to break the legs of women who went to the literacy classes conducted by a local NGO (nongovernmental organization), "We do not listen to the *mullahs* any more. They did not give us even a quarter kilo of rice."[4]

The situation of women in the contemporary world calls urgently for moral standtaking. Women, a majority of the world's population, receive only a small proportion of its opportunities and benefits. According to the *Human Development Report*, in no country in the world is women's quality of life equal to that of men, according to a complex measure that includes life expectancy, educational attainment, and GDP (gross domestic product) per capita.[5] Some countries have much larger gender disparities than others. (Among prosperous industrial countries, for example, Spain and Japan perform relatively poorly in this area; Sweden, Denmark, and New Zealand perform relatively well.[6]) If we now examine the Gender Empowerment Measure, which uses variables chosen explicitly to measure the relative empowerment of men and women in political and economic activity,[7] we find even more striking signs of gender disparity. Once again, the Scandinavian nations do well; Japan and Spain do relatively poorly.[8]

If we turn our attention to the developing countries we find uneven achievements but, in the aggregate, a distressing situation. On average, employment participation rates of women are only 50% those of men (in South Asia 29%; in the Arab states only 16%).[9] Even when women are employed, their situation is undercut by pervasive wage discrimination and by long hours of unpaid household labor. (If women's unpaid housework were counted as productive output in national income accounts, global output would increase by 20–30%.) Outside the home, women are generally employed in a restricted range of jobs offering low pay and low respect. The percentage of earned income that goes to women is rarely higher than 35%. In many nations it is far lower: in Iran, 16%; Belize, 17%; Algeria, 16%; Iraq, 17%; Pakistan, 19%. (China at 38% is higher than Japan at 33%; highest in the world are Sweden at 45%, Denmark at 42%, and the extremely impoverished Rwanda at 41%, Burundi at 42%, and Mozambique at 42%.) The situation of women in the workplace is frequently undermined by sex discrimination and sexual harassment.

Women are much less likely than men to be literate. In South Asia, female literacy rates average around 50% those of males. In some countries the rate is still lower: in Nepal, 35%; Sierra Leone, 37%; Sudan, 27%; Afghanistan, 32%.[10] Two-thirds of the world's illiterate people are women. In higher education, women lag even further behind men in both developing and industrial nations.[11]

Although some countries allowed women the vote early in this century, some still have not done so. And there are many informal obstacles to women's effective participation in political life. Almost everywhere, they are underrepresented in government: In 1980, they made up only around 10% of the world's parliamentary representatives and less than 4% of its cabinet officials.[12]

As Metha Bai's story indicates, employment outside the home has a close relationship to health and nutrition. So too, frequently, does political voice. And if we now turn to the very basic issue of health and survival, we find compelling evidence of discrimination against females in many nations of the world. It appears that when equal nutrition and health care are present women live, on average, slightly longer than men—even allowing for a modest level of maternal mortality. Thus, in Europe the female/male ratio in 1986 was 105/100, in North

America 104.7/100.[13] But it may be objected that for several reasons it is inappropriate to compare these developed countries with countries in the developing world. Let us, therefore, with Jean Drèze and Amartya Sen, take as our baseline the ratio in sub-Saharan Africa, where there is great poverty but little evidence of gender discrimination in basic nutrition and health.[14] The female/male ration in 1986 was 102.2/100. If we examine the sex ratio in various other countries and ask the question, "How many more women than are now in country C would be there if its sex ratio were the same as that of sub-Saharan Africa?," we get a number that Sen has graphically called the number of "missing women." The number of missing women in Southeast Asia is 2.4 million; in Latin America, 4.4; in North Africa, 2.4; in Iran, 1.4; in China, 44.0; in Bangladesh, 3.7; in India, 36.7; in Pakistan, 5.2; in West Asia, 4.3. If we now consider the ratio of the number of missing women to the number of actual women in a country, we get, for Pakistan, 12.9%; for India, 9.5%; for Bangladesh, 8.7%; for China, 8.6%; for Iran, 8.5%; for West Asia, 7.8%; for North Africa, 3.9%; for Latin America, 2.2%; for Southeast Asia, 1.2%. In India, not only is the mortality differential especially sharp among children (girls dying in far greater numbers than boys), the higher mortality rate of women compared to men applies to all age groups until the late thirties.[15]

Poverty alone does not cause women to die in greater numbers than men. This is abundantly clear from comparative regional studies in India, where some of the poorest regions, for example, Kerala, have the most equal sex ratios, and some far richer regions perform very poorly.[16] When there is scarcity, custom and political arrangement frequently decree who gets to eat the little there is and who gets taken to the doctor. And custom and political arrangement are always crucial in deciding who gets to perform wage labor outside the home, an important determinant of general status in the family and the community. As Sen has argued, a woman's perceived contribution to the well-being of the family unit is often determined by her ability to work outside, and this determines, in turn, her bargaining position within the family unit.[17] Custom and politics decree who gets access to the education that would open job opportunities and make political rights meaningful. Custom and politics decree who can go where in what clothing in what company. Custom and politics decree who gets to make what sorts of protests against ill treatment both inside and outside the family and whose voice of protest is likely to be heard.

Customs and political arrangements, in short, are important causes of women's misery and death. It seems incumbent on people interested in justice, and aware of the information about women's status that studies such as the *Human Development Reports* present, to ask about the relationship between culture and justice and between both of these and legal-political arrangements. It then seems incumbent on them to try to work out an account of the critical assessment of traditions and political arrangements that is neither do-gooder colonialism or an uncritical validation of the status quo.

One might suppose that any approach to the question of quality of life assessment in development economics would offer an account of the relationship between tradition and women's equality that would help us answer these questions. But in fact such an account is sorely lacking in the major theoretical approaches that, until recently, dominated the development scene. (Here I do not even include what has been the most common practical approach, which has been simply to ask about GNP (gross national product) per capita. This crude approach does not even look at the distribution of wealth and income; far less does it ask about other constituents of life quality, for example, life expectancy, infant mortality, education, health, and the presence or absence of political liberties, that are not always well correlated with GNP per capita.[18] The failure to ask these questions is a particularly grave problem when it is women's quality of life we want to consider. For women have especially often been unable to enjoy or control the fruits of a nation's general prosperity.)

The leading economic approach to the family is the model proposed by Nobel Prize–winning economist Gary Becker. Becker assumes that the family's goal is the maximization of utility, construed as the satisfaction of preference or desire, and that the head of the household is a beneficent altruist who will adequately take thought for the interests of all family members.[19] In real life, however, the economy of the family is characterized by pervasive "cooperative conflicts," that is, situations in which the interests of members of a cooperative body split apart, and some individuals fare well at the expense of others.[20] Becker deserves great credit for putting these issues on the agenda of the profession in the first place. But his picture of male motivation does not fit the evidence, and in a way substantial enough to affect the model's predictive value—especially if one looks not only at women's stated satisfactions and preferences, which may be deformed by intimidation, lack of information, and habit,[21] but at their actual functioning.[22] Furthermore, the model prevents those who use it from even getting the information about individual family members on which a more adequate account might be based.[23]

Suppose we were to retain a utilitarian approach and yet to look at the satisfactions of all family members—assuming, as is standardly done in economics, that preferences and tastes are exogenous and independent of laws, traditions, and institutions rather than endogenously shaped by them. Such an approach—frequently used by governments polling citizens about well-being—has the advantage of assessing all individuals one by one. But the evidence of preference endogeneity is great, and especially great when we are dealing with people whose status has been persistently defined as second class in laws and institutions of various sorts. There are many reasons to think that women's perception even of their health status is shaped by traditional views, such as the view that female life is worth less than male life, that women are weaker than men, that women do not have equal rights, and so forth. In general, people frequently adjust their expectations to the low level of well-being they think they can actually attain.[24] This approach, then, cannot offer a useful account of the role of tradition in well-being, because it is bound by its very commitments to an uncritical validation of the status quo.

More promising than either Becker's model or the standard utilitarian approach is one suggested by John Rawls's liberalism, with its account of the just distribution of a small list of basic goods and resources.[25] This approach does enable us to criticize persistent inequalities, and it strongly criticizes the view that preferences are simply given rather than shaped by society's basic structure. But in one way the Rawlsian approach stops short. Rawls's list of "primary goods," although it includes some capacity-like items, such as liberty and opportunity, also includes thing-like items, particularly income and wealth, and it measures who is least well off simply in terms of the amount of these thing-like resources an individual can command. But people have varying needs for resources: a pregnant woman, for example, needs more calories than a nonpregnant woman, a child more protein than an adult. They also have different abilities to convert resources into functioning. A person in a wheelchair will need more resources to become mobile than a person with unimpaired limbs; a woman in a society that has defined employment outside the home as off limits to women needs more resources to become a productive worker than one who does not face such struggles. In short, the Rawlsian approach does not probe deeply enough to show us how resources do or do not go to work in making people able to function. Again, at least some of our questions about the relationship between tradition and quality of life cannot be productively addressed.

Workers on such issues have therefore increasingly converged on an approach that is now widely known as "the capabilities approach." This approach to quality-of-life measurement and the goals of public policy[26] holds that we should focus on the question: What are the people of the group or country in question actually able to do and to be? Unlike a focus on opulence (say, GNP per capita), this approach asks about the distribution of resources and opportunities. In principle, it asks how each and every individual is doing with respect to all the functions deemed important. Unlike Becker's approach, the capability approach considers people one by one, not as parts of an organic unit; it is very interested in seeing how a supposed organic unit such as the family has constructed unequal capabilities for various types of functioning. Unlike a standard utilitarian approach, the capability approach maintains that preferences are not always reliable indicators of life quality, as they may be deformed in various ways by oppression and deprivation. Unlike the type of liberal approach that focuses only on the distribution of resources, the capability approach maintains that resources have no value in themselves, apart from their role in promoting human functioning. It therefore directs the planner to inquire into the varying needs individuals have for resources and their varying abilities to convert resources into functioning. In this way, it strongly invites a scrutiny of tradition as one of the primary sources of such unequal abilities.[27]

But the capabilities approach raises the question of cultural universalism, or, as it is often pejoratively called, "essentialism." Once we begin asking how people are actually functioning, we cannot avoid focusing on some components of lives and not others, some abilities to act and not others, seeing some capabilities and functions as more central, more at the core of human life, than others. We cannot avoid having an account, even if a partial and highly general account, of what functions of the human being are most worth the care and attention of public planning the world over. Such an account is bound to be controversial.

II. Anti-Universalist Conversations

The primary opponents of such an account of capability and functioning will be "antiessentialists" of various types, thinkers who urge us to begin not with sameness but with difference—both between women and men and across groups of women—and to seek norms defined relatively to a local context and locally held beliefs. This opposition takes many forms, and I shall be responding to several distinct objections. But I can begin to motivate the enterprise by telling several true stories of conversations that have taken place at the World Institute for Development Economics Research (WIDER), in which the anti-universalist position seemed to have alarming implications for women's lives.[28]

At a conference on "Value and Technology," an American economist who has long been a leftwing critic of neoclassical economics delivers a paper urging the preservation of traditional ways of life in a rural area of Orissa, India, now under threat of contamination from Western development projects. As evidence of the excellence of this rural way of life, he points to the fact that whereas we Westerners experience a sharp split between the values that prevail in the workplace and the values that prevail in the home, here, by contrast, exists what the economist calls "the embedded way of life," the same values obtaining in both places. His example: Just as in the home a menstruating woman is thought to pollute the kitchen and therefore may not enter it, so too in the workplace a menstruating woman is taken to pollute the loom and may not enter the room where looms are kept. Some feminists object that this example is repellant rather than admirable; for surely such practices both degrade the women in question and inhibit their freedom. The first economist's collaborator, an elegant French anthropologist (who would, I suspect, object violently to a purity check at the seminar room door), replies: Don't we realize that there is, in these matters, no privileged place to stand? This, after all, has been shown by both Derrida and Foucault. Doesn't he know that he is neglecting the otherness of Indian ideas by bringing his Western essentialist values into the picture?[29]

The same French anthropologist now delivers her paper. She expresses regret that the introduction of smallpox vaccination to India by the British eradicated the cult of Sittala Devi, the goddess to whom one used to pray to avert smallpox. Here, she says, is another example of Western neglect of difference. Someone (it might have been me) objects that it is surely better to be healthy rather than ill, to live rather than to die. The answer comes back; Western essentialist medicine conceives of things in terms of binary oppositions: life is opposed to death, health to disease.[30] But if we cast away this binary way of thinking, we will begin to comprehend the otherness of Indian traditions.

At this point Eric Hobsbawm, who has been listening to the proceedings in increasingly uneasy silence, rises to deliver a blistering indictment of the traditionalism and relativism that prevail in this group. He lists historical examples of ways in which appeals to tradition have been politically engineered to support oppression and violence.[31] His final example is that of National Socialism in Germany. In the confusion that ensues, most of the relativist social scientists—above all those from far away, who do not know who Hobsbawm is—demand that Hobsbawm be asked to leave the room. The radical American economist, disconcerted by this apparent tension between his relativism and his affiliation with the left, convinces them, with difficulty, to let Hobsbawm remain.

We shift now to another conference two years later, a philosophical conference on the quality of life.[32] Members of the quality-of-life project are speaking of choice as a basic good, and of the importance of expanding women's sphere of choices. We are challenged by the radical economist of my first story, who insists that contemporary anthropology has shown that non-Western people are not especially attached to freedom of choice. His example: A book on Japan has shown that Japanese males, when they get home from work, do not wish to choose what to eat for dinner, what to wear, and so on. They wish all these choices to be taken out of their hands by their wives. A heated exchange follows about what this example really shows. I leave it to your imaginations to reconstruct it. In the end, the confidence of the radical economist is unshaken: We are victims of bad universalist thinking, who fail to respect "difference."[33]

The phenomenon is an odd one. For we see here highly intelligent people, people deeply committed to the good of women and men in developing countries, people who think of themselves as progressive and feminist and antiracist, people who correctly argue that the concept of development is an evaluative concept requiring normative argument[34]—effectively eschewing normative argument and taking up positions that converge, as Hobsbawm correctly saw, with the positions of reaction, oppression, and sexism. Under the banner of their fashionable opposition to universalism march ancient religious taboos, the luxury of the pampered husband, educational deprivation, unequal health care, and premature death.

Nor do these anti-universalists appear to have a very sophisticated conception of their own core notions, such as "culture," "custom," and "tradition." It verges on the absurd to treat India as a single culture, and a single visit to a single Orissan village as sufficient to reveal its traditions. India, like all extant societies, is a complex mixture of elements[35]: Hindu, Muslim, Parsi, Christian, Jewish, atheist; urban, suburban, rural; rich, poor, and middle class; high caste, low caste, and aspiring middle caste; female and male; rationalist and mystical. It is renowned for mystical religion but also for achievements in mathematics and for the invention of chess. It contains intense, often violent sectarianism, but it also contains Rabindranath Tagore's cosmopolitan humanism and Mahatma Gandhi's reinterpretation of Hinduism as a religion of universal nonviolence. Its traditions contain views of female whorishness and childishness that derive from the Laws of Manu[36]; but it also contains the sexual agency of Draupadi in the *Mahabharata,* who solved the problem of choice among Pandava husbands by taking all five, and the enlightened sensualism and female agency of the *Kama Sutra,* a sacred text that foreign readers wrongly interpret as pornographic. It contains women like Metha Bai, who are confined to the home; it also contains women like Amita Sen (mother of Amartya Sen), who fifty years ago was among the first middle-class Bengali women to dance in public, in Rabindranath Tagore's musical extravaganzas in Santiniketan. It contains artists who disdain the foreign, preferring, with the Marglins, the "embedded" way of life, and it also contains Satyajit Ray, that great Bengali artist and lover of local traditions, who could also write, "I never ceased to regret that while I had stood in the scorching summer sun in the wilds of Santiniketan sketching *simul* and *palash* in full bloom, *Citizen Kane* had come and gone, playing for just three days in the newest and biggest cinema in Calcutta."[37]

What, then, is "the culture" of a woman like Metha Bai? Is it bound to be that determined by the most prevalent customs in Rajasthan, the region of her marital home? Or, might she be permitted to consider with what traditions or groups she wishes to align herself, perhaps forming a community of solidarity with other widows and women, in pursuit of a better quality of life? What is "the culture" of Chinese working women who have recently been victims of the government's "women go home" policy, which appeals to Confucian traditions about woman's "nature"?[38] Must it be the one advocated by Confucius, or may they be permitted to form new alliances—with one another, and with other defenders of women's human rights? What is "the culture" of General Motors employee Mary Carr? Must it be the one that says women should be demure and polite, even in the face of gross insults, and that an "unladylike" woman deserves the harassment she gets? Or might she be allowed to consider what norms are appropriate to the situation of a woman working in a heavy metal shop, and to act accordingly? Real cultures contain plurality and conflict, tradition, and subversion. They borrow good things from wherever they find them, none too worried about purity. We would never tolerate a claim that women in our own society must embrace traditions that arose thousands of years ago—indeed, we are proud that we have no such traditions. Isn't it condescending, then, to treat Indian and Chinese women as bound by the past in ways that we are not?

Indeed, as Hobsbawm suggested, the vision of "culture" propounded by the Marglins, by stressing uniformity and homogeneity, may lie closer to artificial constructions by reactionary political forces than to any organic historical entity. Even to the extent to which it is historical, one might ask, exactly how does that contribute to make it worth preserving? Cultures are not museum pieces, to be preserved intact at all costs. There would appear, indeed, to be something condescending in preserving for contemplation a way of life that causes real pain to real people.

Let me now, nonetheless, describe the most cogent objections that might be raised by a relativist against a normative universalist project.

III. The Attack on Universalism

Many attacks on universalism suppose that any universalist project must rely on truths eternally fixed in the nature of things, outside human action and human history. Because some people believe in such truths and some do not, the objector holds that a normative view so grounded is bound to be biased in favor of some religious/metaphysical conceptions and against others.[39]

But universalism does not require such metaphysical support.[40] For universal ideas of the human do arise within history and from human experience, and they can ground themselves in experience. Indeed, those who take all human norms to be the result of human interpretation can hardly deny that universal conceptions of the human are prominent and pervasive among such interpretations, hardly to be relegated to the dustbin of metaphysical history along with recondite theoretical entities such as phlogiston. As Aristotle so simply puts it, "One may observe in one's travels to distant countries the feelings of recognition and affiliation that link every human being to every other human being."[41] Kwame Anthony Appiah makes the same point, telling the story of his bicultural childhood. A child who visits one set of grandparents in Ghana and another in rural England, who has a Lebanese uncle and who later, as an adult, has nieces and nephews from more than seven different nations, finds, he argues, not unbridgeable alien "otherness," but a great deal of human commonality, and comes to see the world as a "network of points of affinity."[42] But such a metaphysically agnostic, experiential and historical universalism is still vulnerable to some, if not all, of the objections standardly brought against universalism.

Neglect of Historical and Cultural Differences

The opponent charges that any attempt to pick out some elements of human life as more fundamental than others, even without appeal to a transhistorical reality, is bound to be insufficiently respectful of actual historical and cultural differences. People, it is claimed, understand human life and humanness in widely different ways, and any attempt to produce a list of the most fundamental properties and functions of human beings is bound to enshrine certain understandings of the human and to demote others. Usually, the objector continues, this takes the form of enshrining the understanding of a dominant group at the expense of minority understandings. This type of objection, frequently made by feminists, can claim support from many historical examples in which the human has indeed been defined by focusing on actual characteristics of males.

It is far from clear what this objection shows. In particular it is far from clear that it supports the idea that we ought to base our ethical norms, instead, on the current preferences and the self-conceptions of people who are living what the objector herself claims to be lives of deprivation and oppression. But it does show at least that the project of choosing one picture of the human over another is fraught with difficulty, political as well as philosophical.

Neglect of Autonomy

A different objection is presented by liberal opponents of universalism. The objection is that by determining in advance what elements of human life have most importance, the universalist project fails to respect the right of people to choose a plan of life according to their own lights, determining what is central and what is not.[43] This way of proceeding is "imperialistic." Such evaluative choices must be left to each citizen. For this reason, politics must refuse itself a determinate theory of the human being and the human good.

Prejudicial Application

If we operate with a determinate conception of the human being that is meant to have some normative moral and political force, we must also, in applying it, ask which beings we take to fall under the concept. And here the objector notes that, all too easily—even if the conception itself is equitably and comprehensively designed—the powerless can be excluded. Aristotle himself, it is pointed out, held that women and slaves were not full-fledged human beings, and because his politics were based on his view of human functioning, the failure of these beings (in his view) to exhibit the desired mode of functioning contributed to their political exclusion and oppression.

It is, once again, hard to know what this objection is supposed to show. In particular, it is hard to know how, if at all, it is supposed to show that we would be better off without such determinate universal concepts. For it could be plausibly argued that it would have been even easier to exclude women and slaves on a whim if one did not have such a concept to combat.[44] On the other hand, it does show that we need to think not only about getting the concept right but also about getting the right beings admitted under the concept.

Each of these objections has some merit. Many universal conceptions of the human being have been insular in an arrogant way and neglectful of differences among cultures and ways of life. Some have been neglectful of choice and autonomy. And many have been prejudicially applied. But none of this shows that all such conceptions must fail in one or more of these ways. At this point, however, we need to examine a real proposal, both to display its merits and to argue that it can in fact answer these charges.

IV. A Conception of the Human Being: The Central Human Capabilities

The list of basic capabilities is generated by asking a question that from the start is evaluative: What activities[45] characteristically performed by human beings are so central that they seem definitive of a life that is truly human? In other words, what are the functions without which (meaning, without the availability of which) we would regard a life as not, or not fully, human?[46] We can get at this question better if we approach it via two somewhat more concrete questions that we often really ask ourselves. First is a question about personal continuity. We ask ourselves which changes or transitions are compatible with the continued existence of that being as a member of the human kind and which are not. Some functions can fail to be present without threatening our sense that we still have a human being on our hands; the absence of others seems to signal the end of a human life. This question is asked regularly, when we attempt to make medical definitions of death in a situation in which some of the functions of life persist, or to decide, for others or (thinking ahead) for ourselves, whether a certain level of illness or impairment means the end of the life of the being in question.[47]

The other question is a question about kind inclusion. We recognize other humans as human across many differences of time and place, of custom and appearance. We often tell ourselves stories, on the other hand, about anthropomorphic creatures who do not get classified as human, on account of some feature of their form of life and functioning. On what do we base these inclusions and exclusions? In short, what do we believe must be there, if we are going to acknowledge that a given life is human?[48] The answer to these questions points us to a subset of common or characteristic human functions, informing us that these are likely to have a special importance for everything else we choose and do.

Note that the procedure through which this account of the human is derived is neither ahistorical nor a priori. It is the attempt to summarize empirical findings of a broad and ongoing cross-cultural inquiry. As such, it is both open-ended and humble; it can always be contested and remade. Nor does it claim to read facts of "human nature" from biological observation; it takes biology into account as a relatively constant element in human experience.[49] It is because the account is evaluative from the start that it is called a conception of the good.

It should also be stressed that, like John Rawls's account of primary goods in *A Theory of Justice*,[50] this list of good functions, which is in some ways more comprehensive than his own list, is proposed as the object of a specifically political consensus.[51] The political is not understood exactly as Rawls understands it because the nation state is not assumed to be the basic unit, and the account is meant to have broad applicablity to cross-cultural deliberations. This means, given the current state of world politics, that many of the obligations to promote the adequate distribution of these goods must rest with individuals rather than with any political institution, and in that way its role becomes difficult to distinguish from the role of other norms and goals of the individual. Nonetheless, the point of the list is the same as that of Rawlsian primary goods: to put forward something that people from many different traditions, with many different fuller conceptions of the good, can agree on, as the necessary basis for pursuing their good life. That is why the list is deliberately rather general.[52] Each of its components can be more concretely specified in accordance with one's origins, religious beliefs, or tastes. In that sense, the consensus that it hopes to evoke has many of the features of the "overlapping consensus" described by Rawls.[53]

Having isolated some functions that seem central in defining the very presence of a human life, we do not rest content with mere bare humanness. We want to specify a life in which fully human functioning, or a kind of basic human flourishing, will be available. For we do not want politics to take mere survival as its goal; we want to describe a life in which the dignity of the human being is not violated by hunger or fear or the absence of opportunity. (The idea is very much Marx's idea, when he used an Aristotelian notion of functioning to describe the difference between a merely animal use of one's faculties and a "truly human use."[54]) The following list of central human functional capabilities is an attempt to specify this basic notion of the good: All citizens should have these capabilities, whatever else they have and pursue.[55] I introduce this as a list of capabilities rather than of actual functionings, because I shall argue that capability, not actual functioning, should be the goal of public policy.

Central Human Functional Capabilities

1. *Life.* Being able to live to the end of a human life of normal length[56]; not dying prematurely or before one's life is so reduced as to be not worth living
2. *Bodily health and integrity.* Being able to have good health, including reproductive health; being adequately nourished[57]; being able to have adequate shelter[58]
3. *Bodily integrity.* Being able to move freely from place to place; being able to be secure against violent assault, including sexual assault, marital rape, and domestic violence; having opportunities for sexual satisfaction and for choice in matters of reproduction
4. *Senses, imagination, thought.* Being able to use the senses; being able to imagine, to think, and to reason—and to do these things in a "truly human" way, a way informed and cultivated by an adequate education, including, but by no means limited to, literacy and basic mathematical and scientific training; being able to use imagination and thought in connection with experiencing and producing expressive works and events of one's own choice (religious, literary, musical, etc.); being able to use one's mind in ways protected by guarantees of freedom of expression with respect to both political and artistic speech and freedom of religious exercise; being able to have pleasurable experiences and to avoid nonbeneficial pain
5. *Emotions.* Being able to have attachments to things and persons outside ourselves; being able to love those who love and care for us; being able to grieve at their absence; in general, being able to love, to grieve, to experience longing, gratitude, and justified anger; not having one's emotional developing blighted by fear or anxiety. (Supporting this capability means supporting forms of human association that can be shown to be crucial in their development.[59])
6. *Practical reason.* Being able to form a conception of the good and to engage in critical reflection about the planning of one's own life. (This entails protection for the liberty of conscience.)
7. *Affiliation.* (a) Being able to live for and in relation to others, to recognize and show concern for other human beings, to engage in various forms of social interaction; being able to imagine the situation of another and to have compassion for that situation; having the capability for both justice and friendship. (Protecting this capability means, once again, protecting institutions that constitute such forms of affiliation, and also protecting the freedoms of assembly and political speech.) (b) Having the social bases of self-respect and nonhumiliation; being able to be treated as a dignified being whose worth is equal to that of others. (This entails provisions of nondiscrimination.)
8. *Other species.* Being able to live with concern for and in relation to animals, plants, and the world of nature[60]

9. *Play*. Being able to laugh, to play, to enjoy recreational activities
10. *Control over one's environment*. (a) *Political*: being able to participate effectively in political choices that govern one's life; having the rights of political participation, free speech, and freedom of association (b) *Material*: being able to hold property (both land and movable goods); having the right to seek employment on an equal basis with others; having the freedom from unwarranted search and seizure.[61] In work, being able to work as a human being, exercising practical reason and entering into meaningful relationships of mutual recognition with other workers.

The "capabilities approach," as I conceive it,[62] claims that a life that lacks any one of these capabilities, no matter what else it has, will fall short of being a good human life. Thus it would be reasonable to take these things as a focus for concern, in assessing the quality of life in a country and asking about the role of public policy in meeting human needs. The list is certainly general—and this is deliberate, to leave room for plural specification and also for further negotiation. But like (and as a reasonable basis for) a set of constitutional guarantees, it offers real guidance to policymakers, and far more accurate guidance than that offered by the focus on utility, or even on resources.[63]

The list is, emphatically, a list of separate components. We cannot satisfy the need for one of them by giving a larger amount of another one. All are of central importance and all are distinct in quality. This limits the trade-offs that it will be reasonable to make and thus limits the applicability of quantitative cost-benefit analysis. At the same time, the items on the list are related to one another in many complex ways. Employment rights, for example, support health, and also freedom from domestic violence, by giving women a better bargaining position in the family. The liberties of speech and association turn up at several distinct points on the list, showing their fundamental role with respect to several distinct areas of human functioning.

V. Capability as Goal

The basic claim I wish to make—concurring with Amartya Sen—is that the central goal of public planning should be the *capabilities* of citizens to perform various important functions. The question that should be asked when assessing quality of life in a country—and of course this is a central part of assessing the quality of its political arrangements—is, How well have the people of the country been enabled to perform the central human functions? And, have they been put in a position of mere human subsistence with respect to the functions, or have they been enabled to live well? Politics, we argue (here concurring with Rawls), should focus on getting as many people as possible into a state of capability to function, with respect to the interlocking set of capabilities enumerated by that list.[64] Naturally, the determination of whether certain individuals and groups are across the threshold is only as precise a matter as the determination of the threshold. I have left things deliberately somewhat open-ended at this point, in keeping with the procedures of the *Human Development Report*, believing that the best way to work toward a more precise determination, at present, is to focus on comparative information and to allow citizens to judge for themselves whether their policymakers have done as well as they should have. Again, we will have to answer various questions about the costs we are willing to pay to get all citizens above the threshold, as opposed to leaving a small number below and allowing the rest a considerably above-threshold life quality. It seems likely, at any rate, that moving all citizens above a basic threshold of capability should be taken as a central social goal. When citizens are across the threshold, societies are to a great extent free to choose the other goals they wish to pursue. Some inequalities, however, will themselves count as capability failures. For example, inequalities based on hierarchies of gender or race will themselves be inadmissible on the grounds that they undermine self-respect and emotional development.

The basic intuition from which the capability approach starts, in the political arena, is that human capabilities exert a moral claim that they should be developed. Human beings are creatures such that, provided with the right educational and material support, they can become fully capable of the major human functions. That is, they are creatures with certain lower-level capabilities (which I call "basic capabilities"[65]) to perform the functions in question. When these capabilities are deprived of the nourishment that would transform them into the high-level capabilities that figure on my list, they are fruitless, cut off, in some way but a shadow of themselves. They are like actors who never get to go on the stage, or a person who sleeps all through life, or a musical score that is never performed. Their very being makes forward reference to functioning. Thus, if functioning never arrives on the scene they are hardly even what they are. This may sound like a metaphysical idea, and in a sense it is (in that it is an idea discussed in Aristotle's *Metaphysics*). But that does not mean it is not a basic and pervasive empirical idea, an idea that underwrites many of our daily practices and judgments in many times and places. Just as we hold that a child who dies before getting to maturity has died especially tragically—for her activities of growth and preparation for adult activity now have lost their point—so too with capability and functioning more generally: We believe that certain basic and central human endowments have a claim to be assisted in developing, and exert that claim on others, and especially, as Aristotle saw, on government. Without some such notion of the basic worth of human capacities, we have a hard time arguing for women's equality and for basic human rights. Think, for example, of the remark of Catharine MacKinnon that I quoted as my epigraph. If women were really just trees or turtles or filing cabinets, the fact that their current status in many parts of the world is not a fully human one would not be, as it is, a problem of justice. In thinking of political planning we begin, then, from a notion of the basic capabilities and their worth, thinking of them as claims to a chance for functioning, which give rise to correlated political duties.

I have spoken both of functioning and of capability. How are they related? Getting clear about this is crucial in defining the relation of the capabilities approach to liberalism. For if we were to take functioning itself as the goal of public policy, the liberal would rightly judge that we were precluding many choices that citizens may make in accordance with their own conceptions of the good. A deeply religious person may prefer not to be well nourished but to engage in strenuous fasting. Whether for religious or for other reasons, a person may prefer a celibate life to one containing sexual expression. A person may prefer to work with an intense dedication that precludes recreation and play. Am I saying that these are not fully human or flourishing lives? Does the approach instruct governments to nudge or push people into functioning of the requisite sort, no matter what they prefer?

Here we must answer: No, capability, not functioning, is the political goal. This is so because of the very great importance the approach attaches to practical reason, as a good that both suffuses all the other functions, making them human rather than animal,[66] and figures, itself, as a central function on the list. It is perfectly true that functionings, not simply capabilities, are what render a life fully human: If there were no functioning of any kind in a life, we could hardly applaud it, no matter what opportunities it contained. Nonetheless, for political purposes it is appropriate for us to shoot for capabilities, and those alone. Citizens must be left free to determine their course after that. The person with plenty of food may always choose to fast, but there is a great difference between fasting and starving, and it is this difference we wish to capture. Again, the person who has normal opportunities for sexual satisfaction can always choose a life of celibacy, and we say nothing against this. What we do speak against, for example, is the practice of female genital mutilation, which deprives individuals of the opportunity to choose sexual functioning (and indeed, the opportunity to choose celibacy as well).[67] A person who has opportunities for play can always choose a workaholic life; again, there is a great difference between that chosen life and a life constrained by insufficient maximum-hour protections and/or the "double day" that makes women in many parts of the world unable to play.

The issue will be clearer if we recall that there are three different types of capabilities that figure in the analysis.[68] First, there are *basic capabilities*: the innate equipment of individuals that is the necessary basis for developing the more advanced capability. Most infants have from birth the basic capability for practical reason and imagination, though they cannot exercise such functions without a lot more development and education. Second, there are *internal capabilities*: states of the person herself that are, as far as the person herself is concerned, sufficient conditions for the exercise of the requisite functions. A woman who has not suffered genital mutilation has the internal capability for sexual pleasure; most adult human beings everywhere have the internal capability to use speech and thought in accordance with their own conscience. Finally, there are *combined capabilities*, which we define as internal capabilities *combined with* suitable external conditions for the exercise of the function. A woman who is not mutilated but is secluded and forbidden to leave the house has internal but not combined capabilities for sexual expression (and work and political participation). Citizens of repressive nondemocratic regimes have the internal but not the combined capability to exercise thought and speech in accordance with their conscience. The aim of public policy is the production of *combined capabilities*. This means promoting the states of the person by providing the necessary education and care; it also means preparing the environment so that it is favorable for the exercise of practical reason and the other major functions.[69]

This clarifies the position. The approach does not say that public policy should rest content with *internal capabilities* but remain indifferent to the struggles of individuals who have to try to exercise these in a hostile environment. In that sense, it is highly attentive to the goal of functioning, and instructs governments to keep it always in view. On the other hand, we are not pushing individuals into the function: Once the stage is fully set, the choice is up to them.

The approach is therefore very close to Rawls's approach using the notion of primary goods. We can see the list of capabilities as like a long list of opportunities for life functioning, such that it is always rational to want them whatever else one wants. If one ends up having a plan of life that does not make use of all of them, one has hardly been harmed by having the chance to choose a life that does. (Indeed, in the cases of fasting and celibacy it is the very availability of the alternative course that gives the choice its moral value.) The primary difference between this capabilities list and Rawls's list of primary goods is its length and definiteness, and in particular its determination to place on the list the social basis of several goods that Rawls has called "natural goods," such as "health and vigor, intelligence and imagination."[70] Since Rawls has been willing to put the social basis of self-respect on his list, it is not at all clear why he has not made the same move with imagination and health.[71] Rawls's evident concern is that no society can guarantee health to its individuals—in that sense, saying that our goal is full combined capability may appear unreasonably idealistic. Some of the capabilities (e.g., some of the political liberties) can be fully guaranteed by society, but many others involve an element of chance and cannot be so guaranteed. We respond to this by saying that the list is an enumeration of political *goals* that should be useful as a benchmark for aspiration and comparison. Even though individuals with adequate health support often fall ill, it still makes sense to compare societies by asking about actual health capabilities, because we assume that the comparison will reflect the different inputs of human planning and can be adjusted to take account of more and less favorable natural situations.

Earlier versions of the list appeared to diverge from the approach of Rawlsian liberalism by not giving as central a place as Rawls does to the traditional political rights and liberties—although the need to incorporate them was stressed from the start.[72] This version of the list corrects that defect of emphasis. These political liberties have a central importance in making well-being human. A society that aims at well-being while overriding these has delivered to its members a merely animal level of satisfaction.[73] As Amartya Sen has recently written, "Political rights are important not only for the fulfillment of needs, they are crucial also for the formulation of needs. And this idea relates, in the end, to the respect that we owe each other as fellow human beings."[74] This idea has recently been echoed by Rawls: Primary goods specify what citizens' needs are from the point of view of political justice.[75]

The capability view justifies its elaborate list by pointing out that choice is not pure spontaneity, flourishing independently of material and social conditions. If one cares about people's powers to choose a conception of the good, then one must care about the rest of the form of life that supports those powers, including its material conditions. Thus the approach claims that its more comprehensive concern with flourishing is perfectly consistent with the impetus behind the Rawlsian project, which has always insisted that we are not to rest content with merely formal equal liberty and opportunity but must pursue their fully equal worth by ensuring that unfavorable economic and social circumstances do not prevent people from availing themselves of liberties and opportunities that are formally open to them.

The guiding thought behind this Aristotelian enterprise is, at its heart, a profoundly liberal idea,[76] and one that lies at the heart of Rawls's project as well: the idea of the citizen as a free and dignified human being, a maker of choices. Politics has an urgent role to play here, getting citizens the tools they need, both to choose at all and to have a realistic option of exercising the most valuable functions. The choice of whether and how to use the tools, however, is left up to them, in the conviction that this is an essential aspect of respect for their freedom. They are seen not as passive recipients of social planning but as dignified beings who shape their own lives.[77]

Let us now return to the Marglins and to Metha Bai. What would this universalist approach have to say about these concrete cases? Notice how close the Marglin approach is, in its renunciation of critical normative argument, to the prevailing economic approaches of which it presents itself as a radical critique. A preference-based approach that gives priority to the preferences of dominant males in a traditional culture is likely to be especially subversive of the quality of life of women, who have been on the whole badly treated by prevailing traditional norms. And one can see this clearly in the Marglins' own examples. For menstruation taboos, even if endorsed by habit and custom, impose severe restrictions on women's power to form a plan of life and to execute the plan they have chosen.[78] They are members of the same family of traditional attitudes that make it difficult for women like Metha Bai to sustain the basic functions of life. Vulnerability to smallpox, even if someone other than an anthropologist should actually defend it as a good thing, is even more evidently a threat to human functioning. And the Japanese husband who allegedly renounces freedom of choice actually shows considerable attachment to it, in the ways that matter, by asking the woman to look after the boring details of life. What should concern us is whether the woman has a similar degree of freedom to plan her life and to execute her plan.

As for Metha Bai, the absence of freedom to choose employment outside the home is linked to other capability failures, in the areas of health, nutrition, mobility, education, and political voice. Unlike the type of liberal view that focuses on resources alone, my view enables us to focus directly on the obstacles to self-realization imposed by traditional norms and values and thus to justify special political action to remedy the unequal situation. No male of Metha Bai's caste would have to overcome threats of physical violence in order to go out of the house to work for life-sustaining food.

The capabilities approach insists that a woman's affiliation with a certain group or culture should not be taken as normative for her unless, on due consideration, with all the capabilities at her disposal, she makes that norm her own. We should take care to extend to each individual full capabilities to pursue the items on the list—and then see whether they want to avail themselves of those opportunities. Usually they do, even when tradition says they should not. Martha Chen's work with widows like Metha Bai reveals that they are already deeply critical of the cultural norms that determine their life quality. One week at a widows' conference in Bangalore was sufficient to cause these formerly secluded widows to put on forbidden colors and to apply for loans; one elderly woman, "widowed" at the age of seven, danced for the first time in her life, whirling wildly in the center of the floor.[79] In other cases, especially when a woman must negotiate a relationship with a surviving husband, it takes longer for her real affiliations and preferences to emerge. Chen's related study of a rural literacy project in Bangladesh[80] shows that it took a good deal of time for women previously illiterate to figure out, in consultation with development workers, that literacy might offer something to their own concrete lives. Nonetheless, what we do not see in any of these cases is the fantasy that the Marglins describe, a cultural monolith univocally repudiating the outsider and clinging to an "embedded way of life." Why should women cling to a tradition, indeed, when it is usually not their voice that speaks or their interests that are served?

VI. Answering the Objections: Human Functioning and Pluralism

We still need to show that this approach has answers to the legitimate questions that confronted it. Concerning *neglect of historical and cultural difference,* we can begin by insisting that this normative conception of human capability is designed to make room for a reasonable pluralism in specification. The capabilities approach urges us to see common needs, problems, and capacities, but it also reminds us that each person and group faces these problems in a highly concrete context. The list claims to have identified in a very general way some components that are fundamental to any human life. But it makes room for differences of context in several ways. First, it is open ended and nonexhaustive. It does not say that these are the only important things, or that there is anything unimportant (far less, bad) about things not on the list. It just says that this is a group of especially important functions on which we can agree to focus for political purposes.

Further, the list allows in its very design for the possibility of multiple specifications of each of the components. Good public reasoning about the list will retain a rich sensitivity to the concrete context, to the characters of the agents and their social situation. Sometimes what is a good way of promoting education in one part of the world will be completely ineffectual in another. Forms of affiliation that flourish in one community may prove impossible to sustain in another. Arriving at the best specification will most reasonably be done by a public dialogue with those who are most deeply immersed in those conditions. We should use the list to criticize injustice, but we should not say anything at all without rich and full information.

We see this, for example, in Martha Chen's account of the Bangladeshi literacy project.[81] An initial approach that simply offered the women adult literacy materials met with no response. It was only after a period of "participatory dialogue," during which the local women told their stories and the development workers gave them rich narrative information about the lives of women elsewhere, that a picture of literacy for these women in these circumstances began to emerge and to make sense. Given the opportunity, they made for themselves a concrete local specification of this vague end. And it was clearly no external imposition: The women's narratives express a joy in self-command and agency that seems to come from something very deep in themselves. Rohima, of the West Shanbandha women's group, comments:

> Even my mother said yesterday: "You did not use to visit others' homes, did not speak to others. How have you learnt to speak so many things?" I said: "Ma, how I have learnt I cannot say. Whenever I am alone I sit with the books." Mother asked: "What do you see in the books?" I said: "Ma, what valuable things there are in the books you will not understand because you cannot read and write." If somebody behaves badly with me, I go home and sit with the books. When I sit with the books my mind becomes better.[82]

The books had to have some relation to the women's concrete situation, but it was equally important that the development workers did not back off when they saw that the women's local traditions contained no history of female literacy.

We can say the same of the related value of autonomy. It would have been very wrong to assume, with the Marglins, that these women did not want separateness and choice, that they really wanted to submerge their own aims in those of husband and family. This, again, emerges retrospectively, in their moving accounts of their newfound feeling of selfhood and mental awareness. "My mind was rusty," says one young wife, "and now it shines." On the other hand, it also would have done no good to go into that village and deliver a lecture on Kant—or on human capabilities! The universal value of practical reason and choice would have meant little in the abstract. To make sense, it had to become concretely situated in the stories they told about themselves and their lives.

If we turn to the difficult story of Metha Bai, something similar emerges. Metha Bai's is the story of age-old traditions regarding widowhood in India.[83] Any approach to her situation would have to be based on an understanding of these traditions and their special connection with issues of caste in an upwardly mobile Hindu family. Talk of "the right to work" would have been no use without a concrete local undertanding. On the other hand, if the workers in the widows project had simply backed off, saying that the local values did not include a value of right to work for widows, they would have missed the depth at which Metha Bai herself longed for choice and autonomy, both as means to survival for herself and her children and as means to selfhood. These are typical examples of the fruitful ways in which an abstract value can be instantiated in a concrete situation, through rich local knowledge.

One further observation is in order. This objector is frequently worried about the way in which universalist projects may erode the values that hold communities together. We have already seen that traditional community values are not always so good for women. We can now add that universalist values build new types of community. All the women studied by Chen stressed the solidarity promoted by the literacy project, the comfort and pleasure they had in consulting with a group of women (some local, some from the development project) rather than each being isolated in the home. Mallika, a young widow in Dapunia, vigorously expresses this idea:

> The group helped us and taught us many things. I have learned how to live unitedly. Before if any rich person abused or criticized, we could not reply. But now if anybody says anything bad, we, the 17 members of the group, go together and ask that person why he or she passed this comment. This is another kind of help we have gotten. Before we did not know how to get together and help each other. . . . Each one was busy with their own worries and sorrows, always thinking about food for their children and themselves. Now we, the 17 members of the group, have become very close to one another.[84]

This story is no isolated phenomenon. In women's groups I have visited in both India and China, the first benefit that is typically mentioned is that of affiliation and friendship with other women in pursuit of common goals. This shows us something highly pertinent to the Marglins' nostalgic tale of embeddedness. We do not have to choose between "the embedded life" of community and a deracinated type of individualism. Universal values build their own communities, communities of resourcefulness, friendship, and agency, embedded in the local scene but linked in complex ways to groups of women in other parts of the world. For these women the new community was a lot better than the one they had inhabited before.

The liberal charges the capability approach with *neglect of autonomy*, arguing that any such determinate conception removes from the citizens the chance to make their own choices about the good life. We have already said a good deal about this issue, but let us summarize, stressing three points. First, the list is a list of capabilities, not a list of actual functions, precisely because the conception is designed to leave room for choice. Government is not directed to push citizens into acting in certain valued ways; instead, it is directed to make sure that all human beings have the necessary resources and conditions for acting in those ways. By making opportunities available, government enhances, and does not remove, choice.[85] It will not always be easy to say at what point someone is really capable of making a choice, especially when there are traditional obstacles to functioning. Sometimes our best strategy may well be to look at actual functioning and infer negative capability (tentatively) from its absence.[86] But the conceptual distinction remains critical. Even in the rare case in which the approach will favor compulsory measures—particularly in primary and secondary education—it does so because of the huge role education plays in opening other choices in life.

Second, this respect for choice is built deeply into the list itself, in the role it gives to practical reasoning, to the political liberties, and also to employment, seen as a source of opportunity and empowerment. One of the most central capabilities promoted by the conception will be the capability of choosing itself.[87]

The examples we have considered show the truth of these claims. In the literacy project, a concern for autonomy was fundamental in the method of participatory dialogue itself, which constructed a situation free from intimidation and hierarchy in which the women's own concerns could gradually emerge and develop on the basis of the information they received. Their ex post facto satisfaction with their new situation, in which life choices were greatly enhanced, indicates, I believe, that the focus on a general capability goal was not a violation of their autonomy. (Rohima comments: "It is good now. . . . As my knowledge and understanding are good now, I will be able to do many things gradually."[88]) Indeed, we can see in the project as a whole the construction of full autonomy out of a more inchoate sense of the self. Metha Bai already had a robust sense of her own interests and how they diverged from the expectations of those around her. But the widows project, which extended her thoughts by providing information and advice, was crucial to the further development of her own conception of life.

Finally, the capability view insists that choice is not pure spontaneity, flourishing independently of material and social conditions. If one cares about autonomy, then one must care about the rest of the form of life that supports it and the material conditions that enable one to live that form of life. Thus, the approach claims that its own comprehensive concern with flourishing is a better way of promoting choice than is the liberal's narrower concern with spontaneity alone, which sometimes tolerates situations in which individuals are cut off from the fully human use of their faculties.

We now face the objection about *prejudicial application*. Catharine MacKinnon once claimed that "being a woman is not yet a way of being a human being."[89] As this remark suggests, most traditional ways of categorizing and valuing women have not accorded them full membership in the human species, as that species is generally defined. If this is so, one might well ask, of what use is it to identify a set of central human capabilities? For the basic (lower-level) capacity to develop these can always be denied to women, even by those who grant their centrality—for example, by denying women "rational nature," or by asserting that they are connected to dangerous or unclean animality. Does this problem show that the human function idea is either hopelessly in league with patriarchy or, at best, impotent as a tool for justice?

I believe that it does not. For if we examine the history of these denials we see, I believe, the great power of the conception of the human as a source of moral claims. Acknowledging the other person as a member of the very same kind would have generated a sense of affiliation and a set of moral and educational duties. That is why, to those bent on shoring up their own power, the stratagem of splitting the other off from one's own species seems so urgent and so seductive. But to deny humanness to beings with whom one lives in conversation and interaction is a fragile sort of self-deceptive stratagem, vulnerable to sustained and consistent reflection, and also to experiences that cut through self-deceptive rationalization. Any moral conception can be withheld, out of ambition or hatred or shame. But the conception of the human being, spelled out, as here, in a roughly determinate way, seems much harder to withhold than others that have been made the basis for ethics, such as "rational being" or "person."

VII. Women and Men: Two Norms or One?

But should there be a single norm of human functioning for men and women? One might grant that human capabilities cross cultures while still maintaining that in each culture a division of labor should be arranged along gender lines.

One such position, which I shall call Position A, assigns to both males and females the same general normative list of functions but suggests that males and females should exercise these functions in different spheres of life: men in the public sphere, for example, and women in the home. The second, which I shall call Position B, insists that the list of functions, even at a high level of generality, should be different: for men, citizenship and rational autonomy; for women, family love and care.

Position A is compatible with a serious interest in equality and in gender justice. For what it says, after all, is that males and females have the same basic needs for capability development and should get what they need. It is determined to ensure that both get to the higher (developed) level of capability with respect to all the central functions. It simply holds that this can (and perhaps should) be done in separate spheres. Is this any more problematic than to say that human functioning in India can, and even should, take a different concrete form from functioning in England? Or that some people can realize musical capacities by singing; others by playing the violin?

The trouble comes when we notice that Position A usually ends up endorsing a division of duties that is associated with traditional forms of hierarchy. Even Mill, who made so many fine arguments against women's subordination, did not sufficiently ask how the very perpetuation of separate spheres of responsibility might reinforce subordination. It is hard to find plausible reasons for perpetuating functional distinctions that coincide with traditional hierarchy. Even in the fourth century B.C.E., Plato was able to see that women's role in childbearing does not require, or even suggest, that women be confined to the home.[90] Advances in the control of reproduction are making this less and less plausible. The disability imposed by childbearing on a member of the labor force is to a large extent socially constructed, above all by the absence of support for child care, from the public sphere, from employers, and from male partners.

Sometimes clinging to traditional divisions is a prudent way of promoting social change. Neither Chen nor her colleagues proposed to jettison all gender divisions within the Bangladeshi villages. Instead, they found "female jobs" for the women that were somewhat more dignified and important than the old jobs, jobs that looked continuous with traditional female work but were outside the home and brought in wages. The "revolution" in women's quality of life never would have taken place but for the caution of the women, who at each stage gave the men of the village reason to believe that the transformations were not overwhelmingly threatening and were good for the well-being of the entire group. But such pragmatic decisions in the face of recalcitrant realities do not tell us how things ought to be. And it is likely that women's subordination will not be adequately addressed as long as women are confined to a sphere traditionally devalued, linked with a low "perceived well-being contribution."[91] The *Human Development Report's* Gender Empowerment Measure rightly focuses, therefore, on the ability of women to win entry into the traditional male spheres of politics and administration.

I turn, then, to Position B, which has been influentially defended by many philosophers, including Rousseau and some of his followers in today's world.[92] Insofar as B relies on the claim that there are two different sets of basic innate capacities, we should insist, with John Stuart Mill, that this claim has not been borne out by any responsible scientific evidence. Experiments that allegedly show strong gender divisions in basic (untrained) abilities have been shown to contain major scientific flaws; these flaws removed, the case for such differences is altogether inconclusive.[93] Experiments that cross-label babies as to sex have established that children are differentially handled, played with, and talked to straight from birth, in accordance with the handler's beliefs about the child's biological sex. It is therefore impossible at present to separate "nature" from "culture."[94] There may be innate differences between the sexes, but so far we are not in a position to know them—any more than we were when Mill first made that argument in 1869.[95]

Second, we should note that even what is claimed in this body of scientific material without substantiation usually does not amount to a difference in what I have been calling the central basic capabilities. What is alleged is usually a differential statistical distribution of some specific capacity for a high level of excellence, not for crossing a basic threshold, and excellence in some very narrowly defined function (say, geometrical ability), rather than in one of our large-scale capabilities such as the capability to perform practical reasoning. Thus, even if the claim were true it would not be a claim about capabilities in our capacious sense; nor, because it is a statistical claim, would it have any implications for the ways in which individuals should be treated. The political consequences of such alleged sex differences in our scheme of things, even had they been established, would be nil.

But we can also criticize Position B in a different way, arguing that the differentiated conceptions of male and female functioning characteristically put forward by B are internally inadequate and fail to give us viable norms of human flourishing.[96]

What do we usually find, in the versions of B that our philosophical tradition bequeaths to us? (Rousseau's view is an instructive example.) We have, on the one hand, males who are "autonomous," capable of practical reasoning, independent and self-sufficient, allegedly good at political deliberation. These males are brought up not to develop strong emotions of love and feelings of deep need that are associated with the awareness of one's own lack of self-sufficiency. For this reason they are not well equipped to care for the needs of their family members or, perhaps, even to notice those needs. On the other hand, we have females such as Rousseau's Sophie,[97] brought up to lack autonomy and self-respect, ill equipped to rely on her own practical reasoning, dependent on males, focused on pleasing others, and good at caring for others. Is either of these viable as a complete life for a human being?

It would seem not. The internal tensions in Rousseau's account are a good place to begin.[98] Rousseau places tremendous emphasis on compassion as a basic social motivation. He understands compassion to require fellow feeling and a keen responsiveness to the sufferings of others. And yet, in preparing Emile for autonomous citizenship, he ultimately gives emotional development short shrift, allocating caring and responsiveness to the female sphere alone. It appears likely that Emile will be not only an incomplete person but also a defective citizen, even by the standards of citizenship recognized by Rousseau himself.

With Sophie, things again go badly. Taught to care for others but not taught that her life is her own to plan, she lives under the sway of external influences and lacks self-government. As Rousseau himself shows in his fascinating narrative of the end of her life,[99] Sophie comes to a bad end through her lack of judgment. Moreover, in the process she proves to be a bad partner and deficient in love. For love, as we come to see, requires judgment and constancy. Thus each of them fails to live a complete human life, and each fails, too, to exemplify fully and well the very functions for which they were being trained, because those functions require support from other functions for which they were not trained. The text leads its thoughtful reader to the conclusion that the capabilities that have traditionally marked the separate male and female spheres are not separable from one another without a grave functional loss. Society cannot strive for completeness by simply adding one sphere to the other. It must strive to develop in each and every person the full range of the human capabilities.

This more inclusive notion of human functioning admits tragic conflict. For it insists on the separate value and the irreplaceable importance of a rich plurality of functions. And the world does not always guarantee that individuals will not be faced with painful choices among these functions, in which, in order to pursue one of them well they must neglect others (and thus, in many cases, subvert the one as well). But this shows once again, I believe, the tremendous importance of keeping some such list of the central functions before us as we assess the quality of life in the countries of the world and strive to raise it. For many such tragedies—like many cases of simple capability failure—result from unjust and unreflective social arrangements. One can try to construct a society in which the tragic choices that faced Emile and Sophie would not be necessary, in which both males and females could learn both to love and to reason.

In April 1994, Metha Bai went to Bangalore for the widows' conference. She met widows from all over India, and they spent a week discussing their common problems. During that week, Metha Bai began to smile a lot. She bought beads in the forbidden color of blue, and she seemed pleased with the way she looked. With advice from a local NGO involved in the conference, she applied for and obtained a loan that enabled her to pay off the mortgage on the small property she still owns. Although her economic situation is not secure and she still does not hold a job outside the home, she has managed to stave off hunger. Like many women all over the world, she is fighting for her life, with resilience and fortitude.

Women belong to cultures. But they do not choose to be born into any particular culture, and they do not really choose to endorse its norms as good for themselves, unless they do so in possession of further options and opportunities—including the opportunity to form communities of affiliation and empowerment with other women. The contingencies of where one is born, whose power one is afraid of, and what habits shape one's daily thought are chance events that should not be permitted to play the role they now play in pervasively shaping women's life chances. Beneath all these chance events are human powers, powers of choice and intelligent self-formation. Women in much of the world lack support for the most central human functions, and this denial of support is frequently caused by their being women. But women, unlike rocks and plants and even horses, have the potential to become capable of these human functions, given sufficient nutrition, education, and other support. That is why their unequal failure in capability is a problem of justice. It is up to all human beings to solve this problem. I claim that a conception of human functioning gives us valuable assistance as we undertake this task.

NOTES

Chapter 1

I have discussed the capabilities approach in several other papers, to which I shall refer: "Nature, Function, and Capability: Aristotle on Political Distribution," *Oxford Studies in Ancient Philosophy* Supplementary Volume 1 (1988), 145–84, hereafter NFC; "Aristotelian Social Democracy," in *Liberalism and the Good*, ed. R. B. Douglass *et al.* (New York: Routledge, 1990), 203–52, hereafter ASD; "Non-Relative Virtues: An Aristotelian Approach," in *The Quality of Life*, ed. M. Nussbaum and A. Sen (Oxford: Clarendon Press, 1993), hereafter NRV; "Aristotle on Human Nature and the Foundations of Ethics," in *World, Mind and Ethics: Essays on the Ethical Philosophy of Bernard Williams*, ed. J. E. J. Altham and Ross Harrison (Cambridge: Cambridge University Press, 1995), 86–131, hereafter HN; "Human Functioning and Social Justice: In Defense of Aristotelian Essentialism," *Political Theory* 20 (1992), 202–46, hereafter HF; "Human Capabilities, Female Human Beings," in *Women, Culture, and Development*, ed. M. Nussbaum and J. Glover (Oxford: Clarendon Press, 1995), 61–104, hereafter HC; "The Good as Discipline, the Good as Freedom," in *The Ethics of Consumption and Global Stewardship*, ed. D. Crocker and T. Linden (Lanham, MD: Rowman and Littlefield, 1998), 312–41, hereafter GDGF; "Capabilities and Human Rights," *Fordham Law Review* 66 (1997), 273–300, hereafter CHR.

1. For this case and others like it, see Martha Chen, "A Matter of Survival: Women's Right to Employment in India and Bangladesh," in *Women, Culture, and Development* (hereafter WCD), ed. M. Nussbaum and J. Glover (Oxford: Clarendon Press, 1995), 37–57. See also M. Chen, *The Lives of Widows in Rural India* (forthcoming).
2. *Bradwell v. Illinois*, 83 U.S. (16 Wall.) 130 (1873).
3. *Carr v. Allison Gas Turbine Division, General Motors Corp.*, 32 F.3d 1007 (1994). Mary Carr won her case on appeal.
4. Martha Chen, *A Quiet Revolution: Women in Transition in Rural Bangladesh* (Cambridge, MA: Schenkman, 1983), 176.
5. *Human Development Report* (New York: United Nations Development Program, 1996) (hereafter *Report*); see also the 1995 *Report*, which focuses on gender. The countries in which women do best in life quality, according to the Gender Development Index (GDI), a measure using the same variables as the HDI (Human Development Index) but adjusted according to disparities between the sexes (see *Report*, 107, for the technical formulation) are, in order, Sweden, Canada, Norway, the United States, Finland, Iceland, Denmark, France, Australia, New Zealand, the Netherlands, Japan, Austria, the United Kingdom, and Belgium.
6. If we subtract the GDI rank from the HDI rank, we get –10 for Spain, –9 for Japan, 8 for Sweden, 10 for Denmark, and 4 for New Zealand.

7. These variables include percentage shares of administrative and managerial positions, percentage shares of professional and technical jobs, and percentage shares of parliamentary seats.

8. The ranking at the top: Norway, Sweden, Denmark, Finland, New Zealand, Canada, Germany, the Netherlands, the United States, Austria, Barbados, and Switzerland. Spain ranks 25; Japan, 37; France, 40; and Greece, 60.

9. These data are from the 1993 report; later reports disaggregate employment data into jobs of various specific kinds and no longer count unpaid agricultural labor as employment.

10. Again, these are 1993 data; the 1996 report gives the absolute percentages, which are, for these examples, Sierra Leone, 16.7%; Afghanistan, 13.5%; Sudan, 32%; Nepal, 13%. Nations in which the female literacy rate is strikingly out of step with the general level of economic development include Saudi Arabia, 47.6%; Algeria, 45.8%; Egypt, 37.0%; Iraq, 42.3%; Pakistan, 23.0%; and India, 36.0%. Striking progress in female literacy, on the other hand, if one can rely on the figures, has been made in Cuba, 94.6%; Sri Lanka, 86.2%; Philippines, 93.9%; most of the former constituent states of the Soviet Union, in the 90s; Vietnam, 89.5%; and China, 70.9%. On the disparity of achievement between China and India, see Jean Drèze and Amartya Sen, *India: Economic Development and Social Opportunity* (Oxford: Clarendon Press, 1996).

11. Numbers of female students in tertiary education per 100,000 people: Hong Kong, 1,022; Barbados, 1,885; Republic of Korea, 2,866; Philippines, 3,140; Egypt, 499; China, 132; Iran, 764; Laos, 60; Pakistan, 149; Ethiopia, 24; and Rwanda, 19.

12. Countries where women hold a high percentage of parliamentary seats: Norway, 39.4%; Sweden, 40.4%; and Denmark, 33.0%. Bangladesh at 10.6% is ahead of the United States at 10.4%, and India at 8.0% is ahead of Japan at 6.7%.

13. The statistics in this paragraph are taken from Jean Drèze and Amartya Sen, *Hunger and Public Action* (Oxford: Clarendon Press, 1989).

14. This is very likely due to the central role women play in productive economic activity. For a classic study of this issue, see Esther Boserup, *Women's Role in Economic Development* (New York: St. Martin's Press, 1970), 2nd ed. (Aldershot: Gower Publishing, 1986). For a set of valuable responses to Boserup's work, see *Persistent Inequalities*, ed. Irene Tinker (New York: Oxford University Press, 1990).

15. See Drèze and Sen, 52.

16. See Drèze and Sen, *India*.

17. See Sen, "Gender and Cooperative Conflicts," in Tinker, 123–49.

18. See Drèze and Sen, *India*, for graphic evidence of the relative independence of educational and health attainment from economic growth, in comparative regional studies.

19. Gary Becker, *A Treatise on the Family* (Cambridge, MA: Harvard University Press, 1981; 2nd ed. 1991).

20. See Sen, "Gender and Cooperative Conflicts"; Partha Dasgupta, *An Inquiry Into Well-Being and Destitution* (Oxford: Clarendon Press, 1993), chap. 11; on food allocation, see Lincoln C. Chen, E. Huq, and S. D'Souza, "Sex Bias in the Family Allocation of Food and Health Care in Rural Bangladesh," *Population and Development Review* 7 (1981), 55–70. Bargaining models of the family are now proliferating; for two valuable recent examples, see Shelly Lundberg and Robert A. Pollak, "Bargaining and Distribution in Marriage," *Journal of Economic Perspectives* 10 (1996), 139–58, and S. Lundberg, R. Pollak, and T. J. Wales, "Do Husbands and Wives Pool Their Resources? Evidence from the U.K. Child Benefit," *Journal of Human Resources* (forthcoming).

21. See, now, Gary Becker, "The Economic Way of Looking at Behavior," the Nobel Address 1992, in *The Essence of Becker*, ed. Ramón Febrero and Pedro S. Schwartz (Stanford, CA: Hoover Institution Press, 1995), 647, on the role of childhood experiences in shaping preferences.

22. Sen, "Gender and Cooperative Conflicts," argues that Becker's account is much stronger as an account of actual preferences in the household than as an account of the real interests (life and death, good and bad health, good and bad nutrition) that underlie the preferences. (He provides evidence that people's perception of their health and nutritional status may be severely distorted by informational deficiencies.)

23. Becker now admits deficiencies in the model: "Many economists, including me, have excessively relied on altruism to tie together the interests of family members." Motives of "obligation, anger, and other attitudes usually neglected by theories of rational behavior" should be added to the models. Becker, "The Economic Way of Looking at Behavior," 648. Elsewhere, Becker mentions guilt, affection, and fear—his example being a woman's habitual fear of physical abuse from men. Ibid., 647. It is unclear whether he still supports an organic one-actor model, with a more complicated motivational structure, or a "bargaining model," of the sort increasingly used by family economists. See Becker, *A Treatise on the Family*.

24. See Sen, "Gender and Cooperative Conflicts"; Jon Elster, *Sour Grapes* (Cambridge: Cambridge University Press, 1993).

25. See John Rawls, *A Theory of Justice* (hereafter TJ) (Cambridge, MA: Harvard University Press, 1970); *Political Liberalism* (hereafter PL) (New York: Columbia University Press, 1993, paper ed. 1996).

26. The "capabilities approach" was pioneered within economics by Amartya Sen and has been developed by both Sen and me in complementary but not identical ways. For an overview, see David Crocker, "Functioning and Capability: the Foundations of Sen's and Nussbaum's Development Ethic," in WCD, 152–98.

27. See Amartya Sen, "Equality of What?," in *Choice, Welfare, and Measurement* (Oxford: Basil Blackwell, 1982), 353–72; and Nussbaum, ASD.

28. Much of the material described in these examples is now published in *Dominating Knowledge: Development, Culture, and Resistance*, ed. Frédérique Apffel Marglin and Stephen A. Marglin (Oxford: Clarendon Press, 1990). The issue of "embeddedness" and menstruation taboos is discussed in S. A. Marglin, "Losing Touch: The Cultural Conditions of Worker Accommodation and Resistance," 217–82, and related issues are discussed in S. A. Marglin, "Toward the Decolonization of the Mind," 1–28. On Sittala Devi, see F. A. Marglin, "Smallpox in Two Systems of Knowledge," 102–44; and for related arguments see Ashis Nandy and Shiv Visvanathan, "Modern Medicine and Its Non-Modern Critics," 144–84. I have in some cases combined two conversations into one; otherwise things happened as I describe them.

29. For Sen's own account of the plurality and internal diversity of Indian values, one that strongly emphasizes the presence of a rationalist and critical strand in Indian traditions, see M. Nussbaum and A. Sen, "Internal Criticism and Indian Relativist Traditions," in *Relativism: Interpretation and Confrontation*, ed. M. Krausz (Notre Dame: Notre Dame University Press, 1989), 299–325 (an essay originally presented at the same WIDER conference and refused publication by the Marglins in its proceedings); and A. Sen, "India and the West," *The New Republic* June 7, 1993. See also Bimal K. Matilal, *Perception* (Oxford: Clarendon Press, 1995) (a fundamental study of Indian traditions regarding knowledge and logic); and B. K. Matilal,

"Ethical Relativism and the Confrontation of Cultures," in Krausz, ed., *Relativism*, 339–62.

30. S. A. Marglin, "Toward the Decolonization," 22–3, suggests that binary thinking is peculiarly Western. But such oppositions are pervasive in Indian, Chinese, and African traditions (see HC). To deny them to a culture is condescending: for how can one utter a definite idea without bounding off one thing against another?

31. See Eric Hobsbawm and Terence Ranger, eds., *The Invention of Tradition* (Cambridge: Cambridge University Press, 1983). In his *New Republic* piece, Sen makes a similar argument about contemporary India: The Western construction of India as mystical and "other" serves the purposes of the fundamentalist Bharatiya Janata Party (BJP), who are busy refashioning history to serve the ends of their own political power. An eloquent critique of the whole notion of the "other" and of the associated "nativism,"where Africa is concerned, can be found in Kwame Anthony Appiah, *In My Father's House: Africa in the Philosophy of Cultures* (New York: Oxford University Press, 1991).

32. The proceedings of this conference are now published as M. Nussbaum and A. Sen, eds., *The Quality of Life* (Oxford: Clarendon Press, 1993).

33. Marglin has since published this point in "Toward the Decolonization." His reference is to Takeo Doi, *The Anatomy of Dependence* (Tokyo: Kodansha, 1971).

34. See S. A. Marglin, "Toward the Decolonization."

35. See Nussbaum and Sen, "Internal Criticism," and A. Sen, "Human Rights and Asian Values," *The New Republic*, July 10/17, 1997, 33–40.

36. See Roop Rekha Verma, "Femininity, Equality, and Personhood," in WCD.

37. Satyajit Ray, "Introduction," *Our Films, Their Films* (Bombay: Orient Longman, 1976, reprinted New York: Hyperion, 1994), 5.

38. Personal communication, scholars in women's studies at the Chinese Academy of Social Sciences, June 1995.

39. Note that this objection itself seems to rely on some universal values such as fairness and freedom from bias.

40. See HF for a longer version of this discussion.

41. Aristotle, *Nicomachean Ethics* VIII.I. I discuss this passage in HN and NRV.

42. "If my sisters and I were 'children of two worlds,' no one bothered to tell us this; we lived in one world, in two 'extended' families divided by several thousand miles and an allegedly insuperable cultural distance that never, so far as I can recall, puzzled or perplexed us much." Appiah, vii–viii. Appiah's argument does not neglect distinctive features of concrete histories; indeed, one of its purposes is to demonstrate how varied, when concretely seen, histories really are. But his argument, like mine, seeks a subtle balance between perception of the particular and recognition of the common.

43. This point is made by the Marglins, as well as by liberal thinkers, but can they consistently make it while holding that freedom of choice is just a parochial Western value? It would appear not; on the other hand, F. A. Marglin (here differing, I believe, from S. A. Marglin) also held in oral remarks delivered at the 1986 conference that logical consistency is simply a parochial Western value.

44. See Noam Chomsky, in *Cartesian Linguistics* (New York: Harper and Row, 1966). Chomsky argues that Cartesian rationalism, with its insistence on innate essences, was politically more progressive, more hostile to slavery and imperialism, than empiricism, with its insistence that people were just what experience had made of them.

45. The use of this term does not imply that the functions all involve doing something especially "active." See here A. Sen, "Capability and Well-Being," in *The*

Quality of Life, ed. M. Nussbaum and A. Sen (Oxford: Clarendon Press, 1993), 30–53. In Aristotelian terms, and in mine, being healthy, reflecting, and being pleased are all "activities."

46. For further discussion of this point, and for examples, see HN.

47. Could one cease to be one's individual self without ceasing to be human? Perhaps, in cases of profound personality or memory change, but I shall leave such cases to one side here. This is ruled out, I think, in Aristotle's conception but is possible in some other metaphysical conceptions.

48. See HN for a more extended account of this procedure and how it justifies.

49. Nor does it deny that experience of the body is shaped by culture. See NRV.

50. Rawls, TJ, 90–95, 396–7.

51. This was implicit in ASD but has become more prominent in recent essays. See A. Sen, "Freedoms and Needs," *New Republic*, January 10/17, 1994, 31–38; Nussbaum GDGF.

52. In ASD I call it "the thick vague theory of the good."

53. Rawls, PL. Note that the consensus is defined in terms of a normative notion of reasonableness. Thus, the failure of some real individuals to agree will not be fatal to the view.

54. On this relationship, see HN.

55. The current version of this list reflects changes suggested to me by discussions during my visits to women's development projects in India. These include a new emphasis on bodily integrity, on employment, on property rights, and on dignity and nonhumiliation.

56. Although "normal length" is clearly relative to current human possibilities and may need, for practical purposes, to be to some extent relativized to local conditions, it seems important to think of it—at least at a given time in history—in universal and comparative terms, as the *Human Development Report* does, to give rise to complaint in a country that has done well with some indicators of life quality but badly on life expectancy. And although some degree of relativity may be put down to the differential genetic possibilities of different groups (the "missing women" statistics, for example, allow that on the average women live somewhat longer than men), it is also important not to conclude prematurely that inequalities between groups—for example, the growing inequalities in life expectancy between blacks and whites in the United States—are simply genetic variation, not connected with social injustice.

57. The precise specification of these health rights is not easy, but the work currently being done on them in drafting new constitutions in South Africa and Eastern Europe gives reasons for hope that the combination of a general specification of such a right with a tradition of judicial interpretation will yield something practicable. It should be noticed that I speak of health, not just health care; and health itself interacts in complex ways with housing, with education, with dignity. Both health and nutrition are controversial as to whether the relevant level should be specified universally, or relatively to the local community and its traditions. For example, is low height associated with nutritional practices to be thought of as "stunting" or as felicitous adaptation to circumstances of scarcity? For an excellent summary of this debate, see S. R. Osmani, ed., *Nutrition and Poverty* (Oxford: Clarendon Press, WIDER series, 1990), especially the following papers: on the relativist side, T. N. Srinivasan, "Undernutrition: Concepts, Measurements, and Policy Implications," 97–120; on the universalist side, C. Gopalan, "Undernutrition: Measurement and Implications," 17–48; for a compelling adjudication of the debate, coming out

on the universalist side, see Osmani, "On Some Controversies in the Measurement of Undernutrition," 121–61.

58. There is a growing literature on the importance of shelter for health; for example, that the provision of adequate housing is the single largest determinant of health status for HIV-infected persons. Housing rights are increasingly coming to be constitutionalized, at least in a negative form—giving squatters grounds for appeal, for example, against a landlord who would bulldoze their shanties. On this as a constitutional right, see proposed Articles 11, 12, and 17 of the South African Constitution, in a draft put forward by the African National Congress (ANC) committee adviser Albie Sachs, where this is given as an example of a justiciable housing right.

59. Some form of intimate family love is central to child development, but this need not be the traditional Western nuclear family. In the development of citizens it is crucial that the family be an institution characterized by justice as well as love. See Susan Moller Okin, *Justice, Gender, and the Family* (New York: Basic Books, 1989).

60. In terms of cross-cultural discussion, this item has proven the most controversial and elusive on the list. It also properly raises the question whether the list ought to be anthropocentric at all, or whether we should seek to promote appropriate capabilities for all living things. I leave further argument on these questions for another occasion.

61. ASD argues that property rights are distinct from, for example, speech rights, in the sense that property is a tool of human functioning and not an end in itself. See also Nussbaum, CHR.

62. Sen has not endorsed any such specific list of the capabilities.

63. See Sen, "Gender Inequality and Theories of Justice," in WCD, 259–73; Becker, "The Economic Way of Looking at Behavior."

64. With Sen, I hold that the capability set should be treated as an interlocking whole. For my comments on his arguments, see NFC.

65. See ibid., with reference to Aristotle.

66. See HN. This is the core of Marx's reading of Aristotle.

67. See chapter 4.

68. See NFC, referring to Aristotle's similar distinctions.

69. This distinction is related to Rawls's distinction between social and natural primary goods. Whereas he holds that only the social primary goods should be on the list, and not the natural (such as health, imagination), we say that *the social basis of* the natural primary goods should most emphatically be on the list.

70. TJ, 62.

71. Rawls comments that "although their possession is influenced by the basic structure, they are not so directly under its control." TJ, 62. This is of course true if we are thinking of health, but if we think of the social basis of health, it is not true. It seems to me that the case for putting these items on the political list is just as strong as the case for the social basis of self-respect. In "The Priority of Right and Ideas of the Good," *Philosophy and Public Affairs* 17 (1988), 251–76, Rawls suggests putting health on the list.

72. See ASD and GDGF.

73. See HN. For the relation of capabilities to human rights, see CHR.

74. Sen, "Freedoms and Needs," 38.

75. PL 187–8.

76. Though in one form Aristotle had it too. See also GDGF; and CHR.

77. Compare Sen, "Freedoms and Needs," 38: "The importance of political rights for the understanding of economic needs turns ultimately on seeing human beings as people with rights to exercise, not as parts of a 'stock' or a 'population' that passively exists and must be looked after. What matters, finally, is how we see each other."

78. Chapter 3 (in this volume) argues that religious norms should not be imposed without choice on individuals who may not have opted for that religious tradition. In that sense, any religiously based employment restriction is questionable.

79. Chen, *The Lives of Widows in Rural India.* Girls in some regions of India are betrothed at a very young age and at that point become members of their husband's family, although the marriage will not be consummated until puberty. Such a girl is treated as widowed even if the male dies before consummation.

80. Chen, *A Quiet Revolution.*

81. Ibid.

82. Ibid., 202. Married at age seven, abandoned by her husband many years later, Rohima lives with her brother. Four of her children have died; one son and one daughter survive. Her son gives her some financial support.

83. See the account of these in Chen, *The Lives of Widows.*

84. Chen, *A Quiet Revolution,* 216.

85. Sen has stressed this throughout his writing on the topic. For an overview, see "Capability and Well-Being." And for some complications, see GDGF.

86. This is the strategy used by Robert Erikson's Swedish team when studying inequalities in political participation. See Robert Erikson, "Descriptions of Inequality," in Nussbaum and Sen, eds., *The Quality of Life.*

87. Rawls proceeds in a similar way, insisting that satisfactions that are not the outgrowth of one's very own choices have no moral worth. He conceives of the "two moral powers" (analogous to our practical reasoning) and of sociability (corresponding to our affiliation) as built into the definition of the parties in the original position, and thus as necessary constraints on any outcome they will select. See ASD.

88. Chen, *A Quiet Revolution,* 199.

89. The remark was cited by Richard Rorty in "Feminism and Pragmatism," *Michigan Quarterly Review* 30 (1989), 263; it has since been confirmed and repeated by MacKinnon herself.

90. Plato, *Republic,* Book V. Although Plato's proposal is theoretical and utopian, it is closely based on observation of the functioning of women in Sparta. See S. Halliwell, *Plato: Republic V* (Warminster: Aris & Phillips, 1994).

91. See Sen, "Gender and Cooperative Conflicts."

92. On Rousseau, see Susan Moller Okin, *Women in Western Political Thought* (Princeton: Princeton University Press, 1979), and Jane Roland Martin, *Reclaiming a Conversation* (New Haven: Yale University Press, 1985). On some related recent arguments, for example, those of Allan Bloom, see Okin, *Justice,* chap. l.

93. See the convincing summary in Anne Fausto-Sterling, *Myths of Gender,* 2nd ed. (New York: Basic Books, 1992).

94. Ibid.

95. John Stuart Mill, *The Subjection of Women* (1869), ed. Susan Moller Okin (Indianapolis, IN: Hackett, 1988).

96. Here I am in agreement with the general line of argument in Okin, *Women,* and Martin, *Reclaiming,* and with the related arguments in Nancy Chodorow, *The Reproduction of Mothering* (Berkeley: University of California Press, 1978).

97. Jean-Jacques Rousseau, *Emile: or On Education,* trans. Allan Bloom (New York: Basic Books, 1979), Book V.

98. See Okin, *Women*; and Martin, *Reclaiming*.
99. See the discussion in Okin, *Women*.

[8]

GENDER, PROPERTY, AND LAND RIGHTS

Bridging a critical gap in economic analysis and policy[1]

Bina Agarwal

> Please go and ask the *sarkar* [government] why when it distributes land we don't get a title. Are we not peasants? If my husband throws me out, what is my security?
>
> (Message conveyed by poor peasant women to the West Bengal government in 1979 through their women representatives on the village council)[2]

Economic analyses and policies concerning women have long been pre-occupied with employment, to the neglect of a crucial determinant of women's situation, namely the gender gap in command over property. This is especially (but not only) true in analyses relating to South Asia. It is argued here that the gender gap in the ownership and control of property is the single most critical contributor to the gender gap in economic well-being, social status and empowerment. In primarily rural economies such as those of South Asia the most important form of property is arable land. A struggle for gender equality in command over landed property will therefore need to occupy center stage in South Asian women's struggle for egalitarian gender relations.

The discussion below is divided into five sections. Section one examines the conceptual links between gender, property, and land rights. Section two elaborates upon why it is important for rural women to have independent rights in land, especially for women's empowerment. Section three looks at gender relations historically in those South Asian communities in which women traditionally enjoyed rights in land. Section four identifies the obstacles women face in realizing effective land rights in most parts of South Asia today, and illustrates how women's command over economic resources is crucially mediated by non-economic factors. Finally, section five highlights some aspects of the interventions needed for change.

EMPOWERMENT OF WOMEN

GENDER, PROPERTY AND LAND: SOME CONCEPTUAL LINKS

In examining the relationship between gender and property, five interrelated issues need particular focus: gender relations and a household's property status; gender relations and women's property status; the distinction between ownership and control of property; the distinctiveness of land as property; and what is meant by rights in land. The first three issues are discussed in the subsection below, and the last two in separate subsections.

Household property and women's property

The links between gender subordination and property need to be sought in not only the distribution of property between households but also in its distribution between men and women, in not only who owns the property but also who controls it, and in relation not only to private property but also to communal property. Further, gender equality in legal rights to own property does not guarantee gender equality in actual ownership, nor does ownership guarantee control. The distinctions between law and practice and between ownership and control are especially critical in relation to women.

This formulation departs significantly from standard Marxist analysis, particularly from that of Engels' ([1884] 1972) still-influential though much criticized exposition, where intra-family gender relations are seen as structured primarily by two overlapping economic factors: the property status of the households to which the women belong, and women's participation in wage labor. Engels argued that in capitalist societies, gender relations would be hierarchical among the property-owning families of the bourgeoisie where women did not go out to work and were economically dependent on men, and egalitarian in propertyless proletarian families where women were in the labor force. The ultimate restoration of women to their rightful status, in his view, required the total abolition of private property (i.e. a move to socialism), the socialization of housework and childcare, and the full participation of women in the labor force[3].

In this analysis, therefore, the presumed equality of gender relations in a working-class family rested on both husband and wife being propertyless and in the labor force, and the inequality in the bourgeois family rested on men being propertied and women being both propertyless and outside the labor force. This underlying emphasis on the relational aspect of gender is clearly important. So is the emphasis on women's economic dependency as a critical constituent of the material basis of gender oppression. However, by advocating the abolition of all private property as the solution, Engels by-passed the issue of women's property rights altogether, and left open the question: what would be the impact on gender relations in propertied households if women too were propertied as individuals? Entry into the labor force is not the only way to reduce economic dependence; independent rights in property would be another, and possibly the more effective way.

Engels' emphasis on women's entry into the labor force as a necessary condition for their emancipation has been enormously influential in shaping the thinking of left-wing political parties and non-party groups, including left-wing women's groups in South Asia[4]. They too give centrality to women's employment, but the necessary accompaniments emphasized by Engels, namely the abolition of private property in male hands and the socialization of housework and childcare, have largely been neglected, as has the question of women's property rights.

A critical additional point (missed in Engels' analysis and associated discussions) is that of property control. Property advantage stems not only from ownership, but also from effective control over it. In societies which underwent socialist revolutions, while private property ownership was legally abolished, control over wealth-generating property remained mainly with men; any positive effects on gender relations that could have stemmed from the change in ownership, if accompanied by gender-egalitarian mechanisms of control, thus went unrealized[5]. Indeed in most societies today it is men as a gender (even if not all men as individuals) who largely control wealth-generating property, whether or not it is privately owned, including as managers in large corporations. Even property that is under State, community, or clan ownership remains effectively under the managerial control of selected men through their dominance in both traditional and modern institutions: caste or clan councils, village-elected bodies, State bureaucracies at all levels[6], and so on. Also in most countries, men as a gender exercise dominance over the instruments through which their existing advantages of property ownership and control get perpetuated, such as the institutions that enact and implement laws[7], the mechanisms of recruitment into bodies which exercise control over (private or public) property, the institutions which play an important role in shaping gender ideology, and so on.

A second issue concerning the relationship between gender and property is: how do we define a woman's class? Marxist analysis, for instance, implicitly assumes that women belong to the class of their husbands or fathers. Hence women of propertied "bourgeois" households are part of the bourgeoisie and those of proletarian households are counted as proletarian. However, there are at least two well-recognized problems with this characterization:

- A woman's class position defined through that of a man is more open to change than that of a man: a well-placed marriage can raise it, divorce or widowhood can lower it.

EMPOWERMENT OF WOMEN

- To the extent that women, even of propertied households, do not own property themselves, it is difficult to characterize their class position; some have even argued that women constitute a class in themselves[8].

In fact, neither deriving women's class from the property status of men nor deriving it from their own propertyless status appears adequate, although both positions reflect dimensions of reality. Women of rich households do gain economically and socially from their parents' or husbands' class positions. But women also share common concerns which cut across derived class privilege (or deprivation), such as vulnerability to domestic violence; responsibility for housework and childcare (even if not all women perform such labor themselves – the more affluent ones can hire helpers); gender inequalities in legal rights; and the risk of poverty if (parental or marital) family support ceases. This ambiguity in women's class position impinges with critical force on the possibilities of collective action among women. On the one hand, class differences among women, derived through men, can be divisive. On the other hand, the noted commonalities between women's situations and the relatively vicarious character of their class privilege make class distinctions between them less sharp than those between men, and could provide the basis for collective action on several counts[9].

A third aspect of the relationship between gender and property concerns the links between gender ideology and property. For instance:

- Gender ideologies can obstruct women from getting property rights. Assumptions about women's needs, roles, and capabilities impinge on the framing and implementation of public policies and property laws. Again, ideas about gender underlie practices such as female seclusion, which restrict women's ability both to exercise their existing property claims and to successfully challenge persisting gender inequalities in law, policy, and practice in relation to such claims. Hence ideological struggles are integrally linked to women's struggles over property rights.
- Those who own and/or control wealth-generating property can directly or indirectly control the principal institutions that shape ideology, such as educational and religious establishments and the media (including newspapers, TV, radio, film, theater, as well as literature and the arts). These can shape views in either gender-progressive or gender-retrogressive directions.
- The impact of gender ideologies can vary by a household's property status. For instance, both propertied and propertyless households may espouse the ideology of female seclusion, but the former group would be in a better economic position to enforce its practice, and in so doing reinforce its emulation by unpropertied households as a mark of social status. At the same time, gender ideologies and associated practices are

not derived from property differences alone, nor can they be seen in purely economic-functional terms. Rather they would tend to shift and change in interaction with economic shifts.

A fourth issue that arises in relation to women and property is the possible links of women's property rights with control over women's sexuality, marriage practices, and kinship structures. For instance, would women with independent property rights be subject to greater or lesser familial control over their sexual freedom than those without them? It would also be important to examine whether societies which historically recognized women's inheritance rights in immovable property, in order to keep the property intact and within their purview, tended to control women's choice of marriage partners and post-marital residence (as discussed later).

The significance of land as property

Thus far we have discussed property in general, but not all forms of property are equally significant in all contexts, nor equally coveted. In the agrarian economies of South Asia, arable land is the most valued form of property, for its economic, political and symbolic significance. It is a productive, wealth-creating, and livelihood-sustaining asset. Traditionally it has been the basis of political power and social status. For many, it provides a sense of identity and rootedness within the village; and often in people's minds land has a durability and permanence which no other asset possesses. Although other types of property such as cash, jewellery, cattle, and even domestic goods (the usual content of, say, dowry in rural India and Nepal) could in principle be converted into land, in practice rural land markets are often constrained, and land is not always readily available for sale (Rosenzweig and Wolpin 1985). In any case, ancestral land often has a symbolic meaning (Selvaduri 1976) or ritual importance (Krause 1982) which purchased land does not. Hence in land disputes people may end up spending more to retain a disputed ancestral plot than its market value would justify. In other words, both the form that property takes and its origin are important in defining its significance and the associated possibility of conflict over it.

What do we mean by rights in land?

Rights are defined here as claims that are legally and socially recognized and enforceable by an external legitimized authority, be it a village-level institution or some higher level judicial or executive body of the State. Rights in land can be in the form of ownership or of usufruct (that is rights of use), associated with differing degrees of freedom to lease out, mortgage, bequeath, or sell. Land rights can stem from inheritance, community membership, transfers by the State, or tenancy arrangements, purchase, and so on. Rights in land also have a temporal and sometimes locational dimension: they may be hereditary, or accrue only for a person's lifetime, or for a lesser period; and they may be conditional on the person residing where the land is located.

As distinct from rights in land, a woman may, in theory, also have "access" to land in other ways, including through informal concessions granted by kin or friends. For instance, a man may allow his sister the use of a plot of his land out of goodwill. But she cannot claim it as a right and call for its enforcement. Having "rights" thus provides a measure of security that other forms of access typically do not.

Four additional distinctions are relevant here. First is the need to distinguish between the legal recognition of a claim and its social recognition, and between recognition and enforcement. A woman may have the legal right to inherit property, but this may remain merely a right on paper if the law is not enforced, or if the claim is not socially recognized as legitimate and family members exert pressure on her to forfeit her share in favor, say, of her brothers. Second is the earlier noted distinction between the ownership of land and its effective control. (Control itself can have multiple meanings, such as the ability to decide how the land is used, how its produce is disposed of, whether it can be leased out, mortgaged, bequeathed, sold, and so on.) It is sometimes assumed incorrectly that legal ownership carries with it the right of control in all these senses. In fact legal ownership may be accompanied by legal restrictions on disposal: for instance, among the Jaffna Tamils in Sri Lanka, under the *Thesawalami* legal code a married woman needs her husband's consent to alienate land which she legally owns. Third, it is important to distinguish between ownership and use rights vested in individuals and those vested in a group. Fourth, one might distinguish between rights conferred via inheritance and those conferred by State transfers of land.

Given the different forms (ownership and usufruct, as vested in individuals or in groups) that land rights can take, and the varying organization of production and distribution that can accompany them, it is not always possible to specify *a priori* what would be the most desirable form for women's land rights to take. But a broad specification can be attempted. When speaking of women having rights in land I mean effective rights, that is rights not just in law but in practice. By "independent" rights I mean rights independent of male ownership or control (that is excluding joint titles with men). Independent rights would be preferable to joint titles with husbands for several reasons: one, with joint titles it could prove difficult for women to gain control over their share in case of marital breakup. Two, women would also be less in a position to escape from marital violence: as some Bihari village women said to me, "for retaining the land we would be tied to the man, even if he beat us." Three, wives may have different land use priorities from husbands which they would be in a better position to act upon with independent land rights. Four, women with independent rights would be better placed to control the produce. Five, with joint titles the question of how the land would be inherited could prove a contentious one. This is not to deny that joint titles with husbands would be better than having no titles at all; but many of the advantages of possessing land would not accrue to women by joint titles alone.

Here the distinctions mentioned earlier between rights vested in individuals and those vested in groups, and between privatized land transfers via inheritance and land transfers by the State, need elaboration. In relation to privatized inheritable landed property, effective land rights would mean inheritance as individuals linked with full rights of control over land use and its produce. In State transfers of land to women, effective rights could either mean individual titles conferring ownership and control rights exactly as with private land; or they could mean rights in land held by a group of women through joint ownership or long lease, and allowing full control over land use and its produce but excluding the right to sell or bequeath it. While individually owned land could be advantageous in distress circumstances in that it can be mortgaged or sold, group rights could protect the land from moneylenders or scheming relatives and enable its more productive use through group investment (as elaborated later).

Some South Asian specificities

With the decline in communal land in South Asia, access to privatized land acquires a critical importance today which it did not have even a century ago. In India, for instance, by a rough estimate, about 85.6 per cent of arable land is likely to be in private hands[10]. Hence the importance of women's land rights spelt out in the next section, while couched in general terms, is especially focussed on rights in privatized land, with two caveats: one, given the importance of communal land (e.g. village commons) to the rural poor, and especially to poor women (who depend on it for firewood, fodder, and other items basic for survival: Agarwal 1992), there is a strong case for protecting the communal nature of any land which still exists in that form. Two, it is necessary to explore the possibilities of new institutional arrangements for jointly owned/controlled land holdings by groups of women, rather than by groups of households (as is the usual focus).

In legal terms women's property rights in South Asia are governed by "personal laws" which vary a good deal by religion and region, forming a complex mosaic. Most of these legal systems give women considerable inheritance rights, and in traditionally patrilineal groups much greater rights than they enjoyed by custom, as a result of legal reform, especially after 1950 (as detailed in Agarwal 1994). But in virtually all the legal systems, some gender inequalities remain. For instance, some systems prescribe lower shares for women (Islamic law, for example, prescribes a daughter's share as half that of a son). Some others restrict the conditions under which women can inherit and retain that inheritance (e.g. the *Maluki Ain* in Nepal only allows unmarried daughters over the age of thirty-five to inherit, and they forfeit their claims on subsequent marriage). Yet other legal systems restrict women's freedom to dispose of their inherited land (as noted for the Jaffna Tamils in Sri Lanka).

Inequalities also stem from gender discriminatory tenurial enactments which affect women's rights specifically in agricultural land. For instance, in India, agricultural land under tenancy is exempt from the scope of the Hindu Succession Act (HSA) of 1956 (which gave Hindu women considerable inheritance rights across India): such land is governed instead by the rules of devolution specified in state-level enactments[11]. In a number of states, mostly in northwest India, these enactments specify succession rules prevailing before the HSA was passed, and which give priority to male agnatic heirs. Again in the fixation of ceilings under land reform laws, many states allow the cultivating household to retain additional land on account of adult sons but not adult daughters. Also, in most states, the holdings of both spouses are aggregated in assessing "family" land, and there is considerable arbitrariness in deciding whose portion will be declared surplus and forfeited. As a result, in several cases the wife's land (and not many women have some) has been declared surplus and taken over by the government, while the husband's land has remained intact (Saradamoni 1983).

Even more critical than the persisting legal inequities is the gap between women's legal rights in land and actual ownership, and between ownership and effective control. Although economic surveys typically do not collect gender-disaggregated data, village studies (especially anthropological accounts) indicate that in most parts of South Asia women do not own land and even fewer are able to exercise effective control over it[12]. These gaps are especially apparent in communities which customarily practised patrilineal inheritance[13]. Communities traditionally practising matrilineal or bilateral inheritance were few and limited to northeast India, parts of south India, and to Sri Lanka. Before examining the nature of gender relations in the latter communities, consider below why having independent rights in land is important for women's well-being and overall empowerment.

WHY WOMEN NEED INDEPENDENT RIGHTS IN LAND

The importance of South Asian rural women having independent rights in arable land rests on several interconnected arguments which can be grouped into four broad categories: welfare, efficiency, equality, and empowerment[14].

OUT OF THE MARGIN

The welfare argument

Especially among poor rural households, rights in land could reduce women's own and, more generally, the household's risk of poverty and destitution. This is due partly to the general positive effect of giving women access to economic resources independently of men; and partly to the specific advantages of possessing land.

Consider first the general case. In large parts of South Asia a systematic bias is noted against women and female children in intra-household access to resources for basic necessities such as health care, and in some degree also food. This is revealed in gender differences in one or more of the following indicators (detailed in Agarwal 1986, 1994): malnourishment, morbidity, mortality, hospital admissions, health expenditures, and female-adverse sex ratios (females per 1,000 males), although the evidence on food allocation *per se* is less conclusive (Harriss 1990). The extent of this anti-female bias varies regionally, but it exists in some degree almost everywhere, particularly as revealed by the sex ratios which are female-adverse across all of South Asia, except Kerala in southwest India. The bias is strongest in northwest India, Pakistan and Bangladesh, and much less stark in south India and Sri Lanka, where the sex ratios, although still female-adverse, are closer to parity.

Further, notable differences have been found in how men and women of poor rural households spend the incomes under their control: women typically spend almost all their incomes on the family's basic needs; men usually spend a significant part on their personal needs (tobacco, liquor, etc.) (Per-Lee 1981; Mencher 1988; Blumberg 1991). Research findings also suggest that children's nutritional status tends to be much more positively linked to the mother's earnings than the father's (Kumar 1978).

In other words, women's and children's risk of poverty and physical well-being could depend significantly on whether or not women have direct access to income and productive assets such as land, and not just access mediated through husbands or other male family members. For female-headed households without adult male support, this link between direct access to economic resources and physical well-being needs no emphasis. Such households constitute an estimated 19–20 per cent of all households in India and Bangladesh[15].

Moreover, as noted earlier, without independent resources even women from rich parental or marital homes can be economically vulnerable, in case of marital breakup or widowhood. In parts of western and northwestern India, not uncommonly, women – divorced, deserted or widowed – can be found working as agricultural laborers on the farms of their well-off brothers or brothers-in-law (Omvedt 1981, and personal observation). Similarly, in east India and Bangladesh, there are many cases of women, married into prosperous households, being left destitute after widowhood

(Cain *et al.* 1979; Vina Mazumdar, personal communication). "This fact," as Omvedt (1981:21) observes, "perhaps . . . more than any other, shows the essential propertylessness of women *as women*."

Within this general argument for women's independent access to economic resources, the case for effective rights in land is especially strong. Consider, for a start, the relationship between land access and poverty at the household level. In India, in 1982, an estimated 89 per cent of rural households owned some land (Government of India 1987:9), and an estimated 74 per cent operated some (Government of India 1986:12)[16]. In Bangladesh, in 1978, the percentage of rural households owning some land (arable or homestead) was 89, and those owning arable land was 67 (Jannuzi and Peach 1980:101). In Sri Lanka, in 1982, 89 per cent of agricultural operators owned some land (including home gardens) (Government of Sri Lanka 1984:17). Although, due to high land concentration, the majority of these households across South Asia only have marginal plots, they face a significantly lower risk of absolute poverty than landless households: several studies note a negative relationship between the incidence of absolute poverty and land access (owned or operated) (Ali *et al.* 1981; Gaiha and Kazmi 1981; Sundaram and Tendulkar 1983). The direct advantages of possessing land (unless the land is of very poor quality) stem from the various production possibilities it provides, such as for growing crops, fodder or trees, keeping a vegetable garden or livestock, practising sericulture, and so on. In addition, land provides indirect benefits, such as increasing access to credit, helping agricultural labor maintain its reserve price and even push up the aggregate real wage rate (Raj and Tharakan 1983) and, where the land is owned, serving as a mortgageable or saleable asset during a crisis. Moreover, for widows and the elderly, ownership of land and other wealth strengthens the support they receive from relatives by increasing their bargaining power within the household. As an old man put it: "without property, children do not look after their parents well" (Caldwell *et al.* 1988:191).

However, given the noted biases in the intra-family distribution of benefits from household resources, exclusively male rights in land, which would render the household less susceptible to poverty by some average measure, will not automatically benefit all its members. And on grounds of both women's and children's welfare, there is a strong case for supporting women's effective rights in private or public land, independently of men. Although such rights are especially important as a poverty alleviation measure for women in poor rural households, they are also relevant, as noted, for women of better-off households, given the risk of poverty that all rural women face without independent resources.

It needs emphasis here that the welfare case for women's land rights stands even if the plot is too small to be economically viable on its own. Indeed those opposing female inheritance in land often emphasize that women might end up inheriting economically non-viable holdings. In my view, this could be a problem where cultivation is seen as the sole basis of subsistence, but not where land-based production is one element (although a critical one) in a diversified livelihood system. For instance, a plot of land which does not produce enough grain for family subsistence could still support trees or provide fodder. Moreover, although forced collective farming is likely to be inefficient, cases of people voluntarily cooperating to undertake land-based joint production and/or investment activities also exist (as elaborated later).

Of course, as the industrial and service sectors of South Asian economies expand, arable land would become a less significant source of livelihood and form of property. But today the majority of South Asia's population still depends on agriculture as a primary or an important supplementary source of sustenance. And, most villagers, even those deriving their income from non-farm activities, depend on village common land and forests for fuel and other basic necessities. Moreover, in none of the South Asian countries do projections predict a rapid absorption of labor (especially female labor) into urban industry in the foreseeable future. Also, since it is predominantly male workers who migrate from rural to urban areas (Bardhan 1977), women's dependence on the rural/agricultural sector remains greater than men's. Although the rural non-farm sector holds potential, its record in providing viable livelihoods has been regionally mixed, with some regions providing high returns/high wages (such as the Indian Punjab), but many others being characterized by low returns and low wages (Islam 1986; Basant and Kumar 1989; Hazell and Haggblade 1990). In particular, women's non-farm earnings appear characteristically low and uncertain (Islam 1987; Singh and Kelles-Vitanen 1987). Hence, although women's earning opportunities in the non-farm sector clearly need strengthening, for most women non-farm livelihoods can at best supplement not substitute for land-based livelihoods. Notably also, those who do well in the rural non-farm sector through self-employment are usually those with land (Islam 1986; Chadha 1992). Effectively, therefore, land will continue to occupy a place of primacy in South Asian livelihoods in general and female livelihood systems in particular, for quite some time to come.

Also, with sectoral shifts, although the importance of land as property may decline, income-generating property *per se* would remain a significant mediator of social relations and an important determinant of social status and political power. Who owns and/or controls property would therefore still be a relevant consideration; and many of the arguments for gender equality in command over landed property would apply to other types of property as well.

EMPOWERMENT OF WOMEN

The efficiency argument

In several contexts, titling women with land could increase output. There are many women operating as household heads with the primary and sometimes sole responsibility for organizing cultivation and ensuring family subsistence, but without titles to the land they are cultivating. For instance, due to long-term male outmigration many women are serving as *de facto* household heads, especially but not only in the hill regions of the subcontinent. Or widows are cultivating plots given to them from joint family estates (as part of their inheritance claims to their deceased husbands' lands), but the plots are still in their in-laws' names. Again, tribal women cultivating communal land rarely get titles to their fields when the land is privatized, since the State typically gives the titles only to male farmers. Titling women in these circumstances and providing them with infrastructural support could increase output by increasing their access to credit[17], and to technology and information on productivity-increasing agricultural practices and inputs (in the dissemination of which both a class and a gender bias prevails)[18].

A more general issue, however, is the likely efficiency effect of women inheriting land. Female inheritance is often opposed in South Asia on the grounds that it will further reduce farm size and increase land fragmentation, and thus reduce output and also marketed surplus. Is this fear valid? Existing evidence indicates otherwise. Small-sized farms typically have a higher value of annual output per unit cultivated area than large-sized ones: this inverse size-productivity relationship which was strong in the 1950s and 1960s (the pre-green revolution period) has sustained in the post-green revolution period, even if somewhat weakened, as studies for India, Bangladesh and Pakistan bear out (Berry and Cline 1979; Agarwal 1983; Boyce 1987). Small farmers have adopted the new technology in most areas where large farmers have done so, although after a time lag (Lipton and Longhurst 1989). The evidence on marketed surplus also does not support the skeptics' claim that this will decline because small farmers will retain a larger percentage for self-consumption[19]. In any case, an improvement in the consumption of the poor in the farm sector cannot, in itself, be seen as an inefficient outcome. Indeed, a dietary improvement may add to labor productivity (Strauss 1986; Deolalikar 1988).

The existing evidence thus gives no reason to expect that land distribution in favor of women would reduce output on account of the size effect. And the problem of land fragmentation can arise equally with male inheritance: in both cases it calls for land consolidation. There could of course be a negative output effect of female inheritance through what I term the "gender-transfer effect" (viz. some of the land which would have gone only to men would now go to women), insofar as women usually face some gender-specific disadvantages as managers of farms, when operating in factor and product markets. But again the answer lies in easing these constraints by institutional support to women farmers, rather than in disinheriting them.

Indeed the experience of non-governmental credit institutions such as the Grameen bank in Bangladesh suggests that women are often better credit risks than men (Hossain 1988). Also, supporting women as farm managers would enlarge the talent and information pool; and in very poor households allocating resources to women could increase their productivity by improving their nutrition.

The provision of land to women could have other indirect benefits as well, such as (a) reducing migration to cities, both by women themselves and by family members dependent on them; and (b) increasing farm incomes in women's hands, which in turn could generate a higher demand for non-farm goods that are produced locally and labor intensively, thus creating more rural jobs[20].

The equality and empowerment arguments

Equality and empowerment concerns, unlike welfare and efficiency considerations, stem less from the implications of land access or deprivation in absolute terms, and more from the implications of men's and women's relative access to land. And they affect particularly women's ability to challenge male dominance within the home and in society.

The equality argument for land rights rests especially on two concerns. One is the larger issue of gender equality as a measure of a just society, in which equality of rights over productive resources would be an important part. The other relates to the specific link between gender equality in land rights and women's empowerment.

Empowerment is defined here as: *a process that enhances the ability of disadvantaged ("powerless") individuals or groups to challenge and change (in their favor) existing power relationships that place them in subordinate economic, social and political positions.* Empowerment can manifest itself in acts of individual resistance as well as in group mobilization. Entitling women with land could empower them economically, as well as strengthen their ability to challenge social and political gender inequities.

A telling illustration is provided by the Bodhgaya movement in Bihar (eastern India) in the late 1970s, in which women and men of landless households participated in an extended struggle for ownership rights in the land they cultivated, held illegally by a *Math* (a temple-monastery complex). During the struggle women demanded independent land rights, not only for reasons of economic security but also because this impinged on marital relations. They feared that if land titles went only to husbands, wives would be rendered relatively even more powerless, and vulnerable to domestic violence. Their fears proved correct. Where only men got titles there was an increase in drunkenness, wife-beating and threats: "Get out of the house, the land is mine now" (Manimala 1983: 15). Where women received titles they could now assert: "We had tongues but could not speak, we had feet but could not walk. Now that we have the land, we have the strength to speak and walk" (Alaka and Chetna 1987: 26). Similar responses were noted in China, when the Chinese Communist Party promulgated the Agrarian Reform law in 1947, which entitled women to hold separate land deeds for the first time (Hinton 1972).

Land rights can also improve the treatment a woman receives from other family members, by strengthening her bargaining power (Dreze 1990, and personal observation in northwest India). Although employment and other means of earning could help in similar ways, in the rural context land usually offers greater security than other income sources – at the very least, a space of one's own. In the Bodhgaya case, for instance, the women being wage laborers were not economically dependent, but their husbands could still threaten them with eviction. Notably too the Bodhgaya women saw intra-household gender relations being affected not just by their own propertyless state, but by their remaining propertyless while their husbands became propertied. In other words, land titles were important to women not only for improving their economic well-being in absolute terms (the welfare argument), but also for improving their relative bargaining position *vis-à-vis* their husbands: their sense of empowerment within the home was linked to economic equality.

Outside the household as well, land ownership can empower women by improving the social treatment they receive from fellow villagers (Mies *et al.* 1986), and by enabling them to bargain with employers from a stronger fall-back position. Land ownership is also widely linked to rural political power (Solaiman and Alam 1977; R. Singh 1988). Although there can be social barriers to women's participation in public decision-making bodies, even for women endowed with land, land rights could facilitate such participation. The support of local women's groups would also help.

Indeed in a limited sense, group action may itself empower women by enhancing their self-confidence and ability to challenge oppression, although in a larger sense it is a means to empowerment, wherein empowerment lies not only in the process of challenging gender inequity but in eliminating it. Collective action is likely to prove a critical means for effecting change toward gender equality in land rights (as elaborated later).

While each of the above arguments for women's independent rights in land is important, it is notable that the welfare and efficiency arguments resonate more with State planners. Why? Part of the answer certainly lies in the fact that these arguments (especially those concerning welfare) focus especially on poor women, and can be subsumed within the poverty alleviation component of planning, with special targeting towards "the most vulnerable" groups, identified as women and female children. But part of the answer must also lie in deep-rooted notions of appropriate gender relations shared by many men who make and implement policy, for whom empowering women to transform those relations into more equal ones would appear inappropriate and even threatening to existing family and kinship structures. Hence it is easier to push for changes where the goal appears to be to give poor women a slightly better deal, than where the goal is to challenge basic inequities in gender relations across classes. It is also the case that programs for health and nutrition are more readily perceived in welfare terms than programs which call for gender-redistributive land reform. It is not a coincidence that land rights have yet to become a necessary component even of women-directed poverty alleviation schemes.

Consider now what can be learnt about the association between land rights and gender relations from traditionally matrilineal and bilateral communities.

GENDER RELATIONS IN TRADITIONALLY MATRILINEAL AND BILATERAL COMMUNITIES

Historically, in some South Asian communities, women enjoyed significant rights in land, and even today do so there more than elsewhere. These are communities traditionally practising matrilineal or bilateral inheritance and concentrated in parts of northeast and south India, and Sri Lanka, as follows:

- Northeast India: the home of three matrilineal tribal communities, the Garos, Khasis, and Lalungs.
- South India: here the Nangudi Vellalars of Tamil Nadu practised bilateral inheritance, and several other groups in and around Kerala practised matrilineal inheritance, including the Nayars of north and central Kerala, the Tiyyars and Mappilas of north Kerala, and the Bants of Karnataka.
- Sri Lanka: here all major communities practised bilateral or matrilineal inheritance – the Sinhalese and Jaffna Tamils were bilateral, and the Muslim "Moors" were matrilineal[21].

Historical and ethnographic evidence (examined in Agarwal 1994) suggests that in regions other than these, inheritance practices were essentially patrilineal.

Women's land rights in the above communities fell broadly into three categories:

- In communities such as the Garos land was a clan's communal property and could not be inherited either by individuals or by joint family units. All clan members resident in the village had use rights to this land as individuals. Responsibility for land management vested with the husband who took up residence with his wife, but a woman's contribution to field labor was substantial and critical, and she controlled the produce.

- In communities such as the Khasis, Nayars, Tiyyars and Mappilas, land, although inherited in the female line, was held as joint family property, and there were no individual rights of alienation. Responsibility for land management vested principally with older men (usually brothers or maternal uncles). However, in decisions concerning the partition or transfer of landed property, women's concurrence was necessary.
- In communities such as the Sinhalese, Jaffna Tamils, and Moors, women had individual inheritance rights in land, and among the former two groups men too held such rights.

The picture we get of gender relations among these groups is a mixed one. On the positive side, women enjoyed considerable social independence and relative equality in marital relations. Indeed, in all the groups, a daughter's rights in land, and the fact that she either remained in her natal home after marriage or had inviolable rights to return to it if she so chose, provided her with a strong fall-back position within marriage. Women could choose their husbands (although heiresses faced some constraints) and initiate divorce. Where uxorilocality or matrilocality was the norm, as it was in many of these groups, marital breakdown led to the husband departing, sometimes (as among the Garos) with only the clothes on his back[22]. (In contrast, in patrilineal, patrilocal contexts, it was women – especially if they violated sexual norms – who faced the very real risk of being evicted and being left destitute.) Norms of sexual behavior outside marriage ranged from relatively gender egalitarian (as among the Sinhalese and the matrilineal tribes of northeast India), to restricted for women (as among the Jaffna Tamils). But in comparison with Hindu and Muslim women of patrilineal groups, especially those shackled by seclusion practices in northwestern South Asia, women among all the matrilineal and bilateral groups enjoyed greater sexual freedom.

They also had considerable freedom of movement and of public interaction. Even among the (Muslim) Moors, Munck (1985:8, 108) remarks: "Women move freely about the village without veils covering their faces. . . . Interaction between men and women is frequent and casual and often sexual comments are exchanged publicly." This is strikingly different from women's situation among most patrilineal Muslims of the subcontinent. Daughters were also specially desired among groups such as the Nayars[23], in marked contrast to the strong son preference among patrilineal communities in northern South Asia.

However, these favorable features were counterbalanced by less favorable ones. First, women's property rights did not alter the overall gender division of labor: domestic work and childcare were still a woman's responsibilities. Second, the range of sexual mores found among these communities indicates that rights in land did not guarantee women the same sexual freedom as men. Third, formal managerial authority over land in a number of matrilineal groups lay with men (as husbands, brothers and maternal uncles). In practice, this would have worked in various ways depending on the role women played in the household's economy, the form (individual or joint) in which property was held, and the size of the estates involved. Where women's role in production and market activities was important (as among the northeastern tribal groups), and/or where women held individual rather than joint property rights (as among Sri Lanka's bilateral groups), they exercised greater control over the land. But where women played little role in farm production, and property was held in large joint family estates collectively owned by several generations of a woman's matrilineal descendants, as among the Nayars of central Kerala and the wealthy Mappilas of north Kerala, men's managerial control over property and their overall authority in intra-household and public dealings appears to have been especially strong. (This also highlights an important difference between matrilineal and patrilineal inheritance systems: in the former there is often a gender divergence between property ownership and its control, while in the latter there is convergence: men (as a gender) own as well as control the property.)

Fourth, most importantly, in all the groups, customary institutions with jural power (such as tribal and caste councils) were monopolized by men and typically excluded women. Among matrilineally inheriting communities, this meant that despite men's restricted access to property ownership, their rights (as a gender) of control over that property on the one hand, and their access to public bodies on the other (with links between the two domains), often enabled them to consolidate social prestige and political power. The Nayar *karanavans*[24] of wealthy households and the Khasi chiefs commanded local influence in ways that the women heiresses of these communities appear not to have done as a rule. Also, among all groups, men's control of the public decision-making domain gave them critical influence over the modification of legal and social rules when external conditions began to change in significant ways, especially under British colonial rule.

In short, ownership rights in landed property clearly conferred important benefits on women, but their virtual exclusion from property management (in some groups) and from jural and overall public authority (in all groups) circumscribed the power they could derive from those rights. This holds lessons for women's struggle for land rights today, namely that women cannot derive the full advantages of land ownership if they continue to be excluded from managerial control and jural authority. And the arenas of contestation over effective land rights for women will therefore need to extend much beyond the courtyards of the household to encompass the complex institutions of community and State – the arenas where legal, social, and political rules are made and unmade. This is further illustrated below.

OBSTACLES TO ACHIEVING EFFECTIVE LAND RIGHTS

Today, most arable land in South Asia (as noted) is in private hands, access to which is mainly through inheritance. Women enjoy considerable property rights in law, but gender inequalities and anomalies in land-related laws remain. Moreover, there is a vast gender gap between law and practice. As noted, most women do not own land; even fewer exercise full control over it. A range of factors – social, administrative and ideological – severely restrict the effective implementation of inheritance laws. These obstacles, (detailed in Agarwal 1994), are summarized below.

First, in most traditionally patrilineal communities, there is a strong male resistance to endowing women, especially daughters, with land. Apart from the reluctance to admit more contenders to the most valuable form of rural property, an important factor underlying such resistance is a structural mismatch between contemporary inheritance laws and traditional marriage practices. Among the matrilineal and bilateral communities discussed earlier, historically families sought to keep the land within the purview of the extended kin either by strict rules against land alienation by individuals, or, where such alienation was possible (as among the bilateral communities), by other means, such as post-marital residence in the village, and often an emphasis on marriage with close kin, especially cross cousins. In fact proximity of the post-marital residence to the natal home appears to have been virtually a necessary condition for recognizing a daughter's share in landed property.

Contemporary laws as framed by the modern State give inheritance rights to daughters as individuals among most communities, including in traditionally patrilineal, patrilocal ones. Marriage customs, however, are still under the purview of the local kin group and, on the relevant counts, have remained largely unchanged. In India this mismatch between inheritance laws and marriage practices is greatest among upper-caste Hindus of the northwest who forbid marriages with close kin and practise village exogamy, preferring marriage alliances in distant villages. Many such communities, moreover, have social taboos against parents drawing on the economic support of married daughters, even during crises. Hence, in the northern states (and especially the northwestern ones) endowing daughters is seen by Hindu parents as bringing no reciprocal economic benefit, while increasing the risk of the land passing out of the hands of the extended family. Resistance to entitling daughters tends to be greatest here. Resistance is less in south and northeast India where marriages within the village and with close kin are allowed and sought, and seeking the help of married daughters during economic crises is also possible.

Second, women in many parts of South Asia tend to forego their shares in parental land for the sake of potential economic and social support from brothers. A visit by a brother is often the only regular link a woman has with her natal home where she is married into a distant village, and especially where social taboos bar parents from accepting a married daughter's hospitality. After the parents' deaths the brother's home often offers the only possibility of refuge in case of marital failure or widowhood. A woman's dependence on this support is directly related to her economic and social vulnerability. Economically, low access to personal property (especially productive assets), illiteracy, limited income-earning skills and earning opportunities, and low wages for available work, can all constrain women's potential for independent economic survival. Socially, women's vulnerability is associated partly with the strength of female seclusion practices and partly with the extent of social stigma attaching to widowhood or divorce. Both economic and social factors vary in strength by community, region, and circumstance, but typically, in anticipation of such support women give up their claims in parental land. Cultural constructions of gender, including the definition of how a "good" sister should behave, the widespread feeling that it is "shameful" for a sister to claim her share, also discourage women from asserting their rights (Hershman 1981). In practice, ethnographies give examples both of brothers helping a sister in need, and of their neglect and duplicity.

Third, dependence on brothers is part of a larger social context in which many aspects of rural women's relationship with the world outside the family is typically mediated through male relatives: fathers, brothers, husbands, and extended male kin. Such mediation is necessitated by a variety of factors, but particularly by the physical and social restrictions on women's mobility and behavior. In many South Asian communities these restrictions are explicit in the norms and ideology of purdah or female seclusion; in many others, they are implicit and subtle, but nevertheless effectively confine women. These restrictions are manifest not just in the veiling of women, but more commonly in the gender segregation of space and the gendered specification of behavior. In fact, strict veiling is limited to some communities and regions – being stronger among Muslims in northern South Asia and among upper-caste Hindus in northwest India, than elsewhere; and even here it varies in extent by the woman's caste, class, and age. More pervasive are the behavioral strictures imposed upon and internalized by women from late childhood, which define where women can go, whom they can speak to and in what manner, how they should dress, and so on. Although such gendering of space and behavior is strongest in communities which explicitly endorse purdah, its more subtle manifestations constitute an implicit code of expected female behavior in large parts of the subcontinent, even where (as in South India and Nepal) purdah is not endorsed. This circumscribes rural women's interaction with men and institutions, their physical and social mobility, their domain of activity and knowledge, and their access to education and to economic (markets, banks, etc.), judicial and administrative institutions. All this severely limits women's ability to claim and control land.

Fourth, male relatives often take pre-emptive steps to prevent women from getting their inheritance. Fathers have been found to leave wills favoring sons and disinheriting daughters; and brothers have been known to forge wills or manipulate statements before the revenue authorities to make it appear that the woman has relinquished her right (Mayer 1960; Alavi 1972; Parry 1979; Jansen 1983). Natal kin are especially hostile to the idea of daughters and sisters inheriting land, since the property can pass outside the patrilineal descent group. A widow's claims to her husband's land are viewed with less antagonism, since there is a greater chance of the land remaining with agnates: she can be persuaded to adopt the son of the deceased husband's brother if she is sonless, or to enter into a leviratic union with the husband's (usually younger) brother, or made to forfeit the property if she remarries outside the family.

Where pre-emptive methods fail, intimidation is attempted. A common tactic is to initiate expensive litigation which few women can financially afford (Kishwar 1987). Some women drop their claims, others press on with the risk of having to mortgage the land to pay legal fees, thus possibly losing the land altogether. Land disputes involving women were rising in parts of the subcontinent even in the late 1950s (Mayer 1960). Today direct violence is also increasingly used to deter women from filing claims, or from exercising their customary rights: beatings are common and murder not unknown. Indeed in eastern and central India, the murder of women who have some land, through accusations of witchcraft, is on the rise (Chaudhuri 1987; Kishwar 1987).

Fifth, the logistics of dealing with legal, economic and bureaucratic institutions are often formidable and work against women staking their claims; and they may only decide to do so if they have male relatives who can mediate. Village women's typically low level of education, and the noted restrictions on their interaction with the extra-domestic sphere and with institutions constituted principally of men, the complicated procedures and red tape involved in dealing with judicial and administrative bodies, and so on, all work to women's disadvantage, as does their relative lack of financial resources. The problem is especially acute in communities with high female seclusion, but it is not absent even where seclusion is not prescribed.

Sixth, local-level (largely male) government functionaries, responsible for overseeing the recording of inheritance shares, often obstruct the implementation of laws in women's favor. Social and official prejudice tends to be particularly acute against inheritance by daughters; widows' claims (as noted) are somewhat better accepted in principle, although often violated in practice.

The gap between legal ownership rights and actual ownership is only one part of the story. The other part relates to the gap between ownership and effective control, especially managerial control, attributable to a mix of factors. Patrilocal marriages in distant villages make it difficult for women to directly supervise or cultivate land they may inherit in the natal village. But problems of directly managing land inherited even in the marital village (say as a widow) are compounded in many areas by factors such as the practice of purdah or the more general (implicit or explicit) gender segregation of public space and social interaction; high rates of female illiteracy; and high fertility (which increases women's childbearing and childcare responsibilities). Moreover, male control over agricultural technology, especially the plough (there are cultural taboos against women ploughing), and the noted male bias in the dissemination of information and technological inputs, disadvantage women farmers and increase their dependence on male mediation. Often added to this is the threat and practice of violence by male relatives and others interested in acquiring women's land. Pressure on women to sharecrop their land to relatives (at below market rates) is usually high, as are the difficulties of ensuring that they get their fair share of the harvest. Some of these factors, such as gender bias in access to production inputs and information, constrain women farmers even in traditionally bilateral and matrilineal contexts.

However, the strength of these constraints on women claiming and managing land varies considerably by region. There are geographic differences in the social acceptance of women's land claims (stemming in part from differences in traditional inheritance rights): in prevailing marriage practices; in the emphasis on female seclusion and control over female sexuality; in women's freedom of movement and labor force participation; in women's literacy and fertility rates; and in the extent of land scarcity. Obstacles stemming from these factors are greatest in northwest India, Bangladesh and Pakistan, and least in south India and Sri Lanka. In fact four geographic zones can broadly be demarcated, ordered in terms of the strength of resistance women are likely to face in exercising their legal rights: Pakistan, northwest India and Bangladesh fall at the high resistance end of the spectrum, and south India and Sri Lanka at the low resistance end; while western, central and eastern India, and Nepal and northeast India, come in between[25].

Over time, gender conflict over private land is likely to increase with its growing scarcity and skewness in distribution. On the one hand male family members will be increasingly reluctant to part with the land. On the other hand, the importance for women of asserting their inheritance rights will grow for several reasons, including the limited expansion of economic opportunities for non-land-related earnings, and the erosion of kin-support systems, as brothers and other relatives become less able or less willing economically to support female kin. In Bangladesh gender conflict over land is already on the rise, with an increasing number of women asserting or planning to assert their claims[26]; and we can expect this also to be the case in other acutely land-scarce parts of South Asia.

In the case of public land, that is land which is under government or community jurisdiction, the obstacles are of a somewhat different nature. Here women's struggle is more directly against the consistent male bias in the distribution of land under land reform programs, resettlement schemes, and various land development projects, and only indirectly against individual family members who may be rival potential beneficiaries. Government officials typically resist the allotment of public land to women on the grounds that allotments can only be made to household heads, whom they assume are men (Lal 1986). This bias is found even when land titles are distributed in traditionally matrilineal and bilateral communities (Schrijvers 1988; Agarwal 1994). And, it is found in the policies and programs of all the political regimes in the subcontinent, including communist ones.

INTERVENTIONS FOR CHANGE: SOME CONSIDERATIONS

The discussion above indicates that today for women to gain effective rights in land will require contestation and struggle in many arenas – the household, the market, the community, and the State – and on diverse aspects: legal, administrative, social, and ideological. Apart from the struggle to establish legal equality, to enhance women's ability to claim and keep control over their rightful inheritance shares will need: establishing the social legitimacy of their claims; reducing gender bias in village land registration practices and village council rulings; increasing women's legal knowledge and literacy; improving women's fall-back position so that they are better able to deal with any associated intra-family conflict, including through external support structures that would reduce women's dependence on brothers and close kin; and so on. Similarly, male bias in government distribution of public land and in infrastructural support for farmers will need contestation.

The ideological struggle to establish women's claims is likely to be especially complex. It is part of an overall struggle for changing perceptions about women's needs, roles, and abilities, in which women's movements, both local and national, even when not focussing on the specific question of land rights, have a critical role to play. This contestation over meanings could take diverse forms, including countering popular arguments against giving women land, such as those relating to land size and fragmentation, questioning the validity of female seclusion and restrictions on women's economic and social participation outside the home, and promoting women's educational programs with an empowerment perspective.

In all this, the role of collective action is likely to be primary. For instance, the local bureaucracy is more likely to accurately register individual women's claims in family land if there were collective pressure on them from say gender progressive groups, especially women's organizations. Such organizations can also play a vital supportive role in providing women with legal information on laws and contacts with lawyers, should legal action be necessary; and in improving effective (not just nominal) female presence in village decision-making bodies. Women elected to all-women panels in village councils in parts of India (especially where supported by local women's organizations), and field-level development administrators in Bangladesh, are found to be more sensitive to women's concerns, and to give priority to local women's needs, in ways that male village council members and bureaucrats typically do not (Goetz 1990; Gandhi and Shah 1991). The presence of women in decision-making roles and positions of authority also has a wider ideological impact; and village women are more likely to take their grievances to female representatives than to all-male bodies.

Local gender progressive organizations could similarly strengthen women's fall-back position in intra-family conflicts over women's land claims, through economic and social support networks and programs which reduce women's dependence on male relatives, especially their brothers in whose favor women usually forfeit their claims. As a woman member of the Bangladesh Rural Advancement Committee (BRAC, a Bangladeshi development NGO which provides credit and technical support to poor village women and men, organized separately into small groups) tellingly asserted: "Well the Samity [organization] is my brother" (Hunt 1983: 38). After joining BRAC women have also been able to challenge purdah practices: "We do not listen to the *mullahs* [Muslim clergy] anymore. They did not give us even a quarter kilo of rice" (Chen 1983: 176). "They said . . . [w]e are ruining the prestige of the village and breaking *purdah*. . . . Now nobody talks ill of us. They say: 'They have formed a group and now they earn money. It is good'" (*ibid.*).

More generally, group support can take at least two forms: through separately constituted groups which provide specialized legal and other services to village women, and through organizations comprised of village women themselves. Initiatives of both kinds would be important not only for women from landed households seeking their inheritance claims, but also for landless women seeking rights in public land by challenging male bias in government land allocations.

In this context, it is worth considering the advantages of land ownership and/or management by groups of women, rather than by women individually. Although individual ownership can allow women the freedom to bequeath, mortgage, or sell the land as they wish, it also carries the risk of the land being appropriated by rapacious moneylenders or male relatives. An alternative arrangement to individual titles in the transfer of State land, or of land acquired by a peasant organization through a land struggle, could be titles held by poor peasant women as a group – each participating woman having use rights in the land but not the right to individually dispose of it. Daughters-in-law and daughters resident in the village could share these usufructuary rights; daughters leaving the village on marriage would lose them, but could reestablish their rights should they need to return to their parental homes on marital failure or widowhood. In other words, land access could be linked formally to residence, as was the case among some tribal communities (such as the Garos), the difference being that here the land would belong not to a clan but to a group of poor women.

Group ownership of land need not, however, imply joint management, just as individual ownership need not preclude joint management. Women holding joint ownership rights could either cultivate separate plots allocated on a household basis, or cultivate collectively as a group with each woman contributing labor time and sharing the returns. Or there could be some combination of individual and group management, such as family-based female cultivation along with joint investment in capital equipment and cooperation in terms of labor sharing and product marketing. Group investment through resource pooling could be advantageous even when women own land individually by reducing the resource crunch they may face at the individual level. In fact, some cases of joint land management and investment by small groups of women already exist in South Asia (see Chen 1983; Lal 1986; N. Singh 1988).

In such initiatives, and more generally to enhance women's ability to function as independent farmers, infrastructural support for women is critical, in the form of access to credit, production inputs, information on new agricultural practices, marketing, and so on. Again, the promotion of women's cooperatives for the provisioning of such services could prove important.

In this context it needs emphasis that it is not just an increase in women's command over economic resources, but also the process by which that increase occurs that has a critical bearing on gender relations. Land rights are not "given" and will not be "provided" to most South Asian women without contestation. As noted, acquiring these rights will require simultaneous struggles on both the economic and non-economic fronts and in several different arenas.

Indeed the theoretical premise of this paper is that gender relations and women's economic, social and political positions are the outcome of processes of contestation and bargaining between the genders (for elaboration, see Agarwal 1994). These processes may not always be explicit but are nonetheless revealed in final outcomes. They involve elements of both cooperation and conflict and take place in various arenas: the household, the market, the community, and the State – arenas which are interlinked in that change in one impinges on the others. For instance, a strengthening of women's bargaining power in the community, say through the formation of a women's organization, has also been found to enhance women's bargaining power within the household.

While it is clear that various forms of collective action will be necessary for empowering women to establish effective rights in land, bringing about collective action is not always easy. A number of complexities (detailed in Agarwal 1994) will need to be addressed, including those posed by class- (and caste-) associated conflict of interests among women, and the fact that even to organize collectively often requires challenging existing social norms, such as breaking the traditional bounds of female seclusion in some communities, for attending group meetings.

Indeed, the issue of gender equality in land rights – not only in law but in practice – calls for a much more multi-pronged and sustained effort than has been attempted so far on any gender-related issue in South Asia. While undoubtedly the noted obstacles appear formidable, their very complexity and range also make land rights a critical entry point for challenging unequal gender relations and power structures at many levels, and gives the struggle to overcome the obstacles a transformative potential.

For this and the other reasons noted, land (and more generally property) has a strategic importance that other gender concerns such as employment do not share in equal measure.

NOTES

1 This paper draws substantially on the author's book, Agarwal (1994). A longer version of it appeared in *World Development* 22 (1), 1994.

2 Personal communication, Vina Mazumdar, Center for Women's Development Studies, New Delhi.

3 This is not meant as a summary of Engels' complex thesis, but merely of one part of it. Critiques of his analysis abound: see especially, Sacks (1975), Delmar (1976), Molyneux (1981) and Sayers *et al.* (1987). In particular, Engels' assumption that gender relations within propertyless groups, such as the industrial proletariat, and under socialism would necessarily be egalitarian has been widely criticized.

4 In socialist countries (including those which were socialist until recently), the influence of Engels' analysis led to a similar preoccupation with women's employment as the major means of eliminating gender oppression (Molyneux 1981).

5 Women's representation in top political and economic decision-making bodies in such countries remained minimal. For instance, in the late 1970s, in the USSR, Czechoslovakia, Poland, and Yugoslavia under 5 per cent of government posts were filled by women (Molyneux 1981).

6 In India, for instance, male dominance is apparent in the judiciary (in 1985

women constituted only 3.6 per cent of the state bar council advocates, and 2.8 percent of High Court and Supreme Court judges), the government administration (in 1987 only 7.4 per cent of the Indian Administrative Service Officers were women), and the legislature (in 1984 only 8 per cent of elected candidates in the Lok Sabha (lower house of parliament) were women). All figures are taken from GOI (1988:119, 126–7, 173).

7 Scandinavian countries have a relatively better record on this: in Norway and Finland, women constituted 34 and 32 per cent of all elected and appointed members of national legislative bodies in 1985–7, in sharp contrast to the 9–10 per cent in India, Bangladesh and Pakistan, and 5–6 per cent in the US and UK (United Nations 1990).

8 Firestone (1970), Millet (1970), and Delphy (1977) all deny the significance of class divisions between women, but from different standpoints.

9 Of course aspects of a person's identity other than class can also be divisive or adhesive, such as caste, ethnicity, and religion.

10 This was calculated from India's land use statistics for 1987–88 (Government of India 1992).

11 In India the term "state" relates to administrative divisions within the country and is not to be confused with "State" used throughout the paper in the political economy sense of the word. In Pakistan and Sri Lanka these administrative divisions are termed provinces.

12 None of the countries in the region, except Sri Lanka, collects gender-disaggregated land ownership and use data in its agricultural and centennial censuses or other large-scale rural surveys. Even in Sri Lanka, such data, collected in the 1981 agricultural census, covered only agricultural operators (that is, cultivators as well as purely livestock and poultry operators) and not all rural households. Also the published data do not give a genderwise breakdown of land ownership even among agricultural operators. Again, most studies of village agrarian structures by economists have confined themselves to the household unit. Hence to gain an idea of where women have been given or have claimed their shares in landed property and under what circumstances, I have drawn on anthropological, historical, and legal sources, supplemented by my fieldwork observations.

13 Ancestral property passes through the male line under patrilineal inheritance, through the female line under matrilineal inheritance, and to and through both sons and daughters under bilateral inheritance.

14 The discussion here concerns land linked to rural livelihoods, especially arable land, but excludes homesites, even though the available data on land ownership do not always separate land under homesites from the rest.

15 See Buvinic and Youssef (1978) for India, and Safilios-Rothchild and Mahmud (1989) for Bangladesh. According to the Indian census some 10 per cent of households are female headed, but this is a significant underestimate (see Agarwal 1985, on reasons for the undercounting).

16 In these estimates, the figure for land ownership covers all land owned by the household, whether or not cultivated, including that used for non-agricultural purposes.

17 There is considerable evidence from Asia that titling can critically enhance farmers' access to credit (in terms of sources, amounts and terms) by enabling them to use land as collateral (see e.g. Binswanger and Rosenzweig 1986; Feder 1989). Also see Saito and Weidenmann (1990) on the problems women farmers face in getting credit in the absence of titles.

OUT OF THE MARGIN

18 For class bias in agricultural extension see Dasgupta (1977) and on gender bias see Kilkelly (1986).

19 For non-food crops the marketed surplus is often very high on farms of all size groups (Lipton 1992) and for food crops the higher productivity on small farms could outweigh their higher propensity-to-consume effect, as found, for instance, in Kenya (Lipton 1992).

20 This is partly because women's lesser mobility would confine them more than men to local markets; and it is partly derivative of the more general observation that villages with greater equality in land (and farm income) distribution in South Asia tend to generate more demand for local non-farm products, especially through consumption linkages (Islam 1986).

21 Although the nomenclature "Moor" (given to the Sri Lankan Muslims under Portuguese rule) has today largely been subsumed under the general category "Muslim," I have retained the term to distinguish the group both from partilineal Sri Lankan Muslims and from matrilineal Indian Muslims (such as the Mappilas) whose inheritance practices were different.

22 Uxorilocality implies that the husband takes up residence with the wife and (with or near) her parental family. Where this is a regular practice dictated by a preferred custom, this results in institutionalized matrilocal residence, where the normal residence of most husbands is with or near the matrilineal kin of the wives. Patrilocal implies that the wife takes up residence with the husband and (with or near) his patrilineal kin.

23 Personal communication, Joan Mencher, New York, 1992.

24 The *karanavan* was the head of the *taravad* and manager of the joint family estate; he was usually the seniormost male member of the *taravad*. *Taravad*: the matrilineal joint family, holding property in common and often sharing a common residence.

25 For maps showing these cross-regional patterns, see Agarwal (1994).

26 See, for example, Abdullah and Zeidenstein (1982); Jansen (1983); Nath (1984).

REFERENCES

Abdullah, T. and Zeidenstein, S.A. (1982) *Village Women of Bangladesh: Prospects for Change*, Oxford: Pergamon Press.

Agarwal, B. (1983) *Mechanization in Indian Agriculture: An Analytical Study of the Indian Punjab*, Delhi: Allied Publishers (repr. 1986).

——— (1985) "Work Participation of Rural Women in the Third World: Some Data and Conceptual Biases", *Economic and Political Weekly* 21 December,: A155–A164.

——— (1986) "Women, Poverty and Agricultural Growth in India", *The Journal of Peasant Studies* July: 165–220.

——— (1992) "The Gender and Environment Debate: Lessons from India", *Feminist Studies* 18, 1: 119–58.

——— (1994) *A Field of One's Own: Gender and Land Rights in South Asia*, Cambridge: Cambridge University Press.

Alaka and Chetna (1987) "When Women Get Land – A Report from Bodhgaya", *Manushi* 40: 25–6.

Alavi, H. (1972) "Kinship in West Punjab Villages", *Contributions to Indian Sociology, New Series* 6, December: 1–27.

Ali, I., Desai, B.M., Radhakrishna, R. and Vyas, V.S. (1981) "Indian Agriculture at

2000: Strategies for Equality", *Economic and Political Weekly* 16, 10–12, March: 409–24.

Bardhan, K. (1977) "Rural Employment, Wages and Labor Markets in India: A Survey of Research", *Economic and Political Weekly* 12, 26–8.

Basant, R. and Kumar, B.L. (1989) "Rural Agricultural Activities in India: A Review of Available Evidence", *Social Scientist* 17, 1–2, January–February: 13–17.

Berry, R.A. and Cline, W.R. (1979) *Agrarian Structure and Productivity in Developing Countries*, Baltimore and London: Johns Hopkins University Press.

Binswanger, H.P. and Rosenzweig, M. (1986) "Credit Markets, Wealth and Endowments in Rural South India", paper presented at the Eighth World Congress of the International Economic Association, New Delhi, 1–5 December.

Blumberg, R.L. (1991) "Income Under Female vs. Male Control: Hypotheses from a Theory of Gender Stratification and Data from the Third World", in R.L. Blumberg (ed.) *Gender, Family and Economy: The Triple Overlap*: 97–127, Newbury Park: Sage Publications.

Boyce, J. (1987) *Agrarian Impasse in Bengal: Institutional Constraints to Technological Change*, Oxford: Oxford University Press.

Buvinic, M. and Youssef, N.H. (1978) "Women-headed Households: The Ignored Factor in Development Planning", Report submitted to AID/WID, International Center for Research on Women, Washington DC, March.

Cain, M.T., Khanam, S.R. and Nahar, S. (1979) "Class, Patriarchy and the Structure of Women's Work in Rural Bangladesh", Working Paper No. 43, New York: Center for Population Studies, The Population Council.

Caldwell, J.C., Reddy, P.H. and Caldwell, P. (1988) *The Causes of Demographic Change: Experimental Research in South India*, Wisconsin: The University of Wisconsin Press.

Chadha, G.K. (1992) "Non-farm Sector in India's Rural Economy: Policy, Performance and Growth Prospects", mimeo, Delhi: Center for Regional Development, Jawaharlal Nehru University.

Chaudhuri, A.B. (1987) *The Santals: Religion and Rituals*, New Delhi: Ashish Publishing House.

Chen, M.A. (1983) *A Quiet Revolution: Women in Transition in Rural Bangladesh*, Cambridge: Schenkman Publishing Co, Inc.

Dasgupta, B. (1977) "Agrarian Change and the New Technology in India", Report No.77.2, Geneva: United Nations Research Institute for Social Development.

Delmar, R. (1976) "Looking Again at Engels's Origin of the Family, Private Property and the State", in J. Mitchell and A. Oakley (eds). *The Rights and Wrongs of Women*, Harmondsworth: Penguin Books.

Delphy, C. (1977) *The Main Enemy: A Materialist Analysis of Women's Oppression*, London: Women's Research and Resources Center.

Deolalikar, A.B. (1988) "Nutrition and Labor Productivity in Agriculture: Econometric Estimates for Rural South Asia", *Review of Economics and Statistics* 70, 4, August: 406–13.

Dreze, J. (1990) "Widows in India", Discussion paper no. DEP 46, London: The Development Economics Research Programme, London School of Economics.

Engels, F.A. [1884] (1972) *The Origin of the Family, Private Property and the State*, Harmondsworth: Penguin Books.

Feder, G. (1989) "The Economics of Land Titling in Thailand", mimeo, Washington, DC: World Bank, April.

Firestone, S. (1970) *The Dialectic of Sex: The Case for Feminist Revolution*, New York: Bantam Books.

OUT OF THE MARGIN

Gaiha, R. and Kazmi, N.A. (1981) "Aspects of Rural Poverty in India", *Economics of Planning* 17, 2–3: 74–112.

Gandhi, N. and Shah, N. (1991) *The Issues at Stake: Theory and Practice in the Contemporary Women's Movement in India*, Delhi: Kali for Women.

Goetz, A.M. (1990) "Local Heroes, Local Despots: Exploring Fieldworker Discretion in Implementing Gender-Redistributive Development Policy", paper presented at the Development Studies Association Conference, Glasgow.

Government of India (GOI) (1986) *Thirty-seventh Round Report on Land Holdings – 2: Some Aspects of Operational Holdings*, Report No. 331, Delhi: National Sample Survey Organisation, Dept. of Statistics.

——— (1987) "A Note on Some Aspects of Household Ownership Holding: NSS 37th Round (January–December 1982)" and "Results on Some Aspects of Household Ownership Holding: NSS 37th Round (January–December 1982)", *Sarvekshana* 11, 2, 33, October: 1–18, S1–S175, Dept. of Statistics, Ministry of Planning.

——— (1988) *Women in India: A Statistical Profile – 1988*, New Delhi: Ministry of Human Resource Development.

——— (1992) "Land Use Statistics, 1987–88", mimeo, Delhi: Directorate of Economics and Statistics, Ministry of Agriculture.

Government of Sri Lanka (1984) *Sri Lanka Census of Agriculture 1982*, Colombo: Dept. of Census and Statistics, Ministry of Plan Implementation.

Harriss, B (1990) "The Intrafamily Distribution of Hunger in South Asia", in J. Dreze, and A.K. Sen (eds) *The Political Economy of Hunger*: 351–424, Oxford: Clarendon Press.

Hazell, P.B. and Haggblade, S. (1990) "Rural-Urban Growth Linkages in India", Working Paper WPS 430, Washington, DC: Agriculture and Rural Development Department, World Bank.

Hershman, P. (1981) *Punjabi Kinship and Marriage*, Delhi: Hindustan Publishing Corporation.

Hinton, W. (1972) *Fanshen: A Documentary of Revolution in a Chinese Village*, Harmondsworth: Penguin Books.

Hossain, M. (1988) "Credit for Women: A Review of Special Credit Programmes in Bangladesh", draft paper, Dhaka: Bangladesh Institute for Development Studies.

Hunt, H.I. (1983) "Intervention and Change in the Lives of Rural Poor Women in Bangladesh: A Discussion Paper", Dhaka: Bangladesh Rural Action Committee, December.

Islam, R. (1986) "Non-farm Employment in Rural Asia: Issues and Evidence", in R.T. Shand (ed.) *Off-Farm Employment in the Development of Rural Asia*: 153–73, Canberra: Australian National University.

——— (1987) "Rural Industrialisation and Employment in Asia: Issues and Evidence", in *Rural Industrialisation and Employment in Asia*: 1–18, New Delhi: International Labor Organisation, Asian Employment Programme.

Jannuzi, F.T. and Peach, J.T. (1980) *The Agrarian Structure of Bangladesh: An Impediment to Development*, Delhi: Sangam Books.

Jansen, E. G. (1983) *Rural Bangladesh: Competition for Scarce Resources*, Oslo: Norwegian University Press.

Kilkelly, K. (1986) "Women's Roles in Irrigated Agricultural Production Systems during the 1985 Yala Season: Parakrama Samudra Scheme and Giritale Scheme, Polonnaruma District", Report, Colombo: United States Agency for International Development (USAID).

Kishwar, M. (1987) "Toiling Without Rights: Ho Women of Singhbhum", *Economic and Political Weekly* 22, 3–5.

EMPOWERMENT OF WOMEN

Krause, I-B.(1982) "Kinship and Economics in North-West Nepal", unpublished PhD dissertation in Social Anthropology, London: London School of Economics, University of London.

Kumar, S. K. (1978) "Role of the Household Economy in Child Nutrition at Low Incomes", Occasional Paper No. 95, Cornell: Dept. of Agricultural Economics, Cornell University.

Lal, I. (1986) "Goats and Tigers", a video film by Ian Lal, Delhi: International Labor Organisation.

Lipton, M. (1992) "Land Reform as Commenced Business: The Evidence Against Stopping", draft paper, Sussex: Institute of Development Studies.

Lipton, M. and Longhurst, R. (1989) *New Seeds and Poor People*, London: Unwin Hyman.

Manimala (1983) "Zameen Kenkar? Jote Onkar: Women's Participation in the Bodhgaya Land Struggle", *Manushi* 14, January–February: 2–16.

Mayer, A.C. (1960) *Caste and Kinship in Central India – A Village and Its Region*, London: Routledge & Kegan Paul.

Mencher, J. (1988) "Women's Work and Poverty: Contribution to Household Maintenance in Two Regions of South India", in D. Dwyer and J. Bruce (eds) *A Home Divided: Women and Income in the Third World*, Stanford: Stanford University Press.

Mies, M., Lalita, K. and Kumari, K. (1986) *Indian Women in Subsistence and Agricultural Labor*, Geneva: International Labor Organisation.

Millet, K. (1970) *Sexual Politics*, New York: Doubleday.

Molyneux, M. (1981) "Socialist Societies Old and New: Progress Towards Women's Emancipation", *Feminist Review* 8, Summer: 1–34.

Munck, V.C. de (1985) "Cross-currents of Conflict and Cooperation in Kotabowa", unpublished PhD dissertation, Riverside: Dept. of Anthropology, University of California at Riverside.

Nath, J.N. (1984) "Dynamics of Socio-economic Change and the Role and Status of Women in Natunpur: Case Study of a Bangladesh Village", unpublished PhD dissertation, Dhaka: Dept. of Sociology, University of Dhaka.

Omvedt, G. (1981) "Effects of Agricultural Development on the Status of Women", paper prepared for the International Labor Office, Tripartite Asian Regional Seminar on Rural Development and Women, Mahabaleshwar, India.

Parry, J.P. (1979) *Caste and Kinship in Kangra*, Delhi: Vikas Publishing House.

Per-Lee, D.A. (1981) "Employment, Ingenuity and Family Life: Rajasthani Women in Delhi, India", unpublished PhD dissertation in anthropology, American University.

Raj, K.N. and Tharakan, M. (1983) "Agrarian Reform in Kerala and its Impact on the Rural Economy – a Preliminary Assessment", in A. Ghose (ed.) *Agrarian Reform in Contemporary Developing Countries*: 31–90, London: Croom Helm.

Rosenzweig, M.R. and Wolpin, K.I. (1985) "Specific Experience, Household Structure, and Intergenerational Transfers: Farm Family Land and Labor Arrangements in Developing Countries, *Quarterly Journal of Economics* 100, supplement: 961–87.

Sacks, K. (1975) "Engels Revisited: Women: The Organization of Production, and Private Property", in R.R. Reiter (ed.) *Toward an Anthropology of Women*: 211–34, New York: Monthly Review Press.

Safilios-Rothschild, C. and Mahmud, S. (1989) "Women's Roles in Agriculture: Present Trends and Potential for Growth", paper produced for the Bangladesh Agricultural Sector Review, UNDP/UNIFEM, Dhaka.

Saito, K.A. and Weidenmann, C.J. (1990) "Agricultural Extension and Women

Farmers in Africa", World Bank Working Paper WPS 398, Washington, DC: Population and Human Resource Department, World Bank.

Saradamoni, K. (1983) "Changing Land Relations and Women: A Case Study of Palghat District, Kerala", in V. Mazumdar (ed.) *Women and Rural Transformation*: 35–171, Delhi: Concept Publications.

Sayers, J., Evans, M. and Redclift, N. (eds) (1987) *Engels Revisited: New Feminist Essays*, London: Tavistock Publications.

Schrijvers, J. (1988) "Blueprint for Undernourishment: The Mahaveli River Development Scheme in Sri Lanka" in B. Agarwal (ed.) *Structures of Patriarchy: State, Community and Household in Modernising Asia*: 29–51, London: Zed Books; New Delhi: Kali for Women.

Selvaduri, A. J. (1976) "Land, Personhood and Sorcery in a Sinhalese Village", in L. Smith (ed.) *Religion and Social Conflict in South Asia*: 82–96, Leiden: E.J.Brill Publishers.

Singh, N. (1988) *The Bankura Story: Rural Women Organise for Change*, New Delhi: ILO.

Singh, R. (1988) *Land, Power and People: Rural Elite in Transition, 1801–1970*, Delhi: Sage Publications.

Singh, A.M. and Kelles-Vitannen, A. (eds.) (1987) *Invisible Hands: Women in Home-based Production*, Delhi: Sage Publications.

Solaiman, M. and Alam, M. (1977) "Characteristics of Candidates for Election in Three Union Parishads in Comilla Kotwali Thana", Comilla: Bangladesh Agency for Rural Development.

Strauss, J. (1986) "Does Better Nutrition Raise Farm Productivity?", *Journal of Political Economy* 94, 2, April: 297–320.

Sundaram, K. and Tendulkar, S. (1983) "Towards an Explanation of Inter-regional Variation in Poverty and Unemployment in Rural India", Working Paper No. 237, Delhi: Delhi School of Economics.

United Nations (1990) *The Situation of Women: Selected Indicators 1990*, Vienna: Dept. of International Economics and Social Affairs, Statistical Office.

[9]

Reflections on Law in the Everyday Life of Women

Catharine A. MacKinnon

For most women, life is little but everyday, a constant cycle of minutiae with few landmarks or dramatic demarcations of time, a litany of needs served but never satisfied, time spent but seldom occupied, lines drawn that, like the horizon, recede on approach. Across time and culture, and in individual biographies, the sameness in women's lives is as striking as the diversity of conditions under which it is lived. Men rise and fall. Their dynasties and revolutions and intellectual fashions come and go. Things happen. In the lives of women, men are served, children are cared for, home is made, work is done, the sun goes down.

Most women will tell you that law has little to do with their everyday lives. They seldom hit walls that look legal—they do not get that far. The lives of women in poverty are circumscribed by rules and regulations that they know are stacked and enforced against them and could be different, but nothing so majestic as "the law" is accessible to them. Many women encounter official obstacles, but few have the law in their hands. If a woman complains to the police of a crime against her, the law is in the hands of the prosecutor. On the civil side, it usually takes money to get the law to work for you in the United States. Even when a woman's injury is recognized by law, which is seldom, most women lack the resources to use it.

To most women, the law is a foreign country with an unintelligible tongue, alien mores, secret traps, uncontrollable and unresponsive dynamics, obscure but rigid dogmas, barbaric and draconian rituals, and consequences as scary as they are incomprehensible. Actually, this is true for most men as well.[1] The difference is that those who can and do make law work for them, those who designed it so it would work for them, as if they were the whole world, are men—specifically, white upper-class men. Women reflect this reality in their view that if you try to use the law, it is as likely to blow up in your face as to help. Law is Kafka's trial, Dickens's *Bleak House.* Mostly women feel that the law is not about them, has no idea who they are or what they face or how they think or feel, has nothing to say to them and can do nothing for them. When the law and their life collide, it is their life that gets the worst of it.

Women in conflict with the law show this relation in highest relief. Most become criminals for responding in kind to male violence against them, for crimes of poverty, for being involved with a man who committed a crime (what the legal system treats as first-degree bad choice of boyfriend), or for prostitution—being sold by men to men for what men value women for, and then being devalued and considered a criminal for it. On my observation, most imprisoned women who are not inside for crimes of self-defense *against* men who batter them are in for crimes committed *with* men who batter them.[2] The law does little to nothing about the crimes against women that position them to commit the crimes that do matter officially. For instance, women's imprisonment by violent men who batter them is not thought official, even though it is widely officially condoned.

The law operates most visibly in the lives of women in such official captivity. They are surrounded, defined, debased, and confined by the law. Their everyday lives are taken over by it. It swallows them up: their liberties, their children, their bodies, their community ties, what initiative and self-respect they had managed to salvage, and sometimes their lives. To be in prison is what it is for women to live their everyday lives entirely inside the law. Even when women criminals do the same things and get the same sentences as men, which is not the norm,[3] their crimes are the crimes of women. They commit them as women, are punished as women, and, when the law

1. See the evocative treatment by Austin Sarat, "'The Law Is All Over': Power, Resistance, and the Legal Ideology of the Welfare Poor," *Yale Journal of Law and the Humanities* 2 (1990): 343–80.

2. I learned this from working with women in prison in the United States and Canada, specifically at Niantic, Conn., and Kingston, Ont.

3. Rita J. Simon and Jean Landis, *The Crimes Women Commit, the Punishments They Receive* (Lexington, Mass.: Lexington Books, 1991).

is finished with them, they are thrown back onto society's trash heap for women.

The law that is applied to them and to all women has not been written by women, white or Black, rich or poor. It has not been based on women's experiences of life, everyday or otherwise. No one represented women's interests as women in creating it, and few have considered women's interests as women in applying it.[4] Unlike men, many of whom are also estranged from the law—especially unlike white upper-class men—no women had voice or representation in constituting this state or its laws, yet we are presumed to consent to its rule. It was not written for our benefit, and it shows.

The exclusion of women from a formative role in the law has meant that much legal intervention in women's lives is unconstructive, to say the least, while most of women's lives is carried out beneath explicit legal notice. Crimes and civil injuries do not imagine most harms distinctive to women, such as the stigma of female sexuality, which pervasively imposes inferiority on women in everyday life. Canons of legal interpretation in laws that might apply to real events in women's lives are shaped to assume the validity of the male point of view. An example in the law of sex discrimination is the "intent" requirement, which bases a finding of discrimination on the perspective of the alleged discriminator rather than on the consequences of his actions for the discriminated against. Burdens of proof and evidentiary standards as well as substantive law tacitly presuppose the male experience as normative and credible and relevant. An example is the mens rea requirement in the law of rape, which bases its determination of rape on the perspective of the accused rapist as opposed to that of the victim. Proceeding by analogy, as the law does, means that new crimes and injuries must be like old ones (read, men's) before they can be recognized as crimes and injuries at all. When a woman tries to raise her voice, precedent often requires decisive deference to a law built on the silence of women, a law that originated when we were not even permitted to vote or to learn to read, in a society premised on our subjection.

No law addresses the deepest, simplest, quietest, and most widespread atrocities of women's everyday lives. The law that purports to address them, like the law of sexual assault, does not reflect their

4. There are striking exceptions like Wanrow v. State of Washington, 88 Wash. 2d 221, 559 P.2d 548 (1977).

realities or is not enforced, like the law of domestic violence. Either the law does not apply, is applied to women's detriment, or is not applied at all. The deepest rules of women's lives are written between the lines, and elsewhere.

Yet the actions and inactions of law construct and constrict women's lives, its consequences no less powerful for being offstage. Focusing on the areas the law abdicates, its gaps and silences and absences, one finds that women's everyday life has real rules, but they are not the formal ones. They have never been legislated or adjudicated. They have not had to be. They effectively prescribe what girls can be, what the community encourages and permits in a woman, what opportunities are available and hence what aspirations are developed, what shape of life is so expected that it is virtually never articulated. These rules go under the heading of socialization, pressure, religion, popular culture, masculinity and femininity, everyday life. The rules of everyday life, in this sense, are that law which is not one, the law for women where there is no law.

The content of the formal legal system, the output of legislatures and courts, has a real effect on these processes, but, from the vantage point of life being lived, it is a distant one. Whether sex discrimination in athletics is illegal, whether women's supposed "interests" make occupational segregation nondiscriminatory,[5] whether pornography is protected by the state,[6] whether legal abortion is available[7]—all deeply shape women's realities, but from high up and a long way off. Women seldom have much say in these matters yet live their consequences every day in factories, behind counters, in beds, in gyms, on streets, in their heads, and in the eyes and at the hands of men, where the everyday lives of most women is largely lived out. Women's exclusion from law and marginality within it does not make the law inactive in women's subordination day to day. The fact that women have nothing to say about a sphere of life does not mean that it does not affect us—to the contrary. Especially if one thinks

5. EEOC v. Sears, 839 F.2d 302 (7th Cir. 1988).

6. Rabidue v. Osceola Refining, 548 F. Supp. 419 (E.D. Mich. 1984); but cf. Robinson v. Jacksonville Shipyards, 760 F. Supp. 1486 (D. Fla. 1991).

7. Roe v. Wade, 410 U.S. 113 (1973) (abortion decriminalized); Webster v. Reproductive Health Services, 492 U.S. 490, 518, 529 (1989) (*Roe*'s decriminalization of abortion questioned). See also Planned Parenthood v. Casey, 112 S. Ct. 2791 (1992) (*Roe*'s fundamental holding affirmed).

of everyday life as not having to be the way it is, the role of law in keeping it the way it is becomes visible, compelling.

Of all of everyday life, sexual relations between women and men may seem the farthest from the reach of law. Sex occurs in private, in presumed consent, in everyday intimacy. Sex is thought of as a sphere to itself with its own rules, written by desire or individual taste or mutual negotiation or tolerance, not by law. Yet the law of sexual assault has a very real everyday impact on sexual life. Rape is supposedly illegal. Yet the rape that the law actually recognizes as illegal is a far cry from the sex forced on women in everyday life. The law's rape is by a stranger, Black, in a strange location, with a weapon, which the woman resisted within an inch of her life. Preferably the woman is white. Most rapes that actually happen are by someone the woman knows, of the same race, often to women of color. Rape happens at home or on a date, without weapons other than hands and a penis, and the woman is too surprised or too terrified or too learned in passivity or wants to get it over with too badly or has heard too much about men who kill women who resist to fight back. Or she does fight back and is not believed, either by the rapist or in court, because sex is what a woman is for.

To the extent your reality does not fit the law's picture, your rape is not illegal. The implications of this for everyday sex life are that any man who knows a woman of the same race can probably get away with raping her. The better he knows her, the more likely he is to get away with it. Married women in states that do not have a law against marital rape are the ultimate example. Until the early seventies, a woman was not considered a reliable witness about her own rape, but the defendant was.[8] Unless someone besides the woman saw it, it was not legally real. Many jurisdictions, like California and Canada and England, still require that the state prove that the accused rapist honestly believed that the woman did not consent, no matter how much force was used.[9]

What does all this mean for having no mean no? When no can legally mean yes, what does yes mean in everyday life? When rape passes legally as intercourse, what is sexual intimacy? The law of

8. Of course, this would only be effective for the defendant permitted to testify in his own defense, a relatively recent development.

9. People v. Mayberry, 15 Cal. 3d 143, 542 P. 2s 1337 (1975); Pappajohn v. The Queen, 11 D.L.R. 3d 1 (1980); DPP v. Morgan, 2411 E.R. 347 (1975).

rape deeply affects sexual intimacy by making forced sex legally sex, not rape, every night. Every day, because women know this, they do not report rapes nine times out of ten.[10] When a woman does report, the media has the legal right to print her name and picture, making her into everyday pornography.[11] The racism of the criminal justice system is an everyday reality for women of color, who do not report their rapes by men of color because of it. In reality, there are no laws against what can be done to them. Many women, no matter how violated they were, do not call what happened to them rape if they do not think a court would agree with them. In this ultimate triumph of law over life, law tells women what happened to them and many of us believe it. When asked, "Have you ever been raped?" many women answer "I don't know."[12]

A similar combination of utter neglect with malignant concern animates the law of reproduction. Women get pregnant every day without wanting to be and at the same time are prevented from having children they want to have. The question here is who controls the reproductive uses of women, a process to which controlling the fetus is instrumental. When a woman is sterilized against her will and even without her knowledge, as has most often been done to women of color and to "mentally disabled" women, no law prohibits it or even compensates it after the fact.[13] Does law then have no relation to each day of the rest of their lives, on which they now cannot have children? If a woman dies from a desperation-induced self-abortion because a funded, safe one is not available by law—and most such women have been Black or Hispanic[14]—did law not end her everyday life?

Pornography suffuses women's everyday life, crisp at child's eye level in the 7-11, hidden at the back of the boss's drawer at work, smack in your face on the wall of the repair shop or the Film Society's

10. Diana Russell, *Sexual Exploitation* (Beverly Hills: Sage Library of Social Research, 1984), 36. ("[O]nly about 1 in 10 nonmarital rapes in the Russell sample were ever reported to the police.")

11. The Florida Star v. B.J.F., 491 U.S. 524 (1989).

12. See, generally, *Senate Judiciary Committee, The Response to Rape: Detours on the Road to Equal Justice*, May 1993.

13. This is documented in Catharine MacKinnon, "Reflections on Sex Equality Under Law," *Yale Law Journal* 100 (1991): 1301 n. 94.

14. See Laurie Nsiah-Jefferson, "Reproductive Laws, Women of Color and Low-Income Women," *Women's Rights Law Reporter* 11 (1989): 15–38.

spring roster at school, soggy under your son's mattress. Under the law of obscenity, pornography is supposed to be against the law. In the real world of everyday life, it is effectively legal because it is pervasively there, available without fear of sanction. This is what a dead-letter law looks like. The combination of pornography being putatively forbidden but totally available, decried in public but permitted and used in private, intrudes the law deeply into women's everyday lives. The allegedly forbidden quality of pornography sexualizes it by surrounding it with power and taboo and makes defending and using it appear to be an act of daring and danger, a blow for freedom against repression. Its actual availability belies the taboo and promotes the power, spreading it and supporting it as a model for women's everyday lives.

The everyday reality of pornography supersedes the formal law against pornography and becomes the real rules for women's lives, the sacred secret codebook with directions about what to do with a woman, what everything she says and does means, what a woman is. All the sexual abuses of women's everyday lives that are not recognized by the law are there in the pornography: the humiliation, the objectification, the forced access, the torture, the use of children, the sexualized racial hatred, the misogyny. As Andrea Dworkin has said, "Pornography is the law for women." Open your mouth this far. Spread your legs this wide. Put your arms like this. Talk dirty to me. Now smile.[15]

In this way, visual and physical intrusion on women—a normative experience of objectification and dehumanization made to seem deviant and marginal when medicalized as voyeurism and other exotic paraphilias—becomes the paradigm for sex. Sex in this sense is not just an activity at a time and place but a pervasive dimension of social life as lived every day. A woman's physical condition (Knocked-Up Mamas, Milky Tits), occupation (lady lawyer, hot housewife), racial or ethnic or religious heritage (Geisha Gashes, Black Bondage, I was a Gestapo Sex Slave), age (Cherry Tarts, Ten), family status (Daddy's Girl), pets (Doggie Girls), facts of everyday life to her, become sex to the consumer in the world pornography creates, along with everyday objects like telephones, cucumbers, beer cans, ropes,

15. Andrea Dworkin said this in many public speeches in 1983 and 1984. The analysis behind it was originally developed in her *Pornography: Men Possessing Women* (New York: G. P. Putnam's Sons, 1979), 70–100.

paper clips, razors, candle wax, police uniforms, plumber's helpers, lollipops, and teddy bears. In this process, the law helps constitute what is called desire by defining what amounts to sexual use and abuse of women and children as illegal and out of bounds and then doing nothing about it. Women realize that reporting sexual assaults is futile because this is a society that considers them freedom. When the state goes a step further and declares that pornography is affirmatively protected after all, and its harm to women is real but does not matter as much as the pornography of us matters,[16] women's despairing relation to the state and its laws—our belief that they will never see us as real—becomes total.

Even in the world pornography has made, it never occurs to most women, living their lives day to day, that having sex with a man to whom one is married is part of being a good mother. The law of child custody in general, of lesbian custody in particular, reveals that there are sexual requirements for the legal adequacy of women's parenting. If a woman has a sexual relationship with a woman, she can lose her children,[17] lesbian being pornography for men, to which they do not think children should be exposed. The everyday sexuality of many women is thus controlled every day through fear due to the recently strengthened possibility of men seeking custody of children.[18] This is not to say that the men actually want the children, although sometimes they do. More commonly, they want to use the threat of challenging custody as a financial lever to reduce support payments, and as control generally. The new norm of joint custody has a similar effect. Day to day, the mother has the major responsibility and does most of the work, but because of joint custody, the father can still control the big decisions. In other words, now not even divorce disturbs the power relation of marriage. And women who were raped in their marriages face sharing custody of their children with their rapist.

Family law keeps a lot of women in place and in line, fearful of

16. Hudnut v. American Booksellers Ass'n., Inc., 771 F.2d 323 (7th Cir. 1985).

17. See Dailey v. Dailey, 635 S.W.2d 391 (Tenn. Ct. App. 1982); Jacobson v. Jacobson, 314 N.W.2d 78 (N.D. 1981); L. v. D., 630 S.W.2d 240 (Mo. Ct. App. 1982); Constant A. v. Paul C.A., 496 A.2d 1 (Pa. Super. Ct. 1985). But cf. S.N.E. v. R.L.B., 699 P.2d 875 (Alaska 1985); Stroman v. Williams, 353 S.E.2d 704 (S.C. App. Ct. 1987). See also Roe v. Roe, 324 S.E.2d 691 (Va. 1985).

18. See Comment, "The Emerging Constitutional Protection of the Putative Father's Parental Rights," *Michigan Law Review* 70 (1972): 1581; Phyllis Chesler, *Mothers on Trial* (New York: McGraw-Hill, 1989).

altering their lives because of how it could be made to look in court. Some do not go public with past abuse through pornography for this reason. Many stay with men who abuse them because they fear the man would try to take their children away, and he would look better under existing legal standards—high income, intact family, white picket fence—than they do. Most women feel they married an individual but find on considering divorce that he represents the law and the law represents him. He is the law of the state in the home.

The realm in which women's everyday life is lived, the setting for many of these daily atrocities, is termed the private. Law defines the private as where law is not, that into which law does not intrude, where no harm is done other than by law's presence. In everyday life, the privacy is his. Obscenity is affirmatively protected in private. Wives are raped in private. Women's labor is exploited in private. Equality is not guaranteed in private. Prostitution, when acts of sex occur out of public view, is often termed private. In private, women who can afford abortions can get them, but those who cannot afford them get no public support, because private choices are not public responsibilities.[19]

Women in everyday life have no privacy in private. In private, women are objects of male subjectivity and male power. The private is that place where men can do whatever they want because women reside there. The consent that supposedly demarcates this private surrounds women and follows us wherever we go. Men reside in public, where laws against harm exist—real harm, harm to men and whoever has the privilege to be hurt like men—and follow them wherever they go. Having arranged the law against rape and battering and sexual abuse of children so virtually nothing is done about them, and having supported male power in the home as a virtual absolute, the law then proclaims its profoundest self-restraint, its guarantee of liberty where it matters most, in "the right to be let alone."[20] This home is the place Andrea Dworkin has described from battered women's perspective as "that open grave where so many women lie waiting to die."[21] As a legal doctrine, privacy has become the affirmative triumph of the state's

19. Harris v. McRae, 448 U.S. 297 (1980).

20. Roberson v. Rochester Folding Box Co., 171 N.Y. 538 (1902); Cooley, *Torts*, 4th ed. sect. 135 (1932). See also Warren and Brandeis, "The Right to Privacy," *Harvard Law Review* 4 (1890): 193; Samuel Hofstadter and George Horowitz, *The Right to Privacy* (New York: Central Book Co., 1964), 1–2.

21. Andrea Dworkin, "A Battered Wife Survives," *Letters from a War Zone* (New York: Dutton, 1988), 100.

abdication of women.[22] Sanctified by the absolution of law, the private is the everyday domain of women in captivity, abandoned to their isolation and told it is what freedom really means.

This is to say that the law is complicit in the impoverishment of the average woman who makes nowhere near the income of the average man,[23] in the everyday aggression against the forty-four percent of women who are victims of rape or attempted rape at least once in their lives,[24] in the assaults of the quarter to a third of women who are battered in their homes,[25] in the denial to women of the choice not to have children and the choice to have children and not to have them stolen, and in every act of violation or second-class citizenship that involves pornography. The law of rape collaborates with rapists to the extent it precludes recognition of the violations it purports to prohibit. The law of discrimination collaborates with perpetrators of discrimination to the extent its doctrines reproduce inequality rather than remedy it, requiring that equality already effectively exist before it can be guaranteed. The law of pornography collaborates with pornographers by protecting their right to abuse women behind the guarantee of freedom of speech, at the same time participating in their marketing strategy of sexualizing pornography by making it seem forbidden. The law of child custody collaborates with patriarchy in imposing male-dominant values on women in the family, and the law of privacy collaborates with whoever has power by guaranteeing spheres of impunity in which the law leaves men to their own devices. Even when the law does nothing—and it does nothing in so many ways—it is responsible for not working for women, whether law permits nothing when it pretends to do some-

22. On the structural level, see, e.g., Harris v. McRae, 448 U.S. 297 (1980); 30Deshaney v. Winnebago County Dep't of Social Services, 489 U.S. 189 (1989). For further discussion, see Catharine MacKinnon, *Toward a Feminist Theory of the State* (Cambridge: Harvard University Press, 1989), chap. 10. For an attempt to reconstruct the privacy right, see Anita Allen, *Uneasy Access: Privacy for Women in a Free Society* (Totowa, N.J.: Rowman & Littlefield, 1988).

23. U.S. Equal Employment Opportunity Commission, *Job Patterns for Minorities and Women in Private Industry 1986,* (1988, occupational segregation by race and sex); Kevin L. Phillips, *The Politics of Rich and Poor* (New York: Random House, 1990), 202–3.

24. Russell, *Sexual Exploitation*, 1984, 50.

25. Harold Lentzner and Marshall DeBerry, *Intimate Victims: A Study of Violence among Friends and Relatives* (Bureau of Justice Statistics, U.S. Dept. of Justice, 1980).

thing, is inadequate, is not enforced, or does not exist at all. If it does not work for women, it does not work.

Those who have power in life have had power in law, and the reverse. This relation is a process, though, not an inert or static fact, as one counterexample serves to reveal. Women have made one law: the law against sexual harassment. Before sexual harassment became actionable as a form of sex discrimination, it was just everyday life. The sex role norm that empowers men to initiate sex to women under conditions of inequality is intensified in sexual harassment. Women are pressured and intimidated into sexual compliance and raped as the price for economic survival. This has been done for centuries with complete impunity. When women's experience was made the basis for the law against sexual harassment, everyday life altered as well. Men kept doing it, but the experience had a name, an analysis that placed it within the collective reality of gender, a forum for confrontation with some dignity and the possibility of relief. Most important, women's own sense of violation changed because it had legal expression and legitimacy and public sanction. Law told them back what they knew was true. Sexual harassment was against the law against treating women as unequals, the law of sex discrimination. This law told the truth: sex inequality is the problem, this problem. In going from everyday life to law, sexual harassment went from a gripe to a grievance, from a shameful story about a woman to actionable testimony about a man. Changing what could be done by law changed the way it felt to live through it in life, and the status of women took a step from victim to citizen.

To wonder whether women will ever become full citizens is partly to ask whether law in women's hands can mean what law in men's hands has meant. For better and worse, probably not. Even when clothed in law, no woman escapes the female body when she is in court, not yet. This may be why sexual harassment complainants still do better on paper than they do on the witness stand. The extent to which law in women's hands could improve upon law in men's is suggested by the pornography example. Obscenity law is men's attempt to regulate pornography. It has been an abject and total failure. It is clear that men do not want to restrict pornography very much or they would treat it seriously, like they treat air traffic control, for instance. In ignoring abuse to women entirely, obscenity law is an invitation to the pornographers to violate women and run, sheltered by the First Amendment. The obscenity definition, which requires the materials be "taken as a whole,"[26] invites the surrounding of abuse with literature, making the abuse look more legitimate. The "community standards" rule invites flooding communities with pornography, so that their standards will come to conform to it. The "prurient interest" requirement invites juries to deny the sexual appeal of the most violent materials, supporting their protection. Even given these built-in difficulties for the successful application of obscenity law to anything, the vagueness of the obscenity definition invites prosecution of nearly anything with sexual content. From the fact that the pornography industry has nearly quadrupled in size since the promulgation of this definition, given the potential scope of the definition, one concludes that men do not want to do anything about pornography. If one assumes that the law can only work as it has worked in men's hands, the failure of obscenity law makes a good case for the limits of the law as such. If one has an alternative, that failure shows that the law is impotent in men's hands when it helps men be potent in everyday life. In other words, men's law has been constructed and applied to conform to a deeper logic, supportive of male power.

The civil rights law against pornography Andrea Dworkin and I proposed, by contrast, puts the legal power to oppose the pornographers in the hands of women. Based on the reality of women's everyday lives, this law gives women the power of law to act against pornography's real abuses. It names the harm: sexual subordination on the basis of gender. It permits women to act without prosecutor's permission or police discretion. It does not forbid pornography, which would keep it sexy; it makes it actionable as a sexualized practice of bigotry, which makes it detumescent. The limits on law encountered with the obscenity approach do not exist here. This is the case both because the law women wrote has a real relation to the lives women live and because, once women are empowered to expose it, there is no place for the abuse to hide, because it needs to use them to exist.

The only question is: will the law permit this? The fact that this law directly confronts male power where it lives means it will be slated for extinction. This does not mean it should not exist, it merely means

26. For further critique of the obscenity definition and detailed citations, see Catharine MacKinnon, *Feminism Unmodified: Discourses on Life and Law* (Cambridge: Harvard University Press, 1987), 152–54.

its existence will be opposed. Making it possible for women to stand against the pornographers in court would be a change in itself. Maybe the lesson here is that law is not monolithic, that what it is depends on *how* it is used, on its social substance and interface. Perhaps equality initiatives are unlike other laws and can confront social inequality more directly and constructively than other laws do.

Among left-leaning academic lawyers, there is a big controversy over whether law matters to life and whether those who care about everyday life should care about law at all. Does life make law or does law make life, they wonder. When men make both, and you are a woman, the distinction may not count for much, except that law purports to have rules other than force and pretends to be accountable, whereas life does not. At this point, the case for giving up on law is even stronger for giving up on life. Women giving up does seem to be the point.

There is a legitimate question, though, about the relation between law and the power that produces it, and the degree to which change in one produces change in the other. Whatever we know about how change is made, we do know that *no* change in one definitely produces no change in the other. Women's experience makes us suspicious of those who seek to make women's legal exclusion and marginalization and invisibility into a radical virtue, even as their antistate position usually stops short of opposing pornography, while the state is clearly for it. Our everyday lives make us suspicious of those who tell us rights do not matter, even as they have them while we do not.[27] Our lives make us suspicious of abdicating the state—in favor of what? those bastions of sensitivity and receptivity to women, the media and organized labor? Besides, what does it mean to abdicate a society you are excluded from but more exclusion? It does not stop affecting you when you stop trying to affect it.

Surely one of the most effective strategies for maintaining a system of dominance is to convince those who seek to end it that the tools of dominance must be left in the hands of the dominant. Women need institutional support for equality, both because of and in spite of the fact that power in women's hands is different from power in men's hands. Getting power is not the same as transforming it, but how are we supposed to transform it if we cannot get it? How

27. For a vivid analysis of this point, see Patricia Williams, "On Being the Object of Property," *Signs* 5 (1988): 5–24.

can it be changed if it is authoritatively defined in male terms and retained in male hands? I am tired of people who have power—whether they identify with it or not—telling women that we can only have power if we transform it. They might begin by insisting it be transformed in the hands of those who already have it. They might also explain how they plan to produce equality without institutional support, indeed while leaving in place present legal structures that enforce women's inequality. It's like telling women we should transform the state in the face of a law that deprives us of the right to vote. What are we supposed to do? Picket and hope they listen? Start a new state? Get the bomb? Why aren't any of these critics doing any of these things or their equivalent? I would also really like to hear their argument against the franchise. Not why it is limited; why its limits mean we should not fight for it and have it at all.

Those who say law cannot make change so we should not try should explain why the law should be exempt in the struggle for social transformation. Some of us suspect that women, in particular, are being told that not much can be done with law because a lot can be. If law were to be made to work for women, the relation of law to life, as well as its content, might have to change in the process. As more women become lawyers and maybe the law starts to listen to women, perhaps the legal profession will decline in prestige and power. Maybe women using law will delegitimize law, and male supremacy—in its endless adaptability and ingenuity—will have to find other guises for the dominance it currently exercises through law.

This is not to urge a top-down model of change or to advocate merely inverting or reshuffling the demographics of existing structures of power, or to say that law alone solves anything. It is to say that putting power in the hands of the powerless can change power as well as the powerless. It is also to urge a confrontational engagement with institutions, one that refuses to let power off the hook. It is a political demand, integral to a larger political movement on all levels, that law recognize that we live here, too. Every day of our lives.

[10]

The "No Problem" Problem

Deborah L. Rhode

Almost two decades have passed since I arrived at Stanford Law School as the second woman on a faculty of some thirty-five men. When I expressed interest in teaching a course on sex discrimination, my colleagues were mainly amused. "Do our students really need a class in that?" "Don't most people manage to discriminate naturally, without formal instruction?" The dean, however, was appalled at the prospect. Not only was it a field he diplomatically described as "mush," it also would "brand me as a woman." "Well," I responded with what I hoped was faint irony, "that probably won't come as a surprise to most of the world. And what, after all, is my alternative?" But to the dean, the issue was academic credibility. And to establish that, I needed a "real" subject; he suggested commercial transactions.

In the years that followed, much changed. But much remained the same. American women no longer confront a deafening silence about gender inequality—what Betty Friedan once labeled a "problem that has no name." But although we have named many problems, we have solved few. Topics such as sexual harassment, the glass ceiling, and date rape have entered our conversations. And women increasingly have entered occupations once reserved for men. Yet ironically enough, this progress has created its own obstacles to further change. Women's growing opportunities are taken as evidence that the "woman problem" has been solved.[1]

This perception has itself become a central problem. The "no problem" problem prevents Americans from noticing that on every major measure of wealth, power, and status, women still are significantly worse off than men. More than 95 percent of corporate executives and 85 percent of elected officeholders are male; more than two-thirds of poor adults are female. For too many women, too many problems are not getting better. Sexual violence, occupational inequalities, and the feminization of poverty remain pervasive, and reproductive freedom is available only to those who can afford it. While we have made considerable progress in encouraging women to pursue traditional male roles, we have been less effective in encouraging men to assume traditional female ones. Women continue to shoulder the vast majority of responsibilities in the home, a burden that limits their opportunities in the world outside it.[2]

Yet despite these patterns, most Americans do not perceive gender inequality as a serious problem. The topic is an unwelcome intruder in most conversations. When speaking of sex, we like to discuss sexual relationships, sexual deviance, and sexual difference; we prefer to avoid sexual inequality and the patterns that sustain it. Even those who share the basic goals of the women's movement fail to give them priority personally, politically, or financially. Few Americans make substantial contributions to candidates or groups focusing on women's issues. Only about a quarter of women say they are very concerned about gender inequality and only about 7 percent of women belong to any organization dedicated to advancing women's interests. The largest of such groups, the National Organization for Women, enrolls only 250,000 of the nation's approximately 90 million adult women.[3]

What accounts for this mismatch between Americans' daily experience and social priorities on gender-related issues? Why do so many individuals fail to see women's inequality as a serious problem? And why do so many fail to see it at all?

Those are the questions that structure this book. Its point is to increase our understanding of denial—of all the ways that we resist acknowledging gender inequalities, as well as our own capacity to address them. Much of our resistance is neither intentional nor overt. Rather, it rests on selective perception, stereotypical assumptions, and unconscious bias.

The dynamics of denial fall into three basic patterns. The first involves denials of gender inequality: many individuals fail to recognize the extent of problems facing women. The second dynamic involves denials of injustice: people often rationalize women's inequality as the result of women's own choices and capabilities. The final pattern involves denials of responsibility: individuals frequently believe that whatever inequality exists, they personally are neither part of the problem nor part of the solution.

Denials of Inequality

Americans' most common response to gender inequality is to deny its dimensions. A widespread perception is that once upon a time, women suffered serious discrimination, but those days are over. Barriers have been coming down, women have been moving up, and full equality is just around the corner. If anything, many men believe that women are now getting undeserved advantages. In a series of recent articles with titles like "The Decline and Fall of the White Male," commentators air their view that "merit is out," "special privileges" are in, and the only group that can't claim equal protection under law is white men. "Pale males eat it again," announces a character in Michael Crichton's popular film *Disclosure*. This perspective is widely shared. According to recent polls, close to half of all men think that they are subject to unfair penalties for advantages that others had in the past. Two-thirds of men and three-quarters of male business leaders do not believe that women encounter significant discrimination for top positions in business, professions, or government.[4]

Such views are difficult to square with the facts. White males account for about 40 percent of the population but about 95 percent of senior managers, 90 percent of newspaper editors, 80 percent of the *Forbes* list of richest Americans, and 80 percent of congressional legislators. Significant sex-based disparities in employment salaries and status persist, even when researchers control for objective factors such as education, experience, and hours worked. As *Newsweek*'s article "White Male Paranoia" points out, the pale male certainly appears to be "holding his own (and most of everybody else's) in the world of hard facts"; it's only in the "world of images and ideas . . . [that] he's taking a clobbering."[5]

What explains this gap between popular perceptions and concrete data on gender inequality? Part of the explanation lies with selective perception. Men often deny bias because they fail to recognize it. They usually don't need to; it does not significantly affect their lives. As with race, part of the privilege of dominance is the privilege of accepting without noticing its benefits.

The legal profession provides a representative example. Until the late 1960s, men constituted 95 percent of all practicing attorneys. Few thought this odd, and most never thought about it at all. Sol Linowitz, a prominent Washington lawyer, recalls that there were only two women in his law school class. Neither he nor most of his male classmates questioned the skewed ratio, although they did feel somewhat uncomfortable when their two female colleagues were around. And, he now acknowledges, "it never occurred to us to wonder whether *they* felt uncomfortable."[6]

Over the last two decades, sensitivity to sex discrimination has greatly increased. However, as a report by the American Bar Association's Commission on the Status of Women tactfully puts it, their agenda remains "unfinished." Three-quarters of female attorneys report experiencing gender bias, while only one-third of men report observing it. The vast majority of male judges are equally unaware of such discrimination, and some cannot recall a single example. Even men who acknowledge bias as a problem often discount its significance. In one recent survey, a Texas attorney summarized widespread views: "Of all the problems we have as lawyers," he noted, "gender discrimination is low on the list of important ones."[7]

To him, perhaps. But not to the female litigators who have to cope with client preferences for male attorneys, or with questions such as, "Do you really understand all the economics involved in this [antitrust] case?" Women of color and lesbian attorneys encounter bias on two fronts. In one telling instance, an African American partner in a major Chicago law firm recently reported that she had been mistaken for a stenographer at every pretrial deposition she had ever attended. Lesbians are routinely hazed, isolated, and denied employment opportunities. They, like Linowitz's classmates, often make others feel "uncomfortable"—and this is viewed as *their* problem, not their colleagues'.[8]

To men who have not been on the receiving end of such discrimination or challenges to their professional competence, this conduct often appears trivial and rarely remains memorable; it seems an isolated incident, not a representative illustration of a broader pattern. By contrast, men are far more likely to notice, recall, and resent bias against their own sex and to invest these incidents with both personal and societal significance. Columbia law professor Patricia Williams describes a typical example. "Nobody's hiring white guys anymore," was the unchallenged conclusion of one participant at a meeting of commercial lawyers. Williams surveyed the room of several hundred attorneys. She spotted one other black woman, no black men, no Hispanics, about ten Asians, and a "modest sprinkling" of white women. "So who is being hired if not white guys?" she wonders. "And if white guys aren't being hired, what on earth makes them think anyone else is?"[9]

Recent data on employment opportunities are more consistent with Williams' perception than with that of her male colleagues. Female lawyers are hired, but not promoted to the most economically rewarding and professionally prestigious positions. Two surveys involving thousands of lawyers with similar backgrounds and work experience found that men were twice as likely as women to have achieved partnership status. The obstacles are even greater for women of color.[10]

Similar patterns of denial are apparent in other employment contexts. One representative survey found that almost two-thirds of men either saw no discrimination against women or believed that it was of minor proportions. In another study, only 2 percent of male supervisors believed that their female subordinates faced any resistance or hostility based on sex; two-thirds of women reported such experiences. What female employees see as demeaning or harassing, their male colleagues often chalk up to "misplaced gallantry" or "harmless flirtation." "I have never been harassed," one male executive informed *Harvard Business Review* researchers, "but I would welcome the opportunity." For many men, it takes some first-hand experience, some observation of a wife or daughter's difficulties, or some exposure to systematic evidence before the cumulative impact of subtle discrimination becomes apparent. In commenting on his own attitude change, a male judge who co-chaired California's Gender Bias Task Force noted, "Until I was on this . . . Task Force, there was never any bias in my court."[11]

For obvious reasons, women are more sensitive to gender inequality than men are, but some perceptual blinders persist among both sexes. Not all women encounter all forms of bias, and those who lack personal experience sometimes fail to appreciate collective problems. What sociologists label the "Queen Bee Syndrome" is common among some professionally successful women. Their attitude is, "I managed, why can't you?"[12]

Many women also are unable to see patterns of discrimination because important parts of the picture are missing or murky. Salary, hiring, and promotion data that compare similarly qualified men and women are hard to come by, and the most overt sexism has gone underground. As a 1989 Supreme Court case revealed, male employers may still penalize a woman who they think needs courses in "charm school." But that is no longer what they say in mixed company or in personnel records. Moreover, gender is only one of the characteristics, and not always the most important one, that disadvantages women. Race, ethnicity, class, disability, and sexual orientation often overshadow or interact with gender.[13]

A wide array of research underscores the difficulties for both men and women in perceiving discrimination when the evidence comes in piecemeal fashion. In one study headed by psychologist Faye Crosby, individuals received information about a hypothetical company in which men earned higher salaries than women with comparable credentials. When participants in the study received information about the company's entire employment history, broken down by gender, they saw discrimination. But when participants looked at the same information case by case, they noticed no bias; each individual decision looked reasonably fair.[14]

The absence of data on collective patterns helps explain why even people who believe that gender bias is a significant problem usually fail to see it in their own workplace settings. As Crosby and her colleagues concluded, "The perception of sex discrimination reminds one of fireflies; one can always see the glow from some distance, but bagging the little critters [individually is far more difficult]."[15]

Self-interest complicates the process. For some men, the increasing unacceptability of sexism, coupled with the inconvenience of eliminating it, encourages various strategies of self-deception. These techniques frequently surface on issues of household work. Employed men, who average only half as much time as employed women on family tasks, generally manage not to notice the disparity. In one recent poll, over two-thirds of surveyed husbands reported that they shared childrearing duties equally with their wives, an assessment wildly inconsistent with that of most wives and virtually all reported research.[16]

Moreover, even men who acknowledge disparities often view women's extra tasks as matters of personal choice, not joint responsibility. Rather than accept an equal division of cleaning, cooking, or childcare obligations, some men redefine their share as unnecessary; they don't mind a little mess or a fast-food dinner, and their infants will do just fine with extra time among their "friends" at daycare. Other men seem not to notice when some of their assigned tasks need doing, or else mismanage key parts of the job. Rather than broadcast constant reminders or complaints, many women simply pick up pieces that their partners don't even realize have been dropped. As one wife wearily noted, "I do my half, I do half of [my husband's half], and the rest doesn't get done."[17]

A related strategy is to divide responsibilities "equally" without noticing that some shares are more equal than others. Surveys consistently find that men have a disproportionate number of the most enjoyable or conveniently scheduled tasks (reading to toddlers, rather than changing their diapers). Part of women's extra burden is invisible but unending "worry work." In the vast majority of households, men "help out," but also opt out of family tasks; women are the planners, the pinch hitters, and the persons ultimately responsible. When difficulties arise, the psychological division of labor remains skewed in ways that many men do not fully appreciate. Standing safely at the sidelines of a domestic crisis, fathers in sociologist Arlie Hochschild's study see themselves as involved and supportive: "Handle it the best way you can, honey, I'm 100 percent behind you." Former congresswoman Pat Schroeder recalls a telling instance of how easily men substitute emotional for actual support. Shortly after her first election, her husband explained in a *Redbook* profile that in the future he would be the one taking the children to the pediatrician. On reading his account, Schroeder immediately telephoned her husband and asked, "For $500, what is the name of the children's pediatrician?" He responded, somewhat sheepishly, that what he had meant was that he would be willing to take the children if she asked.[18]

Schroeder's story, and variations on its theme, often prompt further denials. Many men resist seeing any similarity between such accounts and their own situation. They can name *their* children's pediatrician, and so can every other father that they know. But discomfort sets in if they are pressed for details such as who takes time off from work for emergency visits. Recent research indicates that when children are ill, mothers stay home about 70 percent of the time. In many of the remaining circumstances, women make alternative childcare arrangements that will not disrupt their husbands' schedules. And when couples divorce, the vast majority of fathers assume few of the daily responsibilities of parenting. Within several years after separation, three-quarters of noncustodial fathers do not have even weekly contact with their children. To be sure, men tend to be more involved in childrearing today than when Schroeder began in Congress. But progress is not parity, and a wide gap persists between fathers' theoretical commitments to shared parenting and the time they actually devote to it.[19]

Part of what keeps men, and often women, from recognizing that gap is their choice of reference groups. Where gender appears to be a relevant characteristic, most individuals compare themselves to members of their own sex. In assessing domestic burdens, husbands look to other husbands or their own fathers rather than to wives. From this perspective, unequal divisions of labor become easy to rationalize because they remain the norm rather than the exception.[20]

Women also tend to compare their family burdens to those of members of their own sex. As a result, many wives deny that their husbands do less than their "fair share" around the home, even when responsibilities are grossly unequal. Cultural attitudes reinforce such perceptions. As Anna Quindlen notes, "When men do the dishes it's called helping. When women do dishes, that's called life." Most women are not fully aware of how much time they or their partners spend on family work and generally believe that their arrangements are far more equal than they truly are.[21]

This is not to imply that women totally fail to notice gender inequalities in household burdens. How much help they receive (or don't receive) from their male partners shows up in opinion surveys as one of the greatest sources of resentment. Yet even women who are most resentful often do not expect an equal division of household work. It is only their partner's refusal to help with particular jobs or his inability to justify refusing, that triggers conflict. And for many women, avoiding conflict is more important than achieving equality. They, like their male counterparts, use selective perception as a form of self-protection.[22]

Similar patterns operate in other contexts. According to workplace surveys, even when women recognize gender discrimination as a problem or where objective evidence points to that conclusion, most individuals still do not believe that they personally have been targets. Although many critics denounce feminism for encouraging women to exaggerate their own victimization, recent research finds that individuals generally are reluctant to see themselves in that light. Acknowledging vulnerability carries a cost: it erodes individuals' sense of control and self-esteem, and involves the unpleasantness of identifying a perpetrator. Many women understandably are unwilling to alienate men whose approval is important personally and professionally.[23]

Although some individuals enjoy nursing grievances and claiming the moral leverage of victim status, most do not. As Hillary Clinton once noted, "Who wants to walk around constantly with clenched fists?" Particularly where women feel powerless to avoid inequality, they are likely to avoid acknowledging it.[24]

Denials of Injustice

A second way of denying inequality as a social problem is to deny that gender disparities reflect social injustice. This strategy builds on broader psychological tendencies. Most people share what social science researchers label "a belief in a just world." We generally want to believe that life follows orderly, predictable, and equitable patterns in which individuals get what they deserve and deserve what they get. To hold on to this view, people often blame women's conduct and women's choices for the problems women experience.[25]

Popular explanations of workplace patterns are a case in point. Despite three decades of equal-opportunity legislation, the employment status of women and that of men remain far from equal. American workplaces are still gender-segregated and gender-stratified, with women of color at the bottom of the occupational hierarchy. Full-time female employees earn less than 75 cents for every dollar earned by men. Hispanic female college graduates average lower salaries than white male high school dropouts. Yet many individuals deny that these gender disparities reflect gender discrimination.[26]

Rather, a common view is that women's choices and capabilities explain women's disadvantages. Differences in biology are often held responsible for differences in status. Many women are thought to lack the technical competence and competitive personality that carry the greatest workplace rewards. Female workers also supposedly choose less demanding and lower-paying jobs in order to accommodate family obligations or noneconomic preferences, such as the desire to work in "touchy-feely" service occupations rather than technical positions.[27]

It is true that women as a group do make workplace choices that are somewhat different from those of men. However, those choices are in part a consequence as well as a cause of gender inequalities. Many researchers find that measurable differences in occupation, education, experience, and hours fail to explain even half of the existing wage gap. The remaining disparity is at least partly attributable to unconscious gender biases and the devaluation of "women's work."[28]

Historical, cross-cultural, and clinical research makes clear that jobs done by women often are undervalued *because* they are done by women. In controlled studies, individuals give lower ratings to the same résumés, scholarly articles, or artistic works when they carry a female rather than a male name. So too, when women are asked how much pay they deserve for performing a certain task, they select lower amounts than men. Gender disparities in salary structures reflect this undervaluation of women's work. Contrary to popular assumptions, many pay scales are impossible to square with merit principles. When childcare attendants earn less than parking-lot attendants, the gap speaks volumes about not only gender inequality but also its distortion of our social priorities.[29]

Assumptions about women's responsibility for "women's problems" are just as apparent in discussions about sexual violence. Although the frequency of rape and domestic assault is difficult to pin down with precision, the seriousness of the problem is not in doubt. America has the highest rate of reported rapes among Western industrialized nations; between a quarter and a half of all women will experience rape or attempted rape. A similar percentage will be assaulted by a spouse or partner. Domestic violence is the leading cause of injury to adult women and cuts across lines of race, class, ethnicity, and sexual orientation.[30]

Yet many Americans are convinced that women both exaggerate and perpetuate the brutality that they experience. According to front-page stories and widely quoted "experts" like Katie Roiphe (a graduate student in English), feminist fanatics use "ludicrously" broad definitions of sexual abuse and discount women's own responsibility for putting themselves at risk. Such perceptions are widely shared. Almost three-quarters of Americans do not view forced sex between acquaintances as rape, even when it falls within statutory prohibitions.[31]

Our desire to hold women accountable for such assaults has deeper cultural roots. For many individuals, sexual abuse appears less threatening if victims are responsible for provoking or inviting it. For women, blaming the victim is a way to deny their own vulnerability and to distance themselves from the problem. For men, such a reallocation of responsibility is a way to minimize their sense of collective culpability and to shift the moral high ground of debate. If feminists have encouraged unreasonable definitions of abuse, then men too can claim to be oppressed.[32]

Our tendency to fault women is apparent in virtually every systematic study of rape. For example, in research giving participants written or filmed accounts of sexual assault, many individuals inaccurately recall that victims behaved provocatively, a strategy that appears preferable to believing that an innocent person has suffered. Similarly, judges and juries often blame rape on women's seductive clothing or reckless conduct. Some courts have even managed to blame children under twelve: in one such case, the trial judge referred to the child as an "unusually promiscuous young lady."[33]

Victims of sexual assault are often victimized twice—first by the abuse and then by the blame that accompanies it. An apt illustration involves the Los Angeles "spur posse," a group of high school students who competed with each other for sexual "conquests." When some of the teens eventually faced criminal charges ranging from sexual molestation to rape, many parents rose to their sons' defense. "Nothing my boy did was anything any red-blooded American boy wouldn't do at his age," explained one father. "What can you do?" asked one boy's mother. "It's a testosterone thing." And another parent noted, "Those girls were trash."[34]

Law enforcement officials often hold similar views. The likelihood that a formal rape complaint will result in conviction and incarceration is only 10 percent. Contrary to critics' assertions about "rape hysteria,"

12 Speaking of Sex

underreporting, not overreacting, is women's most common response to sexual assaults. Fear, humiliation, and lack of confidence that their case will be treated fairly deter an estimated four-fifths of victims from filing criminal charges.[35]

Many Americans similarly hold battered women responsible for their own abuse—for provoking, tolerating, or declining to prosecute assaults. One judge summarized prevailing sentiments: "Why don't [women] just get up and leave? All they have to do is get out of the house." What people too seldom ask is whether women have somewhere safe to go, and whether they will be able to support themselves and their children. In most cases of family violence, the answers are scarcely reassuring. Nearly three-quarters of all reported assaults, half of all interspousal homicides, and most serious injuries occur after the abused woman tries to "just get up and leave."[36]

Most individuals at risk of violence are entitled to protective orders, but these orders are routinely violated and violations are rarely prosecuted. In some jurisdictions, protective mandates are not even available for same-sex partners. Despite recent improvements, domestic-violence programs still come nowhere close to meeting crucial needs for housing, child care, employment assistance, and related social services. America has more than twice as many shelters for animals as for battered women.[37]

Nicole Brown Simpson's experience was all too typical, except in the amount of publicity that it belatedly attracted. Despite her repeated calls for help, those in positions of power denied the seriousness of her injuries. "This is just a family matter," O. J. Simpson informed the police, who finally arrested him for an obviously brutal assault. "Why are you making a big deal of it?" In fact, the police didn't. Neither did the Hertz Corporation, which continued to employ him as a spokesperson. Nor did the judge, who imposed a sentence requiring no jail time—only community service, together with counseling sessions that could be completed by telephone.[38]

Such tendencies to forgive and forget are by no means unusual. Fewer than 10 percent of domestic abuse cases result in significant sanctions. Most are dismissed, dropped to misdemeanor status, or diverted to counseling and mediation programs that often trivialize the offense. This nation pays an appalling price for its attitudes toward family violence. The American Medical Association, hardly a captive of feminist fanatics, estimates the cost at between $5 billion and $10 billion a year in health care, workplace absences, litigation, and incarceration. The irrationality of our current priorities emerged clearly in a Massachusetts case where a woman sought a protective order after suffering repeated assaults. The presiding judge declared that if she and her husband wanted to "gnaw" at each other, "fine," but they "shouldn't do it at taxpayers' expense." A year later the woman was dead and the husband was on trial for murder, also at taxpayers' expense.[39]

Denials of Responsibility

A final way that we avoid confronting gender inequality as a problem is to relocate responsibility for finding solutions. Our most common strategy is to individualize the issues. Whatever the cause of such inequality, we make individual women responsible for the remedy. Alternatively, even in contexts where we recognize the need for societal responses, we overstate our progress in achieving them and understate the gap between formal rights and actual practices. And when all else fails, we fall back on biological excuses for sex-based inequalities. Since men and women just *are* different, we cannot expect society to equalize their status.

Our insistence on personal solutions for societal problems reflects broader cultural values. The American ethic exalts individual achievement, not collective action. Influential bestsellers offer cautionary tales of both success and failure, but their underlying message is much the same. Their topic could be the "managerial mother" and how she manages, the rules for catching "Mr. Right" and keeping him caught, or "women who can't say no and the men who control them," but the moral is similar: most solutions for women's problems lie with individual women. It is a matter of choosing the right man, cosmetics, career sequence, or time-budgeting techniques. Women's liberation appears more a matter of self-transformation than of political struggle.[40]

By the same token, increasing numbers of middle- and upper-income women assume that they can "purchase an exit visa" from problems stemming from inadequate public policies and unequal family roles. So, for example, individuals who can afford to hire domestic help can afford to tolerate the lack of government support for childcare and the lack of husbands' willingness to evenly share childcaring responsibilities. For many women, the feminist rallying cry of the 1970s—"the personal is political"—has been reversed. The political is personal and *only* personal.[41]

This individualist ethic emerges clearly in sociologist Ruth Sidel's study of young, unmarried women. Cutting across boundaries of race, class, and ethnicity is a shared assumption that they can "have it all" without the support of government, communities, or an extended family. The "all" is not a modest vision. Nor for most of these women is it a remotely realistic one. What they typically expect is a successful career, a happy marriage, well-adjusted children, and plenty of money; what they lack is any appreciation of the broader cultural changes that such a vision would require.[42]

Women with more life experience are more likely to recognize the inadequacy of individual solutions to shared problems. But what they fail to see—often with good reason—is any way to secure an effective response. Women working a double shift at home and on the job are generally reluctant to take time for political action. And female employees in unsympathetic workplaces may feel too vulnerable to raise gender-related concerns. In Susan Gordon's representative study, almost none of the women who talked about such issues privately were willing to do so publicly. Many were wary of jeopardizing their own situation. Others had found prior efforts at workplace organizing to be futile; male employees were entrenched in their positions and female colleagues were unwilling to make waves. As a result, many women found "no place to go on record with either [their] sympathies or complaints." So too, in Sherrye Henry's and Roberta Siegel's recent surveys, most working women saw unequal opportunity as a problem, but were "not aroused enough or economically secure enough to combat it personally . . . Discrimination was like bad weather. You endured it because you couldn't change it."[43]

In some sense, the American women's movement is a victim of its own success. Its accomplishments have undercut the urgency of further struggle. Feminism's insistence on equal opportunity is widely shared, but its call to common action is widely resisted. The women's movement has created aspirations to gender equality but not the collective commitment necessary to realize them.

What also stands in the way is the failure even to recognize certain problems as problems. An example involves the constraints of femininity. The difficulty here is that many traits traditionally valued in women also perpetuate women's inequality. These traits include sensitivity, warmth, self-sacrifice, nurturance, and physical attractiveness. Most Americans believe that women *should* exhibit those qualities, and a majority of women view "being feminine" as central to how they define themselves. Yet few individuals realize how often these expectations restrict women's opportunities for self-fulfillment and for making their own decisions about what they find fulfilling.[44]

Our recent progress in expanding women's choices has magnified these constraints. We increasingly expect women to achieve in multiple arenas with conflicting demands. Personal qualities that attract workplace rewards—drive, competitiveness, and self-promotion—are at odds with the characteristics that men most value in women, and that many women value in themselves. Female employees are caught in a double bind. They are vulnerable to criticism for being "too feminine" or "not feminine enough"; what is assertive in a man may seem abrasive in a woman. Moreover, the time and effort required for success in the workplace compete with the time and effort necessary for satisfaction in the home and for meeting standards of sexual attractiveness in the culture generally. Yet as long as we insist that these tradeoffs involve matters of individual choice, we divert attention from the social conditions that restrict the choices available. As a result, too many women too much of the time end up with unsatisfying compromises. Wherever they are putting their energy, they worry that it should be going somewhere else.

Physical appearance is an issue that we seldom link to inequality. Because women enjoy many activities associated with maintaining a feminine image, they often discount the personal costs that societal expectations impose. And men who don't pay that price are even less conscious of its magnitude. But in subtle ways, our prevailing double standards institutionalize inequality. Our ideals of attractiveness are much more demanding for women than for men, and we punish women's deviations much more severely. Recent studies consistently find that females are far less satisfied with their appearance than males, as well as far less concerned about their partner's appearance. As Gloria Steinem has noted, it seems that "men are almost always okay no matter how they look, while women are rarely okay no matter how they look, and thus feel constantly in need of 'fixing.'" Women spend over $50 billion a year in efforts to slim down and measure up through diets, cosmetics, and "corrective" surgery. Virtually every part of the female body, from eyebrows to toenails, is a target of opportunity and therefore of potential anxiety.[45]

We punish women not only for failing to meet cultural expectations, but sometimes just for trying. That double bind was apparent at a recent meeting of several hundred public utility executives. When one of the few women in the group missed a session, a male colleague speculated audibly that "there must be a sale at Saks." Yet even harsher judgments await the executive who does not look as if she shopped, and shopped well, at Saks.

Hillary Clinton has been in similar no-win situations. Often mocked for looking "frumpy," she has done no better attempting to look glamorous. Her constantly changing hairstyles, fashion-conscious press releases, and seductively posed magazine profiles earn widespread ridicule. As one commentator put it, "She might as well be selling moisturizing cream." For many women, the middle ground between trying too hard and not hard enough seems always out of reach.[46]

Among those committed to women's rights, the entire question of appearance is deeply problematic. We worry about how we look and we worry about worrying. Appearance is an important source of women's self-expression as well as subordination. How to value one without perpetuating the other is by no means self-evident. In one of Nicole Hollander's cartoons, the main character fantasizes about what the world would be like without men: "No crime and lots of happy, fat women." We need other ways to advance in that general direction.

Of course, on some issues of inequality, Americans generally recognize that responsibility cannot lie entirely with individual women. In the past quarter-century America has adopted an increasing array of legal decisions, public policies, and employer initiatives that seek to ensure equal opportunity. But this progress carries a double edge. Once we pass a law or institute a policy, we often believe that we've done our bit for women and move on to other issues. The result is that we settle for equality in form rather than equality in fact. Alternatively, even when we acknowledge that some gender inequalities remain unsolved, we often put responsibility for addressing them anywhere and everywhere else.

Our willingness to accept partial policies or symbolic victories is not, of course, unique to gender-related issues. Yet this tendency creates particular problems for women, who are a diffuse and divided constituency. Their mobilization becomes increasingly difficult once policymakers have addressed the most obvious needs.

A recent illustration involves family and medical leave. After a decade of struggle, the women's movement finally won federal legislation guaranteeing twelve weeks of unpaid leave after childbirth or adoption. However, the statute provides least for those who need help most. It exempts small businesses and recently hired or part-time employees, leaving about half of American workers unprotected. Moreover, unpaid time-off benefits only those who can afford to take it, and twelve weeks falls far short of what virtually all child development experts consider appropriate. Childbirth leave is also just one part of what Americans need in order to juggle work and family responsibilities. A majority of employees lack opportunities for flexible schedules, decent part-time positions, and quality child care. The costs of these policy failures are greatest for low-income women, who are disproportionately women of color. Yet even those who acknowledge such policy limitations often duck any responsibility for filling the gaps. Male government leaders look to employers, employers look to government, and both look to families. Within those families, husbands look to wives, and wives too often simply stop looking.[47]

Managers would like to help their workforce balance job and family responsibilities, but . . . There is usually a long list of buts. From the perspective of employers, flexible schedules or reduced hours appear impractical for most jobs. Managers assume that colleagues, clients, and customers won't tolerate the inconvenience, or that the work requires total commitment. Extended family leave appears equally infeasible. It seems a largely pointless gesture for men, who rarely take advantage of even the limited policies available. Women, on the other hand, supposedly grab as much as they can, which makes such options prohibitively expensive. Yet missing from this balance sheet are the less visible costs of failing to accommodate work/family conflicts: lower morale and higher stress, absenteeism, and job turnover.[48]

Although most husbands observe such problems, many resist contributing to the solution. From their vantage point, any major shift in *their* worklife is simply not an option. After all, a demanding job is a demanding job. Yet missing from this world view is any acknowledgment of the inequalities that result when men take their own aspirations and constraints as given, while assuming that women's are negotiable.[49]

So too, on many other gender-related issues, we overstate our partial progress and overlook the problems that remain. Reproductive choice is an obvious example of how readily we deny the gap between formal rights and daily experience. Prevailing Supreme Court decisions hold that individuals have a constitutional right to end a pregnancy without "undue burdens" by the State. Yet that standard has permitted a wide range of restrictions, including extended waiting periods, expensive testing, and prohibitions on the use of public funds or facilities. Such limitations, together with inadequate responses to "pro-life" terrorism, curtail the number of abortion providers and increase the risks and costs associated with the procedure. More than four-fifths of all U.S. counties have no facility offering abortions, and clinics providing such services run constant risks of harassment, arson, and assault.[50]

Such limitations on access have the greatest impact on low-income, minority, and adolescent women—those who are least able to bear the costs of an unwanted child. The result, as feminist law professor Catharine MacKinnon notes, is that only "women with privileges get rights." Constitutional rulings may guarantee reproductive choice, but our law enforcement and health care systems do not.[51]

A final way of denying responsibility is to assume that sex-based disparities reflect sex-based differences that we cannot or should not alter. Many Americans believe that certain inequalities are biologically rooted. Even more believe that gender stereotypes may contribute to gender differences, but that the responsibility for perpetuating those stereotypes lies somewhere else. As columnist Dave Barry observes, "Any parent will tell you that girl babies will generally display a wide-eyed curiosity about the world, whereas boy babies will generally try to destroy it." The reason, we suppose, lies with hormones, brain structures, and other influences beyond our control. Parents blame schools, toys, television, and other children. Media leaders blame families, and teachers blame everyone but themselves.[52]

In fact, there is plenty of responsibility to go around, and biology should by no means bear most of it. Children absorb traditional images of masculinity and femininity at early ages. Our culture encourages gender roles that are separate and, in important respects, unequal. We now have unisex books with titles like *Maybe You Should Fly a Jet, Maybe You Should Be a Vet,* but we still give girls dolls and boys planes. And we still have a society in which about 95 percent of licensed pilots are men, and a similar proportion of childcare workers are women. When toys talk, their messages, both literal and symbolic, reaffirm traditional gender roles. That point came through clearly in a recent hoax by a group calling itself the Barbie Liberation Organization. Group members bought several hundred Barbie and GI Joe dolls and switched their voice boxes. The result was a mutant colony of Barbies that roared, "Vengeance is mine!" and a battalion of Joes that twittered, "Will we ever have enough clothes?"[53]

The point of the hoax was to encourage parents to challenge traditional sex-based stereotypes. But even adults who join that effort may be unconscious of their own roles in perpetuating traditional gender messages. One mother who insisted on supplying her daughter with tools rather than dolls finally gave up when she discovered the child undressing a hammer and singing it to sleep. "It must be hormonal," was the mother's explanation. At least until someone asked who had been putting her daughter to bed.

Whatever their biological predispositions, children receive strong cultural signals about sex-appropriate tasks and behaviors. Much of their learning comes from unintended or indirect messages. If, as is still the case, most men don't make the beds they sleep in and parents assign more homemaking chores to daughters than to sons, children will learn what is "women's work."[54]

The Unfinished Agenda

Achieving true equality between the sexes will require fundamental changes in what we hold responsible for our distance from that goal. We need to recast the gender roles that children learn in homes, schools, and the media. We must also address the social policies, workplace structures, and family patterns that obscure and institutionalize injustice.

Of course, not all Americans have the same vision of what full equality would look like. Should our destination be a society where sexual identity has little relevance and where neither women nor men dominate particular social roles? Or do we want a world where sex continues to matter, but where men and women have genuinely equal opportunities, and their roles assume truly equal value?

On these questions, our society offers no simple or single answers. But we need not reach consensus in order to make substantial progress. Although we may not agree about what gender would mean in an ideal society, we know more than enough about what it would not mean. No just society could tolerate the inequalities that women now experience in status, income, power, and physical security.

The challenge remaining is to make those inequalities visible and to translate our personal aspirations into political commitments. A half-century ago, William Allen White counseled women to "raise more hell and less dahlias."[55] This book suggests why and how.

Notes

1. The "No Problem" Problem

1. Betty Friedan, *The Feminine Mystique* (New York: Norton, 1964), 15–32.
2. Federal Glass Ceiling Commission, *Good for Business: Making Full Use of the Nation's Human Capital,* Fact-Finding Report, Bureau of National Affairs, Daily Labor Report (17 March 1995), 528, 541, 634–639 (executives). See the sources cited in Chapter 5 (sexual violence); Chapter 7 (poverty, family responsibilities, reproductive freedom); Chapter 6 (employment, work/family conflicts); and Chapter 9 (elected officials).
3. Contributions to women's causes and candidates have dramatically increased in the last decade but still account for only a small percentage of charitable and political contributions. And just over 5 percent of foundation support goes to issues involving women and girls. See National Council for Research on Women, "Women and Philanthropy," *Issues Quarterly* 1 (1994): 13. For polls on women's concerns, see Roper Organization, *The 1990 Virginia Slims Opinion Poll,* 11, 22. For women's membership data, see Harris Associates, *Women's Equality Poll* (New York: Feminist Majority Foundation, April 1995), 9.
4. Paul Craig Roberts, "The Decline and Fall of the White Male," *San Francisco Examiner,* 9 January 1996, A13 (discussing "special privileges"); David Gates, "White Male Paranoia," *Newsweek,* 29 March 1993, 48 (citing poll on unfair penalties). For surveys on perceptions about discrimination, see Federal Glass Ceiling Commission, *Good for Business,* 528, 541, 634–639; sources cited in Deborah L. Rhode, "Gender and Professional Roles," *Fordham Law Review* 63 (1994): 39, 64; and Lisa Grunwald, "If Women Ruled America?" *Life,* April 1992, 44.
5. For the percentage of white males in positions of status and wealth, see Federal

Glass Ceiling Commission, *Good for Business,* 634–637; Gates, "White Male Paranoia," 48, 49. For sex-based disparities in pay and promotion, see American Bar Association [ABA] Commission on the Status of Women, *Unfinished Business: Overcoming the Sisyphus Factor* (Chicago: American Bar Association, 1995) (lawyers); Sarah Boxer, "Mr. and Ms. Doctor," *New York Times,* 14 April 1996, E2 (academics and physicians); Jane Frieson, "Alternative Economic Perspectives on the Use of Labor Market Policies to Redress the Gender Gap in Compensation," *Georgetown Law Journal* 82 (1993): 31, 41–42. See also the sources cited in Chapter 6. For male perceptions, see Gates, "White Male Paranoia," 49.

6. Sol Linowitz and Martin Mayer, *The Betrayed Profession* (New York: Scribner's, 1994), 6.
7. ABA Commission, *Unfinished Business.* For differing reports of male and female attorneys, see Ann J. Gellis, "Great Expectations: Women in the Legal Profession: A Commentary on State Studies," *Indiana Law Journal* 66 (1991): 941, 971; and Rhode, "Gender and Professional Roles," 826. For judicial perceptions, see *Preliminary Report of the Ninth-Circuit Gender Bias Task Force* (Seattle: United States District Court, Western District of Washington, 1992). For Texas survey results, see Diane F. Norwood and Arlette Molina, "Sex Discrimination in the Profession: 1990 Survey Results Reported," *Texas Bar Journal* (January 1992): 50, 51.
8. See sources cited in Rhode, "Gender and Professional Roles," 66 (antitrust example); American Bar Association Multicultural Women Attorneys' Network, *The Burdens of Both, the Privileges of Neither* (American Bar Association: Chicago, 1994), 1 (stenographer example); "Los Angeles County Bar Association Committee Report on Sexual Orientation Bias," reprinted in *Southern California Review of Law and Women's Studies* 4 (1995): 295, 441–449, 471 (sexual-orientation examples). See also Chapter 6.
9. Patricia J. Williams, *The Rooster's Egg* (Cambridge, Mass.: Harvard University Press, 1995), 97.
10. For partnership data, see ABA Commission, *Unfinished Business;* Rhode, "Gender and Professional Roles," 58–59; American Bar Association Young Lawyers Division, *The State of the Legal Profession, 1990* (1991), 54, 63–64. For barriers facing women of color, see American Bar Association Task Force on Minorities and the Justice System, *Achieving Justice in a Diverse America: Report of the ABA Task Force on Minorities and the Justice System* (1992); ABA Multicultural Women's Network, *Burdens of Both.*
11. For survey data, see Roberta A. Sigel, *Ambition and Accommodation: How Women View Gender Relations* (Chicago: University of Chicago Press, 1996), 145; and Sherrye Henry, *The Deep Divide: Why Women Resist Equality* (New York: Macmillan, 1994), 4. For the trivialization of sexual harassment, see *Sand v. Johnson,* 33 Fair Employment Practice Cases (BNA) 716 (E. D. Mich., 1982); cases cited in Chapter 5; cases cited in Deborah L. Rhode, "Sexual Harassment," *University of Southern California Law Review* 65 (1992): 1459,

1461; and Eliza G. C. Collins and Timothy B. Blodgett, "Sexual Harassment: Some See It . . . Some Won't," *Harvard Business Review* 59 (March–April 1981), 92. For attitudes on bias, see David Rothman, quoted in Ninth-Circuit Gender Bias Task Force, *Discussion Draft* (U.S. Court of Appeals for the Ninth Circuit, 1992), 171.

12. Ann Wilson Schaff, *Women's Reality* (New York: Harper and Row, 1981), 44.
13. *Price Waterhouse v. Hopkins,* 490 U.S. 228 (1989), discussed in Chapter 6.
14. Faye J. Crosby, Ann Pufall, Rebecca Claire Snyder, Marion O'Connell, and Peg Whalen, "The Denial of Personal Disadvantage among You, Me, and All the Other Ostriches," in Mary Crawford and Margaret Gentry, eds. *Gender and Thought: Psychological Perspectives* (New York: Springer Verlag, 1989), 79.
15. Ibid., 80, 94. See also Rhoda Unger and Mary Crawford, eds., *Women and Gender: A Feminist Psychology* (New York: McGraw-Hill, 1992), 182–184.
16. For the division of work, see Juliet B. Schor, *The Overworked American* (New York: Basic Books, 1991); Scott J. South and Glenna Spitze, "Housework in Marital and Nonmarital Households," *American Sociological Review* 59 (1994): 337; and Colleen O'Connor, "Women, If You Think You Have No Time to Relax, You're Probably Right," *San Jose Mercury News,* 8 August 1994, E1. For husbands' perceptions, see Michalene Busico and Lori Eickmann, "Families Searching for Fair Workloads," *San Jose Mercury News,* 24 February 1992, A8. See also the sources cited in note 17 below and in Chapter 6.
17. For men's attitudes and their wives' responses, see Arlie Hochschild with Ann Machung, *The Second Shift* (New York: Viking, 1989), 43, 259; and Lillian B. Rubin, *Families on the Fault Line* (New York: Harper Collins, 1994), 86–89. According to demographer Martha Farnsworthe Riche, "The great lesson of the past 15 to 20 years is that men don't care if the house is clean and neat, by and large"; quoted in Barbara Vobejda, "Children Help Less at Home, Dads Do More," *Washington Post,* 24 November 1991, A1. For further discussion of men's avoidance strategies, see Vobejda, "Children Help Less," A1; Linda C. Thompson, "Family Work: Women's Sense of Fairness," *Family Issues* 12 (1991): 181, 186.
18. For research on men's tasks and attitudes, see Janet Saltzman Chafetz, *Gender Equity: An Integrated Theory of Stability and Change* (Beverly Hills: Sage, 1990), 50; Rubin, *Families,* 86, 88; and Hochschild with Machung, *The Second Shift,* 90. For women's responsibilities, see Thompson, "Family Work," 190–191; O'Connor, "Women," 6E; Patricia Schroeder, Public lecture, Stanford University, 2 April 1992.
19. For responsibilities concerning sick children, see William T. Gormley, Jr., *Everybody's Children: Child Care as a Public Problem* (Washington, D.C.: Brookings Institute, 1995), 19, n. 12. For responsibilities following divorce, see Frank Furstenberg, Jr., "History and Current Status of Divorce in the United States," *The Future of Children* 4 (1994): 29, 37; Ross Thompson, "The Role of the Father after Divorce," *The Future of Children* 4 (1994): 210, 223.

20. For tendencies toward same-sex comparison, see Faye Crosby, *Relative Deprivation and Working Women* (New York: Oxford University Press, 1982), 94; Rubin, *Families,* 89; Jerry Suls, "Comparison Processes in Relative Deprivation: A Life-Span Analysis," in *Relative Deprivation and Social Comparison: The Ontario Symposium,* vol. 4, ed. James Olson, C. Herman, and Mark Zanna (Hillsdale, N.J.: Erlbaum, 1986), 95, 97. For men's comparisons concerning family tasks, see Hochschild and Machung, *The Second Shift,* 51; Thompson, "Family Work," 196.
21. For women's assessments of family burdens, see Alison Cowan, "Poll Finds Women's Gains Have Taken Personal Toll," *New York Times,* 21 August 1989, Al, A4; Judith Lorber, *Paradoxes of Gender* (New Haven: Yale University Press, 1991), 190; Anna Quindlen, "Abhors a Vacuum," *New York Times,* 9 September 1992, A21. For women's misperceptions of burdens, see Thompson, "Family Work," 184; O'Connor, "Women," Al; Lorber, *Paradoxes of Gender,* 189.
22. For women's perceptions of fairness, see Roper Starch Worldwide, Inc., *1995 Virginia Slims Opinion Poll* (Storrs, Conn.: Roper Center for Public Opinion Research), 80–81 (56 percent of employed women and 49 percent of nonemployed women resent how little their partner does around the house, and two-thirds of women feel that men are not doing their fair share of family labor); Carol Tavris, *The Mismeasure of Woman* (New York: Simon and Schuster, 1992), 33. For expectations of inequality and behaviors provoking conflict, see Thompson, "Family Work," 185–186; Kathleen Gerson, "Men's Influence on Women's Work and Family Choices," in Michael Kimmel, ed., *Changing Men* (Newbury Park, Calif.: Sage, 1987), 115, 120–122; See also Henry, *The Deep Divide,* 95.
23. For women's reluctance to view themselves as victims, see Crosby, *Relative Deprivation,* 13–18, 65–67, 94–115; Kristin Bumiller, *The Civil Rights Society: The Social Construction of Victims* (Baltimore: Johns Hopkins University Press, 1988), 81–95; Sigel, *Ambition and Accommodation,* 83–94; Jackson, "Relative Deprivation and the Gender Wage Gap," *Journal of Social Issues* 4 (1989): 117, 119–120; and Rita J. Simon and Jean M. Landis, "The Polls—A Report: Women's and Men's Attitudes about a Woman's Place and Role," *Public Opinion Quarterly* 53 (1989): 265. For claims that feminism encourages women to exaggerate their victimization, see Katie Roiphe, *The Morning After: Sex, Fear, and Feminism on Campus* (Boston: Little, Brown, 1993); Naomi Wolf, *Fire with Fire* (New York: Random House, 1993); and sources discussed in Chapters 5 and 8.
24. For discussion of the appeal of victim status, see Martha Minow, "Surviving Victim Talk," *University of California Law Review* 40 (1993): 1411. For women's desire to avoid victim status, see Bumiller, *The Civil Rights Society;* Crosby, *Relative Deprivation;* Crosby, Pufall, Snyder, O'Connell, and Whalen, "The Denial of Personal Disadvantage"; Hillary Clinton, quoted in Wolf, *Fire with Fire,* 304.

25. Isaac M. Lypkus, "A Heuristic Model to Explain Perceptions of Unjust Events," *Social Justice Research* 5 (1992): 359, 361–362. Melvin Lerner, *The Belief in a Just World: A Fundamental Delusion* (New York: Plenum, 1980), vii–viii.
26. President Bill Clinton, Proclamation 6883, National Pay Inequity Awareness Day, 1996, published in *Weekly Compilation of Presidential Documents* 32 (April 11, 1996): 651; Jocelyn C. Frye, "Affirmative Action: Understanding the Past and Present," in Cynthia Costello and Barbara Kivimae Krimgold, eds., *The American Woman, 1996–1997* (New York: Norton, 1996): 33, 38.
27. See "Women's Choices, Not Bias, Blamed for Lower Earnings," *Los Angeles Times,* 15 December 1995, A43; and sources cited in Chapter 6.
28. For the wage gap, see Chapter 6. For gender bias and the devaluation of female labor, see Crosby, *Relative Deprivation,* 3–5; Bumiller, *The Civil Rights Society,* 26–30; and note 29 below.
29. For summaries of research on undervaluation, see Barbara Reskin, "Bringing the Men Back In: Sex Differentiation and the Devaluation of Women's Work," *Gender and Society* 2 (1988): 58; Michele A. Wittig and Rosemary H. Lowe, "Comparable Worth Theory and Practice," *Journal of Social Issues* 45 (1989): 233; Brenda Major, "Gender Differences in Comparisons and Entitlement: Implications for Comparable Worth," *Journal of Social Issues* 45 (1989): 99–106. For studies finding lower ratings for female work and résumés, see Michele Paludi and Lisa Strayer, "What's in an Author's Name? Differential Evaluations of Performance as a Function of Author's Name," *Sex Roles* 12 (1985): 353; Richard F. Martell, "Sex Bias at Work: The Effects of Attentional and Memory Demands on Performance Ratings of Men and Women," *Journal of Applied Social Psychology* 21 (1991): 1939. For women's sense of fair pay scales, see Linda A. Jackson and Severin V. Grabski, "Perceptions of Fair Pay and the Gender Wage Gap," *Journal of Applied Social Psychology* 18 (1986): 606; Alice Eagly, *Sex Differences in Social Behavior: A Social-Role Interpretation* (Hillsdale, N.J.: Erlbaum, 1987), 111; Major, "Gender Differences," 105. For examples of biased salary structures, see sources cited in Deborah L. Rhode, *Justice and Gender* (Cambridge, Mass.: Harvard University Press, 1989), 193, 199; and the discussion in Chapter 6.
30. For statistics on rape, see National Victim Center and the Crime Victim Research and Treatment Center, *Rape in America: Report to the Nation* (Arlington, Va.: National Victim Center, 1992); Patricia A. Harney and Charlene Muehlenhard, "Rape," in *Sexual Coercion: A Sourcebook on Its Nature, Causes, and Prevention,* ed. Elizabeth Grauerholz and Mary A. Koralewski (Lexington, Mass.: Lexington Books, 1991), 3; Mary P. Koss and Mary R. Harvey, *The Rape Victim: Clinical and Community Interventions,* 2nd ed. (Newbury Park, Calif.: Sage, 1991), 27–29, 262–263; and Chapter 5, below. For statistics on domestic violence, see Committee on the Judiciary, United States Senate Majority Staff Report, *Violence against Women: A Week in the Life of America,* 102nd Congress, 2nd Session, October 1992; also sources cited

in "Developments: Legal Responses to Domestic Violence," *Harvard Law Review* 106 (1993): 1498, 1501; Antonio C. Novello, "From the Surgeon General: A Medical Response to Violence," *Journal of the American Medical Association* 267 (1992): 3132; and Chapter 5.

31. For critiques of feminists, see Roiphe, *The Morning After;* Warren Farrell, *The Myth of Male Power* (New York: Simon and Schuster, 1993), 329; Rene Denfeld, *The New Victorians: A Young Woman's Challenge to the Old Feminist Order* (New York: Warner, 1995), 61, 63. For perceptions of acquaintance rape, see Robin Warsaw, *I Never Called It Rape: The "Ms." Report on Recognizing, Fighting, and Surviving Date and Acquaintance Rape* (New York: Harper and Row, 1988); Koss and Harvey, *The Rape Victim.*
32. Lisa Maria Hogeland, "A Fear of Feminism," *Ms.* (November–December 1994): 18; Crosby, Pufall, Snyder, O'Connell, and Whalen, "The Denial of Personal Disadvantage," 82; Minow, "Surviving Victim Talk."
33. For exaggerations of victims' responsibility, see Melvin J. Lerner, *The Belief in a Just World* (New York: Plenum, 1980), 21, 109–110, 123; Robert Garcia, "Rape, Lies, and Videotape," *Loyola Law Review* 25 (1992): 711. For a landmark study, see Apsler and Friedman, "Chance Outcomes and the Just World: A Comparison of Observers and Recipients," *Journal of Personality and Social Psychology* 31 (1975): 887. For judicial and juror attitudes, see *Report of the Florida Supreme Court Gender Bias Study Commission,* March 1990, 140–141 (reporting widespread belief that sexual-molestation victims precipitate abuse); and sources cited in Chapter 5. For blame of children, see Lynn Hecht Schafran, "Documenting Gender Bias in the Courts: The Task Force Approach," *Judicature* 70 (1987): 280, 289 n. 17.
34. Jill Smolowe, "Sex with a Scorecard," *Time,* 5 April 1993, 41; Emily Yoffe, "Girls Who Go Too Far," *Newsweek,* 22 July 1991, 58.
35. Majority Staff Report, Committee on the Judiciary, U.S. Senate, 103rd Congress, 1st Session, *The Response to Rape: Detours on the Road to Equal Justice* (Washington, D.C.: Government Printing Office, 1993), 8, 12.
36. The judge is quoted in "Report of the New York Task Force on Women and the Courts," *Fordham Urban Law Journal* 15 (1986–1987): 32. For similar views, see Naomi R. Cahn and Liz Herman, "Prosecuting Woman Abuse," in Michael Steinman, ed., *Woman Battering: Policy Responses* (Highland Heights, Ky.: Academy of Criminal Justice Sciences, 1991), 95–96; Martha Mahoney, "Legal Images of Battered Women: Redefining the Issue of Separation," *Michigan Law Review* 90 (1991); and sources cited in Chapter 5. For statistics on assaults and homicide, see Mahoney, "Legal Images," 64–65; and Tamar Lewin, "The Terror of a Stalker's Threat," *New York Times,* 8 February 1993, A1.
37. For protection orders, see Peter Finn, "Civil Protection Orders: A Flawed Opportunity for Intervention," in *Woman Battering,* 80, 155–159; Ruthann Robson, "Lavender Bruises, Intra-Lesbian Violence, Law, and Lesbian Theory," *Golden Gate Law Review* 20 (1990): 567, 576–581. For other assistance,

see Margi Laird McCue, *Domestic Violence: A Reference Handbook* (Santa Barbara, Calif.: ABC-CLIO, 1995), 119; "Developments," 1510; Robson, "Lavender Bruises," 576–581; and Chapter 5.

38. O. J. Simpson, quoted in Barbara Vobejda, "Allegations Focus National Attention on Society's Response to Spouse Abuse," *Washington Post,* 19 June 1991, A18.
39. For the infrequency of serious sanctions, see sources cited in Chapter 5 and in "Developments," 1585–1586; Lisa Lerman, "Mediation of Wife Abuse Cases: The Adverse Impact of Informal Dispute Resolution on Women," *Harvard Women's Law Journal* 7 (1990): 57. For the costs of violence, see NOW Legal Defense Fund, *Stop Violence against Women: Strategies for Ending Violence against Women* (New York: NOW Legal Defense Fund, 1994); Novello, "Surgeon General." For the Massachusetts case, see Ellen Goodman, "Equal Rights Award," *Boston Globe,* 25 August 1982, A11.
40. Phyllis Schneider, "The Managerial Mother," *Working Woman,* December 1987, 117; Kevin Leman, *The Pleasers: Women Who Can't Say No and the Men Who Control Them* (New York: Dell, 1987); Ellen Fein and Sherrie Schneider, *The Rules: Time-Tested Secrets for Capturing the Heart of Mr. Right* (New York: Warner, 1996). For Americans' general tendency to see individual, not structural, causes of inequality, see James R. Kluegel and Eliot R. Smith, *Beliefs about Inequality* (New York: Aldine de Gruyter, 1986), 223–225.
41. For discussion of "exit visas," see Suzanne Gordon, *Prisoners of Men's Dreams: Striking Out for a New Feminine Future* (Boston: Little, Brown, 1991), 283.
42. Ruth Sidel, *On Her Own: Growing Up in the Shadow of the American Dream* (New York: Penguin, 1990).
43. Gordon, *Prisoners of Men's Dreams,* 108–111; Henry, *The Deep Divide,* 108; Sigel, *Ambition and Accommodation,* 53, 83–95.
44. For qualities associated with femininity, see Chapter 2. For the value placed on femininity, see Henry, *The Deep Divide,* 39, 55.
45. For research on the relative importance of appearance for males and females, see Gloria Steinem, *The Revolution from Within* (Boston: Little, Brown, 1992), 299; Jane E. Smith, V. Ann Waldorf, and David L. Trembath, "Single White Male Looking for Thin, Very Attractive . . .," *Sex Roles* 23 (1990): 675. For women's concerns and purchases, see Steinem, *Revolution from Within,* 299; and Naomi Wolf, *The Beauty Myth* (New York: William Morrow, 1991), 17.
46. Maureen Dowd, "Hillary Rodham Clinton Strikes a New Pose and Multiplies Her Images," *New York Times,* 12 December 1993, E3. See also the discussion of media coverage of Clinton in Chapter 4.
47. For discussion of exemptions in the Family and Medical Leave Act of 1993, 3 U.S.C. § 2601, 2631, 2651, see Commission on Family and Medical Leave, *A Workable Balance: Report to Congress on Family and Medical Leave Policies* (Washington, D.C.: Women's Bureau, U.S. Department of Labor, 1996), 61–65. For recommendations of child development experts, see "Recommendations of Yale-Bush Child Center, Advisory Committee on Infants," in *The*

Parental Leave Crisis: Toward a National Policy, ed. Edward F. Zigler and Meryl Frank (New Haven: Yale University Press, 1988), 343–346. For the inadequacies in childcare and work/family policies, see Gormley, *Everybody's Children* (1990): 431; Rhode, *Justice and Gender,* 172–173; and Chapter 6.

48. Commission on Family and Medical Leave, *A Workable Balance,* 11, 144–245; Rosalind Barnett and Caryl Rivers, *He Works / She Works* (New York: Harper Collins, 1996).
49. Hochschild with Machung, *Second Shift,* 113.
50. For the "undue burden" standard, see *Planned Parenthood of Southeastern Pennsylvania v. Casey,* 112 S. Ct., 2791, 2820–2821 (1992). For restrictions, see *Webster v. Reproductive Health Services,* 492 U.S. 490, 511, 520 (1989); *Harris v. McRae,* 448 U.S. 297, 326 (1980); Charlotte Rutherford, "Reproductive Freedom and Afro-American Women," *Yale Journal of Law and Feminism* 4 (1992): 255. For other barriers, harassment, and terrorism, see Chapter 7, below. For the lack of providers, see Gina Kolata, "RU 486: It Isn't Just Popping a Pill," *New York Times,* 28 July 1996, E14; Center for Reproductive Law and Policy, *Ensuring Reproductive Freedom* (New York: Center for Reproductive Law and Policy, 1993); and Chapter 7.
51. Catharine MacKinnon, "*Roe v. Wade:* A Study in Male Ideology," in *Abortion: Moral and Legal Perspectives,* ed. Jay L. Garfield and Patricia Hennessey (Amherst: University of Massachusetts Press, 1984), 43, 52.
52. Dave Barry, *Complete Guide to Guys* (New York: Random House, 1995), 36; and Chapter 2, below.
53. Angela Lau, "More Women Are Pilots, but They're Still in Minority," *San Diego Union Tribune,* 14 February 1994, B1; Avid Firestone, "While Barbie Talks Tough, G.I. Joe Goes Shopping," *New York Times,* 31 December 1993, A12.
54. For men and beds, see L. M. Boyd, "Grab Bag," *San Francisco Chronicle,* 8 March 1986. For parents and children, see Chapter 3, below.
55. William Allen White, quoted in Anna Quindlen, *Thinking Out Loud: On the Personal, the Political, the Public and the Private* (New York: Random House, 1993), epigraph.

[11]

The Right to Care

Robin West

Do individuals have a fundamental *right,* in liberal societies that protect individual rights, to care for their dependents? And if they do, does that right imply a "nested" right to some measure of state, social, or community support for caregiving labor, so that caregiving does not impoverish the caregiver, leaving her, and her dependents, unduly vulnerable? To use Eva Kittay's term for the social support needed to ensure a caregiver's well-being, do caregivers have a right to *doulia*?[1] Caregiving is obviously crucial labor, both to the cared-for individual and to the society and species of which the individual is a part: Without minimal care in infancy, none of us would survive, and without decent care during our extended childhoods, none of us would flourish. It is also crucial to the survival of political liberalism, no matter how that ideal is defined. Without care, and a lot of it, we would have virtually no chance of becoming either the autonomous individuals honored by liberal philosophers, and protected, at least in theory, by liberal rights, or the responsible, civic-minded political actors, committed to and interested in the common good and the public square, so valued by modern civic republicans.[2] Nor would we become the productive, or creative, or iconoclastic, artists, musicians, artisans, and freethinkers, so esteemed by libertarians, or the reliable producers or consumers of wealth so valued by liberal economists. Without care, we would not become liberal individuals, wealth-maximizing entrepreneurs, iconoclastic thinkers, or public-spirited communitarians, in any of the exalted senses of those phrases intended by our contemporary, liberal philosophers. Without the provision of care in infancy, childhood, and old age, the species would simply die out, as would liberalism, along with all else we collectively cherish.

Furthermore, while virtually all of us receive care for a substantial portion of our childhood, most of us, even in liberal societies that obsessively honor and reward heroic individualism, will spend a good part of our adult lives providing care to dependents, either infants, children, or the aged, and sometimes all three simultaneously. For many of us, this caregiving labor (and its fruits) is the central adventure of a lifetime; it is what gives life its point, provides it with meaning, and returns to those who give it some measure of security and emotional sustenance. For even more of us, whether or not we *like* it and regardless of how we regard it, caregiving labor, for children and the aged, is the work we will do that creates the relationships, families, and communities within which our lives are made pleasurable and connected to something larger than ourselves. Thus, caring labor is not only essential to the survival and flourishing of the individual cared for and vital to the well-being of the community. It is also a substantial part of adult identity.

It is also clear, however, that in a market-oriented, social world, caregiving labor leaves the caregiver profoundly vulnerable, and when the caregiver is vulnerable, so are the dependents for whom she cares. In part because of our patriarchic history, and the embeddedness of that history in our current markets, caregiving labor, largely done by women, is either totally unpaid or poorly underpaid labor. A woman caring for her own dependents is not compensated for the work she is doing, and a woman caring for the dependents of others is at best poorly compensated. Even caregivers who are also employed in some additional salaried or wage-earning work, however, will feel the brunt of this history. Employers, for the most part, are neither expected to nor required to accommodate caregiving obligations. As a consequence, caregiving employees will be adversely affected by this history of nonaccommodation: absences related to caregiving exigencies, for example, may lead to loss of pay or termination of the employment, part-time employment lacks benefits crucial to the well-being of oneself and one's dependents, and in salaried work, shortened work hours due to the necessities of caregiving will disparately affect income, benefits, and opportunities for advancement.

Thus, caregivers who lack support, or *doulia*, run the risk of serious impoverishment. Furthermore, without assistance, a caregiver may be politically disempowered as well: She will have neither time nor resolve to immerse herself in affairs of state. Likewise, while giving care, a caregiver is also largely precluded by the demands of her dependents from participation in the community's shared culture: As Harriet Beecher Stowe once remarked, in explaining why *Uncle Tom's Cabin* was not a better book, it is hard to produce high quality art when there are children's needs to which one *must*—and will—attend.[3] As essential as care is to the nurturance and maturation of individuals who will themselves, possibly, become liberal individuals and responsible, public-spirited, republican citizens, so the provision of care—the doing of care labor—seems to be strikingly incompatible with those very identities, at least as our current work world is now constructed. Putting it a little differently, whoever does the caregiving work in a liberal society, if that work is done without support, will be, for that very reason, disabled from participating as a liberal equal in the larger society of which she is a member. Whatever class of persons does the caregiving work will likewise be precluded as a class from that equal liberal citizenship.

We are left, then, with this problem: Caregiving labor is an essential, foundational, precondition of liberal society, but the market and political economy long associated with liberalism leave those who provide the care vulnerable and leave the class of persons who provide it—generally, women—disproportionately, or unequally so. It would be fair to surmise, given this state of affairs, that in a liberal world that depends crucially upon caregiving labor, and employs rights to assure the conditions of liberalism, that rights to care, as well as rights to the *doulia*, or support, that would protect the caregiver would be given a very high priority. Nevertheless, and without a doubt, the traditional liberal answer to the question posed herein has been a resounding "no." Rights, in liberal societies, protect individuals' autonomy, will, choices, plans of life, contracts, property, and conscience. Women give birth to and then provide care to children who mature into those rights-bearing autonomous adult individuals and then often provide the care for those adults when they have reached an age such that they yet again require full-time caregiving assistance. But no regime of rights protects caregivers or caregiving labor. Rights have never been viewed, within liberalism, as a source of support for caregivers.

This is not to say that liberal rights in toto have been of no use to women, or even of no use to women who are, have been, or might become caregivers. Rather, rights, in contemporary liberal societies, have helped women no less than men, when women, whether or not they are caregivers, acting as individuals, have sought to limit state involvement in their individualistic and atomistic lives. Thus, women, like men, enjoy rights of autonomy, conscience, speech, movement, association, contract, property, and religion. Women also, like men, now enjoy "nondiscrimination" rights: rights not to be irrationally categorized, or classified, by the state, and, within limited conditions, by private entities as well, according to unrealistic, stereotypical notions of women's nature—a stereotype generally garnered from their caregiving role.[4] Thus women cannot be irrationally precluded from jury duty, military service, employment opportunities, or political office solely by virtue of being women, on the specious grounds that because they are women, their caring nature or their caregiving obligations per se incapacitate them for such service, labor, or public role. Women have *rights* not to be so precluded, and even not to be so precluded on precisely that ground: that is, a woman has a right not to be stereotypically presumed to be a caregiver, and if she is a caregiver, she has a right not to be stereotypically presumed to have certain traits, such as an inability to engage in market wage labor or fulfill political, civic roles, because of her caregiving work.[5] Furthermore, in almost all contemporary liberal societies, so-called privacy rights typically protect women who, acting individualistically, decide *not to be* caregivers or to limit their caregiving obligations: thus, rights now guarantee many, perhaps most, women in liberal societies with nonconsensual pregnancies the freedom to abort the pregnancy (though only if they can pay for the procedure) and more broadly, the right to use contraception so as to prevent pregnancy.[6] And lastly, and as I will discuss in a little more detail further on, caregivers who are parents, including women, at least so long as they are in financially secure and relatively traditional families, have very limited, negative "parental rights," rooted in norms of familial autonomy, to make decisions regarding their children's education and upbringing, and to make those decisions free of state interference (although, again, not a positive right to actually *obtain* high-quality public education, health care, or any other material assistance requisite to that upbringing). Thus, and as the Court has recently reconfirmed, parents, including mothers, in traditional and independent families, have negative rights to keep intermeddling states, bureaucrats, departments of education, social workers, grandmothers, grandfathers, and other unwanted relatives and strangers out of the privacy of their home and away from their children, should the parents, acting as parents, deem it in the best interest of their children to do so.[7] Parents may, for example, to take a final example, "homeschool" their children, and in any language they choose, without state interference.[8] They have a "right" to do so and have had such a right for almost one hundred years.

But neither nondiscrimination rights not to be precluded from public life on the basis of false generalities regarding the nature of caregiving work, privacy rights not to become a caregiver if one chooses not to, nor parental rights to be free of excessive interference by the state in the raising and educating of one's children have ever been extended to include, or interpreted so as to imply, a right to material support from the state for the caregiving labor itself. Caregivers—whether or not they choose to become such, whether or not they are parents, and whether they are men or women—enjoy no rights *of support*. There is no right to the doulia of which Eva Kittay speaks. Caregivers do not have rights to either the financial or the in-kind assistance that would guarantee them some measure of security in their caregiving work. Nor do they have rights to help with the work itself, which would in turn free them to participate in political and cultural life.

In a modern liberal world that purports to value both the care that is a requisite of healthy, adult, liberal society and gender equality, the exclusion of caregiving and caregivers from the protective domain of rights looks downright anomalous. When viewed in light of other protections for caregiving and family autonomy, the omission requires justification. For roughly the first two centuries of liberal theory and politics, the exclusion of caregiving and caregivers from the protective embrace of rights, and hence from liberalism, was justified explicitly by reference to the differences between male and female nature, and the ill-suitedness of women for the realms of life from which caregiving seemed to preclude them.[9] The modern liberal account of the exclusion is harder to construct, but it presumably rests not on the imperatives of "women's nature," but rather, perhaps, on a reliance on "women's choice." What caregivers *should* do, on this constructed vision, in a post–welfare reform *and* post–formal equality liberal world, is raise children with the economic support of a husband, even if that means she risks becoming economically dependent upon him and vulnerable to his exploitation or abuse. But, it is important to realize, women are by no means *required* to do so. A woman can, after all, choose not to become a caregiver at all—she has that right. Just as important, she has the choice to be a caregiver and raise her children outside of marriage. Consequently, if a woman "chooses" to raise her children outside of traditional marriage, then her impoverishment and struggle to parent without social supports by virtue of that choice were just that—her choice—and therefore her own responsibility. Thus, so long as women are free to choose to become or not to become mothers, and free to choose whether to do so within or outside of marriage, then their relative impoverishment and lack of support should they choose to do so outside of marriage, once they are immersed in caregiving labor, are simply of no moment, even if the exclusion does seem to differentially create hardships for women. To paternalistically protect women from the consequences of their own choices—choices available, after all, at least in theory, to either sex—would do nothing but interfere with women's autonomy. No one, so might go the argument, after all, is *forced* to mother, and no one is forced to mother outside of marriage—at least so long as adoption is an available option for the fruits of nonconsensual pregnancies, and abortion is legal. Women are not conscripted into involuntary, nonmarital mothering. That the decision to mother, when voluntarily made, has economic consequences—that it has "opportunity costs"—does not in any fundamental way distinguish it from any other chosen lifestyle: The decision to mother might well diminish one's life's earnings, but so might the decision to sail around the world. So long as both are freely chosen, there is no greater reason to support the former than the latter with a regime of rights.

Thus, within contemporary liberalism, the tension between liberal individualism and formal equality, on the one hand, and the demands of caregiving, on the other, is resolved by reference to women's choice, rather than to women's nature—a woman might choose to mother within a traditional marriage, she might choose not to mother at all, or she might choose to mother outside of marriage. If caregiving is chosen rather than imposed, and open to all rather than only to women, then the anomaly noted previously—that egalitarian liberalism requires cared-for individuals, but caregivers are rendered unequal by a social structure that refuses any rights of support for caregiving labor—more or less disappears. After all, this state of affairs is chosen; it is the cumulative result of individual choices. It is no longer the result of "stereotype," or social pressure, or traditional gender-role indoctrination. Choices that impoverish us—so long as they are free—do not make us unequal. They just represent our freely preferred styles of life. If I choose not to work very hard and play a lot of pickup basketball or sail around the world instead, I can hardly complain that I am not supported by the state in my leisure, or even that I am "impoverished"; likewise, if I choose to mother outside of marriage, I can hardly complain that if the state denies me income supports, I am thereby "impoverished." A choice is a choice is a choice. Liberalism protects our choices through a regime of rights. It is not required to protect us from the consequences—and particularly the economic consequences—of those choices.

This more contemporary-sounding justification for the exclusion of caregiving, however—we might call it the "women's choice" justification—is surely as strained and unacceptable as its nineteenth-century, "women's nature" counterpart. First, of course, not all abortions are legal, and for many poor or geographically isolated women facing nonconsensual and unwanted pregnancies, they are in practice unobtainable. Furthermore, for many women and girls, motherhood is in no meaningful sense a choice at all: Women are still quite routinely implicitly pressured, and still oftentimes explicitly trained, to embrace careers of dependent domesticity. But as important, whether chosen or not, once embarked upon, pregnancy, childbirth, and caregiving potentially impoverish the caregiver whether or not motherhood is consensually chosen, for a reason that quite sharply distinguishes it from other "chosen" paths of life: As Kittay so carefully argues, caregivers, because of both moral and emotional imperatives, are unlikely, either as individuals or as a group, to use traditional levers of economic struggle to remedy the risks of impoverishment and diminished opportunities brought on by this labor. Unpaid caregiving is not work that caregivers simply abandon, or should simply abandon, when an equal or more rewarding opportunity presents itself. It is not, in other words, nor should it be, regarded as "*employment at will*," to use the legal term of art for wage labor that is nonunionized, typically undercompensated, and unprotected, but that is theoretically justified by the fact that the autonomous, "at will" employee, no less than the "at will" employer, can terminate the employment at any time, should a better opportunity come along. Caregivers, like "employees-at-will," are undercompensated and unprotected, but unlike employees-at-will, they enjoy no such "autonomy" freeing them to leave the job at any point (and thereby exert some pressure, by virtue of their legal freedom to walk off the job, to improve working conditions). Rather, caregivers virtually *by definition* are emotionally and ethically committed to the work of caring for their dependents. They don't unionize, walk off the job, or strike for better working conditions. They don't individualistically keep an eye out for the better entrepreneurial opportunity just around the corner. They don't, in short, commodify their labor. Quite the contrary. Consequently, caregivers receive all the vulnerability but none of the solace and certainly none of the security from the "at will" aspect of their employment. Their "autonomy" does not protect them. If caregiving is not to impoverish or diminish the opportunities of those who engage in it, they need familial, community, or state support, whether or not the decision to embark on the caregiving path was voluntarily taken.

And caregivers continue to have no rights to support, just as the public will to provide that support is eroding, both nationally and globally, and just as the need for it increases. To be sure, even in the United States, where such support has historically been miserly compared with other wealthy industrialized democracies, Congress and state legislatures have been moved, from time to time, to provide some level of support for caregiving labor. In the early part of the twentieth century, state legislatures passed legislation protecting, first, war widows, and then eventually all widows, with dependent children.[10] At midcentury, with Depression-era memories still fresh, that legislation was expanded into an entitlement to economic assistance provided to all poor mothers without husbands, regardless of whether or not widowed.[11] This is even the case for the Family and Medical Leave Act of 1993,[12] which essentially protects (some) caregivers from losing their jobs after giving birth to newborns, taking on the care of an adopted child, or faced with a family health crisis demanding their care and time, but makes no provision for *paid* leaves. But in all of these cases, the assistance provided by these bits of legislation has been regarded as, in effect, state-sponsored charity; as fulfilling, at most, a state's or a community's duty to provide assistance to its weaker citizens. That assistance is decidedly not perceived as the provision of a level of support to which citizens doing vital work are entitled *as a matter of right*. Likewise, when the state withdraws support, as the U.S. Congress did in the 1996 Personal Responsibility and Work Opportunity Reconciliation Act,[13] which effectively ended the federal guarantee of support for poor women with dependent children, it is viewed as, at worst, a breach of a moral obligation or perhaps an unwise matter of policy. It is most assuredly not viewed as an infringement of anyone's civil, individual, human, or constitutional rights.

What have feminists made of this enduring refusal of liberal theory and liberal societies to construct, recognize, or embrace rights of care? Two related lines of analysis have emerged. First, over the last twenty years, a number of feminists in a range of disciplines, including Martha Fineman in law[14] and Eva Kittay in philosophy,[15] have argued that the incompatibility of caregiving labor on the one hand, and liberal rights on the other, implies neither the peculiar illiberalism of women's nature, nor even (or only) the need for greater reproductive choice, but rather, the inadequacies of liberal theory itself. Liberalism, not women, according to this now quite fully developed "dependency critique," is what is flawed. Liberalism, and the rights culture it has fostered, fails to even acknowledge, much less address, the brute facts of human dependency, the societal as well as individual need for extensive caregiving labor that that fact of dependency demands of us, the disproportionately female labor that constitutes "dependency work," the inequalities that gendered division of labor fosters, and the inhumane consequences for children, as well as women, of the false view of human nature on which liberal regard and solicitude for robust individualism rests. What we should conclude from this incompatibility is not that women are distinctively illiberal, according to Fineman, Kittay, and other dependency critics, or that the human relations within the private sphere must by definition be beyond the state's reach, or even that women must be free not to be caregivers. Rather, what we should conclude is that liberalism, and the legal institutions that rest on it, are just plain starkly inhumane: They do not well serve the human community. Because they exclude from consideration the nature of our extended dependency upon others in infancy and old age both, they do not accurately reflect our humanity, and because they do not accurately reflect our humanity, they cannot adequately serve our human and social needs.

Other feminists and women's studies scholars, including notably Carol Gilligan in psychology[16] and Nel Noddings in philosophy,[17] have argued that the apparent incapacity of liberalism to embrace dependency work reflects an even larger incongruence: The ethic of rights, Gilligan and Noddings argue, has been constructed in a way that is not just hostile to, but diametrically antithetical to, an ethic of caregiving. If so, then it is not at all surprising that rights have not been reconfigured so as to protect the vulnerabilities to which caregiving leads: The modes of thought to construct the former are radically at odds with the modes of being central to the doing of the latter. Liberal rights fail to protect caregivers, in essence, because the "rights mentality" is at war with caring labor. Like the dependency critique developed by Fineman and Kittay, then, the ethical critique suggested in the work of Gilligan and Noddings (and others) seemingly concludes that liberalism and the rights at its core are in some fundamental way incompatible with the work of caregiving. According to both of these lines of analysis, the exclusion of caregivers—overwhelmingly women—from liberalism's domain is structural, and even definitional. It will not be overcome by insisting on the formal equality of women to men, or the equal availability to all of previously gendered roles, either in the world of wage work or domestic labor. Caregivers will continue to be excluded, regardless of whether or not women are welcomed to liberalism's domain, and regardless of whether it is women or men doing the caregiving work.

What has not been systematically explored, to date, in either the liberal and constitutional literature on rights, or the philosophical writing on the ethic of care, is the possibility of constructing liberal rights so as to protect the interests, needs, material security, and aspirations of caregivers. Liberalism has unquestionably, to date, been hostile to caregivers and caregiving labor, but it may be unduly pessimistic to assume, on that ground alone, that liberalism is monolithically and even definitionally configured so as to exclude the natures of caregivers or the work they do. Liberalism, and rights, may prove more malleable than that. It is not, at any rate, obvious that a generous and reconfigured liberalism, understood as a philosophical guide to political choice, is dependent upon a false and counterexperiential account of human nature. Perhaps what we ought to conclude, from the inhumane failure of the liberal rights tradition, to date, to extend protective rights to the needs of caregivers, is that liberalism needs to be amended. At any rate, it seems to me that the most "natural" conclusion to draw from both Gilligan and Noddings's demonstration of our rights culture's failure to acknowledge the ethical dimension of care, and Fineman's and Kittay's critique of liberalism's failure to protect the caregiving labor required by our human condition, is that liberalism ought be expanded so as to embrace a right to care—and that it ought to do so, furthermore, with all deliberate speed.

CONSTRUCTING LIBERAL RIGHTS TO CARE

Rights, in liberal constitutional democracies, are widely understood as imperative constraints upon or guides for representative politics, justified by some aspect of our universally shared human nature. Thus, the consequence of having a right is that the state *must* either take, or not take, some action: Rights are imperatives that states must heed, not suggestions. We have the rights we have in a liberal society, however, because of our understanding of *who we are* and who we ideally wish to be. We have various autonomy rights, for example, which means that the state must refrain from actions that infringe upon our autonomy, because we believe, rightly or wrongly, that our nature is such that we flourish when left free to decide matters of conscience, religion, or belief, for ourselves. We also have various property rights, which means that the state must protect our property from infringement and may not itself confiscate it without compensation, because we believe, rightly or wrongly, that our nature is such that we are made secure and thus better off through private ownership of possessions. We have privacy rights, because we believe that we need a sphere of untrammeled privacy, or intimacy, in order to thrive; we have contract rights, because we believe we are creatures who benefit from unregulated bargains; we have nondiscrimination rights, because we believe we have a shared nature that belies stereotyped differences. All of these rights, presumably, either stay or guide the state's hand, and all of them, by virtue of doing so, presumably, benefit us both collectively and individually, even where and when our representative lawmakers, speaking for a temporal majority of us, believe otherwise. And they do so, finally, because they protect some sphere of life (such as personal intimacy or economic markets) or some activity (such as expression or religious worship) or some source of identity (such as ethnicity or sexual orientation) that we have come to believe is essential for our ability to flourish.

Why, though, and when, are rights necessary? Why won't standard politics protect those spheres of life necessary for flourishing? Essentially, rights are necessary, in liberal societies, when, for some reason, the sphere of life, service, freedom, activity, or identity that is protected by the right, and so necessary to flourishing, might nevertheless be systematically undervalued, underappreciated, or underprotected by standard political processes. Thus, we enjoy rights of expression, rather than simply whatever expressive freedoms are from time to time granted by the state, because we suspect that without the right, expressive freedom will be unduly curtailed—temporal political passions will silence the voice of dissenters, and although there may be palpable short-term gains from that censorship, in the long run, we believe, we would all lose by the silencing. We enjoy a right to vote, or to be free of enslavement, because we suspect that without such a right, conditions might impel a political repeal of such freedoms. We enjoy rights to privacy likewise because we fear the censorial hand of an oppressively judgmental state moved by temporal and impassioned moral majorities more than we fear the consequences of private immorality. In some liberal societies (not this one), there exist rights to a living wage, to labor, to shelter, and to food, and again, these "welfare rights," where they exist, are justified, in part, by the awareness that the standard tools of political or economic reform will not readily yield them: There is no economic or political imperative forcing the employer's or the state's hand. But here as elsewhere, we construct and then enjoy rights when we come to understand, in what Bruce Ackerman calls a "constitutional moment,"[18] that we must have them in order to thrive and that the political process is unlikely to confer them.

There are (at least) two further reasons we sometimes construct antimajoritarian rights, according to standard liberal theory, worth mentioning here. First, at least sometimes in the United States and elsewhere, we construct rights when we have reason to believe that a particular practice or activity, if unchecked, will have a severe and adverse affect on a subgroup that has historically been subordinated. Thus, we have rights of nondiscrimination in employment, housing, and public accommodations, in part, because we believe that those private markets will adversely impact upon racial minorities, even where such discriminatory practices would be inefficient as well as unfair, and we have rights against de jure laws that delineate between us on the basis of race because of a similar suspicion regarding our political processes. And lastly, here and elsewhere, at least on occasion, we construct rights to underscore our most fundamental and most shared intergenerational values. The panoply of rights we protect expresses our social self-understanding, and more specifically, it expresses a self-understanding meant to endure even in times of its political neglect. It is not surprising, then, that the construction of a right requires intergenerational cooperation. The need for the right is most visible when the practice it would protect is most vulnerable, and when the political will to actually create it is accordingly lacking.

Does this widely shared, and I think, noncontroversial understanding of the various rationales for rights suggest a basis for a right to give care and a right to the doulia needed to support it? I think so. Clearly, our nature is such that we thrive when cared for. Our nature is also such that our period of infantile need is extended over time, and likewise is our period of caregiving labor. We flourish both individually and communally when decent care is provided, and we suffer when it is not. The better the care for infants and children, the more they will thrive, and the more likely they will mature to become liberal and equal citizens who can themselves provide care, as well as fulfill responsibilities of citizenship in a liberal society. The better the care we receive during our declining years, the less likely we are to feel cheated out of the rewards for years of labor. The better the care that is provided in cases of disease and disability, the greater the sense of comfort that we will not be abandoned, should we find ourselves critically ill or disabled. And, the more demanding and consuming is the care, the harder it is to provide without support.

Furthermore, we have very good reason to think that standard political and economic tools will not generate market or political protections for this labor or for those who provide it. Caregivers do not, as a rule, willy-nilly abandon infants or dependents, even under very harsh conditions. A pressing moral imperative to perform the work uninterruptedly once it is undertaken, together with the emotional attachment of caregiver and cared-for that results from caregiving labor, strongly suggest that the work will be less supported than it should be in democratic, market economies. There is no political will or need to support caregiving labor if it is going to be performed in any event, and no organizational ability to confront that lack of will with some set of non-negotiable "caregivers' demands," so long as caregivers continue to provide the services regardless of whether those "demands" are met, enduring either impoverishment or dependency as the cost of doing so. We therefore have good reason to believe that familial and economic institutions, if unchecked, will continue to undercompensate caregiving labor, and that women will be adversely impacted, as a group, by that practice. For this utterly unexceptional reason, deeply familiar to liberal theorists, we need rights of care, then, to protect caregivers against the pendulum swings of public support and neglect for their work.

Likewise, we need rights of care to protect women and men from the inegalitarian consequences of that neglect, just as we need rights of nondiscrimination to protect potential employees from the adverse consequences of irrational racism or sexism, and lastly, we need a right of care and a right to supported caregiving labor to better express our self-understanding as a species for whom caregiving is a central life activity. Thus, all three rationales for rights—the dysfunction of political and economic processes for protecting caregiving labor; the inegalitarian consequences for a historically subordinated group of not doing so, and our self-understanding that successful caregiving is indispensable to a liberal state, as well as to a full conception of persons—point in the direction of care and doulia rights. Whether we are presently in a "constitutional moment" that might support the creation of such a right is, of course, an open question: We may now be in a period when the political will to support caregiving labor in any way other than through traditional family structures is at an all-time low. But we are also in a period when the need for such a right is increasingly vividly clear to many people who historically have had no sense of it whatsoever: men, because of feminist advances and rising feminist consciousness, are actually *doing* caregiving labor and consequently experiencing some of the risks of that work.[19] Women and men who are caring for dependents know they need support, and they also increasingly know that complete economic dependency upon a marital partner in an unequal economic relationship is not a viable long-term solution. A right to support for caregiving labor might, then, express that quite fundamental shift in our collective and social self-understanding.

CONSTITUTIONAL AUTHORITY FOR A RIGHT TO CARE

Does the U.S. Constitution authorize recognition of a right to care, and of the doulia necessary to protect it? The document, of course, nowhere speaks of a "right to care," but that silence is clearly not determinative: The Constitution doesn't speak of a "right to privacy," or of the "separation of powers," or of an "exclusionary rule," or of a "right to parent" either. Of greater consequence than the document's silence is the Supreme Court's interpretations and actions, and here, the story is somewhat more complicated. On the one hand, and perhaps needless to say, the Court has never made mention of a right to care. Nor has the Court *ever* interpreted the Constitution as requiring even minimal state obligations to provide material support for poor people, or for that matter for anyone. Further, in the pivotal 1989 case *DeShaney v. Winnebago County Department of Social Services*, the Court stated flatly, albeit in dicta, that the Constitution across the board excludes even a hint of such positive state obligations or positive individual or citizen rights.[20] There is no sign, finally, that the Court will change course either now or in the near future, even should the Court become a somewhat more liberal institution than its recent and current personnel permit it to be.

On the other hand, it is not at all hard to find, in the Court's two centuries of constitutional interpretation, authority for the existence of a right to care. During the first half of the twentieth century, in a wave of libertarian judicial activism, the Supreme Court interpreted the Fourteenth Amendment's notoriously vague and open-ended "due-process clause," which simply denies states the power to deprive citizens of "life, liberty, or property without due process of law," as implicitly protecting not only these "procedural rights" to some sort of process, as the language of the clause most transparently suggests, but also a panoply of *unenumerated*, substantive rights—or, as they came to be called, "fundamental" rights—against pernicious legislation.[21] The Court, in that activist and libertarian era, went on to hold that the fundamental, unenumerated rights protected by the so-called substantive prong of the due-process clause include not just fundamental rights to contract and property, to be enjoyed free of interfering state regulation, but also the rights of parents to educate and raise their children as they saw fit, free of state interference.[22] At that time, the activist Court spoke confidently of the centrality of both the institution of the family *and* the importance of caregiving and child raising to adult life, and the need to somehow acknowledge that centrality in our foundational political institutions, and it was quite willing to use its powers of constitutional interpretation and the open-ended "liberty" phrase in the Fourteenth Amendment to do so. Thus, the Court "freely" interpreted the "liberty" protected by the due-process clause against unwise legislation, as incorporating the liberty to educate and raise children in a manner chosen by the parents. It accordingly found a number of laws, including laws requiring English-language instruction and mandatory public education, to be unconstitutional.

Although those cases are now viewed as important primarily for the claim that the due-process clause protects substantive, unenumerated, fundamental rights against pernicious legislation—rather than protecting only the right to not be summarily deprived of property or liberty without "legal process"—their particular holdings regarding parental rights continue to be good law. Just this past term, the Court reinvoked the "parents' rights" line of authority, while striking a state law that apparently gave judges wide latitude in awarding visitation rights to grandparents, over the objections of parents.[23] The antiactivist Rehnquist Court did so, furthermore, unambiguously, under the so-called substantive prong of the liberty clause, using the 1930s parents' rights cases as precedential authority. Parents' rights, and more generally parents' rights jurisprudence, are alive and well, even in the hands of a strict constructionist, originalist, and relatively conservative Supreme Court.

And, at least arguably, these parents' rights cases provide some precedential support for the notion that the Constitution can be read as requiring the state to guarantee that parenting, or caring, be effective, and to do so through the provision of doulia. Clearly, the parents' rights as originally envisioned in the first part of the century by the Supreme Court were regarded as individual, and indeed patriarchal, rights, which were generally justified by, and in sync with, the states' and community's interest in maintaining strong traditional families that would in turn produce robust healthy citizens—and *not* justified by the community's interest in an ethic of doulia more broadly conceived. Nevertheless, rights evolve, as our understanding of their ethical roots evolves. Parents' rights today might profitably be viewed as justified by the states' and community's interest in ensuring the well-being of all caregivers. We now realize that not only children in traditional families, but all of us at various points in our lives, require intense full-time care, and that not only traditional mothers in nuclear families, but again many or perhaps all of us at some point, will be called upon to provide that care. Our understanding, in other words, of the community's interest, that both bolsters and grounds this right, has deepened, and so then might our understanding of the contours of the right itself.[24] To put the argument in classic, analogic form, surely, if state legislation permitting visitation by grandparents against the will of the parents so interferes with a parent's right and responsibility to parent as to be unconstitutional, then social institutions or laws that impoverish caregivers, and so interfere with a caregiver's ability to provide care, ought be under a constitutional cloud as well. That those social institutions continue to adversely impact women likewise leads support to the conclusion that since the 1970s, the Court has at least been constitutionally concerned, as the Court a century ago most assuredly was not, with conditions that systematically disadvantage women. Putting the point metaphorically, one might say that the old "family rights" cases from the first half of the twentieth century, particularly if intertwined with the Court's equality jurisprudence from the second half, imply the groundwork, or the roots, of a twenty-first-century constitutional right of care. The recognized rights of parents to provide for, raise, and educate their children, when combined with a premise of equality (rather than with the premise of patriarchy quite explicitly embraced by the early-twentieth-century Court) strongly suggest the existence of a fundamental right to care, a core right, furthermore, to which parental rights of authority might properly be viewed as "merely" penumbral.

Of course, this constructed, precedential argument for a presently existing constitutional right to care is (*in one sense* of what it means to "do" constitutional law, or what it means to say what our current constitutional law "is") baldly counterhistorical, even wildly so. After all, instead of looking at what could happen to the family rights cases of the 1930s, just look at what *did* happen, and what did not: The "family rights" or "parents' rights" first articulated in the 1930s never developed, in the Court's jurisprudence, into a right to care; they never even took the first baby step. Rather, the Court's first major expansion of the parent's rights precedents came in 1964, in *Griswold v. Connecticut*,[25] when the Court reasoned from the old "parents' rights" logic, to a more general right of marital "privacy," which in turn encompassed a right of married persons to contraception. This was followed a short time later with *Eisenstadt v. Baird*,[26] which importantly extended the logic of *Griswold* to single people, thus obliterating the connection—albeit tenuous—still recognized in *Griswold* between the family rights logic of the early cases and the institution of marriage. The Court next decided *Roe v. Wade*,[27] which established a right to an abortion, and did so using exactly the same line of cases. In all of these 1960s and 1970s "reproductive rights" cases, the Court relied heavily on its parents' rights decisions of a half century earlier, first for the general proposition that the Fourteenth Amendment's due-process clause contains within it substantive, unenumerated, fundamental rights that cannot be constitutionally infringed upon by legislation, and second, for the more specific proposition that the "right to privacy" within which to make decisions whether or not to have children is one such right. Thus, the right to raise one's family, and particularly the right to educate one's children, free of interference from the state—first put forward in the 1920s and 1930s—was invoked, in the 1960s and 1970s, as the precedential support for the mid- and late-century right to purchase and use contraception, and then the right to purchase an abortion.[28] Rather than a right to care, in other words, the right to parent became essentially the right *not* to parent, or put more crudely, but possibly more accurately, the right to have heterosexual sex without reproductive consequences. It became a negative and quite limited right to be free of state involvement in matters pertaining to reproductive freedom.

Such a privacy right, or liberty right, to "heterosexual sex without babies," as its critics might put it, has been unquestionably of great importance in securing fundamental rights of privacy and liberty for women. But nevertheless, the "privacy jurisprudence" developed by the Court has proven to be a mixed blessing for caregivers. Once parents' rights to rear children are transformed into a privacy right to be free of parental or caring obligations, it is much harder to argue that these same rights can or should embrace a robust right to care, much less a right to doulia: Indeed, arguably, by freeing women *not* to parent, or to parent only "at will," the Court's privacy jurisprudence *undercuts*, rather than supports, such a claim. I think it's fair to say that the Fourteenth Amendment due-process "right to parent," as the Court's decision during this term regarding the constitutional limits on grandparents' visitation permitted by states attests, *in the Court's collective consciousness*, now consists of, at most, on the one hand, a negative right to use contraception or procure abortions (within limits) free of state interference, and on the other hand, an autonomy right of parents to be free of either state or third-party interference in their decisions regarding their children's upbringing, should they freely decide to have them. Some of the language of the decisions, particularly the early decisions, supports the idea of a right to care. But the case law the Court has developed from that early language by no means unambiguously implies the existence of such a right, and the language of the later cases, particularly taken in conjunction with the Court's insistence in other contexts that the Constitution consists solely of negative rights, seriously undermines it.

So where does this history of judicial interpretation leave the constitutional status of a right to care? To summarize so far: The Constitution nowhere mentions a right to care, but it does guarantee that "life, liberty or property" cannot be taken away without due process of law, and the Court has, for a hundred years now, and as recently as last term, affirmed that that right consists of not just rights to be protected by legal process, but also of fundamental unenumerated rights that cannot be infringed upon by pernicious legislation. Furthermore, the Court has consistently interpreted those fundamental, unenumerated rights as including a "right to parent." The Court *could* conceivably expand, or reinterpret, such a right as protecting a more general, as well as more generous, "right to care"; this would surely be no more or less "activist" than its construction of rights to contraception and abortion services. It has not, however, done so, and it is extremely unlikely that it will do so in the foreseeable future; indeed, at least the current Court is increasingly disinclined to interpret fundamental rights as including *any* positive right against a state, or imposing any positive duty upon a state. A blanket prohibition of positive rights leaves little room for a judicially recognized right to care.

However, it would be a grave mistake to imply from even a confident prediction that the Supreme Court will not, in the foreseeable future, interpret the Constitution as protecting a right to care, that we do not have one. There are several reasons not to read too much into predictions about what the Court will or won't do, when specifying the case for or against a constitutional right. First, of course, predictions can always be wrong; the Court's interpretation of the Constitution evolves, and evolves to fit a changing social self-identity. That the Court has never located in the Fourteenth Amendment, or any other constitutional source, authority for a right to care does not mean that it could not do so in the future, and should it do so, such a right would be no less constitutionally "authorized" than the right to integrated schooling, the right to be read one's Miranda warnings, the right to procure first-term abortions, or the right to raise one's children free of the meddling interference of unwelcome grandparents, none of which is mentioned in the Constitution, but all of which are now recognized as constitutionally mandated rights. And at least arguably, such an evolution would be a seemingly *more* natural, not less natural, extension of the parental rights cases that eventually became the cornerstone of our reproductive freedom jurisprudence. The early parental rights cases, after all, relied heavily on the importance of parenting to adult life, which would also be one of the cornerstones of the modern right to care. The privacy and reproductive freedom cases, by contrast, obviously suggest very much the opposite, although they manage to judiciously avoid saying as much.

The second reason we should not read too much into the Court's failure to construct a right to care is simply that we should be careful not to overstate the Court's institutional role in our constitutional system of government, or its generative role in our system of constitutional meanings. The U.S. Constitution is not the only source of constitutional authority, and the U.S. Constitution is not the only constitution with which courts grapple. States have constitutions as well, and many of them contain language that could readily suggest a right to care, and without the history of hostile judicial interpretation to weigh it down. Furthermore, the Supreme Court is not the only arbiter, even assuming it is the final arbiter, of constitutional wisdom, even in the federal system. State courts, state legislators, Congress, the executive branches at both the state and federal level, and, most important, citizens, all have constitutional obligations and responsibilities, including the responsibility to interpret both state and federal constitutions. This is particularly important in the context of a right to care. A right to care, if it exists, is unquestionably a positive, as well as negative, right: If it exists, it requires states and legislatures and Congress to do something, not just refrain from doing the impermissible.[29] If a right to care can fairly be implied from our constitutional history, it will fall to state and federal legislators, not to courts, to enact legislation to give it meaning. Thus, it is legislators, not courts, that need to be convinced of the existence of such rights, as it is legislators, not courts, that ought to legislate on the basis of it.

But last, and most important, we should not overstate the importance of the judicially interpreted Constitution, or mistake it for "the" meaning of the Constitution, because to do so misstates and misunderstands the function of constitutionalism itself. If we have a constitutional right to care, then we have it regardless of whether or not the Supreme Court has yet recognized it—this is the consequence of "taking rights seriously," to use Ronald Dworkin's fecund phrase.[30] If we have a right, we have it because such a right is morally justified and because it is a part of the way we have come to "constitute" ourselves as a people, as in part—but only in part—evidenced by our constitutional documents, and by our evolving and interpretive constitutional law. To enact laws pursuant to such a right, and to refrain from passing laws that would violate such a right, are legislative tasks and responsibilities. Such legislation, prompted by the imperative dimension of a right, is neither conditioned upon nor triggered by any judicial pronouncement regarding the status of the right. It is conditioned upon—and triggered by—political will.

LIBERAL, CRITICAL, AND CONSERVATIVE OBJECTIONS

Let me conclude by cataloging and then briefly responding to the most salient objections, or worries, that might be posited to a constructed right to care, by liberal legal and constitutional theorists, critical legal scholars, and conservative legal thinkers, respectively. Liberal legalists might pose three related objections. First, it might be objected that a positive right to support for caregiving labor flies in the face of now conventional understandings of liberal, constitutional rights, at least as that tradition has been understood in the United States. U.S. constitutional rights, whatever might be the case elsewhere, are now widely understood to be necessarily "negative": Rights give us a shield of protection against an overly intrusive state, but they do not entitle us to any sort of positive state action. A state that overlegislates, or irrationally legislates, runs the risk of running afoul of constitutional understandings, and a court might accordingly strike the errant legislation as unconstitutional. A state that underlegislates—that passively or irrationally refuses to enact law—might be in breach of moral or political duties, but it has not breached any constitutional obligations or infringed upon any constitutional rights. Even a state that failed to legislate against violently criminal activity, thus leaving citizens at the mercy of undeterred private violence, according to the current Supreme Court, would breach no right—we do not have a right, as the Court famously claimed ten years ago, to a police force or to any other governmental service.[31] The Constitution does not require the state to do anything on behalf of our rights; it only forbids the state from acting in certain ways. We have rights only to keep the state out of our affairs where it has no business meddling. We do not have rights to state services, protection, or provisions. A right to support for caregiving labor would unquestionably be a positive right; it would require the state to support the work of caregiving with either financial assistance, assistance in kind, or some combination. As such, it is antithetical to our constitutional scheme.

Relatedly, it might be objected, rights, as understood in the liberal constitutional tradition, are functionally protected by the courts, through adjudication, against recalcitrant legislators and pernicious legislation; they do not and should not compel or guide legislation. Thus, we have a right to free expression, and what that means, pragmatically, is that a law that infringes upon it will be struck by a court as unconstitutional; it does not mean that legislators are constitutionally bound to pass legislation that will protect the conditions for the free interchange of ideas. Rights are shields against unconstitutional state action; they do not provide protection against unconstitutional social conditions, which then must be rectified through legal action. We do not have "rights," against "society," to be protected by laws passed by legislators so as to protect those rights; rather, we have "rights" against the "state," and against the pernicious and overreaching laws it passes, to be protected, in turn, by court action. Rights constrain states or sovereigns. They do not *guide* them.

And lastly, rights, conventionally understood in liberal legal discourse, protect our robust, autonomous, heroically independent, and fiercely individualistic selves. They do not nor should not protect our dependent, relational, communitarian, duty-bound selves; in fact, if anything, rights exist precisely so as to ensure that such relational duties and dependencies do not overburden us. Rights protect our freedoms to think whatever we think, express ourselves as we wish, worship whom we please, own property, and enter into contracts according to our own rights. A right to care and a right to supported caregiving, from a conventional, liberal-constitutional perspective, are virtually oxymoronic. Rights protect our freedom to differentiate, divorce from, and distance ourselves from others: I have a right to privacy in my home, to school my children as I wish, to utter hateful utterances or absorb pornographic images, to lock my door and keep my neighbors at arm's length, and to secure my possessions, views, and entitlements from the prying eyes of states, communities, and others. Rights of free speech and rights to be free of arbitrary arrest might protect the panhandler against state harassment when he stands on the street and asks for change, but far more clearly, rights unambiguously protect my right to avert my eyes from his and keep my wallet in my pocket as I walk by. They protect my freedom *not* to teach my children lessons in civic obligation. They protect my freedom *not* to provide blood, kidneys, or reproductive services to anyone, notably including my dependents. They protect my right to "bowl alone" if I wish, and more generally, they protect my right to be "left alone." Rights limit our obligations, they do not create obligations, and they assuredly do not protect us within relationships created through those obligations, or more specifically protect us against the exploitative potential created by our obligatory commitments. They do not protect our vulnerability brought on us by virtue of our human dependencies or our communitarian interdependencies. We are, from a liberal perspective, essentially, autonomous and independent selves who thrive when "left alone" to explore our individuality apart from the constraining and distorting influences of others. A right to care is oxymoronic, then, because it protects us in our weakness, rather than promoting, celebrating, and protecting our individualistic strength.

A quite different set of objections might be posed by radical legal scholars, and particularly critical legal scholars influenced by the "rights critique"[32] developed in American and English law schools during the 1980s and 1990s. There are basically two such objections, I think, both of which are at heart strategic, or pragmatic, rather than theoretical. The first such objection goes to the danger of "co-optation." Even if rights are not necessarily negative or individualistic, the tendency to cast them as such in capitalist and liberal societies is overwhelming, and in light of that history, any attempt to construct a positive and nonindividualistic right is likely to be worse than futile. A right, then, even if initially posed, or desired, as a positive and communitarian right can be easily transformed through judicial interpretive processes into a negative right, often used against the very group that urged the right's construction. Thus, a positive right to be free of white racism, for example, which would clearly require the state to act so as to address the problem and consequences of white racism, becomes, instead, in the hands of judicial interpreters, a negative right to be free of discriminatory, racially motivated state legislation, and eventually a "right" to color-blind legislation, and finally a right *of whites* to be free of the burdens of affirmative action. Similarly, a "right," say, to meaningful political participation becomes a right to be free of state censorship, and then eventually a right to influence, even with vast and disproportionate wealth, political processes, and outcomes. A "right to work," urged as a positive citizenship right in the post–Civil War era, becomes a negative "antipaternalism" right to set terms of employment contracts that are free of state efforts to raise minimum wages or impose maximum hours constraints. This list could be extended quite easily; there are plenty of reasons to be legitimately worried that in capitalist societies rights tend to backfire against progressive causes. The co-optation danger, in this context, is that a right to care, even if crafted as a positive right to material support in caregiving labor, might quickly become nothing more than a negative right to either stay home and raise one's children oneself or to hire a nanny of one's choice, free of regulatory constraints such as mandated labor conditions, social security payments, or minimum-wage laws. The right to care could in rather short order become a rhetorical justification for policies that could well make life harder rather than easier for caregivers.

The second worry prompted by the rights critique is that a right to care, even if secured, would benefit only a few and would further legitimate the continuing structural injustices that plague our contemporary world. A right not to be discriminated against by the state on the basis of race, for example, does more than simply fail to address the problems created by white racism in the private sphere: It exacerbates them, and it exacerbates them by legitimating them. It falsely suggests that the problem of racism is one of state racism and then falsely promises that by forbidding it, it has addressed every legitimate problem of justice suffered by nonwhites. The harms caused by private white racism are thereby erased, minimized, or perversely valorized. Likewise, a right to purchase an abortion does more than simply fail to address the real reproductive health problems of poor women; it suggests, wrongly, that the primary constraint on reproductive freedom is moralistic legislation, rather than poverty, and then promises, cruelly, that a right to purchase an abortion is all that women facing unwanted pregnancies have a right to expect abortion from a just state. Likewise here, a right to supported caregiving would do more than simply fail to address the material needs of poor people. It would suggest wrongly that the only problem of poverty that is a problem of justice is the inability to provide adequate care without support. It would then promise, again cruelly, that a right to such support is all that is needed to rectify the injustices of poverty.

Finally, we can readily fashion the outlines of a conservative, traditionalist objection. A right to supported care, even if required by justice, might be disastrous for the human community it supposedly serves. Dependents, caregivers, and those who support them might all be better off within the confines of traditionally understood marital compacts: The caregiver—generally but not necessarily a woman—cares for dependents, and her husband, or spouse, supports her. She is dependent upon and therefore subservient to his benign authority. In a well-functioning family unit, no right is necessary to protect the position of caregivers, while actually providing a right is worse than unnecessary: It holds out incentives that would encourage, or at least not discourage, child raising outside of marriage. Children raised outside of marriage face higher risks of poverty, criminality, learning disabilities and low education rates, and a host of additional social disabilities. What we need to do to address these social ills is attack their cause, and their cause is the flight from marriage, stability, and responsibility that married life entails. A caregiver's right to social or state support would perversely worsen the conditions it set out to address.

RESPONSES

Let me take these objections in order—liberal, critical, and conservative. First, on the negativity and atomism of rights, the negativity of rights even in U.S. constitutional law is easily overstated. Any number of positive rights have in fact been recognized, at one time or another, by the Supreme Court, including not just the rights of criminal defendants to a court-appointed lawyer and the right to Miranda warnings, but also the right of all of us to vote.[33] Outside of the United States, it is quite clear that liberal societies can and do honor, recognize, and in some cases constitutionalize positive rights and do not noticeably sacrifice their liberality by doing so.[34] Furthermore, at the center of a Hobbesian and Lockean understanding of the liberal state, surely a theoretical cornerstone of American constitutionalism, is a distinctly positive right: the right to protection, by the state, against private violence, and a positive duty of the state sovereign to provide that protection. Notwithstanding the Court's logic in *DeShaney*, individuals, so said Hobbes, give up the right of self-help and self-defense in the state of nature when entering the civil compact, and what they get in exchange for that concession is the right, clearly positive, to enjoy the protection of the sovereign against private aggression. The U.S. Constitution both explicitly recognizes and even expands this positive, Hobbesian right to protection: The Fourteenth Amendment, passed in part to assure that freed slaves would be protected against white violence and vengeance, guarantees not only protection of the law, but equal protection of the law. The Supreme Court and liberal constitutional commentators are simply wrong to insist that the American constitution is one of "negative" rights only.

To be sure, a right to protection against private violence is not the same thing as a right to supported caregiving. Nevertheless, neither the existence of, nor the case for the latter, is undercut by its positivity. Positivity is by no means either a necessary feature of the rights protected by liberalism or a compelling, structural feature of American constitutionalism. Furthermore, if we were to recognize a positive right to protection against private violence and exploitation as at the heart of our constitutional scheme of government—and again, concededly, we currently do not—we could, possibly, envision a quite different set of penumbra rights emanating from that core, just as we now envision penumbral, unenumerated rights emanating from our core, negative right to be left alone. A right to the equal protection of the law against private violence, for example, if recognized as guaranteeing a positive right to protection against violence (as its roots in the antilynching campaigns of the amendment period suggest it should be) and not just a nondiscrimination right to equal, even if inadequate, protection, might not just more clearly impose duties of protection on states, but might also project a "gravitational pull" on the meaning of other phrases, to use a popular constitutional metaphor. The phrase most likely impacted by such a pull would surely be the substantive prong of the due-process clause. If that prong does indeed imply substantive, unenumerated rights, and if those rights might be positive in character, and if we are right to be constitutionally concerned about societal conditions that reinforce gendered inequality, then the case for a "penumbral," unenumerated right to care looks quite solid indeed.

Relatedly, there is nothing about a right, and at the end of the day nothing about American constitutionalism, that suggests that rights are *only* what courts are inclined to protect. Rather, the insistence of some American liberal constitutionalists that courts, and not legislators, enforce rights, and that rights therefore provide protection only against states and state action, rather than against private or social wrongs, seems deeply mistaken. The constitutionalists' focus on judicial control of the creation of rights, for example, flies in the face of powerful and general jurisprudential understandings of rights, which in turn ground rights in entitlements and expectations individuals hold vis-à-vis and against social equals, to be protected by law, not just entitlements and expectations individuals hold vis-à-vis states.[35] There is similarly nothing in the United States' constitutional tradition to suggest such a narrow and cramped understanding. Most assuredly, judicial review, and, therefore, judicial supremacy regarding constitutional interpretation, is unquestionably a part of our tradition. The Court gets the last word. It doesn't follow, however, from the Supreme Court's authority as the final arbiter of constitutional meaning that it is the exclusive interpreter: As mentioned, legislators, executives, and citizens all have constitutional obligations, and such obligations logically entail the necessity of constitutional interpretation as well. Nor does it follow from judicial supremacy that courts, and only courts, are constitutionally obligated to protect and take action to protect the rights of citizens. Legislators, too, take an oath to uphold the constitution; legislators, too, are required to do so.

Nor is there anything intrinsic to the rights tradition that weds it to a falsely atomistic conception of our nature. Rights and the liberal tradition that fosters them have changed, sometimes dramatically, to reflect changing understandings of our nature, no less than changing circumstances: We now accord rights to classes of people routinely denied them at the birth of liberal theory, and we have done so explicitly on the basis of changing understandings of the universality of fundamental attributes. We have created rights to reproductive decision making, although in the past reproduction was relegated to fate rather than to choice, and we have done so because of our belief that autonomy regarding reproduction better suits our nature. We have created rights of nondiscrimination, and we have vastly expanded the scope of our rights of free expression, well beyond anything that could conceivably have been intended by the framers, and we have done so largely because of changing accounts of who and what we are. There is no reason that liberal theory, and the rights it supports, could not transform itself so as to meet the "dependency critique." One way to do so, although there could well be others, would be to fashion liberal rights of care and, in so doing, both protect and acknowledge the caring labor that makes liberalism and all else possible.

And what of the critics' worries of co-optation and legitimation? Rights are indeed often co-opted, and negative rights do tend to legitimate the injustice that they either insulate or fail to address. But we should be careful not to throw the baby out with the bath water. That rights can be co-opted does not distinguish them from other legal or political tools of progressive reform, and that they legitimate what they fail to address might simply be a cost worth absorbing or a risk worth taking. While a right to care might legitimate the poverty it leaves untouched, it touches quite a lot. Furthermore, abandoning rights, as the critics would apparently have us do, and attempts to improve social conditions through rights, carries its own strategic costs and they are substantial: Rights, should progressives abandon the project of constructed, describing, and defending rights, would then become the sole province of the libertarian and conservative right. The end result of a world in which progressives, but not others, have abandoned rights, is dystopic, in the extreme: It is a world in which we have rights to property, guns, privacy, contract, and employment at will, but no rights to a clean environment, a decent education, support in caregiving labor, a good job, protection against violence, exploitation, or subordination, shelter, food, or a living wage. There are powerful forces afoot in our contemporary globalized Zeitgeist to produce just such a dystopic world. But feminists, progressives, and leftists shouldn't embrace it, or unwittingly support such a paradigm shift, because of a too-ready acquiescent fear that liberal rights are too dangerous a means of establishing social progress. Rights wedded without dissent to a market-economic vision of a night-watchman state is the risk incurred by doing so.

And finally, would a right to care only exacerbate social ills currently caused by child raising outside of marriage? There is no space here to rehearse the long-standing debates over welfare policy, much of which centers on this question. However, it is worth noting that marriage itself might look very different—and more appealing—if it were itself nested within, and justified by, a fundamental right to care, rather than a right to privacy or even a right to parent. If individuals have a right to provide care without being made unduly vulnerable by virtue of doing so—a right to doulia—a marriage, ideally, both could and should be understood as meeting the right by providing the support. For marriage to actually be a form of doulia, however, rather than a form of exploitation, the institution of marriage would have to be reconceived, and the various panoply of laws that regulate marriage would have to be modified to reflect that new direction. Some reforms toward this reconstruction would be modest. The income produced in the labor market by one partner, for example, could be required, by law, to be given to both partners. The future needs of the caregiving partner could be fully recognized and protected through equalizing the social security entitlements of both partners. Fathers could be expected or required—not just permitted—to take extended leaves from work to provide hands-on support for caregivers upon the birth or adoption of a child . . . and so on. More fundamentally, and more drastically, laws aimed at protecting women and caregivers within marriages from abuse and exploitation would have to be strengthened, and with the goal of protecting the caregivers' rights—an understanding, it's worth noting, diametrically contrary to the current Court's understanding of congressional attempts to address domestic violence. Were marriage to be so understood, and the laws sustaining it reformed to reflect that understanding, it would itself constitute a form of doulia and would satisfy any right to doulia a caregiver within a marriage might have.

Were marriage to be so constructed, or reconstructed, would the existence of a right to doulia nevertheless create an undesirable incentive to avoid marriage altogether? Again, wouldn't this simply exacerbate the social ills caused by out-of-wedlock births, and really for no good reason, were marriage to be reformed so as to make it a more desirable form of doulia? There are two responses. First, it is altogether possible that the social ills of poverty, higher infant mortality rates, lower birth weights, less and lower quality education, poorer nutrition, higher rates of criminality, higher rates of incarceration, and greater health risks, all suffered by children of single mothers, and all lamented by social conservatives, are "caused" less (if at all) by the marital status of the single mother than by the lack of the right to supported care proposed here; The impoverished single mother, after all, currently lacks both a husband and a right to doulia. But more important, there is no reason to think that a right to doulia would create perverse incentives to pursue viable, healthy marriages. The claim that it would, I think, both understates the value of marriage and overstates the worth of the doulia right: Marriage supplies warmth and companionship, the sharing of daily responsibilities and decisions, as well as support, while the doulia right is only to the latter.

The right proposed here—a right to doulia, or supported caregiving—would mean that the single mother would be guaranteed a level of material, financial support, of in-kind assistance, and of help with the caregiving itself, so as to assure that she can provide adequate care without endangering herself and her dependents. Even if we accept *arguendo* the conservative's judgment that marriage is the best institutional context within which to care for dependents, there is no reason to think that such a right would supplant marriage. If it is truly the case that marriage—understood as available to all, regardless of sexual orientation—really is a better way, emotionally, morally, and financially, to live one's adult life, a right to doulia surely constitutes no threat to it. Nor is there any reason to think that such a right would or should supplant public efforts to encourage marital lifestyles as a socially preferred means of assuring adequate care. It would mean, however, that our priorities would shift. Our rights would, as they should, expand so as to protect that which makes social life possible—caregiving—while our policies, such as our current policy preference for marriage, would reflect our current sense of the best means of providing care. It would mean that women, along with their dependents, who cannot or choose not to raise children or care for elderly or disabled dependents' marriages, but nevertheless care for dependents, are not punished for doing so. Children and their mothers, and more generally dependents and their caregivers, both inside and outside of marriage, would enjoy public support, rather than contempt or neglect, and they would enjoy that public support because they have a right to it, not because from time to time and under limited circumstances they spark our pity. It would mean that we would no longer perceive caregivers in need as contemptible, or at best pitiful, and above all, as lacking rights. It would mean that we would quit blinding ourselves—quite *willfully* blinding ourselves, because we all know better—to the necessity and importance of the work they do. We would quit viewing caregivers—when we view them at all—as nothing but a burden; as nothing but dependent upon us.

NOTES

1. Eva Feder Kittay, *Love's Labor: Essays on Women, Equality, and Dependency* (New York: Routledge, 1999), 68. Kittay states the principle of *doulia* in this way: "Just as we have required care to survive and thrive, so we need to provide conditions that allow others—including those who do the work of caring—to receive the care they need to survive and thrive."

The word *doulia* is Kittay's improvisation of the Greek word *doula*, which designates a postpartum helper assigned to assist a new mother as she takes charge of her newborn infant. *Doulia*, then, designates the "arrangement by which service is passed on so that those who become needy by virtue of tending to those in need can be cared for as well." Kittay goes on to explain *doulia*'s ethic as being rooted in an extended, social reciprocity: "*Doulia* is part of an ethic that is captured in the colloquial phrase 'what goes around comes around.' If someone helps another in her need, someone, in turn, will help the helper when she is needy—whether the neediness derives from her position as caregiver or from circumstances that pertain to health or age." Kittay, at 107 (footnotes omitted).

2. Linda MacClain, "Care as a Public Value: Linking Responsibility, Resources, and Republicanism," *Chicago-Kent Law Review* 76, no. 3 (2001): 1673.

3. Tillie Olsen, *Silences* (New York: Delacorte, 1978), 204–05.

4. Mary Becker et al., *Cases and Materials on Feminist Jurisprudence: Taking Women Seriously* (St. Paul, Minn.: West Publishing, 1994), chapters. 2, 9–11.

5. See, e.g., *Virginia Military Inst. v. U.S.*, 508 U.S. 946 (1993); International Union, *UAW v. Johnson Controls, Inc.*, 499 U.S. 187 (1991); *Price Waterhouse v. Hopkins*, 490 U.S. 228 (1989); *California Savings and Loan Ass'n v. Guerra*, 479 U.S. 272 (1987); *Wimberly v. Labor and Indus. Relations Comm'n of Mo.*, 479 U.S. 511 (1987); *Rostker v. Goldberg*, 453 U.S. 57 (1981); *Orr v. Orr*, 440 U.S. 268 (1979); *Personnel Adm'r of Mass. v. Feeney*, 442 U.S. 256 (1979); *Craig v. Boren*, 429 U.S. 190 (1976); *Geduldig v. Aiello*, 417 U.S. 484 (1974); *Frontiero v. Richardson*, 411 U.S. 677 (1973); *Reed v. Reed*, 404 U.S. 71 (1971).

6. See *Planned Parenthood of Southeastern Pa. v. Casey*, 505 U.S. 833 (1992); *Roe v. Wade*, 410 U.S. 113 (1973); *Eisenstadt v. Baird*, 405 U.S. 438 (1972); *Griswold v. Conn.*, 381 U.S. 479 (1965).

7. See *Troxel v. Granville*, 530 U.S. 120 S. Ct. 2054 (2000). As Jill Hasday has recently argued, the situation is very different for single mothers dependent on state assistance, who must tolerate, as a condition of receiving that assistance, considerable inference with their decision-making authority within their families by a wide range of social-service providers. See Jill Elaine Hasday, "Parenthood Divided: A Legal History of the Bifurcated Law of Parental Relations," *Georgetown Law Journal* 90, no. 2 (2002): 299.

8. See *Meyer v. Nebraska*, 262 U.S. 390, 399 (1923).

9. See *Bradwell v. Illinois*, 83 U.S. (16 Wall.) 130 (1873), for a classic example of how this understanding infected the Supreme Court's interpretation of the Constitution.

10. See Becker, supra note 4, at 888. See also Kittay, supra note 1, at 124–31.

11. See Social Security Act, chapter 531, §§ 401–06, 49 Stat. 620, 627–29 (1935). See also Becker, supra note 4, at 888; Sylvia A. Law, "Women, Work, Welfare, and the Preservation of Patriarchy," *University of Pennsylvania Law Review* 131 (1983): 1249, 1254–61.

12. Family and Medical Leave Act of 1993, Pub. L. No. 103-3, 107 Stat. 6 (codified as amended in scattered sections of 2 U.S.C., 5 U.S.C., and 29 U.S.C.).

13. Personal Responsibility and Work Opportunity Reconciliation Act of 1996, Pub. L. No. 104-193, 100 Stat. 2105 (codified as amended in scattered sections of 7 U.S.C., 8 U.S.C., 21 U.S.C., 25 U.S.C., and 42 U.S.C.).

14. Martha A. Fineman, *The Neutered Mother: The Sexual Family and Other Twentieth Century Tragedies* (New York: Routledge, 1995).

15. Kittay, supra note 1.

16. Carol Gilligan, *In a Different Voice: Psychological Theory and Women's Development* (Cambridge, Mass.: Harvard University Press, 1982).

17. Nel Noddings, *Caring: A Feminine Approach to Ethics and Moral Education* (Berkeley: University of California Press, 1984).

18. Bruce A. Ackerman, *We the People* (Cambridge, Mass.: Belknap Press of Harvard University Press, 1991).

19. And, of course, businesses are increasingly dependent on noncaregiving female labor and may be starting to see the advantages of a gender-integrated workforce. All who profit from those businesses—owners, managers, employees, and customers and consumers—have a stake in facilitating the participation of women in them and therefore of strengthening the position of caregivers, both male and female, so as to better enable that participation.

20. See *DeShaney v. Winnebago County Department of Social Services*, 489 U.S. 189 (1989). In *DeShaney*, a four-year-old boy and his mother sued the Winnebago County Department of Social Services for failing to adequately protect him against the abusive violence of his father, which was so severe as to leave him profoundly brain-damaged. The Court held that the plaintiffs had failed to show that the county's social services department was sufficiently involved in the boy's case so as to pass the requisite level of "state action" needed to trigger constitutional guarantees; the Constitution protects us against the actions of states, not private parties.

The Court then went on to claim, although it was not necessary to the "state action" holding, that the Constitution is one of "negative liberties" only, and that for that reason as well, the state had no affirmative obligation to protect Michael DeShaney against private violence. Even if the state of Wisconsin had no police force, the Court claimed, there would be no violation of Michael's or anyone else's constitutional rights to liberty—the Constitution provides only negative rights of protection against excessive state action, not positive rights to some minimal degree of state support or protection.

21. See, generally, Paul Brest and Sanford Levinson, *Processes of Constitutional Decisionmaking: Cases and Materials*, 3d ed. (Boston: Little, Brown, 1992), chapters 9, 11; Geoffrey R. Stone et al., *Constitutional Law*, 3d ed. (Boston: Little, Brown, 1996), chapter 6; *Lochner v. New York*, 198 U.S. 45 (1905); *Hammer v. Dagenhart*, 247 U.S. 251 (1918); *A.L.A. Schechter Poultry Corp. v. United States*, 295 U.S. 495 (1935); *Carter v. Carter Coal Co.*, 298 U.S. 238 (1936).

22. See, e.g., *Prince v. Massachusetts*, 321 U.S. 158, 166 (1943); *Pierce v. Society of the Sisters of the Holy Names of Jesus and Mary*, 268 U.S. 510, 534 (1925); *Meyer v. Nebraska*, 262 U.S. 390, 399 (1923).

23. See *Troxel v. Granville*, 530 U.S. 120 S. Ct. 2054 (2000).

24. The Supreme Judicial Court of Massachusetts' notoriously antimaternalist and antiparentalist reasoning in *Upton v. JWP Businessland* throws even the limited understanding of the social interest in parenting in doubt. In *Upton v. JWP Businessland*, the Court held that it was not a violation of public policy for Businessland to discharge Joanna Upton, an at-will employee, because she was a single mother unwilling to work newly imposed long hours because of her need to care for her young son. See *Upton v. JWP Businessland*, 425 Mass. 756, 757, 682 N.E.2d 1357 (1997). A right to care, if one can be defended, highlights that case's flaws.

25. 381 U.S. 479 (1965).

26. 405 U.S. 438 (1972).

27. 410 U.S. 113 (1973).

28. Again, it is important to note that the right established in *Roe*, *Casey*, and the later "reproductive rights" cases is not the right to have an abortion; it is the right to contract for abortion services, free of undue state interference. It is not a right to the funding necessary to obtain an abortion.

29. It should be noted that other countries embracing a rights tradition, as well as international organizations such as the United Nations, enumerate and attempt to protect

positive rights. The United States' hostility to the possibility of protecting positive rights through constitutional mechanisms can fairly be described as extreme. See generally, Robin West, "Revitalizing Rights," in *Rights*, Robin West, ed. (Burlington: Ashgate, Dartmouth, 2001).

30. Ronald Dworkin, *Taking Rights Seriously* (Cambridge, Mass.: Harvard University Press, 1977).

31. DeShaney, supra note 27, at 195–96.

32. See Morton J. Horwitz, "Rights," *Harvard Civil Rights-Civil Liberties Law Review* 23 (1988): 393; Mark V. Tushnet "An Essay on Rights," *Texas Law Review* 62 (1984): 1363

33. See Susan Bandes, "The Negative Constitution: A Critique," *Michigan Law Review* 88 (1990): 2271.

34. See Mary Ann Glendon, "Rights in Twentieth Century Constitutions," *University of Chicago Law Review* 59 (1992): 519.

35. See Richard S. Markovits, "Legitimate Legal Argument and Internally-Right Answers to Legal-Rights Questions," *Chicago-Kent Law Review* 74 (1999): 415, 426–27.

Part III
Family

[12]

Relational Rights and Responsibilities: Revisioning the Family in Liberal Political Theory and Law

MARTHA MINOW and MARY LYNDON SHANLEY

This article discusses three main orientations in recent works of legal and political theory about the family—contract-based, community-based, and rights-based—and argues that none of these takes adequate account of two paradoxical features of family life and of the family's relationship to the state. A coherent political and legal theory of the family in the contemporary United States requires recognition of the relational rights and responsibilities intrinsic to family life.

Family policy issues in the late twentieth century magnetically collect concerns about the quality of both intimate and civic life. What do people owe one another as family members and as citizens? What are the prospects for sexual equality within the family, and what does such equality have to do with other areas of life? What constellations of people should count as families in the eyes of the law? Should family members be entrusted with life and death decisions such as abortion and euthanasia, and if not, then who should be? Does anyone outside the family, including government, bear responsibility for the health and welfare of children, people with disabilities, and the elderly? These questions have arisen due to changing social mores and practices, new developments in medical and reproductive technologies, and shifting macro-economic patterns. In addition, the collapse of the common law paradigm of the patriarchal family has left political and legal theory with a plethora of competing accounts about the nature of family relationships and of the family's relation to the state. This article examines some of those accounts, and tries to set forth what we see as principles that should guide a family law that respects sexual equality and diversity of family forms, takes seriously the responsibilities generated by family relationships, and recognizes the role of the larger society in sustaining viable and vibrant families.

Martha Minow and Mary Lyndon Shanley 5

The common law understanding of the family, like that of liberal political theory in general, traditionally rested on a particular understanding of the relationship of family members to one another and to the state. That vision of familial and political order regarded the family as a natural, prepolitical, hierarchical, indissoluble, and private association made up of a heterosexual couple and their biological children. Although this view was already under attack by the mid-nineteenth century, and although in the twentieth century families have undergone tremendous sociological changes, neither political and legal theorists nor legislators and judges have agreed on a consistent grounding for family law to take its place.

In surveying recent works of legal and political theory about the family, we find three main orientations—contract-based, community-based, and rights-based—each of which attempts to provide an adequate foundation to replace the reliance on the natural and patriarchal approach of the common law. Contract-based theories respond to the collapse of the hegemony of the traditional model of "family" by suggesting that the law treat the family as a contractual association, allowing the partners to a marriage to set whatever terms to the relationship they choose as long as they provide for the support, education, and well-being of their children (Becker 1981; Kymlicka 1991; Shalev 1989; Shultz 1982; Weisbrod 1994; Weitzman 1974). Community-based theories maintain that the moral standards of the community—whether traditional or newly articulated—delineate boundaries of what will "count" as a family for purposes of receiving recognition from the state and of what practices among people will be protected or supported as appropriate to family life (Elshtain 1991, 1995; Galston 1991; Glendon 1987; Regan 1993; Sandel 1982). Rights-based theories attempt to derive general principles to guide family law, starting from a commitment to equal freedom and opportunity for every individual in society (Okin 1989; Radin 1987, 1995; Hunter 1991).

None of these approaches, in our view, takes adequate account of two paradoxical features of family life and of the family's relation to the state. First, family members are individuals, but they are individuals who are in part defined by their relationships with others. Second, while loving and committed relationships might presumably exist without the state, there are in fact no family or family-like relationships that are not shaped by social practices and state action. Contract-based and many rights-based theories emphasize the individual and so tend to encompass only the first prong of each of these paradoxes; community-based theories emphasize the role of the state and traditional communities in defining family relationships and so tend to encompass the second prong.

We suggest that political theory and family law alike must embrace these paradoxes in their entirety, regarding people simultaneously as individuals and as persons deeply involved in relationships of interdependency and mutual responsibility, and regarding families both as private associations and as entities shaped by social policy and state action. Too often disputes among family members pit the claim of one individual against another without adequate attention to the web of relationships that is not reducible to individual claims. And, as recent contributions of those developing an "ethic of care" have shown, human interdependence may create claims not only on family members and intimate associates but on the public, perhaps acting through government, to provide the material conditions necessary to sustain care-giving relationships essential to human physical and emotional well-being (Gilligan 1982; Ruddick 1989; Tronto 1993; Young 1995). Their insights, we believe, can best be translated into public policy through a concept of relational rights and responsibilities (Burtt 1994; Horsburgh 1992; Minow 1985, 1990).

Theorists and practitioners alike must acknowledge that any resolution of the tension inherent in these paradoxes must inevitably be tentative and temporary, open to discussion and renegotiation. Liberal theory has not traditionally acknowledged the extent to which family policy and family law inevitably reflect political decisions and choices. Yet while family law in the United States gives great importance to individual freedom and equality, these concepts as well as such fundamental issues as the definition of "family" are hotly contested. In shaping law that can deliver justice in the absence of universal agreement, it is not enough to try to take the interests and values of minorities (of race, religion, national origin, sexual orientation, poverty) into account, but to have individuals with those reference points articulate and represent their interests and values themselves. The reshaping of family law and public policy will require not only our best thinking about family life but also a serious democratization of political and legal discussion and decision-making.

CHANGES IN FAMILY LIFE AND LAW FROM THE NINETEENTH CENTURY TO THE MID-TWENTIETH CENTURY

By "liberal" political theory and law we refer to those principles of limited government and individual rights that undergird U.S. political culture and jurisprudence. Although there have always been significant differences among liberal thinkers concerning the nature of the family and its relation to civil society and although the actual provisions of family law have varied over time and in different jurisdictions, certain general features of liberal theory's understanding of proper family relationships and of the relation between the family and the state infused works of liberal theorists and lawyers from the seventeenth century through the nineteenth (see, for example, John Locke [1690], J. S. Mill [1869]). The family was a natural and therefore a "private" association, consisting of a male, a female, and their biological children. In this family the husband/father exercised authority over his wife and children (and in many instances his servants, tenants, and slaves), was responsible for the economic support of members of the household, and represented them in the public sphere. The mother/wife was responsible for managing household life and expenditures, seeing to the physical care of household residents, and providing emotional support and nurture to family members. The responsibility for both the moral education and the economic support of children fell to their parents (but servants, tenants, and slaves did not have claims for such support and education).

This depiction of the family as a natural association that gave authority over children to their parents and over servants to the head-of-household was deeply gendered: the husband had authority over the wife, and the father was the head-of-household. Liberal theory also assumed that there was a clear division between the private realm of the family, created by nature through human sexual mating and reproduction, and the public realm of politics, created by convention through the social contract. Hence at one and the same time liberalism assumed that government authority and law properly regulated public, but not private, matters, and that the representative of the household in the public realm—the citizen—was male (Pateman and Brennan 1979).

There were, of course, always disjunctures between the picture of family in political theory and law and the actual lives of families. In the United States, domestic relations law until the mid-nineteenth century did not encompass the family life of slaves, who instead were governed by slave codes and property laws (Burnham 1987). Neither biological nor affective ties altered slaves' primary legal status as property, even when they were the offspring of the master. Like slaves, children born out-of-wedlock, widows, and abandoned wives and their children as well as those who explicitly rejected conventional family life and instead pursued solitary or communal households fell outside the legal norms of the patriarchal family in nineteenth-century U.S. law (Grossberg 1985; Hartog 1991; Minow 1985; Weisbrod 1980).

The disjunction between the picture of the family in political theory and law and many people's lived or desired experiences grew especially pronounced in the mid-nineteenth century (Minow 1985). Abolitionist efforts before the Civil War brought the experiences of slaves into debates over political rights; the restrictions on marriage, the separation of mothers and children, and the rape of African American women figured prominently in assaults on the institution of slavery. At the same time, both experience in abolition activities and analogies to them enabled white women reformers to seek changes in the legal status of married women and to seek direct political participation through the vote (Yellin 1989). In both respects the women's rights reformers rejected the picture of the wife's legal personality as subsumed in the husband's and instead sought to secure her independent rights to hold property, enter into contracts, and express political preferences. The notion of romantic love and the propriety of individual choice of marriage partner eventually affected views of divorce; lawyers reasoned that if marriage was created by the consent of the parties to live in a certain way, and if one of them violated that agreement, then their union could be dissolved once such "fault" was proved (Grossberg 1985; May 1980). The growing acceptance of formal legal adoption from the mid-nineteenth century on reflected the notion that binding relationships between parent and child could be created by volition and consent as well as by biology, although adoption did try to mirror the "natural family" through efforts to match race and religion as well as to seal from view the adoptee's family of origin (Zainaldin 1979).

Legal and political struggles responded to changing work patterns, tides of immigration, and continuing racial tensions. As unmarried women and immigrant women sought waged work in rapidly urbanizing and industrial America, their activities challenged the seeming inevitability of the male-headed household. More-privileged women who participated in volunteer and club activities similarly explored public spaces and addressed public policy issues in ways that belied the image of women as exclusively "domestic" creatures. In addition, the campaign for prohibiting liquor reflected efforts to bring state power to bear on violence against women and children, and states began to establish foster care, orphanages, and juvenile courts in the early twentieth century. Antiracism efforts first against lynching and then against racial segregation laid the foundations for challenges to antimiscegenation laws and race-matching in adoption by the middle of the twentieth century. Massive migrations from rural to urban areas and from the South to the North, along with continuing streams of immigration, produced countless communities of diversity and enormous personal experiences with change. World War II drew many women into traditionally male employment roles and also gave many African American and other minority men experiences serving the country that contrasted sharply with their continuing treatment as second-class citizens at home. All these experiences created a cauldron for social experimentation and reform movements by midcentury, including the black civil rights movement and the women's liberation movement.

By the mid-1960s, the emergence of a second wave of feminism, critiquing in particular the middle-class nuclear family, underscored the depth of challenge to the conception of the male-headed nuclear family as "natural." The power of husbands over wives was no longer treated as natural and increasingly faced serious challenges in both public and private settings. Egalitarian notions also affected popular and legal views of children. In place of earlier practices that treated children as analogous to property controlled by parents, laws and judicial decisions restricted the power of parents over children in areas such as child labor, extended a certain set of fundamental liberties to children, and invited children's views in matters such as custody following divorce.

Cumulatively, these developments have a common theme: political theorists could no longer view the family as a prepolitical sphere, and legal theorists faced complicated judgments over the extent to which families were private and immune from the intervention of the state. Reformulations led from libertarian or anarchist assertions that the state had no business regulating the terms of interpersonal associations to calls for more stringent restrictions on divorce. The various conceptualizations of family underlying many of the debates on family law and policy reflect the complexity of human aspirations that include the desire to enjoy both autonomy and interrelationship, to savor both independence and intimacy. But while the challenge to the notion that the family is a natural and private association of a heterosexual couple and their biological children was widespread, scholarship did not arrive at consensus on any alternative legal understanding of "family." In the section that follows we survey the three major legal approaches that have attempted to deal with these complexities of family life and family law during the past twenty-five years.

Alternative Views of "The Family" in Contemporary Liberal Theory and Law

Contract-Based Theories: The Primacy of Individual Volition

Ever since Sir Henry Maine characterized the development of modern law as a movement from status to contract, these concepts have been juxtaposed as competing bases for legal regimes: one must choose between ascriptive roles and obligations, on the one hand, or freely chosen roles and obligations, on the other. Hence proponents of a contractual ordering of family life point out the consistency between their views and many of the deepest aspirations of liberal society: the right of individuals to have their freedom limited only by self-assumed obligations.

Given the burdens that ascriptive notions about women's "nature" and proper roles have placed on women seeking equality in both the family and public life, it is not surprising that some feminists see contract as an instrument to provide women greater freedom, self-determination, and equality without subjecting either women or men to traditional sex roles (Fineman 1995; Kymlicka 1991; Shalev 1989; Shultz 1982, 1990; Weisbrod 1994; Weitzman 1974, 1981, 1985). Unlike traditional marriage law's assumptions about the sexual division of labor in both household and larger society, contractual ordering could allow spouses to decide for themselves how to order their personal as well as their financial relationship during their marriage and in the event of divorce. Contracts could also provide for pluralism and a diversity in family life impossible to achieve under a uniform domestic relations law. If marriage were regulated by contract, for example, there would seem to be no reason why two individuals of the same sex should be prohibited from entering such a contract. Arguing both for contractual ordering and for legal recognition of same-sex marriage, Lenore Weitzman asserts that "there is a serious question as to whether the state has any legitimate interest interfering with contracts regarding non-commercial sexual relations between consenting adults," although she acknowledges that legal recognition of same-sex marriages might be hampered by the fact that homosexual relations are "still prohibited by the criminal codes of most states" (Weitzman 1974, 1275 and n. 479). Marjorie Shultz finds that the repeated refusals by the states to formalize unions of same-sex couples by legal marriage "reflect a hesitancy to pursue fully the implications of pluralism and privacy. Where diverse individual outcomes are valued and pluralism is necessary, some form of private ordering of conduct and values is the appropriate regulatory structure" (Shultz 1982, 248). The point of marriage is to create clear expectations and binding obligations to promote stable interpersonal relationships. It is reasonable to ask the state to enforce agreements that would underpin the material aspects of such relationships, but it is not a legitimate concern of the state who may marry whom, or how they should order the personal and material aspects of their relationship.

Proponents of contractual ordering of reproduction see it, like contract marriage, as a way of breaking down gender stereotypes and increasing the scope of human choice in establishing families. Contracts could facilitate diverse ways of bringing children into a family, including children born through contract pregnancies ("surrogate mother" arrangements) and through sperm donation from known donors; a contract might regulate the degree of contact between biological parent(s) and offspring in open adoptions; and in some accounts, it would make adoption a market transaction (Shalev 1989; Robertson 1989; Caplan 1990; Posner 1992). Some feminists welcome contract pregnancy as a way to illustrate that childbearing and child rearing are quite distinct human functions and that child rearing need not be and should not be assigned exclusively to the woman who bears the child (or to women rather than men, for that matter) (Shultz 1990, 304; Shalev 1989, 121). From this perspective, contract pregnancy seems to expand choice for both the woman who bears the child and for the commissioning parent(s). Carmel Shalev argues that one aspect of autonomy is "the deliberate exercise of choice with respect to the individual's reproductive capacity," and that pregnancy contracts should be strictly enforced out of respect for women's decision-making capacity (Shalev 1989, 103).

Contract pregnancy also would allow women who cannot bear children to become parents either alone or with a partner. They could also become parents through foster care and adoption, of course, but a contract pregnancy would allow a couple to become parents without relying on adoption agencies and state departments of social services, to take responsibility for a child even before conception, and sometimes for one or both of them to have a genetic relationship to the child (Shalev 1989; Shultz 1990). Contract pregnancy might also enable a gay couple to have a child to which one of them was biologically related. A contract might allow a lesbian couple wishing to have a child with a known sperm donor to stipulate the nature and degree of his involvement with the child. Contracts could also permit adults who were not in a sexual relationship to share responsibility for child rearing (Young 1995).

While private ordering has liberating aspects, it also entails more worrisome implications. The assumption that bargains will be freely struck masks configurations of social power that provide the backdrop to any contracts. Generations of labor leaders have pointed out the fallacy of assuming that workers and employers were equally free bargaining agents. With respect to the marriage contract, one of John Stuart Mill's great insights in *The Subjection of Women* was his observation that the decision to marry for the vast majority of women could scarcely be called "free." Given women's low wages, scarcity of jobs, and lack of opportunity for higher or even secondary education, marriage was for them a "Hobson's choice": that or none (Mill [1969]). Even the "I do" of someone very much in love and desirous of marriage does not in-and-of-itself guarantee freedom. With respect to contract pregnancy, the notion that the "labor" of pregnancy and childbirth can be sold like any other bodily labor sweeps away "any intrinsic relation between the female owner, her body, and reproductive capacities" (Pateman 1988, 216). As Pateman points out, this objectification of women's bodies and reproductive labor could be more alienating than liberating for many. Furthermore, to depict a woman who agrees to bear a child because it is the only way to bring her household income above the poverty line as exercising her "freedom" ignores the restraints or compulsions of economic necessity.

If contract provides no advantage over public law with respect to enhancing the freedom of parties to either marriage or pregnancy contracts, it similarly offers no guarantee of an equal relationship between the parties to the contract. Leaving decisions about property distribution to contracts between the marriage partners carries no guarantee that such agreements will be more fair than statutory stipulations regarding equitable distribution. Similarly, descriptions of contract pregnancy as nothing more than womb rental in a supposedly neutral market masks the profoundly gendered nature of the structures that surround such transactions. Contractual ordering does not alter those background economic and social conditions that curtail the freedom of some and enhance that of others, that create relationships of domination and subordination between men and women as well as between rich and poor.

Contractual ordering also fails to deal with the fact that certain dependencies that develop in intimate relationships can not be adequately addressed by contract. Persons who may be considered independent actors at the time a contract is signed make whole series of decisions—not only career decisions but other life choices as well—the consequences of which can neither be anticipated nor allocated between the parties when they occur. "Surrogate" mothers who attempt to revoke their agreements often describe the emergence of an unanticipated sense of relationship that emerged unbidden during the course of pregnancy. To speak of the "freedom" of the contracting woman as residing in her intention as an "autonomous" agent misunderstands the relationship between woman and fetus, and the influence of that relationship on the woman's sense of herself (Young 1990, 167; Rich 1976, 47).

The model of the individual on which proposals for contracts-in-lieu-of-marriage and contract pregnancy rests—that of a self-possessing individual linked to others only by agreement—fails to do justice to the complex interdependencies involved in family relations and child rearing. Proposals to replace family law by private ordering reflect the serious limitations of a version of liberalism that understands freedom as the ability to determine and pursue one's goals without interference from government or other individuals, and obligation as arising only from specific acts of the will. It also does away with any recognition of a public interest in the ordering of family relationships. Contractual ordering regards individuals as what Hegel called "immediate self-subsistent persons," abstracted from their social relationships (quoted in Pateman 1983, 95). The bases of marriage, reproductive activity, and family life thus become indistinguishable from those of civic and economic association. From this perspective, as Carole Pateman has pointed out, "Marriage and the family are . . . treated as if they were an extension of civil society and so constituted by, and their relationships exhausted by, contract" (Pateman 1983, 82). Contractual ordering is not so much a movement away from status as its negation or mirror image: "The undifferentiated social bonds of a hierarchy of ascription are replaced by the undifferentiated, universal bond of contract" (Pateman 1983, 95).

In its capacity to replace the outmoded, hegemonic, and frequently oppressive understandings of gender norms of traditional statutory and common law rules infusing family law, contract seems to many advocates of gender equality and pluralism of family forms a tool of liberation. But this tool is too crude to deal with the complex relationships of family life. Although persons may freely decide to marry, marriage itself is a social practice; stipulations governing the rights and responsibilities of spouses and parents reflect shared understandings of propriety and fairness which may be subject to debate, but should not be set aside by idiosyncratic agreements. Too often other people are deeply affected by the contracts over whose terms they have no say. Rejecting the contractarians' notion of marriage as a partnership to be shaped by the wills of the parties, genetic material and babies as marketable resources, and gestation as comparable to any other waged labor, other legal and political theorists emphasize the socially constructed nature of both families and their individual members.

Community-based Theories: The Importance of Social Norms and Traditions of the Good

Unlike contract-based theorists, who leave family definition and responsibilities to the private ordering of individuals, community-based theorists regard families as expressions of personal and social relationships larger than individuals and not resting primarily on agreement (Elshtain 1991, 1995; Galston 1991; Glendon 1987, 1991; Regan 1993; Sandel 1982; Walzer 1983). Community-based theorists reject the picture of the self adopted by contractarians, who start with the autonomous individual and neglect both the context of larger social relationships and "communal notions of equity and responsibility" in relationships (Regan 1993, 42, 168, 125). These theorists all emphasize that families are not simply private associations but also crucial institutions that help compose civil society and the polity.

Some community-based theorists turn to traditional sources to articulate the content of social norms and the shape of relationships endorsed by the community (Glendon 1987, 1991; *Michael H. v. Gerald D.*, opinion for the Court by Justice Antonin Scalia). Others stress a commitment by the society to pursue the common good rather than a regime of entirely private, individual choices (Selznick 1994, 26-28). Some expressly embrace the title "communitarian" in search of public values larger than the preferences of individuals and more than a mere aggregation of those preferences (Galston 1991; Etzioni 1993). They value civil society and criticize liberalism's tendency to ignore or reject history, tradition, or collective decisions about the good life.

Community-based theorists stress that no person becomes autonomous without first going through an extended period of dependency. "Selves" are formed through the intense relationships of infancy and childhood. Community-based theorists also remind us that individuals are shaped by membership in particular ethnic, regional, and religious communities whose values may depart from the values of society's majority. Where contract-based theories would urge freedom for individuals to embrace their own values under a state neutral about all values except individuals' freedom to contract, community-based theories regard it as neither possible nor desirable "that the state should refrain from coercive public judgments about what constitutes the good life for individuals" (Galston 1991, 14).

Many feminists endorse at least parts of the community-based critiques of contractarian versions of liberal individualism. They agree with the critique of autonomous individualism that neglects or distorts how human identities are formed; they add that this picture is deeply gendered in both imagining a male self and neglecting historically female work in nurturing children and dependents (Benhabib and Cornell 1987, 12; Held 1987, 113). In a moving essay on family life Jean Elshtain points out the way in which the notion of the autonomous individual has not only denied the importance of community but has also denigrated women's traditional sphere of activity and ignored the contribution "women's work" has made to sustaining both families and civil society. Any viable human community, she notes, must include persons "devoted to the protection of vulnerable human life. That, historically, has been the mission of women. The pity is not that women reflect an ethic of social responsibility but that the public world has, for the most part, repudiated such an ethic" (Elshtain 1995, 268).

Feminist community-based theorists agree that political life should hold more than the fulfillment of ends chosen independently by individuals (Weiss 1995, 176), and that more than calculated self-interest can and should bind together the political community (Friedman 1993, 285). But while they join other communitarians in the critique of marriage as merely a contract, they are skeptical about turning to traditional articulations of "shared norms about how spouses should act toward one another" as a basis for understanding spousal responsibilities (Regan 1993, 143). These shared norms have been too thoroughly permeated by gender inequality to act as a model for contemporary marriage law. In such discussions, feminists no less than other community-based theorists face difficult disagreements about which norms and values the community should endorse and law should enforce.

These disagreements do not simply track debates over tradition versus change, or social control versus private individual choice. William Galston rejects the assumption that the only political alternatives are liberal neutrality and antiliberalism. There is, he argues, "a third way: a nonneutral, substantive liberalism committed to its own distinctive conception of the good, broadly (though not boundlessly) respectful of diversity, and supported by its own canon of the virtues" (Galston 1991, 44). For Galston, these values include self-restraint, self-transcendence, tolerance, the work ethic, a capacity for moderate delay of gratification, adaptability, the "disposition and the capacity to engage in public discourse," and the "disposition to narrow the gap between principles and practices in liberal society" (Galston 1991, 213-27).

Yet once the topic for debate is the content of values deserving public endorsement and enforcement, disagreements can grow intense even among people who share a critique of the excesses of individualism. Elshtain, for example, argues not only that "the family is a prerequisite for any form of social life" but also that "a particular ideal of the family is imperative to create a more humane society" (Elshtain 1995, 268). Much contemporary debate over families involves disagreements about what precisely the terms of that particular ideal should be, and whose intimate relationships should be excluded from public support or even punished.

Consider the question whether same-sex couples should be allowed to marry. Community-based theorists join in agreeing that this is not a question to be left to the parties themselves, as contractarians would have it. Nor do community-based theorists ask, as rights-based theorists do, whether individuals regardless of sexual orientation should enjoy a right against state control over intimate relationships. Community-based theorists instead view questions such as same-sex marriage as questions for the community to decide, based on tradition, normative theories of the good, or other collective judgments. The result is considerable disagreement.

Jean Elshtain opposes gay and lesbian marriage. She argues that maintaining marriage as a heterosexual union crucially emphasizes the link between sexual expression and procreative activity. The commitments entailed in marriage stand, and should stand, in contrast to unrestrained, public, and commercial sex and the ethos of the " 'wanting' self" so familiar in the world of contract. Although not all families will raise children, "the symbolism of marriage-family as social regenesis is fused in our centuries-old experience with marriage ritual, regulation, and persistence." Because there is great social value in preserving the family as an institution "framed within a horizon of intergenerationality," Elshtain is willing to privilege "a restrictive ideal of sexual and intimate relations" (Elshtain 1991, 686). She would not leave same-sex couples unprotected; she favors ordinances that allow unmarried couples to register as domestic partners and to assume mutual financial responsibility for each other and receive recognition as a couple for certain purposes such as certain insurance and housing. She would, nonetheless, restrict marriage to heterosexual couples in order to emphasize that "marriage is not, and never has been, primarily about two people . . . [but] about the possibility of generativity" (Elshtain 1991, 686).

In contrast, other community-based theorists argue in favor of legalizing marriage for same-sex couples. To do so, they argue, would express the value to society of stable, committed adult relationships, particularly where children are involved. Michael Sandel argues that legal recognition of same-sex marriage would reaffirm the state's interest in protecting the social institution of marriage. Homosexual marriage would reinvigorate "failing public norms of monogamy, loyalty, and mutual care." It would "cultivat[e] the disposition to cooperation rather than competition without which democratic community is unthinkable" (Sandel 1989). Milton Regan favors legalizing gay and lesbian marriage because doing so would recognize "the role of marriage in promoting a relational sense of identity," that is, it would emphasize society's commitment to a noncontractarian view of commitment and responsibility (Regan 1993, 121). Theorists with this perspective would endorse the substantive ends of intimate relationships rather than merely a right of choice in intimate settings.

The arguments on both sides refer to values, traditions, and substantive ends, many of which overlap and converge; nothing internal to this debate can resolve it. Community-based theorists invite and indeed prescribe such debates given their commitment to the substantive good. They further present conflicts over how to ground the values that should prevail and even how to justify critiques of the excesses of individualism. Some, such as Glendon, would combat excessive individualism by norms of individual responsibility and state obligation to protect families (Glendon 1987, 134). Others, such as Galston, pursue community-based norms from a functional or instrumental perspective; social power should be deployed to reduce divorce, for example, in order to lessen the chances that children of divorce fail to grow into independent and contributing members of the society, economic community, and polity (Galston 1991, 287). Still others focus on the violation of traditions of human integrity presented by market approaches, such as contract pregnancy (Rhode 1989, 225), or on the need to revitalize traditions such as the centrality of status (Regan 1993, 151-53).

Having embraced as a political task the substantive choices about families and intimate roles and duties, community-based theorists have to confront deep divisions about policy choices and the values implicated by them. Religious and cultural views and practices vary regarding what kind of family form is desirable, who is a good parent, what range of choice should be granted over reproduction and to whom, and what duties adult children owe their parents. The community-based theories lack the easy accommodation for pluralism afforded by contract-based theories that leave many such matters to private agreement; they also lack a similar accommodation for pluralism afforded by rights-based theories that endorse individual freedoms.

The community-based theories proceed instead with the view that one way of life is to be preferred or some are to be disfavored. Not only does this view run counter to the liberty and tolerance usually advocated in pluralist societies, it also invites potentially unresolvable and intense conflicts about what should and should not be preferred. For forcing authoritative decisions about the issues that contract-based and rights-based theorists would reserve to private individuals, community-based theorists may exacerbate social and political divisions along religious and cultural lines. A response to similar conflicts prompted the development of individual rights frameworks in eighteenth-century Europe, and many legal and political theorists seize the vision of individual freedoms and equality in a third, rights-based approach to family law.

Rights-based Theories: The Tension Between Individualism and Family Relationship

Community-based theories seem to invite disputes over what kinds of families and family values society should endorse, whereas contract-based approaches seem to promote pluralism of family forms and intimate choices yet simultaneously fail to protect individuals against oppressive bargains and ongoing patterns of social inequality. Advocates of rights-based approaches to family law seem to hope that they will be able to promote pluralism while also putting forward as societal values certain basic freedoms guaranteed to each individual. Such approaches are rooted both in classical liberalism and in U.S. constitutionalism.

Extending individual rights to the realm of families is a relatively new phenomenon: prior to the mid-twentieth century, the Supreme Court seldom confronted disputes claiming constitutionally protected rights associated with family formation or dissolution, definitions of kinship or affiliation, and obligations of care and support based on family ties. Instead, those matters remained subject to state regulation, and often the states in turn relied on traditions, religious or otherwise. The states did define terms for family formation and dissolution but also tended to exempt families from otherwise prevailing rules of contract, tort, and criminal law. In these respects, U.S. courts followed a tradition of noninterference in family lives, at least when that tradition coincided with state purposes and values. Notable exceptions required parents to comply with compulsory school laws for their children, and subjected, in particular, poor, immigrant, African American, and Native American families to surveillance, which at times led to the removal of children from their family homes.

In the mid-twentieth century, litigation involving various "rights" of family members began to impart a federal, constitutional dimension to family law. The Supreme Court pronounced constitutional bases for a right to marry (*Loving v. Virginia* 1967); the right to procreate (*Skinner v. Oklahoma* 1942; *Griswold v. Connecticut* 1965); the right not to procreate (*Griswold v. Connecticut* 1965; *Eisenstadt v. Baird* 1972; *Roe v. Wade* 1973); the right to retain or establish parental ties (*Stanley v. Illinois* 1972; *Lehr v. Robertson* 1983). The Court rejected claims for a right to engage in consensual homosexual activity (*Bowers v. Hardwick* 1986), and restricted claims of parental status outside of marriage (*Lehr v. Robertson* 1983; *Michael H. v. Gerald D.* 1989). The Court also recognized as worthy of constitutional protection certain claims of parental decision-making power (*Wisconsin v. Yoder* 1972; *Parham v. J.R.* 1979) and family privacy (*Moore v. City of East Cleveland* 1977).

Two fundamental conceptions of rights undergird these decisions. The first views the family as a unitary entity, entitled to protection from state scrutiny or interference; the second locates rights in distinct individuals who should be guarded from state obstruction in intimate choices and behaviors (Hearst 1995; Minow 1988). Both approaches offer a critical purchase on otherwise prevailing governmental actions, but the second in particular begins to challenge legal assumptions about proper family relationships. Elizabeth Schneider has documented efforts to marshal individual rights against assault by spouses, and against the screen of family privacy that had shielded such practices from arrest, prosecution, and punishment (Schneider 1985, 1992). Nan Hunter, Sylvia Law, and more recently William Eskridge have asserted individual rights to marry that should extend to couples of the same sex, in part to counter gender hierarchies that hurt women even in heterosexual marriages (Hunter 1991; Law 1988; Eskridge 1993). The prevalence of constitutional theories about marriage prompts one commentator to label his criticism of such theories a "dissenting view" (Maltz 1992). Nancy Polikoff argues that courts should recognize that both partners in a lesbian couple should have parental rights with regard to children living in their household (Polikoff 1990).

Commentators using rights discourse are not always in agreement over what rights are relevant and which should prevail in any particular case. John Robertson advocates recognition of a right to use medical technology and to purchase genetic and gestational services from others (Robertson 1983, 1989). In contrast, Margaret Jane Radin invokes rights of individuals to resist the incursions of the market especially in the context of genetic material and "surrogate", or contract mother arrangements (Radin 1987, 1995).

The most pronounced conflict, however, pits the vision of individuals enjoying rights against the picture of the family as a unitary entity entitled to rights against state intrusion. Many of the asserted individual rights specifically prevail upon the state to pry behind closed doors to family homes either to protect individuals from harm or to enable them to alter the otherwise prevailing pattern of relationships. Thus, the right to be free from abuse in marriage brings the state into the household by justifying actual police investigations and more basically by instituting a norm of mutual respect between spouses. The right to choose contraception or abortion enables not just a couple but an individual to make choices without the interference of others, including the intimate partner.

Although John Rawls notably neglects the internal ordering of families, his work has strengthened the intellectual resources for rights-based theories. *A Theory of Justice* develops a strong foundation for notions of individual rights even when they challenge traditions and conventions. Rawls's work has also led to debates about what the rights pertaining to family members might be, and whether a rights-based discourse is, in the end, adequate for a political or legal theory of the family. Notably, Susan Okin criticizes Rawls for failing to take gender seriously in formulating the principles of justice and for failing to carry these principles fully into the context of families (Okin 1989, 89-109). Attacking the common law notion that the family is a unitary entity that should be shielded from the state's prying eye, Okin argues that the traditional liberal defense of family privacy has made it difficult to recognize the gender inequality that permeates social and legal arrangements affecting women's lives in both families and civil society. Okin maintains further that when Rawls identifies "the monogamous family" as one of the major social institutions that is to be guided by his two principles of justice, he fails to acknowledge that most families violate the principle of equal liberty and the principle that any inequalities should work to the benefit of the least well-off. No one uncertain about what sex he or she will have, Okin argues, would accept the prevailing gender structures of society and the family as just.

This argument by Okin makes tremendous strides toward a theory of justice addressing families. It demands that such a theory explore the ways that gender-based practices affect the distribution of power and goods both in families and in larger social institutions, and in the interaction between both realms. Similarly, Okin opens the way toward consideration of state recognition for relationships between same-sex couples as part of a larger effort to eliminate the significance of gender roles (Okin 1996).

Eva Kittay similarly sets forth grounds for rejecting Rawls's assumptions about families. Like Okin, she rejects his assumption that heads-of-households can be understood as mutually disinterested decision-makers except regarding intergenerational ties (Okin 1989; Kittay 1995, 13). Missing from Rawls's view is attention to those relationships of care-giving and dependency that exist not simply between generations, but among those living at the same time. Dependency may arise from youth or age, disability or illness, or mutual reliance; neither dependent people nor those who care for them conform to the model of the self-sufficient, autonomous individual presumed by liberal theorists such as Rawls (Kittay 1995, 14-16).

In this respect, Kittay, along with others, criticizes the very conception of liberal rights insofar as it neglects the significance of care and relationships of care to both a theory of justice and an ideal way of life. Kittay joins others such as Annette Baier, Carol Gilligan, Virginia Held, Sara Ruddick and Joan Tronto who regard it as a moral imperative that all people should benefit from conditions for continuous care and connection (Baier 1985; Gilligan 1982; Held 1987; Ruddick 1989; Tronto 1993). An ethic of care that values the efforts of continuous attention and help must find a place in any adequate account of family lives and in any just family law. The work of theorists who explore an ethic of care tends to expose a conceptual limitation in rights, conventionally conceived, as a basis of thinking about families: whether assigned to individuals or to families as entities, rights may fail to highlight, protect, or define relationships of moral connection. Yet so many rights associated with family life—the rights to marry, to divorce, to receive child support, to procreate—involve not individuals per se but the claims, responsibilities, and boundaries of particular human relationships. Defining such rights requires articulation of the moral predicates and scope of such relationships (Minow 1990; Kiss forthcoming).

In their rejection of the model of the self-sufficient and self-interested individual, community-based theorists critical of the liberal tradition do not distinguish contractarian from rights-based approaches in political theory and law. We agree that a political theory inattentive to the connections between and among people can never adequately address themes and issues facing families, but we think it important to distinguish contractarian and rights-based views. Contractarian views acknowledge human relationships but treat them all as chosen and susceptible to market or market-like bargains. Little scope for public articulation of values persists in a contract-based regime beyond preservation of the institution of contract and perhaps rejection of extreme bargains. Rights-based views instead require public articulation of the kinds of freedoms that deserve protection and the qualities of human dignity that warrant societal support.

Moreover, whether acknowledged or not, rights articulate relationships among people. Every freedom of action guaranteed to an individual demands as a correlate constraints of respect by other individuals (Minow 1990; Kiss forthcoming). In the context of family matters, rights-based theories need to acknowledge more fully their relational dimensions and draw on the insights of those who study caretaking.

This route—enriching rights-based theories with strong attention to relationships and their preconditions—holds more promise for family law than the other approaches surveyed here. Contract-based theories promote individual freedoms but neglect social values and concerns about inequality and dignity; community-based theories articulate shared values but risk constraining individual freedoms and social pluralism while prompting greater social conflict. Rights-based theories invigorate as social values respect for certain individual freedoms, but they historically lack a rich understanding of relationships, including their preconditions, their responsibilities, and their consequences. In the next section we consider whether and how a notion of relational rights, informed by theories of caretaking and moral relationships, might address a variety of difficult issues confronting family policy and law.

Elements of an Adequate Theory of Family Law: Relational Rights and Responsibilities

This discussion of three contemporary approaches to family law illuminates the difficulty of framing family law in the face of both vast social changes and the collapse of the common law paradigm of the family as a unitary, hierarchical, and indissoluble entity. Difficult policy issues demand answers and simultaneously reveal the inadequacy of current normative resources undergirding family law. Among these issues are those concerning:

> —the place of biology in reproduction: What, if any, claims should those with biological ties have regarding the conception, gestation, birth, and custody of a child?

—sexual orientation: What relations between adult homosexual partners, and among homosexual parents and minor children, should the state permit or promote?

—the preference or privilege that might attach to families formed according to legal formalities compared with families formed informally: Should those in legally executed marriage and adoption receive benefits denied to those in informal arrangements?

—the role of the market in forming family relationships: Should people be able to contract for the conception and/or gestation of a child? for a child available for adoption? for sexual services? for spouses?

—the role of government money in providing support for families: Should government subsidize child care, respite care, care of ill or disabled family members?

—the relationship of the workplace to family life: Should workplaces be structured to favor or support one or more types of families? Should work loads in the paid labor force be rendered more flexible to accommodate demands of children, elderly relatives, or other family duties?

—the relative power of family members in family-related decision-making: Is there any legal or philosophical basis for granting greater power to one member of an adult partnership, such as in decisions over abortion and child custody? In decisions about custody, how (if at all) should decision-making power be allocated between parents and children? In medical treatment decisions, how should the views of patients, spouses, and other relatives be collected and given force?

—racial and religious identities: Is there any place for racial or religious identity as a basis for decision-making by the state in disputes over child custody or rules governing foster care, adoption, marriage, divorce, and medical treatment?

—dependency, disability, and illness: Who is responsible for the daily care and financial support of dependents such as children, elderly people, and people with severe disabilities or illnesses? What degree of family relationship establishes such responsibilities?

Each of these issues has arisen because of new technologies, changing social practices, and conflicts among normative or ethical perspectives. The hard choices each poses for policymakers indicate the extent to which family law and family policy reflect both human social practices and institutions, and conscious political choices. These choices require argument, debate, and continual assessment and reassessment in light of experience and values.

But to say that family law is properly the product of political discussion and negotiation is not to say that it cannot be based on principle. It is, rather, to say that in a world in which social and material conditions change over time, the way in which law reflects fundamental principles will change too.

We believe that any adequate family law must be based on principles that take account of two paradoxical characteristics of family life and the family's relationship to the state. First, the individual must be seen simultaneously as a distinct individual and as a person fundamentally involved in relationships of dependence, care, and responsibility. For example, a woman who agrees to bear a child for someone else must be viewed both as a responsible agent and as someone who, after bearing a fetus to term, has established some relationship to the child. A court deciding who shall have custody of the child she has borne and now wishes to keep must neither reduce the case to the enforcement of a contract nor regard the fact of childbearing alone as determining parental claims (Shanley 1993; see also Shanley 1995). Similarly, when either same-sex or heterosexual couples who share custody of children separate or divorce, rulings determining financial support and child custody or visitation must consider each party to such actions both as separate adults and as individuals-in-relationship. The law must allow parents to resume their independence and to remarry or form new relationships if they wish, but the law must also enforce the continuing obligations each has to their children. Those obligations are not only for financial support, but may also include requirements that one parent not take actions that would jeopardize the possibility of a continuing relationship between the other parent and the child.

Second, family law and political theory must take account of the additional paradox that family relationships are simultaneously outside of and yet shaped by the political order. Even confining our view to Western societies, the forms family associations take are clearly affected by law. People's views of who might be a possible marriage partner are shaped by the prohibited degrees of kinship and bans on same-sex and polygamous marriages. Laws also have affected who were regarded as parents and children; legal adoption allowed the creation of nonbiological family ties, while bastardy statutes denied any legal significance whatsoever to the biological tie between offspring and parents (Grossberg 1985). Yet families were clearly not creatures of the state like joint-stock companies and limited partnerships. With the exception of bastardy statutes, the biological tie between an adult and his or her offspring has been taken to establish prima facie parental rights and obligations; few have proposed that children, at birth, be assigned to the best possible caretaker, rather than to their biological parents.

Moreover, peoples' lives as family members are importantly framed and influenced by practices and decisions of the larger society. Some of those practices and decisions impose burdens and allocate benefits according to generally held views about acceptable family and public behaviors; for example, nepotism laws both reflected and enforced norms against married women's working outside the home. Others reflect matters including but not limited to macroeconomic policies that set the acceptable level of unemployment, and therefore the availability of jobs; resources devoted to public transportation; and employment practices that affect equal opportunity regardless of gender, race, or other characteristics. The current practice of contract pregnancy in the United States, for example, is shaped by cultural norms that link maternity and womanhood very closely and that regard biological ties to the children one raises as highly desirable, and by economic structures that have made paid gestational labor an attractive job relative to other available options for some women and couples.

We have argued that neither a contract-based approach nor a community-based approach takes adequate account of these two paradoxical aspects of family life. While a contractarian view of marriage emphasizes the need to accommodate differences among individuals and within relationships, it encompasses only the first part of each paradox, ignoring responsibilities that may not be readily dealt with by contract and the social and economic contexts that influence the choices made by family members. While community-based theories understand the importance of tradition and social context in shaping individuals and their relationships, they risk marginalizing perspectives of members of nontraditional groups that have not historically had strong political representation. A conception of relational rights and responsibilities, we believe, would not regard "rights" as belonging to individuals and arising from the imperative of self-preservation, but rather would view rights as claims grounded in and arising from human relationships of varying degrees of intimacy, what Kenneth Karst has called "intimate associations" (Karst, 1980).

Relational rights and responsibilities should draw attention to the claims that arise out of relationships of human interdependence. Those claims entitle people to explore a range of relationships and in so doing to draw sustenance from the larger community. A focus on relational rights and responsibilities might examine the legality of same-sex marriage by considering the place of such proposed relationships in the lives of those immediately involved and those in the surrounding community. Similarly, in thinking about cases in which a gestational mother who is party to a pregnancy contract wishes to keep the child rather than turn him or her over to the other contracting party, attention to relational rights and responsibilities requires consideration of the relationship between the gestational mother and the baby, the potential relationship between the commissioning parent(s) and the baby, and the baby's need for ongoing relationships with adults who assume full parental responsibilities. The issues for resolution thus are not simply the rights of adults who entered a contract, nor of community standards about contracts in such circumstances, but the moral and psychological dimensions of persons whose claims arise out of actual and potential relationships. In other disputes concerning child custody, a focus on relational rights and responsibilities would give great weight to preserving some continuity of relationships.

An adequate theory of family law would also have to recognize the relationship between family life and the political and economic order. Here again a vital conception of relationships and responsibilities would help. Each intimate relationship is in turn embedded in relationships of neighbors, religious and ethnic groups, and even relationships of strangers, all deeply affected but not entirely determined by the political system and economic circumstances. Connecting these relationships to a vibrant sense of responsibility would engage wide circles of people, including even public-policymakers and voters who would need to consider what social and economic structures are necessary to permit continuous, caring human relationships especially responsive to those most dependent on such care. As Kittay argues, "A society cannot be well-ordered, that is, it cannot be one in which all its members are sustained and included within the ideal of equality, if it fails to be a society characterized by care" (Kittay 1995, 24). The polity cannot presuppose the contribution made by caregivers to maintaining the social and political order, but "must take upon itself the primary responsibility of maintaining structures that will support the principles of care" (Kittay 1993, 7b).

Expanding our understanding of the individual to encompass relationships of interdependency would invigorate private and public responses to family issues. Acknowledging the interdependence of family members and the larger polity itself is crucial, although this is simply a beginning, not an end, of the analysis. For then the society, whether through law or other means, must still address what criteria should be used to resolve disputes over what should count within the very definition of "family" and what constellation of intimate relations should receive the special resources of public approval and recognition. The resolution of such issues, we argue, requires not only reasoned deliberation but also politics and a political practice revised along the principles of justice aimed to produce participation by the full variety of human being in the society.

A satisfactory theory of family law would thus have to reach the operations of the political and legal systems that generate and implement family law. The theory would need to justify reforms so that people who are presently marginalized could come to participate effectively in the debates and decisions that frame entitlements essential to sustaining viable family lives.

This last point connects families and politics more directly than the familiar but still important point that families prepare new generations of political actors (Tocqueville 1954; Mill [1969]; Chodorow 1978; Okin 1989; Sennett 1977). That important fact does justify greater public attention to the work of families and greater public resources to support that work. More basically, however, families cannot fully teach justice in the absence of a just family law. The creation of a just family law requires reform not only of family law itself but also of the larger political and legal processes by which family law is created and applied. If the political process employed to explore and debate the nature and status of family life itself does not redress the structures of hierarchy that have permeated the family, then the resulting political choices about family are suspect. Exclusions and disadvantages on the basis of gender, race, ethnicity, religion, and class have rendered problematic the conventional conception of family in political and legal discourse. If those same exclusions and disadvantages characterize the political process intended to rectify these shortcomings, political constructions of the family cannot be deemed legitimate according to the criteria of a liberal democracy. For this reason, an adequate political and legal theory of the family must include attention to the political process through which choices about family status and family relations are produced. In particular, an adequate political theory of the family cannot presuppose equality and full and fair representation in the political process. We suggest that the United States cannot claim to have a legitimate family policy unless and until the political process that produces it is more inclusive and trustworthy than it is at present.

A political and legal theory that took into account the two paradoxical aspects of family membership in a liberal society to which we have called attention here would not provide ready, easy, or generally acceptable answers to difficult questions such as those we raise at the beginning of this section. It would, however, provide the analytic, intellectual, and rhetorical resources for approaching such questions. It would help to ensure that the contractarian models of economic life do not take over all other areas of public life or of family relationships, and that a search for common norms does not eliminate pluralism or curtail privacy. It would also put the prerequisites of relationships of care at the center of concern, rather than treat them as incidental effects of individual choices or needs. A theory of relational rights and responsibilities would encompass not only individual freedoms but also rights to enter and sustain intimate associations consistent with public conceptions of the responsibilities those associations entail, underscoring the connection between families and the larger community. Progress in thinking about and addressing the complex issues concerning family life that have arisen from the demise of the common law model of the patriarchal family, sociological changes in family structures, and developments in reproductive technology seems most likely to develop from a political and legal theory that focuses on the relationships that constitute family life and the preconditions necessary to sustain such relationships.

NOTE

We gratefully acknowledge the help of Alice Hearst, Uma Narayan, the anonymous reviewers, and the editors of this issue on an earlier version of this essay.

REFERENCES

Baier, Annette. 1985. Caring about caring. In *Postures of the mind: Essays on mind and morals*. Minneapolis: University of Minnesota Press.
Bartlett, Katharine. 1984. Rethinking parenthood as an exclusive status: The need for legal alternatives when the premise of the nuclear family has failed. *Virginia Law Review* 70(5): 879-963.
Becker, Gary S. 1981. *A treatise on the family*. Cambridge: Harvard University Press.
Benhabib, Seyla, and Drucilla Cornell. 1987. Introduction: Beyond the politics of gender. In *Feminism as critique*, ed. Seyla Benhabib and Drucilla Cornell. Minneapolis: University of Minnesota Press.
Burnham, Margaret. 1987. An impossible marriage: Slave law and family law. *Journal of Law and Inequality* 5(2): 187-225.
Burtt, Shelley. 1994. Reproductive responsibilities: Rethinking the fetal rights debate. *Policy Science* 27(2-3): 179-96.
Caplan, Lincoln. 1990. *An open adoption*. New York: Farrar, Strauss and Giroux.
Chodorow, Nancy. 1978. *The reproduction of mothering: Psychoanalysis and the sociology of gender*. Berkeley: University of California Press.
Cohen, Joshua. 1992. Okin on justice, gender, and the family. *Canadian Journal of Philosophy* 22(2): 263-86.
Elshtain, Jean Bethke. 1991. Accepting limits. *Commonweal* 18(20) (22 November): 685-86.
———. [1982] 1995. Feminism, family, and community. In *Feminism and Community*, ed. Penny Weiss and Marilyn Friedman. Philadelphia: Temple University Press.
Elshtain, Jean Bethke et al. 1993. A communitarian position on the family. *National Civic Review* (Winter): 25-35.
Eskridge, William. 1993. A history of same-sex marriage. *Virginia Law Review* 79(7): 1419-1513.
Etzioni, Amitai. 1993. *The spirit of community: Rights, responsibilities, and the communitarian agenda*. New York: Crown Publishers.
Fineman, Martha Albertson. 1991. *The illusion of equality: The rhetoric and reality of divorce reform*. Chicago: University of Chicago Press.
———. Review of *Justice, gender, and the family*. Ethics 102(3): 647-49.
———1995. *The neutered mother, the sexual family, and other twentieth-century tragedies*. New York: Routledge.

Friedman, Marilyn. 1993. Feminism and modern friendship: Dislocating the community. In *Friendship: A philosophical reader*, ed. Neera Kapur Badhwar. Ithaca: Cornell University Press.

Galston, William. 1991. *Liberal purposes: Goods, virtues, and diversity in the liberal state.* Cambridge: Cambridge University Press.

Gilligan, Carol. 1982. *In a different voice.* Cambridge: Harvard University Press.

Glendon, Mary Ann. 1987. *Abortion and divorce in Western law.* Cambridge: Harvard University Press.

———. 1991. *Rights talk: The impoverishment of politics.* Cambridge: Harvard University Press.

Grossberg, Michael. 1985. *Governing the hearth: Law and family in nineteenth-century America.* Chapel Hill: University of North Carolina Press.

Hartog, Hendrick. 1991. Marital exists and marital expectations in 19th century America. *Georgetown Law Journal* 80(October): 95-129.

Hearst, Alice. 1995. Domesticating reason: Families and good citizens. Paper presented at Law and Society Association Conference, Toronto, Ontario, 3 June.

Held, Virginia. 1987. The non-contractual family: A feminist view. *Canadian Journal of Philosophy*. Supplementary 13.

Holmes, Stephen. 1993. *The anatomy of anti-liberalism.* Cambridge: Harvard University Press.

Horsburgh, Beverly. 1992. Redefining the family: Recognizing the altruistic caregiver and the importance of relational needs. *University of Michigan Journal of Law Reform* 25(2): 423-564.

Hunter, Nan. 1991. Marriage, law, and gender: A feminist inquiry. *Law and Inequality* (1): 9-ff.

Karst, Kenneth L. 1980. The freedom of intimate association. *Yale Law Journal* 89(4): 624-92.

Kiss, Elizabeth. forthcoming. Alchemy or fool's gold? Assessing feminist doubts about rights. *Contentious concepts: feminist perspectives on political theory*, ed. Mary Lyndon Shanley and Uma Narayan. Cambridge: Polity Press.

Kittay, Eva Feder. 1993. Taking dependency seriously: Equality, social cooperation, and The Family and Medical Leave Act considered in light of the social organization of dependency work. Paper delivered at Conference on Feminism and Social Action, University of Pittsburgh, November.

———. 1995. Taking dependency seriously: The Family and Medical Leave Act considered in the light of the social organization of work and gender equality. *Hypatia* 10(1): 8-30.

Kymlicka, Will. 1991. Rethinking the family. *Philosophy and Public Affairs* 20(1): 77-98.

Law, Sylvia. 1988. Homosexuality and the social meaning of gender. *Wisconsin Law Review* 2: 187-235.

Littleton, Christine. 1987. Equality across difference: A place for rights discourse? *Wisconsin Women's Law Journal* 3: 189-212.

Locke, John. [1690] 1980. *Second treatise of government.* Ed. C. B. Macpherson. Indianapolis: Hackett.

Maltz, Earl M. 1992. Constitutional protection for the right to marry: A dissenting view. *George Washington Law Review* 60(4): 949-68.

May, Elaine Tyler. 1980. *Great expectations: Marriage and divorce in post-Victorian America.* Chicago: University of Chicago Press.

Mill, John Stuart. [1869] 1988. *The subjection of women*. Ed. Susan Moller Okin. Indianapolis: Hackett.
Minow, Martha. 1985. "Forming under everything that grows": Toward a history of family law. *Wisconsin Law Review* 4: 819-98.
———. 1988. We, the family: Constitutional rights and American families. In *The Constitution and American life*, ed. David Thelen. Ithaca: Cornell University Press.
———. 1990. *Making all the difference: Inclusion, exclusion, and American law*. Ithaca: Cornell University Press.
Okin, Susan Moller. 1989. *Justice, gender, and the family*. New York: Basic Books.
———. 1996. Sexual orientation, gender, and families: Dichotomizing differences. *Hypatia* 11(1): 30-48.
Pateman, Carole. 1983. The shame of the marriage contract. In *Women and men's wars*, ed. Judith Stiehm. New York: Pergamon Press.
———. 1988. *The sexual contract*. Stanford: Stanford University Press.
Pateman, Carole, and Teresa Brennan. 1979. "Mere auxiliaries to the commonwealth": Women and the origins of liberalism. *Political Studies* 27(2): 183-200.
Polikoff, Nancy. 1990. This child does have two mothers: Redefining parenthood to meet the needs of children in lesbian-mother and other non-traditional families. *Georgetown Law Review* 78(3): 459-575.
Posner, Richard. 1992. *Sex and reason*. Cambridge: Harvard University Press.
Radin, Margaret J. 1987. Market inalienability. *Harvard Law Review* 100(8): 1849-1937.
———. 1995. What, if anything, is wrong with baby-selling? *Pacific Law Journal* 135-45.
Rawls, John. 1971. *A theory of justice*. Cambridge: Harvard University Press.
Regan, Milton C. 1993. *Family law and the pursuit of intimacy*. New York: New York University Press.
Rhode, Deborah. 1989. *Justice and gender: Sex discrimination and the law*. Cambridge: Harvard University Press.
Rich, Adrienne. 1976. *Of woman born: Motherhood as experience and as institution*. New York: Norton, Bantam.
Robertson, John. 1983. Procreative liberty and the control of contraception, pregnancy, and childbirth. *Virginia Law Review* 69(3): 405-62.
———. 1989. Embryos, families, and procreative liberty. *Southern California Law Review* 59(5): 939-1041.
Ruddick, Sara. 1989. *Maternal thinking*. Boston: Beacon Press.
Sandel, Michael J. 1982. *Liberalism and the limits of justice*. Cambridge: Cambridge University Press.
———. 1989. Moral argument and liberal toleration: Abortion and homosexuality. *Californial Law Review* 77(3): 521-38.
Schneider, Elizabeth M. 1986. The dialectic of rights and politics: Perspectives from the women's movement. *New York University Law Review* 61: 589-ff.
———. 1992. Particularity and generality: Challenges of feminist theory and practice in work on woman-abuse. *Brooklyn Law Review* 67(3): 520-68.
Selznick, Philip. 1994. Foundations of communitarian liberalism. *The responsive community* 4(4) (Fall): 16-28.
Sennett, Richard. 1977. *The fall of public man*. New York: Knopf.
Shalev, Carmel. 1989. *Birth power*. New Haven: Yale University Press.
Shanley, Mary Lyndon. 1995. Fathers' rights, mothers' wrongs? Reflections on unwed fathers' rights and sex equality. *Hypatia* 10(1): 74-103.

———. 1993. "Surrogate mothering" and women's freedom: A critique of contracts for human reproduction. *Signs* 18(3): 618-39.

———. 1989. *Feminism, marriage, and the law in Victorian England, 1850-1895.* Princeton: Princeton University Press.

Shultz, Marjorie Maguire. 1982. Contractual ordering of marriage: A new model for state policy. *California Law Review* 70(2): 204-334.

———. 1990. Reproductive technology and intention-based parenthood: An opportunity for gender neutrality. *Wisconsin Law Review* 2: 297-398.

Tocqueville, Alexis de. 1954. *Democracy in America.* New York: Vintage Books.

Tronto, Joan. 1993. *Moral boundaries: A political argument for an ethic of care.* New York: Routledge.

Walzer, Michael. 1983. *Spheres of justice: A defense of pluaralism and equality.* New York: Basic Books.

Weisbrod, Carol. 1980. *The boundaries of utopia.* New York: Pantheon.

———. 1994. The way we live now: A discussion of contracts and domestic relations. *Utah Law Review* 2: 777-815.

Weiss, Penny A. 1995. Feminism and contractarianism: Comparing critiques of liberalism. In *Feminism and community*, ed. Penny A. Weiss and Marilyn Friedman. Philadelphia: Temple University Press.

Weitzman, Lenore. 1974. Marriage contracts. *California Law Review* 62(4): 1169-1258.

———. 1981. *The marriage contract: Spouses, lovers, and the law.* New York: Free Press.

———. 1985. *The divorce revolution: Unexpected social and economic consequences for women and children in America.* New York: Free Press.

Weston, Kath. 1991. *Families we choose: Lesbians, gays, kinship.* New York: Columbia University Press.

Williams, Patricia. 1991. *The alchemy of race and rights.* Cambridge: Harvard University Press.

Yellin, Jean F. 1989. *Women and sisters: The antislavery feminists in American culture.* New Haven: Yale University Press.

Young, Iris. 1995. Mothers, citizenship, and independence: A critique of pure family values. *Ethics* 105(3): 535-56.

———. 1990. Pregnant embodiment: Subjectivity and alienation. In *"Throwing like a girl" and other essays in feminist philosophy and social theory.* Bloomington: Indiana University Press.

Zainaldin, Jamil S. 1979. The emergence of a modern American family law: Child custody, adoption, and the courts, 1796-1851. *Northwestern University Law Review* 73(6): 1038-89.

[13]

Group Identity and Women's Rights in Family Law: The Perils of Multicultural Accommodation*

AYELET SHACHAR
Legal Ethics, Yale Law School

In 1941, Julia Martinez, a full-blooded member of the Santa Clara Pueblo tribe and a citizen of the United States who resided on the Santa Clara Reservation in Northern New Mexico, married a non-tribal husband and gave birth to a daughter named Audrey. Audrey was brought up on the Pueblo, spoke the Tewa language, participated in its life, and was culturally, for all practical purposes, a Santa Claran Indian. However, according to Pueblo personal status law, she was not an Indian by "blood." Membership in the tribe was granted either to children whose parents were both Pueblo members or to children of *male* members who married outside the tribe; membership, however, was denied to children of *female* members who married outside the tribe. After unsuccessful efforts to persuade the tribe to change its gender-discriminatory membership rule, Julia and Audrey Martinez filed a lawsuit in a federal court, seeking declaratory and injunctive relief which would enable Audrey and similarly situated children to acquire tribal membership. In 1978, the equal protection claim raised by Martinez was rejected by the US Supreme Court on the basis of a "non-intervention" rationale.[1] Thus, while the *Martinez* case strengthened the autonomy of the Pueblo vis-à-vis the state,[2] it also, like many other instances of multicultural accommodation, perpetuated the systematic intra-group maltreatment of a particular category of insider (in this case, women who married non-tribal husbands and the children born of those unions) *in accordance with their group's accommodated traditions.*

The *Martinez* case and other legal cases from countries such as Israel and India, which have already implemented accommodationist policies in the family

*As ever, I am indebted to Ran Hirschl for his keen critiques. His comprehensive involvement and enthusiasm made the writing of this article possible. I would also like to thank Bruce Ackerman, Jack Balkin, Joe Carens, Jay Katz, Chandran Kukathas, Will Kymlicka, Reva Siegel, Joseph Weiler, Rachael Wilson and the anonymous readers for helpful comments. Special thanks to Bob Goodin for his invaluable advice and suggestions. I gratefully acknowledge the support of the W.M. Keck Foundation and the Yale Law School.

[1]Santa Clara Pueblo v. Martinez, 436 US 49 at 52, 54, 62–5 (1978) [hereinafter the *Martinez* case]. For a thorough exploration of the *Martinez* case, see Resnik (1989).

[2]My usage of the term "state" here and throughout the article is interchangeable with the term "central government."

law arena, challenge the presumption that group-differentiated rights, which aim to eradicate inequality between identity groups and the larger society, are "primarily a matter of external protections."[3] An examination of practical legal experiences from these countries shows that the external aspects of multicultural accommodationist policies cannot be considered without regard to the policies' internal impacts.[4]

"Accommodation," in the multicultural context, refers to a wide range of state attempts to facilitate identity groups' practices and norms, for example, by exempting group members from certain laws, or by awarding identity groups some degree of self-governance.[5] Multicultural accommodation, in its various legal manifestations, generally aims to ensure that identity groups have the option to maintain what Robert Cover calls their *nomos*: the normative universe in which law and cultural narrative are inseparably related.[6] Multicultural accommodation presents a problem, however, when pro-identity group policies improve the status of identity groups but worsen the status of less powerful group members.[7]

Schematically, six prototypical legal conflicts can arise under a multicultural legal system: individual vs. individual; individual vs. state; identity group vs. identity group; identity group vs. state (the most-often discussed legal conflict under multiculturalism); nonmember (or outsider) vs. identity group (as, for

[3]See Kymlicka 1996, p. 160.

[4]See e.g. the case of Mohd. Ahmed Khan v. Shah Bano Begum and others, AIR 1985 S.C. 945. Shah Bano, a seventy-three-year-old Moslem woman, was thrown out of her husband's house (after forty-three years of marriage); she was later unilaterally divorced by her husband in accordance with Moslem personal status law (by a *talaq* divorce). She then turned to a state court in order to obtain alimony payments from her former husband, although by Moslem personal law she had no right to alimony payments beyond the *iddat* period (the first three months after the dissolution of marriage). The case reached the Indian Supreme Court, which upheld Shah Bano's claim and imposed maintenance payments upon her husband. Because the *Shah Bano* case was politically debated as an "external protections" confrontation between majority and minority interests, the Supreme Court's decision created a furore so great that in 1986 the Indian Parliament passed the Muslim Women (Protection of Rights on Divorce) Act (No. 25 of 1986). This Act withdrew Muslim women's right to appeal for maintenance under state law; hence imposing a strict "non-intervention" policy on Moslem-Indian marriage and divorce affairs. For further discussion, see Diwan and Diwan (1994) and Mahmood (1986). Similarly, in Israel, respect for the different religious communities' personal status laws is inscribed in state law, hence emphasizing the external protections on family law even at the cost of legitimizing internal restrictions, such as the "anchoring" of a wife by her husband in accordance with Halakhic law (Shiloh 1970).

[5]The move toward the legal recognition of identity groups as entities deserving special or "differentiated" rights is thoroughly discussed in Kymlicka (1995); see also Spinner (1994),Taylor (1994, pp. 25–73) and Young (1990).

[6]Cover 1983.

[7]I use the term "identity groups" to refer to religious, ethnic and tribal groups which are recognizable as groups by virtue of their *nomos*. Although what constitutes an identity group is a controversial question, we will propose for the purposes of this discussion that such groups are marked by a unique history, a distinct "text" of shared legal and social traditions, collective memories, or an experience of maltreatment by mainstream society. I focus my analysis on identity groups that raise claims for recognition and enforcement of their traditions in certain legal arenas, such as family law. See Levy 1997, pp. 36–40.

example, in affirmative action cases[8]); and individual member (or insider) vs. identity group. My analysis focuses on the final category of legal conflict: that which occurs between a group member and her own identity group. That is, I address the intra-group maltreatment of certain less powerful group members, in this case, women, as *sanctioned* by group practices, which takes place against the background of multicultural accommodation policies that delegate legal powers from the state to identity groups. More specifically, my discussion interrogates the injurious effects of accommodated family law policies on the female members of identity groups. Ultimately, the paper outlines several viable legal paradigms which could gird a reshaped, less problematic multicultural model.

I. THE PERILS OF ACCOMMODATION

From a legal perspective, multicultural accommodation policies which delegate powers from the state to identity groups raise complex questions about the appropriate relationships between "inside" courts and "outside" authorities, particularly with regard to the protection of group members' basic individual rights in intra-group spheres. I refer to this set of concerns as the *trichotomy* question: that is, can the multicultural state allocate jurisdiction to identity groups in certain fields of law while simultaneously protecting group members' individual rights as citizens?[9]

Advocates of accommodation policies offer two answers to the trichotomy question, representing what I call a "strong version" and a "weak version" of the multicultural model. The strong version argues that identity groups should be given a strong formal and legal recognition and be permitted to govern their members "in accord with their customs and views."[10] The weak version also justifies granting self-governance rights to identity groups, however these "differentiated rights" are viewed as supplementing, not replacing, the universal rights assigned to all citizens by virtue of their membership in the state.

The strong multicultural model is based on the notion that the constitution (and the individual rights it protects) are, as James Tully puts it, "an imperial yoke, galling the necks of the culturally diverse citizenry."[11] Under the strong model, the state should free identity groups from the injustice of an alien form of rule by two means: first, by creating islands of self-governance for identity

[8]In such cases, an outsider challenges the criteria which define an identity group or the legitimacy of distributing benefits to group members based on those criteria for membership. See e.g. Regents of the University of California v. Bakke, 438 US 265 (1978).

[9] I address the tension between multiculturalism and citizenship in greater detail in Shachar 1998. At minimum, the state is required to provide its citizens with equal protection of their bodily integrity and life. Indeed, one of the only uncontested objectives of political order is the *protection of its citizens*. Interpretations vary as to the scope of this protection, however. See e.g. Nedelsky 1996.

[10]Tully 1995b, p. 4; 1995a, p. 114.

[11]Tully 1995b, p. 5.

groups; and second, by officially including the "different" voices of identity groups within the constitutional framework and within public discourse.[12]

The strong model, however, focuses almost exclusively on the problem of inter-group injustice. Hence, in its crusade to integrate identity groups into the public sphere in a fair and equal manner, respecting their differences, the strong multicultural model fails to effectively address the phenomenon of intra-group oppression.[13] This makes the strong multicultural citizenship model troubling from the standpoint of the trichotomy question, precisely because it obscures the power relations *within* identity groups while highlighting the conflicts that exist *among* identity groups or *between* identity groups and the state. A weak version of the multicultural citizenship model, on the other hand, more effectively addresses the question of intra-group effects of multicultural accommodation: it acknowledges the potential tension between recognizing different cultures and protecting the rights of group members as citizens.[14]

Although proponents of the weak multicultural model argue about the normative justifications for adopting accommodation policies (these justifications vary from "autonomy-based/valorization of choice" arguments to "tolerance/respect for diversity" reasoning), they agree that a morally adequate treatment of identity groups must seek ways to provide accommodation *without* abandoning the protection of individual rights. Will Kymlicka, a prominent representative of the weak version, expresses this goal in the following way: "A comprehensive theory of justice in a multicultural state will include both universal rights, assigned to individuals regardless of group membership, and certain group-differentiated rights or 'special status' for minority cultures."[15] Moreover, Kymlicka argues that the real test of the multicultural model of citizenship lies in its ability to "explain how minority rights coexist with human rights, and how minority rights are limited by principles of individual liberty, democracy, and social justice."[16]

The strong multicultural model fails Kymlicka's test because it emphasizes only the rights of identity groups. In contrast, the weak version aims to mediate among the components of the trichotomy, and therefore offers a more compelling

[12]See e.g. Young 1989, p. 259.

[13]Chandran Kukathas (1992, p. 127; 1997), for example, supports a policy of "non-intervention" in the affairs of identity groups (so long as individuals have a right of exit), even if the consequences of this accommodationist policy may mean that some groups adopt practices which are harmful to a certain category of insider, e.g. women.

[14]See e.g. Galston 1995.

[15]Kymlicka 1995 p. 6. Note that Kymlicka's (1995, pp. 26–33) multicultural model takes as its paradigmatic case the experience of countries like Canada, Australia and the United States, which typically have to deal with claims raised either by "newcomers" or by indigenous peoples. In other parts of the world, however, particularly in deeply divided societies, the motivation for adopting accommodationist policies is neither compensatory, as it is with indigenous peoples, nor inclusionary, as it is with immigrants' customs. Rather, in deeply divided societies such as Israel and India, the more common motivation for granting nomoi groups a limited sphere of autonomy in matters crucial for their self-definition is that of maintaining the social and political peace, preserving a *modus vivendi* of mutual existence in a shared political community.

[16]Kymlicka 1995, p. 6.

multicultural model. As I show in the next sections, however, the weak multicultural model contradicts its own central tenet—that "minority rights are limited by principles of individual liberty, democracy, and social justice"—because there are circumstances under which it upholds multicultural accommodation even in cases where "external protections" are used to justify "internal restrictions."[17]

Family law is an ideal arena in which to test my hypothesis that multicultural accommodation is never solely a matter of dispute between the group and the state. Clearly, when the state awards self-governance power over members' marriage and divorce affairs to identity groups, it enhances their autonomy. At the same time, this delegation of legal authority also exposes insiders who belong to traditionally subordinated classes, such as women, minorities within the group, and children, to what I call *the paradox of multicultural vulnerability*. These group members may accrue some benefit from the transfer of legal powers from the state to their identity groups, but as individuals with "other" identities they bear disproportionate costs for their group's *nomos*. Moreover, unlike other situations in which self-governance powers are awarded to identity groups, violations of individual rights in the family law arena are systematic rather than accidental, and thus legal arrangements that aim to relieve inter-group inequalities will almost certainly have detrimental *intra*-group effects on a specific category of insider, namely women.

To illustrate this last point, consider the following two situations in which the multicultural state might grant identity groups self-governance powers over certain legal arenas. In situation A, the state grants an identity group full discretion over matters of resource developments in the community, as part of its multicultural accommodationist policy.[18] Such an allocation of powers from the state to the group strengthens the group's autonomy vis-à-vis the state, because decisions regarding resource development will be made by the majority in the group in accordance with its own decision-making mechanisms. If the state transfers exclusive powers to the group, however, there is the possibility that some individual members of the group will be worse off, in comparison with their situation under state law. Assume that an Indian tribe has been awarded full discretion over matters of resource development, and its members have decided to open a gambling facility on the territory under the tribe's jurisdiction. Also assume that a similar decision could not have been made under state law because state law prohibits gambling activities.

The tribe's decision could succeed or fail to develop the tribe's resources. The justifications for adopting the decision, however, are not dictated by the group's

[17]Kymlicka (1996), however, recognizes the potential tension between inter-group accommodation (or "external protections"), and intra-group violations of insiders' basic rights by their own group (or "internal restrictions"). Yet, as above mentioned, Kymlicka views group differentiated rights as "primarily a matter of external protections."

[18]This is one of the examples given by Kymlicka (1995, p. 30), who discusses powers which are being gradually transferred by the United States and Canada to North American tribal/band councils.

authoritative texts or traditions. In other words, providing gambling opportunities to the tribe and its visitors is not an identity-preserving imperative dictated by the group's authorities or inside courts in the name of preserving the tribe's *nomos*.

The tribe's decision to open a gambling facility will no doubt have both an economic and a social impact on tribe members. Although a successful casino would accrue financial benefits for tribe members, certain insiders (compulsive gamblers, for example) might be better off if the gambling facility is not opened. Thus majority policy decisions can potentially injure certain group members. However, the infringements upon certain group members are in such cases accidental rather than encoded within a group's sanctioned traditions which systematically impose violations of individual rights upon a certain category of insider, as in the following situation B.

In situation B, a group is awarded exclusive jurisdiction over matters that are important for its self-definition, such as family law. Such accommodation not only grants the group more autonomy vis-à-vis the state, but also awards it substantive legal powers with which to define its own membership boundaries (for example, to decide who by marriage or by birth is eligible for group membership), and to shape legal relations between spouses in intra-group spheres. In other words, what is granted in situation B is not a policy issue which is to be determined by the group's decision-making mechanism, such as whether or not to open a gambling facility. Instead, a well defined "text" of social and legal norms and practices (that is, parts of the group's self-determined essential traditions) is given authoritative status.[19] Thereafter, group members are bound by the state to have their personal affairs adjudicated by inside courts which apply the group's essential traditions, even if, as individuals, they would have preferred to have such matters adjudicated by outside courts which apply state laws. In situation B, self-governance powers, combined with a state "non-interventionist" policy, might expose certain insiders (women undergoing divorce proceedings, for example) to intra-group violations of their individual rights because such violations are enshrined in the group's essential traditions.[20]

While the intra-group effects in situation A might be waived because they impose "random" costs upon certain insiders (for example, the compulsive gamblers), the intra-group effects in situation B are quite different in nature. When restrictions upon a certain category of insider are *built into* an identity

[19]Religiously-defined identity groups generally have a recognized textual corpus (e.g. holy scripts and their authoritative interpretations), which encode their marriage and divorce laws, while ethnic and tribal groups might only have unwritten customary rules by which they regulate their members' behavior. My reference to "text" in this context, however, also relates to customary family law rules.

[20]What constitutes an identity group's "essential tradition" is never fully fixed or immune from change. However, at any given period a group's textual interpreters have emphasized specific norms and practices as having a dominant (or in my terminology, "essential") status. Thus "essential traditions," in religious groups, for example, usually consist of a recognized corpus, which is in turn subject to reinterpretation by the group's recognized religious leaders or inside courts.

group's family law practices, as in situation B, the multicultural state permits the de facto imposition of these internal restrictions. Thus, in situation B, the "external" and "internal" aspects of multicultural accommodation are mistakenly considered separate: in other words, the *disproportionate injury* imposed on certain group insiders is *directly related* to the ways in which the *state accommodates their identity groups.* In such instances, the state's multicultural policies conflate the language of "respect to groups" with a license to subordinate specific group members.

The tension between "external" and "internal" impacts of multicultural family law arrangements is evident in the practical legal experience of countries like Israel and India, which have already adopted accommodation policies with reference to the personal status affairs of their citizens. All Israeli citizens, for example, must have their marriage and divorce disputes resolved by religious courts of their respective communities.[21] The Israeli religious courts, which have been awarded different degrees of exclusive jurisdiction over matters of family law, are in principle immune from state intervention,[22] even if they uphold group traditions which expose certain insiders, particularly women undergoing divorce proceedings, to maltreatment.[23]

Under Halakhic law, for example, the giving and accepting of the *get* (divorce decree) is a private act between the spouses, which takes place under the supervision of a rabbinical court. Unless both spouses agree to the divorce, the ultimate power to decide whether or not to dissolve the marriage remains in the husband's hands: until he declares that he is willing to grant his wife the *get*, there is no way in which she may be released from the marriage bonds.[24] Because such maltreatment of women is sanctioned by (state-authorized) rabbinical courts, Israel's multicultural accommodation policy does more than recognize the autonomy of religious courts in the family law arena. In effect, it also grants these "inside" courts a *carte blanche* license to subordinate certain group members. Not only Jewish women, but also Moslem, Christian and Druze women are potentially subject to intra-group controls by their own group's traditions under the auspices of Israel's accommodationist family law policy.[25]

[21]In Israel, when both spouses belong to the same religious community, they must, by state law, pursue matters of marriage and divorce in a religious "inside" court. Thus, no "unified" (civil) law applies to all Israeli citizens in matters of personal status. Instead, each community's religious court applies its personal law (i.e., the group's "essential traditions"). Therefore, "[i]n matters affecting their families, Israelis *must* function as Jews, Muslims, Druzes, etc." Edelman (1994, p. 121, emphasis added); see also, Shiloh (1970).

[22]See Basic Law: Judicature, Laws of the State of Israel, 38, 101–6, articles 15 (c)-(d)(3)-(4); Women's Equal Rights Law, 1951, Laws of the State of Isarel 5, 171–2, article 5.

[23]For further discussion, see Raday (1992).

[24]Rabbinical courts in Israel have not yet found a solution to this problem of intra-group oppression. For a clear summary of Halakhic divorce law, see Bayer (1968); see also Bleich (1981).

[25]Moslem *Sahri'a* courts, for example, have exclusive jurisdiction over *all* matters of personal status of Moslem Israeli citizens. This wide jurisdiction, of course, brings up a host of other problems that cannot be addressed here. For a concise account of Moslem personal status laws, see al-Hibri (1992); for further analysis of the status of women under Islamic family law, see Hijab (1988, pp. 9–37) and Nasir (1994).

II. FAMILY LAW, COLLECTIVE IDENTITY AND THE MALTREATMENT OF WOMEN

Family law fulfills important social and legal functions in nomoi groups: on the one hand, family law is a crucial venue for preserving collective identities and, on the other, a means by which power inequalities between men and women are maintained within the group. In order to understand the centrality of family law to preserving a group's membership boundaries, we need briefly to examine the two basic means through which collective identities are maintained. The two means, which are often intertwined, are generally categorized as: "the racial, ethnic, biological and territorial, on the one hand, and the ideological, cultural and spiritual on the other."[26] Anne McClintock stresses the former, emphasizing that collective identities "are frequently figured through the iconography of familial or domestic space."[27] She also observes that even the term nation derives from *natio*: "to be born,"[28] and that communities are also symbolically figured as *domestic genealogies*.[29] Benedict Anderson also suggests that communities are best viewed as akin to families or religious orders.[30] Such communities are understood by their members as having "finite, if elastic, boundaries."[31] Defined in this fashion, group membership derives its meaning from a system of "differences," which must be demarcated by membership boundaries.[32]

Nomoi groups demarcate their boundaries by engaging in sorting processes which define who is inside and who is outside the group. Nomoi groups, however, unlike nation-states, lack the institutional authority to formally determine who belongs to the political community (for example, they lack the sovereignty which would permit them to define citizenship or legal residency). Moreover, groups struggling to preserve their differences within a nation-state—that is, under a common citizenship status—lack the institutional means to oblige members to claim membership. Nomoi groups cannot issue formal documents of membership or force members to contribute taxes to the collective. Instead, they attempt to maintain their membership boundaries by employing biological-descent and cultural-affiliation criteria. Some groups, for example, define themselves primarily in cultural or linguistic terms. These groups are less exclusive than those which define themselves solely in terms of biological descent. These more exclusive nomoi groups often use *family law* as a central tenet in the

[26]Ben Israel 1992, p. 393.
[27]McClintock 1993, pp. 62–3.
[28]Note that the analogy I propose here between identity groups and nations is limited to the "mechanisms" of biological and cultural reproduction. As I explained earlier, I focus here on the situation of identity groups which exist within the framework of a larger political entity (the state). I will not examine the claims of groups seeking national independence/sovereignty, or secession from the larger body politic. Rather, the identity groups which I analyze seek accommodation for their differences within the boundaries of a state which is composed of a diverse citizenry.
[29]McClintock 1993.
[30]Anderson 1991.
[31]Anderson 1991, p. 7.
[32]This demarcation of differences *among* groups does not imply, however, that actual inequality and exploitation do not prevail *within* groups, as Anderson himself observes.

construction of their membership boundaries, and in asserting and preserving their differences.[33]

The emphasis in more exclusive nomoi groups on marriage and membership by birth,[34] which I call family law's "demarcating function," provides a strong impetus for the group to develop various, often detrimental, social and legal mechanisms for controlling the personal status, sexuality and reproductive activity of women—for women have a central and potentially powerful role in procreating the collective. Intra-group policing of women,[35] if encoded in the group's essential traditions, is achieved partially via the implementation of personal status laws which clearly define how, when and with whom women can give birth to children so as to ensure that those children become legitimate members of the community.[36] Thus, precisely because of women's important role in reproducing a group's membership boundaries, they are subject to strict legal regulation, particularly at the junctures of marriage and divorce.

More exclusive religious groups often highlight women's responsibilities as the reproducers of legitimate children in accordance with the group's personal status laws and as primary socializers of the young.[37] This understanding of women's contribution to the collective, developed, glorified and maintained by the group's authorities, is borne out, for example, by Orthodox Jewish perceptions of the family.[38] The recognition that women contribute to the group as bearers of the collective might, in theory, grant women a powerful position within their group; in practice, however, in Orthodox Jewish groups, as in many other religious communities, this conceptual deification of the female role of wife–mother–homemaker has done exactly the opposite.

Under Halakhic law, for example, a husband's refusal to grant his wife a divorce decree (or *get*) results not only in the wife's inability to remarry but also in severe restrictions on her sexuality and procreative activity. For example, if she were to have a sexual relationship with another man she would be considered a *moredet* (rebellious wife) and, as such, may lose her rights to child custody and

[33]Accordingly, family law loses its distinct role in setting the legal terms for defining membership if the group permits anyone interested in joining the group to become a full member.

[34]Obviously there are other ways of establishing membership in nomoi groups (e.g., by religious conversion). However, most nomoi groups (and nations) acquire members first and foremost by birth. For a position which advocates a transition from a model of citizenship as birthright into a model of political membership by consent, see Schuck and Smith (1985).

[35]Men, too, are controlled by such laws, but not in a similar, discriminatory and subordinating, fashion.

[36]Legitimacy, in this context, refers not to the traditional common-law definition (i.e. a child born in a legal marriage), but to granting membership by birth only to a child born in accordance with the group's specific personal status laws and lineage rules. For these purposes, legal marriage is often a necessary but not sufficient condition. See e.g. the case of *Santa Clara Pueblo v. Martinez*.

[37]See e.g. Anthias and Yuval-Davis 1989. Note, however, that Anthias's and Yuval-Davis's analysis of women's unique position does not aim to essentialize their role as reproducers of collective identities (that is, primarily as mothers). Anthias and Yuval-Davis therefore differ from cultural feminists who on the normative level glorify mothering as the epitome of an ethics of care. Compare with West (1988).

[38]See e.g. Berman (1973) and Meiselman (1978).

spousal alimony; moreover, if she were to have a child by another man while still considered legally married to her imprisoning husband, that child would be considered a *mamzer* and would be doomed to exile from the Jewish community for ten generations while bearing the shameful status of a bastard.[39]

Marriage and divorce laws not only determine personal status, however. They also define the rights and duties of spouses during a marriage and, in the event of divorce, determine the economic and parental consequences of this change in personal status. In this sense, a group's governing essential traditions shape the "distribution" of resources and obligations between ex-husband and ex-wife, and play a crucial role in maintaining power inequalities between men and women within the community.

Given the *distributing and demarcating* functions of family law, nomoi groups predictably express a strong interest in having *exclusive* control over their members' marriage and divorce affairs. In moving toward a multicultural citizenship model, family law has therefore become a contested field in which the state and nomoi groups vie for control. That nomoi groups should struggle for autonomy in the family law arena is not surprising. Yet, as I have noted, family law policies in more exclusive nomoi groups have a particular, often detrimental, effect on women, who stand at the fulcrum of legal rules and policies encoded in their groups' essential traditions.[40] Precisely because family law partakes in shaping internal restrictions within a given group, the multicultural state cannot treat the delegation of legal powers in the family law arena solely as a matter of external protections. Rather, the multicultural state must recognize the tensions inherent in any accommodationist policy in the family law arena.

Moreover, as matters of family law are rarely, if ever, open to public deliberations, self-governance powers are transferred from the state to the group's members only in theory. In practice, accommodation in the family law arena gives full discretion to a group's acknowledged spokespersons—most often male members who are involved in some form of politics, law or religion—to implement "inside" laws over group members.[41] Such accommodation can create a *disincentive* for the group's elite to relieve internal restrictions against women,

[39]The threat of exclusion from the Jewish community in the case of the *agunah*'s illegitimate children is not merely theoretical. In fact, rabbinical courts in Israel maintain "blacklists" of persons who are barred from marriage to Jews (*psuley hitun*), among them the *mamzerim*.

[40]Clearly, however, not all women within a given identity group encounter intra-group injuries, even if they are subject to the same family law code. This is partly because women in religious or ethnic communities, as elsewhere, differ along lines such as social status, wealth or age.

[41]Note, however, that the self-governance powers granted to religious courts in Israel and in India over members' family law affairs are not as expansive as those granted to Indian tribes in the United States.

for example, by reworking family law practices in a less discriminatory way *within* the group.[42]

We should note, however, that even when the multicultural state changes the "background rules" affecting the status of nomoi groups by granting religious "inside" courts jurisdiction over their members in matters of family law, nomoi groups, and especially their leaders, are never fully independent of "outside" authorities. Significantly, the ultimate power to define the criteria by which groups are recognized, accommodated and awarded some degree of self-governance powers remains in the hands of the state.

For example, even under the Ottoman *millet* system, which nowadays is presented in the multicultural literature as a model of religious pluralism and tolerance,[43] the Ottoman authorities did not award *millet* leaders *carte blanche* jurisdiction over all internal legal matters. Rather, the extent of the self-governing power of each religious community (or *millet*) was specifically indicated in the different Imperial charters issued by Ottoman authorities (in our modern terminology, the state) to the official leaders of each *millet* from time to time.[44] These leaders were required to be subjects of the Ottoman empire; moreover, their status as leaders of particular *millets* had to be approved by "outside" authorities. Approved *millet* system leaders "were to govern, make laws for, judge, tax and punish the rayahs of their religion." Moreover, they were "responsible with their heads for the maintenance of order within their communities."[45] In return, these leaders had the authority to govern their religious communities via inside courts, in accordance with the laws of those communities.[46]

The Ottoman state, however, reserved for itself the power either to refuse to recognize the whole body of rules comprised in a *millet*'s system of personal law, or to recognize only the rules relating to certain limited matters (for example, marriage).[47] Moreover, the power of execution of religious courts' decisions was left in the hands of the Ottoman authorities, so that the application of the "inside" courts' decisions was never fully separate from the state. Thus the Ottoman state never relinquished its dominant position in relation to the *millets*,

[42]One example of an *internal* reinterpretation of existing essential traditions is offered by Moslem women's groups which suggest the inclusion of specific stipulations in the Islamic marriage contract. Such stipulations safeguard the legal rights of the signatories and can serve as a legal tool to preclude the abuse of women. For example, stipulations can specify that a wife cannot be removed from an agreed upon locality, that she has a right to divorce if her husband takes another wife, or that she may work outside the home. Such stipulations are legally binding (by Islamic law and by state law) if signed by the spouses and registered *before* the officiating person signs the marriage certificate. For further details, see Alkateeb (1996).

[43]See e.g. Sigler 1983.

[44]Vitta 1970, p. 173.

[45]Goadby 1926, p. 102.

[46]The scope of jurisdiction awarded by the Ottomans to "inside" courts normally included "jurisdiction over the clergy, and jurisdiction in matters of family law (marriage, divorce, alimony, etc.), wills, and inheritance over the laity" (Goadby 1926, p. 102).

[47]Vitta 1970, p. 192.

even when it granted the *millets* certain powers of self-governance. Likewise, if the contemporary multicultural state hopes to provide relief to citizens whose rights are violated by their groups' traditions, then theorists and legislators must recognize that the state should not fully relinquish its power over identity groups. Rather, the real challenge lies in envisioning a new, reshaped multicultural model which allocates legal authority to both the state and identity groups.

III. TOWARD A RESHAPED MULTICULTURAL MODEL

A reshaped multicultural model geared toward resolving, or at least mitigating, the injurious intra-group effects of "external protections" must begin with an *intersectionist* understanding of the position of identity group members in the multicultural state. The intersectionist view takes into account the conception of personal identity as fragmented, discursive, positional, and imbued with multiple ascriptions.[48] As Pierre Birnbaum observes, in contemporary multicultural theory "individuals . . . are [mistakenly] understood as the bearers of a single oppressive and quasi-essentialist idealized cultural identity from which no escape is possible. Such an immutable collective identity is not compatible with the expression of other identities (sexual, religious, etc.) in which some might wish to recognize themselves at certain moments of their existence."[49] The intersectionist view of identity, on the other hand, would acknowledge the *multidimensionality* of insiders' experiences and would capture the potential double or triple disadvantages that certain group members are exposed to given their *simultaneous belongings*.[50]

Moreover, an intersectionist view would recognize that group members are *always* caught at the intersection of multiple affiliations.[51] They are group members (perhaps holding more than one affiliation) and, at the same time, citizens of the state.

A reshaped multicultural model should therefore reject the "either/or" understanding of identity and the oversimplified perception of allocation of legal authority it entails, that is, either *all* powers are granted to the state or to the group. The more complex question, of course, is how to allocate legal authority over these individuals with multiple affiliations, in ways which "accommodate" their *simultaneous belongings* and provide adequate safeguards for attending to the interests of less powerful group members. In the following pages I utilize the example of family law to illustrate the contours of an "intersectionist" approach to multicultural accommodation—one which aims to respect the the centrality of

[48]See e.g. Alcoff 1988.

[49]Birnbaum 1996, p. 41.

[50]Unfortunately, most proponents of group-differentiated rights fail to notice the vulnerability of women to intra-group maltreatment because they view them simply as *group members*.

[51]By thinking about the internal restrictions caused by accommodation, and by adding gender as a relevant category of analysis, we can begin to recognize the 'intersecting' disadvantages that erode the citizenship status of female group members. See e.g. Crenshaw 1989.

family law in preserving collective identities yet which does not grant nomoi groups a *carte blanche* power to systematically subordinate a specific category of insiders, namely women.

An intersectionist approach will present an alternative to two existing paradigms: the model of hierarchical imposition and the model of fragmentation.[52] The model of hierarchical imposition entails the enforcement of various state laws upon all citizens, demanding conformity with dominant norms and failing to respect group-based traditions. The model of fragmentation, on the other hand, gives *carte blanche* legal authority to nomoi groups to pursue their own traditions, even at the cost of legitimizing systematic intra-group oppression. Neither of these paradigms succeeds in recognizing nomoi groups' essential traditions without compromising group members' state-guaranteed individual rights. Both paradigms are the result of a dichotomous understanding of legal authority: under both these models, *either* the state *or* the group would exclusively govern insiders' legal affairs. As I have shown, however, even when the state formally refrains from intervening in a group's essential traditions, it in fact partakes in solidifying the power-relations encoded in these traditions. In other words, by accommodating inter-group differences, the multicultural state inevitably finds itself shaping, at least in part, intra-group relations.

A reshaped multicultural model must therefore rest on the acknowledgment that interaction between the "external" and "internal" effects of accommodation is inevitable. In contrast to approaches driven by the hierarchical imposition and fragmentation models, an intersectionist approach would seek to design legal policies for multicultural accommodation which do not deny the potentially negative implications of delegating legal power to nomoi groups. That is, an intersectionist multicultural accommodation policy would permit identity groups a maximum degree of autonomy while still protecting insiders who are put at risk by their own groups' accommodated traditions. A crucial question remains, however: how should the interests of identity groups, individuals and the state be balanced in practice? What would an intersectionist multicultural accommodationist policy actually look like?

A. Horizontal Priority Models

A first possibility is to divide legal authority along the lines of what I call "horizontal priority." Under this approach, legal controls over group members' activities are devised in accordance with different layers of authority, one on top of the other, which means that identity groups are granted primary and original jurisdiction over certain legal arenas while still remaining subject to some form of residuary or appellate jurisdiction by state courts. Under the horizontal priority approach, the main question to be resolved is how to allow identity groups, as

[52]See Cover and Aleinikoff 1977, pp. 1046–52.

smaller governmental units, to determine matters affecting their collective identity, and still to preserve the power of the state to impose compliance with basic constitutional principles, for example, citizens' rights to bodily integrity, autonomy, and self-determination. Various models might fulfill this requirement.

The first possibility is what I call "regulated accommodation." Under this option, the state would allow identity groups self-governance powers in certain legal arenas but it would also provide *direct legal access* to state courts for occasion when the group systematically injures the state-guaranteed rights of a particular category of insider. Contemporary invocations of the usage of international law in domestic affairs, for example, would approximate this model, particularly with regard to the expansion of individuals' standing vis-à-vis their own states in international courts.[53]

This model has major drawbacks, however. For example, the burden of initiating the legal process against an identity group falls on the weaker party (the insider who claims her state-guaranteed rights were violated). Hence the insider is potentially exposed to severe pressures to withdraw the legal claim in order to protect the group. Similar pressures are imposed on abused children or spouses who dare turn to the legal system and seek retribution against their alleged perpetrators. This tension could, to some degree, be mitigated by granting *amici curiae* standing to administrative bodies or non-governmental organizations, which might aid the injured insider. From an identity group's perspective, however, this model is problematic because it leaves underdetermined the scope of *in potentia* state intervention. Given that any sanctioned group tradition which contradicts state laws could, in theory, be overturned or circumscribed by individual group members who seek remedy against the group, the regulated accommodation model could extensively limit the autonomy of identity groups.

Another possibility is a model of "conditional accommodation." Here the state would grant *exclusive* jurisdiction to a nomoi group over certain legal arenas *without* providing direct venues in which insiders could challenge their group's practices in state courts. Yet the allocation of legal authority, under this model, would be *conditional*; the group, and particularly its inside courts, as state-authorized institutions with public powers (for example, to solemnize marriages and divorces), would have to comply with certain due process and equal treatment requirements. This model therefore leaves it to the group to "sort out" its own discriminatory practices. However, the group (or, rather, its public officials) would have to at least comply with the state's licensing terms or it would face the prospect of losing its legal authority entirely.

[53]The analogy of international intervention in domestic affairs, however, raises grave concerns that violations of women's rights, e.g. rape or spousal beating and killing, would not be considered violations of human rights that merit outside intervention in intra-group spheres. Are violations against women, for example, included in Kymlicka's (1995, p. 169) definition of situations that merit outside intervention, "such as slavery or genocide or mass torture and expulsions"? For a critique of the lack of protection of women's rights in international law, see MacKinnon (1994).

From the legal perspective, this model is problematic because it does not provide legal certainty since the identity group's jurisdiction is always conditional. Moreover, it does not allow group members to *directly* impact the state's policy with regard to their own identity group. In this sense, this model reflects a semi-corporatist stance, in which "business" is assumed to take place only between state officials and the groups' leaders. If, however, an identity group is governed by an elite which holds that any "submission" to change is a threat to their group's *nomos*, then the conditional accommodation model becomes useless. In such a case, this model would only aggravate the tensions already at play within a given community: for example, it could force women to demonstrate their group loyalty by giving up their quest to alter a gender-discriminatory reading of their group's family law traditions, and it could create greater resistance to whatever is perceived as reflecting "outside" norms (for example, gender equality). In short, if a conditional accommodation solution is seen by group leaders as an instance of intolerable (indirect) intervention in their group's practices, it will, probably, fail to provide a solution to the problem of sanctioned intra-group maltreatment.

B. The Vertical Priority Model

An altogether different and better way to divide legal authority in the family law arena, which I call the intersectionist "joint-governance" approach, allocates legal powers based on a subject-matter jurisdiction, or along lines of vertical priority. In other words, instead of operating on the basis of a layered division of authority between a group's essential traditions and the state's laws, as the above models suggest, the joint-governance approach assumes that *mixed standards* would simultaneously govern group members' legal affairs.

As I have shown, identity groups are inevitably dependent upon the state for their legal recognition and accommodation. Moreover, given that most fields of human activity in the modern state are already governed by a complex and often overlapping mosaic of various legal regulations deriving from more than one source, it is both unrealistic and undesirable to assume that the recognition of identity groups' essential traditions can reverse this trend. If anything, multicultural accommodation would add to this plurality of legal sources. The main idea behind an intersectionist joint-governance approach to accommodation, then, is to permit input from two legal systems—a group's essential traditions and the state's laws—to resolve a single dispute, for example, a divorce proceeding. In the family law arena, this translates into seeking legal arrangements which provide greater possibilities for women to define their personal status and to shape the economic and parental consequences of divorce, without undermining their group's controls over the definition of its membership boundaries.

As I explained earlier, family law serves at least two important functions: it *demarcates* membership boundaries by defining who is an insider by virtue of marriage and birth in accordance with the group's specific personal status laws and lineage rules, and it *distributes* rights, duties, and ultimately power, between men and women within the community.

Unfortunately, most existing accommodationist policies overlook the fact that family law has two functions, rather than only one. An intersectionist joint-governance approach, on the other hand, utilizes this distinction by providing nomoi groups' greater autonomy over their membership boundaries while, at the same time, providing female group members with greater bargaining powers in the event of divorce.

More specifically, an intersectionist joint-governance approach to family law would by and large grant nomoi groups jurisdiction over marital status definitions because such decisions determine, among other things, who can become a group member through marriage, and under which conditions divorced group members can marry within the faith and have children who will be considered full and legitimate members of the community. Thus self-governance over marital status decisions is important if more exclusive nomoi groups are to maintain their membership boundaries. A delegation of legal power from the state to nomoi groups over family law's *demarcating* function would therefore permit more exclusive groups to preserve a crucial aspect of their *nomos*.[54]

A similar justification for accommodation, however, does not stand with regard to nomoi groups' control over family law's *distributing* function. Disputes between divorcing spouses over issues of alimony, property division or child support are not concerns unique to group members. All state citizens potentially face similar disputes when dissolving a marriage. Granting recognition to identity groups' essential traditions which systematically disadvantage divorcing women would provide husbands within accommodated groups with sanctioned extortive powers to settle (status-related) property disputes in ways which disenfranchise women from state-guaranteed protections.[55] These protections were in the first place designed to help the formerly economically dependent spouse avoid destitution when the marriage came to an end.[56] Given the fact that in many religiously-defined nomoi groups women are already in a disadvantaged position vis-a-vis their husbands due to their group's (gender-discriminatory) marital status definitions, it would be absurd to further disadvantage them by taking

[54]Cleveland (1925, p. 1095) writes, "From the time of clan and kin communities to the twentieth century status is the true expression of the fact that there are different ideas about fundamental relations... Status is still a serene monument to the originality of [different] political communities." Note, however, that Cleveland's definition of status is wider than the definition I suggest, which relates only to marriage and divorce in the context of preserving a group's membership boundaries.

[55]This distinction between marital status and marital property issues is not altogether new. It can be traced to the common-law division of authority between ecclesiastical courts and chancery courts in England. See Vestal and Foster 1956, pp. 23–31.

[56]For further discussion, see e.g. Singer (1992).

away whatever property rights and protections other divorcing women are entitled to—as citizens—in accordance with state laws.

The intersectionist joint-governance approach therefore acknowledges that power relations exist not only *among* groups but also *within* groups, and that the protective shield of state accommodation could potentially be used as a weapon against less powerful insiders. This approach respects the crucial identity-preserving function of family law while intervening to protect group members against certain intra-group violations which are indirectly condoned under the accommodationist pretext of respecting identity groups' essential traditions.

We should note, however, that state laws have themselves historically maintained the power hierarchies between men and women via legal policies that define women's marital status and shape the rights, duties and powers "connected" to marriage and divorce.[57] Only quite recently, largely due to the feminist movement, have explicit gender biases been removed from various state laws regulating the family. However, even if state laws imperfectly address women's interests in the family law arena, women's interests are still generally better protected under a joint-governance approach than under identity groups' essential traditions. A recent Israeli family law case, *Bavli v. Rabbinical High Court*, illustrates this last point.

In 1992, in the *Bavli* case, a Jewish woman turned to the Israeli Supreme Court seeking remedy against a rabbinical court's decision given in connection with a divorce dispute. The decision held that in accordance with Halakhic law the wife was not entitled to any share in the property acquired during the couple's twenty-nine years of marriage, although by state law she was entitled to an equal share of that property.[58] This decision was not unusual; on average, rabbinical courts impose lower alimony payments on husbands and grant women fewer marital property rights than do state courts.[59] To deal with this problem, the Israeli Supreme Court held in *Bavli* that while all religious communities in Israel (that is, Jewish, Moslem, Christian and Druze courts) have jurisdiction over their members' marital *status*, these courts have no similar authority to impose their essential traditions on *property* matters "connected" with a divorce dispute. Instead, these issues must be resolved by the more egalitarian principles entrenched in state laws.[60]

[57]In the tradition of the English common law, a woman, by marrying, immersed her own legal individuality in the person of her husband (Blackstone 1765, vol.1, p. 430). The English common law set the basis for legal practices concerning married women in the new United States. Through the 19th century and into the 20th the legal handicaps imposed on wives by the common law gradually were eliminated; and wives were given an economic and legal individuality in the eyes of the law.

[58]H.C. 1000/92 Bavli v. Rabbinical High Court 48 (2) P.D. 221.

[59]Alimony payments ordered by rabbinical courts are matters "connected" to the divorce suit and are 30% lower on average than alimony payments which are ordered by state laws. See survey no. 115, Israel Social Security Institute, "Women Who Received Alimony Payments via the Social Security Institute," pp. 2, 16, 19 (1994, in Hebrew).

[60]The *Bavli* decision, however, leaves room for each community's religious courts to reach these distributive decisions based on a reinterpretation of their own essential traditions.

The *Bavli* decision has set an important legal precedent in that it has allowed women to overcome some of the gender biases encoded in their identity groups' family law traditions, while still preserving nomoi groups' legal authority to demarcate membership boundaries.[61] This decision thus demonstrates, that in countries such as Israel and India, where accommodationist family law arrangements have already been adopted, religious divorce disputes could be resolved more fairly if the extortive powers of the stronger party were limited by the subject-matter allocation of jurisdiction between the state and identity groups.[62]

C. The Martinez Case Revisited

The intersectionist joint-governance approach to multicultural accommodation, which provides less powerful insiders with access to state laws in debates involving the property aspects of status disputes, which motivated the decision in *Bavli*, could also have better resolved the above mentioned *Martinez* case. In the *Martinez* case, Julia Martinez's daughter Audrey was denied the right to "remain on the reservation in the event of [her] mother's death, or to inherit her mother's home or her possessory interests in the communal lands." According to tribal personal status law, children of *male* Pueblos who marry outside the tribe are extended tribal membership, whereas children of *female* Pueblos who marry outside the tribe are excluded from membership. Having been unsuccessful in their efforts to persuade the Pueblo to change its membership rules, Julia Martinez and her daughter filed an equal protection lawsuit against the tribe. The case eventually reached the US Supreme Court, which held that it had no authority to intervene against the tribe's gender-biased membership rules, because judicial review of claims such as those raised by Julia and Audrey Martinez would undermine tribal sovereignty and self-governance. Although the

[61]My intersectionist joint-governance approach refers to a legal scenario in which identity groups have already been granted legal powers over matters of both marriage and divorce. Different legal solutions to the problem of intra-group oppression are required, however, when the state permits identity groups to perform legally binding marriages but reserves for itself the exclusive power to regulate acts of divorce. For further discussion of this last point, see Syrtash (1992).

[62]Not surprisingly, however, *Bavli* and other such cases were severely criticized by the religious communities involved. Authorities from the respective communities argued that state courts were intervening in groups' family law affairs in ways which would eventually have a "homogenizing" effect on their traditions, threatening their survival as distinct cultural entities. This is a legitimate concern which the intersectionist joint-governance approach addresses by respecting the identity-preserving function of family law while providing legal venues to better protect the interests of those insiders who are put at risk by their own groups' family law practices, for example, by granting women more leverage in negotiating the economic and parental consequences of a religious divorce. Even with recourse to state laws, however, women are still vulnerable to group-sanctioned maltreatment. While state regulation of family law can, for example, assist a Jewish *agunah* if her husband uses the *get* as a tool for extortion and blackmail, an intersectionist joint-governance approach less effectively assists an anchored wife whose husband refuses to grant a *get* in order to impose pain or to prevent her from marrying another man. Yet because many *gets* are indeed refused as a bargaining tool, the intersectionist joint-governance approach would effectively resolve many of the *agunah* cases.

Court correctly recognized that the membership rules "were 'no more or less than a mechanism of social...self-definition,' and as such were basic to the tribe's survival as a cultural and economic entity,"[63] it erred in leaving Martinez's daughter, Audrey, and similarly situated children who were put at risk by the tribe's accommodated traditions, *without legal remedy*.

An intersectionist joint-governance approach would have resolved the *Martinez* case differently. It would have recognized that the tribe's membership rule had both demarcating *and* distributing effects (for example, tribal status definitions served as a basis for entitlement to land use rights).[64] Given these two functions of Pueblo family law, an intersectionist joint-governance approach would not have interfered with the tribe's control over the *demarcation* of its boundaries, yet it would have provided *distributive* remedies for injuries sanctioned by the tribe's accommodated traditions. More specifically, in respecting the Pueblo's "attempt to secure the survival of a culture for which land is life,"[65] intersectionist distributive remedies, allocated on the basis of subject matter, could not have granted Audrey a possessory right to tribal communal lands if no other "outsiders" were permitted to own a share in such lands. However, other distributive remedies could have been provided for the excluded children. For example, the Pueblo might have been ordered to establish educational or loan funds for Audrey and other such children who would eventually be forced to leave the reservation because the maltreatment of certain women, their mothers, is encoded in the tribe's family law traditions.[66]

IV. CONCLUSION

An intersectionist joint-governance approach to multicultural accommodation in the family law arena thus allocates self-governance powers to identity groups with regard to membership issues, while trying to minimize the discrimination perpetuated by gender biases inscribed in the groups' traditions. Although the model I have begun to sketch here citing the recent Israeli *Bavli* case and an alternative, hypothetical solution to the *Martinez* case is still rough, and not without shortcomings, it takes into account all three elements of the trichotomy, recognizes group members' multiple affiliations and effectively addresses the two functions of family law. Hence, this developing model can begin to resolve, or at least alleviate, the degree of injury which women in particular suffer in the context of their groups' essential traditions. The intersectionist joint-governance solution, while it is far from fully resolving *the paradox of multicultural vulnerability*, at least seeks to overcome the *Catch* 22 situation in which intra-

[63] *Martinez*, at p. 54.
[64] For further details, see Resnik (1989, pp. 719–22).
[65] See MacKinnon 1987, p. 67.
[66] Of course, details need to be specified, for example, as to the degree of de facto tribal membership that would justify distributive remedy to these children.

group oppression is propagated by the very accommodationist policies which seek to mitigate cultural biases in the multicultural state.

REFERENCES

Alcoff, Linda. 1988. Cultural feminism versus post-structuralism: the identity crisis in feminist theory. *Signs*, **13**, 405–36.
al-Hibri, Aziza. 1992. Marriage laws in Muslim countries. *International Review of Comparative Public Policy*, **4**, 227–44.
Anderson, Benedict, 1991. *Imagined Communities*. Rev. edn. London: Verso.
Bayer, Menachem M. 1968. The role of Jewish law in pertaining to the Jewish family. Pp. 1–43 in Jacob Freid, ed., *Jews and Divorce*. New York: Ktav Publishing House.
Ben Israel, Hedva. 1992. Nationalism in historical perspective. *Journal of International Affairs*, **45**, 367–97.
Berman, Saul J. 1973. The status of women in Halakhic Judaism. *Tradition*, **14**, 5–28.
Birnbaum, Pierre. 1996. From multiculturalism to nationalism. *Political Theory*, **24** , 33–45.
Blackstone, William. 1765. *Commentaries on the Laws of England*. Oxford: Clarendon Press.
Bleich, J. David. 1981. Modern-day *agunot*. *Jewish Law Annual*, **4**, 167–87.
Cleveland, Richard F. 1925. Status in common law. *Harvard Law Review*, **38**, 1074–95.
Cover, Robert M. and T. Alexander Aleinikoff. 1977. Dialectical federalism: habeas corpus and the court. *Yale Law Journal*, **86**, 1035–102.
Cover, Robert M. 1983. Forward: *Nomos* and Narrative. *Harvard Law Review*, **97**, 4–68.
Crenshaw, Kimberle. 1989. Demarginalizing the intersection of race and sex: a black feminist critique of antidiscrimination doctrine, feminist theory, and antiracist politics. *The University of Chicago Legal Forum*, 1989, 139–67.
Diwan, Paras and Peeyushi Diwan. 1994. *Women and Legal Protection*. New Delhi: Deep & Deep Publications.
Edelman, Martin, 1994. *Courts, Politics, and Culture in Israel*. Charlottesville: University Press of Virginia.
Galston, William A. 1995. Two concepts of liberalism. *Ethics*, **105**, 516–34.
Goadby, Frederic M. 1926. *International and Inter-Religious Private Law in Palestine*. Jerusalem: Hamadpis Press.
Hijab, Nadia. 1988. *Womanpower*. Cambridge: Cambridge University Press.
Kukathas, Chandran. 1992. Are there any cultural rights? *Political Theory*, **20**, 105–39.
Kukathas, Chandran. 1997. Cultural toleration. Pp. 69–104 in Ian Shapiro and Will Kymlicka, eds, *Ethnicity and Group Rights*. New York: New York University Press.
Kymlicka, Will, 1995. *Multicultural Citizenship: A Liberal Theory of Minority Rights*. Oxford: Clarendon Press.
Kymlicka, Will. 1996. Three forms of group-differentiated citizenship in Canada. Pp. 153–70 in Seyla Benhabib, ed., *Democracy and Difference*. Princeton, N.J.: Princeton University Press.
Levy, Jacob T. 1997. Classifying cultural rights. Pp. 22–53 in Ian Shapiro and Will Kymlicka, eds, *Ethnicity and Group Rights*. New York: New York University Press.
MacKinnon, Catharine A. 1987. Whose culture? A case note of Martinez v. Santa Clara Pueblo. Pp. 63–9 in MacKinnon, *Feminism Unmodified*. Cambridge, Mass.: Harvard University Press.
MacKinnon, Catharine A. 1994. Rape, genocide, and women's human rights. *Harvard Women's Law Journal*, **17**, 5–16.
Mahmood, Tahir, 1986. *Personal Laws in Crisis*. New Delhi: Metropolitan Book Co.
McClintock, Anne. 1993. Family feuds: gender, nationalism and the family. *Feminist Review*, **44**, 61–78.
Meiselman, Moshe. 1978. *Jewish Woman in Jewish Law*. New York: Yeshiva University Press.

Nasir, James J. 1994. *The Status of Women Under Islamic Law and Under Modern Islamic Legislation*. London: Graham & Trotman.

Nedelsky, Jennifer. 1996. Violence against women: challenges to the liberal state and relational feminism. Pp. 454–97 In Ian Shapiro and Russell Hardin, eds, *Political Order*. New York: New York University Press.

Raday, Frances. 1992. Israel—the incorporation of religious patriarchy in a modern state. *International Review of Comparative Public Policy*, 4, 209–25.

Resnik, Judith. 1989. Dependent sovereigns: Indian tribes, states, and the federal courts. *University of Chicago Law Review*, 56, 671–759.

Schuck, Peter H. and Rogers M. Smith. 1985. *Citizenship Without Consent: Illegal Aliens in the American Polity*. New Haven, Conn.: Yale University Press.

Shachar, Ayelet. 1998. The paradox of multicultural vulnerability: identity groups, the state, and individual rights. Forthcoming in Christian Joppke and Steven Lukes, eds, *Multicultural Questions*. Oxford: Oxford University Press.

Shiloh, Isaac S. 1970. Marriage and divorce in Israel. *Israel Law Review*, 5, 479–98.

Sigler, Jay, 1983. *Minority Rights: A Comparative Analysis*. Westport, Conn.: Greenwood Press.

Singer, Jana A. 1992. The privatization of family law. *Wisconsin Law Review*, 1992, 1443–1567.

Spinner, Jeff. 1994. *The Boundaries of Citizenship: Race, Ethnicity and Nationality in the Liberal State*. Baltimore, Md.: Johns Hopkins University Press.

Syrtash, John Tibor. 1992. *Religion and Culture in Canadian Family Law*. Toronto: Butterworths.

Taylor, Charles. 1991. Shared and divergent values. Pp. 53–76 in Ronald L. Watts and Douglas M. Brown, eds, *Options for a New Canada*. Toronto: University of Toronto Press.

Taylor, Charles. 1994. The politics of recognition. Pp. 25–73 in Amy Gutmann, ed., *Multiculturalism: Examining the Politics of Recognition*. Princeton, N.J.: Princeton University Press.

Tully, James. 1995. Cultural demands for constitutional recognition. *Journal of Political Philosophy*, 3, 111–32.

Tully, James, 1995. *Strange Multiplicity: Constitutionalism in an Age of Diversity*. Cambridge: Cambridge University Press.

Vestal, Allan D. and David L. Foster. 1956. Implied limitations on the diversity jurisdiction of federal courts. *Minnesota Law Review*, 41, 1–41.

Vitta, Edoardo, 1970. The conflict of personal laws: part I. *Israel Law Review*, 5, 170–202.

West, Robin. 1988. Jurisprudence and gender. *University of Chicago Law Review*, 55, 1–72.

Young, Iris Marion. 1989. Polity and group difference: a critique of the ideal of universal citizenship. *Ethics*, 99, 250–74.

Young, Iris Marion. 1990. *Justice and the Politics of Difference*. Princeton, N.J.: Princeton University Press.

Yuval-Davis, Nira and Floya Anthias. 1989. *Woman–Nation–State*. London: Macmillan.

[14]
Vulnerability by Marriage

Susan Moller Okin

As the preceding chapters made clear, major contemporary theories of social justice pay little or no attention to the multiple inequalities between the sexes that exist in our society, or to the social construct of gender that gives rise to them. Neither mainstream theorists of social justice nor their critics (with rare exceptions) have paid much attention to the internal inequalities of the family. They have considered the family relevant for one or more of only three reasons. Some have seen the family as an impediment to equal opportunity. But the focus of such discussion has been on class differentials among families, not on sex differentials within them. While the concern that the family limits equality of opportunity is legitimate and serious, theorists who raise it have neglected the issue of gender and therefore ignored important aspects of the problem. Those who discuss the family without paying attention to the inequalities between the sexes are blind to the fact that the gendered family radically limits the equality of opportunity of women and girls of all classes—as well as that of poor and working-class children of both sexes. Nor do they see that the vulnerability of women that results from the patriarchal structure and practices of the family *exacerbates* the problem that the inequality of families poses for children's equality of opportunity. As I shall argue in this chapter, with the increasing prevalence of families headed by a single female, children suffer more and more from the economic vulnerability of women.

Second and third, theorists of justice and their critics have tended either to idealize the family as a social institution for which justice is not an appropriate virtue, or, more rarely, to see it as an important locus for the development of a sense of justice. I have disagreed strongly with those who, focusing on an idealized vision of the family, perceive it as governed by virtues nobler than justice and therefore not needing to be subjected to the tests of justice to which we subject other fundamental social institutions. While I strongly support the *hope* that families will live up to nobler virtues, such as generosity, I contend that in the real world, justice is a virtue of fundamental importance for families, as for other basic social institutions. An important sphere of distribution of many social goods, from the material to the intangible, the family has a history of distributing these goods in far from just ways. It is also, as some who have overlooked its internal justice have acknowledged, a sphere of life that is absolutely crucial to moral development. If justice cannot at least begin to be learned from our day-to-day experience within the family, it seems futile to expect that it can be developed anywhere else. Without just families, how can we expect to have a just society? In particular, if the relationship between a child's parents does not conform to basic standards of justice, how can we expect that child to grow up with a sense of justice?

It is not easy to think about marriage and the family in terms of justice. For one thing, we do not readily associate justice with intimacy, which is one reason some theorists idealize the family. For another, some of the issues that theories of justice are most concerned with, such as differences in standards of living, do not obviously apply among members of a family. Though it is certainly not the case in some countries, in the United States the members of a family, so long as they live together, usually share the same standard of living. As we shall see, however, the question of who earns the family's income, or how the earning of this income is shared, has a great deal to do with the distribution of power and influence within the family, including decisions on how to spend this income. It also affects the distribution of other benefits, including basic security. Here, I present and analyze the facts of contemporary gender-structured marriage in the light of theories about power and vulnerability and the issues of justice they inevitably raise. I argue that marriage and the family, as currently practiced in our society, are unjust institutions. They constitute the pivot of a societal system of gender that renders women vulnerable to dependency, exploitation, and abuse. When we look seriously at the distribution between husbands and wives of such critical social goods as work (paid and unpaid), power, prestige, self-esteem, opportunities for self-development, and both physical and economic security, we find socially constructed inequalities between them, right down the list.

The argument I shall make in this chapter depends to a large extent on contemporary empirical data, but also reflects the insights of two theorists, moral philosopher Robert Goodin and economist Albert O. Hirschman. Neither has used his argument to make a case about the injustice of the gender-structured family, but both establish convincing arguments about power and vulnerability that will be invaluable as we look at the data about contemporary marriage.

Goodin's recent book *Protecting the Vulnerable* discusses the significance of socially caused vulnerability for issues of justice. He argues that, over and above the general moral obligations that we owe to persons in general, "we bear special responsibilities for protecting those who are particularly vulnerable to us."[1] His major aim is to justify the obligations that welfare states place on citizens to contribute to the welfare of their more vulnerable fellow citizens. But his arguments can be employed to shed light on a number of other important social issues and institutions, including marriage and the family. Goodin's theory is particularly applicable to marriage because of its concern not only with the protection of the vulnerable but also with the moral status of vulnerability itself. Obviously, as he acknowledges, some cases of vulnerability have a large natural component—the vulnerability of infants, for example, although societies differ in how they allocate responsibility for protecting infants. Some instances of vulnerability that may at first appear "natural," such as those caused by illness, are in fact to a greater or lesser extent due to existing social arrangements.[2] And "some of the most important dependencies and vulnerabilities seem to be *almost wholly social in character*" (emphasis added).[3] Because asymmetric vulnerabilities create social obligations, which may fail to be fulfilled, and because they open up opportunities for exploitation, Goodin argues that insofar as they are alterable they are morally unacceptable and should be minimized. In this, he cites and follows the example of John Stuart Mill, who complained about the "great error of reformers and philanthropists [who] . . . nibble at the consequences of unjust power, instead of redressing the injustice itself."[4] As Goodin concludes, in the case of those vulnerabilities that are "created, shaped, or sustained by current social ar-

Vulnerability by Marriage

rangements . . . [w]hile we should always strive to protect the vulnerable, we should also strive to reduce the latter sort of vulnerabilities insofar as they render the vulnerable liable to exploitation."[5]

One of the tests Goodin employs to distinguish such unacceptable relations of asymmetrical vulnerability from acceptable relations of mutual vulnerability or interdependence is to examine the respective capacities of the two parties to withdraw from the relationship. Even if there is some degree of inequality in a relationship, Goodin says, "as long as the subordinate party can withdraw without severe cost, the superordinate cannot exploit him."[6] As I shall argue, the differing respective potentials for satisfactory withdrawal from the relationship is one of the major elements making marriage, in its typical contemporary manifestations in the United States, a morally unacceptable relationship of vulnerability.

The idea that the mutuality or asymmetry of a relationship can be measured by the relative capacities of the parties to withdraw from it has been developed extensively by Albert O. Hirschman, in two books written many years apart. In his 1970 book entitled *Exit, Voice and Loyalty*, Hirschman makes a convincing connection between the influence of voice by members within groups or institutions and the feasibility of their exit from them. There is a complex relation, he argues, between voice and exit. On the one hand, if the exit option is readily available, this will "tend to *atrophy the development of the art of voice*." Thus, for example, dissatisfied customers who can easily purchase equivalent goods from another firm are unlikely to expend their energies voicing complaints. On the other hand, the nonexistence or low feasibility of the exit option can impede the effectiveness of voice, since the *threat* of exit, whether explicit or implicit, is an important means of making one's voice influential. Thus "voice is not only handicapped when exit is possible, but also, though in a quite different way, when it is not." Because of this, for members' influence to be most effective, "there should be the possibility of exit, but exit should not be too easy or too attractive."[7] Hirschman concludes that institutions that deter exit by exacting a very high price for it, thereby rendering implausible the threat of exit, also repress the use and effectiveness of voice. Thus both potential modes of influence for combating deterioration are rendered ineffective.

Because the subjects of Hirschman's attention in *Exit, Voice and Loyalty* are groups with many members, his concern is with the power of the members vis-à-vis the institution, rather than with the power of the members relative to one another. But in the case of a two-member institution, such as marriage, special dynamics result from the fact that exit by one partner does not just weaken the institution, but rather results in its dissolution. Whether or not the other party wishes to exit, he or she is effectively expelled by the decision of the other to exit. Because of this, the *relative* potential of the exit option for the two parties is crucial for the relationship's power structure. Hirschman had made this argument, in the context of international relations, in a book published twenty-five years earlier, *National Power and the Structure of Foreign Trade*.[8] There he showed how state A can increase its power and influence by developing trading relations with state B, which is more dependent on the continuance of the trading relationship than A is. While both states gain something from the trade, the gain is far more significant in the one case than in the other. Thus the less dependent state's greater potential for exiting unharmed from the relationship gives it power or influence that can be used (through explicit or implicit threat of withdrawal) to make the more dependent state comply with its wishes. In addition, because of the extent of its dependence on trade with A, state B may alter its economic behavior in such a way that it becomes even more dependent on its trade with A.[9] Power (which may or may not remain latent) is likely to result from dependencies that are entered into voluntarily by parties whose initial resources and options differ, and in such circumstances the asymmetric dependency may well increase in the course of the relationship.

How do these principles apply to marriage? Few people would disagree with the statement that marriage involves, in some respects, especially emotionally, *mutual* vulnerability and dependence. It is, clearly, also a relationship in which some aspects of unequal vulnerability are not determined along sex lines. For example, spouses may vary in the extent of their love for and emotional dependence on each other; it is certainly not the case that wives always love their husbands more than they are loved by them, or vice versa. Nevertheless, as we shall see, in crucial respects gender-structured marriage *involves women in a cycle of socially caused and distinctly asymmetric vulnerability*. The division of labor within marriage (except in rare cases) makes wives far more likely than husbands to be exploited both within the marital relationship and in the world of work outside the home. To a great extent and in numerous ways, contemporary women in our society are *made* vulnerable by marriage itself. They are first set up for vulnerability during their developing years by their personal (and socially reinforced) expectations that they will be the primary caretakers of children, and that in fulfilling this role they will need to try to attract and to keep the economic support of a man, to whose work life they will be expected to give priority. They are rendered vulnerable by the actual division of labor within almost all current marriages. They are disadvantaged at work by the fact that the world of wage work, including the professions, is still largely structured around the assumption that "workers" have wives at home. They are rendered far more vulnerable if they become the primary caretakers of children, and their vulnerability peaks if their marriages dissolve and they become single parents.

Part of the reason that many nonfeminist social theorists have failed to recognize this pattern is that they confuse the socially caused (and therefore avoidable) vulnerability of women with the largely natural (and therefore largely unavoidable) vulnerability of children. This goes along with the usually unargued and certainly unfounded assumption that women are inevitably the primary caretakers of children. But as I shall show, women are made vulnerable, both economically and socially, by the interconnected traditions of female responsibility for rearing children and female subordination and dependence, of which both the history and the contemporary practices of marriage form a significant part.

It may be argued that it makes no sense to claim that something as ill-defined and variable as "modern marriage" is unjust, since marriages and families take so many forms, and not all marriages result in the dependence and vulnerability of their female members. There is some validity to this objection, and I shall try to counter it by making qualifications and pointing out exceptions to some of the general points I shall make. Part of the peculiarity of contemporary marriage comes from its very lack of definition. The fact that society seems no longer to have any consensual view of the norms and expectations of marriage is particularly apparent from the gulf that exists between the continued *perception* of most men and women that it is still the primary responsibility of husbands to "provide for" their wives by participating in wage work and of wives to perform a range of unpaid "services" for their husbands, and the *fact* that most women, including mothers of small children, are both in the labor force *and* performing the vast majority of household duties. In addition, the persistent perception of the male as provider is irreconcilable with both the prevalence of separation and divorce and the fact that, more and more, women and children are *not* being provided for after divorce. Between the expectations and the frequent outcome lies an abyss that not only is unjust in itself but radically affects the ways in which people behave within marriage. There is no way to alleviate the continuing inequality of women without more clearly defining and also reforming marriage. It seems evident, both from the disagreements between traditionalists and feminists and from the discrepancy between people's expectations of marriage and what in fact often happens to those who enter into it that there exists no clear current consensus in this society about what marriage is or should be.

Marriage has a long history, and we live in its shadow. It is a clear case of Marx's notion that we make our history "under circumstances directly encountered, given and transmitted from the past."[10] Certainly, gender is central to the way most people think about marriage. A recent, detailed study of thousands of couples, of different types—married and unmarried, heterosexual, gay and lesbian—confirms the importance of gender to our concept of marriage. Philip Blumstein and Pepper Schwartz's findings in *American Couples* demonstrate how not only current family law but the traditional expectations of marriage influence the attitudes, expectations, and behavior of married couples. By contrast, the lack of expectations about gender, and the lack of history of the institution of marriage, allow gay and lesbian couples more freedom in ordering their lives together and more chance to do so in an egalitarian manner. As the study concludes: "First, while the heterosexual model offers more stability and certainty, it inhibits change, innovation, and *choice* regarding roles and tasks. Second, the heterosexual model, which provides so much efficiency, is predicated on the man's being the dominant partner." The unmarried couples interviewed did not, in general, assume so readily that one partner would be the primary economic provider or that they would pool their income and assets. Homosexual couples, because of the absence of both marriage and the "gender factor," made even fewer such assumptions than did cohabiting heterosexual couples. They were almost unanimous, for example, in refusing to assign to either partner the role of homemaker. By contrast, many of the married respondents still enthusiastically subscribed to the traditional female/male separation of household work from wage work. While the authors also found the more egalitarian, two-paycheck marriage "emerging," they conclude that "the force of the previous tradition still guides the behavior of most modern marriages."[11]

It is important to recollect, in this context, how recently white married women in the United States have begun to work outside the home in significant numbers. Black women have always worked, first as slaves, then mostly—until very recently—as domestic servants. But in 1860, only 15 percent of all women were in the paid labor force and, right up to World War II, wage work for married women was strongly disapproved of. In 1890, only 5 percent of married women were in the labor force, and by 1960 the rate of married women's labor force participation had still reached only 30 percent. Moreover, wage work has a history of extreme segregation by sex that is closely related to the traditional female role within marriage. The largest category of women workers were domestic servants as late as 1950, since which time clerical workers have outnumbered them. Service (mostly no longer domestic) is still very predominantly female work. Even the female-dominated professions, such as nursing, grade-school teaching, and library work, have been "pink-collar labor ghettos [which] have historically discouraged high work ambitions that might detract from the pull of home and children." Like saleswomen and clerical workers, these female professionals "tend to arrive early in their 'careers' at a point above which they cannot expect to rise."[12] In sum, married women's wage work has a history of being exceptional, and women's wage work in general has been—as much of it still is—highly segregated and badly paid.

The traditional idea of sex-differentiated marital responsibility, with its provider-husband and domestic-wife roles, continues to be a strong influence on what men and women think and how they behave. Husbands, at least, tend to feel this way even when their wives *do* work outside the home; and when there is disagreement about whether the wife should work, it is more often the case that she wants to but that he does not want to "let" her. Thirty-four percent of the husbands and 25 percent of the wives surveyed by Blumstein and Schwartz did not think that couples should share the responsibility for earning a living. These percentages rise sharply when children are involved: 64 percent of husbands and 60 percent of wives did not think that the wife should be employed if a couple has small children.[13] Given the emphasis our society places on economic success, belief in the male provider role strongly reinforces the domination of men within marriage. Although, as we shall see, many wives actually work longer hours (counting paid and unpaid work) than their husbands, the fact that a husband's work is predominantly paid gives him not only status and prestige, both within and outside the marriage, but also a greater sense of entitlement. As a consequence, wives experiencing divorce, especially if they have been housewives and mothers throughout marriage, are likely to devalue their own contributions to the marriage and to discount their right to share its assets. "Many divorcing women still see the money their husbands have earned as 'his money.'"[14] In ongoing marriages too, it is not uncommon for husbands to use the fact that they are the primary breadwinners to enforce their views or wishes.[15]

JUSTICE, GENDER, AND THE FAMILY

Vulnerability by Anticipation of Marriage

In many respects, marriage is an institution whose tradition weighs upon those who enter into it. The cycle of women's vulnerability begins early, with their anticipation of marriage. Almost all women and men marry, but marriage has earlier and far greater impact on the lives and life choices of women than on those of men.* Socialization and the culture in general place more emphasis on marriage for girls than for boys and, although people have recently become less negative about remaining single, young women are more likely than young men to regard "having a good marriage and family life" as extremely important to them.[17] This fact, together with their expectation of being the parent primarily responsible for children, clearly affects women's decisions about the extent and field of education and training they will pursue, and their degree of purposiveness about careers. It is important to note that vulnerability by anticipation of marriage affects at least as adversely the futures of many women who do *not* marry as it affects those who do. This is particularly significant among disadvantaged groups, particularly poor urban black women, whose actual chances of marrying and being economically supported by a man are small (largely because of the high unemployment rate among the available men), but who are further burdened by growing up surrounded by a culture that still identifies femininity with this expectation.

Even though the proportion of young women who plan to be housewives exclusively has declined considerably,[18] women's choices about work are significantly affected from an early age by their expectations about the effects of family life on their work and of work on their family life. As is well known, the participation of women in the labor force, especially women with small children, has continued to rise.† But, although a small minority of women are rapidly increasing the previously tiny percentages of women in the elite professions, the vast majority of women who work outside the home are still in low-paying jobs with little or no prospect of advancement. This fact is clearly related to girls' awareness of the complexity they are likely to face in combining work with family life.[20] As the authors of one study conclude: "the occu-

*For the past century, nearly 90 percent of women have married by the age of thirty and between 80 percent and 90 percent have become mothers by the age of forty. In 1986, only 4.7 percent of women and 5.7 percent of men aged 45-54 in the U.S. had never married.[16]

†The labor force participation rate of U.S. women has risen steadily for three decades, from 35 percent (of those aged sixteen or more) in 1960 to 57 percent in 1986. Roughly 70 percent of women between the ages of twenty and thirty-four were employed in 1983, including (in 1983 and 1986) more than 50 percent of married women with children under the age of six.[19]

pational aspirations and expectations of adolescents are highly differentiated by sex . . . [and this] differentiation follows the pattern of sexual segregation which exists in the occupational structure." They found not only that the high school girls in their large-scale study were much less likely than the boys to aspire to the most prestigious occupations, but that the girls who had such aspirations displayed a much lower degree of confidence than the boys about being able to attain their goals.[21]

As the women Kathleen Gerson recently studied looked back on their girlhood considerations about the future, virtually all of them saw themselves as confronting a choice: *either* domesticity and motherhood *or* career.[22*] Given the pervasiveness of sex-role socialization (including the mixed or negative messages that girls are often given about their future work lives), the actual obstacles that our social structures place in the way of working mothers, and the far greater responsibility, both psychological and practical, that is placed on mothers than on fathers for their children's welfare, it is not surprising that these women perceived a conflict between their own work interests and the interests of any children they might have.[23] While many reacted against their own mothers' domestic lives, very few were able to imagine successfully combining motherhood with a career. And those who did generally avoided confronting the dilemmas they would have to face.[24] But most grew up with the belief that "a woman can have either a career or children, but not both."[25] Not surprisingly, many of them, assuming that they would want to have children, followed educational and work paths that would readily accommodate the demands of being a primary parent. The only way that those who were career-oriented came to believe that they might avoid the difficult choice, and even attempt to combine their work with mothering, was by deciding to be trailblazers, rejecting strongly ingrained beliefs about the incompatibility of the two.

Needless to say, such a choice does not confront boys in their formative years. *They* assume—reasonably enough, given our traditions and present conditions and beliefs—that what is expected of them as husbands and fathers is that, by developing a solid work life, they will provide the primary financial sup-

*Though Gerson's sample includes no women of color, it represents in other respects a wide range of class backgrounds and present situations. Gerson presents a number of surprising findings. One is that more of the women in her sample *changed* their orientation—from domestic to nondomestic or vice versa—than maintained their original orientation. What happened within their marriages and in their work lives was clearly influential here. Another is that many (45%) of her sample started out with nondomestic orientations, at a time when few of their mothers presented role models for this choice (p. 61). As Gerson shows, reaction against mothers' choices and situations was just as likely to influence daughters' choices as was identification with them.

port of the family. Men's situation can have its own strains, since those who feel trapped at work cannot opt for domesticity and gain as much support for this choice as a woman can.[26] For those who become unemployed, the conflict of their experience with society's view of the male as provider can be particularly stressful. But boys do not experience the dilemma about work and family that girls do as they confront the choices that are crucial to their educations, future work lives and opportunities, and economic security.

When women envisage a future strongly influenced by the demands on them as wives and particularly as mothers, they are likely to embark on traditionally female fields of study and/or occupational paths. The typical route for women is still to finish their education with high school and to marry and have children in their early twenties, though a growing minority are continuing their education, establishing themselves in careers, and marrying later.[27] Some of those who are primarily family-oriented foresee their wage work as temporary or intermittent, while some envisage trying to combine some continued work in the marketplace with traditionally female family responsibilities. But whether such women enter clerical, sales, or service work, or train for one of the predominantly female professions such as teaching or nursing, they are heading not only for the relatively more flexible hours or greater replaceability that most of these jobs afford but also for low pay, poor working conditions, and, above all, blocked mobility. In 1987, women who worked year-round at full-time jobs earned a median wage of $15,704—71 percent of the $22,204 earned by full-time working men.[28] The fact that women's educational achievement is becoming equal to men's, through the level of master's degrees, is clearly affecting women's *participation* in the work force.[29] But, though it could also potentially affect their earnings relative to men's, it has done so very little up to now, in part because the professional and service occupations that are more than two-thirds female—such as education, humanities, home economics, library science, and health science—are far worse paid than those that are still more than two-thirds male—such as science and engineering.[30] Occupational sex segregation cancels out women's educational advances: in 1985, the average full-time working white woman with a college degree or higher earned $2,000 less than the average white man who had only a high-school diploma; and the average black woman with some college education earned slightly less than the average white man who had only an elementary school education.[31]

Regardless of educational achievement, women are far more likely than men to work in administrative support jobs, as a secretary, typist, or bookkeeper, for example, which in most cases hold no prospects for advancement. Almost 30 percent of employed women worked in this category in 1985, compared with fewer than 6 percent of men.[32] A study of workplaces during the late 1960s and the 1970s (*after* the 1963 Equal Pay Act and Title VII of the 1964 Civil Rights Act) found the sex segregation of specific jobs and occupational ladders in both manufacturing and nonmanufacturing firms to be so pervasive that more than 90 percent of women would have had to change jobs in order for women to share equally the same job titles as men. Frequently, workplaces had only one or two job titles that included members of both sexes. On top of all this, recent research has shown that large discrepancies exist between male and female wages for the same job title. While female secretaries earned a median wage of $278 per week in 1985, the median for male secretaries was $365; moreover, in twenty-four other narrowly defined occupations in which females earned *less* than they would have as secretaries, males earned *more* in every case than a female secretary. Indeed, some firms designate particular jobs as male and others designate the same jobs as female, and the wage rates differ accordingly. It seems, therefore, that "the wage level for a particular job title in a particular establishment is set *after the employer decides whether those jobs will be filled by women or men*."[33] Barbara Bergmann's detailed study of sex segregation in the workplace leads her to conclude:

> Women are fenced off from a disproportionate share of what we might call "labor-market turf." . . . [Thus] the supply and the demand in the markets for men's and women's labor are powerfully affected by discrimination. . . . The exclusion of women from a big share of all of the jobs in the economy is what creates two labor markets where there should be only one. The discriminatory assignment of jobs to one sex or the other is what sets the level of demand in each market . . . [and] force[s] women to have to sell their labor at a low price.[34]

Thus workplace discrimination *per se* is very significant. In addition, as I have suggested, some of the segregation of wage work by sex is attributable to the individual choices that women and men make in the context of their own socialization and with knowledge of the gender structure of the family in particular. M. Rivka Polatnick has recently summarized the situation:

> Not only during the period of childrearing do women become economically or professionally disadvantaged vis-à-vis men; most women's lives have already been constructed in anticipation of that period. "Helpful advice" from family, friends, and guidance counselors, and discriminatory practices in schools and in the job

market steer women toward jobs and interests compatible with a future in childrearing.[35]

It is no wonder, then, that most women are, even before marriage, in an economic position that sets them up to become more vulnerable during marriage, and most vulnerable of all if their marriage ends and—unprepared as they are—they find themselves in the position of having to provide for themselves and their children.

Vulnerability Within Marriage

Marriage continues the cycle of inequality set in motion by the anticipation of marriage and the related sex segregation of the workplace. Partly because of society's assumptions about gender, but also because women, on entering marriage, tend already to be disadvantaged members of the work force, married women are likely to start out with less leverage in the relationship than their husbands. As I shall show, answers to questions such as whose work life and work needs take priority, and how the unpaid work of the family will be allocated—if they are not simply assumed to be decided along the lines of sex difference, but are live issues in the marriage—are likely to be strongly influenced by the differences in earning power between husbands and wives. In many marriages, partly because of discrimination at work and the wage gap between the sexes, wives (despite initial personal ambitions and even when they are full-time wage workers) come to perceive themselves as benefiting from giving priority to their husbands' careers. Hence they have little incentive to question the traditional division of labor in the household. This in turn limits their own commitment to wage work and their incentive and leverage to challenge the gender structure of the workplace. Experiencing frustration and lack of control at work, those who thus turn toward domesticity, while often resenting the lack of respect our society gives to full-time mothers, may see the benefits of domestic life as greater than the costs.[36]

Thus, the inequalities between the sexes in the workplace and at home reinforce and exacerbate each other. It is not necessary to choose between two alternative, competing explanations of the inequalities between men and women in the workplace—the "human capital" approach, which argues that, because of expectations about their family lives, women *choose* to enter lower-paid and more dead-end occupations and specific jobs,[37] and the workplace discrimination explanation, which blames factors largely outside the control of female employees. When the pivotal importance of gender-structured marriage and the expectation of it are acknowledged, these explanations can be seen, rather, as complementary reasons for women's inequality. *A cycle of power relations and decisions pervades both family and workplace, and the inequalities of each reinforce those that already exist in the other.* Only with the recognition of this truth will we be able to begin to confront the changes that need to occur if women are to have a real opportunity to be equal participants in either sphere.[38]

Human capital theorists, in perceiving women's job market attachment as a matter of voluntary choice, appear to miss or virtually to ignore the fact of unequal power within the family. Like normative theorists who idealize the family, they ignore potential conflicts of interest, and consequently issues of justice and power differentials, *within* families. This means that they view the question of whether a wife works solely in terms of the total aggregate costs and benefits for the family unit as a whole.[39] They assume that if a wife's paid work benefits the family more (in terms, say, of aggregate income and leisure) than her working exclusively within the household, her rational choice, and that of her husband, will be that she should get a job; if the reverse is true, she should not. But this simplistic attention to the family's "aggregate good" ignores the fact that a wife, like a husband, may have an independent interest in her own career advancement or desire for human contact, for example, that may give her an incentive to work even if the family as a whole may on that account find its life more difficult. Further, the human capital approach overlooks the fact that such goods as leisure and influence over the expenditure of income are by no means always equally shared within families. It also fails to recognize that the considerable influence that husbands often exert over their wives' decisions on whether to take paid work may be motivated not by a concern for the aggregate welfare of the household but, at least in part, by their desire to retain the authority and privilege that accrues to them by virtue of being the family's breadwinner.[40] Thus the decisions of married women about their participation in the job market, even when they *are* choices, may not be such simple or voluntary choices as human capital theory seems to imply.

In addition, those who seek to explain women's comparative disadvantage in the labor market by their preference for domestic commitments do not consider whether at least some of the causality may run in the opposite direction. But there is considerable evidence that women's "choices" to become domestically oriented, and even whether to have children, may result at least in part from their frequently blocked situations at work. Kathleen Gerson's study shows that, though they usually did not notice the connection, many of the women in her sample decided to leave wage work and turn to childbearing and domesticity coincidentally with becoming frustrated with the dead-end nature of their jobs. Conversely, she found that some women who had initially thought of themselves as domestically oriented, and who had in many cases chosen traditionally female occupations, reversed these orientations when unusual and unexpected opportunities for work advancement opened up to them.[41]

Even if these problems with the human capital approach did not exist, we would still be faced with the fact that the theory can explain, at most, half of the wage differential between the sexes. In the case of the differential between white men and black women, 70 percent of it is unexplained. At *any* given level of skill, experience, and education, men earn considerably more than women. The basic problem with the human capital approach is that, like much of neoclassical economic theory, it pays too little attention to the multiple constraints placed on people's choices. It pays too little attention to differentials of power between the sexes both in the workplace and in the family. It thus ignores the fact that women's commitment and attachment to the workplace are strongly influenced by a number of factors that are largely beyond their control. As we have seen, a woman's typically less advantaged position in the work force and lower pay may lead her to choices about full-time motherhood and domesticity that she would have been less likely to make had her work life been less dead-ended. They also give her less power in relation to her husband should she want to resist the traditional division of labor in her household and to insist on a more equal sharing of child care and other domestic responsibilities. Those who stress the extent to which both husbands and wives cling to the "male provider/female nurturer" roles as unobjectionable because efficient and economically rational for the family unit need to take a step back and consider the extent to which the continued sex segregation of the work force serves to perpetuate the traditional division of labor within the household, even in the face of women's rising employment.

Vulnerability by Marriage

HOUSEWORK AND THE CYCLE OF VULNERABILITY

It is no secret that in almost all families women do far more housework and child care than men do. But the distribution of paid and unpaid work within the family has rarely—outside of feminist circles—been considered a significant issue by theorists of justice. Why should it be? If two friends divide a task so that each takes primary responsibility for a different aspect of it, we would be loath to cry "injustice" unless one were obviously coercing the other. But at least three factors make the division of labor within the household a very different situation, and a clear question of justice. First, the uneven distribution of labor within the family is strongly correlated with an innate characteristic, which appears to make it the kind of issue with which theorists of justice have been most concerned. The virtually automatic allocation to one person of more of the paid labor and to the other of more of the unpaid labor would be regarded as decidedly odd in any relationship other than that of a married or cohabiting heterosexual couple.* One reason for this is that, as we shall see, it has distinct effects on the distribution of power. While the unequal distribution of paid and unpaid work has different repercussions in different types of marriages, it is always of significance. Second, though it is by no means always absolute, the division of labor in a traditional or quasi-traditional marriage is often quite complete and usually long-standing. It lasts in many cases at least through the lengthy years of child rearing, and is by no means confined to the preschool years. Third, partly as a result of this, and of the structure and demands of most paid work, the household division of labor has a lasting impact on the lives of married women, especially those who become mothers. It affects every sphere of their lives, from the dynamics of their marital relationship to their opportunities in the many spheres of life outside the household. The distribution of labor within the family by sex has deep ramifications for its respective members' material, psychological, physical, and intellectual well-being. One cannot even begin to address the issue of why so many women and children live in poverty in our soci-

*Blumstein and Schwartz's comparisons of homosexual couples (male and female) with heterosexual couples (cohabiting and married) demonstrate vividly the extent to which the division of labor in the household is affected by sex difference. In all but about 1 percent of contemporary homosexual households, they found that the homemaker/provider division of roles is avoided. Even when one partner is not working, and is in fact doing more of the housework, the tendency is to think of him or her as "temporarily unemployed" or "a student." Lesbians take particular care to distribute household duties equitably. And yet, contrary to what one might expect on the basis of some arguments (including that of economist Gary Becker), such households seem to be managed with considerable efficiency. Blumstein and Schwartz, *American Couples*, pp. 116, 127–31, 148–51.

ety, or why women are inadequately represented in the higher echelons of our political and economic institutions, without confronting the division of labor between the sexes within the family. Thus it is not only itself an issue of justice but it is also at the very root of other significant concerns of justice, including equality of opportunity for children of both sexes, but especially for girls, and political justice in the broadest sense.

The justice issues surrounding housework are not simply issues about who does *more* work. However, on average, wives living with their husbands *do* now work slightly more total hours than their husbands do.[42] In addition, this averaging obscures a great variety of distributions of both quantity and type of work within marriages. For the purposes of this discussion, it will be helpful to separate couples into two major categories: those in which the wife is "predominantly houseworking" (either a full-time housewife or employed part-time) and those in which the wife is "predominantly wage-working" (employed full-time or virtually full-time).[43] Within each category, I shall look at issues such as the distribution of work (paid and unpaid), income, power, opportunity to choose one's occupation, self-respect and esteem, and availability of exit. As we shall see, wives in each category experience a somewhat different pattern of injustice and vulnerability. But, except in the case of some of the small number of elite couples who make considerable use of paid help, the typical divisions of labor in the family cannot be regarded as just.

Predominantly Houseworking Wives

When a woman is a full-time housewife—as are about two-fifths of married women in the United States who live with their husbands—she does less total work, on average, than her employed husband: 49.3 hours per week, compared with his 63.2. This is also true of couples in which the wife works part-time (defined as fewer than thirty hours per week, including commuting time), though the average difference per week is reduced to eight hours in this case.[44] This is, of course, partly because housework is less burdensome than it was before the days of labor-saving devices and declining fertility. Not surprisingly, however, during the early years of child rearing, a nonemployed wife (or part-time employed wife) is likely to work about the same total number of hours as her employed husband. But the *quantity* of work performed is only one of a number of important variables that must be considered in order for us to assess the justice or injustice of the division of labor in the family, particularly in relation to the issue of the cycle of women's vulnerability.

In terms of the quality of work, there are considerable disadvantages to the role of housewife.[45] One is that much of the work is boring and/or unpleasant.

Vulnerability by Marriage

Surveys indicate that most people of both sexes do not like to clean, shop for food, or do laundry, which constitute a high proportion of housework. Cooking rates higher, and child care even higher, with both sexes, than other domestic work.[46] In reality, this separation of tasks is strictly hypothetical, at least for mothers, who are usually cleaning, shopping, doing laundry, and cooking at the same time as taking care of children. Many wage workers, too, do largely tedious and repetitive work. But the housewife-mother's work has additional disadvantages. One is that her hours of work are highly unscheduled; unlike virtually any other worker except the holder of a high political office, she can be called on at any time of the day or night, seven days a week. Another is that she cannot, nearly as easily as most other workers, change jobs. Her family comes to depend on *her* to do all the things she does. Finding substitutes is difficult and expensive, even if the housewife is not discouraged or forbidden by her husband to seek paid work. The skills and experience she has gained are not valued by prospective employers. Also, once a woman has taken on the role of housewife, she finds it extremely difficult, for reasons that will be explored, to shift part of this burden back onto her husband. Being a housewife thus both impairs a woman's ability to support herself and constrains her future choices in life.[47]

Many of the disadvantages of being a housewife spring directly or indirectly from the fact that all her work is unpaid work, whereas more than four-fifths of her husband's total work is paid work. This may at first seem a matter of little importance. If wives, so long as they stay married, usually share their husbands' standards of living for the most part, why should it matter who earns the income? It matters a great deal, for many reasons. In the highly money-oriented society we live in, the housewife's work is devalued. In fact, in spite of the fact that a major part of it consists of the nurturance and socialization of the next generation of citizens, it is frequently not even acknowledged as work or as productive, either at the personal or at the policy level. This both affects the predominantly houseworking wife's power and influence within the family and means that her social status depends largely upon her husband's, a situation that she may not consider objectionable so long as the marriage lasts, but that is likely to be very painful for her if it does not.[48]

Also, although married couples usually share material well-being, a housewife's or even a part-time working wife's lack of access to much money of her own can create difficulties that range from the mildly irritating through the humiliating to the devastating, especially if she does not enjoy a good relationship with her husband. Money is the subject of most conflict for married couples, although the issue of housework may be overtaking it.[49] Bergmann reports that in an informal survey, she discovered that about 20 percent of the housewife-mothers of her students were in the position of continually having to appeal to their husbands for money. The psychological effects on an adult of economic dependence can be great. As Virginia Woolf pointed out fifty years ago, any man who has difficulty estimating them should simply imagine himself depending on his wife's income.[50] The dark side of economic dependence is also indicated by the fact that, in the serious predivorce situation of having to fight for their future economic well-being, many wives even of well-to-do men do not have access to enough cash to pay for the uncovering and documentation of their husband's assets.

At its (not so uncommon) worst, the economic dependence of wives can seriously affect their day-to-day physical security. As Linda Gordon has recently concluded: "The basis of wife-beating is male dominance—not superior physical strength or violent temperament . . . but social, economic, political, and psychological power. . . . Wife-beating is the chronic battering of a person of inferior power who for that reason cannot effectively resist."[51] Both wife abuse and child abuse are clearly exacerbated by the economic dependence of women on their husbands or cohabiting male partners. Many women, especially full-time housewives with dependent children, have no way of adequately supporting themselves, and are often in practice unable to leave a situation in which they and/or their children are being seriously abused. In addition to increasing the likelihood of the more obvious forms of abuse—physical and sexual assault—the fear of being abandoned, with its economic and other dire consequences, can lead a housewife to tolerate infidelity, to submit to sexual acts she does not enjoy, or experience psychological abuse including virtual desertion.[52] The fact that a predominantly houseworking wife has no money of her own or a small paycheck is not necessarily significant, but it can be very significant, especially at crucial junctures in the marriage.

Finally, as I shall discuss, the earnings differential between husband and housewife can become devastating in its significance for her and for any dependent children in the event of divorce (which in most states can now occur without her consent). This fact, which significantly affects the relative potential of wives and husbands for exit from the marriage, is likely to influence the distribution of power, and in turn paid and unpaid work, *during* the marriage as well.

Vulnerability by Marriage

Predominantly Wage-Working Wives and Housework

Despite the increasing labor force participation of married women, including mothers, "working wives still bear almost all the responsibility for housework." They do less of it than housewives, but "they still do the vast bulk of what needs to be done," and the difference is largely to be accounted for not by the increased participation of men, but by lowered standards, the participation of children, purchased services such as restaurant or frozen meals, and, in elite groups, paid household help. Thus, while the distribution of paid labor between the sexes is shifting quite considerably onto women, that of unpaid labor is not shifting much at all, and "the couple that shares household tasks equally remains rare."[53] The differences in total time spent in all "family work" (housework and child care plus yard work, repairs, and so on) vary considerably from one study to another, but it seems that fully employed husbands do, *at most*, approximately half as much as their fully employed wives, and some studies show a much greater discrepancy.

Bergmann reports that "husbands of wives with full-time jobs averaged about two minutes more housework per day than did husbands in housewife-maintaining families, hardly enough additional time to prepare a soft-boiled egg."[54] Even unemployed husbands do much less housework than wives who work a forty-hour week. Working-class husbands are particularly vocal about not being equal partners in the home, and do little housework. In general, however, a husband's income and job prestige are *inversely* related to his involvement in household chores, unless his wife is employed in a similarly high-paid and prestigious job. Many husbands who profess belief in sharing household tasks equally actually do far less than their wives, when time spent and chores done are assessed. In many cases, egalitarian attitudes make little or no difference to who actually does the work, and often "the idea of shared responsibility turn[s] out to be a myth."[55]

Some scholars are disinclined to perceive these facts as indicating unequal power or exploitation. They prefer to view them as merely embodying adherence to traditional patterns, or to justify them as efficient in terms of the total welfare of the family (the husband's time being too valuable to spend doing housework).[56] There are clear indications, however, that the major reason that husbands and other heterosexual men living with wage-working women are not doing more housework is that *they do not want to, and are able, to a very large extent, to enforce their wills*. How do we know that the unequal allocation of housework is not equally women's choice? First, because most people do not like doing many of the major household chores. Second, because almost half of wage-working wives who do more than 60 percent of the housework say that they would prefer their husbands to do more of it.[57] Third, because husbands with higher salaries and more prestigious jobs than their wives (the vast majority of two-job couples) are in a powerful position to resist their wives' appeal to them to do more at home, and it is husbands with the highest prestige who do the least housework of all. Even when there is little conflict, and husbands and wives seem to agree that the woman should do more of the housework, they are often influenced by the prevailing idea that whoever earns less or has the less prestigious job should do more unpaid labor at home. But since the maldistribution of wages and jobs between the sexes in our society is largely out of women's control, even *seemingly nonconflictual* decisions made on this basis cannot really be considered fully voluntary on the part of wives.[58] Finally, the resistance of most husbands to housework is well documented, as is the fact that the more housework men do, the *more* it becomes a cause of fighting within couples. Examining factors that caused the breakup of some of the couples in their sample, Blumstein and Schwartz say:

> Among both married and cohabiting couples, housework is a source of conflict. . . . *[A] woman cannot be perceived as doing less housework than her partner wants her to do without jeopardizing the relationship*. However, a man, who is unlikely to be doing even half the work, can be perceived as doing less than his fair share without affecting the couple's durability. *It is difficult for women to achieve an equal division of housework and still preserve the relationship*[59] [emphasis added].

As a result, in many of the households in which men and women both work full-time—those for which much paid household help or reliance on other purchased services is not a practical option—the unequal distribution of housework between husbands and wives leads to gross inequities in the amount and type of work done by each. "Drudge wives," as Bergmann has recently termed women in such households, do more total work than their husbands, averaging 71.1 hours a week to the husband's 64.9. But of greater overall significance is the fact that a vastly higher proportion of the wife's than of the husband's work is unpaid. She averages 28.1 hours of unpaid "family" work to 43 hours of paid work, whereas he averages only 9.2 hours of family work to 55.8 hours of paid work.[60] One important effect of unequal sharing of housework and other family work within dual working couples is that the amount of time and energy the wife has left to commit to her wage work is

Vulnerability by Marriage

considerably more limited than her husband's. It used to be assumed, in the days when the full traditional division of labor in the family prevailed, that any job requiring responsibility and commitment was incompatible with day-to-day responsibilities for home and children. This was why, or so it was argued, men could not, and should not be expected to, share in these tasks.[61] But now many women, whether forced by economic need or refusing to accept the choice between parenthood and career that men have never had to make, are trying to do both.[62] Their chances of success are significantly affected by the fact that, although they are likely to expend significant amounts of time on their homes and children, they must compete at work, not only with men from families like their own, who do significantly less family work than they do, but also with men whose wives are full-time housewives or work only part-time.

WIVES AND WAGE WORK

While theorists of justice have largely ignored it, women's double burden and its effects have long been recognized by feminists. Largely because of the unequal distribution of housework and child care, married women's opportunities in the work force are considerably more constrained than men's. As Gerson notes, "the simple fact of [women's] working . . . does not by itself entail significant social change." Though women are now less inclined than they were a generation ago to be part-time and sporadic workers, there is a wide gap between the increase in their labor force participation and their labor force attachment and position.[63] Because of their lower level of labor force attachment, their tendency to work part-time and at jobs that in other respects bend to meet the needs of the family, and their propensity to accommodate their own employment to their husbands', women's wages become lower in relation to men's as they get older. Whereas the ratio between an average full-time working woman's earnings and a full-time working man's is 83:100 between the ages of twenty-one to twenty-nine, the wage gap by ages forty-five to sixty-four has increased to 60:100.[64]

The constraints placed on wives as workers are strengthened by the fact that many full-time employers assume, in innumerable ways, that "someone" is at home at least part-time during the day to assume primary responsibility for children. The traditional or quasi-traditional division of labor is clearly assumed in the vast discrepancy between normal full-time working hours and children's school hours and vacations. It is assumed by the high degree of geographical mobility required by many higher-level management positions. It is also implicit in the structure of the professions, in which the greatest demands are placed on workers at the very peak of the child-rearing years. Academia and the law are two clear examples; both tenure and partnership decisions are typically made for a person between the ages of thirty and thirty-five, with obvious discriminatory implications for the professional parent (almost always a woman) who does not have a partner willing to assume the major responsibility for children.

Because the structure of most wage work is inconsistent with the parenting responsibilities chiefly borne by women, far fewer women (especially married women) than men *do* work full-time. Only 27 percent of all wives in families with children worked full-time year-round in 1984, compared with 77 percent of husbands.[65] Some mothers conclude that, given the demands of their work, the only reasonable answer to the needs of their children is to take time out of the workplace altogether. Others work part-time. But the repercussions of either of these choices, given the current structure and attitudes of the workplace, are often serious and long-lasting. The investment in career assets is by far the most valuable property owned by most couples. To the extent that wives work part-time or intermittently, their own career potential atrophies, and they become deeply dependent on their husbands' career assets. Even when a wife maintains her career, her husband's work needs—in terms of time, freedom from other preoccupations, education and training, and geographical mobility—usually take priority. This is often the case even with dual-career couples who are similarly qualified and claim to be committed to an egalitarian ideology.[66] In relation to the outside world of employment, therefore, the notion that husbands and wives are equals is myth. Typically, women as workers are disadvantaged by marriage itself, and the more so the longer the duration of the marriage.[67]

POWER IN THE FAMILY

There are very few studies of power within marriage. Of those few, the one most frequently cited until recently—Robert O. Blood, Jr., and Donald M. Wolfe's 1960 *Husbands and Wives*—though informative, is now outdated and unreliable in the way it interprets its own findings.[68] The study in itself is of considerable interest for the question of power and gender, given its influential character, not only because of what it purports to discover but also because these findings are both distorted and blurred by the authors' initial assumption that a moderate degree of male dominance is the desirable norm within families.* This assumption leads them to define what their own scale indicates to be moderate male dominance as "relative equalitarianism" in family decision making. When reinterpreted in the absence of this sexist normative assumption, we find that what Blood and Wolfe's study of married life in the 1950s discovered was not, as they claimed, that "the American family has changed its authority pattern from one of patriarchal male dominance to one of equalitarian sharing," but rather that male dominance was still the norm, though its extent varied in accordance with a number of factors.[69] The most important of these was the discrepancy in income and wage-work success between the husband and the wife.

As Blood and Wolfe report their findings about what variables affect family power, they are again misleading, due to their implicit assumptions. They conclude that the distribution of power, and its ebb and flow during the course of a marriage, vary with the "resources" that each spouse contributes to the family. But they completely fail to notice that the only resources that affect marital power are those—such as income, success, and prestige—that are valued in the world *outside* the marriage. Resources such as domestic services and childbearing and child-rearing capacities, skills, and labor are not only not positively correlated with marital power but are in fact *negatively* correlated with it. While Blood and Wolfe note that the housewife with preschool children is at the least powerful point in her marriage, and that her power decreases as the number of children rises, they do not question why she should be so powerless at a time when she is contributing so much to the family. Because of their unstated sexist assumptions about what constitutes a "resource," they explain her lack of power in terms of her extreme financial dependence on her husband, and fail to perceive her husband as dependent on *her* for any resources at all.[70]

Only recently, with the publication of Blumstein and Schwartz's *American Couples*, have we had a large-scale and more neutral account of the power picture behind decision making by couples. They asked thousands of couples to respond on a scale of 1 to 9 (with 5 defined as "both equally") to the question: "In general, who has more say about important decisions affecting your

*Blood and Wolfe's study is based on interviews with the wives (only) in 731 city (Detroit) and 178 farm families, during the 1950s. The authors' biases are apparent throughout, from their labeling of the less powerful husband "Caspar Milquetoast" to their pronouncement that families ranging from husband-dominance to "extreme equalitarianism" are "appropriate," but that wife-dominance is a "deviant" and "not normal" reversal of marital roles. *Husbands and Wives*, pp. 11, 45.

relationship, you or your partner?" Clearly, what this new study reveals about married couples confirms the major findings that Blood and Wolfe's earlier study discovered but obscured. First, though the number of marriages in which spouses consider that they share decision-making power relatively equally has increased considerably, the tendency in others is still distinctly toward male rather than female dominance.[71] Second, it is still clearly the case that the possession by each spouse of resources valued by the *outside* world, especially income and work status, rather than resources valuable primarily within the family, has a significant effect on the distribution of power in the relationship.

Blumstein and Schwartz preface their findings about couples, money, and power by noting that they are not likely to accord with "cherished American beliefs about fairness and how people acquire influence in romantic relationships." Perhaps this is why, as they point out, although "economic factors tend to be involved in every aspect of a couple's life," standard textbooks on marriage and the family are unlikely to devote more than five pages to this subject. Just as political and moral theorists have been extremely reluctant to admit that questions of justice pertain to family life, a similar tendency to idealize—and to conceal dominance—has apparently characterized sociologists of the family until recently, too. But Blumstein and Schwartz's study establishes quite decisively that "in three out of four of the types of couples . . . studied [all types except lesbian couples], . . . the amount of money a person earns—in comparison with a partner's income—establishes relative power."[72] Given that even the 26 percent of all wives who work full-time earn, on average, only 63 percent as much as the average full-time working husband, and the average wife who works for pay (full- or part-time) earns only 42 percent as much, it is therefore not at all surprising that male dominance is far more common than female dominance in couples who deviate from a relatively egalitarian distribution of power.[73] When women are employed, and especially when their earnings approach those of their husbands, they are more likely to share decision-making power equally with their husbands and to have greater financial autonomy. In marriages in which the husband earned over $8,000 more than the wife (more than half the marriages in the Blumstein and Schwartz sample), the husband was rated as more powerful (as opposed to an equal sharing of power or to the wife's being more powerful) in 33 percent of cases. In marriages in which the incomes of husband and wife were approximately equal, only 18 percent of the husbands were rated as more powerful. The workplace success of wives, then, helps considerably to equalize the balance of power within their marriages and gains them greater respect from their husbands, who often have little respect for housework. Success at work, moreover, can reduce the expectation that a wife will do the vast bulk of family work.[74] Nevertheless, the full-time employment, and even the equal or greater earnings, of wives do not guarantee them equal power in the family, for the male-provider *ideology* is sometimes powerful enough to counteract these factors.[75]

Given these facts about the way power is distributed in the family, and the facts brought out earlier about the typical contentiousness of the issue of housework, it is not difficult to see how the vulnerability of married women in relation to the world of work and their inequality within the family tend to form part of a vicious cycle. Wives are likely to start out at a disadvantage, because of both the force of the traditions of gender and the fact that they are likely to be already earning less than their husbands at the time of marriage. In many cases, the question of who is responsible for the bulk of the unpaid labor of the household is probably not raised at all, but *assumed*, on the basis of these two factors alone. Because of this "nondecision" factor, studies of marital power that ask only about the respective influence of the partners over *decisions* are necessarily incomplete, since they ignore distributions of burdens and benefits that may not be perceived as arising from decisions at all.[76]

However, there *is* often conflict about how much time each partner should devote to wage work and how much to family work. This may include disagreement over the issue of whether the wife should have a job at all, whereas this is almost always taken for granted (a "nondecision") in the case of the husband. Since the partner whose wage work is given priority and who does far less unpaid family work is likely to increase the disparity between his and his spouse's earnings, seniority, and work status, his power in the family will tend to grow accordingly. Hence if, as is likely, he wishes to preserve a traditional or semitraditional division of labor in the family, he is likely to be able to do so. This need not involve constant fighting, with the man always winning; his "man" power and his earning power combined may be so preeminent that the issue is never even raised. Either way, his wife is likely to find it difficult to reallocate the family work so as to make him responsible for more of it so that she can take a job or expend more time and energy on the one she has. In addition, the weight of tradition and of her own sex-role socialization will contribute to her powerlessness to effect change.

Vulnerability by Separation or Divorce

The impact of the unequal distribution of benefits and burdens between husbands and wives is hardest and most directly felt by the increasing numbers of women and children whose families are no longer intact. In 1985, 28 percent of ever-married white women and 49 percent of ever-married black women in the United States were separated, divorced, or widowed.[77] Marital disruption through the death of a spouse, divorce, or separation is consistently rated as the most psychologically stressful life event for men and women alike.[78] But in women's lives, the personal disruption caused by these events is frequently exacerbated by the serious social and economic dislocation that accompanies them.

Every year, divorce disrupts the lives of more than three million men, women, and children in the United States.[79] The annual divorce rate per 1,000 married women increased from 9.2 in 1960 to 22.6 in 1981; it has leveled off and even declined slightly during the 1980s. Half of all marriages contracted in the 1970s are projected to end in divorce, and between 50 and 60 percent of the children born in the early 1980s are likely to experience the breakup of their parents' marriage by the age of eighteen. Rates of separation and divorce are much higher for black than for white women: in 1983 there were 126 divorced white women for every 1,000 married women; for black women, the ratio was 297 to 1,000.[80] In 1985, about 23 percent of children under the age of eighteen lived with only one parent—in about 90 percent of cases, the mother. Contrary to popular prejudice, female-maintained families with children consist in only a fairly small percentage of cases of never-married women raising children alone. They are in the vast majority of cases the result of separation or divorce.[81]

Not only has the rate of divorce increased rapidly but the differential in the economic impact of divorce on men and women has also grown. Divorce and its economic effects contribute significantly to the fact that nearly one-quarter of all children now live in single-parent households, more than half of them, even after transfer payments, below the poverty level. Moreover, partly because of the increased labor force participation of married women, there has been a growing divergence between female-maintained families and two-parent families.[82] These dramatic shifts, with their vast impact on the lives of women and children, must be addressed by any theory of justice that can claim to be about all of us, rather than simply about the male "heads of households" on which theories of justice in the past have focused.

Vulnerability by Marriage

There is now little doubt that, while no-fault divorce does not appear to have caused the increasing rate of divorce, it has considerably affected the economic outcome of divorce for both parties.[83] Many studies have shown that whereas the average economic status of men improves after divorce, that of women and children deteriorates seriously. Nationwide, the per-capita income of divorced women, which was only 62 percent that of divorced men in 1960, decreased to 56 percent by 1980.[84] The most illuminating explanation of this is Lenore Weitzman's recent pathbreaking study, *The Divorce Revolution*. Based on a study of 2,500 randomly selected California court dockets between 1968 and 1977 and lengthy interviews with many lawyers, judges, legal experts, and 228 divorced men and women, the book both documents and explains the differential social and economic impact of current divorce law on men, women, and children. Weitzman presents the striking finding that in the first year after divorce, the average standard of living of divorced men, adjusted for household size, increases by 42 percent while that of divorced women falls by 73 percent. "For most women and children," Weitzman concludes:

> divorce means precipitous downward mobility—both economically and socially. The reduction in income brings residential moves and inferior housing, drastically diminished or nonexistent funds for recreation and leisure, and intense pressures due to inadequate time and money. Financial hardships in turn cause social dislocation and a loss of familiar networks for emotional support and social services, and intensify the psychological stress for women and children alike. On a societal level, divorce increases female and child poverty and creates an ever-widening gap between the economic well-being of divorced men, on the one hand, and their children and former wives on the other.[85]

Weitzman's findings have been treated with disbelief by some, who claim, for example, that California, being a community property state, is atypical, and that these figures could not be projected nationwide without distortion. However, studies done in other states (including common law states and both urban and rural areas) have corroborated Weitzman's central conclusion: that the economic situation of men and that of women and children typically diverge after divorce.[86]

The basic reason for this is that the courts are now treating divorcing men and women more or less as equals. Divorcing men and women are not, of course, equal, both because the two sexes are not treated equally in society and, as we have seen, because typical, gender-structured marriage makes women socially and economically vulnerable. The treatment of unequals as if they were equals has long been recognized as an obvious instance of injustice. In this case, the injustice is particularly egregious because the inequality is to such a large extent the result of the marital relationship itself. Nonetheless, that divorce as it is currently practiced in the United States involves such injustice took years to be revealed. There are various discrete parts of this unjust treatment of unequals as if they were equals, and we must briefly examine each of them.

The first way in which women are unequally situated after divorce is that they almost always continue to take day-to-day responsibility for the children. The increased rate of divorce has especially affected couples between the ages of twenty-five and thirty-nine—those most likely to have dependent children. And in approximately 90 percent of cases, children live with mothers rather than fathers after divorce. This is usually the outcome preferred by both parents. Relatively few fathers seek or are awarded sole custody, and in cases of joint custody, which are increasing in frequency, children still tend to live mainly with their mothers. Thus women's postdivorce households tend to be larger than those of men, with correspondingly larger economic needs, and their work lives are much more limited by the needs of their children.[87]

Second, as Weitzman demonstrates, no-fault divorce laws, by depriving women of power they often exerted as the "innocent" and less willing party to the divorce, have greatly reduced their capacity to achieve an equitable division of the couple's tangible assets. Whereas the wife (and children) typically used to be awarded the family home, or more than half of the total tangible assets of the marriage, they are now doing much worse in this respect. In California, the percentage of cases in which the court explicitly ordered that the family home be sold and the proceeds divided rose from about one-tenth of divorces in 1968 to about one-third in 1977. Of this one-third, 66 percent had minor children, who were likely on this account to suffer significantly more than the usual dislocations of divorce. James McLindon's study of divorcing couples in New Haven, Connecticut, confirms this effect of no-fault divorce. In the case of an older housewife, forced sale of the family home can mean the loss of not only her marriage, occupation, and social status, but also her home of many years, all in one blow.[88] Whether what is supposed to be happening is the "equal" division of property, as in the community property states, or the "equitable" division, as in the common law states, what is in fact happening is neither equal nor equitable. This is partly because even when the division of *tangible* property is fairly equal, what is in fact most families' principal asset is largely or entirely left out of the equation. This leads us to the third component of injustice in the current practice of divorce.[89]

As we have seen, most married couples give priority to the husband's work life, and wives, when they work for wages, earn on average only a small fraction of the family income, and perform the great bulk of the family's unpaid labor. The most valuable economic asset of a typical marriage is not any tangible piece of property, such as a house (since, if there is one, it is usually heavily mortgaged). In fact, "the average divorcing couple has less than $20,000 in net worth." By far the most important property acquired in the average marriage is its career assets, or human capital, the vast majority of which is likely to be invested in the husband. As Weitzman reports, it takes the average divorced man only about *ten months* to earn as much as the couple's entire net worth.[90] The importance of this marital asset is hard to overestimate, yet it has only recently begun to be treated in some states as marital property for the purposes of divorce settlements.[91] Even if "marital property" as traditionally understood is divided evenly, there can be no equity so long as this crucial piece is left in the hands of the husband alone. Except for the wealthy few who have significant material assets, "support awards that divide income, especially future income, are the most valuable entitlements awarded at divorce."[92] Largely because of the division of labor within marriage, to the extent that divorced women have to fall back on their own earnings, they are much worse off than they were when married, and than their ex-husbands are after divorce. In many cases, full-time work at or around the minimum wage, which may be the best a woman without much job training or experience can earn, is insufficient to pull the household out of poverty. As Bianchi and Spain state, "women's labor market adjustments to accommodate children, which are often made within a two-parent family context and seem economically rational at the time, cause difficulty later when these same women find themselves divorced and in great need of supporting themselves and their children."[93]

For reasons that seem to have been exacerbated by no-fault divorce laws, most separated or divorced women *do* have to fall back on their own earnings. These earnings—as opposed to spousal support payments or public transfer payments—make up the major portion of the income of female-maintained families. In 1980, they constituted the entire income of almost half such households.[94] The major reason for this is that, loath to recognize that the husband's earning power, and therefore his continuing income, is the most important asset of a marriage, judges have not been dividing it fairly at the time of divorce. As Weitzman summarizes the situation, "Under the new divorce laws, . . . a woman is now expected to become self-sufficient (and, in many cases, to support her children as well)."[95] Alimony and child support are either not awarded, not adequate, or not paid, in the great majority of cases. For many separated or divorced women, as for most single mothers, the idea of the male provider is nothing but a misleading myth that has negatively affected their own work lives while providing them with nothing at all.

In many divorces, there is inadequate income to support two households, with the paradoxical result that poor women with dependent children are even less likely than others to be awarded child support. But even in the case of families who were comfortably off, judges frequently consider what proportion of his income the husband will need to maintain his own standard of living (and even that of his hypothetical future family) before considering the needs of his wife and children. Instead of thinking in terms of compensating wives for all the unpaid effort that most have expended on the home and children, judges are thinking in terms of "what she can earn, and what he can pay."[96] On top of this, they are often misled by the fact that many women are now in the labor force into assuming that wives who have spent many years predominantly as mothers and homemakers will suddenly be able to support themselves.[97]

Contrary to popular belief, alimony has always been awarded rarely, only to the ex-wives of middle- and upper-class men— a small minority of the divorcing population.[98] While this situation has not changed, what *has* changed is the nature of alimony, which under no-fault practices has become in almost all cases a short-term "transitional" award, designed to help divorced women become self-sufficient as rapidly as possible. The burden of proof is now distinctly on the woman to show that she cannot support herself. In Weitzman's sample, only 17 percent, or roughly one-sixth, of divorcing wives were awarded alimony in 1978. The average amount awarded was $350 a month in 1984 dollars, for a median length of twenty-five months. Partly because of the shorter duration of their marriages, the incidence of alimony awards to mothers of preschool children was even lower than the average—only 13 percent. Even in cases in which a husband's high earning capacity has clearly resulted in large part from his wife's financial and/or domestic support during marriage, judges have been extremely reluctant to require him to continue to share it with her in order to allow her to complete a comparable education or training herself. Since about 1985, however, there has been a trend in some

Vulnerability by Marriage

states toward reversing time limitations on alimony after long-term traditional marriages.[99]

The phenomenon of shrinking alimony is exacerbated by the paucity of child support. David Ellwood reports that nationwide, as of 1985, 82 percent of divorced custodial mothers of children under twenty-one were awarded child support but only 54 percent received any, and the average received amounted to $2,538 per year, or just over $200 a month. Separated and never-married women are awarded and receive child support less frequently and in lesser amounts.[100] A 1982 Census Bureau survey reported over eight million women raising at least one child without the father in the home. Of these, the court had ordered support in only five million cases. The average annual payment ordered was $2,180 for white women, $2,070 for Hispanic women, and $1,640 for black women. Weitzman's California-based research showed that a divorced man is rarely (and only in the lowest earning groups) ordered to pay more than a third of his net income in *total* support payments to his former wife and children.[101]

The inadequate levels of child support ordered are only part of the problem. A nationwide survey showed that, in 1981, the ordered amounts were paid in full in less than one-half of cases. Approximately one-quarter of mothers awarded support received partial payment, and one-quarter received no payment at all.[102] In general, except in the case of fathers earning more than $50,000, who comply in more than 90 percent of cases, nonpayment of child support bears little relation to the father's income. One of the major problems appears to be the ineffectiveness or lack of enforcement procedures.[103] With the Child Support Enforcement Amendments of 1984, the problem has now been addressed by federal legislation mandating the withholding of payments from the father's paycheck. Even when paid in full, however, the amounts of alimony and child support that are being awarded are grossly unfair, given the unequal situations in which marriage leaves men and women. The effect of judges' tendency to regard the husband's postdivorce income as first and foremost *his* is that they "rarely require him to help [his former wife and children] sustain a standard of living *half as good as his own*"[104] (emphasis added).

Another reason that divorced women are likely to have to rely on their own, often inadequate earnings is that they are much less likely than their ex-husbands to remarry. The reasons for this are almost all socially created and therefore alterable. In the vast majority of cases, a divorced mother continues to take primary responsibility for the children, but she has lost to a very large extent the financial resources she had within marriage, making her a less attractive marital partner than the typical divorced man. Custody of children is known to be a factor that discourages remarriage. Men who divorce in their thirties and forties are typically noncustodial parents, and are often at the height of their earning power—not an insignificant factor in attracting a subsequent, sometimes much younger wife. Such a couple will not be affected by the social disapproval attached to a woman who marries a much younger man, in the rare case that she does so. Whereas increasing age is not much of an impediment for a man seeking to remarry, it seriously affects a woman's chances, which decrease from 56 percent in her thirties to less than 12 percent if she is in her fifties or older when divorced. This is largely, of course, because so much more emphasis is placed on youth and good looks as constituting attractiveness in women than in men. And ironically, success at work, highly correlated with remarriage for men, is inversely correlated for women.[105]

By attempting to treat men and women as equals at the end of marriage, current divorce law neglects not only the obvious fact that women are *not* the socioeconomic equals of men in our society, but also the highly relevant fact that the experience of gendered marriage and primary parenting greatly exacerbates the inequality that women already bring with them into marriage. To divide the property equally and leave each partner to support himself or herself and to share support of the children might be fair in the case of a marriage in which the paid and unpaid labor had been shared equally, and in which neither spouse's work life had taken priority over that of the other. However, as we have seen, such marriages are exceedingly rare. Traditional or quasi-traditional marriages are far more common, even in the case of the many wives who currently work full-time outside the home. A wife who has contributed at least her fair share in a gender-structured marriage, by undertaking virtually all of the unpaid family work while her husband pursues his work life, meanwhile greatly enhancing his actual and prospective earnings, is by no means treated equally if, at the time of divorce, she is almost entirely cut off from the benefits of his enhanced economic position. But in the typical divorce today, this is exactly what happens.

Clearly, the prospects of a divorcing woman, particularly if she is a custodial parent, are in many ways much bleaker than the prospects of a divorcing man. For the many reasons discussed, the economic costs of divorce fall overwhelmingly on women and children, and not on men. Along with these costs go great social and psychological costs, associated with the greater dislocation of their lives and the stress that accompany economic loss. It is highly significant that, unlike men, both women and children experience economic loss as the worst dimension of divorce. Moreover, recent research has shown that, due to the inadequacy in amount and duration of child support, even children of middle-class divorced parents often experience serious and long-term disadvantage and loss of opportunity.[106]

This implies, of course, that social reform could significantly alter the negative impact of divorce on those who suffer most from it. The important lesson is that women's vulnerability within marriage and their disadvantaged position in the case of marital breakdown are intimately linked. Women are made vulnerable by anticipation of gendered marriage, and are made more vulnerable by entering into and living within such marriage. But they are *most* vulnerable if they marry and have children, but then the marriage fails. Surely women's awareness of this situation has some effects on their behavior and on the distribution of power within marriage itself.

Exit, Threat of Exit, and Power in the Family

At the beginning of this chapter, I summarized Goodin's argument that socially created asymmetric vulnerability is morally unacceptable, and should be minimized. I also referred to Hirschman's arguments about the effects of persons' relative potentials for exit on their power or influence within relationships or groups. Neither of these theorists considers the institution of contemporary marriage an example of such power imbalance.[107] But the evidence presented here suggests that typical, contemporary, gender-structured marriage is an excellent example of socially created vulnerability, partly because the asymmetric dependency of wives on husbands affects their potential for satisfactory exit, and thereby influences the effectiveness of their voice within the marriage.

There has been virtual silence among theorists about the dimension of power in the family that accrues to the spouse who would lose less by exiting from the marriage—a dimension that those who study it seem loath to recognize, partly, no doubt, because it ill accords with society's beliefs about how intimate or romantic relationships are conducted. Three rare scholars who have explicitly applied the notion that potential for exit affects power of voice within marriage are Heer, critiquing Blood and Wolfe's distorted theory of family power, and Bergmann and Fuchs in their recent studies of women's continuing inequality.[108] All three make brief but succinct and lucid arguments that are clearly further validated by the evidence presented here—that marriage is a clear case of asymmetric vulnerability, in which not only power to make decisions but also power to prevent issues from becoming objects of decision is related to the spouses' relative opportunities to exit satisfactorily from the relationship. More typically, marriage is not treated as a situation to which the general theory of the effects of unequal dependency and potential for exit on power applies. Blood asserts, for example, that Heer's "exit" theory is rendered implausible by the fact that "*only* 37 percent" of the couples questioned in a 1939 study of marital success or failure had ever contemplated separation or divorce.[109] Surely this is a remarkably high percentage, especially given the far lower divorce rate then than now.

Of course, the family and other personal relations are special cases of this theory, as of so many others. But the aspects of families that make them different from other institutions such as political parties, schools, and so on, to which theories about the effect of different potentials for exit on power have typically been applied, do not render these theories inapplicable to them. Families are typically held together by strong ties of loyalty, and separation or divorce represents a drastic "solution" to their conflicts. But, particularly now that one in two marriages is expected to end in divorce, it is simply unrealistic to suggest that the threat of exit is absent, especially at times of marital conflict, or that the different abilities of spouses implicitly or explicitly to call on this threat are not likely to affect power and influence in the relationship. Ending a marriage usually causes pain and dislocation for both adults as well as for any children involved. However, the argument presented in this chapter has demonstrated clearly that, in all the ways that are affected by economic deprivation, women and children are likely to suffer considerably more than men from marital dissolution. It is highly probably that most wives, well aware of this fact, take it into consideration in deciding how firm a stand to take on, or even whether to raise, important issues that are likely to be conflictual. We cannot adequately understand the distribution of power in the family without taking this factor into account, and the idea that marriage is a just relationship of mutual vulnerability cannot survive this analysis.

If we are to aim at making the family, our most fundamental social grouping, more just, we must work toward eradicating the socially created vulnerabilities of women that stem from the division of labor and the resultant division of power within it. As I shall argue in the final chapter, in order to do anything effective about the cycle of women's socially created vulnerability, we must take into account the current lack of clarity in law, public policy, and public opinion about *what marriage is*. Since evidently we do not all agree about what it is or should be, we must think in terms of building family and work institutions that enable people to structure their personal lives in different ways. If they are to avoid injustice to women and children, these institutions must encourage the avoidance of socially created vulnerabilities by facilitating and reinforcing the equal sharing of paid and unpaid work between men and women, and consequently the equalizing of their opportunities and obligations in general. They must also ensure that those who enter into relationships in which there is a division of labor that might render them vulnerable are fully protected against such vulnerability, both within the context of the ongoing relationship and in the event of its dissolution.

Notes

1. Robert E. Goodin, *Protecting the Vulnerable: A Reanalysis of Our Social Responsibilities* (Chicago: University of Chicago Press, 1985), p. 109. He specifies, further: "Vulnerability amounts to one person's having the capacity to produce consequences that matter to another. Responsibility amounts to his being accountable for those consequences of his actions and choices" (p. 114).

2. Ibid., p. 190. This is so in at least two respects: *who* becomes disabled by illness or accident is affected by social inequalities and working conditions, and the extent to which physical or mental disabilities render one vulnerable is partly a factor of social provisions (for example, wheelchair ramps) for the less able.

3. Ibid., p. 191.

4. John Stuart Mill, *Principles of Political Economy* (London: Parker and Son, 1848), bk. 5, chap. 11, sec. 9; cited by Goodin, *Protecting the Vulnerable*, p. 189.

5. Goodin, *Protecting the Vulnerable*, p. xi. This succinct statement of the position (argued in his chap. 7) is quoted from Goodin's synopsis.

6. Ibid., *Protecting the Vulnerable*, p. 197.

7. Albert O. Hirschman, *Exit, Voice and Loyalty: Responses to Decline in Firms, Organizations, and States* (Cambridge: Harvard University Press, 1970), pp. 43, 55, 83.

8. Albert O. Hirschman, *National Power and the Structure of Foreign Trade* (Berkeley: University of California Press, 1945; expanded ed. 1980). See pp. vi–viii of the expanded edition for a summary of the original argument, as well as some later reservations of the author about his failure to try to find a remedy for the asymmetrical dependency he had uncovered.

9. Ibid., *National Power*, p. 31.

10. Karl Marx, *The Eighteenth Brumaire of Louis Bonaparte*, in *Selected Works* (Moscow: Progress Publishers, 1969), vol. 2, p. 378.

11. Philip Blumstein and Pepper Schwartz, *American Couples* (New York: Morrow, 1983), pp. 324, 115.

12. Quotations are from Kathleen Gerson, *Hard Choices: How Women Decide About Work, Career, and Motherhood* (Berkeley: University of California Press, 1985), p. 209. For sources of this data, see also Jacob Mincer, "Labor Force Participation of Married Women: A Study of Labor Supply," in *Aspects of Labor Economics: A Conference of the Universities—National Bureau Committee for Economic Research* (Princeton: Princeton University Press, 1962), p. 64; Ruth Sidel, *Women and Children Last: The Plight of Poor Women in Affluent America* (New York: Viking, 1986), esp. pp. 50–56, 60; Suzanne M. Bianchi and Daphne Spain, *American Women in Transition* (New York: Russell Sage, 1986), p. 196. Gerson places "careers" in quotation marks here because she and her respondents understand the word to mean "not mere labor force participation, but rather long-term, full-time attachment to paid work with the expectation, or at least the hope, of advancement over time" (p. 126*n*1). It does not imply any differentiation between manual and intellectual, or professional and nonprofessional work. I shall use *career* in this nonelitist sense.

13. Blumstein and Schwartz, *American Couples*, pp. 52, 118–125, 560*n*2. See also the Nye study cited there, which concludes that "both married men and married women still feel it is the husband's responsibility to provide for his wife." In Gerson's study, too, even among the nontraditional women, who placed great emphasis on self-sufficiency, "few expressed a willingness to provide full economic support for their partners or to indulge male partners who might prefer total domesticity to paid work" (*Hard Choices*, p. 113*n*4; see also pp. 174–75). Beliefs about the desirability of wives' not working for wages are lagging behind actual social behavior.

14. Lenore J. Weitzman, *The Divorce Revolution: The Unexpected Social and Economic Consequences for Women and Children in America* (New York: The Free Press, 1985), pp. 315–16.

15. Blumstein and Schwartz, *American Couples*, pp. 51–111 passim, esp. pp. 58–59, 82.

16. Bianchi and Spain, *American Women*, p. 2; U.S. Bureau of the Census, *Statistical Abstract of the U.S.: 1986* (Washington, D.C.: 1987), p. 40.

17. Bianchi and Spain, *American Women*, p. 9, quoting Arland Thornton and Deborah Freedman, "Changing Attitudes Toward Marriage and Single Life," *Family Planning Perspectives* 14 (November–December 1982): 297–303.

18. Bianchi and Spain report that between 1969 and 1975, the proportion of women in their early twenties who planned to be housewives (versus working outside the home) declined from about half to one-quarter among whites and from about half to one-fifth among blacks. This decline was especially marked among those with the most education. *American Women*, p. 18.

Notes

19. Victor Fuchs, *Women's Quest for Economic Equality* (Cambridge: Harvard University Press, 1988), pp. 11–13, 77–78 (the 51 percent reported on p. 12 appears to be a misprint, since the 1983 figure was 53 percent; David Ellwood, *Poor Support: Poverty in the American Family* (New York: Basic Books, 1988), pp. 47–49.

20. Gerson, *Hard Choices*. Other studies of the cross-pressures relating to sex roles that many women experience when planning their educations and work lives include: Bernard C. Rosen and Carol S. Aneshensel, "Sex Differences in the Educational-Occupational Expectation Process," *Social Forces* 57, no. 1 (1978): Nira Danziger, "Sex-Related Differences in the Aspirations of High School Students," *Sex Roles* 9, no. 6 (1983): Larry C. Jensen, Robert Christensen, and Diana J. Wilson, "Predicting Young Women's Role Preference for Parenting and Work," *Sex Roles* 13, nos. 9–10 (1985): and Margaret Mooney Marini and Ellen Greenberger, "Sex Differences in Occupational Aspirations and Expectations," *Sociology of Work and Occupations* 5, no. 2 (1978).

21. Marini and Greenberger, "Sex Differences," 147–48, 157. Only 47 percent of the girls but 75 percent of the boys with the highest aspirations expected to reach them. The girls' levels of ambition were less affected than the boys' by either socioeconomic background or academic achievement. See also "In Career Goals, Female Valedictorians Fall Behind," *New York Times*, November 8, 1987, sec. 12, p. 7.

22. Gerson, *Hard Choices*, esp. pp. 136–38.

23. On female socialization, see Nancy Chodorow, *The Reproduction of Mothering* (Berkeley: University of California Press, 1978); Lenore J. Weitzman, "Sex-Role Socialization," in *Women: A Feminist Perspective*, 2nd ed., ed. Jo Freeman (Palo Alto: Mayfield, 1979). On the practical conflicts faced by wage-working mothers, see, for example, Linda J. Beckman, "The Relative Rewards and Costs of Parenthood and Employment for Employed Women," *Psychology of Women Quarterly* 2, no. 3 (1978); Mary Jo Frug, "Securing Job Equality for Women: Labor Market Hostility to Working Mothers," *Boston University Law Review* 59, no. 1 (1979).

24. In Gerson's sample, only 14 percent of the respondents' own mothers had worked during their preschool years, and 46 percent had mothers who had never worked outside the home until their children left (p. 45). On avoidance of the conflict between wage work and motherhood, see Gerson, *Hard Choices*, pp. 64–65.

25. Ibid., p. 137.

26. Moreover, the support that *women* can expect for this choice is now waning. See, for example, Gerson, *Hard Choices*, pp. 77–80, 212.

27. Bianchi and Spain, *American Women*, chaps. 1 and 4.

28. As recently as 1984, full-time working women earned on average $14,780, only 64 percent of men's $23,220. Thus the very recent closing of the gap was as much due to the approximate $1,000 *drop* in the average man's annual wage as to the $1,000 rise in the average woman's. (Sources: *Employment and Earnings*, U.S. Department of Labor, Bureau of Labor Statistics, (Washington D.C.: Government Printing Office, July 1987); U.S. Bureau of the Census, Current Population Reports, Series P–60, no. 149, *Money Income and Poverty Status of Families and Persons in the United States: 1984* (Washington, D.C.: Government Printing Office, 1985), p. 2.

29. In May 1987, 87.7 percent of all women with a college degree were employed, compared with 33.7 percent of women who had not completed high school. Of women with a college degree, 81.6 percent were employed *full-time*, compared with only 23.6 percent of those who did not complete high school (*Employment and Earnings*).

30. In 1987 (Second quarter), men in "service" occupations had an average salary of $15,912, compared with an average of $10, 244 for women in "service" occupations; the average man in a "professional specialty" earned $32,552, compared with the average "professional" woman's $23,348 (*Employment and Earnings*).

31. *Women in the American Economy*, Current Population Reports, Special Studies, U.S. Department of Commerce, Bureau of the Census (Washington, D.C.: Government Printing Office, 1986).

32. *Current Population Reports*, Population Profile of the United States 1984–85, U.S. Department of Commerce, Bureau of the Census. Samuel Cohn's recent study of occupational sex-typing examines in detail the feminization of clerical work within two large British firms. He concludes that the discrepancy in job status and rates of pay between the sexes is largely the result of the concentration of women in clerical jobs from which there is virtually no possibility of promotion, and their exclusion from supervisory positions. *The Process of Occupational Sex-Typing* (Philadelphia: Temple University Press, 1985).

33. Barbara R. Bergmann, *The Economic Emergence of Women* (New York: Basic Books, 1986), esp. chap. 6 (statistics and quotation are from pp. 121 and 133). Bergmann acknowledges (p. 122) that some of the differential may be due to men's working more overtime than women; she does not, however,

Notes

mention the fact (influenced by sex roles within marriage) that men average longer tenure in the same job than women, which is also likely to affect their rates of pay. See also Bianchi and Spain, *American Women*, p. 165; William T. Bielby and James N. Baron, "A Woman's Place Is with Other Women: Sex Segregation Within Organizations," in *Sex Segregation in the Workplace: Trends, Explanations, Remedies*, ed. Barbara F. Reskin (Washington, D.C.: National Academy Press, 1984); Francine Blau, *Equal Pay in the Office* (Lexington, MA: D.C. Heath, 1977); and Fuchs, *Women's Quest*, pp. 32–44.

34. Bergmann, *Economic Emergence*, pp. 125–26. See also Gerson, *Hard Choices*, p. 220.

35. M. Rivka Polatnick, "Why Men Don't Rear Children: A Power Analysis," in *Mothering: Essays in Feminist Theory*, ed. Joyce Trebilcot (Totowa, N.J.: Rowman and Allanheld, 1983), p. 28. See also Sidel, *Women and Children*, pp. 29–33, on women's socialization into the expectation of economic dependence on a man and of motherhood. Victor Fuchs reports that "the more children a woman expects to have, the less likely she is to invest in market-related human capital while in school and during the first few years of paid work." "Sex Differences in Economic Well-Being," *Science* 232, no. 4749 (1986): 463.

36. Gerson, *Hard Choices*, chap. 5 and pp. 130–31.

37. Key articles contributing to this argument are Jacob Mincer, "Labor Force Participation of Married Women"; Jacob Mincer and Solomon Polachek, "Family Investment in Human Capital: Earnings of Women," in *Marriage, Family Human Capital, and Fertility*, ed. Theodore W. Schulz (Chicago: University of Chicago Press, 1974); Jacob Mincer and Haim Ofek, "Interrupted Work Careers: Depreciation and Restoration of Human Capital," *Journal of Human Resources* 17 (Winter 1982); Solomon Polachek, Occupational Self-Selection: A Human Capital Approach to Sex Differences in Occupational Structure," *Review of Economics and Statistics* 63 (February 1981). Gary Becker's *A Treatise on the Family* (Cambridge: Harvard University Press, 1981) also belongs within this general mode of thinking.

38. Works in which these interconnections are best recognized and analyzed include Bianchi and Spain, *American Women*, pp. 188–95; Bergmann, *Economic Emergence;* Fuchs, *Women's Quest;* Gerson, *Hard Choices;* Heidi Hartmann, "Capitalism, Patriarchy, and Job Segregation by Sex," *Signs* 1, no. 3 (1976); and Sylvia Walby, *Patriarchy at Work: Patriarchal and Capitalist Relations in Employment* (Minneapolis: University of Minnesota Press, 1986), pp. 71–74. Fuchs concludes: "There is prejudice, and there is exploitation [in the workplace], but the enormous amount of sex segregation by occupation and industry, the huge gap in wages, and the unequal burdens in the home are mostly attributable to other factors. . . . [W]omen's weaker economic position results primarily from conflicts between career and family, conflicts that are stronger for women than for men" (*Women's Quest*, pp. 4–5).

39. See, for example, Becker, *A Treatise on the Family*.

40. See Walby, *Patriarchy at Work*, p. 73, and Blumstein and Schwartz, *American Couples*, pp. 131–35, for examples of this influence.

41. Gerson, *Hard Choices*, chaps. 5 and 6. Of those who found themselves trapped in female labor market ghettos, she says: "Previous ambivalences toward motherhood subsided, and domesticity became more attractive than it had earlier appeared. . . . [T]he decision to have a child typically coincided with mounting frustration at work. . . . The experience of blocked work mobility, although not the only factor, was a major contributing factor in this group's decision to become mothers" (pp. 107–8). "Blocked mobility triggered a downward spiral of aspirations and gave childbearing a liberating aura by comparison. . . . In important respects, women's work is organized to promote this turn toward a home-centered life" (p. 110).

42. Victor Fuchs, *Women's Quest*, pp. 77–78. This represents a change from previous findings, and is due to women's increased hours of paid work. Between 1960 and 1986, Fuchs reports, "on average, wives increased their total work load by four hours per week while husbands decreased theirs by two and a half hours" (p. 78). Cf. Barbara Bergmann, *Economic Emergence*, p. 263, who reports (based on 1975–76 data) husbands' averaging approximately one hour per day more of total work time than wives.

43. Since it is the most recently completed large-scale study of housework available, I use the 1975–76 Michigan Survey Research Center's statistics as analyzed by Bergmann (pp. 261–66). However, I conflate some of her many categories into fewer categories, for the sake of clarity and brevity. My reason for combining part-time employed wives with housewives rather than with fully employed wives is that part-time work is usually badly paid, insecure, dead-ended, and undervalued.

44. Bergmann, *Economic Emergence*, p. 263, table 11-2, using University of Michigan 1975–76 data. Note that, given Fuch's findings, these figures may well have changed, since women working part-time are likely to be working longer hours.

45. See Bergmann, *Economic Emergence*, chap. 9, "The Job of Housewife." One indicator that the homemaker role involves considerable disadvantages is the extremely small number of men who choose it. Blumstein and Schwartz say that despite recent media interest in househusbands, "try as we might, . . . we could not find a significant number" of them. "Only 4 of 3,632 husbands describe their work as taking care

Notes

of the house full-time" (*American Couples*, pp. 146, 561*n*11). Bergmann reports: "In January 1986, 468,000 men were estimated to be out of the workforce because they were 'keeping house,' 22 percent more than in 1980" (*Economic Emergence*, p. 259, citing U.S. Bureau of Labor Statistics, *Employment and Earnings* (February 1986), p. 15. Another factor influencing this, however, as both Blumstein and Schwartz and Gerson note, may be the fact that few married women wish to undertake the full provider role.

46. Bergmann, *Economic Emergence*, p. 267.

47. See Weitzman, *The Divorce Revolution*, esp. pp. xi, 35.

48. See Gerson, *Hard Choices*, pp. 211–12, for a good summary of how "work associated with child rearing and the private sphere has been systematically devalued," and the current effects of this on domestically oriented women. See also Polatnick, "Why Men Don't Rear Children." Studies such as Blumstein and Schwartz's cite examples of husbands using in arguments the fact that their wives do not earn money: "If you're so smart, how come you don't earn anything?" (*American Couples*, pp. 58–59). See Weitzman, *The Divorce Revolution*, pp. 315–16, on divorcing housewives' devaluing of their work, and pp. 334–36, on how their identification by their husbands' social status can lead to a loss of sense of identity by wives after divorce. At the public policy level, the lack of recognition of the economic value of housewives' work is indicated by the fact that housework is included in the GNP only if it is paid work done by a housekeeper. The old story about the parson who lowers the GNP by marrying his housekeeper still holds true, in spite of the fact that it has been estimated that, if it *were* included, unpaid housework done in the industrialized countries would constitute between 25 and 40 percent of the GNP. Debbie Taylor et al., *Women: A World Report* (Oxford: Oxford University Press, 1985).

49. Blumstein and Schwartz say: "Money matters are the most commonly discussed issues among married couples. In study after study, going back several decades, between one quarter and one third of all married couples ranked money as their primary problem" (*American Couples*, p. 52). Fuchs reports that, according to Morton H. Shaevitz, an expert on gender relations, "Arguments about housework are the leading cause of domestic violence in the United States" (*Women's Quest*, p. 74, citing *Healthcare Forum* 1987, p. 27).

50. Bergmann, *Economic Emergence*, pp. 211–12; Virginia Woolf, *Three Guineas* (London: Harcourt Brace, 1938), p. 110; see also pp. 54–57.

51. Linda Gordon, *Heroes of Their Own Lives* (New York: Viking, 1988), p. 251.

52. Bergmann, *Economic Emergence*, pp. 205–6; Sidel, *Women and Children*, pp. 40–46. See also Lenore Walker, *The Battered Woman* (New York: Harper & Row, 1979). Fears stemming from economic dependence seem to be just beneath the surface, with many housewives, and ready to emerge at the hint of a sympathetic ear. Gerson occasionally reports this (e.g., p. 115), and I have heard the same fears of being left, expressed by acquaintances who are economically dependent wives, since I told them of my work on this book. Chapter 8 of Lillian Rubin's *Worlds of Pain* (New York: Basic Books, 1976) is an excellent source on the effects of the relative powerlessness and dependence of working-class housewives on their unwilling compliance with their husbands' sexual demands. Blumstein and Schwartz discuss at some length the relationship between power and sexual initiation, refusal, consideration of each partner's needs, and satisfaction (*American Couples*, pp. 206–306 passim).

53. See Bergmann, *Economic Emergence*, chap. 11; Bianchi and Spain, *American Women*, pp. 231–40; Blumstein and Schwartz, *American Couples*, pp. 144–48; Gerson, *Hard Choices*, p. 170. Quotations are from Blumstein and Schwartz, p. 144, and Gerson, p. 170. There is broad agreement on this issue, though some studies find that, in very recent years, male participation in housework and child care appears to be slightly on the rise. Bergmann reports that when some of the couples who participated in the 1975–76 University of Michigan Study were resurveyed in 1981–82, it appeared that "these husbands had increased their contributions by about an hour per week over the six-year interval" (p. 266). On the other hand, she finds that "younger husbands appear to do even less housework than their older counterparts, although neither group of men averages as much as half an hour per day" (p. 264).

54. Bergmann, *Economic Emergence*, p. 263. She defines as "housewife-maintaining" "those families in which the wives devoted five or fewer hours a week to paid employment" (p. 62*n*). Sharon Y. Nickols and Edward Metzen, in "Impact of Wife's Employment upon Husband's Housework," *Journal of Family Issues* 3 (June 1982), found on the basis of a time-allocation study from 1968 to 1973 that when wives became employed their average hours per week spent in housework dropped from thirty-five to twenty-three, but that their husbands' average contribution stayed at two hours per week.

55. Blumstein and Schwartz, *American Couples*, p. 145. They find that, among full-time employed married couples who profess strongly egalitarian attitudes about housework, 44 percent of wives compared with 28 percent of husbands do more than ten hours of housework per week. Also, some of the examples

Notes

they cite suggest that the "egalitarianism" of these professed attitudes may be rather superficial; as one wife says of her husband's cleaning the floors and oven: "He takes care of that *for me*" (p. 142, emphasis added). See also Shelley Coverman, "Explaining Husbands' Participation in Domestic Labor," *The Sociological Quarterly* 26, no. 1 (1985); Bianchi and Spain, *American Women*, p. 233.

56. For recent examples, see Becker, *A Treatise on the Family*; and Jonathan Gershuny, *Social Innovation and the Division of Labour* (Oxford: Oxford University Press, 1983), p. 156.

57. Bergmann, *Economic Emergence*, pp. 267–68 and refs., p. 350*n*9.

58. Blumstein and Schwartz, *American Couples*, pp. 139–54, esp. 151–54. See below on the importance of "nondecisions" in studying power.

59. Blumstein and Schwartz, *American Couples*, p. 312. They also say: "It seems to be a cultural given in America that growing up female makes housework something women do . . . [whereas] growing up male in this country causes even liberal men to reject household tasks" (p. 148). On the issue of income differential and housework, Bianchi and Spain conclude: "In two-parent families, until such time as wives command salaries equal to their husbands' salaries, on average, it is unlikely that men will devote as much time and energy to the nurturance of the family" (*American Women*, p. 243). On conflict, Blumstein and Schwartz report that, in their large sample, the amount of fighting that took place about housework increased with the amount of housework the husband did (*American Couples*, pp. 146, 562*n*32).

60. Bergmann, *Economic Emergence*, table 11.2, p. 263.

61. For example, in a 1960 passage defending the traditional division of labor between the sexes as "pragmatic and nonideological," two prominent sociologists of the family wrote: "Whether working late at the office, figuring in his study, or puzzling over a problem in his easy chair, the responsible executive is unavailable for housework. The more responsible he is, the less available he becomes—for the means to promotion is overtime work, and the consequence of promotion is more overtime work." Robert O. Blood, Jr., and Donald M. Wolfe, *Husbands and Wives: The Dynamics of Married Living* (New York: The Free Press, 1960), p. 59. Given that she has little chance of becoming "less available" for housework, the responsible female executive who does not wish to forgo parenthood is more likely to puzzle over problems at the washing machine than in an easy chair.

62. Bergmann points out that, though "substantial . . . [t]he disadvantages of the employed wife—loss of leisure, increased management difficulties, a more harried and difficult schedule—must be preferable to the disadvantages of the housewife, or fewer women would have made the trade" (*Economic Emergence*, pp. 257–58). In lower-income families with "drudge wives," however, the trade is likely to be made mostly in order to improve the family's standard of living.

63. Gerson, *Hard Choices*, pp. 128–29.

64. U.S. Bureau of the Census 1986 data, cited in the *New York Times*, September 14, 1987, p. A13.

65. Ellwood, *Poor Support*, table 5.1, p. 33 (tabulated from U.S. Bureau of the Census Current Population Survey, March 1985).

66. Barbara Strudler Wallston, Martha A. Foster, and Michael Berger, "I Will Follow Him: Myth, Reality, or Forced Choice—Job Seeking Experiences of Dual Career Couples," in *Dual Career Couples*, ed. Jeff Bryson and Rebecca Bryson (New York: Human Sciences Press, 1978). A recent study of couples with more or less equal corporate careers demonstrates both their extreme dependence on the flexible, low-paid labor of other women, usually immigrants, and the fact that even in this group "wives . . . are the ones who really provide their husbands with continuous flexibility [whereas] the housekeeper provides the wife with flexibility." Nevertheless, these dual-career couples appear to make career decisions more equitably than those in the earlier study. See Rosanna Hertz, *More Equal Than Others* (Berkeley: University of California Press, 1986), p. 189 and chap. 5 on housework and child care; chap. 2 on career decisions.

67. See Weitzman, *The Divorce Revolution*, pp. xi–xviii, chaps. 5, 7, and 11 passim.

68. Blood and Wolfe, *Husbands and Wives*. For critiques of this study, see David M. Heer, "The Measurement and Bases of Family Power: An Overview," *Marriage and Family Living* 25, no. 2 (1963); Constantia Safilios-Rothschild, "Family Sociology or Wives' Family Sociology? A Cross-Cultural Study of Decision Making," *Journal of Marriage and the Family* 31, no. 2 (1969); and Dair Gillespie, "Who Has the Power? The Marital Struggle," *Journal of Marriage and the Family* 33, no. 3 (1971).

69. Ibid., p. 47 and chap. 2. To measure relative influence in family decision making, Blood and Wolfe develop a scale from 1 to 10 on which, for some unexplained reason, 4 represents equal decision making by husband and wife. They then define as "relatively equalitarian" *not* those marriages that fall within the 3 to 5 range, as one might expect, but those that fall within the 4 to 6 range. Discovering that the average among the families in their sample is 5.09, they conclude that American families are equalitarian, rather than moderately male dominant—as their own data would seem to demonstrate.

Notes

70. This is pointed out by Heer, "The Measurement and Bases: An Overview," pp. 137–38. In response, Blood basically concedes the point, agreeing that the original study failed to specify that "resources" was being employed to refer only to those "drawn from the external system," such as income, social status, education, and participation in the work force. "The Measurement and Bases: a Rejoinder," *Marriage and Family Living* 23, no. 4 (1963): 475–76.

71. Blumstein and Schwartz, *American Couples*, figs. 1 and 2 and text, pp. 54, 57. The most male-dominant category of marriage that they identify is that in which husbands and wives believe in the male provider role. Of these, about 40 percent consider their relationship to be male-dominated, five times more than consider it female-dominated. But even among these couples, slightly more than half believe that their relationships are equal in terms of power.

72. Blumstein and Schwartz, *American Couples*, pp. 53, 52.

73. Bianchi and Spain, *American Women*, p. 202. In 1986, working wives contributed about 28 percent to family income. Congressional Caucus for Women's Issues: *Selected Statistics on Women*, July 1988, p. 3.

74. Blumstein and Schwartz, *American Couples*, pp. 53–93 passim and 139–44. See also Polatnick, "Why Men Don't Rear Children," esp. pp. 23–25.

75. Blumstein and Schwartz, *American Couples*, pp. 56–57.

76. See Peter Bachrach and Morton S. Baratz, "The Two Faces of Power," *American Political Science Review* 56 (1962): 947–52, on the importance of taking account of "nondecisions" when studying the distribution of power. Unfortunately, the phrasing of the question about power that Blumstein and Schwartz posed to their respondents does not allow us to look at nondecisions. It seems very likely, given the strongly gendered traditions of marriage, that many married couples would not have regarded "Who will be the primary parent?" or "Who will do the housework?" as "important decision[s] affecting [the] relationship," since they would not have regarded them as things to be decided at all. An ongoing study includes a question that addresses this issue: *Study of First Years of Marriage* (Survey Research Center, Institute for Social Research, University of Michigan, Ann Arbor, 1986), question D6, p. 28.

77. U.S. Bureau of the Census, Current Population Reports: *Marital Status and Living Arrangements*, March 1985 (Washington, D.C.: Government Printing Office).

78. Weitzman, *The Divorce Revolution*, p. 349 and refs.

79. Ibid., p. xvii, citing Arland Thornton and Deborah Freedman, "The Changing American Family," *Population Bulletin* 38, no. 4 (1983): 7.

80. Bianchi and Spain, *American Women*, pp. 21–25.

81. Although households maintained by never-married women increased eightfold between 1960 and 1980, they still constituted only 800,000 or 17 percent of female-maintained households with children. In 1980, 15 percent of never-married black women were raising one or more children, compared with 1 percent of whites (Bianchi and Spain, *American Women*, pp. 103–8; also *New York Times*, April 30, 1987). By 1987, never-married women headed 23 percent of female-maintained households with children under eighteen. See chap. 1 note 3 in this volume.

82. Ellwood, *Poor Support*, chap. 5; Sidel, *Women and Children*, p. xvi. For female-headed households in 1984, the poverty rate was 34.5 percent. Of children in female-maintained households, 53.9 percent were poor. The poverty line income for a family of four in 1984 was $10,609, which allows $2.43 per person per day for food, and leaves $589.40 per month for all the family's other needs. See Bianchi and Spain, *American Women*, p. 207, on the growing economic discrepancy between two-parent families and female-maintained families, and p. 211 on the chronicity of poverty of the latter.

83. Bianchi and Spain, *American Women*, p. 26, citing numerous studies. See also James B. McLindon, "Separate But Unequal: The Economic Disaster of Divorce for Women and Children," *Family Law Quarterly* 21, no. 3 (1987). However, cf. Herbert Jacob's dissenting argument in "Another Look at No-Fault Divorce and the Post-Divorce Finances of Women," *Law and Society Review* 23, no. 1 (1989). Beginning with California in 1970, all states except South Dakota now have some form of no-fault divorce law. Twenty-two states still have fault-based divorce as well as no-fault. Most of the pure no-fault states allow unilateral divorce by one party without the consent of the other. Weitzman, *The Divorce Revolution*, pp. 41–43, 417–19.

84. Bianchi and Spain, *American Women*, pp. 30–32 and refs., 205–7, 216–18; Gerson, *Hard Choices*, pp. 221–22 and refs. As Bianchi and Spain comment, "although female-maintained families have become more middle class—at least as indexed by the educational attainment of the householder—their income situation relative to husband-wife households has deteriorated" (p. 207).

85. Weitzman, *The Divorce Revolution*, p. 323. See esp. introduction and chaps. 2 and 10. See also Saul Hoffman and John Holmes, "Husbands, Wives, and Divorce," in *Five Thousand American*

Notes

Families—Patterns of Economic Progress, ed. Greg J. Duncan and James N. Morgan (Ann Arbor, Mich.: Institute for Social Research, 1976); and Judith Wallerstein and Joan Kelly, *Surviving the Breakup: How Children and Parents Cope with Divorce* (New York: Basic Books, 1980). This last study, of the effects of divorce in an affluent community (Marin County, California), reports that three-quarters of the divorced women experienced a significant decline in their standard of living, and for one-third this change was sudden and severe. As Weitzman points out, census figures corroborate the findings of these researchers: "In 1979, the median per capita income of divorced women who had not remarried was $4,152, just over half of the $7,886 income of divorced men who had not remarried" (p. 343).

86. A study of all the divorce cases that closed in a five-month period (1982–83) in four counties in Vermont shows a 120 percent gain in postdivorce *per capita* income for men, a 25 percent drop for children, and a 33 percent drop for women (assuming that all support ordered is paid). Heather Ruth Wishik, "Economics of Divorce: An Exploratory Study," *Family Law Quarterly* 20,no. 1 (1986). A study of divorce in New Haven, Connecticut, comparing a sample of 102 cases from the fault-based period (1970–71) with a sample of 100 from the no-fault period (1982–83) shows that the frequency, amount, and duration of alimony awarded has decreased, and that women are now less likely to be awarded the family home and much more likely to work for wages. Although 61 percent of the 1980s divorced women worked full-time and another 17 percent worked part-time, "the husband's average postdivorce per capita income surpassed that of his wife and children overall and in every income group . . . [averaging] $333 to [his wife's and each child's] $122 per week." McLindon, "Separate But Unequal," p. 391. See also Rosalyn B. Bell, "Alimony and the Financially Dependent Spouse in Montgomery County, Maryland," *Family Law Quarterly* 22, no. 3 (1988), esp. 279–84; and the excellent discussions in Mary Ann Glendon, *Abortion and Divorce in Western Law* (Cambridge: Harvard University Press, 1987), chap. 2; and Herma Hill Kay, "Equality and Difference: A Perspective on No-Fault Divorce and Its Aftermath," *University of Cincinnati Law Review* 56, no. 1 (1987).

87. Weitzman, *The Divorce Revolution*, pp. xiii–xiv and chaps. 8, 9; Blumstein and Schwartz, *American Couples*, pp. 33–34. Gerson says: "Although joint custody arrangements are on the rise, Hacker (1982) reports that the number of divorced fathers with sole custody of their children has actually decreased in the last decade" (*Hard Choices*, p. 221). See also Clair Vickery, "The Time-Poor: A New Look at Poverty," *Journal of Human Resources* 12 (Winter 1977), on the extra time demands on custodial mothers.

88. Weitzman, *The Divorce Revolution*, pp. 78–96; McLindon, "Separate But Unequal," pp. 375–78. It is no wonder that, as Weitzman reports, "many women who have lived through and for their husbands say that the loss of the role of wife is tantamount to 'losing a part of myself'" (p. 335).

89. Weitzman, *The Divorce Revolution*, chap. 4.

90. Ibid., pp. 53, 60.

91. Some changes have been occurring; most states now regard pensions and other retirement benefits as marital assets, but far fewer are viewing other career assets, such as professional degrees, training, or goodwill, this way. Weitzman, *The Divorce Revolution*, p. 47 and chap. 5. See also Doris Jonas Freed and Timothy B. Walker, "Family Law in the Fifty States: An Overview," *Family Law Quarterly* 28, no. 4 (1985): 411–26.

92. Weitzman, *The Divorce Revolution*, p. 61; see also pp. 68–69.

93. Bianchi and Spain, *American Women*, p. 243; see also pp. 207–11.

94. Ibid., p. 206. See also McLindon, "Separate But Unequal." Weitzman reports that about 14 percent of the women in her weighted sample resorted to welfare in the first year after divorce (*The Divorce Revolution*, p. 204); and that the structure of the job market is such that only half of all full-time female workers earn enough to support two children above the poverty line without supplemental income from either their father or the government (p. 351).

95. Weitzman, *The Divorce Revolution*, p. 143.

96. Ibid., p. x.

97. Bianchi and Spain, *American Women*, p. 213. Weitzman points out that among those in her interview sample, of those men earning less than $20,000 a year (83 percent of those divorcing), only 15 percent were required to pay alimony, compared with 62 percent of those earning more than $30,000. The implication is that men earning less than $20,000 can ill afford to spare any of their earnings. But on the other hand, once a wife earns $10,000, her chances of being awarded alimony decline precipitously, with the implication that a woman (who is much more likely to have children living with her) can get along on half of what it takes a man to live (*The Divorce Revolution*, pp. 178–82). In cases where mothers of young children *were* awarded alimony and/or child support, the husband was rarely ordered to part with more than one-third of his income. Again, the implication is either that the wife and children can live on half of

Notes

what he requires, or that she should immediately go out to work and somehow try to pay for adequate child care.

98. In 1968, before no-fault divorce, fewer than 20 percent of divorcing wives in California were awarded alimony. Nationwide, only 14 percent of divorced women questioned in a 1978 census survey reported being awarded alimony. Even in 1919, when far fewer wives were in the labor force, a L.A. County study shows that only 32 percent of divorcing wives were awarded alimony (Weitzman, *The Divorce Revolution*, pp. 144, 167–68).

99. On limited alimony, see ibid., pp. 32–36 and chaps. 6–7. On recent appellate decisions cases in which time-limited alimony orders have been reversed, see Joan M. Krauskopf, "Rehabilitative Alimony: Uses and Abuses of Limited Duration Alimony," *Family Law Quarterly* 21, no. 4 (1988). In Weitzman's interviews, judges were asked about a hypothetical case: a twenty-nine-year-old nurse had supported her husband through eight years of college, medical school, internship, and residency. Fewer than one-third of the judges said they would require her ex-husband to support her through four years of medical school. The others "did not think it fair to saddle her husband with her 'optional expenses' since she was clearly capable of supporting herself" (p. 35).

100. David Ellwood, *Poor Support*, p. 158.

101. Weitzman, *The Divorce Revolution*, pp. 264–76. She suggests that judges are grossly ignorant about how much it costs to raise a child, and points out that the levels of child support ordered rarely cover the average cost of day care alone. This suggests that judges are making the sex-biased assumption that child care costs nothing, at the same time assuming that the mother should go out to work full-time!

102. Bianchi and Spain, *American Women*, pp. 212–14; Sidel, *Women and Children*, p. 103. The level of noncompliance among Weitzman's California interviewees was even higher. She reports that only one-third of the wives awarded child support said they received the full amounts during the first year after divorce, and that 43 percent received little or nothing (*The Divorce Revolution*, p. 283).

103. Weitzman, *The Divorce Revolution*, pp. 295–300, esp. table 25, p. 296.

104. Ibid., p. 183. See also Ellwood, *Poor Support*, pp. 158–60. Glendon and Weitzman are hopeful that the new enforcement measures will help alleviate custodial mothers' poverty. Glendon, *Abortion and Divorce*, pp. 88–89, 110–11; Weitzman, *The Divorce Revolution*, pp. 307–9.

105. On custody as a factor affecting remarriage, see, for example, Becker, *A Treatise on the Family*, p. 225. On women's work success, see Blumstein and Schwartz, *American Couples*, pp. 32–33.

106. Weitzman reports that "what women say they miss most about marriage is the husband's income." What men report missing most is "having a sexual partner . . . , and having a partner in life." As for children, though researchers have shown that preschool children of divorced families with inadequate income had significantly higher levels of anxiety-depression than other preschoolers, "when family income is adequate, there are no differences in anxiety-depression levels between [preschool] children in divorced families and those in intact families" (*The Divorce Revolution*, pp. 348, 354). On both the feelings of emotional deprivation and the diminished opportunities of middle-class children of divorce, see Judith S. Wallerstein and Shauna B. Corbin, "Father-Child Relationships After Divorce: Child Support and Educational Opportunity," *Family Law Quarterly* 20, no. 2 (1986).

107. Goodin refers to marriage in the past as an institution of exploitation and domination but, because he thinks that "the traditional division of marital labor . . . is surely dead or dying," he concludes that "modern marriage relations . . . embody . . . a morally desirable sort of 'symmetry and complementarity'" (*Protecting the Vulnerable*, pp. 72–79, 196). When Hirschman rarely and briefly refers to the family in the course of his arguments about the effect of exit potential on influence, what he says indicates that he is thinking almost entirely about families of origin, rather than families created by marriage (*Exit, Voice and Loyalty*, pp. 33, 76). In the only place in the book where he exhibits any interest in the applicability of his argument to families by marriage, he briefly comments that the high costs (in energy and emotional expenditure as well as money) of obtaining a divorce may act as an incentive to the use of the voice option in resolving marital disputes (p. 79). However, in a recent paper, Hirschman argues that no-fault divorce law "undercuts the recourse to voice" in resolving marital difficulties. He suggests that those who framed the new laws "probably did not realize the extent to which the earlier obstacles to divorce indirectly encouraged attempts at mending the so easily frayed marital relationship and how much the new freedom to exit would torpedo such attempts." Citing Weitzman's work, he also makes brief reference to the differential impact of divorce on the two parties. "Exit and Voice: An Expanding Sphere of Influence," in A. O. Hirschman, ed., in *Rival Views of Market Society and Other Recent Essays*, (New York: Viking, 1986), pp. 96–98.

108. Bergman, *Economic Emergence*, pp. 269–70; Fuchs, *Women's Quest*, pp. 71–72; Heer, "The Measurement and Bases of Family Power: An Overview," p. 138.

Notes

109. Blood, "The Measurement and Bases of Family Power: A Rejoinder," p. 476*n*12 (emphasis added).

[15]

Comparative Law and the Same-Sex Marriage Debate: A Step-by-Step Approach Toward State Recognition

William N. Eskridge, Jr.*

On December 20,1999, the Vermont Supreme Court ruled in *Baker v. Vermont*[1] that the state's different treatment of lesbian and gay couples under its marriage law violated the Vermont Constitution.[2] In April 2000, the Vermont legislature responded by creating a new institution of "civil unions" for same-sex couples. In June 1999, the government of the Netherlands introduced legislation to recognize same-sex marriages.[3] In one sense, a race has commenced: the Vermont plaintiffs and the Dutch government are each striving to make their jurisdiction the first in recent Western history to provide full, formal recognition to same-sex unions as legal marriages entailing the same rights and obligations as different-sex marriages.

In another sense, this may be a race without a winner. Pragmatists caution that Denmark moved to the brink of same-sex marriage in 1989 and the state of Hawaii seemed to be on the verge of recognizing same-sex marriage in 1993, yet both have hesitated in the face of popular criticism. Most fundamentally, moralists on both the right and left insist that this is a race that ought to have no winners. Both quail at the thought of legally recognized same-sex marriages or even civil unions: conservatives fear that *gay* marriage will constitute a state stamp of approval on homosexuality and sodomy, which should instead be considered flawed (at best) or evil (at worst) alternatives to preferred heterosexuality and procreative intercourse, while progressives fear that gay *marriage* will constitute a queer stamp of approval on the gendered and sex-negative features of middle-class family values.

I have discussed the conservative and progressive critiques of same-sex marriage in prior publications and have maintained that neither progressives nor conservatives have yet produced a convincing response to my argument that the principle of *formal equality* requires the state to recognize same-sex unions on the

---

* John A Garver Professor of Jurisprudence, Yale Law School. J.D., Yale Law School, 1978; M.A., Harvard University, 1974; B.A., Davidson College, 1973. This essay was originally presented at the University of Pacific, McGeorge School of Law in 1999 as part of McGeorge School of Law's Distinguished Speaker Series. I am grateful for the excellent research help provided by Joshua Stehlik.

1. 744 A.2d 864 (Vt. 1999).

2. *Id.* at 867.

3. *See* Kees Waaldijk, University of Leiden, *The Latest About Lifting the Ban on Marriage for Same-Sex Couples in the Netherlands* (visited Oct. 1999) <http://www.coc.nl/index.html?file=marriage> (copy on file with the *McGeorge Law Review*) (describing the Marriage Bill, which was formally introduced in the Netherlands' Parliament in June of 1999).

same terms as which it recognizes different-sex unions.[4] In this Essay, I not only demonstrate how the events in Vermont and Hawaii link up with those in the Netherlands and Denmark, but I also correlate those events with the broader constitutional and theoretical debates as well. My general thesis is that not only does comparative law reveal the current plurality of legal regulatory regimes, but it also suggests the likelihood of that pluralism's progressing, slowly but surely, to state recognition of same-sex unions, and to a pluralism of options for same-sex partners within most countries. My specific thesis is that comparative international and domestic experience suggests that, even if some conservative and progressive criticisms of same-sex marriage end up being true in the short term, most will not be borne out in the long term. Not only are the expressed fears of the religious right and radical queer theorists greatly overstated, but they are mutually offsetting as well.

I. THE SAME-SEX MARRIAGE DEBATE

In *Loving v. Virginia*,[5] a unanimous United States Supreme Court invalidated Virginia's law prohibiting different-race marriages. Part I of Chief Justice Earl Warren's opinion ruled that denying a black-white couple a marriage license that would be given to a similar black-black couple is race discrimination in violation of the Equal Protection Clause of the United States Constitution.[6] The Hawaii Supreme Court in *Baehr v. Lewin*[7] applied this same kind of analysis to the State's bar to same-sex marriages.[8] Specifically, the court in *Baehr* held that denying a female-female couple the marriage license that would be given to a similar female-male couple is discrimination on the basis of sex, in the same way that denying a black-white couple a marriage license that would be given to a black-black couple is discrimination on the basis of race.[9] In the latter case, the classification (the variable item) is the race of one partner; in the former case, the classification (the variable item) is the sex of one partner. Like the United States Constitution, the Hawaii Constitution makes sex a classification that cannot be used to confer legal disadvantages unless there is a compelling justification.[10] That justification cannot be state encouragement of "natural" gender roles (husband and wife), because

4. The arguments are in WILLIAM N. ESKRIDGE, JR., THE CASE FOR SAME-SEX MARRIAGE (1996) [hereinafter ESKRIDGE, THE CASE FOR SAME-SEX MARRIAGE], and WILLIAM N. ESKRIDGE, JR., GAYLAW: CHALLENGING THE APARTHEID OF THE CLOSET chs. 6, 8 (1999) [hereinafter ESKRIDGE, GAYLAW].

5. 388 U.S. 1 (1967).

6. *Id.* at 7-12; U.S. CONST. amend. XIV, § 1.

7. 852 P.2d 44 (Haw. 1993).

8. *Id.* at 59-67.

9. *Id.* at 68.

10. HAW. CONST. art. I, § 5 ("No person shall be deprived of life, liberty, or property without due process of law, nor be denied equal protection of the laws, nor be denied the enjoyment of the person's civil rights or be discriminated against in the exercise thereof because of race, religion, sex or ancestry.").

heightened scrutiny of sex-based classifications rests upon the idea that state insistence on rigid gender roles ordinarily limits individual choice without serving valid public goals.

Part II of *Loving* briefly presented an independent ground for striking down Virginia's law against different-race marriage:

> The freedom to marry has long been recognized as one of the vital personal rights essential to the orderly pursuit of happiness by free men. . . . To deny this fundamental freedom on so unsupportable a basis as the racial classifications embodied in these statutes . . . is surely to deprive all the State's citizens of liberty without due process of law.[11]

The United States Supreme Court in *Zablocki v. Redhail*[12] applied this holding of *Loving* to invalidate a state bar to remarriage by people with outstanding child or spousal support obligations.[13] Justice Thurgood Marshall's opinion for the Court ruled that no state restriction of the "'freedom of personal choice in matters of marriage and family life'" can be sustained unless the state can show that its restriction is narrowly drawn to serve a compelling social purpose.[14] Because there was no suspicious classification in *Zablocki* comparable to the race-based classification in *Loving*, the stricter judicial scrutiny applied in *Zablocki* was justified solely on its restriction of the right to marry.[15]

Zablocki involved an equal protection challenge and established a doctrinal structure logically applicable to other cases: a state law or practice that places a "direct legal obstacle in the path of persons desiring to get married" denies those persons the equal protection of the laws unless the state policy is "supported by sufficiently important state interests and is closely tailored to effectuate only those interests."[16] A further implication of *Zablocki* is that the denial of state recognition of same-sex marriages on the same terms as different-sex marriages is a denial of *formal equality* that must be specially justified by the state. The legal consequences of state-recognized marriage in this country are vast—including duties of support and fidelity, presumptions of spousal authority and agency in the event of disability or death, rights against state or private interference in the spousal relationship, and more than a thousand duties and rights under federal law. There is serious debate

11. *Loving*, 388 U.S. at 12.
12. 434 U.S. 374 (1978).
13. *Id.* at 377.
14. *Id.* at 385-87 (quoting Cleveland Bd. of Educ. v. LaFleur, 414 U.S. 632, 639-40 (1974)). Justice Lewis Powell concurred only in the Court's judgment, in large part because he believed the implications of the majority opinion would also support a right to same-sex marriage. *Id.* at 396-406 (Powell, J., concurring). Chief Justice Burger and Justice Stewart concurred only in the Court's result, while Justice Rehnquist dissented. *Id.* at 391 (Burger, C.J., and Stewart, J., concurring); *id.* at 407 (Rehnquist, J., dissenting).
15. *Id.* at 383-87.
16. *Id.* at 387 n.12, 388.

regarding whether the state over-rewards marriage or over-protects marital relations. However that debate is resolved, many legal consequences of marriage that are unequally apportioned in our society will remain. The principle of formal equality demands that couples wishing to assume these rights and duties ought to be allowed to do so, unless there is a neutral state justification for excluding them.

This principle of law is also a principle of common sense. Assume you are running a household of three children, and you set different groundrules as to important matters for different children, perhaps to the disadvantage of one particular child.[17] Such a regime is a bad one: you are not only needlessly hurting the disfavored child, but you are likely spreading discord among the children and perhaps even spoiling the preferred children. A regime of unequal treatment invites jealousy and bad feelings. In this way, the principle of formal equality is a rule supported by practical experience as well as by the more abstract idea of the equal dignity and personhood of each human subject. This principle does not insist that everyone always be treated exactly the same—only that differences in treatment be justified neutrally and purposively.

The principle of formal equality means that the burden of persuasion as to same-sex marriage lies with the opponents. The issue should not be "Why gay marriage?" but should instead be "Why *not* gay marriage?"

At first, traditionalist opponents argued that different treatment is justified by the nature of marriage, which inevitably situates same-sex couples outside of it. For these critics, same-sex marriage is an oxymoron; such relationships, they argue descriptively, have never been recognized as *marriages*,[18] and, they argue prescriptively, ought not be so recognized, because marriage ought to involve a man and a woman at least theoretically capable of having procreative sex.[19] The descriptive argument is factually oversimple: societies in history, including many Native American tribes in this country, have recognized same-sex unions as marriages.[20] It also begs the question: How should our society structure the legal institution of marriage? The prescriptive argument tries to answer that question, but is too dogmatic by demanding that procreation be an essential goal of marriage.

---

17. I am thinking of rules for which the different ages of the children do not make a difference. Thus, if Martha is taught how to drive at age fifteen and then gets her license at age sixteen, then thirteen-year-old Sally will expect the same treatment—not to be taught how to drive at age thirteen, but to be taught the way Martha was when she reaches age fifteen. Moreover, the rule of formal equality needs to be understood in light of context, which might be materially different for the two children. If Sally were blind, she should not be treated the same. Finally, formal equality can be sacrificed for a neutral reason, especially one related to the activity being regulated. If Sally proves herself to be a reckless driver during lessons at age fifteen, her parent(s) may justifiably postpone her applying for a license until she receives further instruction or proves herself more careful.

18. *See, e.g.*, Baker v. Nelson, 191 N.W.2d 185, 186-87 (Minn. 1971) (holding that statute governing marriage does not authorize marriage between persons of the same sex, and such marriages are prohibited).

19. *See, e.g.*, John M. Finnis, *Law, Morality, and "Sexual Orientation,"* 69 NOTRE DAME L. REV. 1049, 1063-76 (1994) (asserting that intercourse between spouses enables them to actualize the blessings of children and mutual affection).

20. *See* ESKRIDGE, THE CASE FOR SAME-SEX MARRIAGE, *supra* note 4, ch. 2.

Should infertile couples, including elderly couples, be disabled from marrying? No state has ever imposed such a requirement, and none could under the Supreme Court's right-to-marry jurisprudence. As the Court officially recognized in its last right-to-marry case, *Turner v. Safley*,[21] the first and, for most people, the most important role of marriage is "expression[] of emotional support and public commitment"—namely, the *unitive* goal of marriage (as opposed to its *procreative* goal).[22]

Moreover, this kind of oppositionist rhetoric buttresses the sex discrimination argument for same-sex marriage by showing how resistance to same-sex marriage rests upon an insistence on rigid gender roles. To tell a woman that she cannot legally marry a woman is to restrict the woman's choice more fundamentally than to tell her she cannot attend the Virginia Military Institute (VMI) or administer her parents' estate.[23] To tell a woman that the state will recognize her committed union only if she agrees to be a *wife* to a wedded *husband* is a more dogmatic insistence on rigid gender roles than is a state's decision to allow eighteen-year-old women, but not eighteen-year-old men, to buy 3.2% beer.[24] If women's exclusion from VMI and state preference in beer sales are both unconstitutional, as the Supreme Court has held,[25] because they limit choice and rest upon rigid gender roles, then refusing to recognize a woman's choice of another woman as her life partner is not only just as unconstitutional, but more deeply so.

Although the definitional argument against same-sex marriage prevailed among judges and legislators before the 1990s, this argument's factual ignorance and normative sexism reinforces the power of my argument of formal equality. The factual ignorance of the definitional argument suggests that other motives were at work. The usual suspect is homophobia, which is inspired not just by the disgust that oral or anal sex arouses in many Americans, but is more fundamentally inspired by women's and men's abandonment of traditional gender roles.[26] The rigid gender roles insisted upon by the definitional argument suggest that ultimately it is sexism

---

21. 482 U.S. 78 (1987) (protecting incarcerated prisoners' right to marry).

22. *Id.* at 95. *Turner* did not change the analytical structure created by *Loving* and *Zablocki*, which requires the state to justify with the strongest policy reasons why it excludes some couples from the marriage rights routinely granted to others. What *Turner* did clarify was the nature of the right itself. *Loving* and *Zablocki* gave some emphasis to the procreative goal of marriage. *Turner*, in contrast, stressed the social, or unitive, goal of marriage, where marriage is an institution of commitment. Because some of the prisoners would never be able to consummate their marriages, the unitive goal was the only one applicable for many in the protected class.

23. *See* Virginia v. United States, 518 U.S. 515 (1996) (public paramilitary college cannot exclude women); Reed v. Reed, 404 U.S. 71 (1971) (state cannot give males a preference in administering estates even if, as implied, men are likely to have more business experience).

24. *Cf.* Craig v. Boren, 429 U.S. 190, 199-210 (1976) (holding it unconstitutional sex discrimination for the state to allow eighteen-year-old women, but not eighteen-year-old men, to buy 3.2% beer, even though there was strong evidence that men were more likely to drink and drive than were women).

25. *See Virginia*, 518 U.S. at 519; *Craig*, 429 U.S. at 199-210.

26. Although adulterous President William Clinton survived the knowledge that he was regularly fellated by White House intern Monica Lewinski, you can be sure the reaction would have been more severe if the President had been fellated by the equally obsequious George Stephanopolous.

that drives this exclusion, thereby mobilizing the moral and political force of sex discrimination jurisprudence. Same-sex couples, and couples that resist easy classification as same- or different-sex, ought to be treated the same as conventional different-sex couples in the eyes of the law.

While the definitional argument against same-sex marriage remains popular, it has been supplemented and, among intellectuals, replaced by other arguments that are explicitly consequentialist. Such arguments focus on assertedly bad social consequences that follow from legal recognition of same-sex marriages. Some conservatives maintain that same-sex marriage would promote *homosexuality* and place a state "stamp of approval" on a status that is either wicked or suboptimal, especially for impressionable adolescents who would otherwise marry, procreate, and raise a family.[27] Some progressives maintain that same-sex marriage would promote patriarchal *marriage* and place a state stamp of approval on assimilation of gay people into the straight mainstream,[28] an assimilation that they view as wicked or suboptimal, especially for impressionable adolescents who might otherwise blaze their own queer paths.[29]

Both critiques of same-sex marriage make unsupported factual assumptions and wantonly speculate about the consequences of same-sex marriage. Also, both critiques cannot be right: many radical progressives would be delighted if same-sex marriage actually did promote homosexuality, and at least some conservatives ought to be satisfied if it gave marriage a helping hand. Relatedly, the newer conservative and progressive critiques help answer one another: conservatives should heed the progressive observation that same-sex marriage is state encouragement of interpersonal commitment most of all, while progressives ought to concede the conservatives' observation that same-sex marriage would contribute to the erosion of traditional gender roles (patriarchy) within the institution of marriage, which promises to open up more choices for women as well as men. Especially as attenuated, neither criticism can trump the principle of formal equality, and critics of both stripes would better focus their time and energy on issues that actually advance the values they advocate; conservatives might spend more energy supporting marriages of all kinds and remedying the tendency of men to dump and pauperize their wives who tend to invest more in the relationship, the children, and even the husbands' careers, while progressives might work toward social and institutional supports for more informal families of choice, such as friendship linkages and community support groups.

27. *E.g.*, RICHARD A. POSNER, SEX AND REASON 311 (1992).

28. *See* Nancy D. Polikoff, *We Will Get What We Ask For: Why Legalizing Gay and Lesbian Marriage Will Not "Dismantle the Legal Structure of Gender in Every Marriage,"* 79 VA. L. REV. 1535, 1536-43 (1993).

29. *E.g.*, Paula L. Ettelbrick, *Since When Is Marriage a Path to Liberation?*, NAT'L GAY & LESBIAN Q., Fall 1989, at 9, 9-12, *reprinted in* WILLIAM N. ESKRIDGE, JR. & NAN D. HUNTER, SEXUALITY, GENDER, AND THE LAW (1997).

One source of insight that is largely absent from the same-sex marriage debate has been comparative law. Six countries—Denmark, Sweden, Norway, Iceland, Greenland, and the Netherlands—have adopted laws endowing registered same-sex partnerships with almost all the legal rights and duties associated with marriage.[30] France has created a new institution, the civil solidarity pact, which includes some of the benefits and duties related to marriage of same-sex couples. Canada and Hungary have allowed same-sex partners all the benefits and obligations legally accorded different-sex cohabiting couples. What lessons does the comparative experience offer the same-sex marriage debate? Surprisingly many.

II. SAME-SEX PARTNERSHIPS IN OTHER COUNTRIES

The tables below set forth basic comparative law information for state regulation of gay people and their unions, including same-sex registered partnerships. These tables tell us nothing about the subjective experience of same-sex couples in any of these countries, and it is too early to tell how state recognition of same-sex partnerships will play out. Nonetheless, these tables do tell us much about the path to legalized same-sex marriage. The path is step-by-step and incremental, inevitable in some jurisdictions, impossible elsewhere in the short term, and sedimentary in the sense that new institutions are being piled on top of old ones. Consider these points in some detail.

A. *The Step-by-Step Principle*

Table 1 sets forth, for selected countries, the dates on which each country adopted a progay change in its law: repealing laws criminalizing consensual sodomy, equalizing the age of consent for same-sex and different-sex intercourse, prohibiting discrimination on the basis of sexual orientation, affording same-sex cohabiting couples the same rights and obligations as different-sex couples, recognizing same-sex unions as "registered partnerships" or the like, and expressly allowing same-sex partners to adopt children on the same terms as married couples. Only Denmark has adopted all these gay-equality measures. Most countries in the table—and a large majority not in the table—have adopted few or none.

The overriding lesson of Table 1 is that legal recognition of same-sex unions—or, ultimately, marriages—comes through a step-by-step process.[31] Such a process is *sequential* and *incremental*: it proceeds by little steps that are taken in

30. References for the laws discussed in this paragraph can be found in Appendix I to this Article.

31. The materials contained in Table 1 are taken from Appendix I, *supra*. *See generally* THE SOCIOLEGAL CONTROL OF HOMOSEXUALITY: A MULTI-NATION COMPARISON (Donald J. West et al. eds., 1997) [hereinafter MULTI-NATIONAL COMPARISON]; International Lesbian and Gay Association, *World Legal Survey* (visited Apr. 2000) <http://www.ilga.org> (copy on file with the *McGeorge Law Review*).

2000 / The Same-Sex Marriage Debate

a particular order.[32] Registered partnership laws, just short of same-sex marriage, have not been adopted until a particular country has first decriminalized consensual sodomy and equalized the age of consent for homosexual and heterosexual intercourse, then has adopted laws prohibiting employment and other kinds of discrimination against gay people, and finally has provided other kinds of more limited state recognition for same-sex relationships, such as the giving of legal benefits to or the enforcing of legal obligations on cohabiting same-sex couples.

The recurrence of the same pattern in country after country suggests this paradox: law cannot move unless public opinion moves, but public attitudes can be influenced by changes in the law. For gay rights, the impasse suggested by this paradox can be ameliorated or broken if the proponents of reform move step-by-step along a continuum of little reforms. There are a number of pragmatic reasons why such a step-by-step process can break the impasse over a period of time. Step-by-step change permits gradual adjustment of anti-gay mindsets, slowly empowers gay rights advocates, and can discredit anti-gay arguments. Consider each.

32. *See* Kees Waaldijk, The "Law of Small Change": How the Road to Same-Sex Marriage Got Paved in the Netherlands 1-3 (July 1999) (unpublished manuscript, on file with the author). This paper was authored for and presented at a conference entitled Legal Recognition of Same-Sex Partnerships: A Conference on National, European, and International Law, in London, England.

Table 1
Progay Laws Outside the USA, Selected Countries

Country	Consensual Sodomy Decrim-inalized	Equal Age of Consent for Same-Sex Relations	First Anti-Discrim-ination Law	Benefits for Same-Sex Cohabiting Couples	Registered Partnership Legislation	Adoption by Same-Sex Partners
Netherlands	1810	1971	1992	Yes	1998	Proposed
Denmark	1930	1976	1987	Yes	1989	1999
Iceland	n.k.	1992	1996	1996	1996	Proposed
Sweden	1944	1978	1987	1987	1995	
Norway	1972	1972	1981	Yes	1993	
Greenland	1930	1978	1987	Yes	1994	
Finland	1971	1998	1995	Yes	Proposed	
Canada	1969	1969	1996	1999		
Spain	1822	1995	1995		Proposed	
Catalonia					1998	
Aragon					1999	
Israel	1988	1988	1992	1994		
France	1791	1982	1985		1998	
Germany	1969	1994			Proposed	
Czech Republic	1961	1990			Proposed	
Hungary	1961			1995		
South Africa	1998	1998	1997	1999		
Belgium	1792	1985	Proposed	1998	Proposed	
Russia	1993	1997				
United Kingdom		Proposed				
England	1967					
Scotland	1980					
N. Ireland	1982					
Ireland	1993		1999			
Brazil	1823	Yes				
China						
India						
Mexico						
Pakistan						

Paul's experience on the road to Damascus is exceptional; human beings rarely change their fundamental attitudes overnight. But one's anti-gay attitudes—or at least one's willingness to give vent to or act on them—can change as the culture changes. If you are a thirty-year-old man who is sickened by the idea of homosexuality or of "homosexuals," you are highly unlikely to support gay marriage, but you might be open to sodomy decriminalization for practical reasons, such as your belief that the state is wasting its time snooping around people's bedrooms. Yet sodomy decriminalization and a lessening of public condemnation of homosexuality will sooner or (probably) later embolden some of your gay friends, family members, and coworkers to come out of their closets. You will probably be shocked at first, and you can assimilate them as exceptions to your dislike of "homosexuals," but there is a good chance that some of your anti-gay attitudes will soften as you enter middle age.[33] Over time, maybe a long period of time, your interaction with gay people might open you up to acquiescing in anti-discrimination laws, for your experience has been that gay coworkers are okay and that anti-gay workers are troublemakers. You could still oppose same-sex marriage, but even this attitude might bend when your daughter partners with another woman and you and your spouse integrate her into your extended family in a variety of ways. Because your other children have long known of your daughter's orientation, they are cool with the issue more generally. As each step in the progression toward gay equality encourages more people to be openly gay, not only can middle-aged homophobic attitudes change, but the attitudes of new generations might start out less homophobic. These changes will support gay equality. The foregoing is, however, only one among several possible scenarios. Because the homophobe may have a traumatic experience that confirms his dislike or simply ignores or denies positive information, his preexisting anti-gay attitudes may be completely resistant to change.[34]

Even if underlying attitudes do not change significantly, legal incrementalism can contribute to gay equality. In this regard, consider not only the information in Table 1, but that in Table 2, on the next two pages.[35] Table 2 sets forth, for all 50 American states and the District of Columbia, the dates on which each state adopted a progay change in its law: repealing laws criminalizing consensual sodomy (or

33. Surveys have found that knowing gay people is negatively correlated with having anti-gay attitudes. *See* Gregory M. Herek, *Beyond "Homophobia": A Social Psychological Perspective on Attitudes Toward Lesbians and Gay Men*, *in* BASHERS, BAITERS & BIGOTS: HOMOPHOBIA IN AMERICAN SOCIETY 1, 13-15 (John P. DeCecco ed., 1985).

34. On the strong persistence of anti-gay attitudes notwithstanding gay liberation and thousands of coming out stories, see ALBERT D. KLASSEN ET AL., SEX AND MORALITY IN THE U.S.: AN EMPIRICAL ENQUIRY UNDER THE AUSPICES OF THE KINSEY INSTITUTE 165-84 (Hubert J. O'Gorman ed., 1989).

35. The information found in columns one, three, and four of Table 2 are taken from ESKRIDGE, GAYLAW, *supra* note 4, at 328-37, 356-61; the data contained in columns three, four, and five is from WILLIAM N. ESKRIDGE, JR. & NAN D. HUNTER, SEXUALITY, GENDER, AND THE LAW 863-68, 949 (1997); the materials found in columns two and six are taken from Appendices II and III, *supra*.

reducing it to a misdemeanor), enhancing defendants' sentences for crimes involving gay-bashing, prohibiting sexual orientation discrimination in public and (then) private employment, allowing a same-sex partner to adopt her partner's children as a "second parent," and extending benefits to state employees who are same-sex "registered partners."

Table 1 and 2 suggest that discriminalization of sodomy might pave the way—and probably is a precondition—for the adoption of anti-discrimination laws. Not only does sodomy repeal remove a popular objection to anti-discrimination laws,[36] but it facilitates the political conditions for such laws. Repeal of sodomy laws not only emboldens some gay people to come out of their closets, but also emboldens the uncloseted to organize themselves politically and press for other equality assurances, such as laws that prohibit discrimination against them in the private as well as public spheres.[37] The more openly gay people there are *and* the better organized they are politically, the greater attention politicians and judges will pay to their arguments for equal legal entitlements, even if popular attitudes are otherwise unaffected. Again, the dynamics might work the opposite way under unfavorable circumstances: if the newly uncloseted were to cause some terrible incident, there could be a backlash not only against further rights for gay people, but also against the new rights that had just been recognized.

36. That is, one can logically object to adopting an anti-discrimination law that protects people whose conduct (such as consensual sodomy) is habitually criminal. How can you protect a status group whose characteristic conduct is felonious? For an argument of this sort, see Romer v. Evans, 517 U.S. 620, 640-43 (1996) (Scalia, J., dissenting).

37. Because members of a potential interest group have incentives to "free ride" on the efforts of others, diminished political activity will ordinarily occur on behalf of that group. For gay people, the free rider problem is particularly severe, because most gay people are closeted. Once uncloseted, gay people's incentives to organize are much greater, but are impeded by threats of losing their jobs or other private as well as public retaliation.

Table 2
Progay Legal Measures, States of the USA

State	Sodomy Decrim.	Hate Crime	Public Emp. Discrim.	Private Emp. Discrim.	Second Parent Adoptions	Registered Partner-ship
Vermont	1977	1989	1991	1991	1993	1998
California	1975	1991	1979	1979	(1980s)	1999
Hawaii	1972		1991	1991		1995
D.C.	1994	1990	1977	1977	1995	1994
New Jersey	1978	1995	1991	1991	1995	
Massachusetts	(1974)	1996	1989	1989	1993	
New York	1980		1983		1995	
Illinois	1961	1991	1996		1995	
Minnesota	(1977)	1989	1986	1993		
Wisconsin	1983	1991	1982	1982		
Connecticut	1969	1990	1991	1991		
New Hampshire	1973	1997	1997	1997		
Nevada	1993	1989	1999	1999		
Rhode Island	1998	1991	1985	1995		
Oregon	1971	1989	1987			
Washington	1975	1993	1985			
Pennsylvania	1980		1975			
Ohio	1972		1983			
Colorado	1971					
Louisiana	1999	1997				
Delaware	1972	1997				
Iowa	1976	1992				
Kentucky	1992	1998				
Maine	1975	1995				
Nebraska	1977	1997				
Florida	(1971)	1991				
Alaska	1978					
Georgia	1998					
Indiana	1976					
Montana	1997					
New Mexico	1975					
North Dakota	1973					
South Dakota	1976					
Tennessee	1996					

Table 2
Progay Legal Measures, States of the USA

State	Sodomy Decrim.	Hate Crime	Public Emp. Discrim.	Private Emp. Discrim.	Second Parent Adoptions	Registered Partner-ship
West Virginia	1976					
Wyoming	1977					
Maryland			1993			
Arizona	(1977)	(1997)				
Arkansas	(1977)					
Kansas	(1969)					
Michigan	(1980)					
Missouri	(1977)					
Texas	(1973)					
Alabama						
Idaho						
Mississippi						
North Carolina						
Oklahoma						
South Carolina						
Virginia						
Utah						

Another way that incrementalism works to facilitate gay equality is even more subtle but is potentially powerful in the long term. Opponents typically argue that pro-gay measures will have catastrophic consequences—rampant promiscuity and public lewdness, predation against children, and erosion of families.[38] These ills do not in fact occur when states adopt gay equality measures, in part because the predictions are irrational and hysterical to start with, and in part because the measures are so incremental. When sodomy laws are repealed, gay people do not drastically change their sexual practices, and only a minority of gay people are encouraged to be bolder in the public arena. The Scandinavian registered partnership laws dramatically illustrate how the persistence of the closet can itself contribute to arguments for gay rights. As Table 3 reveals,[39] few same-sex couples have registered under Scandinavian partnership laws offering them almost all the benefits and obligations pertaining to different-sex married couples. Not only have

38. *E.g.*, GEORGE GRANT & MARK A. HORNE, LEGISLATING IMMORALITY: THE HOMOSEXUAL RIGHTS MOVEMENT COMES OUT OF THE CLOSET (1993). See also ESKRIDGE, GAYLAW, *supra* note 4, ch. 3, for examples of exaggerated predictions made by opponents of gay rights in the 1970s.

39. Table 3 is taken from materials distributed at the Conference on Legal Recognition of Same-Sex Partnerships organized by Professor Robert Winterute (Kings College) for July 1999.

2000 / The Same-Sex Marriage Debate

few couples registered under these laws, but observation by scholars in those countries has detected no significant effects, good or bad, for the society as a whole. The incrementalism—indeed, the sloth-like pace—by which social practices and law have changed undermines the apocalyptic rhetoric of anti-gay groups. The homophobes who cried wolf against sodomy repeal lose some credibility when they cry wolf again during debates about anti-discrimination laws and measures recognizing same-sex unions.

Table 3
Partnership Registration in Five Countries, 1990-98

	Denmark	Norway	Sweden	Iceland	Netherlands
1990 (MM/FF)	746 (573/173)	n.s.	n.s.	n.s.	n.s.
1991 (MM/FF)	258 (171/87)	n.s.	n.s.	n.s.	n.s.
1992 (MM/FF)	218 (139/79)	n.s.	n.s.	n.s.	n.s.
1993 (MM/FF)	185 (124/61)	n.s.	n.s.	n.s.	n.s.
1994 (MM/FF)	197 (105/92)	294 (203/91)	n.s.	n.s.	n.s.
1995 (MM/FF)	194 (119/75)	98 (64/34)	333 (249/84)	n.s.	n.s.
1996 (MM/FF)	199 (106/93)	127 (80/47)	160 (101/59)	n.s.	n.s.
1997 (MM/FF)	178 (101/77)	118 (75/43)	131 (79/52)	33 (16/17)	n.s.
1998 (MM/FF)	197 (84/113)	n.a.	125 (79/46)	12 (5/7)	5217 (1860/1487)
Total (MM/FF)	2372 (1498/874)	674 (442/232)	749 (508/241)	45 (21/24)	5217 (1860/1487)

B. The Progressivity Thesis

The foregoing incremental and sequential process is also *progressive*: each step in this process is a step toward formal equality for lesbians, gay men, bisexuals, and possibly transgendered people. While recognition of same-sex unions is impossible and barely conceivable until other anti-discrimination measures have been adopted, and anti-discrimination laws are usually not possible until sodomy has been decriminalized, the decriminalization of sodomy makes it easier to adopt anti-discrimination laws, which in turn make it easier to recognize same-sex unions, for the reasons developed above. Once same-sex unions are euphemistically recognized as "registered partnerships," and modest numbers of people take advantage of the new institution to formalize their well-ordered middle-class unions, it would then be, I hypothesize, a smaller step to recognize same-sex marriage. The implication is that recognition of same-sex marriage is likely, so long as: (1) the preparatory steps are followed; (2) gay people come out of their closets and insist on equal rights; and (3) society does not perceive disastrous consequences flowing from the steps it has already taken.

This is a breathtaking thesis only if viewed in the short term. Fifty years ago, it would have been preposterous to think that consensual sodomy would be widely decriminalized in the United States, as it is today (Table 2). Thirty years ago, extending antidiscrimination protections to gay people in the workplace would have been unthinkable almost anywhere in the Western world, whereas today such protections are commonplace (Tables 1 and 2). Fifteen years ago, it would have been visionary to think that a Western state would create a registry and benefits for same-sex partnerships, such as now exist in seven countries (Tables 1 and 3) and the state of Vermont, and insane to believe that same-sex marriages would be seriously debated all over Europe and the United States, as they are today. Yet the beginning of the millennium bears witness to the seriousness of this debate. The Netherlands or Vermont may or may not recognize same-sex marriages in the next few years, but some state will in the foreseeable future. Once that happens, and God fails to send the locusts down on that state,[40] other states will follow along. This process might take years, it might take decades, but it will take place.

A skeptic can reasonably object that this is the sort of progressive, whiggish approach to history that has repeatedly been undone by the unpredictability of human events. Depressions, wars, and technological developments—to identify only the most obvious monkey-wrenches—can derail this train of legal innovation. I agree and argue only that external shocks can accelerate, as well as derail, the progression. Moreover, the critical long-term social trends work in favor of expanding gay rights. Consider what it is that distinguishes the most pro-gay countries and states in Tables 1 and 2 from the most anti-gay countries and states. An obvious variable is relative urbanization. In general, the countries and states with large rural and small-town populations are less open to gay equality than those whose populations are concentrated in large cities and their suburbs. Urbanization correlates positively with gay equality for a variety of reasons: gender-benders and sexual minorities have greater freedom in big cities to form subcultures, a phenomenon which in turn draws such people away from rural areas; urban life discourages large families and offers women more opportunities outside the home, which undermines traditional gender roles (woman gives birth to and cares for children, man earns money); and as procreation declines and social opportunities multiply in urban settings, sex for pleasure becomes relatively more acceptable. In the United States, the most pro-gay states are those of the urbanized Northeast corridor, those ringing Lake Michigan, and the West Coast states; the least pro-gay

40. Indeed, it is much more likely that the "first move" on same-sex marriage will reap economic benefits, rather than the Wrath of God. *See* Jennifer Gerarda Brown, *Competitive Federalism and the Legislative Incentives to Recognize Same-Sex Marriages*, 68 S. CAL. L. REV. 745 (1995).

states tend to be the more rural ones of the South, Great Plains, and Rocky Mountains (Table 2).

Whatever the precise fate of big cities, clustering of human beings in urban suburban, and exurban (suburban-urban) areas appears to be a robust trend in industrialized, technology-driven modern states. That social trend undercuts attitudes that form the basis for homophobia: namely, gender rigidity and sex negativity.[41] Thus, even without a step-by-step approach to gay equality, popular attitudes ought to evolve in gay-friendly ways because of urbanization alone. An increasingly urbanized population will be increasingly receptive to the incremental campaign for full gay equality.

That legal recognition of same-sex marriage is probable does not mean that such recognition will be universal. Tables 1 and 2 suggest that, even if the Netherlands and Vermont were to legalize same-sex marriage, other countries and states would not, either in the short term or in the long term. States like Mississippi and Idaho, and countries like the United Kingdom and Argentina, would be unprepared to follow Vermont and the Netherlands, to the extent that those jurisdictions continue to criminalize gay people for their consensual intimacy. However long it takes to recognize same-sex marriage in the Netherlands and Vermont, it will take much longer to do so in the United Kingdom and Mississippi. Although I think same-sex marriage is an idea whose time has come, I also think that it will not come to some jurisdictions for a long time, if ever. Countries in Northern Europe and states in the Northeastern United States are most likely to lead the way, given their readiness under the step-by-step principle, but it is really unclear how many countries or states would recognize same-sex marriage even in the medium term and even if urbanizing trends continue.

There is another variable that makes the matter even less predictable. Return to Tables 1 and 2, which show that urbanization does not perfectly correlate with advances in gay rights. This variable hardly explains why the Netherlands is more gay-friendly than the United Kingdom or why Vermont is much more gay-friendly than Michigan. Utah, Virginia, and Texas are extremely anti-gay, yet are more urbanized than Vermont and are not much less urbanized than such pro-gay meccas as Oregon and Wisconsin. Internationally, the big puzzle is why the Scandinavian countries are so much more pro-gay than comparably urbanized countries like Switzerland and, most strikingly, the United Kingdom. A secondary variable is whether fundamentalist religion plays an important role in the public culture of a Western-acculturated country or state.[42] In America, states where the aggressively anti-gay Southern Baptist Convention and the Church of Jesus Christ of Latter-Day Saints have the most members are, generally speaking, the most anti-gay in their

41. *See* ESKRIDGE, GAYLAW, *supra* note 4, ch. 6; KLASSEN ET AL., *supra* note 34, at 225-27, 240-41.

42. *Cf.* KLASSEN ET AL., *supra* note 34, at 227-28, 238-39 (explaining that religious devoutness, especially when fundamentalist Protestant, most accurately predicts anti-homosexual attitudes).

policies. Internationally, countries where organized religion has become politically domesticated (Scandinavian nations and the Netherlands) are most likely to have pro-gay policies. Countries where religious involvement in politics is viewed with suspicion (France, Belgium) are likely to have intermediate policies, and countries with active involvement of religions in politics (Latin America and the United States) will have anti-gay policies.

Unlike increasing urbanization, which seems predictable in the medium term, the role of fundamentalist religion in public culture is much less predictable. To my knowledge, no one has ever successfully predicted the trajectory of religious enthusiasm.[43] Indeed, that trajectory might be influenced by gay people's efforts to secure equal rights. As gay rights and openly gay people have become part of the public culture, fundamentalist religions in the United States have not only been energized in their efforts to confront that development, but have reordered their religious beliefs to make homophobia doctrinally central. Thus, it is quite possible that recognition of same-sex marriages in one or a few jurisdictions could massively reenergize religious fundamentalism and trigger a national or transnational backlash against gay rights. If that were to occur, the United States and the world could end up with a long-term division between jurisdictions recognizing same-sex unions or marriages and those not recognizing such unions or marriages. If most states did adopt same-sex union or marriage statutes, however, the U.S. Supreme Court would probably require all states to do so as a matter of constitutional equal protection—just as it did a generation ago for different-race marriage in *Loving v. Virginia.*

C. The Sedimentary Precept

Each step toward same-sex marriage is typically *sedimentary:*[44] rather than displacing earlier reforms, the new reform simply adds another legal rule or institution on top of the earlier one. In this way, the same-sex marriage movement has contributed to a transformation in the options the state offers to different-sex as well as same-sex couples. Thus, when Denmark enacted its registered partnership law, it did not revoke the legal rights of cohabiting same-sex couples. In 1998, the Parliament in the Netherlands enacted a law recognizing registered partnerships, granting to such unions most of the rights, benefits, and obligations of marriage (but not the name "marriage"). Unlike Denmark's pioneering law, the Dutch law made registered partnerships available to different-sex as well as same-sex couples, and about a third of the registrants have been different-sex couples (Table 3). This

43. Indeed, so predicting is even more treacherous than predicting the weather. Zealots and officials who were confident that the cult of Jesus could be extinguished by crucifying its leader are only the most famous example of the way in which conventional judgment fails to account for religious movements. Who would have predicted in the 1960s that the "religious right" would be an important player in national politics in the 1980s?

44. *Cf.* Barry Friedman & Scott B. Smith, *The Sedimentary Constitution*, 147 U. PA. L. REV. 1 (1998).

example suggests that the experimentation in social policy triggered by the same-sex marriage movement can, and perhaps ought to, create new institutions available to all kinds of couples, not just same-sex couples. Consistent with the sedimentary precept, the 1999 bill to recognize same-sex marriages in the Netherlands would not displace registered partnerships, which would remain available for different-sex as well as same-sex couples even if same-sex marriage were recognized.

The same-sex marriage movement is part of a larger evolution in the way the state regulates human coupling. Today in the Netherlands, and tomorrow in many other jurisdictions, couples of all kinds will have a *menu of options*:

- *Dating (Tort/Criminal Law).* Couples can just date and be intimate friends. Such a relationship can be important for the couple, as some people do not want any further level of commitment. These relationships are regulated by law, primarily to protect each partner against actionable wrongs committed against her by the other partner. Criminal and civil tort law prohibit sexual assault, libels, theft or conversion of assets, blackmail, and the like. This is admittedly a minimalist level of regulation.
- *Cohabitation (Contract Law).* Almost all couples start by dating; some of those couples then decide to cohabit. This move not only signals a closer relationship, but in Western polities often entails more legal obligations. In addition to the obligation not to commit torts or crimes, the United States, Canada, and most Western European countries impose some contractual obligations on the partners as a matter of law or implied contract. Not only will the state enforce explicit promises made to induce cohabitation and a particular sharing of duties, but the state will also protect the reliance interests of partners and protect against unjust enrichment of one partner at the expense of the other. Thus, cohabiting partners may have duties of mutual maintenance and support; a partner who furthers his career while his cohabitant maintains the household may be held financially accountable in the event of a breakup.
- *Cohabitation Plus (Unitive Benefits).* Some countries, such as Canada and the Netherlands, not only enforce tort law and expansive contract principles to protect cohabiting partners, but also offer the partners some specific benefits. I call them "unitive" benefits, because they typically involve rules treating the partners as coupled and granting them financial and other benefits that reflect their unity, at least as to some matters. In the United States and France, cohabitation plus is accomplished through *domestic partnership* and *civil solidarity pacts*, respectively. Under the new French law, civil partners can file joint tax returns, the state makes it easier for a noncitizen partner of a French

citizen to immigrate to France, and employers are required to make allowances for partners' vacation plans.[45] American domestic partnership laws usually just allow formal registration and provision of fringe benefits to partners of state employees.

- *Registered Partnership (Regulatory Benefits and Duties).* After or instead of cohabiting, many couples decide to commit to a longer-term partnership. The Netherlands and the Scandinavian countries allow these couples to register as partners. Registered partners are not only governed by tort law and contract precepts, and not only have some unitive benefits granted by the state, but also have a whole range of duties as well as benefits under state law. The only benefits usually not allowed are those relating to children, such as marital preferences in adoption and presumptions that children born in the relationship are the biological children of the couple. (The Netherlands has already dropped this exception, and other countries will likely do so as well.)
- *Marriage (Regulatory Benefits and Duties).* The traditional way couples commit to a long-term relationship is, of course, through marriage. Under the sedimentary precept, the state will continue to support, as well as recognize, marriage, with all the rights and duties entailed in registered partnerships as well as the children-related rights noted above. It is also possible that the state will re-think its regulatory regime, and add or subtract rights and duties to meet the social needs or preferences of the twenty-first century.

Note that each regime incorporates the rules in prior regimes and adds to them. Thus, marriage includes the criminal restrictions of the dating regime, the contract precepts of cohabitation regime, the unitive benefits of cohabitation plus, and all the benefits and duties of registered partnerships—as well as rights to adoption and the symbolic tie to Western marriage traditions. This phenomenon is consistent with the principle of sedimentation.

III. COMPARATIVE LAW AND THE THEORETICAL DEBATE

Even if I am *descriptively* right that some jurisdictions will accept the principle of formal equality and legally recognize same-sex marriages as part of the foregoing menu of options, I might be *prescriptively* wrong that this is a beneficent, or at worst neutral, development. The comparative law experience provides important but provisional support for the proposition that formal equality is a

45. *See* Proposition de Loi Adoptée par L'Assemblé Nacionale en Première Lecture, relative au pacte civil de solidarité, No. 207, 9 Dec. 1998 (visited May 2000) <http://www.senat.fr/leg/taan98-207> (copy on file with the *McGeorge Law Review*).

worthwhile goal for both gay people and for the polities in which they live. *First*, the step-by-step process has revealed that same-sex unions, and potentially marriages, are not an oxymoron.[46] Lesbians, gay men, and bisexuals can pair up with people of the same sex and form productive unions. As Table 3 shows, the numbers are quite modest, but there is reason to believe that the unions are admirable ones. The evidence from Denmark, which has had a registered partnership law since 1989, is that most of the registered couples have stayed together (the divorce rate is quite low so far). While it is too early to compare the break-up rates for same-sex and different-sex couples, such a comparison would be beside the point, for the point is that such couples undermine stereotypes about unreliable or promiscuous "homosexuals." It is also significant, and may explain the low rates of registration, that couples registering under the partnership laws are coming out *as couples*, and not just as individuals. Thus, the laws facilitate an intriguing new phase in the history of "coming out of the closet."[47]

Second, the legal recognition of same-sex unions that is best supported by principles of justice and equality can, and perhaps usually does, have benign or good consequences. Denmark, Sweden, and the Netherlands have given almost complete recognition to same-sex unions, without malign consequences: there are no reports, even from traditionalists in those countries, that different-sex families have been weakened or that unhealthy promiscuity or sexually transmitted diseases have become a problem. Indeed, the scanty evidence supports the opposite hypotheses thus far. Not only have same-sex couples been able to solidify their conception of family through registering as partners, but new family-forming opportunities have been offered for different-sex couples.[48] The pro-family and anti-discrimination policies of these countries have contributed modestly to campaigns to prevent the spread of sexually transmitted diseases, most prominently AIDS.[49]

Moreover, there is no evidence that legal recognition of same-sex unions has contributed to a decline in the institution of marriage. Reports from Denmark suggest that the opposite may be the case; in the ten years since same-sex couples have been able to register, the marriage rate for different-sex couples has been stable, and their divorce rate has declined.[50] I am dubious that there is a causal link,

46. Recall, however, that legally recognized same-sex unions are by no means unprecedented in world history. *See, e.g., supra* text accompanying note 20 (recounting the historical acceptance of same-sex unions in some cultures).

47. Of course, one does not need such a law to come out in this way. The highest ranking openly gay judicial official in the world, Justice Michael Kirby of Australia's High Court, came out publicly by identifying his spouse as Jan.

48. By the end of 1998, for example, 2,372 couples had registered under the Danish law and 5,217 under the Dutch law; 1,870 of the Dutch couples were different-sex. *Supra* Table 3.

49. *See* Benny Henriksson & Hasse Ytterberg, *Sweden: The Power of the Moral(istic) Left*, *in* AIDS IN THE INDUSTRIALIZED DEMOCRACIES: PASSIONS, POLITICS, AND POLICIES 317, 321-22 (David L. Kirp & Ronald Bayer eds., 1992).

50. *See* Darren Spedale, Nordic Bliss: The Danish Experience with "Gay Marriage" (1999) (unpublished manuscript, copy on file with author).

for the same reasons I question opponents' confidence that same-sex marriage will ruin the institution, but the correlation between the opening up of marriage to same-sex couples and a (perhaps temporary) halt in the institution's erosion for different-sex couples ought to expose the element of hysteria and irresponsibility in opponents' predictions. Furthermore, no evidence exists to show that the Danish experience caused significant distress for homophobes, and it seems extremely unlikely that any distress that has been felt by homophobes approaches the suicidal distress that anti-gay policies and attitudes have created among adolescents in this country. To be sure, the low levels of distress might owe something to the small number of same-sex couples who have registered under these laws: 2,372 after nine years of the Danish law, 674 after four years of the Norweigan law, 749 after four years of the Swedish law, 45 after two years of the Icelandic law, and 5,217 after one year of the Dutch law (Table 3). This phenomenon again illustrates how the incrementalism of gay-equality makes legal reform easier over time, but at the cost of real equality for gay people.

Third, and most interestingly, the comparative experience has much to suggest about the consequences of same-sex marriage for the law's regulation of the family. To begin with, some of what the experience teaches is consistent with conservative and progressive criticisms of same-sex marriage. Most strikingly, early experience is consistent with the feminist argument that same-sex marriage will be a means by which white male couples will align themselves with mainstream society and distance themselves from working class couples, female couples, and couples of color or of different races.[51] As Table 3 shows, all the countries but Iceland have seen male couples take advantage of partnership registration at much higher rates than female couples, in some years at double or triple the rates. It may be significant, however, that the ratio of male to female couples has drastically fallen over time in Denmark, from 3:1 in 1990 to 1.3:1 in 1997 and 0.8:1 in 1998 (the later statistic shows more female than male couples registered), and began at 1.3:1 in the Netherlands. There are many possible explanations for the early disparity and the recent narrowing of the gender gap, but the evidence thus far lends tentative but modest support to this progressive criticism.

The comparative experience cuts against the progressive criticism that same-sex marriage will channel gay people into a patriarchal institution. Apart from the notion that same-sex marriage contributes to the delinking of marital partnership from gendered roles (husband = breadwinner, wife = housekeeper and child-rearer), the struggle for same-sex marriage has already yielded new civil institutions within which couples can choose to formalize their relationships—the Danish and Dutch registered partnerships, the American domestic partnerships, and the French civil solidarity pacts—and an expanded *menu of options* described above. Such a menu could support the traditionalist argument that same-sex marriage undermines the

51. *See* Ettelbrick, *supra* note 29, at 8-12.

institution of marriage itself. In the Netherlands, cohabitation and registered partnerships are available to different-sex as well as same-sex partners. The principle of formal equality insists that options available to same-sex couples presumptively be available to different-sex couples. Hence, different-sex couples in the Netherlands ought to and will have the same menu of choices, thereby providing them with options short of marriage and arguably drawing some couples away from that institution. Note, however, that traditionalists have helped create their own *bête noire*: by opposing same-sex marriage, traditionalists have forced proponents to move more incrementally than they otherwise would and, therefore, to seek institutions short of marriage. That those institutions short of marriage have become open to different-sex couples ought not be surprising, given the gay rights movement's general commitment to the principle of formal equality and the demand for such institutions by straight and bisexual people. Likewise, the tactics of some progressive critics of same-sex marriage may make their prophecies self-fulfilling. By insisting that same-sex marriage will domesticate gay radicalism and marginalize unpartnered lesbians, gay men, and bisexuals, these critics are contributing to a discourse of self-marginalization rather than exploring the new opportunities opened up by the *menu of options* I describe.

IV. Conclusion

Conservatives and progressives will continue to be frustrated by the forward march of the same-sex marriage movement, but their frustration lies in the nature of our dynamic yet pragmatic society. Urbanization and associated developments are pressing the industrialized world toward same-sex marriage or its functional equivalent, and traditionalist resistance is either futile or counterproductive. The more traditionalists holler and obstruct, the more they will press the law to create new institutions responsive to different-sex as well as same-sex desires for union. Progressive objections to using marriage as a vehicle for gay rights are equally futile in the short term, for the simple reason that marriage has long been a focal point for desire and aspiration in our culture, and apparently for reasons that remain popular. That not only makes it an attractive aspiration for many same-sex couples, but also makes it a convenient target for gay rights activism, even in countries or states where activists have to accept compromises. In the longer term, though, I think progressive critiques will grow more persuasive, and Western polities will have to think more deeply about how best to structure the options on the menu of interpersonal commitment.

Appendix I
Country-by-Country Survey of Laws Relating to Sexual Minorities

Belgium

Sodomy and Age of Consent. Sodomy was discriminalized during the French occupation of what is now Belgium (1792), but for most of Belgium's independent history (after 1830) there were different ages of consent. Section 372 of Penal Code, prohibiting homosexual contact between persons over 18 and consenting partners under 18, was repealed in 1985, equalizing age of consent to 16 for both homosexuals and heterosexuals. *See* International Lesbian and Gay Association, *World Legal Survey: Belgium* (visited April 2000) <http://www.ilga.org> [hereinafter cited as ILGA, *World Legal Survey*].

Cohabiting Couples. The Belgian legislature adopted the Law of 23-11-98 which extended legal benefits to cohabiting same-sex couples. The law is expected to be implemented in the year 2000. *See* ILGA, *World Legal Survey: Belgium.*

Brazil

Sodomy and Age of Consent. Since 1823, homosexual behavior between consenting adults has been legal—unless the adults are both soldiers. The age of consent for both homosexual and heterosexual activities is 14 years. Nonetheless, police harass gay people under "public decency" and "outrageous behavior" laws. *See* ILGA, *World Legal Survey: Brazil.*

Canada

Sodomy. Criminal Code § 159(1) makes it an offense to engage in an act of anal intercourse. Section 159(2)(a) exempts private, consensual anal sex between husband and wife. Section 159(2)(b) exempts private, consensual anal sex between any two persons 18 years or older.

Age of Consent. Criminal Code §§ 151 (sexual interference with child) and 153(1)(a) & (b) (sexual exploitation of young person) are written in gender neutral terms.

Anti-Discrimination Law. Canadian Human Rights Act (a federal act), RSC 1985, c. H-6, was amended in 1996 to include sexual orientation, effective June 20, 1996, Bill C-33. In *Haig and Birch v. Canada,* (1992), 9 OR (3d) 495, Ontario Court of Appeals had held that Charter of Rights and Freedoms required that sexual orientation be read into Canadian Human Rights Act as prohibited grounds of discrimination. Federal Government did not appeal, so Canadian Human Rights Commission began applying the Canadian Human Rights Act throughout Canada

2000 / The Same-Sex Marriage Debate

as though sexual orientation were listed. *Accord, Vriend v. Alburta*, [1998] 1 S.C.R. 493 (Sup. Ct. Can. 1998).

Same-Sex Benefits. In *Attorney General v. M. and H.*, [1999] S.C.R. (March 18, 1999), the Supreme Court of Canada ruled that provinces having laws conferring benefits on cohabiting different-sex partners had to extend those laws to same-sex partners as well. In February 2000, the federal government introduced legislation to create nationwide parity of benefits for same-sex couples and different-sex common law couples.

Adoption. Provincial law neither prohibits, nor expressly permits, adoption by lesbians, gay men, or same-sex couples. The effect of legislation is typically to exclude same-sex couples from adopting, while permitting single gay men or lesbians to adopt. Most adoption legislation restricts step-parent adoption to opposite sex couples, and in some jurisdictions, to married couples, making it impossible for lesbians or gay men to adopt their partner's child. *See* DONALD G. CASSWELL, LESBIANS, GAY MEN, AND CANADIAN LAW 290 (1996).

China

No specific statement in Criminal Code about homosexual status, but: Criminal Law Art. 106 says: "All hooliganism should be subject to arrest and sentence." In practice, hooliganism has included homosexual behavior. *See* THE SOCIOLEGAL CONTROL OF HOMOSEXUALITY: A MULTI-NATION COMPARISON 63 (Donald J. West et al., eds., 1997) [hereinafter cited as MULTI-NATION COMPARISON].

Czech Republic

Sodomy. Consensual homosexual behavior between adults was decriminalized in 1961 (Law 140/1961).

Age of Consent. In 1990, Law175/1990 equalized the age of consent for heterosexual and homosexual partners by repealing section 244 of the Penal Code. *See* MULTI-NATION COMPARISON 246.

Denmark

Sodomy and Age of Consent. Denmark's reform of its Penal Code in 1930 dropped sodomy laws but left many discriminations in place. In 1976, the same age of consent (15 years) was adopted for both homosexual and heterosexual relations. *See* ILGA, *World Legal Survey: Denmark.*

Anti-Discrimination. In 1987, sexual orientation was added to the anti-discrimination clause contained in Penal Code (Art. 266) and to the Anti-Discrimination Act of 1971.

Registered Partnerships. Act No. 372 of 7 June, 1989 permitted partnership registration for two persons of the same sex. Partners need not live together or have sexual relations, although one must be a Danish citizen. Regulation has the same legal effect as marriage, except where otherwise provided by legislation. References to "marriage" or "spouse" in Danish law automatically include registered partnerships, except that parties in registered partnerships cannot adopt a child and cannot have joint custody (as of 2000). *See* FAMILY LAW IN EUROPE 58 (Carolyn Hamilton et al. eds., 1995).

England

Sodomy. The Sexual Offenses Act of 1967 decriminalized private, consensual homosexual acts between men over the age of 21.

Age of Consent. Criminal Justice and Public Order Act of 1994 lowered age of consent for male homosexuals to 18 years (see § 145). Note, however, that present law sets the age of consent for heterosexual and lesbian contact at 16 years.

Finland

Sodomy and Age of Consent. Sodomy was discriminalized in 1971, but it was not until June 1998 that Parliament equalized the age of consent for homosexual and heterosexual relations. *See* ILGA, *World Legal Survey: Finland.*

Anti-Discrimination. The Constitution as amended by Law 17 July 1995/969 prohibits discrimination on account of sex, age, etc., or "any other reason related to the person," which is accepted as including sexual orientation. Law 21 April 1995/578 prohibits "sexual preference" discrimination in public accommodations and employment. *See* ILGA, *World Legal Survey: Finland.*

France

Sodomy and Age of Consent. The French Revolution's criminal code of 1791 dropped the crime against sodomy, and it was never reinstated. The age of consent was equalized at age 15 in 1987. *See* ILGA, *World Legal Survey: France.*

Anti-Discrimination. In 1985, the Prohibition of Discrimination (Art. 187-1, 187-2, 416, and 416-1) of the Penal Code was expanded to include discrimination on grounds of "moral habits," which includes homosexuality. *See* Loi no. 85-772 du 25 juliet 1985.

Pactes Civiles. In 1998, France adopted legislation creating new *pactes civiles de solidarité* for same-sex couples. *See* Proposition de Loi Adoptée par L'Assemblé Nacionale en Première Lecture, relative au pacte civil de solidarité, No. 207, 9 Dec. 1998 (visited May 2000) <http://www.senat.fr/leg/taan98-207>.

2000 / The Same-Sex Marriage Debate

Germany

Sodomy and Age of Consent. Federal Republic: Criminal Law Reform Act of 1969 decriminalized homosexual sex if partners were over the age of 21 (lowered to 18 soon thereafter).

German Democratic Republic: Art. 151, passed in 1968, deleted the simple crime of homosexuality, but penalized sexual acts carried out by an adult with a juvenile under the age of 18 who is of the same sex. After a Supreme Court decision in 1989, the East German parliament deleted Art. 151 from the Penal Code, equalizing the age of consent laws.

Unification: In 1994, Germany voided Article 175 of Penal Code, which made punishable sex between males if one of them is under the age of 18, while the opposite sex age of consent was 14. The new Article 182 of Penal Code equalized the age of consent. *See* MULTI-NATION COMPARISON 262.

Greenland

Greenland is a self-governing dependency of Denmark, most of whose laws apply to Greenland as well. The main exception is that Greenland did not accept the 1989 Danish Registered Partnership Law until 1994. Such partnerships became effective in Greenland in 1996. *See* ILGA, *World Legal Survey: Greenland.*

Hungary

Sodomy and Age of Consent. In 1961, Hungary descriminalized homosexual acts between consenting adults if they were both older than 20 years. In 1967, the age of consent for same-sex intimacy was lowered to 18 years—in contrast to the age of 14 years for different-sex intimacy. *See* Lilla Farkas, "Nice on Paper: Legislation vs. Practice in Hungary" (1999).

Cohabitation. In its decision 14/1995, on the legal equality of same-sex partnerships, the Hungarian Constitutional Court ruled that the state could refuse to recognize same-sex marriage but was required to recognize same-sex cohabiting relationships in the same way it recognized different-sex cohabiting relationships. Parliament enacted legislation to that effect in 1996.

Iceland

Age of Consent. In July 1992, the Icelandic parliament equalized the age of consent at 14 years for both homosexual and heterosexual relations. *See* ILGA, *World Legal Survey: Iceland.*

Anti-Discrimination. In 1996, the Icelandic parliament amended the country's penal code to prohibit antigay hate speech and discrimination in sales or service. *See* ILGA, *World Legal Survey: Iceland.*

Registered Partnerships. In 1996, the Icelandic parliament adopted the Registered Partnership Law. Similar to that adopted in Denmark, Norway, and Sweden, the Icelandic law also gives lesbian and gay couples joint custody of the children either partner brings to the family. *See* ILGA, *World Legal Survey: Iceland.*

Ireland

Sodomy. The Criminal Law (Sexual Offences) Act, 1993, repealed the complete prohibition on al sexual acts between males, and legalized private, homosexual acts so long as both parties are at least age 17 and neither is mentally impaired.

Anti-Discrimination. An Employment Equality Bill was adopted in 1999 that protects against workplace discrimination. *See* ILGA, *World Legal Survey: Ireland.*

Israel

Sodomy and Age of Consent. In 1988, the Knesset repealed § 351 of the Penal Code, which made male sodomy a crime. The minimum legal age for homosexual and heterosexual relations was equalized at age 16. *See* ILGA, *World Legal Survey: Israel.*

Anti-Discrimination. In 1992, the Knesset approved a law prohibiting job discrimination on the basis of sexual preference. *See* ILGA, *World Legal Survey: Israel.*

Cohabiting Partners. In *El-Al Israel v. Danilowitz* (May 1994), the Supreme Court of Israel interpreted the equality provisions of Israel's Labor Code to require employers to treat same-sex cohabiting partners similar to different-sex spouses for purposes of employment.

Mexico

Sodomy. No state Penal Code considers homosexual contact in itself a criminal offense, except that Article 201 of Penal Code of Federal District (which includes Mexico City) states: anyone "who facilitates corruption of a minor under 18 years of age . . . by inducing to the practice of begging, alcoholism, to the consumption of narcotic drugs, to the practice of prostitution, homosexualism . . . the punishment will be an imprisonment of 5 to 10 years" (Penal Code, 1995).

2000 / The Same-Sex Marriage Debate

Netherlands

Sodomy and Age of Consent. Section 248 of Criminal Code set age of consent at 21 for homosexuals, while heterosexual age of consent was much lower. This distinction was repealed by the Law of April 8, 1971, Staatsblad [the official law gazette of the Netherlands] 212.

Anti-Discrimination. Since 1992, anti-discrimination provisions of Criminal Code that ban racial discrimination have been expanded to include homosexual preference. Section 429 quater prohibits workplace discrimination. *See* MULTI-NATION COMPARISON 303-05.

Registered Partnerships. The Netherlands adopted a Partner Registration Act in 1998. Different-sex as well as same-sex couples can register as partners and are entitled to all the benefits and duties of marriage, but not the right to adopt children. Also, divorce is easier for registered partners. *See* ILGA, *World Legal Survey: Netherlands.*

Norway

Sodomy and Age of Consent. Norway in 1972 repealed Penal Code § 213, which prohibited sexual acts between men. Following repeal, the age of consent has been the same for homosexual as for heterosexual relations, age 16. *See* ILGA, *World Legal Survey: Norway.*

Anti-Discrimination. Section 135(a) prohibits discrimination against gay men and lesbians. Section 349a prohibits discrimination in business or similar activities. Both laws were adopted in 1981.

Registered Partnerships. Act of Registered Partnerships of April 30, 1993, No. 40 gives homosexuals the right to registered partnerships (see para XX), which has the same legal effect as marriage, except for right to adopt children. *See* Marianne Roth, *The Norwegian Act on Registered Partnership for Homosexual Couples*, 35 J. FAM. L. 467 (1997).

Pakistan

Sodomy. Section 377 of the Penal Code of the Islamic Republic of Pakistan prohibits "carnal intercourse against the order of nature with any man." Such acts carries with it a punishment of up to 100 lashes and from two years to life imprisonment. *See* MULTI-NATION COMPARISON 120.

Russia

Sodomy. Art. 121.1 of the Russian Federation Criminal Code was repealed in 1993 as part of wide-ranging reform law. This article had made muzhelozhstvo (sex between men) punishable by imprisonment for up to 5 years. Article 121.2, in cases of sex between men involving threat or physical force, remains in effect. *See* MULTI-NATION COMPARISON 229-30.

Scotland and Northern Ireland

Sodomy. The English Sexual Offences Act of 1967 did not apply to Scotland, and male homosexual conduct, which remained illegal until the Criminal Justice (Scotland) Act of 1980. Following a judgment by the European Court of Human Rights (*Dudgeon v. UK*, 4 EHRR 149 (1981)), the provisions were extended to Northern Ireland in 1982.

Age of Consent. The Criminal Justice and Public Order Act of 1994 lowered the age of consent for private homosexual acts from the age of 21 (in section 80 of the Criminal Justice (Scotland) Act 1980 and in Article 3 of the Homosexual Offences (Northern Ireland) Order 1982) to the age of 18.

South Africa

Sodomy. The Constitutional Court of South Africa invalidated the nation's sodomy, gross indecency, and other homosexual offense laws under the 1996 and 1997 Constitutions. *See National Coalition for Gay and Lesbian Equality v. Minister of Justice* (Judgment of Oct. 9, 1998).

Anti-Discrimination. Section 9(3) the South African Constitution of 1997 prohibits the state from discrimination against anyone on the basis of sexual orientation; § 9(4) extends the anti-discrimination duty to private actors as well.

Partnership Benefits. The Constitutional Court of South Africa required the government to grant the same benefits to same-sex partners that its immigration laws extends to different-sex "spouses." *See National Coalition for Gay and Lesbian Equality v. Minister of Home Affairs* (Judgment of Dec. 2, 1999).

Spain

Sodomy and Age of Consent. Sodomy has not been a crime in Spain since 1822 (although "habitual homosexual acts" were criminal in 1928-32). Spain's new Criminal Code, adopted November 24, 1995, eliminated distinctions in age of consent, which is 12 years for homosexual as well as heterosexual relations. *See* ILGA, *World Legal Survey: Spain*.

2000 / The Same-Sex Marriage Debate

Anti-Discrimination. Article 14 of the 1978 Constitution prohibits discrimination on the basis of sex, age, religion, creed, political ideology, or "whatever other social or personal circumstance." Courts have usually fit sexual orientation under this residual category. The Law of 16-11-1995 bans sexual orientation discrimination in housing, employment, public services, and professional activities. *See* ILGA, *World Legal Survey: Spain.*

Partnership. The government has proposed a partnership law, but it has been stalled since 1997. Partnership laws were adopted at the regional level in Catalonia on 30 June 1998 and Aragon on 12 March 1999. *See* ILGA, *World Legal Survey: Spain.*

Sweden

Sodomy and Age of Consent. Same-sex intimacy was discriminalized in 1944, and the age of consent was equalized at age 15 in 1978. *See* ILGA, *World Legal Survey: Sweden.*

Anti-Discrimination. In 1987, the Parliament amended Ch. 16, par. 9 of the Penal Code to make sexual orientation a ground for unlawful discrimination in employment and provision of service to the public. An omnibus workplace anti-discrimination law went into force on 1 May 1999. *See* ILGA, *World Legal Survey: Sweden.*

Cohabitation. The Unisexual Cohabitees Act (Lag 1987:813) prescribes that the Cohabitees (Joint Homes) Act is applicable to homosexual cohabitees. This Cohabitees Act states that on the dissolution of the cohabitation, an equal division of the value of the home and household goods which have been acquired for common use shall take place. On death of a party, surviving party has right to equal division of common household goods and joint dwelling to retain as much of the property as equals twice the base sum applicable under the National Insurance Act at date of death. *See* ILGA, *World Legal Survey: Sweden.*

Registered Partnerships. Lag 1994: 1117, Om Registrerat Partnerskap, adopted June 1, 1994, effective January 1, 1995, provides a registration procedure whereby same-sex partners can obtain all the obligations and benefits of marriage, except that same-sex couples cannot (1) adopt children, (2) have access to state-provided artificial insemination, or (3) have the benefit of certain state-provided benefits. *See* ILGA, *World Legal Survey: Sweden.*

Appendix II
States that Include Sexual Orientation in their Penalty-Enhancement Statutes

Vermont: VT. STAT. ANN. tit. 13, § 1455 (1993)

California: CAL. PENAL CODE § 422.75 (West 1997)

District of Columbia: D.C. CODE ANN. § 22-4003 (Supp. 1994)

New Jersey: N.J. STAT. ANN. § 2C:12-1(e) (West Supp. 1994)

Massachusetts: MASS. ANN. LAWS ch. 265, § 39 (West 1999)

Illinois: 720 ILL. COMP. STAT. 5/12-7.1 (West Supp. 1996)

Minnesota: MINN. STAT. ANN. § 609.2231 (West Supp. 1996)

Wisconsin: WIS. STAT. § 939.645 (1998)

Connecticut: CONN. GEN. STAT. ANN. § 53(a)-181(b) (West Supp. 1994)

New Hampshire: N.H. REV. STAT. ANN. § 651:6(g) (1997)

Nevada: NEV. REV. STAT. § 207.185 (Supp. 1995)

Rhode Island: R.I. GEN. LAWS § 11-5-13 (1995)

Oregon: OR. REV. STAT. § 166.155 (1995)

Washington: WASH. REV. CODE ANN. § 9A.36.080 (West Supp. 1994)

Louisiana: LA. CODE tit. 14, § 107.2 (West Supp. 2000)

Delaware: DEL. CODE ANN. tit. 11, § 1304 (1994)

Iowa: IOWA CODE ANN. § 729A.2 (West 1992)

Kentucky: KY. REV. STAT. ANN. § 532.031 (Michie 1990 & Supp. 1998)

Maine: ME. REV. STAT. ANN. tit. 17-A, § 1151 (West 1997)

2000 / The Same-Sex Marriage Debate

Nebraska: NEB. REV. STAT. § 28-111 (1997)

Florida: FLA. STAT. ANN. § 775.085 (West 1992)

Arizona: ARIZ. REV. STAT. § 41-1822 (West 1999) (collecting hate crime data)

Appendix III
States Recognizing Domestic Partners

Hawaii: HAW. REV. STAT. § 572C1 (Reciprocal Beneficiaries Law)

California: CAL. FAM. CODE § 297 (West Supp. 2000)

District of Columbia: D.C. CODE ANN. § 36-1402 (1981)

Vermont: Vermont Labor Relations Board decision, Grievance of B.M., S.S., C.M., and J.R., Docket No. 92-32, extends medical and dental benefits to domestic partners of state employees.

Part IV
Violence

[16]

IDENTITY WITHIN: CULTURAL RELATIVISM, MINORITY RIGHTS AND THE EMPOWERMENT OF WOMEN

RADHIKA COOMARASWAMY*

I. INTRODUCTION

For the last three decades, the concept of "identity" has taken center place in political, social, and cultural debates. Charles Taylor has conceptualized identity as the search for the authentic self.[1] Anthony Appiah has argued that identity involves the playing out of narrative scripts that we have learned from childhood.[2] Whether we root out identity within the essence of the human personality or in the constructions of social life, identity politics has certainly conditioned many of the modern debates about rights, politics, and justice. Identity is not an essential, immutable, permanent status, it has many constituent elements. Future experiences often transform the nature and direction of personal identity. Identity is often composite, made up of multiple selves, often contesting, contradicting, and transforming the other. Identity therefore reconstitutes itself, reacting to and negotiating ideology and lived experience.

The subjective identities that philosophers explore must come to terms with the objective reality of identity as it plays out in the real world. In all societies, as the Census and Statistics departments will attest, people are categorized and identified by a social identity, especially as it is expressed in religious, ethnic, or tribal terms. These group-based identities often help determine our position in the social and political hierarchy of a society and also condition people's attitudes and perceptions toward us as we go about our daily business. These stereotypes and homogenous characterizations create obstacles for the realization of equality. They are also the substance of discrimination and often the basis for power and privilege. Our subjective sense of identity is greatly determined by

---

* Radhika Coomaraswamy received her B.A. from Yale, her J.D. from Columbia University and her L.L.M. from Harvard University. She is the Director of The International Center for Ethnic Studies in Colombo, Sri Lanka and The United Nations Special Rapporteur on Violence Against Women

1. CHARLES TAYLOR, THE ETHICS OF AUTHENTICITY 44 (1991).
2. Kwame Anthony Appiah, *Identity, Authenticity, Survival: Multicultuiral Societies and Social Reproduction*, *in* MULTICULTURALISM 149 (Amy Gutman ed., 1994).

this objective experience as it interacts with our everyday life and conditions the way we think about ourselves. Our group-based identity often goes to the core of our sense of self and our desire for dignity.

For many women, their sense of identity arises as a result their experience as women, living within groups primarily governed by men. Though their sense of self and dignity comes from how the wider society treats women, they often have to face discrimination within local groups. They may have to submit to discriminatory practices and laws, as well engage in rituals, customs, and habits that reinscribe the subordinate status of women within the hierarchy of their religious, ethnic, or tribal identity. Many women acquiesce because they see their group identity as the most important aspect of their lives. Others resist, only to be branded as traitors or "bad women" who bring the group into disrepute.

For outsiders, especially women's activists interested in pursuing gender equality, discrimination within minority groups and third world societies poses a profound set of challenges. On the one hand, the feminist movement has always seen itself as an ally of third world societies and minority groups in their fight for equality and struggle against discrimination and prejudice. On the other hand, as a movement for the recognition of personal choice, it has sought to maximize individual freedom and creativity even at the expense of the group. Fighting prejudice against underprivileged groups while struggling for women's empowerment goes to the heart of the modern dilemma between the universalism of human rights and the particularity of cultural experience. In a world where western imperialism has historically been the champion of third world females in Asia or Africa, the struggle for women's rights acquires another dimension. How does one fight for women's rights without being complicit in the racism and prejudice that characterizes Northern attitudes toward Southern countries or the majority-minority dynamics within particular societies?

II. The Legacy of Colonialism

The historical legacy of colonialism points to the third world female as being an important part of the encounter between the West and third world societies. The colonial powers acted as catalysts in the emergence of a new relationship between the sexes. By highlighting the position of women in colonial societies to denigrate the third world "other," the colonial powers served to focus attention on certain cultural practices that discriminated against women. As a result, according to Kumari Jayawardena, the early nationalist movements in many societies sought to improve the position of women in their societies by trying to eliminate the practices that they saw as inimical to their standing.[3] They sought to regain the moral high ground by standing for women's equality and by combating practices harmful to women.[4]

Nowhere is this legacy more visible than in India, where British social reform of the nineteenth century focused entirely on Indian females, especially Indian girls and Indian widows. In 1870, the British Colonial regime enacted the Special Act of 1870, which eradicated the practice of female infanticide in the Northwest provinces.[5] Census data gathered from the 1840s shows startling imbalances in sex ratios, indicating that the practice was widespread.[6] The British government took draconian measures to curtail the practice, including criminalization, surveillance, registering births, monitoring pregnancies, and putting parents in jail. By 1906 they withdrew the law because it had been so effective in the provinces under consideration—Rajasthan, the Punjab, and the Northwest Frontier. The British made it clear that the British colonial regime had the monopoly on violence, and that it alone could determine issues of life and death.

The practice of child marriage also earned the ire of the British. Among Brahmins of India, during this period girls customarily married between the ages of five and ten. Cases of young brides dying because of sexual intercourse with much older men resulted in the 1872 Native Marriage Act that established 14 as the age of consent.[7] The case of Rakhmabhai received international attention during this period. Rakhmabhai was a brilliant student who lived with her educated parents. She was, however, also a child bride of an uneducated, unemployed relative. On her matriculation, her husband brought a suit for the restitution of conjugal rights to have Rakhmabhai come and live with him or be sent to prison. She responded by engaging in a debate on child marriage in the papers and in public fora. The Hindu Orthodox institutions reacted strongly to her intervention and even a British Court upheld her husband's right with a technical interpretation of the law. An out-

3. Kumari Jayawardena, Feminism and Nationalism in the Third World 12 (1986).
4. *Id.* at 78.
5. Janaki Nair, Women and Law in Colonial India 84 (1996).
6. *Id.* at 85.
7. *Id.* at 72.

of-court settlement saved her from what would have been for her a fate worse than death; she went on to become India's first woman doctor.[8] But her case was not in vain. The early Indian nationalists were greatly moved by her agitation. Reformers such as Vidyasagar, Ranade, and Roy took up the cause of preventing child marriage. Indian women of Gandhi's Congress in 1929 managed to get Indian nationalists to push for the Child Marriage Restraint Act without much opposition.[9] Because of women like Rakhmabai, the Indian nationalist movement had a social reform component that stressed elimination of this discriminatory practice.[10]

Another cause celebre for the social reform movement of the nineteenth century in India was that of widows. The British took drastic measures to prevent Sati (widow immolation) and received support from Hindu reformers. In the late nineteenth century, a law against Sati was passed as a major component of colonial social reform.[11] Where the issue did not involve violence, however, but only discriminatory laws such as the remarriage of widows, the British sided with the traditional elite over the rights of women. In Hindu societies widows were not allowed to remarry men of their choosing. They often remained at the mercy of the men in their families and had to marry the brother of their husbands. Rich widows in the Punjab who had a British education began agitating for widow remarriage to anyone of her choosing. Fearing the extensive partition and alienation of land and family property, the British sided with the men and endorsed the practice of Karewa—levirate marriage of the widow to one of the men of her dead husband's family.[12] This was the other reality of colonialism. The Colonial powers championed the third world female when it involved issues of violence, as this challenged their monopoly and authority over life and death issues. Other questions of equality that involved the

8. Meera Kosambi, *Gender Reform and Competing State Controls Over Women – The Rakhmabai Case, in* Social Reform, Sexuality and The State 274 (P. Uberoi ed., 1996) [hereinafter Social Reform].

9. *Id.* at 122-145.

10. *See, e.g.*, Partha Chatterjee, *The Nationalist Resolution of the Women's Question in* Recasting Women: Essays, *in* Indian Colonial History 246 (K. Sangari et al. eds., 1991) (stating that women like Rakhmabai provided contrast to those nationalists who claimed that women should remain in traditional roles).

11. A law against Sati was passed in 1829 by the British Administration in India. *See generally* Ashis Nandy, *SATI- A Nineteenth Century Tale of Women, Violence and Protest in* At the Edge of Psychology: Essays in Politics and Culture (1980) (discussing the reform movement).

12. Prem Chowdhry, *Contesting Claims and Counter Claims: Questions of the Inheritance and Sexuality of Widows in a Colonial State, in* Social Reform, *supra* note 8 at 73.

stability of the local order and the terms of collaboration with the feudal elite were ignored. The colonial power would insist that they were only respecting local customs and practices.

The colonial legacy of western powers championing the cause of third world women conditions the debate on women's equality in many parts of the world. This was also rendered possible by what Partha Chatterjee calls the resolution (Chatterjee Resolution) of the woman question within the nationalist movement of India and probably in many other societies affected by colonialism.[13] Early nationalists influenced by the British social reform movement called for reform from within and for the protection of the rights of women.[14] Later nationalists moved away from the early focus on social reform to emphasizing the preservation of the Indian identity and tradition.[15] Seizing on the public/private distinction that provided the basis for the colonial common law, these conservative groupings took control of nationalist movements.[16] The private was seen as the space for women who would keep the family insulated from the pressures of the public colonial world. Women then became the custodians of the culture of ethnic, religious, and tribal groups. While men began to don suits and move into the modern public space, women were expected to carry the cultural markers and make the home the traditional space to nurture and pass on ethnicity and symbols of identity to future generations.[17] Although the British brought women into the public discourse in the nineteenth century, the late nationalists returned women to the home and made them the caretakers of the very culture that often discriminates against them.[18]

Any movement for women's international human rights must recognize this historical colonial legacy. Because of this legacy, any struggle for women's equality and dignity in third world and minority cultures is seen as the secret weapon of western imperialism. Strategies aimed at improving women's rights have to take this inevitable fact into consideration. Secondly, the Chatterjee Resolution points to the fact that women have been socialized to believe that they are the custodians of the very laws, rituals, and practices

13. Chaterjee, *supra* note 10, at 233.

14. *Id.* at 240-43.

15. *Id.* at 244-49.

16. *Id.*

17. *Id.* at 243. ("The home was the principal site for expressing the spiritual quality of the national culture, and women must take the main responsibility of protecting and nurturing this quality").

18. *Id.* at 250.

that discriminate against them.[19] In addition, women in many societies believe that their dignity is intricately linked to the identity of the group. They see any attack on that identity as an assault on their own dignity. Although there are exceptional women who have moved away from strong cultural ties to the community of their birth, the vast majority feel a deep connection to group identity.[20] Any attempt to fight for women's rights must keep this symbiosis in mind.

III. The International Framework

The international human rights framework attempts to deal with concepts of culture and cultural relativism through the prism of the rights of minorities.[21] Since World War II, the international community has attempted to come to terms with the issue of minority rights.[22] When the Human Rights Commission was created, the issue of human rights was a central part of its mandate. Furthermore, the Sub-Commission on Minorities was created with independent experts as a means of ensuring its impartiality and objectivity.[23] There have been only a few actual legal developments with regard to minorities since its inception, however, such as the Convention on the Elimination of Racial Discrimination in the 1960s[24] and, in the 1990s, the Declaration on the Rights of Persons Belonging to National or Ethnic, Religious and Linguistic Minorities.[25] In addition, The Human Rights Commission in Geneva created the Working Group on Minorities in the late nineties to allow for more focused attention on the rights of minorities. The World Conference on Racism, to be held in South Africa, will be another watershed event, however, but there was no agreement on any final course of action.

Article 27 of the International Covenant on Civil and Political Rights (ICCPR) contains the essence of minority rights as recog-

19. *Id.* at 249-52.

20. *Id.* at 235-36.

21. Henry Steiner & Philip Alston, International Human Rights in Context 597 (1993).

22. *Id.*

23. *Id.*

24. Convention on the Elimination of All Forms of Racial Discrimination, Mar. 7, 1966, 660 U.N.T.S. 195, G.A. Res. 2106, U.N. GAOR, 20th Sess., Agenda Item 58, U.N. Doc. A/Res/2106 (1966) (reprinted in 5 I.L.M. 352) (entered into force Jan. 4, 1969).

25. Declaration on the Rights of Persons Belonging to National or Ethnic, Religious and Linguistic Minorities, G.A. Res. 47/135, U.N. GAOR, 47th Sess., Annex, U.N. Doc. A/RES/47/135/Annex (1992) [hereinafter DRPBN].

nized by the international community.[26] It gives minorities the right to enjoy their own culture, to profess and practice their own religion, and to use their language.[27] The Declaration on the Rights of Minorities (Minorities Declaration) gives minorities the right of survival and the right to promote their identity.[28] The Minorities Declaration also gives minorities the right to enjoy their own culture, religion, and language and to effectively participate in political decision-making.[29] The State has an affirmative obligation to grant minorities equality and to create conditions that will enable minorities to develop their culture, language, and religion.[30]

The situation for women from minority groups and diverse ethnic and indigenous groups is more complex. One must read the provisions on group rights together with the existing body of international law that guarantees the human rights of women. The international framework on the international human rights of women accepts equality as a guiding principle.[31] Article 3 of the International Covenant on Civil and Political Rights requires states to undertake measures to ensure the equal right of men and women to the enjoyment of all civil and political rights.[32] A similar provision exists with regard to the International Covenant on Economic, Social and Cultural Rights (ICESCR).[33] The Convention on the Elimination of All Forms of Discrimination Against Women (CEDAW) condemns discrimination against women in all its forms and obligates states to pursue by "all appropriate means and without delay" a policy of eliminating discrimination against women.[34] International standards also recognize the concept of patriarchy and the historical discrimination that women have suffered around the world. The United Nations Declaration on the Elimination of Violence Against Women states in its preamble that "violence

26. International Covenant on Civil and Political Rights, Dec. 19, 1966, art. 3, 999 U.N.T.S. 171, 6 I.L.M. 368 (1967) [hereinafter ICCPR].

27. *Id.* art. 27.

28. DRPBN, *supra* note 25 art. 1.

29. *Id.* art. 2.

30. *Id.* art. 4.

31. *Id.* art. 3.

32. *Id.*

33. International Covenant on Economic, Social and Cultural Rights, G.A. Res. 2200, U.N. GAOR, 21st Sess., Annex, Supp. No. 16, art. 3, U.N. Doc. A/6136 (1967) [hereinafter ICESCR] ("The States Parties to the present Covenant undertake to ensure the equal right of men and women to the enjoyment of all economic, social and cultural rights set forth in the present covenant").

34. Convention on the Elimination of All Forms of Discrimination Against Women, Dec. 18, 1979, art. 2, 1249 U.N.T.S. 20378 [hereinafter CEDAW].

against women is a manifestation of historically unequal power relations between men and women, which have led to domination over and discrimination against women by men."[35]

In addition, international human rights standards with regard to women are comprehensive and involve the accountability of state and non-state actors. CEDAW obligates states to remove all forms of discrimination against women by "any person, organization or enterprise."[36] Article 5 of CEDAW requires state parties to take all appropriate measures

> to modify the social and cultural patterns of conduct of men and women, with a view to achieving the elimination of prejudices and customary and all other practices which are based on the idea of the inferiority or the superiority of either of the sexes or on stereotyped roles for men and women.[37]

International standards recognize the transforming nature of the project at hand.

IV. Manifestations of the Tension Between Women's Rights, Cultural Relativism, and Minority Rights

The tension between the rights of groups to practice their culture and the rights of women under international human rights norms plays itself out in the everyday life of women across the globe. The controversy surrounding female genital mutilation (FGM) provides one example of this tension. In 1990 Fuambai Ahmadu, an African scholar from Sierra Leone spoke these emotional words before the American Anthropological Association.

> It is difficult for me, considering the number of ceremonies I have observed, including my own, to accept that what appear to be expressions of joy and ecstatic celebrations of womanhood in actuality disguise hidden experiences of coercion and subjugation. Indeed, I offer that the bulk of Kono women who uphold these rituals do so because they want to . . . they embrace the legitimacy of female authority, and particularly, the authority of their mothers and grandmothers.[38]

This statement contrasts with the courageous work of African feminists such as Nawal El Saadawi and Asma El Dareer, doctors who brought the plight of FGM before a world audience. Focusing on the health hazards, they painted a horrendous picture of women's

35. Declaration on the Elimination of Violence Against Women, G.A.Res. 104, U.N. GAOR, 48th Sess., Supp. No. 49, U.N. Doc. A/48/49 (1993) [hereinafter DEVAW].

36. CEDAW, *supra* note 34, art. 2.

37. *Id.* art. 5.

38. Richard A Shweder, *What About Female Genital Mutilation? And Why Understanding Culture Matters in the First Place*, 129 Daedalus 209, 210 (2000).

genitalia being mutilated by broken glass and crude implements, of lifelong health problems, of painful sexual relations, and sometimes of death.[39] Joined by western feminists such as Alice Walker and human rights crusaders such as Fran Hosken and Equality Now, they have managed to garner worldwide revulsion against this cultural practice.

FGM comes in various forms.[40] The first, pharonic infibulation is the most drastic, involving the removal of the clitoris, labia minora, and the labia majora.[41] The second, an intermediate form, involves the removal of the clitoris and the labia minora.[42] The third contains the removal of only the clitoris.[43] There is a fourth type of symbolic practice that sometimes involves placing a knife on the genitalia, but no cutting.

Very little debate exists about the nature and hazards of FGM. The health hazards are particularly appalling and forced the World Health Organization to make a concerted intervention against FGM.[44] But sometimes the more difficult questions relating to female sexuality had to be raised, including, for example, when Egypt decided to allow hospitals to perform FGM.[45] Even if an FGM operation is performed without health hazards, the net result is that women will not feel sexual pleasure after the operation. Sexual relations for women who have undergone the operation will always be uncomfortable and sometimes painful. Problematically, international standards with regard to the right to sexuality remain slightly ambiguous. The Beijing Declaration recognizes the right to reproductive health that in its definition includes the right of individuals to a safe and satisfying sex life.[46] The right to sexuality and sexual choice as an explicit right in and of itself, however, has yet to be recognized and endorsed at the international level.

---

39. *See* Asma El Dareer, Woman, Why Do You Weep? (1983).

40. *Id.* at 1.

41. *Id.*

42. *Id* at 3.

43. *Id* at 2.

44. World Health Organization, Female Genital Mutilation (2001), *at* http://www.who.int/frh-whd/FGM/.

45. *See* ReligiousTolerance.org, Female Genital Mutilation, *at* http://www.religioustolerance.org/fem_cirm.htm.

46. Beijing Declaration and Platform for Action, U.N. Fourth World Conference on Women, Sept. 4-15, 1995, art. 94, U.N. Doc. A/Conf. 177/20 (1995) [hereinafter Beijing Declaration]; Report of the International Conference on Population and Development, ch. vii ¶ 7.2, U.N. Doc. A/CONF.171/13 (1994) [hereinafter International Conference Report].

For some anthropologists, the emphasis on rights and sexuality are misplaced and are part of a legacy of neocolonialism. Some argue that FGM is about "being human the African way;" that it is about the notion of a rite of passage to adulthood, integrally linked to concepts of symbolic birth and African ideas about women and womanhood. FGM is seen as a great moment in the life of women, a celebration, a wedding, women's space.[47] While earlier feminists and nationalists accepted the western critique and tried to move forward, many of the young African anthropologists question the critique itself.[48] Concepts of right and wrong, good and bad, are thrown up for grabs in a world with no moral anchor and where human rights is seen as the last outreach of the Enlightenment project.

The debate concerning FGM therefore becomes a conversation about colonialism and imposed western values.[49] More importantly African anthropologists react to the way western feminists struggle against FGM, who place much emphasis on morality and self-righteousness.[50] The United States has banned the practice under federal law[51] and has made loans to African states conditional on measures taken to fight FGM.[52] African scholars bristle at this type of intervention. They believe that FGM has become the vehicle for "the arrogant gaze" through which the west looks at and passes judgment on other cultures. Therefore, the legal imperative of rights discourse sometimes gets lost in the larger politics of the post-colonial era.

And yet, as much as these scholars disturb the complacency of the western worldview, individual African women disturb their romanticization of FGM as a celebrated practice of being a woman the African way. The case of Fauzia Kasinga highlights the injustice involved in turning a blind eye to FGM.[53] Fauzia was from Togo and her parents initially spared her the experience of FGM. After her father died, though, she was placed under the authority of the patriarch of the family who asked her to marry a forty-year-old man

47. Sylvia Wynter, "*Genital Mutilation or Symbolic Birth?" Female Circumsicion, Origins and the Acculturalism of Feminist/Western Thought*, 47 CASE W. RES. L. REV. 501, 502 (1997).

48. *Id.*

49. *Id.*

50. *Id.*

51. 18 U.S.C.A. §116 (1997).

52. *Id.* (U.S. representatives in international financial institutions are required to oppose loans to countries that do not take measures to eradicate female genital mutilation).

53. *See generally* FAUZIYA KASSINDJA, DO THEY HEAR YOU WHEN YOU CRY? (1998).

and made arrangements to have her circumcised. Fauzia, with the help of her mother and sister, fled the country and came to the United States to seek asylum. After a long struggle and a terrible experience in U.S. asylum centers, she received her vindication. She was given asylum as the United States recognized the imminent threat of FGM as a ground for gender-based persecution.[54] Since her case, Togo has banned FGM and her own patriarch has become a convert in the struggle against FGM.

While African anthropologists react to disorder in their symbolic universe, many women activists in Kenya, Senegal, and Egypt have begun door-to-door campaigns to fight FGM at the grassroots level.[55] Isabelle Gunning captures the majority viewpoint in her article on the best strategy to fight FGM.[56] In it, she warns against the arrogant gaze of imperialism and finds that the best way to fight FGM is through education and health programs supported by the international community.[57] Recognizing that FGM is a violation of a woman's rights and dignity, she suggests the best strategy is teaching the community.[58]

For many others, however, such as the feminist pioneers Nawal el Sadaawi,[59] banning the practice and imposing criminal sanctions is an essential element in fighting these practices. A ban imposed by law also represents state recognition that it will not tolerate such practices. In addition, one of the reasons why women perpetuate the practice is that they feel that their daughters will become unmarriageable unless circumcised. Unless the practice is banned, parents do not have an excuse to prevent their daughters from being subjected to the practice. Many campaigners argue that mothers often tell them that they are relieved when the practice is banned because they then have an excuse not to comply with cruel cultural practices.[60]

In deciding which cultural practices deserve international attention and agitation and which practices require criminalization, it is important to consider the nature of the practice. FGM, for example, appears to require concerted campaigning. Given the irreversi-

---

54. *Id.*

55. *See* Equality Now, Awaken FGM Newsletter, *available at* http://www.equalitynow.org/brochure_eng_hub.html.

56. Isabelle R. Gunning, *Arrogant Perceptions, World Travelling and Multicultural Feminism: The Case of Female Genital Surgeries*, 23 Colum. Hum. Rts. L. Rev. 189 (1991).

57. *Id.*

58. *Id.*

59. *See* Dr. Nawal el Saadawi, *at* http://www.nawalsaadawi.net/index.html.

60. *See generally*, http://www.equalitynow.org.

bility of FGM, its intrinsically violent nature rooted in the sexual subjugation of women, and the fact that it involves a child who cannot exercise choice, many human rights activists around the world feel that there should be a two-pronged attack in fighting the practice of FGM. The attack would include banning the practice, which would serve a summons on society that such practices are unacceptable, as well as education and health programs involving African women that will try and engage the community in a discussion about why this practice is harmful to their women. But Gunning's caution that all this should be done without the arrogant gaze of the outsider is essential if rights discourse is to win the ideological battle. The full participation and consultation of women and men living in these societies must be the ultimate goal.

FGM is in the genre of violations against women that deserves international attention framed in terms of the rights discourse. It is violent, it causes severe pain and suffering, it is irreversible, and it shocks the conscience of everyone who does not perpetrate the practice. The shocks-the-conscience test of all outsiders (not only the West) is not always negative. It may actually be a reflection of international consensus in the making. Such practices deserve international agitation, international legal sanctions, and international programs and policies to combat the practices so that girls are spared this violence of the most intimate sort, which prevents them from being human in the most wholesome way.

Other cultural practices that fall into this type of genre are, for example, Sati in India or honor crimes practiced in many Arab and Mediterranean societies. The question of Sati in India raised many of the same debates as FGM, but this time between the central government of India and the government of the region where the practice was taking place. The issue came to a head in India when in the late 1980s Roop Kanwar committed Sati on her husband's pyre.[61] The Central government and the Rajasthani government acted swiftly to outlaw the practice and to bring in strong measures against those that aid, abet, or watch such a spectacle. Nevertheless, thousands of Rajasthanis gathered to protest these measures as violating the traditional customs of the Rajputs.

Among scholarly circles the debates were often acrimonious. Some scholars argued that the ideology of Sati, a story of heroic death, should not be challenged, even if modern day practices

61. Radhika Coomaraswamy, *To Bellow Like a Cow: Women, Ethnicity and The Discourse of Rights*, *in* Human Rights of Women 39 (Rebecca Cook ed., 1994) [hereinafter *To Bellow Like a Cow*].

were going to be banned. Sati was an aspect of religious mythology, a story of sacrifice and resurrection. Moreover, it was strongly argued that the beliefs of the community should not be brought into question.[62] Women who really wanted to commit Sati should be allowed to do so and what should be prevented are forced Satis.

More nuances exist, however, when evaluating social and economic data. A political-economic analysis of Sati, devoid of mythological significance, shows that Sati provided a means of dealing with the unwanted widow. Allowing Sati would result in great pressure being put on women to commit Sati, pressures they may not be able to resist.[63] If "true" Sati was allowed, the ideological pressure on a young woman would compel her to give in to family demands to commit Sati. She would have no bargaining power in such a context, surrounded by her husband's family. To prevent this social pressure, most writers felt that Sati should be banned both at the center and the periphery. A widow who truly loved her husband could find other means through which to express her grief.

As with FGM, little disagreement existed that the modern practice should be discouraged. But people did call into question the arrogance of the central government and feminists in passing judgment on the beliefs and practices of a community. The vernacular press in India demonized the feminist groups that led the attack on the practice.[64] Sati as a practice thrived in the same part of the country where female infanticide thrived during the time of the British. Though the mythology of Sati depicts a poignant story, the actual fact is that it is practiced in the area of the country where a female life is greatly undervalued and where violence against women and girls is widespread. The practice reflects this misogyny and not an isolated religious belief. Feminist militancy in this regard may therefore be justified. Few further cases of Sati have been recorded in Rajasthan since the government took this strong action with regard to Sati after Roop Kanwar's case.

Another cultural practice that falls within the "severe pain and suffering" genre of women's human rights violations is the practice of honor killings, practiced in Arab countries, Turkey, Northern Pakistan, and other countries of Mediterranean heritage. In addi-

62. Ashis Nandy, *Sati in Kali Yuga: Public Debate on Roop Kanwar's Death*, *in* THE SAVAGE FREUD (Sherry B. Ortner et al. eds., 1995).

63. Kumkum Sangari & Sudesh Vaid, *Institutions, Beliefs, Ideologies: Widow Immolation in Contemporary Rajasthan*, *in* GENDER AND POLITICS IN INDIA (Nivedita Menon ed., 1999).

64. *To Bellow Like a Cow*, *supra* note 61, at 49-50.

tion, immigrant communities in western countries may also engage in this kind of behavior, especially when women or girls refuse to marry men of their parents choosing.[65] In honor killings, family members kill women or girls for destroying the honor of the family. The type of behavior that can bring on this type of gruesome death could be adultery, falling in love, wanting a divorce, asking to choose one's own marriage partner, or mere allegations of illicit sexual conduct.[66] The manner of death is often horrendous, involving stoning or being ritually stabbed and killed in public. Despite its gruesome nature, there is general community support for honor killings in the societies where it is practiced. Mothers interviewed after the death of their daughters often shed no tears, saying that their daughters deserved the death.[67]

The case of Samia Sarwar in Pakistan brought international attention to the practice of honor killings.[68] Samia was a married woman from a powerful landowning family in Peshawar, Pakistan. She wanted a divorce from her abusive husband who was also a relative. There were also hints of her being in love with someone else. Finally, after months of disagreement during which Samia had to be hidden in a shelter by women's groups, her family agreed to the divorce. Her mother, uncle, and an unidentified man came to the office of Samia's lawyers to work out the details of her divorce. Before the discussions could proceed, the man who accompanied her family suddenly pulled out a gun and shot Samia dead. The aftermath of the shooting was equally disturbing. The State only reluctantly prosecuted members of Samia's family though there were many witnesses. Attempts to bring legislation against honor killings failed because many of the legislators did not want to take a stand against them.

The concept of honor is integrally linked to notions of public esteem and private shame. Sri Lankan anthropologist Gananath Obeyesekere speaks of lajja Bhaya, fear and shame, as the primary means of control in feudal societies.[69] When a daughter or a wife acts in a manner that would bring the family into disrepute, many societies sanction violence against the woman concerned. In some

65. *See* Working Group on Forced Marriages, A Choice by Right, Home Office Communications Directorate (2000).

66. *See* Amnesty International, Pakistan: Violence Against Women in The Name of Honor (1999).

67. *Id.*

68. *Id.*

69. Gananath Obeyesekere, Medusa's Hair: An Essay on Personal Symbols and Religious Experience 83 (1981).

ways all societies allow men the right to kill their wives if their honor is at stake. Feminists analyzing the doctrine of provocation in Brazilian criminal law have argued that provocation essentially equals the honor defense.[70] A man who catches his wife committing adultery is allowed a greater license to commit violence than the average citizen committing an ordinary crime.[71] The reverse is not necessarily true. Provocation is rarely used to defend women who kill their husbands. The notion that men can commit violence against women who shame them in any way serves as an underlying assumption in many legal systems.

Honor in the family, like FGM, is closely linked to the control of female sexuality and movement. Honor is a code that ensures that women will behave in a manner that preserves their chastity and their obedience. If they dare to cross the boundaries, violence will be their fate. In Brazil, honor was seen as a matter of self defense.[72] To shame a man was to attack his person and property.[73] In addition, masculinity and machismo as they are played out in some societies have an undercurrent of violence, and honor is the excuse for its manifestation.[74]

V. Torture-Like Practices

FGM, Sati, and honor killings are the type of women's human rights violations that most resemble torture. The prohibition against torture is jus cogens, a norm of international law that cannot be derogated from by nation states. It is well recognized that the prohibition against torture is now an important principle of international law. State practice in the international arena reflects a consensus that all states recognize that torture violates international law. Though many human rights laws and regulations are contested, all commentators and jurists agree that torture and genocide form the genre of human rights violations that have acquired jus cogens status. The Convention on Torture (Torture Convention) requires the following elements: infliction of severe pain and suffering, or the intent to inflict severe pain and suffer-

70. *See* Human Rights Watch, Criminal Injustice: Violence Against Women in Brazil [hereinafter Criminal Injustice] (Oct. 1991).

71. Pakistan: Violence Against Women in the Name of Honor, Amensty International – USA, *at* http://www.amnesty-usa.org/countries/pakistan/reports/honour/overview2.html (Feb. 2, 2002).

72. *See* Criminal Injustice, *supra* note 70.

73. *Id.*

74. *See* Nancy Lindisfarne, *Variant Masculinities, Variant Virginities: Rethinking Honour and Shame, in* Dislocating Masculinity 82-97 (Andrea Cornwall et al. eds.).

ing, for a specified purpose that includes punishment and discrimination, and done with the consent or acquiescence of a public official.[75]

The practices in the area of violence against women outlined above are exceptional human rights practices because they most resemble torture. They involve "severe pain and suffering," and this aspect puts them in a separate category from other human rights abuses. One of the prohibited purposes of torture is discrimination, and one may argue that the above practices constitute an attempt to discriminate. One could also argue that state inaction and complicity in these cases involving violence against women meets the public official and acquiescence requirement of the Torture Convention. Because these cultural practices resemble torture, universal human rights must be seen to easily trump cultural relativist arguments that foster these particular practices. Minorities or majorities that engage in such practices arguably violate some of the most fundamental principles of international law and international human rights law.

In deciding which cultural practices existing in the world require international action and agitation, one must surely consider those practices that most resemble torture. States have taken firm action against FGM, Sati, and honor killings.[76] Footbinding in China provides another similar example. Michel Foucault and others have argued that modern law finds physical violence against the integrity of the body totally unacceptable.[77] The public spectacle killings in ancient societies that were so gruesome as to strike terror in the hearts of the public are no longer tolerated. Other forms of violence, however, do not receive as much consideration. Whatever the criticism, Foucault's argument that violence against the integrity of the body that causes "severe pain and suffering" is the type of human rights abuse that immediately receives censure must be seen as a reflection of an international consensus.[78] Cultural practices that challenge this norm must therefore receive the maximum degree of international scrutiny.

In arguing for maximum international scrutiny for "severe pain and suffering" violations of human rights, it is not necessary that

75. Convention Against Torture and Other Cruel, Inhuman or Degrading Treatment or Punishment, Dec. 10, 1984, art. 1, para. 1, G.A. Res. 39/46, 39 U.N. GAOR, Supp. No. 51, U.N. Doc. A/RES/39/708 (1984) [hereinafter Torture Convention].

76. *See, e.g.*, CEDAW, *supra* note 34 (including any sex-based distinction that prevents women from enjoying basic human rights in the definition of discrimination).

77. Michel Foucault, Discipline and Punish: The Birth of the Prison 7 (1979).

78. *Id.* at 25.

such scrutiny adopt the posture of "the arrogant gaze." Many groups in the countries in question campaign against these forms of violence. One should enter into partnership with these organizations and assist them in their attempts to fight these practices. These organizations have to win the ideological battle in their own societies to eliminate these practices.

VI. Discriminatory Laws

Short of inflicting violence and severe pain and suffering, many other customary and religious laws and practices also violate women's human rights. These usually deal with family law and the relationship between men and women within the family. In this area, a different approach aimed at balancing international women's rights with the rights of minorities may be necessary from a strategic viewpoint. Cultural practices relating to polygamy, inheritance rights, maintenance, consent at the time of marriage, child custody, child marriage, and others are among the issues that women's advocates raise in their fight for equality within the family.[79] CEDAW article 16 is very clear about the nature and structure of marriage: there must be free and full consent of the spouses at the time of marriage and full equality between the partners during the marriage and at its dissolution.[80] Many customary and religious systems around the world contest this recognition of freedom and equality as the principles on which to base marriage.

Sandra Lovelace was a Canadian-Indian born in New Brunswick on the Tobique Indian reserve.[81] She married a non-Indian, went out of the reserve, and had a son.[82] The marriage broke up and she came back to the reserve.[83] The elders informed her that once she married a non-Indian she lost all rights and returns to the reserve as a stranger.[84] As a result, they denied her housing and other benefits allowed on the reserve.[85] Men who marry outsiders, however, retain their status within the reserve.[86]

In many ways this form of discrimination violates the spirit of Article 9 of CEDAW. The Article declares that "[s]tate Parties shall

79. CEDAW, *supra* note 34, art. 16.
80. CEDAW, *supra* note 34, art. 16.
81. Anne Bayefsky, *The Human Rights Committee and The Case of Sandra Lovelace*, 120 Canadian Y.B. Int'l L. 244 (1982).
82. *Id.*
83. *Id.* at 249.
84. *Id.* at 244.
85. *Id.*
86. *Id.*

grant women equal rights with men to acquire, change or retain their nationality. They shall ensure in particular that neither marriage to an alien nor change of nationality by the husband during marriage shall automatically change the nationality of the wife."[87] This type of provision is not peculiar to the Tobique Indians. Though many laws have been changed recently, most systems in the world link the domicile of the wife to the domicile of the husband and the nationality of the wife and children to the nationality of the husband and father. Family integrity was the argument usually put forward by these systems that also recognize the father's bloodline as the only legitimate bloodline.[88]

Sandra Lovelace took her case to the Canadian courts and then to the Human Rights Committee in Geneva. The Canadian government defended itself by relying on section 4 of the Indian Act, which placed these matters squarely within the jurisdiction of Indian Councils that run the reservations. They argued that this related to Article 27 of the Universal Declaration of Human Rights and the ICCPR that states clearly: "In those States in which ethnic, religious or linguistic minorities exist, persons belonging to such minorities shall not be denied the right, in community with the other members of their group, to enjoy their own culture, to profess and practice their own religion, or to use their own language."

When the case came up before the Human Rights Committee, commentators were eager to see how the Committee balanced the right to equality guaranteed to women in Article 3 of the ICCPR with the right to enjoy one's culture, a central dilemma for those fighting for women's rights internationally. They were sorely disappointed. The Committee disregarded the equality argument and claimed that Article 27 gave Sandra Lovelace the right to enjoy her identity as a Tobique Indian and the present practice prevented her from enjoying that right. They held for her but without dealing with the issues of discrimination or women's equality.

The reluctance of the Committee to delve into issues that would require the right to equality on the part of women to trump the right to culture indicates the complexity raised by this question. For indigenous people, there exists a serious question of survival. Free marriage across boundaries may result in their assimilation and disappearance. Tribes have tried to control this possibility by limiting the marriage options of their women. The limited nature

87. CEDAW, *supra* note 34, art. 9.

88. *See* Human Rights Watch, Botswana Second Class Citizens: Discrimination Against Women under Botswana Citizenship Act (1994).

of land and resources on the Indian reservation provides another reason why the tribal leaders want to limit the numbers and the possibilities. Therefore, they see outsider men as far more threatening to the tribe than outsider women who would probably not claim resources and benefits from the tribal leaders.

In this context the rights of indigenous women to equality has been a question of great debate in Canada. Indigenous women often frame their rights within the discourse of the rights of the Indian people. Their dignity as women requires that others recognize and respect their status as Indians.[89] But they believe that according women equality within that framework would not disrupt tribal realities. Many of them feel that the best strategy is to work with tribal leaders to get them to change their minds and change their laws. Others, like Lovelace, feel that the Canadian government should intervene and ensure women's rights even at the expense of going against the wishes of the tribal leaders.

A similar dilemma emerges when one deals with the Shah Bano case in India. Shah Bano was a seventy-year-old woman whose husband unilaterally divorced her and refused to pay her maintenance. The Muslim personal law in India sanctions both unilateral divorce and non-payment of maintenance.[90] Shah Bano sued her husband under a provision of general criminal law that allowed destitute wives to sue their husbands for maintenance. The Indian Supreme Court held with her, but her case led to a great deal of Muslim unrest in India and the political leaders decided to change the law so that women in her situation would not have the criminal law recourse in the future.[91]

The Muslims are a minority in India and, many commentators argue, a minority that lives with a great deal of hostility because of India's relationship with its neighbor, Pakistan. Moreover, the Hindu Nationalist parties have roused a great deal of feelings against the Muslim presence in India. The destruction of the mosque in Ayodhya provides one example of this discrimination. Any change in the status of the personal law is seen as an assault on the Muslim community and therefore Shah Bano's actions raised many issues. She herself was somewhat disturbed by the intensity of feelings and the politicization of her case. Both Hindu extremists

89. M.A.J. Guerrero, *Civil Rights vs. Sovereignty: Native American Women in Life and Land Struggle in* FEMINIST GENEALOGIES, COLONIAL LEGACIES, DEMOCRATIC FUTURES (M.J.J. Alexander et al. eds., 1997).

90. Mohammed Ahmed Khan v. Shah Bano Begum, A.I.R. 1985 S.C. 945.

91. *Id.*

as well as feminists supported her. This confrontation made many feel that the only way forward was reform from within the community instead of reform imposed by the Indian Supreme Court or any other outside force.

At the international level, the Shah Bano case raises questions of a woman's right to equality but it also raises the dilemma of article 18 of the Universal Declaration of Human Rights and the ICCPR. Article 18 states that

> everyone shall have the right to freedom of thought, conscience, and religion. The right shall include freedom to have or adopt a religion or belief of his choice, and freedom, either individually or in community with others and in public or private, to manifest his religion or belief of his choice.[92]

This provision arguably gives protection to religious law on personal matters; if people do not agree with the laws, they can change their religion.

Others such as Courtney Howland have argued strongly against this position. Howland argues that systematic sex discrimination violates the U.N. Charter. Using the judgment of the International Court of Justice on apartheid, she argues that systematic sex discrimination should receive the same treatment, and that countries that engage in such discrimination should receive the same treatment as apartheid-dominated South Africa.[93] She points out that the U.N. Charter governs countries joining the United Nations and that Article 55 clearly states that one of the purposes of the United Nations is "universal respect for and observance of Human Rights and Fundamental Freedoms for all without distinction as to race, sex, language or religion."[94] In addition she notes that Article 56 requires all states to pledge themselves to the purposes of the United Nations, including those set out in Article 56. She goes on to point out that the International Court of Justice has held that Article 56 imposes a legal obligation on states. Howland's main argument rests on the premise that when states join the United Nations and sign onto the Charter they are legally obligated to respect the observance of Human Rights and Fundamental Freedoms without distinction as to sex.

In relation to the Shah Bano case, it is also interesting to note what exactly is meant by Freedom of Religion in terms of actual

92. ICCPR, *supra* note 26, art. 18.

93. Courtney W. Howland, *The Challenge of Religious Fundamentalism to the Liberty and Equality Rights of Women: An Analysis Under The United Nations Charter*, 35 Colum. J. Transnat'l L. 271-377 (1997).

94. U.N. Charter art 1, para. 3.

state practice. The U.N. General Assembly passed a Declaration on the Elimination of Religious Intolerance and Discrimination.[95] The declaration makes it clear that international law protects the manifestations of religious belief related to worship, maintaining places of worship, charitable institutions, articles for rites and customs, publication of materials, teaching the religion, soliciting funds, religious holidays, and communicating with others. It does not include as a protected aspect of religious worship religious laws that discriminate against women.

Regardless of the international legal status of the relevant religious law in Shah Bano's case, the practical reality was very different. The Indian Supreme Court held for her, but ethnic riots and political bargaining got in the way of her remedy. In this political context, the search for solutions other than top-down legal impositions by courts of law, which may be insensitive to minority sentiments, may have to evolve for women to truly receive the benefits of the international rights and remedies articulated in the international human rights instruments.

The dilemma between international rights and local realities also manifests itself in customary law and inheritance practices in Africa. Land is the most valuable economic resource in the Third World but, due to inheritance laws in these societies, a great disparity exists between male and female access to land.[96] Under customary legal regimes in Sub-Saharan Africa, women do not inherit any land, and only enjoy the land through their husbands and sons. Unmarried women and young widows without sons have little access to family resources. Old widows with sons and young widows with young sons have to live at the mercy of their sons or under the guardianship of their husband's brothers. Though a few tribes use a matrilineal system, the vast majority of tribes in Africa greatly restrict women's rights to inherit and use land.

Due to these practices, women have no material assets and are devalued within the family. They have little bargaining power and the position of widow is often unenviable. In India, the lack of widow's inheritance is one of the reasons for the practice of Sati. Widows, divorcees, and neglected first wives often find themselves in a situation of poverty. They either have to labor on the field of

95. U.N. Declaration on the Elimination of Religious Intolerance and Discrimination, G.A. Res. 36/55, U.N. GAOR, 36th Sess., Supp. 51, U.N. Doc. A/36/51 (1981).

96. Gita Gopal, World Bank, Gender Related Legal Reform and Access to Economic Resources in Eastern Africa 2 (1999).

their brothers-in-law or migrate to societies where young women often become victims of trafficking.[97]

Women's lack of inheritance is central to the practices of patriarchy and the belief that the continuity of the family depends only on father and son, that women are only a means by which to continue this line. Such beliefs often underpin customary law and even immigration law, which automatically gives women the domicile, residence, and nationality of their husbands. In addition, the belief that male labor is bread-winning, while female labor in the home is only supportive, justifies many of these inheritance laws as fruits of the labor of male members of the household. Practically speaking, societies also encourage these inheritance practices to prevent fragmentation of the land into too many parts.

Increasingly, development support groups argue for changing these inheritance laws and giving women greater access to land. The current practices flagrantly violate CEDAW, especially Article 13, which states clearly "[s]tate Parties shall take all appropriate measures to eliminate discrimination against women in other areas of economic and social life in order to ensure, on a basis of equality of men and women, the same rights, in particular the right to family benefits."[98] In addition, women's equality will only come about with women's economic independence and, therefore, access to land rights is imperative with regard to other areas of women's rights. For example, domestic violence might decrease if women have their own plot of land and their own economic resources. Women's access to land will also give access to credit, information, and technology to work the land. Access to land also provides security against poverty in old age. With access to land, women's status and bargaining power will increase dramatically.

Recently, non-governmental organizations (NGOs) and aid agencies have found that women often enhance the welfare of the family if given control of the family finances.[99] Studies have shown that husbands often keep up to 90% of their earnings for their own consumption, while a wife and mother would likely spend the majority of her earnings on the children.[100] The success of the Gramyn bank in Bangladesh and women's credit schemes in other parts of the developing world has led many organizations to

97. Bina Agarwal, A Field of One's own: Gender and Land Rights in South Asia 214 (1994).

98. CEDAW, *supra* note 34, art. 13.

99. Bina Agarwal, *supra* note 97, at 27-33.

100. *Id.*

rethink the concept of head of the household, which once automatically implied the male husband, and to invest more money in women's potential.

Rethinking inheritance rights in Sub-Saharan Africa implies restructuring customary law to ensure greater equality for women. This has become a heated issue, especially in South Africa. Many scholars have resisted any attempt to reform customary law, viewing it as an attempt to westernize and destroy the African family.[101] In 1998, South Africa promulgated a new law called The Recognition of Customary Law Act, which kept provisions of the family law but took away some provisions that accentuated inequality between the sexes.[102]

In South Africa, kings and chiefs head a large number of traditional groups, all of which have their own customary law. Despite minor differences, however, they are all premised on certain common practices. The first is the practice of "lobolo," where the husband's family negotiates with the parents of the bride to be, and an agreement is made regarding a payment by the bride's family to the groom's family. This payment could be in the form of cattle, money, or, in urban areas, other forms of amenities. In all of the systems, the wife leaves to live with the husband's family; she has no right to inheritance or to custody of the children, and her husband can practice polygamy. Widows are at the mercy of the male members of the husband's family and sometimes have to marry another male member in a levirate marriage. Native courts headed by the chiefs and kings of the traditional groups often enforce these customary laws.

The South African Constitution guarantees full equality for women and prohibits "the state or any person from unfairly discriminating . . . against anyone on the grounds of . . . gender, sex, pregnancy, marital status, etc."[103] This article, with its strong language about equality that covers public and private actors, forms part of the most progressive bill of rights in constitutional history. At the same time, the South African Constitution guarantees the rights of tribal and cultural groups,[104] by directing courts to apply customary law when that law clearly applies.[105] It makes clear, how-

101. *See, e.g.*, M. MAHMOOD MAMDANI, CITIZEN AND SUBJECT (1997) (discussing changes in customary law in Aftrican countries).

102. *See* David Chambers, *Civilizing The Natives: Marriage in Post-Apartheid South Africa*, 129 DAEDALUS 101, 112-13 (2000).

103. S. AFR. CONST. art. 9(3)-(4).

104. *See id.* art. 30.

105. *Id.* art. 211(3).

ever, that "no one exercising these rights may do so in a manner inconsistent with any provision of the Bill of Rights."[106]

The South African Law Commission (SALC) engaged in an interesting process in dealing with this contradiction.[107] The feminists in South Africa were pushing for some form of uniform civil law that would incorporate the provisions of CEDAW as the only family law in the country. The tribal chiefs wanted the courts to recognize customary law. They were ready to agree to allow couples to choose the law that would govern their marriage, but wanted to ensure that all customary marriages, past and future, would be seen as valid.

The SALC engaged in an open process to discover the best method to reconcile these opposing viewpoints. It received communication from all manner of sources and advice from individuals and experts around the world. Ultimately, the SALC decided that all couples should have the option of choosing between having their marriages governed by the customary law or by the general law.[108] In addition, the Recognition of Customary Marriages Act (Marriages Act) provides a minimum core of required provisions that apply to all marriages.[109] These provisions require that all marriages be freely chosen and consensual.[110] Unless a prenuptial contract exists, all property acquired during marriage is community property.[111] This provision strikes at the heart of the inheritance regime that discriminates against women. Under the Marriages Act, married women may also acquire and dispose of assets and enter into contracts.[112] Couples must register marriages and only a civil family law court judge can permit a divorce.[113] In this context, the judge uses the general law to divide the property, award alimony, and determine the custody of children.[114]

In many ways this law gives women the right to economic independence and provides for equality in marriage. Certain practices, resting on the notion of informed consent on the part of the woman, however, are allowed to continue.[115] The "lobolo" practice

106. *Id* art. 30.
107. *See* David Chambers, *supra* note 1022, at 111.
108. *Id.* at 112.
109. *Id.* at 113.
110. *Id.*
111. *Id.*
112. *Id.*
113. *Id.*
114. *Id.*
115. *Id.*

may continue if the daughter consents.[116] In addition, a polygamous marriage is valid if the first wife consents, and a written contract with the first wife divides the property accrued to that point.[117] Levirate marriages may also continue if the widow consents to marrying the brother of her deceased husband.[118] Some may argue that "consent" in this context is a misplaced concept, but the SALC believed that agency is possible and that women may wish to conform to traditional practices. The SALC also focused on the freedom to choose partners as an essential aspect of the minimum core of rights and took steps to protect the economic and material interests of the woman in marriage. Recognizing the centrality of women's economic independence to equality, the SALC ensured that customary law did not take away their economic rights.

The passage by Parliament of the Marriages Act did not please everyone, but it did gain general acceptance. The colonial powers and the apartheid regime always gave communities maximum space and control over family lives. The independent South African government dismantled this system of deference to tradition, keeping in mind the Bill of Rights and the equality of women. They were successful because they engaged in a consultative process and because socio-economic realities of urban South Africa required a reassessment of marriage practices.[119]

VII. Toward a Resolution

While the legal paradigm of torture helps us sort out those cultural practices that deserve international attention, the South African experience may assist us in determining those aspects of customary and religious law that require amendment so that the ideal of the universality of human rights retains some significance for women in their every day life. In determining those aspects of cultural practice that do not withstand human rights scrutiny, general principles underlying international human rights law may prove useful.

The rights of children demonstrates one area of international human rights that has near universal recognition and approval.

116. *Id.* at 103, 113. The "lobolo" or bridewealth that the groom will convey to the parents of the bride is agreed upon during stylized negotiations between the groom or members of his family and the parents of the bride.

117. *Id.* at 113.

118. *Id.*

119. *Id.* at 114-15.

The Convention on the Rights of the Child (CRC) is the most widely ratified convention in history; only two countries (Somalia and the United States) have not yet signed it.[120] In some sense, Courtney Howland's argument that countries signing international documents are bound by the standards and principles set forth in those documents has special significance in this area. Unlike in the case of the Universal Declaration of Human Rights, state parties to the CRC had all achieved independence when they signed and, therefore, made affirmative decisions to be bound by the CRC. This worldwide consensus, with few reservations on substantive articles, must reflect the fact that countries are ready to accept international scrutiny with regard to the rights of the child.

The CRC precludes those aspects of customary and religious law and practice that violate the rights of the child. This would include provisions relating to child marriage[121] as well as any practice that prevents the education of girls.[122] In addition, those practices that result in health hazards for girls would also open a country to international scrutiny.[123] In all these areas customary and religious law and practice must give way to international standards. Countries or minority groups with their own customary laws must bring these laws and practices into conformity with international norms and principles reflected in the CRC.

In practical terms, asserting the rights of the child often conflicts with the important concept of parental authority and decision making. Scholars such as Martha Minow have argued that one should view the problems of children through the concept of relationships and not through the prism of rights.[124] From this perspective, parents should get maximum discretion and any changes should be attempted through discussion and dialogue with the parents.[125] In terms of outlining effective strategies this may be the better approach. It is only in a climate of nurture and care that children can be protected, not in the crossfire of rights and freedoms. The popularity of the Convention, however, demonstrates

120. *See* Cynthia P. Cohen, ACLU International Civil Liberties Report, The United States and Somalia Bar Universal Ratification of The U.N. Convention on The Rights of the Child 46 (1998).

121. The Convention stipulates eighteen as the age when a child becomes an adult. Convention on the Rights of the Child, Nov. 20, 1989, art. 1, U.N. Doc. A/RES/44/25 (1989), *reprinted in* 28 I.L.M. 1457, 1459 (1989). [hereinafter the CRC].

122. *Id.* art. 28

123. *Id.* art. 3.

124. Martha Minow, *About Women, About Culture, About Them, About Us*, 129 Daedalus 125, 138-39 (2000).

125. *Id.*

that the welfare of children is of national and international concern and reflects an international consensus. The space for the justification of cultural relativism is, therefore, somewhat limited. The strategies used to implement this concern, however, may differ.

Other principles may also assist us in determining how to resolve issues relating to cultural relativism in family law. For example, unlike the Covenant on Civil and Political Rights, the ICESCR defines its provisions in terms of the progressive realization of rights within available resources.[126] This type of framework allows us to see rights in a more fluid sense, without immediate resolution. General Comment Number Three of the Covenant on Economic Social and Cultural Rights Committee (ICESR Committee) argues that, although these rights are not necessarily immediately realizable, a minimum core of rights should be immediately granted.[127] Immediate rights include the right to primary education or the right to safe childbirth.

In the case of women's rights within a given cultural context, this framework of progressive realization over a period of time may prove the best approach in the long term. Though torture-like practices require immediate action, provisions relating to family law may be more effective if they are modeled on the ICESCR approach. Progressive realization of equality propelled by women's groups working on the ground may actually result in more lasting and effective solutions. Committees such as CEDAW can also push governments to comply with their international obligations. As suggested in General Comment Number Three by the ICESCR Committee,[128] in the short term, governments should ensure that women receive a minimum core of rights within the family and the community.

In attempting to identify which aspects of customary and religious law and practice deserve this minimum core approach, the principle of autonomy may prove a guiding principle. Pursuing the principle of autonomy would imply removing those aspects of customary and religious law and practice that prevent women from being in a position to make decisions about their lives. In some ways the concept is related to choice, but the principle of autonomy recognizes social, economic, and political constraints and attempts to maximize women's power within those realities. In addition, the term autonomy recognizes that it is not only choice in

126. ICESCR, *supra* note 33, art. 2.
127. *Id.* at cmt. 3 para. 9-10.
128. *Id.*

an abstract political sense but choice in terms of economic and social reality that matters. For this reason, the concept of autonomy is also concerned with economic and social rights of women as a way of ensuring meaningful choice in everyday life. In some ways the SALC that inquired into customary law accepted this principle of autonomy as its guiding principle. It required that women have freedom of choice when it comes to marrying and accepting polygamy, and that women's economic independence be assured through the removal of provisions that prevented them from enjoying the economic resources of the family.[129]

The principle of autonomy is integrally linked to concepts of freedom and choice that underpin what is loosely called a western epistemology. The project of the Enlightenment enshrined these concepts in law and practice. Individual men became the centerpiece of the universe, not God. Many of the struggles of the twentieth century have been to expand the beneficiaries of the Enlightenment project to include women and non-western males. But writers such as Michel Foucault have deconstructed this ideal in its many manifestations and have proven to the world that this framework, with its façade of respectability, masks a cruel and ruthless system of power.[130] Writers such as Edward Said[131]and other young post-colonial scholars have shown how this model applied to the colonies and how it operated to subjugate and victimize people of color.[132] Their studies provide convincing portrayals of the Enlightenment project as an arrogant, western system of belief that destroyed everything in its path.

At some point, however, a leap of faith must occur. In a globalized world where economies and cultures meet, interact, and transform each other, we must develop a set of standards that have international recognition and durability. It would be naïve to assume that these interactions and transformations take place at random. There is an imposition of will by international media and business conglomerates that manipulate our tastes and our assumptions. Globalization may not be an equitable process, but it has also led to something else: the growth of international civil society. Groups and organizations have gathered around the concept of human rights as a mobilizing force against social justice and inequity. While only a few of these voices are heard globally, there

129. *See* Chambers, *supra* note 102, at 112-13.

130. *See* Michel Foucault, The Archaeology of Knowledge (1972).

131. *See* Edward Said, Culture and Imperialism (1994).

132. *See* Gananath Obeyesekere, The Apotheosis of Captain Cook (1992).

is no doubt that there is "globalization from below," and that third world groups are active members of this community.[133] These groups dialogue with one another, often at world conferences, and there is an informal consensus has developed to their approach.[134] Central to their consensus is the importance and primacy of the concept of democracy; not democracy in the narrow sense of western representative government, but democracy in a more inchoate sense of the need to include people of all groups and communities in a process of participation and decision-making.

If one were to read the many declarations and resolutions of the United Nations, one would see that democracy and participation by individuals and groups at all levels is a central animating tenet. Except for the documents dealing with peace and security or the economy, the political and civil documents of the United Nations make democracy and participation their central political concept. Therefore, it may be said that democracy as a general principle, even if not in its specific western manifestation, is part of an international consensus and is the underlying principle of organizations like the United Nations. Though it has not been recognized as jus cogens, the development of international norms since the end of the Second World War does point to democracy in a general sense as an emerging norm.

For democracy to be meaningful in the lives of individual women, these women must have the opportunity to make choices and decisions. Therefore, those aspects of customary religious law and practice that completely preclude them from making important decisions about their lives should be brought under scrutiny by national and international regimes. Provisions that deny women the right to give their consent to marriage or to leave an abusive relationship must surely be contested. In addition, provisions that deny women economic independence, such as those relating to her right to own property, enter into contracts, or receive inheritance, should also deserve intensive scrutiny.

Central to this regime of choice is the right to choose the person you wish to marry and the context in which such a marriage will operate. The U.N. Convention on Consent to Marriage, Minimum Age of Marriage and Registration of Marriage,[135] as well as

133. *See, e.g.*, GLOBALISATION AND GENDER, 26 SIGNS 4, 944 (2001).

134. Beijing Declaration, *supra* note 46, ch. 5.

135. Convention on Consent to Marriage, Minimum Age of Marriage and Registration of Marriage, G.A. Res. 1763/S, U.N. GAOR, 521 U.N.T.S. 7525, 231.

CEDAW,[136] recognizes the right to freely choose the partner and the context of one's marriage. Choosing to deny oneself the rights given by international standards is a different matter than recognizing the fact that such standards do exist and those who prefer such standards should be given the right to be governed by them. Therefore, central to the question of discriminatory laws under custom and tradition is the issue of optionality. All married couples on the date of their marriage should have the right to choose the system of laws that should govern their marriage. This protects the right of free choice central to international standards and documents of human rights. Some feminists have suggested that there be a "reverse optionality," that everyone is born into the general law but can choose to opt for a customary or religious system of law on their wedding day.[137]

In addition, an approach to cultural practice that takes autonomy as a central guiding principle would require national governments to engage in a process much like the proceedings of the South African Commission.[138] National governments should sift through their family and personal laws and identify a minimum core of provisions common to all legal systems. This minimum core would protect the rights of the child and the basic autonomy of the woman so that she could make decisions about her life. Couples on their wedding day could then choose which system of law should govern their marriage, legal provisions drafted in accordance with CEDAW or legal provisions relating to their own customary or religious law.[139]

VIII. Learning from Below

In pushing for these changes as the basic minimum obligations of states to international standards relating to women's rights, advocates should pursue sensitive strategies to ensure their success. Increasingly in the South and within certain minority groups there is a civil society that is responsive to these international concerns. None of the societies or groups under consideration are monoliths with a singular purpose of oppressing women. As many anthropologists have depicted, all these societies have ways and means of

136. CEDAW, *supra* note 34, art. 16.

137. *See* Madhu Kishwar, Religion at the Service of the Nation and Other Essays 233-248 (1998).

138. *See* Chambers, *supra* note 102, at 101.

139. Abdullahi Ahmed An-Na'im, *State Responsibility Under International Human Rights Law to Change Religious and Customary Law, in* Human Rights of Women 167, 176 (Rebecca Cook ed., 1994).

expressing women's liberation and emancipation. Reformists who try to improve the situation of women always exist within each tradition.[140]

Women's groups have become increasingly active and involved. Where such groups exist, leadership on these issues at the national and international level should come from them.[141] Any strategy should be formulated after full consultation and discussion with these groups because they are aware of the ground realities and the cultural and economic sensitivities. Only where such groups do not exist and where there is a situation of terror, such as in Taliban-ruled Afghanistan, should one consider direct international action. Action such as denying aid to governments or imposing penalties on third world states or communities for violation of women's rights should only be considered if the space does not exist for internal change and transformation and if local groups call for such intervention.

The specter of the Enlightenment-gone-wrong in the colonies still exists. The legacy of a colonial paternalism that posits the third world female as victim still triggers a great deal of resentment even among those who are generally favorable to women's rights. Insensitive strategies coupled with the arrogant gaze will only do greater harm and de-legitimize the very groups fighting for these causes in countries and minority groups. At the same time, however, people should recognize that internationally accepted standards and norms do exist, in defiance of post-modernist tendencies. Being sensitive to cultural relativism cannot imply putting hard-won battles on human rights up for grabs. There is a shared history and a collective memory at the international level. What must be seen as negotiable are the strategies of enforcement and implementation and not the bottom line concept of a woman free and equal.

140. *Id.* at 168.
141. *Id.* at 169.

[17]

LAW AS A TROJAN HORSE:

UNINTENDED CONSEQUENCES OF RIGHTS-BASED INTERVENTIONS TO SUPPORT BATTERED WOMEN

Renée Römkens†

I. INTRODUCTION

The call to law and legal rights and their concomitant progress narratives figure centrally in late modern society. This pull is particularly characterized by an appeal to law as an instrument to bring about recognition of various social and political problems as civil rights issues. In many respects, domestic violence can be considered the premier civil rights issue in this context. After thirty years of feminist advocacy and politics, a small but historic change has taken place: domestic violence has entered mainstream international and national politics as a matter of legitimate public concern and has become the subject of various legal regulations in the United States, notably the provision of rights to support and protect victims.[1] Domestic violence has been constructed as a respectable legal domain where, both nationally and internationally, substantial lawmaking takes place that reflects interesting political and cultural differences.[2] In the field of

---

† Visiting Professor at Columbia University, Department of Sociology and Institute for Research on Women and Gender and Associate Professor at Utrecht University, the Netherlands (Dept. of General Social Sciences). Different versions of this paper have been presented at the Annual Law & Society Meeting in Miami, Florida (May 26-29, 2000) and at the Women and the Welfare State Conference at Hebrew University, Jerusalem (June 5-6, 2000). For suggestions and comments on earlier drafts of this paper, I am grateful to Martha Ertman, Katherine Franke, James Jacobs, Holly Maguigan, Martha Mahoney, Linda Mills, Julie Nice, Selma Sevenhuijsen, and Joan Tronto. While working as a Visiting Scholar at New York University's Global Law Program in 2000-2001, I have particularly benefitted from discussions with colleagues at the Center for Research in Crime and Justice at NYU Law School.

1. For the United States, the Violence Against Women Act ("VAWA") is the most recent example of federal regulation. Note that the civil rights remedy it contained has recently been declared unconstitutional in *U.S. v. Morrison*, 529 U.S. 598 (2000). In his recent essay on changes in the past fifty years in criminal law, Sanford Kaddish views the influence of feminism on criminal law as a "social development to be remembered." Sanford Kaddish, *Fifty Years of Criminal Law: An Opinionated Review*, 87 CAL. L. REV. 943, 981 (1999). He points in particular to the changes in rape law and in the law of self-defense. *Id.* at 975-79.

2. International regulation of domestic violence is most notably reflected in the U.N. Convention on the Elimination of All Forms of Discrimination Against Women, G.A. Res. 34/180, U.N. GAOR, 34th Sess., Supp. No. 46, at 193, U.N. Doc. A/RES/34/180 (1979) [hereinafter CEDAW]. *See also* Declaration of Basic Principles of Justice for Victims of Crime and Abuse of Power, G.A. Res. 40/34, U.N. GAOR, 40th Sess., at 213, U.N. Doc. A/RES/40/34 and /36. It is important to bear in mind that there are profound international differences in the translation of this public concern into legal regulation. For example, despite the fact that various West European countries, such as Great Britain, the Netherlands and Germany, started shelters for battered women as early as the United States did and have meanwhile developed a strong shelter movement, the amount and level of civil and/or criminal legal regulation in these countries varies substantially. *See* Liz Kelly, Renée Römkens & Elizabeth Stanko, *Guest Editors' Introduction*, 7 VIOLENCE AGAINST WOMEN 727, 729 (2001). Within the European Union, efforts are being undertaken to harmonize future legislation in this area among member countries. *Id.*

domestic violence against adult women, for example, the level of both criminal and civil legal regulation in most West European countries is not as widely developed as in the United States (both on the national and state levels). This seems to reflect a general cultural difference in the way law figures much less prominently in European as compared to American culture as the primary device to call upon when resolving or handling social conflicts. Further international comparative research is necessary to gain more insight into this cultural-legal aspect.[3] It is interesting to note that in Dutch, the expression "American situations" (*Amerikaanse toestanden*) is commonly used in an unequivocally pejorative sense to indicate America's cultural preoccupation with issues of liability and the tendency to sue, usually for excessive amounts of monetary compensation, for any form of sustained damage or suffering. From a Dutch (European) perspective, this is generally considered to be an objectionable use of law that reflects the status of (if not obsession with) law in a liberal society as one of the most powerful cultural instruments that can be called upon to serve individual interests under the guise of pursuing legal justice. However, the development toward juridification of the issue of domestic violence inevitably invokes new social and legal disputes, both in civil and criminal law. In particular, the ongoing debate focuses on the questions of whether and how the fact that violence in the home is a matter of public concern translates into an affirmative obligation of the state to protect victims of family violence.[4] It is interesting to note that from a constitutional law perspective, the plight of the state is usually emphasized within feminist legal debates and the predominant negative liberties approach in the United States has been severely criticized.[5] From a criminal legal perspective, however, there is a growing acknowledgment among feminist legal scholars that mandatory arrest and prosecution policies

3. *See, e.g.*, Susan L. Miller & Rosemary Barberet, *A Cross-cultural Comparison of Social Reform: The Growing Pains of the Battered Women's Movements in Washington, D.C., and Madrid, Spain*, 19 L. & SOC. INQUIRY 923 (1994) (concluding that criminal justice respondents in the United States advocated arrest in conjunction with social services, while in Spain, these respondents were more reluctant to endorse criminal sanctions).

4. According to current constitutional legal doctrine in the United States, the state—notably the police—has no affirmative duty to protect women (and children) because the source of harm of such violence is considered private. *See* DeShaney v. Winnebago County Dep't of Soc. Serv., 489 U.S. 189, 195-97 (1989) (ruling that the state lacks any affirmative obligation to prevent domestic violence or to protect individuals against it, if the source of harm is private). For a recent critique of this ruling, see G. Kristian Miccio, *Notes from the Underground: Battered Women, the State, and Conceptions of Accountability*, 23 HARV. WOMEN'S L.J., 133, 135 (2000) ("After DeShaney and its progeny, conceptions of state accountability for domestic violence have been eradicated from rights discourse."). Miccio discusses the consequences of the doctrine of the "special relationship" as it relates to a 1999 California case, *Benavidez v. San Jose Police Dept.*, 71 Cal. App. 4th 853 (1999). In this case, the court ruled that police did not owe the victim a duty of care and did not negligently perform their duties by leaving the victim in her home when injured by violence commited by her boyfriend, despite their violation of San Jose Police Department Order § L2194.40, which gives detailed instructions to provide "all forms of help" to victims of domestic violence.

5. Elizabeth Schneider, *The Dialectic of Rights and Politics: Perpsepctives from the Women's Movement*, 61 N.Y.U. L. REV. 589 (1986). *See also* G. Kristian Miccio, *With All Due Deliberate Care: Locating the Contours of State Responsibility for Violence Against Mothers in the Age of* DeShaney, 29 COLUM. HUM. RTS. L. REV. 164 (1998) (arguing from a human rights perspective that a state pattern of nonfeasance in domestic violence disputes makes the state as culpable as private actors and that using the public/private dichotomy to defend the absence of an obligation to protect victims creates the impression that the state is morally condoning abuse).

invoke dilemmas and problems that deserve critical attention when developing policies to help protect victims.[6]

Against the background of this discourse on domestic violence and legal rights, and drawing from critical feminist and legal theory, I will focus in this article on the paradoxical, contingent and even contradictory implications of the recognition of rights.[7] Once law is invoked, a powerful institution and accompanying discourses are unleashed that often stretch far beyond the instrumental and politically inspired goals that underlie this appeal to law in order to bring about social justice. In practice, legal regulation to support individuals who have suffered domestic violence is a double-edged sword. The law inevitably controls, monitors and potentially punishes, at the same time that it empowers, protects and enhances freedom. The shift of domestic violence into the legal and public policy domain creates a need to establish and define general categories that fit the bureaucratic administrative system, while working with limited budgets to answer the question, "Which victims deserve support?" The invocation of law as a categorizing mechanism to identify rights bearers—through criminal law or welfare law—engages a powerful regulatory mechanism that might be at odds with the emancipatory goals in mind when invoking the law. Contrary to what liberal legal theory suggests, rights are not only "trumps."[8] In this paper I will explore the flip side of rights as trumps as exemplified by recent developments in creating rights and special provisions for battered women.

Legal rights do not operate in a vacuum where only law rules. The enactment and impact of rights are dependent upon and influenced by the wider political, cultural and social contexts. For a better understanding of the ways in which rights do or do not serve the complex and often contradictory interests of battered women, it is important to situate them in the specific social-cultural and political discursive contexts in which rights operate. Therefore, I will start by presenting two empirical examples of legal and policy regulation to support and/or protect battered women. I have chosen two cases from different countries and legal systems to illustrate empirically how the invocation of law, regardless

6. *See* Linda Mills, *Killing Her Softly: Intimate Abuse and the Violence of State Intervention*, 113 HARV. L. REV. 550 (1999) (arguing that mandatory interventions of the criminal justice system can equally result in imposing "state violence" onto abused women). *See also infra* note 66 on mandatory arrest policy, effectiveness and issues of women's agency.

7. A large volume of feminist work has documented and theorized the impact of gender, race and class biases in law, notably to the detriment of women. *See generally, e.g.*, Kimberlé Crenshaw, *Mapping the Margins: Intersectionality, Identity Politics, and Violence Against Women of Color*, *in* THE PUBLIC NATURE OF PRIVATE VIOLENCE 93 (Martha A. Fineman & Roxanne Mykitiuk eds., 1994); IDENTITIES, POLITICS, AND RIGHTS (Austin Sarat & Thomas R. Kearns eds., 1995); TAMAR PITCH, LIMITED RESPONSIBILITIES: SOCIAL MOVEMENTS & CRIMINAL JUSTICE (John Lea trans., 1995); THE PUBLIC NATURE OF PRIVATE VIOLENCE (Martha A. Fineman & Roxanne Mykitiuk eds., 1994); Judith Resnik, *Asking About Gender in Courts*, 21 J. WOMEN CULTURE & SOC'Y 952 (1996); CAROL SMART, FEMINISM AND THE POWER OF LAW (1989).

8. RONALD DWORKIN, TAKING RIGHTS SERIOUSLY xi (1977) ("Rights are political trumps held by individuals. Individuals have rights when, for some reason, a collective goal is not sufficient justification for denying them what they wish, as individuals to have or to do."), *quoted in* IDENTITIES, POLITICS, AND RIGHTS, *supra* note 7, at 2 n.8.

of the specific legal or policy regimes they represent, can have not only unintended, but also institutionally subversive consequences.

I will present in Part II an example from American policy and administrative regulation. I will argue that the provision within American welfare law to support battered women, usually referred to as the Family Violence Option, so far seems to be unsuccessful in achieving its aim of providing support to battered women. Based on a discussion of the initial rhetoric surrounding welfare reform in the mid-nineties, I will argue that the Family Violence Option, although intended to exempt battered women with dependent children from some of the severe cutbacks in welfare, was at odds with the socially and politically dominant rhetoric that underlay the general welfare reform—rhetoric that stigmatizes battered women. Not surprisingly, this underlying contradiction is revealed in a failure in the implementation of the legal-administrative provision. I will analyze data from a recent study on the use of the Family Violence Option in New York City that documents how the majority of battered mothers on welfare are excluded from support. In Part III, I will present a case from the criminal justice domain about a program developed to respond more effectively to victims of domestic violence and stalking in the Netherlands. I will show how the implementation of the program manifests a shifting of priorities from protection of the victim to prosecution of the offender. In the end, this means that the majority of victims are effectively excluded from entering the program.

In Part IV I will reflect on several questions: What is problematic about rights? What happens if we create a special category of women—in this case, battered women—based upon current or past harms? What cultural notions underlie our system of legal categorizing? Despite the fact that both examples come from very different regulatory regimes and are initial studies that deserve to be replicated and/or updated, they provide unique and valuable information on the impact and limited effectiveness of creating specific provisions for groups of women. I will reflect upon how the cases can further our theoretical understanding of how law operates as a regulatory device that evokes not only unforeseen and contradictory, but also self-defeating, consequences. These cases illustrate the regulatory work of law and the social and cultural categories it builds upon, which the law subsequently transforms and reifies into legal identities. It is not my intention to take a position for or against law as a strategic instrument. Rather, it is my goal to critically analyze whether legal regulations and legal rights work the way we want them to, and to assess how they work within different regulatory regimes that could illuminate the unintended effects of law. As I will show, legal regulation excludes many battered women from protection or support precisely at the moment when it announces its desire to support and protect them through inclusion in law.

II. THE AMERICAN CASE: FAILURE OF THE FAMILY VIOLENCE OPTION IN WELFARE REFORM

A. *Welfare Reform, Domestic Violence and the Rhetoric of Responsibility*

The relationship between welfare and domestic violence has only gradually become the subject of critical attention, particularly in the United States, within the context of the mid-1990s welfare reforms.[9] Given the prevalence, nature and consequences of domestic abuse, chronic violence can substantially increase the chances that its victims—mostly women—will end up in poverty.[10] More generally, poverty is a highly racialized and gendered problem, in that it affects Black and Latina women much more than white women.[11] There are various links between domestic violence and welfare need.[12] A woman may divorce and subsequently face daunting impediments to finding employment, such as a lack of childcare providers. Alternatively, a woman may go on welfare in order to be financially able to leave her abuser but may be unable to leave welfare because her abuser sabotages her attempts to pursue education, training or employment. She may experience difficulties at work, lose her job or drop out of school due to the controlling, abusive and harassing behavior of her ex-spouse.[13] Conservative

9. *See* Jody Raphael, *Domestic Violence and Welfare Receipt: Toward a New Feminist Theory of Welfare Dependency*, 19 HARV. WOMEN'S L.J. 201, 208 (1996) (arguing that "[b]ecause domestic violence experts have been historically disconnected from feminist welfare policy analysts and academics, the issue of domestic violence has failed to inform the policy debates about welfare"); Peter Margulies, *Representation of Domestic Violence Survivors as a New Paradigm of Poverty Law: In Search of Access, Connection and Voice*, 63 GEO. WASH. L. REV. 1071, 1071 (1995) (noting that "traditional poverty scholars have ignored how domestic violence exacerbates poverty and causes homelessness. Rather than integrating domestic violence issues into a richer conception of poverty law, traditional scholars have marginalized domestic violence into the gendered ghetto of family law and the exotica of criminal law defenses."); *see, e.g.*, ANNE MARIE CAMMISSA, FROM RHETORIC TO REFORM? WELFARE POLICY IN AMERICAN POLITICS (1998). Wwhile providing an excellent perspective on the general political and historical developments animating American welfare policy, Cammissa makes no mention at all of specific provisions in the welfare reforms for battered women or women in general. This failure to address the gendered impact of welfare is interesting given the dearth of socio-historical research that has documented how welfare is crucial in the social support and regulation of women's lives in particular. *See* MIMI ABRAMOVITZ, REGULATING THE LIVES OF WOMEN: SOCIAL WELFARE POLICY FROM COLONIAL TIMES TO THE PRESENT (1996); LINDA GORDON, PITIED BUT NOT ENTITLED: SINGLE MOTHERS AND THE HISTORY OF WELFARE, 1890-1935 (1994); WOMEN, THE STATE, AND WELFARE (Linda Gordon ed., 1990). For an excellent contribution on the implications of recent developments in welfare in the United States, particularly regarding issues of domestic violence in relation to welfare, see BATTERED WOMEN, CHILDREN AND WELFARE REFORM: THE TIES THAT BIND (Ruth A. Brandwein ed., 1999).

10. JODY RAPHAEL & RICHARD TOLMAN, TAYLOR INSTITUTE, TRAPPED BY POVERTY, TRAPPED BY ABUSE: NEW EVIDENCE DOCUMENTING THE RELATIONSHIP BETWEEN DOMESTIC VIOLENCE AND WELFARE 3 (1997). *See also* Erin Meehan Richmond, Note, *The Interface of Poverty and Violence Against Women: How Federal and State Welfare Reform Can Best Respond*, 35 NEW ENG. L. REV. 569, 570-576 (2001) (providing a recent review of studies documenting the relationship between poverty, welfare and domestic violence).

11. Susan L. Thomas, *"Ending Welfare as We Know It," or Farewell to the Rights of Women on Welfare? A Constitutional and Human Rights Analysis of the Personal Responsibility Act*, 78 U. DET. MERCY L. REV. 179, 183 (2001) (quoting 1997 U.S. Census Bureau data, she reiterates that poverty is a woman's problem; 95% of welfare recipients in the United States are women. Poverty is also racially skewed: Black female heads of a household have higher poverty rates than white women, 39.8% vs. 27.7% respectively.).

12. *See, e.g.*, Ruth A. Brandwein, *Family Violence, Women and Welfare*, *in* BATTERED WOMEN, CHILDREN AND WELFARE REFORM: THE TIES THAT BIND 3, 10 (Ruth A. Brandwein ed. 1999).

13. Jody Raphael, *Domestic Violence and Welfare Receipt: The Unexplored Barrier to Employment*, 3 GEO. J. ON FIGHTING POVERTY 29, 31 (1995).

estimates indicate that between fourteen and thirty-two percent of welfare recipients in the United States are abused by their current partners.[14]

Drastic welfare reforms in 1996 in the United States—under the ominous name of the Personal Responsibility and Work Opportunity Reconciliation Act of 1996 (hereinafter PRA)—instituted major cutbacks and brought "an end to welfare as we knew it."[15] Some of the major changes include the five-year limit on receiving benefit, the requirement to secure paid employment after two years ("from welfare to work"),[16] and the tougher child-support requirements. These changes imply severe limits on available resources for welfare and particularly affect the most vulnerable social groups in society—notably battered and single women with children.[17] To understand how this reform affects battered women, it is important to remember that the political debates justifying welfare reform were characterized by a highly moralistic rhetoric of personal responsibility for sustaining oneself and one's children. This easily paved the way for a rhetoric of individual failure, blame and stigmatization of those in need of public support in times of increasing job-insecurity and the basic uncertainty flowing therefrom.[18] Joan Tronto has pointed out how the debates surrounding American welfare reform generally deploy the standpoint of work ethic.[19] Among other things, the work ethic assumes a simple and direct relationship between effort and desert and uses a tautological account of desert and success: those who work hard earn a lot; those who are poor are lazy and do not work hard enough. In its "methodological individualism" the work ethic underlying American welfare reform reduces all complex social and political issues into simple and straightforward issues of desert with highly moral overtones: those who work will be successful and deserve good, those who do not work are the poor and lazy failures. It is this rhetoric of success (no matter how elusive that turns out to be for most of those who work hard) and failure that is a recurring theme in the

14. MARCELLENE E. HEARN, NOW LEGAL DEF. & EDUC. FUND, NEW YORK CITY'S FAILURE TO IMPLEMENT THE FAMILY VIOLENCE OPTION 12 (2000) (citing RAPHAEL & TOLMAN, *supra* note 10); *see also* Raphael, *supra* note 9, at 205. As these figures relate to women with a partner, these percentages do not include the women who ended up on welfare due to divorce from an abusive partner.

15. With this wide-ranging and politically charged terminology, President Clinton in 1992 announced plans to change existing American welfare laws. CAMMISSA, *supra* note 9, at 63-93.

16. Note that in this political rhetoric, domestic work, care providing and/or child rearing work is *not* considered "work." Only paid work is considered to be real work.

17. *See* Wendy Pollack, *Twice Victimized—Domestic Violence and Welfare "Reform,"* 30 CLEARINGHOUSE REV. 329 (1996).

18. *See* ZYGMUNT BAUMAN, IN SEARCH OF POLITICS 5 (1999). Bauman recently argued that "uncertainty, insecurity and unsafety" are "the most sinister and painful of contemporary troubles." *Id.* In particular, he talks about economic insecurity and uncertainty as a consequence of the casualization of work and the decrease of employment that prevents an increasing number of people from gaining access to a structural and secure income to sustain themselves. *Id.* at 9-58. He strongly criticizes the welfare-to-work program because of the short term and generally low qualified jobs people end up in. This program "leads from lesser to greater insecurity." *Id.* at 180. He makes a case for a basic income as a human rights issue: "(T)he right to stay alive which precedes and conditions all choice is the inalienable property of all human beings, not something to be earned." *Id.* at 181.

19. *See* Joan Tronto, What's Wrong With the Work Ethic? (1997) (unpublished manuscript) (on file with author). *See generally* MAX WEBER, THE PROTESTANT ETHIC AND THE SPIRIT OF CAPITALISM (1930) (pointing to the profound connection between Calvinist work ethos as a pre-condition for the explosive economic growth and the development of Western capitalism in the nineteenth and early twentieth centuries).

welfare debate. "[It] posits welfare recipients as defective citizens, and then passing judgment on which defects are legitimate and which ones are not, we give ourselves license not to listen to welfare recipients themselves but to pass judgement on them based on whatever little information we may have." [20] Martha Fineman observed quite poignantly that we all live subsidized lives, whether the subsidy comes from government in the form of direct assistance to poor families or indirectly in the form of tax exemptions: "The question is why we stigmatize some subsidies, but not others."[21] Several critics of the PRA pointed out that welfare reform induced a rhetoric of *irresponsibility* and in so doing provided the narrative that allows the association between dependency on welfare with illegal behavior. Poverty was re-framed as more of a moral than an economic problem.[22]

B The Family Violence Option to Support Battered Women on Welfare

In the debates leading up to the welfare reform, there was a growing awareness, fueled by emerging research, on the relationship between domestic violence and poverty.[23] It became obvious that the welfare reform as described in the aforementioned requirements would severely impact battered women with dependent children.[24] Although the PRA did provide a general "hardship exemption," a special amendment was introduced to address the special hurdles, related to income and safety issues, that battered women face in successfully moving from welfare to work. The 104th American Congress eventually unanimously adopted an amendment to the PRA called the Family Violence Option (hereinafter FVO), that allowed states to provide flexible waivers to exempt battered women from certain requirements of the bill.[25]

20. *Id.* at 11.

21. Martha Fineman, *The Nature of Dependencies and Welfare "Reform,"* 36 SANTA CLARA L. REV. 287, 290 (1996). In a similar vein, David Greenberg documents recent increases in disproprotianility in tax benefits for lower income, compared to middle- or high-income American households. "Constant exposure to condemnations of welfare for the poor makes it easy to forget that there are large (and largely unpublicized) subsidies to middle- and upper-income groups." David Greenberg, *Punishment, Division of Labor and Social Solidarity*, *in* THE CRIMINOLOGY OF CRIMINAL LAW 284, 294 (Advances in Criminological Theory Series, Vol. 8, 1999.

22. For a recent contribution to the debate that explicitly addresses the gender and racialized dimensions of this reformulation process, see Lisa A. Crooms, *The Mythical, Magical "Underclass": Constructing Poverty in Race and Gender, Making the Public Private and the Private Public.* 5 J. GENDER RACE & JUST. 87, 91 (2001) (providing an analysis of how the legal welfare reform privatizes public poverty, which permits poverty to be cast as a private matter caused by individual irresponsibility and immorality).

23. The various reports from the Taylor Institute, notably from Jody Raphael, have been crucial in this respect. *See* Wendy Pollack & Martha F. Davis, *The Family Violence Option of the Personal Responsibility and Work Opportunity Act of 1996: Interpretation and Implementation*, CLEARINGHOUSE REV., 1079-1100 (1997). *See also* Richmond, *supra* note 10, at 579.

24. *See, e.g.*, Sheryl L. Howell, *How Will Battered Women Fare Under the New Welfare Reform?* 12 BERKELEY WOMEN'S L.J. 140, 149 (1997).

25. According to Pollack and Davis, the fact that a special provision for battered women was created is the result of successful cooperation of "women's rights, welfare and domestic violence advocates and intelligent legislators." Pollack & Davis, *supra* note 23, at 1080. The authors note that advocates "consider the creation of separate state-funded programs for other populations of public assistance recipients" who cannot comply with PRA requirements, such as a head of household with a disability who is not eligible for Supplemental Security Income or people who must provide care to a disabled child.

The FVO enables states to temporarily waive the work requirement, or to extend the period during which battered women can receive welfare when the requirements would unfairly penalize them or put them or their families at risk of further harm. It also enables them to waive the work requirements or other criteria if they would make it more difficult for the spouse to leave the abusive situation.[26] The FVO has been adopted by forty-one states.[27] In order to identify the women in need of special support through the FVO, the FVO requires that the agency administering welfare screen and provide referrals to victims of domestic violence. This creates an affirmative obligation to notify every welfare applicant of the availability of domestic violence services and the procedure for obtaining a protective order, to screen every welfare applicant or recipient for domestic violence, and to refer anyone who identifies herself in writing as a victim of domestic violence to a specialized domestic violence liaison at the welfare agency, who will subsequently handle the case to see whether a waiver is appropriate and meets the requirements for a federally recognized good cause domestic violence waiver.[28] After referral takes place, a specialized domestic violence liaison is responsible for assessing the applicant's credibility, before deciding about the type of appropriate waiver. In this process, the law states that, at a minimum, the liaison officer has to get a sworn statement from the victim alleging the abuse. In addition, other documentation of the abuse of a legal or social nature, such as protective orders, hospital records, and letters from social service providers, can be used to establish credibility.[29] On paper, the law seems to support welfare recipients who are victims of domestic violence, presenting them as deserving special support.

In the spring of 2000, a research report was released analyzing the way this law has been implemented in New York City. It revealed that the City of New York failed quite dramatically to meet any of the mentioned legal requirements and in many instances violates state law. In summary:

No systematic notification of services takes place. A majority of applicants and recipients that were interviewed for the New York study were not informed at all about any domestic violence services or of the waivers available according to the FVO.

There is no systematic screening of potential victims of domestic abuse. The majority of applicants and recipients of welfare were not questioned at all about any experiences with domestic violence.

No systematic referrals take place. Of applicants and recipients who were screened and said in writing that they were experiencing domestic violence, only

26. 42 U.S.C. 602 (a)(7) (2000).

27. *See* JODY RAPHAEL & SHEILA HAENNICKE, KEEPING BATTERED WOMEN SAFE THROUGH THE WELFARE TO WORK JOURNEY: HOW ARE WE DOING? A REPORT ON THE IMPLEMENTATION OF POLICIES FOR BATTERED WOMEN IN STATE TEMPORARY ASSISTANCE FOR NEEDY FAMILY PROGRAMS (1999), *quoted in* HEARN, *supra* note 14, at 4.

28. *See* HEARN, *supra* note 14, at 5.

29. N.Y. COMP. CODES R. & REGS. tit. 18, § 351.2 (l) (2001). Finally, a waiver must contain a services plan to count as "good cause waiver" that meets federal legal standards. *See* HEARN, *supra* note 14, at 8.

half were referred to a domestic violence liaison officer. Of those who orally presented themselves as victims, not one received an appropriate referral.[30]

In some cases where the applicant presented the caseworker with evidence of domestic violence, such as an order of protection, the applicant was actively denied a special referral. The caseworker thought there was no longer any danger since she did not live with the batterer anymore. The report clearly indicates that many caseworkers lacked any knowledge of domestic violence, and that domestic violence is not considered a serious issue to take into consideration. In New York City, between 25,000 and 57,600 welfare recipients were estimated to be eligible to meet with a domestic violence liaison officer in 1999. Only 3,023 actually did so. Of those, only about one-third (thirty-six percent) obtained any type of waiver (mostly child support waivers or a partial employment waiver). The domestic violence liaison officers attributed this low referral rate to the non-specialized caseworkers' "lack of knowledge" and lack of "proper training" regarding their legal obligation.

Addressing a conference in 1998, Jason Turner, one of the welfare agency's commissioners in charge of implementing the FVO, urged caution in its implementation. He advised "not to let domestic violence inadvertently become a designation which permits individuals to not take responsibility for their lives." Domestic violence should never become "an exemption from obligation."[31] It seems from the empirical data on the administration of the FVO that this advice has been taken to heart by the welfare agencies.

C Family Violence Option: From Support to Exclusion

These data tell an old and familiar story: the impact of any law depends upon its implementation in day-to-day practice, as well as on its political support, or lack thereof.[32] Various factors influence its success, including available expertise

30. HEARN, *supra* note 14, at 1-2. All empirical data on the FVO in New York City presented here are from this report.

31. *Id.* at 3.

32. Interestingly, the Amendment to the Personal Responsibility Act was passed unanimously by Congress in 1996 without any substantial debate. Pollack & Davis, *supra* note 23, at 1085. The implementation of the FVO set off defensive media coverage of the topic, emphasizing that it was not unfair to create these provisions for battered women. *See generally, e.g.*, Jennifer Gonnerman, *Welfare's Domestic Violence: The Rules Ending Welfare As We Knew It Will Trap Women in Abusive Situations*, THE NATION, Mar. 10, 1997, at 21. Gonnerman interviewed the proponents of the FVO, allowing them to respond to the measure's criticism. She recorded their justifications as to why the entrapment of battered women requires temporary measures to support and protect women, and noted their contention that the goal of the FVO was not to exempt battered women permanently from the new work requirements. Likewise, the proponents of the FVO asserted that it did not provide an alibi for women to stay on welfare. *Id. See also* Leslye Orloff, *Lifesaving Welfare Safety Net Access for Battered Immigrant Women and Children: Accomplishments and Next Steps*,7 WM. & MARY J. WOMEN & L. 597 (2001). Orloff, citing portions of the Illegal Immigration Reform and Immigrant Responsibility Act of 1996 (IIRIRA), argues that although these provisions are intended to support battered women, they create severe obstacles in practice that keep many battered women and childresn from accessing the public benefits they are entitled to receive. *Id.* at 621-656 (citing 8 U.S.C. §§ 1182(a)(4), 1631(a), (e)-(f) and 1641 (1994 & Supp. V 1999). These provisions are intended to grant access to public benefits for certain battered immigrants, yet at the same time they severely limit that access. The author argues that battered immigrant women must be exempted from the five-year bar from welfare provisions and must be granted access to food stamps and SSI. *Id.*at 643-44.

and material support. The use of the FVO shows what some critics predicted from the very start: without training for the appropriate people within the welfare agencies, the implementation of the provision is doomed to fail.[33] Furthermore, the lack of substantial supplemental funding remains one of the major obstacles.[34] Given the shift toward more punitive welfare regulations in the United States, and the preexisting bureaucratic nature of welfare agencies that in the nineties became structurally understaffed, the already limited willingness and ability of these agencies to support the people receiving or applying for welfare benefits became all the more exaggerated.[35]

It is interesting to note the development in recent policies regarding financial support for social and therapeutic services in the field of domestic violence. Under the Family Violence Prevention and Service Act, states are provided assistance in order to increase public awareness about family violence and to provide immediate shelter and related assistance to victims of family violence. The Act also provides for technical assistance and training related to family violence programs. This does not, however, cover training of caseworkers in welfare agencies.

A closer look reveals that there is also a gendered dynamic that illuminates why the implementation of a provision designed to support battered women became an opportunity to punish in practice. First, the work ethic underlying the welfare reform is deeply gendered and facilitates the onset of an "othering" dynamic toward welfare recipients, women, and people of color.[36] In its standard of economic success, the traditional work ethic excludes all unpaid labor, including the care work that is done at home by women[37] or by highly underpaid

33. *See also* Elizabeth Watson et al., *Reports of Regional Activism*, 7 GEO. J. ON POVERTY L. & POL'Y 231, 232 (2000) (citing warnings from workers and advocates in the field of welfare reform, that the FVO becomes meaningless if caseworkers do not know of this law, or do not know how to apply it). The authors stress the importance of training caseworkers to ask their clients about domestic violence and to respond usefully to a client who is abused.

34. *See* Howell, *supra* note 24, at 149 (noting that the Welfare Act actually provides a financial disincentive because states may only grant the exception to twenty percent of families on public assistance). Given that the percentage of abused women among welfare recipients is most probably higher than 20%, this implies that the FVO excludes a substantial number of women from the promised support. *See* RAPHAEL & TOLMAN, *supra* note 10; Howell, *supra* note 24, at 149. Furthermore, Howell notes that many women will not come forward with their experiences of abuse out of shame and fear of retaliation. *Id.*, at 143-45, 149.
Donna Coker criticizes this consistent lack of funding, especially given that the criminalization of domestic violence, while well-funded, does not effectively empower women. Donna Coker, *Crime Control and Feminist Law Reform in Domestic Violence Law: A Critical Review*, 4 BUFF. CRIM. L. REV. 801, 802-05 (2001). Coker has also argued that the litmus test for effective laws or policies for battered women should be whether legal or social service interventions enhance women's access to material resources. *See generally* Donna Coker, *Shifting Power for Battered Women: Law, Material Resources, and Poor Women of Color*, 33 U.C. DAVIS L. REV. 1009 (2000).

35. The quality of service provided to the public by the Social Security Administration has deteriorated in recent years, according to recent reports of the Federal Social Security Advisory Board. "The number of Social Security employees has dropped 22 percent in the last 15 years, to 65,048, from 83,505 in 1985 . . . . But the number of beneficiaries in programs run by Social Security increased by 26 percent in those years, to 51.7 million, from 41.1 million." Robert Pear, *Federal Panel Warns Bush of Social Security Problems*, N.Y. TIMES, Feb. 19, 2001, at A11.

36. *See* Family Violence Prevention and Services Act, 42 U.S.C.A. §§ 10, 401-10, 418 (West 1995 & Supp. 1999); *ee* Crooms, *supra* note 22, at 89-95; Tronto, *supra* note 19, at 9.

37. *See* Fineman, *supra* note 21, at 305-06.

(mostly female and often minority) domestic servants. Through their unpaid or underpaid, and thus undervalued care work, with its concomitant positions of powerlessness and lack of privilege, those who perform this work easily become essentially "different." The structural obstacles to getting or holding a paid job on top of domestic care-taking and child-rearing responsibilities are constructed as individual problems of defective citizens. This rhetoric creates a narrative within which the welfare recipient figures as the "other" who is the one to be blamed.[38] Within American welfare reform, the divorced or single woman who lives outside heterosexual marriage and the hierarchical family, especially if she is a racial or ethnic minority, is treated as a social problem in need of regulation because she does not fit within the mythical, idealized marriage and nuclear family in our society.[39]

Subsequently, the battered woman has become particularly vulnerable to this stigmatizing othering mechanism because the abused woman who does not leave is in the context of welfare law a defective citizen par excellence. In dealing with domestic violence, the obsession of various professional disciplines with the idea of leaving the abusive relationship, disregarding all the social-economic and psychological complexities at stake, is striking.[40] There is abundant research illustrating how leaving a violent relationship is an outcome of a long trajectory, complicated by myriad struggles related to systemic social and economic obstacles and by psychological limitations due to the severe consequences of chronic trauma that most abused women have experienced.[41] Furthermore, leaving the relationship is the most dangerous period in which she runs the greatest risk of being killed.[42] All this is widely known; in fact, it formed the basis for the FVO provision to support battered women on welfare. But interestingly, this social scientific and clinical knowledge seems not to have had any substantial influence on policymakers or administrators charged with implementing the FVO. This is another example of the general and often

38. Tronto, *supra* note 19, at 9.

39. Fineman , *supra* note 21, at 310-11 (underlining the normativity of the family ideology in welfare law); Crooms, *supra* note 22, at 88-89 (pointing more explicitly to the fact that the PRA imposes a strict heterosexual gender regime and and punishes those women and unmarried mothers who do not conform to that regime and do not perform gender in the correct way). Thomas argues that the PRA is inherently discriminatory in various ways because it is explicitly based on the model of the traditional, heterosexual, two-parent family. She contends that it violates several human rights provisions and several constitutional rights of women, such as the right to make their own decisions about marriage, procreation and parenting. It infringes both the spirit and the letter of women's human rights declarations as codified in various articles in CEDAW. *Supra* note 2. Because the PRA will have a disparate impact on Black, Latina and other non-white communities who suffer more from poverty, Thomas believes that the PRA violates the International Convention on the Elimination of All Forms of Racial Discrimination (CEAFRD). Thomas, *supra* note 11, at 182-85, 200-01.

40. *E.g., generally*, Martha Mahoney, *Exit: Power and the Idea of Leaving in Love, Work, and the Confirmation Hearings*, 65 S. CAL. L. REV. 1283 (1992); Mills, *supra* note 6, at 551.

41. Renée Römkens, *Het Onbehagen over Geweld Tegen Vrouwen. Projectie en Internalisering van Verantwoordelijkheid en Schuld* [Violence Against Women and its Discontents: Projection and Internalisation of Responsibility and Guilt], *in* AGRESSIE: DETERMINANTEN, SIGNALERING EN INIERVENTIE 211-27 (P.B. Defares and J. D. van der Ploeg, eds.); *see also* Mahoney *supra* note 40; Howell, *supra* note 24.

42. *See* Mahoney (1992), *supra* note 40; *see also* M..I. Wilson & M. Daly, *Who Kills Whom in Spouse Killings? On the Exceptional Sex Ratio of Spousal Homicides* CRIMINOLOGY 189-215 (1992); M.I. Wilson, & M. Daly, *Spousal Homicide Risk and Estrangement,* VIOLENCE AND VICTIMS 3-16 (1993).

dramatic gap between science and policy development that subverts the latter.[43] The battered woman surfaces in this welfare discourse as the one who (at least potentially) is to be blamed—if not for the violence, then certainly for not "taking responsibility" for leaving. This is the new politically correct language to reframe the complex issue of exit from a violent relationship as a matter of individual (ir)responsibility.[44] In the context of welfare reform, the female victim of domestic violence emerges as a threatening cultural icon of failure: failure of marriage and heterosexual romance, failure to protect her children,[45] and more importantly failure to take responsibility and leave. Even after she leaves, the battered mother has failed and runs the risk of being punished. By reformulating the issue of not leaving a violent relationship as "not taking responsibility," battered women, more than any other recipients of welfare, are constructed within the discursive context of welfare reform as *undeserving* welfare

43. Martha Minow, in a critical analysis of the much debated gap between policy makers and social scientists, attributes this gap to the "rejection of social action" by the social sciences and concludes in general terms that there is a loss of "commitment to action and reform." Martha Minow, *Learning from Experience: The Impact of Research about Family Support Programs on Public Policy*, 143 U. PA. L. REV. 221, 251 (1994). Although I certainly agree with the author's observation that policy development is often uninformed by social science, her attribution of the cause to the loss of commitment among the social scientists is contestable. Certainly the assertion that this loss of commitment is due to their "search for validity as an objective methodology" is far from clear—validity is a characteristic of data presented as a result of the use of a method, but can never be a methodology. *Id.* at 252. More importantly it simplifies the socio-economic, cultural, political, and often highly gendered power dynamics at stake that influence which scientific knowledge is taken into consideration in the decision making process that underlies policy development. The FVO case in this article is clearly an example of the minimization and ignorance of abuse of women, if not the arrogance of policy makers in the face of overwhelming data that point in the opposite direction.

44. *See* Crooms, *supra* note 22.

45. Regardless of any actions that battered mothers may have taken to protect their children, they can be found guilty of neglect or abuse under a strict liability standard, because of their "failure to protect" their children against the harm that results from exposure to domestic violence. Most recently even women who had left their abusers but had admitted to the social workers that they had been beaten while pregnant, were punished. Their newborn children were removed after birth because of the mother's failure to protect them. *See* Rachel Roth, *Adding Insult to Injury*, *at* http://www.salon.com/mwt/feature/2000/09/14/battered_mothers/print.html (Sept. 14, 200). Amy R. Melner concludes that there is a "lack of empathy" apparent in the treatment of abused mothers in the judicial system. Women may face criminal or civil liability, they may lose custody for their failure to protect their children, or the court may terminate their parental rights for abuse and neglect. Amy R. Melner, *Rights of Abused Mothers vs. Best Interest of Abused Children: Courts' Termination of Battered Women's Parental Rights Due to Failure to Protect Their Children from Abuse*, 7 S. CAL. REV. L. & WOMEN'S STUD. 299, 300 (1998). *See also* V. Pualani Enos, *Prosecuting Battered Mothers: State Laws' Failure to Protect Battered Women and Abused Children.* 19 HARV. WOMEN'S L.J. 229 (1996); Jane C. Murphy, *Legal Images of Motherhood: Conflicting Definitions from Welfare Reform, Family, and Criminal Law*, 83 CORNELL L. REV. 688 (1998).

Since 1996, the New York State Legislature has attempted to afford additional protection to domestic violence victims and their children by mandating consideration of domestic violence when determining the best interests of the child in custody and visitation cases. Susser argues that this new law "is clearly meant to impose restrictions on visitation and custody for one parent who has been found to have committed violence against the other parent" and reports that in practice the legislative findings meant to help battered mothers in custody disputes, are used by courts and child protective officials *against* them in accusing them of neglect. Kim Susser, *Weighing the Domestic Violence Factor in Custody Cases: Tipping the Scales in Favor of Protecting Victims and Their Children*. FORDHAM URB. L. J., 875, 878 (2000). Schernitzki argues that the label of "failure to protect" reflects the double standard society uses for mothers and fathers in holding mothers primarily if not exclusively accountable, not so much for their own affirmative actions, but for the violent conduct of their husbands and boyfriends. Rebecca Ann Schernitzki, *What Kind of Mother are You? The Relationship Between Motherhood, Battered Woman Syndrome and Missouri Law*, 56 J. MO. B. 50 (2000).

recipients, precisely at the moment they have entered as a social and legal category to be specifically "protected" or "supported."

When the FVO was enacted in 1996, it was strongly critiqued for the way it represented women. Martha Mahoney, though certainly not opposing this exception, criticized the problematic images that underlie this provision. She indicated that it might lead to a particularly unhelpful competition among women based on the violence they experienced and the status that it would give them. She feared a development in which feminists would try to emphasize battering experiences. In the end, Mahoney argued, the "battered woman" would end up as a more "worthy" recipient of special support, which would implicitly create an image that might be detrimental to the "regular" and "less worthy" welfare mother who was supposed to be able to get a job or leave the unhappy marriage since she was not battered.[46] The portrayal of abused women could lead to a divide-and-conquer strategy: abused women would become the new deserving recipients of less harmful welfare policies, and implicitly all others would be undeserving recipients for whom the punitive new directions in welfare reform are acceptable, so the argument went. This has not happened. On the contrary, creating two symbolic and paradigmatic categories of welfare recipients—the single or divorced mother as the "regular" welfare client and the battered woman who deserves an exception—has in fact amplified the marginalization of the battered woman and has undermined her entitlement to welfare until she proves that she is a responsible woman in the eyes of the law. American discourse on the right to welfare is essentially connected to a discourse on responsibilities (as the new euphemism for obligations). It is precisely this convergence of the discourse of responsibilities with the discourse on violence and exit from abusive relationships that seems to have made the battered woman into a less deserving welfare recipient.

The FVO's failure illustrates how the granting of a legal provision through an appeal for group-based rights has not brought the kind of support that the FVO amendment to the welfare law intended. The very creation of special rights for battered women created an opportunity for the offensive rhetoric of stigmatization and inaugurated a policy that in fact led to the *exclusion* of the majority of battered women on welfare and in need of special assistance who were the initial target of the provision.[47]

---

46. Martha Mahoney, Images of Battered Women, Presentation at the Law & Society Meeting in Glasgow (July 1996); e-mail from Martha Mahoney (Oct. 11, 2000) (on file with author).

47. Maurice Goldman gives a recent example of how the Personal Responsibility and Work Opportunity Reconciliation Act of 1996 (the "Welfare Reform Act") and the Illegal Immigration Reform and Immigrant Responsibility Act of 1996 ("IIRIRA") particularly exclude battered immigrant women from support they were initially provided with under the Violence Against Women Act of 1994. Both the Welfare Reform Act and IIRIRA prevent immigrant women from collecting any federal aid unless they fall within specific exceptions. Because of these statutes, an abused immigrant who leaves her spouse will be homeless and without economic support. Maurice Goldman, *The Violence Against Women Act: Meeting its Goal in Protecting Battered Immigrant Women*, 37 FAM. & CONCIL. CTS. REV. 375 (1999).

III. THE DUTCH CASE: LIMITED PROTECTION OF BATTERED AND STALKED WOMEN

A. *AWARE: Electronic Alarms to Protect Victims of Stalking*

As an attempt to better protect battered women who are stalked by their former partners, technological developments in the private commercial domain in electronic alarm systems have found their way into the criminal justice system, both in the United States and in Europe.[48] In this section I will focus on a project called AWARE (Abused Women's Active Response Emergency). In this project, the home of the woman—who no longer lives with the abuser—is secured by an electronic alarm system that she can set off at home by pushing a button when her ex-partner approaches and/or threatens her. The woman also receives a remote pendant that she can carry with her, and it enables her to set off the alarm up to 300 feet around the house, in cases the abuser stalks her in the street around the victim's house. The alarm is connected to the security company who immediately inform the police upon receiving the alarm. Once the police are informed, the policy is to immediately send a patrol car to the woman's house in order to arrest the perpetrator. In 1991, the first AWARE project started in Winnipeg, Canada. As of 2001, AWARE has been implemented in 160 cities in the United States.[49] So far, no empirical research has been done in the United States nor in Canada into the effectiveness of the AWARE program. In the Netherlands the first pilot project was launched in 1998 by the Rotterdam police in conjunction with various social services and a women's health care center. During the project's pilot stage, we conducted an exploratory in-depth study into the system's implementation.[50] Given that this study provides the only and most recent data available internationally, in this part I will present some core data from that study.[51] Although generalizations must be limited, such data nonetheless can provide insights into certain problems that are indicative of wider underlying issues concerning the invocation of the criminal legal system

48. *See also* DAVID GARLAND, THE CULTURE OF CONTROL: CRIME AND SOCIAL ORDER IN CONTEMPORARY SOCIETY (2001) (pointing out that increasing cooperation between the private sector and criminal justice system is one of the ways in which the rapidly developing culture of crime control over the past decades manifests itself).

49. *See* ADT, AWARE PROGRAM LOCATIONS, *at* http://www.adt.com/divisions/residential/in_your_community/aware_locations.cfm (last visited Nov. 13, 2001). In 1995, a comparable project started for the first time in Europe, in Great Britain (where the project is called Linkline) and two years later in the Netherlands. *See* RENÉE RÖMKENS & SYLVIA MASTENBROEK, DAN HOOR JE DE VISSEN ADEMEN: OVER BELAGING EN BEDREIGING VAN VROUWEN DOOR HUN EX-PARTNER EN DE BEVEILIGING DOOR HET AWARE-SYSTEEM [THEN YOU HEAR FISH BREATHE: ON STALKING OF WOMEN BY THEIR EX-PARTNERS AND PROTECTION THROUGH THE AWARE-SYSTEM] 10-11 (1999). These projects implement the electronic alarm system in all kinds of variations. What varies in particular are the conditions for the alarm connection, who wears the pendant, the period of connection and the degree to which the multi-disciplinary approach has been implemented in order to both support and protect the women and to criminally sanction and treat the perpetrator.

50. RÖMKENS & MASTENBROEK (1999), *supra* note 49. *See also* Renée Römkens, *De Paradox van Bescherming en Bestraffing* [The Paradox of Punishment and Protection], NEMESIS 79 (2000).

51. The author is currently engaged in research into the implementation of the AWARE-program in the Domestic Violence Bureau of the District Attorney's Office in King's County, New York. The project is in its earliest stage of data collection. First results will be published in 2002.

to resolve social problems. Here I will focus on essential aspects of the program that are comparable to the way the system is implemented in the United States. I will indicate where the data are specifically relevant within the Dutch criminal legal system (as in the inquisitorial system, without a jury, unlike the American adversarial jury system).

The basic aim of the AWARE project is to provide protection to victims through swift intervention focused on arresting and prosecuting the perpetrators.[52] In order for women to be eligible for the alarm system, the Dutch Selection Committee agreed to use what they labeled as "objective and independent criteria": first, the woman is de facto separated from her partner and maintains no voluntary contact with him; second, she has a restraining or civil protection order; third, there is a police record available indicating earlier assaults; and fourth, the woman is willing to follow through with a criminal prosecution against her ex-partner upon his arrest.[53] These four qualifications show that legal criteria or information from the police were the defining indicators for the seriousness of the violence and stalking. One of the reasons for the Committee to be very strict in selecting which women were provided with the electronic alarm system was what they considered to be the severe character of the criminal justice response (arrest and prosecution).[54] It should be handled carefully to avoid the possibility that women could use the system as a means of retaliation, according to the Committee. The Committee emphasized that it was reluctant to adopt liberal criteria because it feared that women might use the alarm to have ex-partners arrested with a push of the button.

Given these concerns and what they reflect about the expected vengeful motivations attributed to the women, it is interesting to see how the system was distributed (or not) and how it was used by the women in day-to-day practice. During the first half-year of the project, 148 women inquired about the system. Eventually thirty-five women applied for the protection system, expecting that they would meet the selection criteria. All thirty-five women had a history of very severe abuse with repeated injuries that sometimes required hospital treatment.[55] The selection procedure turned out to be highly exclusionary in its

52. A parallel aim is to offer counseling and social services to the victim and to provide treatment to the perpetrator.

53. In the United States the security company that installs the system (ADT) suggests similar criteria for implementing the AWARE program. Most importantly, there must be an imminent danger of attack, the woman must have obtained a restraining order, and she must be willing to prosecute and testify against the batterer. ADT, THE ADT AWARE® PROGRAM: PROTECTION FOR ABUSED WOMEN, *at* http://www.adt.com/divisions/residential/in_your_community/aware.cfm (March 17, 2000).

54. *See* RÖMKENS & MASTENBROEK, *supra* note 49, at 29-38.

55. On average, the women in this study had been divorced for three years. The stalking behavior they were suffering from on and off during most of that time varied from following the woman in the street; violently attacking her in a public space; harassing her and her family members at home or at work with phone calls, letters, or threats to her and the children; or damaging property (car, garden, house), often at night. Two-thirds of the women had fled to a shelter at least once. One in six women moved permanently to escape the stalking, though in most cases the abuser tracked down her new address. This group of applicants without exception experienced severe, chronic traumatization, which caused numerous psychosomatic complaints and depressive symptoms. *Id.* at 108-116.

effect. Of the thirty-five applicants, only one in four women received the alarm system.[56] Two legal criteria turned out to be the biggest obstacles.

First, obtaining the required civil protection order created a high threshold.[57] One in four women withdrew their applications because they were too traumatized and were psychologically not in a condition to deal with all the efforts and paperwork it would take to start the legal procedures to get a protection or restraining order. Some of these women went into hiding while their applications were pending. Further, one in four applicants eventually did not dare to apply for a civil protection order out of fear of retaliation (given that the system would not yet be in place at the time the woman applied for a civil protection order).[58] Women's reluctance to apply for civil protection orders was read as a signal that their ex-partner's behavior was not serious. The underlying notion is that if the violence is really severe, any woman would always want a legal protection order. Calling upon the law becomes then the self-evidentiary proof of seriousness, unlike the victim's own narrative and her perceptions of estimated risks. [59] Of all applicants who eventually did register for protection orders, one in seven was rejected or suspended. There was a great disparity between civil judges' decisions as to when to grant civil protection orders.[60] These data clearly put the assumed objectivity and neutrality of judges' decisions in a different light.[61] An application for a civil protection order is not only a risky enterprise for some battered and stalked women but is an endeavor with an uncertain outcome.

Second, the requirement to show police records as objective evidence regarding the partner's previous abuse and/or stalking behavior created difficulties. Often, women had not reported to the police for fear of revenge from their ex-partners. Several women indicated that in the past the police had advised them to not report abuse or file a complaint because prosecution was not feasible due to lack of evidence, and therefore filing a complaint would be of no use. This left these women, who eventually refrained from applying for AWARE, without so-called objective legal evidence. Further, the qualification of police

---

56. *Id.* at 39-56.

57. Under Dutch civil law, it is a time-consuming and complicated process to obtain a civil order of protection in domestic violence cases. In this study we found that it usually took at least two months for women to receive a civil protection order, which delayed the connection to the AWARE system and enhanced the safety problems. As of now there are no specific legal provisions in the Netherlands, unlike in many states in the United States, that facilitate the issuance of protection orders in cases of domestic violence. *Id.* at 43.

58. Karla Fischer & Mary Rose, *When "Enough is enough": Battered Women's Decision-Making Around Court Orders of Protection*, 41 CRIME & DELINQUENCY 414 (1995).

59. *Id.*

60. *See also* Tatia Jordan, *The Efficacy of the Californian Stalking Law: Surveying its Evolution, Extracting Insights from Domestic Violence Cases*, 6 HASTINGS WOMEN'S L.J. 363, 377 (1995).

61. *See also* Katherine E. Mahoney, *The Myth of Judicial Neutrality: The Role of Judicial Education in the Fair Administration of Justice*, 32 WILLAMETTE L. REV. 785 (1996); J. St. Joan, *Sex, Sense and Sensibility: Trespassing into the Culture of Domestic Abuse*, 20 HARV. WOMEN'S L.J. 263 (1997).

records as more objective than other evidence is questionable, considering the overwhelming data on bias in police records on domestic violence.[62]

A comparison of the nine cases of women who eventually did get the AWARE alarm system and the twenty-seven women who did not indicated that there were no significant differences in severity of abuse or how recent threats were. One must therefore conclude that the legal criteria for eligibility excluded more severely endangered women in need of protection than it included.

B. AWARE and Legal Exclusionary Dynamics

This mostly unintended exclusionary effect was a direct consequence of the enforcement of legalistic criteria, but was masked by invoking ideological notions regarding the "neutrality" and "objectivity" of these criteria. Information on the abuse provided by the applicant herself or evidenced by non-legal documents—even medical records—was explicitly considered to be more subjective and therefore not only insufficient but also less reliable. This illustrates the ease with which law can endow itself with the mantle of power and situate itself as a producer of a superior kind of knowledge, where concepts like "neutrality" and "objectivity" are taken as flowing self-evidently from the praxis of the legal system. In doing so, law turns out to be an impaired instrument with an inherently limited capacity to validate women's experiences.[63] It comes as no surprise, then, that law excludes many women from the protection it purports to offer.

This exclusionary effect is related to the shift that took place in the implementation of the project—from protecting the victim to prosecuting the perpetrator as the central goal. We might consider this as a highly ironic example of what Reva Siegel has identified as "preservation through transformation" (i.e., the preservation and perpetuation of the privileged status of men that can be observed in several legal reforms in the United States in the area of domestic violence).[64] This shift to prioritizing prosecution is an unintended consequence of providing support to victims within the criminal legal context that is by definition primarily oriented toward the perpetrator. If criminal law defines the conditions under which protection to the victim is offered, it will do so on its terms. For police and prosecutors, numbers of arrests and convictions count as material proof of their success. They measure their production by arrest and conviction rates, not by a victim's increased feelings of safety. So when determining a woman's eligibility for the alarm system, estimating the chances for a successful prosecution of the perpetrator seems to be a primary goal. This is

62. The records of earlier police interventions retrieved in this study most often showed clear tendencies of minimization of violence (e.g., referring to "marital quarrel" or "relational problems"). *See* Ruth E. Fleury et al., *What Happened Depends on Whom You Ask: A Comparison of Police Records and Victim Reports Regarding Arrests for Woman Battering*, 26 J. CRIM. JUST. 53 (1998).

63. *Id.* at 58.

64. Reva Siegel, *"The Rule of Love": Wife Beating as Prerogative and Privacy*, 105 YALE L.J. 2117, 2118 (1996).

paradoxical because after all, the AWARE system could serve as a deterrent, since the ex-partner might refrain from further stalking in order to avoid being arrested. Furthermore, the reason for prioritizing police documentation and civil protection orders was that they provided the "objective" data necessary to build a criminal case that might take place in the future. From the very beginning, achieving the goal of a successful prosecution overshadowed the related goal of providing protection to women. Although there is no reason to position prosecution and protection in opposition to each other since the one does not necessarily exclude the other, the question remains: Why should prosecution of the defendant count as a primary goal if it is to be achieved at the expense of the protection of many victims?[65]

In a project unequivocally aimed at protecting and supporting battered and stalked women, the law does so on its own conditions. It is constructed according to the terms of a dominant legal culture that does not necessarily take into account the woman's best interests. It is illuminating to note that the Dutch women whose houses were eventually secured with the alarm system were reluctant to use it. The women want to get protection and safety from the alarm system, yet they do everything possible to avoid a full-blown intervention of the criminal justice system which would force them to play the assigned role of testifying victims in a regime that they dislike for a variety of reasons.[66] This illustrates that women are in fact trying to be creative in using the alarm and the criminal justice system connected to it, in their own way, which does not necessarily fit the criminal justice logic of trigger-happy law enforcement. The women prioritize protection and peace of mind for themselves and their children, and knowing they can set off the alarm if necessary meets their primary need—to get protection. Punishment or prosecution of ex-partners does not seem to be a priority for the victims. This calls into question the presumed vengefulness of battered women that caused the Selection Committee to be so strict in assigning the system. The fact that women rarely use the alarm also raised the question among the legal professionals involved in the AWARE program as to whether the system is successful.[67] Again we see the criminal legal system defines

---

65. *See* JEFFREY FAGAN, NATIONAL INSTITUTE OF JUSTICE, THE CRIMINALIZATION OF DOMESTIC VIOLENCE: PROMISES AND LIMITS 39 (1996) (noting that the double goals of punishment of offenders and protection of victims "may be reciprocal as policy but may be in conflict at the operational level").

66. *See* RÖMKENS & MASTENBROEK, *supra* note 49, at 57-61. In order to protect women, a powerful and normative intervention is invoked that affects both women's privacy and agency. *See* Sally Engle Merry, *Wife Battering and the Ambiguities of Rights*, *in* IDENTITIES, POLITICS, AND RIGHTS, *supra* note 7, at 271-306; Donna Coker, *Crime Control and Feminist Law Reform in Domestic Violence Law: A Critical Review*, 4 BUFF. CRIM. L. REV. 801, 814-20 (2001); Linda Mills, *Mandatory Arrest and Prosecution Policies for Domestic Violence: A Critical Literature Review and the Case for More Research to Test Victim Empowerment Approaches*, 25 CRIM. JUST. & BEHAV. 306 (1998). Empirical research illustrates that in calling upon the law for protection we run the risk of invoking interventions that might even harm women in order to end domestic violence. *See* Mills, *supra* note 6. Recent empirical findings again demonstrate that the deterrent effect of arrest on future violence by the perpetrator is virtually absent. *See* Judith McFarlane et. al., *Women Filing Assault Charges on an Intimate Partner: Criminal Justice Outcome and Future Violence Experienced*, 6 VIOLENCE AGAINST WOMEN 396 (2000).

67. Preliminary data from the Brooklyn DA's Office in Kings County, New York on the experiences with the AWARE electronic alarm system confirms this picture. Since the start of the AWARE program in Brooklyn in 1995, 242 women have been in the program, 54 of whom are currently active. Only five activations of the alarm

success within its own paradigm and exclusively on its own criminal legal terms (e.g., arrests and prosecutions) not in terms of increased safety for the victims. Based on the research findings partly presented here, the Rotterdam police have expressed a willingness to reconsider a less stringent enforcement of legal criteria for entering the program, notably the civil protection order.

IV. THEORETICAL REFLECTIONS AND DISCUSSION

There are many differences between the two projects, and the qualitative and exploratory nature as well as the limited numbers of women involved in each of the studies urges appropriate caution in drawing broad conclusions. Despite the fact that part of the problem relates to shortcomings in the implementation of regulations underlying both programs, administrative improvements would not resolve the underlying cause of the problems. These examples illustrate several more structural dynamics inherent in legal regulation and legally-based policy developments that can inform further reflection on how group-based laws work when implemented on an individual level in domestic violence cases.

Both projects show several paradoxes that law as a regulatory mechanism implies. Most notably they illustrate that the invocation of law can be more detrimental and less emancipatory than its advocates had hoped. Legal rights do not merely provide entitlements for individual subjects that stand above and outside politics. As much as rights can emancipate, they regulate and can constrain at the same time. As Michel Foucault has argued, in law's regulatory work, its subversion is implied.[68] Unlike what early feminist activism suggested (equating the personal as political and vice versa), there certainly can be a dilemma at stake between satisfying "personal" and "political" needs. From a political point of view, group rights—in this case rights for battered women—are grounded in legal and political recognition because they serve the primary aim of a political strategy. However, successful campaigns in the politics of recognition win on terms set not by the rights holders but by larger institutional forces.[69] The political interests and values of these institutions do not always converge with the individual's, and thus the demand for recognition often entails damaging "misrecognition" by others.[70] Let me emphasize again that the question is not whether we should be for or against rights or special provisions for battered women. Instead, we should focus on the following: How emancipatory and effective are rights in terms of bringing justice to and supporting women? Where can rights go wrong? Which cultural and political contexts impact the law? How can representations of battered women help explain the unforeseen impacts of regulations that were intended to provide legal support?

---

resulted in an arrest. The number of alarm activations by women that did not result in an arrest is fewer than ten. Interview with Deidre Biallo-Padin, Chief, Domestic Violence Bureau, in Brooklyn, NY (Nov. 9, 2001).

68. *See generally* MICHEL FOUCAULT, THE HISTORY OF SEXUALITY: AN INTRODUCTION (1974).

69. Charles Taylor, *The Politics of Recognition*, *in* MULTICULTURALISM: EXAMINING THE POLITICS OF RECOGNITION, 25 (Amy Gutman ed., 1994).

70. *Id.*

I will reflect upon two dynamics that seem to play a crucial role in understanding the potential counterproductive effect of legal regulation: the impact of legalizing the social identity of the battered woman and the impact of legalizing a complex social and personal conflict like violence against women in intimate relationships.

A. Legalizing Social Identities and Essentializing Social Ills

Both cases exemplify a paradoxical shift in the representation of the victim of domestic violence. While there is a growing social and political awareness of the epidemic of abuse of women, that informed both initiatives, in their day-to-day practice both projects move toward a more restrictive definition of the "real" or "worthy" victim who deserves compassion, support, and protection through the criminal justice and welfare systems. Well-meaning policy has excluded many battered women from support under the FVO and from the protection of the alarm system. The legal categorization of "battered women"—or any other identity category for that matter—defines the class of rights holders in terms that are deeply normative, not just descriptive. Thus, all who seek the law's protection and legal recognition must conform their identities to that regulatory, normative frame. The paradoxical and inevitable result is that, precisely when the abuse of women shifts from a private into a public issue, many women are excluded from the benefits that are attached to that official category of battered woman. Both cases exemplify that political or legal strategies always have meanings that exceed their original purposes, and exclusion might be an unintended yet significant meaning.

The category of the battered woman is necessarily reified into a legal identity, of which women must prove themselves to be members. In both cases a profound distrust of the battered woman's own narrative operates in combination with the legal ideology of objectivity, rendering it difficult to prove membership in this category for those who appeal to law for protection against domestic violence. This paradox exemplifies the principal constraint of emancipatory politics in late modernity: subjects and practices are always at risk of being resubordinated and disciplined through the discourses naming and politicizing them.[71] While striving toward visibility and acceptance, the legal language of recognition can become the language of constraint.[72] Battered women are no exception to this power dynamic. Law making and policy development rest on the assumption of a paradigmatic victim. This is inevitably a stereotypical victim who rarely exists in everyday life. Legal rights are by definition generalized, abstract provisions and their ability to meet the concrete needs of individuals is therefore structurally constrained and certainly not guaranteed.

The legal category of the battered woman is based on past or current injury that law seeks to remedy. We might therefore look to the debate on law and

71. *See* FOUCAULT, *supra* note 68.

72. WENDY BROWN, STATES OF INJURY (1995).

identity politics. In rights regimes, law creates a politicized identity as a vehicle for protection or support, and this identity is both regulatory and controlling in its unintended consequences. As Wendy Brown observed: "The emancipatory function of rights cannot be adjudicated in abstraction from the judicial apparatus through which they are negotiated . . . . Rights may subject us to intense arms of bureaucratic domination and regulatory power even at the moment that we assert them in our own defense."[73] We could say that the welfare state produces welfare subjects through various categories of need, of which the victim of domestic violence is one. In that context, the battered woman has become "a normativized social identity that is manageable by regulatory regimes."[74]

By creating specific categories to include victims of domestic violence and battered women in the groups that are provided rights or benefits such as welfare and protection, the law invariably invokes exclusionary mechanisms to limit the number of women to whom the rights are granted, and in doing so it tends to undermine the values that motivated inclusion. This limitation is inherent in law's individualizing nature, even when law-makers are motivated by concern for battered women and a desire to actively assume responsibility for their support. One of the discursive powers of law is that it recasts social dynamics as characteristics of individuals.[75] In the realm of domestic violence, legal regulations seem particularly likely to have this individualizing and exclusionary effect. In both of the projects I discuss, creating the legal category "the victim of domestic violence" both reflects and reinforces ambivalence about the complex constraints on choices that battered women face. Male violence toward women in intimate heterosexual relationships touches upon deeply rooted cultural ambiguities regarding the recognition of domestic violence as a social and political harm rather than an individual's bad fate.[76]

Several authors have noted that in the debate on the current crisis in the welfare state, there is a tendency to essentialize social ills into individual failure to provide an illusion of certainty and normalcy to the wider population in current society.[77] Jock Young has labeled one aspect of this process "the vendetta

73. *Id.* at 120-21.

74. *Id.* at 59.

75. *See id.* at 128.

76. For a clear example of this cultural ambivalence regarding the social nature of family violence, see *DeShaney v. Dept. of Soc. Serv.*, *supra* note 4. In the context of a discussion on the recent increase in use of shelters by women and children in New York City during the winter of 2001, Mayor Giuliani of New York City stated that "many people fabricate stories of domestic violence in order to get into a shelter." National Public Radio (March 5, 2001). This was the Mayor's response to a reporter's suggestion that the increase might have reflected the impact of a publicity campaign that ran in the winter of 2001 in the subways of NYC, urging battered women to seek help earlier. This statement reflects the profound and pervasive disbelief about wife abuse that coexists with the urge to help battered women. This cultural amibguity leads to a classic double bind for many battered women who are urged to speak out and seek help: damned if you do, damned if you do not. For a more extensive discussion of cultural ambiguities, see Part IV.B.

77. *See, e.g.*, JOCK YOUNG, THE EXCLUSIVE SOCIETY (1999); *see also* BAUMAN, *supra* note 18.

against the single mother."[78] Like the single mother, the divorced or single battered woman is often characterized as an individual who fails to take responsibility. In this way, the battered woman becomes a social and normativized identity that is managed by the current welfare regime in the United States. In both cases discussed in this paper, one's membership in the legal category is proven through formal legal documentation; the presumed lack of credibility, reliability or responsibility of domestic abuse victims explicitly justifies the need for such proof. The category of the battered woman triggers archetypal notions about blame, revenge and responsibility—or more accurately, the lack thereof. The representation of the battered woman, and more generally of the domestic violence victim, regularly shifts from a group category of "deserving victims" during the stage of lawmaking, to a category of potentially flawed, unreliable, irresponsible, exaggerating, and undeserving individuals in its day-to-day legal implementation of laws that were originally intended to protect and support women.

B. Legalizing Social Conflicts and Cultural Ambivalences

Very specific socio-political motives informed feminist strategies from the beginning of the 1970s in the appeal to the law to legitimate domestic violence as a social and political problem and to lay a solid foundation for the state's responsibility to ensure and protect battered women's rights. However, the strategic focus on the problem by activists and policy makers alike as one that demands a legal solution can also be understood as reflecting a more general social trend in late modernity toward an increasing juridification—certainly in the United States through civil law—of the interaction between individual citizens. Some theorists relate this to increasing individualization and to a decrease of social cohesion and a loss or diminishment of traditional social support structures on a community level that might be helpful in creating extralegal solutions to conflicts.[79] Social and cultural changes toward a more atomized society have increased the need for impersonal ways to effectuate our rights and resolve conflicts. At the same time we witness the increasing enforcement of criminal laws as well as the criminalization of behaviors that formerly were considered to be social ills at worst. Local and national governments, notably in the United States, have increasingly embraced the ideology of "law and order," which sets off a rhetoric that associates poverty

78. YOUNG, *supra* note 77, at 197. It is important to note that the category of "single mother" is overdetermined by race in the United States more than in the United Kingdom, where Young's analysis is primarily situated.

79. *Id. See also* Robert D. Putnam, *Bowling Alone: America's Declining Social Capital*, 6 J. DEMOCRACY 65 (1995). Jeffrey Rosen commented recently on the "litigation explosion" in the United Staets and particularly on the increasing reliance on the vocabulary of law in everyday interaction. According to Rosen this signals a social transformation due to "a breakdown of traditions of trust and manners." "As traditional authorities find themselves under siege, citizens increasingly turn to laws and legalisms to resolve their social and political disputes." Jeffrey Rosen, *In Lieu of Manners*, N.Y. TIMES MAGAZINE, Feb. 4, 2001 at 6:46.

with criminality and in effect monitors and controls people living in lower class neighborhoods.[80] The two cases presented here illustrate the unholy marriage of the declining welfare state and an increasing reliance on the criminal justice system to monitor and regulate society.[81]

Within a legalistic approach, domestic violence is inevitably framed in a discourse of rights and responsibilities, which is often based on an unproblematized distinction between the private and public realm. There is a clear distinction assumed between domestic violence as a private issue, and therefore predominantly a matter of individual responsibility, and domestic violence as a part of the social and public domain, and therefore the state's responsibility. Violence against women defies this conceptualization of the private-public opposition, and certainly defies a logical conceptualization of the problem in terms of a right to respect of bodily integrity. A battered woman's ambivalence about leaving a violent relationship is experienced not as conflicting rights between her and her partner, but as conflicting responsibilities and conflicting desires to care for herself and her children on the one hand and for her partner on the other. The rhetoric and ethics of rights and legal responsibilities have severe limitations because they fail to capture the paradoxes these women face.[82]

The problems that arise when domestic violence is defined as a social conflict that enters into the legal realm illustrate some of the limitations inherent to the politics of law. The legal context in which support for battered women is framed usually offers an inflexible and limited set of tools that is not well equipped to deal with ambivalence. And it is ambivalence that pervades all aspects of domestic violence, not only among the victims. The responses that battered women's experiences evoked during the implementation of the legal provisions I presented revealed a deeply-ingrained ambivalence in society toward domestic violence generally, and toward the category of battered women in particular, that undermines support for battered women. In the past decades a shift has taken place toward a more principled rejection of the use of violence in intimate relationships. In the abstract we abhor domestic violence and have made it into an illegal act, a crime for which the perpetrators can be held accountable, be arrested, put in jail, or subjected to treatment programs, and for which the victims deserve our support. In spite of these political commitments, publicity

80. Zygmunt Bauman argues that in the postmodern era of globalization most nation-states have two faces. On the one hand there is the "Social State," which guarantees minimal securities for its citizens but increasingly serves only the middle class, especially in the United States. On the other hand there is the "Charitable State," which through the use of law and order supports and also controls the poor population, notably African-Americans. This "charitable" aspect of the state is based on a moralizing conception of poverty. ZYGMUNT BAUMAN, GLOBALIZATION: THE HUMAN CONSEQUENCES 103 (1998).

81. *See also* GARLAND, *supra* note 48.

82. *See* Römkens (1991), *supra* note 41 (arguing that an ethics of care might offer a theoretical and political framework to reflect upon the role of the state in providing care to citizens or creating the conditions under which (female) citizens are better equipped to take care of themselves and others). *See also* CAROL GILLIGAN, IN A DIFFERENT VOICE: PSYCHOLOGICAL THEORY AND WOMEN'S DEVELOPMENT (1982) (distinguishing between a "voice of justice" and a "voice of care" in moral reasoning and arguing that these different ethical voices reflect attention to rights versus responsibilities, respectively); Tronto *supra* note 19.

campaigns, shelters, and various legal policies that express support for battered women, the attitude toward individual victims in the implementation of law and policy remains at best ambiguous. The construction discussed above of the battered woman as a moral failure reflects this clearly. From a cultural-psychological perspective the battered woman almost needs to be othered[83] into the stereotypical lower-class and racialized (black) "helpless" victim, with no alternative but to go to a shelter. That popular representation protects the (white) middle- and upper-class self-image that rests upon the assumption so crucial to Western civilization that "we" are in control of our aggression and violence.[84] No matter how we as a society want to recognize battering as a social problem, the othering of the battered woman persists because domestic violence is so prevalent that it is too close for comfort.[85] The image of battered women as a typical lower class problem allows the association of domestic violence with poverty, hence with irresponsibility and lack of credibility, as we saw in both projects. This othering and moralizing approach to the battered woman is most blatantly visible in the cultural obsession with the issue of exit and the rhetorical question that is always at hand: that "we" do not understand why battered women do not leave and that "we" would most certainly leave if this would happen to us—thereby positioning the author of the question on the right side of

83. *See* Yael Danieli, *Countertransference in the Treatment and Study of Holocaust Survivors and their Children*, 5 VICTIMOLOGY: AN INT'L. J. 355 (1980) (describing how countertransference mechanisms are common in the treatment and study of Jewish Holocaust survivors and are reflected in the defensive grouping of clients into a larger social category (e.g., "passive Jews"). Doing so enables therapists to distance themselves from their individual clients' suffering when that resonates with undealt-with pain for the therapist, particularly when the therapist is Jewish. Danieli suggests that these dynamics are often also at stake among researchers vis-a-vis their research subjects.).

84. *See* NORBERT ELIAS, UEBER DEN PROZESS DER ZIVILIZATION [THE CIVILIZING PROCESS] (1939) (analyzing the development of "etiquette" in Western Europe and arguing from a sociological and psychoanalytic perspective that controlling and ritualizing public display of violence has been crucial to Western civilization and the self-image of Western individuals).

85. A comparison of data from reliable representative surveys reveals that at least one in eleven women in Western Europe and North America has been severely and repeatedly abused by a male partner at some point in her life, and this abuse has resulted in injuries that required medical treatment. *See generally* Malcom Gordon, *Definitional Issues in Violence Against Women*, 6 VIOLENCE AGAINST WOMEN 747 (2000); Carol Hagemann-White, *European Research on the Relevalence of Violence Against Women*, VIOLENCE AGAINST WOMEN 732 (2001).

A Dutch national survey on domestic violence conducted in 1985 was one of the first that provided representative data indicating that abuse of women is not statistically correlated to any socio-economic class. Renée Römkens, *Prevalence of Wife Abuse in the Netherlands. Combining Quantitative and Qualitative Methods.* JOURNAL OF INTERPERSONAL VIOLENCE 99 (1997). *See also* Holly Johnson, *Rethinking Survey Research on Violence Against Women, in* RETHINKING VIOLENCE AGAINST WOMEN 23. (R. Emerson Dobash, R. Dobash eds., 1998). For estimates on violence in same-sex relationships see SAME-SEX DOMESTIC VIOLENCE (Beth Leventhal & Sandra Lundy eds.,1999). An unintended effect of the battered women's movement is that in the public discourse on battering a stereotype of domestic violence has been created that facilitates this othering dynamic. The public image of the battered woman is based on the representation of those few women who are visible: battered women who turn to the police or live in shelters, who are virtually always poor and with few social resources. (Incidental "celebrity cases" that catch the media's attention, such as the abuse and alleged homicide of Nicole Brown Simpson by OJ Simpson in the early nineties, hardly seem to affect the dominant image of battering as a lower-class problem). *See, e.g.* DONNA FERRATO, LIVING WITH THE ENEMY (1991) (portraying pictures of predominantly poor, lower-class women who experienced abuse from their husbands or boyfriends). The book contains only one story of a relatively wealthy couple in which the wife was severely abused, and one on "the wife of a top government official . . . puncturing the myth that only the poor get battered." *Id.* at 131.

the dividing line because s/he knows when to leave, s/he is not a victim and silencing in shame those addressed who might be a victim. The confrontation with domestic violence inevitably triggers profound, albeit mixed, feelings of discomfort, disengagement, pain, sadness, confusion or anger, all of which consciously or subconsciously fuel our judgment and our response to these situations. It requires intense training to be aware of the complexities at stake, both from the perspective of professionals and from the victims' perspectives, in order to develop a well-informed, open-minded and supportive attitude.[86] Without proper training the day-to-day decision making used in implementing law or policies reveals highly individual prejudices, biases and moral judgements. When dealing with violence in intimate relationships, the rush to judgment on an individual level fits neatly with the cultural ambivalence, and subsequently the limit of our tolerance and support is easily revealed. As we saw in these projects and their underlying aim, the battered woman is considered to be deserving of compassion as a victim of a violent crime, yet the violence is minimized when she does not translate it into legal actions like filing a complaint or applying for a protection order. She is held morally responsible for her victimization, at least partly, as long as she does not leave; and she can simply leave, "because every house has a front door you can walk through," as I heard a judge once say in court to a battered woman who had killed her spouse. She bears responsibility for her victimization simply because it takes place in an intimate relationship. In the political and legal rhetoric we see the language of choice creeping in, "masking coercion as private desire." [87] The liberal legalistic distinction between the private and public domain has come full circle, disguising the many structural constraints battered women may face, and de facto excluding them from the very provisions intended to support them.

V. CONCLUSION

Recognition of the public nature of private violence against women has been achieved to some degree, as has the recognition of the public obligation that flows therefrom. [88] However, the shift from abuse of women as a "private" into a "public" issue is not without ambivalence and social resistance.[89] Too often the public obligation and/or public responsibility in the case of domestic violence is read as a need of *legal* regulation as if the law would provide a solid enough power basis to overcome that resistance. Within feminist legal theory there are ample reasons to keep reflecting on whether and how law operates and under

86. Immediately after the FVO was launched it was stressed that an essential element of successful implementation of the FVO was educating applicants and recipients of public assistance about domestic violence. Another key element was training for all personnel on domestic violence and its effects on victims and survivors. *See* Pollack and Davis, *supra* note 23, at 1087.

87. BROWN, *supra* note 72, at 123.

88. *See* Jane Maslow Cohen, *Private Violence and Public Obligation: The Fulcrum of Reason, in* THE PUBLIC NATURE OF PRIVATE VIOLENCE 349 (Martha A. Fineman & Roxanne Mykituk eds., 1994).

89. *See generally* ELIZABETH M. SCHNEIDER, BATTERED WOMEN AND FEMINIST LAWMAKING (2000).

what conditions it can be an empowering tool to support or protect women's safety. The suggestion that there exists a "dialectic relationship" between politics and feminist lawmaking in the field of domestic violence,[90] often seems to be premised upon the optimistic assumption that political struggles and the struggle for rights inform each other in a way that leads to progress or will at least bring more social justice. Without denying or minimizing that the entrance of domestic violence into the arena of law has brought about legal provisions and social changes that can support and empower women, the intervention of law also often takes its toll. Law can have a beneficial effect, but only for a limited number of women and at a considerable price. This exemplifies how law in its implementation can be violent in and of itself.[91]

The legal interventions and projects as described in this paper give reason for skepticism given the powers that the law invokes, that are *inherent* in the law and that undermine the intended goal of the intervention. When calling upon the law it is important that we acknowledge the paradoxical effects and the dilemmas at stake which might not be easy or even possible to resolve, but which might protect us against naive optimism. Law can disappoint us because it is often ineffective, or even damaging, precisely because it operates within a self-proclaimed rational, and certainly dichotomous and adversarial style that is not able to deal with complex and conflicting realities that battered women confront. This raises the question of how the emancipatory goal of a law surfaces in the face of other goals the law shares, as law in its implementation is embedded and operates as part of powerful institutionalized regimes, such as the bureaucracy of a welfare regime, that impose ideologies of their own. In a culture that values law as the ultimate instrument to protect and deliver "justice," "freedom" and "liberty," and in which political problems are thought best resolved by legal solutions, it is difficult to fundamentally question law.[92] If the law indeed can help to legitimate or even might ease human suffering, we should not forget the "juridogenic" characteristics of law that can make things worse.[93] If we appeal to law, we sometimes call upon a Trojan horse: when we invite law in, law re-invites itself time and again, but on its own terms and with its own agenda.

---

90. *Id.* at 6.

91. *See* Robert M. Cover, *Violence and the Word,* 95 YALE L. J. 1601-29 (1986); LAW'S VIOLENCE (Austin Sarat & Thomas R. Kearns eds., 1992).

92. *See, e.g.,* Naomi Cahn, *Policing Women: Moral Arguments and the Dilemmas of Criminalization,* 49 DEPAUL L. REV. 817, 825 (2000) (critiquing criminal law's limited ability to support victims, and pleading to make more use of civil law).

93. *See* CAROL SMART, supra note 7 at 12 ("Just as medicine is seen as curative rather than *iatrogenic,* so law is seen as extending rights rather than creating wrongs. It is perhaps useful to coin the term *juridogenic* to apply to law as a way of conceptualizing the harm that law may generete as a consequence of its operations.")

[18]

(MIS)IDENTIFYING CULTURE: ASIAN WOMEN AND THE "CULTURAL DEFENSE"

Leti Volpp

17 *Harv. Women's L.J.* 57 (1994) (Excerpts)

I. INTRODUCTION

The "cultural defense"[1] is a legal strategy that defendants use in attempts to excuse criminal behavior or to mitigate culpability based on a lack of requisite mens rea.[2] Defendants may also use "cultural defenses" to present evidence relating to state of mind when arguing self defense or mistake of fact. The theory underlying the defense is that the defendant, usually a recent immigrant to the United States, acted according to the dictates of his or her "culture," and therefore deserves leniency.[3] There is, however, no formal "cultural defense"; individual defense attorneys and judges use their discretion to present or consider cultural factors affecting the mental state or culpability of a defendant.[4] In my discussion of this strategy, I focus on the significance of its use for Asian women.

When examining the "cultural defense" and its effect on Asian women, I write from the subject position of an Asian American woman.[5] I also write with the benefit of collective insight of Asian American women working with the Asian Women's Shelter in San Francisco, who created the "Cultural Defense" Study Group.[6] The Study Group arose from concern about the use of the "cultural defense" and from the pressing need for Asian American women to articulate a position on its use.

The "cultural defense" presents several complex problems inherent in essentializing a culture and its effect on a particular person's behavior. I analyze the use of the defense in two cases in order to illustrate problems with the defense and situations in which allowing cultural information into the courtroom might be appropriate. I argue that any testimony about a defendant's cultural background must embody an accurate and personal portrayal of cultural factors used to explain an individual's state of mind and should not be used to fit an individual's behavior into perceptions about group behavior.

Presentation of cultural factors must also be informed by a recognition of the multiple, intersectional layers of group-based oppression that may be relevant to understanding any particular case. The concept of intersectionality, which in this context refers to the interplay of racism and sexism in the experiences of women of color, provides a useful analytical tool.[7] Because of our identity as both women and persons of color within discourses shaped to respond to one categorization or the other, women of color exist at the margins of both discourses.[8] Because intersectionality is a methodology that disrupts the categorization of race and gender as exclusive or separable,[9] I argue that an intersectional analysis is essential to an understanding of the relationship of the "cultural defense" to Asian women.

I also explore why the choice of whether or not to support the use of the "cultural defense" is difficult and suggest a strategy for making this choice. I ultimately argue that the value of antisubordination should be used to mediate between a position that totally rejects the defense and a position that embraces a formalized "cultural defense" from the perspective of cultural relativism. I conclude that the formalization of a "cultural defense" should not be promoted, and that a commitment towards ending all forms of subordination should inform the decision of whether or not to support the informal use of cultural information on behalf of a defendant in a given case.

I discuss two cases, *People v. Dong Lu Chen*[10] and *People v. Helen Wu*,[11] in detail because they are representative of the two kinds of cases in which "cultural defenses" involving Asian women have most often been attempted.[12] The first type of case, exemplified in *Chen*, involves an Asian man seeking a "cultural defense" for his violence towards an Asian woman.[13] The second factual pattern, seen in Wu, features an Asian woman seeking to admit cultural factors to explain her mental state when she attempted to commit parent-child suicide.[14]

Both of the cases I examine involve Chinese Americans. I hesitate to focus on these cases because Chinese Americans are frequently used to synecdochically represent all Asian Americans, and I repeat that process here by describing my project as one about "Asian women."[15] Yet, paradoxically, because of the homogeneity into which the dominant community crushes the vast diversity of Asian America,[16] the legal system's treatment of two cases affecting Chinese Americans does reflect popular and legal conceptions of other Asian American communities.[17]

I use the terms "Asian" and "Asian American" at different points throughout this piece in order to emphasize how communities are identified in different contexts. The concept of a "cultural defense" rests on the idea of a community not fully "integrated" into the United States and assists "Asians in America," or "immigrants," as opposed to "Asian Americans." Asian Americans are those whom American society generally assumes to have assimilated into "American culture"[18] to the extent that we do not require a special defense.[19]

Drawing this distinction relies on the problematic positioning of recent immigrants from Asia as "not American." Reserving the term "American" for those who seem fully assimilated erases two important and related factors. The first is the fluid and shifting nature of American identity. The second is the fact that both immigrant and Asian experiences are integral and formative components of American identity. This failure to acknowledge the multiplicity of American identity leaves American identity, and specifically the identity of United States law, a neutral and unquestioned backdrop.[20] One is left with an image of a spoonful of cultural diversity from immigrants ladled onto a flat, neutral base. Creating a "cultural defense" for immigrants in the United States thus rests on the implication that U.S. law is without a culture.[21]

The flawed conception, inherent in a "cultural defense," that recent immigrants have a "culture" while U.S. law does not, promotes an anthropological relationship between the court and the immigrant defendant. The court, through testimony of "experts," conducts an examination of communities not considered to "fit" within the borders of U.S. law. This anthropological relationship is characterized by "expert" presentations of Asian culture that depict Asian communities as static, monolithic and misogynist. This dynamic distances the subject of study by creating an unrecognizable "other" and allows the dominant anthropologist "expert" to subordinate members of the foreign culture through descriptive control.

This Article begins by examining the use of the "cultural defense" in a case that clearly demonstrates its potential to render Asian women invisible by ignoring factors of subordination within their own communities. In Part II, I narrate the case *People v. Dong Lu Chen*.[22] In that case, an Asian woman, Jian Wan Chen, was murdered by her husband. Dong Lu Chen, the defendant, successfully used a "cultural defense" that presented essentialized notions of "Chinese culture" to excuse his actions. By analyzing the expert testimony and decision of the trial judge, I show how the "cultural defense" in that case used a description of "culture" that obliterated any notion of gender oppression.

In Part III, I analyze the response to the *Chen* case among white feminist organizations and Asian American community organizations, which paradigmatically illustrates the tensions that exist between these groups regarding the use of the "cultural defense." I survey reactions to the "cultural defense" both within these communities and within legal literature. I conclude that a new approach to the "defense" is necessary, both to guide appropriate presentations of cultural information within the courtroom, and to inform the choice of whether and when to support admission of a defendant's cultural background.

I examine in Part IV the case of *People v. Helen Wu*,[23] in which the state of California convicted an Asian woman of killing her son. This case illustrates that, despite the problematic positioning of "immigrant," "culture" and "America" inherent in the "cultural defense," many cases will present compelling fact patterns that encourage allowing cultural evidence into the courtroom to explain the defendant's actions as shaped by her particular experiences. But *People v. Helen Wu* also exemplifies the problem of cultural determinism inherent in the use of a "cultural defense": the defense rests on the notion that one's behavior is determined by one's identity. Because what defendants frequently present as "culture" in "cultural defenses" is static and particular, if a defendant's behavior does not sufficiently match what experts describe as "traditional" cultural behavior, she may lose the opportunity offer testimony as to her cultural background.

In Part V, I explain why a formal "cultural defense" would be problematic and why allowing informal testimony is preferable. As an instructive parallel that argues against the creation of a formalized "cultural defense," I describe difficulties engendered by a formalized battered women's syndrome. I explain the importance of an intersectional analysis to understanding how "cultural defenses" impact Asian women and discuss the utility of "strategic essentialism" in determining when to allow "cultural" evidence.

I conclude by describing in Part VI an approach to the "cultural defense" that supports what may appear to be the contradictory interests of Jian Wan Chen, "victim," and Helen Wu, "defendant." I argue that the value of antisubordination should be factored into the decision of whether or not to support use of the defense and that a commitment to antisubordination must entail a simultaneous recognition of material and descriptive oppression based on factors such as race, gender, immigrant status and national origin.[24]

II. INVISIBLE WOMAN: THE *PEOPLE v. DONG LU CHEN*[25]

In 1989, Brooklyn Supreme Court Justice Edward Pincus sentenced Chinese immigrant Dong Lu Chen to five years probation for using a claw hammer to smash the skull of his wife, Jian Wan Chen.[26] The defense sought to demonstrate that the requisite state of mind was lacking by introducing evidence about Chen's cultural background. After listening to a white anthropologist "expert," Burton Pasternak, provide a "cultural defense" for Dong Lu Chen, Pincus concluded that traditional Chinese values about adultery and loss of manhood drove Chen to kill his wife.

The defense introduced most of the information about Dong Lu Chen's cultural background through Pasternak's expert testimony. Defense Attorney Stewart Orden presented Pasternak with a lengthy hypothetical designed to evoke a response about the "difference" between how an "American" and a "Mainland Chinese individual"[27] might respond to a particular set of events. This hypothetical was in fact a history of Dong Lu Chen and provided the defense's explanation for why he killed Jian Wan Chen.[28]

As Orden set forth in this "hypothetical," Dong Lu Chen was fifty-four years old at the time of trial. Since 1968 Dong Lu Chen believed he was hearing voices around him; doctors told him there was something wrong with his mind.[29]

In September, 1986, the Chen family immigrated to the United States. While Dong Lu Chen worked as a dish washer in Maryland, Jian Wan Chen and the three children stayed in New York.[30] During a visit when Jian Wan Chen refused to have sex with him and "became abusive," Dong Lu Chen became suspicious she was having an affair. He returned to Maryland, burdened with the stress of his wife's assumed infidelity.[31]

In June, 1987, Dong Lu Chen moved to New York.[32] On August 24 he rushed into his wife's bedroom and grabbed her breasts and vaginal area. They felt more developed to him and he took that as a sign she was having affairs.[33] When he confronted her the next day, she said she was seeing another man.[34] On September 7, when he again confronted her and said he wanted to have sex, "she said I won't let you hold me because I have other guys who will do this."[35] His head felt dizzy, and he "pressed her down and asked her for how long had this been going on. She responded, for three months."[36] Confused and dizzy, he picked something up and hit her a couple of times on the head. He passed out.[37]

After presenting the above "facts" as part of his hypothetical, Orden asked Pasternak if this history was consistent with reactions "under normal conditions for people from Mainland China."[38] Pasternak responded:

> Yes. Well, of course, I can't comment on the mental state of this particular person. I am not a psychiatrist. I don't know this particular person. But the events that you have described, the reactions that you have described would not be unusual at all for Chinese in that situation, for a normal Chinese in that situation. Whether this person is normal or not I have no idea.... If it was a normal person, it's not the United States, they would react very violently. They might very well have confusion. It would be very likely to be a chaotic situation. I've witnessed such situations myself.[39]

Orden also asked Pasternak to verify that a "normal Chinese person from Mainland China" would react in a more extreme and much quicker way than an "American" to the history as given in the hypothetical.[40] Pasternak answered:

> In general terms, I think that one could expect a Chinese to react in a much more volatile, violent way to those circumstances than someone from

our own society. I think there's no doubt about it.[41]

This initial testimony highlights some important issues. First, the distinction Orden and Pasternak draw between "American," "someone from our own society," and "Chinese" implies that "Chinese" and "American" are two utterly distinct categories: "American" does not encompass immigrant Chinese.[42] This dichotomy rests on the lingering perception of Asians in America as somehow "foreign," as existing in "America" while not being "American."[43] Importantly, the perspective that Chinese living in the United States are not "American" is the very basis for the assertion of the "cultural defense," on the grounds that someone from a distinctly "non-American" culture should not be judged by "American" standards.

Perceiving Chinese living in the United States as American, as part of our policy, significantly affects our responses to Dong Lu Chen. Referring to Dong Lu Chen's identity as a hyphenated identity — Asian American — recognizes the specific histories of people of color in the United States while emphasizing the existence of a community of other Asian Americans that is best situated to evaluate and judge his actions. For reasons discussed further below, members of Asian American communities, particularly community organizations aware of internal power dynamics, should determine the use and content of the "cultural defense."[44]

After dichotomizing "American" and "Chinese," Orden and Pasternak's second step in creating a "cultural defense" was to assert that a man considered "normal" in the category "Chinese" would react very differently from someone in the category "American" to the belief that his wife was having an affair.[45] Their third step collapsed the history of a particular person with specific mental problems into the category "normal person from Mainland China."[46] Finally, Orden's and Pasternak's description of Dong Lu Chen's reaction was predicated on the "stress theory" of violence: abuse happened because the batterer experienced stress. This is a theory much criticized by battered women's advocates who note that batterers choose to abuse power over their victims and that violence is not an automatic stress-induced response beyond batterers' control.[47] As the prosecuting attorney pointed out, Chen waited from August 25, when he was allegedly informed by his wife that she was having an affair, until September 7 to confront his wife violently.[48]

To bolster Pasternak's assertions about Dong Lu Chen's behavior, Orden asked him to testify about the particularities of family life in China. Pasternak spoke of the "extraordinary" difference between "our own" ability and the ability of "the Chinese" to control the community through social sanctions.[49] He added to the "voices" that Dong Lu Chen heard in his head, earlier presented as a sign of mental difficulties, another set of "voices" controlling Chen.[50] Pasternak testified that his "Chinese friends" often said "there is no wall that the wind cannot penetrate," meaning that the voices of social control "will be heard everywhere."[51] Orden and Pasternak repeated these "voices of the community" throughout the trial to signify that in a tradition-bound society like Mainland China, social control is more strict and unchanging than in the West, and that a "Chinese individual" carries these "voices" of social control wherever he goes.

Continuing his description of Chinese familial life and values, Pasternak asserted that "casual sex, adultery, which is an even more extreme violation, and divorce" are perceived as deviations from these social mores.[52] "In the Chinese context," adultery by a woman was considered a kind of "stain" upon the man, indicating that he had lost "the most minimal standard of control" over her.[53] Pasternak contrasted the condemnation of adultery in China with the United States, "where we take this thing normally in the course of an event."[54] He claimed that the Chinese woman was likely to be "thrown out" and that both parties would have difficulty remarrying.[55]

Pasternak proceeded to delineate the ramifications of a woman's adultery for the Chinese man and Chinese woman in the context of the United States.[56] Pasternak relied on his perception of the prevalence of "yellow fever" among white males and the desexualization of Asian men in America to assert that a Chinese "adulteress" would have no problem establishing a relationship with a white man, while the Chinese male cuckold would have no chance of finding a white woman. The Chinese male would be considered a "pariah" among Chinese women because he would be viewed as having been unable to "maintain the most minimal standard of control" within his family.[57]

Pasternak's bizarre portrayal of divorce and adultery in China in fact had little basis in reality.[58]

When Assistant District Attorney Arthur Rigby pressed Pasternak for his sources during cross-examination, Pasternak mentioned fieldwork he did between the 1960s and 1988 (he could not remember the title of his own article), incidents he saw, such as a man chasing a woman with a cleaver, and stories he heard.[59] He admitted he could not recall a single instance in which a man in China killed his wife or having ever heard about such an event, yet he suggested that this was accepted in China.[60] Pasternak's description of "Chinese society" thus was neither substantiated by fact nor supported by his own testimony. The description was in fact his own American fantasy.

During his cross-examination of Pasternak, Rigby attempted to undermine Chen's "cultural defense" by deconstructing Pasternak's identification of "American," his description of Chinese as insulated from Western influence and his depiction of Chinese Americans as completely non-assimilated. Rigby began his questioning by asking, "What would you consider your average American?" Pasternak responded, "I think you are looking at your average American."[61]

With this statement Pasternak situated his own subjective position as the definition of the "average American." In other words, Pasternak defined the "average American" to be a white, professional male. By situating himself as the "average American," Pasternak exposed his subjective identification as the "average American" against whom the "foreigner," Dong Lu Chen, was to be compared. He also demonstrated his identification with masculinity. He thereby abandoned any pretensions towards "objectivity" he might have claimed as an anthropologist and revealed his personal investment in his identity as dominant anthropologist[62] and white male, vis a vis the subordinated Chinese male and female objects of study.

When Rigby pressed Pasternak about whether he meant "Anglo Saxon male" by "average American," Pasternak responded by positioning "us"/"American" and "them"/"Chinese" as "two extremes."[63] When asked to identify what he meant by "American," he replied by describing American as not "Chinese."[64] With this explanation, Pasternak followed a tradition, identified as Orientalism, of dichotimizing the human continuum into "we" and "they" and essentializing the resultant "other."[65] When a dominant group essentializes a subordinated group by focusing on selected traits to describe the group as a whole, the dominant group defines its own characteristics in contrast to the subordinated group.[66] This fetishization of "difference" enabled Pasternak's creation of a "cultural defense" for Dong Lu Chen by depicting gender relations in China as vastly different from gender relations in the United States. The resulting image erased the prevalence of gendered violence in the United States and distanced the United-States-based spectator from both Dong Lu Chen and Jian Wan Chen in a way that rendered them unrecognizable and inhuman.

After challenging Pasternak's definition of "average American," Rigby attacked his depiction of Chinese culture as insular and impermeable by outside influence. Rigby asked whether in the last ten years, since Nixon opened relations with China, China had "embraced Western culture" and if this had a "liberalizing" or "awakening" effect. "No," said Pasternak.[67] This question demonstrated that Rigby as well as Pasternak accepted a construction of China as a "closed" or "conservative" nation slumbering away, as compared to the "advanced" West. Rigby's method of attack thus depended in part on the same stereotypes he attempted to undermine.

Rigby, trying another approach, then asked:

> "Now in a situation where someone from China comes to the United States, let's say, for instance, comes to New York City, how quickly do they assimilate, if at all, the American culture?" Pasternak answered, "Very slowly, if ever.... Of all the Asians who come to this country, from my experience,... the people who have the hardest time adjusting to this society are Chinese. The Japanese do a lot better."[68]

Pasternak's statement obviously served his construction of Dong Lu Chen as inassimilable alien. His response failed to problematize the concept of assimilation, and its complete lack of historical or contextual specification unmasked ludicrous generalizations. Which "Chinese" was Pasternak referring to? Which "Asians?"[69]

Although Orden attempted to point out some of the flaws inherent in Pasternak's characterizations of Chinese culture and its relationship to Jian Wan Chen's death, Justice Pincus was swayed by the "persuasiveness" of Pasternak's testimony about the "cultural" roots of Dong Lu Chen's actions. He held:

> Were this crime committed by the defendant as someone who was born and raised in America, or born elsewhere but primarily raised in America, even in the Chinese American community, the Court [sic] would have been constrained to find the defendant guilty of manslaughter in the first degree. But, this Court[sic] cannot ignore...the very cogent forceful testimony of Doctor Pasternak, who is, perhaps, the greatest expert in America on China and interfamilial relationships.[70]

Pincus specifically found significant Pasternak's testimony that Chen lacked a Chinese community to act as a "safety valve" to keep Chen from killing his wife.[71] Yet the alleged motivation for Chen's actions was his "shame" and humiliation before this very same community. The inconsistency in this reasoning is self-evident.[72]

Pincus attempted to incorporate his newly acquired, inaccurate and essentialized understanding of Chinese culture into his sentencing decisions. At the probation hearing Pincus tried to integrate these lessons about the "Chinese" and how a "Chinese" is motivated by "honor" and "face":

> And I must have a promise from the defendant on his honor and his honor of his family he will abide by all of the rules and conditions that I impose.... And if he does not obey and he violates any of these conditions, not only does he face jail, but this will be a total loss of face.[73]

In his decision to grant probation rather than impose a jail sentence, Pincus also took other unrelated "cultural" considerations into account. Pincus believed that the possible effect of Chen's incarceration on his daughters' marriage prospects should be a factor in determining Chen's sentence. Pincus told a reporter, "Now there's a stigma of shame on the whole family. They have young, unmarried daughters. To make them marriageable prospects, they must make sure he succeeds so they succeed."[74] In the sentencing colloquy Pincus indicated that he also learned that Dong Lu Chen was a "victim":

> Based on the cultural background of this individual he has also succeeded in partially destroying his family and his family's reputation.... There are victims in this case: The deceased is a victim, her suffering is over. The defendant is a victim, a victim that fell through the cracks because society didn't know where or how to respond in time.[75]

Thus Pincus was able to justify his probationary sentencing: Dong Lu Chen did not serve time for killing his wife because in balancing this action and the surrounding circumstances he was just as much a "victim" as she was.[76]

But where was Jian Wan Chen in this story? The defense strategy rendered her invisible. She was most notably present in the testimony as a dead body[77] and as a reputed "adulteress," bringing a "stain" upon her husband.[78] Jian Wan Chen did not exist as a multi-faceted person but was instead flattened into the description "adulteress." Any discussion of her at trial was premised upon her characterization as a woman who provoked her husband into jealousy. How should this flattening be interpreted? This invisibility and erasure of the woman, Jian Wan Chen?

Jian Wan Chen's invisibility involved more than the disappearance of a victim in a trial focused on the guilt or innocence of a defendant. The defense presented a narrative that relied on her invisibility as an Asian woman for its logical coherence. This invisibility was manifest through the absence of Jian Wan Chen as a subject, a void that was filled only by stereotypes of the sexual relationships of "Chinese women" and an image of her silent physicality. She appeared as an object, whose silence devalued her humanity to the extent that the taking of her life did not merit a prison sentence.

Jian Wan Chen's invisibility is a legacy of an intersection of race and gender that erases the existence of women of color from the popular consciousness.[79] Because white male citizens personify what is considered "normal" in the United States, a status as "other" that is more than one deviation away from the "norm" rarely exists in popular consciousness.[80] The exclusion of Jian Wan Chen exemplifies the difficulty that women of color have when attempting to express themselves as holistic subjects, as Asian women whose identity lies at the intersection of multiple forms of subordination.[81]

Applying an intersectional analysis, it is clear that what Pasternak presented as "Chinese culture" privileged race over any consideration of gender oppression. Pasternak's perspective was "male," obviating the possibility that a woman, and specifically a Chinese immigrant woman, might describe divorce, adultery and male violence within "Chinese culture" very differently. The perspective, was, of course, also "white." The "whiteness" of Pasternak's perspective allowed him to situate Dong Lu Chen in a category labelled "Chinese" diametrically opposite to Pasternak's own "average," white, male citizen position. Yet this placement ignored that Jian Wan Chen was, in fact, the person categorically opposite to Pasternak: she was Chinese, immigrant and female. Thus, the "cultural defense" served in this case to legitimize male violence against women by glossing over the gendered aspects of Pasternak's testimony about "culture."

The *Chen* trial suffered from a complete absence of any female perspective: Dong Lu Chen, Pasternak, Orden, Rigby and Pincus were all male. Jian Wan Chen was dead, symbolizing how ideologies that subordinate groups of people literally transpire over the body of an "other." Thus, Jian Wan Chen's invisibility is not only the product of the racist notion that "Asian life is cheap,"[82] it also is a remnant of the indifference with which many in the United States treat the epidemic of violence against women.[83] Furthermore, the complete disregard for her life also reflected the way racism and sexism intersect to render insignificant violence against women of color, and here specifically, Asian immigrant women.

The impact of the trial and probationary sentencing resonated beyond the courtroom, sending a message to the wider community. Jian Wan Chen's life was not valued; her life was worth less than other lives; her murderer did not deserve punishment in jail. Other Chinese immigrant women living with abuse at the hand of their partners and husbands identified with Jian Wan Chen and clearly understood that violence against them by their partners and husbands had the implicit approval of the state.[84]

The Chen decision sent a message to battered immigrant Asian women that they had no recourse against domestic violence. One battered Chinese woman told a worker at the New York Asian Women's Center, "Even thinking about that case makes me afraid. My husband told me: 'If this is the kind of sentence you get for killing your wife, I could do anything to you. I have the money for a good attorney.'"[85] In other words, her husband could afford to hire someone to testify as an expert to bolster a "cultural defense" that legitimized his violence.[86] The New York Asian Women's Center co-director reported that battered women who had previously threatened their husbands with legal sanctions also lost this threat as a means to stop the abuse: "For some women this has worked, but no more. They tell me their husbands don't buy it anymore because of this court decision."[87]

III. RESPONSE TO THE CASE: LIMITED POSITIONS

After Pincus's decision in the *Chen* case, a coalition of Asian American community activists and white feminists protested and planned to file a complaint against Pincus with the state Commission on Judicial Conduct.[88] The coalition, however, rapidly fragmented. White feminists like Elizabeth Holtzman[89] and the National Organization for Women wanted to completely ban any consideration of culture from the courtroom, while Asian American activists from the Organization of Asian Women, the Asian American Legal Defense and Education Fund and the Committee Against Anti-Asian Violence were unable to agree with that position.[90] Asian American groups wanted to be able to retain the possibility of using the "cultural defense" in other contexts. Francoise Jacobsohn, president of the New York City National Organization for Women chapter, said that she understood the concerns of the Asian American organizations but felt frustrated:

> They were afraid that we were going to go around with a battering ram and destroy the whole concept of a cultural defense. But the judge needed to know that we did not find his statements acceptable.[91]

The philosophical division that fragmented this coalition is symptomatic of the split that exists between white feminists and feminists of color. White feminists saw the case as indicating that a defendant's cultural background should never be taken into account in deciding a sentence: according to Holtzman, we should have only "one standard of justice."[92]

Holtzman's position is one example of a number of different responses to the "cultural defense" taken by legal scholars. As yet, none have effectively navigated between the extremes of condemning the defense in all cases or promoting the defense in the interest of cultural pluralism. Neither of the extremes is satisfying because they both fail to acknowledge that the multiple subordinations existing within immigrant communities are relevant to the choice of whether to support the use of the "cultural defense" in any one case.

* * * *

V. THE RISK OF A FORMALIZED DEFENSE

* * * *

Discourse about "race" or "culture" must not obliterate the intersectional oppressions of Asian women, who exist at a nexus of societal racism and sexism in multiple contexts. "Cultural defenses" that focus solely on "cultural difference" with no analysis of gender subordination serve to block out gender oppression and gender difference within Asian American communities. Thus, in the Chen case, the "cultural defense" masked the fact that Jian Wan Chen suffered subordination as a woman and as a victim of gendered violence. The deployment of the "cultural defense" where gender subordination is at issue requires that we examine not only the way that "cultural practices" among Asian men and Asian women are an expression of particular power arrangements, but also the different means by which these practices are maintained and legitimated.[158]

For example, the fact that domestic violence in Asian communities is frequently explained by both Asians and non-Asians as caused or promoted by "Asian culture"[159] is particularly troublesome. This explanation was precisely the "cultural defense" given to Dong Lu Chen. Popular conception in the United States too often understands Asians to be governed by cultural dictates. This misconception is related to the association of "Asian" with "foreign" and "culture" with "other," and leads to dehumanizing descriptions of Asians.[160] I do not mean to deny that there is something we can call "culture" that may explain behavior. My concern is that domestic violence among Asian American communities is explained as "cultural," when a similar description is rarely given to domestic violence in the heterosexual white community. This masks the severity of violence against Asian women by describing it as a "practice" rather than as a political problem. Moreover, to explain behavior as "cultural" implies that it is insular to Asian communities and that the dominant society bears no relationship to that behavior.[161] This hides the fact that Asian women are also subject to oppression from forces outside of Asian communities.

While a formalized "cultural defense" is problematic because it will force defendants' actions to be defined through a group-based identity and reify cultural stereotypes, in some circumstances a defense that presents cultural background will be appropriate. In formulating a legal recourse to the predicament of a particular individual whose behavior was influenced by forces such as racism, sexism and subordination in the form of violence, admission of cultural factors should not function as a reductive "explanation" of that individual's actions as fitting into group behavior or "culture." Rather, the choice to provide an individual defendant with cultural information should be made for the purpose of explaining that individual's state of mind, in much the same way that the criminal law allows other information about a defendant's life history to mitigate sentences or charges in a criminal trial. Even when we attempt to use cultural information to explain an individual's oppressions or her state of mind, we are forced to label and define, in other words, to essentialize, certain behavior as "cultural." This can be done in the spirit of what might be called "strategic essentialism"[162] — consciously choosing to essentialize a particular community for the purpose of a specific political goal.[163] Strategic essentialism ideally should be undertaken by the affected community, which is best situated to undertake the process of selecting the appropriate circumstances in which to offer cultural information.

The defendant's community may be an important resource to provide the court with a "subjective" perspective that serves to explain her actions in the context of their own norms. In *State v. Chong Sun France*,[164] for example, a Korean woman who left her small children alone at night and returned to find one dead was sentenced to twenty years for second degree murder and felonious child abuse. The trial transcript demonstrates a hearing rife with gender, race, and cultural biases, as well as incredible communication difficulties between France and the court.[165] Throughout the hearing, the prosecution portrayed France as a bad mother — irresponsible and negligent

— and as an opportunistic and promiscuous immigrant woman. The court found France guilty, adopting the prosecution's argument that she deliberately placed her son in the bureau drawer and shut him inside, crushing him.[166]

Chong Sun France would have benefitted from "cultural information" from her community. Expert testimony could have provided information to the judge and jury, interpreting her actions as those of a caring but poor Asian woman with few resources to adequately care for her children. France was released on parole on December 31, 1992, after a massive campaign organized by Korean women, who pointed out the lack of culturally specific information in her representation. The campaign's petition provides "cultural information" explaining France's actions from the perspective of other Korean immigrant women and offering information about child care in Korea.[167] While the community's presentation of cultural information runs the risk of essentializing Korean immigrant women in the eyes of the court and of popular culture, the risk can be justified in that it was the affected community of Korean immigrant women who made that strategic choice and also made the choice of what characteristics to present as "cultural information."

VI. MOVING TOWARDS HOME

The juxtaposition of the cases of Dong Lu Chen and Helen Wu flushes into view what may seem to be a number of contradictions. How can one argue that the "cultural defense" for Dong Lu Chen was inappropriate while approving the use of cultural information for women like Helen Wu? Both defendants were accused of killing someone over whom they had power. Both alleged feelings of great stress. Both pointed to cultural determinants as a reason for their actions. I reconcile my divergent positions on the two cases by proposing that the value of antisubordination must be a criterion in the decision as to when and how cultural factors should be presented as a defense.

Antisubordination is a value that the legal system must factor into whether to present testimony as to a defendant's cultural background.[168] Valuing the principle of antisubordination is more than a game of hierarchical rankings of "who's most oppressed"; it means a serious commitment to evaluating and eradicating all forms of oppression.[169] In the cases of Helen Wu and Dong Lu Chen, it can involve making identity-based claims to knowledge about the appropriate political choices to make in balancing the risks of perpetuating stereotypes against fairness to the parties involved. As described above, this process can be called strategic essentialism.

Antisubordination does not posit that those who suffer oppressions lack agency due to their victimization and therefore are not responsible for their crimes. Rather, the agency of an Asian American woman, or of anyone who is the subject of multiple oppressions, exists within a complex arena of fractured structural forces and pressures. A fair presentation of her situation should evaluate her agency within this context. In cases like Chen and Wu, such an evaluation reveals these to be cases about Jian Wan Chen and Helen Wu, both subordinated on the basis of gender as well as impacted by dynamic forces from within and without their communities. The point of antisubordination is not to read every story as a "subordinated woman's story"; rather, it is that one must never explain or close off any story into being just one story.[170]

One step in an antisubordination analysis can be to examine whether the defendant acted with a consciousness of her position within the social structure of her community. Helen Wu resisted what she perceived as subordination out of a set of very narrowly defined choices; Dong Lu Chen acted to constrain his wife's choices further. Understanding someone's location as marginal is crucial to understanding her actions.[171] While I do not intend to justify Helen Wu's killing her son, an antisubordination analysis would consider her position in relation to her family and the narrow options she perceived to ameliorate her suffering.[172]

Antisubordination, as premised on the vastness of oppression along unidirectional lines, such as male oppression of women, and xenophobic oppression of immigrants, must be the value on which we base our choices of whether to support the use of cultural factors in a defense and what information should be presented. Because the use of a "cultural defense" reflects the myriad problems of identity politics, including the perpetuation of stereotypical notions that can operate to exclude other people from benefitting from its use, this tactic will be a complex one to follow. Using a goal of antisubordination, however, to evaluate the appropriateness of these factors both combats decision-making premised on problematic descriptions of Asian women, and reflects a normative vision of what is valuable in our communities. Such a framework will also help dislodge the backdrop of "neutrality" as it exposes the relationship between the dominant and immigrant communities. The baseline from which the "uses and abuses" of "culture" are evaluated must be examined: we must question the unstated presuppositions about the American political and cultural character.

A coherent position on the presentation of "cultural information" that highlights its effect on Asian women thus requires an intersectional analysis, which implicates the use of antisubordination as a value to determine how the defense should be presented and when it should be used. Questions of identity and assimilation, of "strategic essentialism" and self-determination are important elements of the discussion. In making choices about the use of cultural testimony it is difficult to maneuver among complicated and sometimes contradictory strategic moves within a system that relies on its lack of flexibility as a means of deriving authority.

Creation of a formalized "cultural defense" will result in fossilizing culture as a reductive stereotype, and lead to inquiries into whether a defendant's identity sufficiently matches that stereotype to merit expert testimony. Cultural information should be allowed only as an informal factor to be considered in deliberations, with the following caveats.

Clearly, an awareness that "culture" is something that affects everybody's actions is essential in consideration of a "cultural defense." There must be an acknowledgement of the fluid and interdynamic nature of cultures.[173] Information that explains the actions of a defendant should be articulated by community members who are sensitive to the dynamics of power and subordination within the community of the defendant. For example, in cases involving women who are abused, such as Jian Wan Chen or Helen Wu, input from organizations that work with battered Asian women is imperative, whether in the form of expert testimony or in amicus briefs. Information about the defendant's culture should never be reduced to stereotypes about a community but rather should concretely address the individual defendant's location in her community, her location in the diaspora and her history. The information should be provided so as to give insight into an individual's thoughts, and should not be used for purposes of explaining how an individual fits into stereotypes of group behavior.

Moreover, advocates should be wary lest the presentation of cultural factors does more harm to Asian women defendants than good, given the ease with which Asian behavior slips into stereotype. There may often be sufficient evidence to show that a defendant lacked the requisite mental state, without admitting special cultural testimony. In fact, a careful distinction must be made between assuming that cultural factors are relevant because Asians are governed by culture, and presenting an individual defendant with pertinent cultural background.

Highlighting the problematic aspects of "cultural defenses" should engender greater awareness of the complications connected to their use. It should also elucidate the difficult yet imperative nature of committing to a future that fights the subordination of Asian women, whether in forms material or descriptive.

Leti Volpp was a Law Clerk to Chief Judge Thelton Henderson, U.S. District Court, Northern District of California; J.D., Columbia University, 1993; M.Sc., University of Edinburgh, 1989; M.S.P.H., Harvard School of Public Health, 1988; B.A., Princeton University, 1986.

Reprinted by permission.

ENDNOTES

1 I put "cultural defense" in quotes since, as discussed throughout the Article, the use of the term is politically problematic and is a misnomer, given the nonexistence of a singular, formalized defense.

2 In many cases the lack of requisite mens rea is argued on the basis of insufficient mental capacity. An impaired mental state defense is based on the idea that the accused is unable to appreciate the wrongfulness of her act or conform her conduct to the requirements of the law because of a mental disease or defect that she was suffering at the time the offense was committed. MODEL PENAL CODE s 4.01(1) (1962).

3 There have also been attempts to use "cultural defenses" for non-immigrant defendants of color. See, e.g., People v. Rhines, 182 Cal. Rptr. 487 (Cal. Ct. App. 1982) (involving the appeal of a Black man, convicted of raping two Black women, who argued that the trial court failed to take into account "cultural differences" between Blacks and whites). For a critique of the "cultural defense" attempted in that case

and of Orlando Patterson's "cultural defense" of Clarence Thomas's "down home style of courting," see Kimberle Crenshaw, Whose Story Is It, Anyway? Feminist and Antiracist Appropriations of Anita Hill, in RACE-ING JUSTICE, EN-GENDERING POWER 422 (Toni Morrison ed., 1992).

The defense strategy in the murder trial of Native American Patrick Hooty Croy was referred to as a "cultural defense." See Denise Ferry, Capitalizing on Race and Culture: The Croy Acquittal and Its Application to Future Minority Cases, 19 CACJ/FORUM 48, 48 (1992); David Talbot, The Ballad of Hooty Croy, L.A. TIMES, June 24, 1990, (Magazine) at 16. The following expert testimony was admitted as relevant to Hooty Croy's argument of self defense: testimony by an expert in Indian history and contemporary affairs about the relationship between Indians and non-Indians in Hooty Croy's county, testimony by experts in anthropological linguistics and eyewitness identification about misunderstanding in language (e.g., "shooting poofitch" — going deer hunting — was reported by the prosecution witness as "shooting the sheriff"), and testimony by an Indian psychologist who had interviewed Hooty Croy over the course of several years. See Ferry, supra, at 50.

4 Cultural factors may be admitted as part of expert testimony at trial or as part of jury instructions. They also may be presented as mitigating factors during the sentencing phase and in the plea bargaining stage.

5 My perspective also derives from my experiences working with Shakti Women's Aid, a resource center and refuge for battered women of color in Edinburgh, Scotland; with the Asian Women's Shelter, which works with battered Asian women in the San Francisco Bay area; and with the New York Asian Women's Center, which works with battered Asian women in the New York City metropolitan area.

6 Jacqueline Agtuca, Inderpal Grewal, Deeana Jang, Mimi Kim, Debbie Lee, Jayne Lee, Lata Mani, Leni Marin, Beckie Masaki, and Alexandra Tantranon-Saur composed the Study Group.

7 I identify this Article as part of a growing body of literature that uses the concept of intersectionality to address how women of color are situated in the law. For examples of other works that use the intersectionality framework, see generally Paulette Caldwell, A Hair Piece: Perspectives on the Intersection of Race and Gender, 1991 DUKE L.J. 365; Kimberle Crenshaw, Demarginalizing the Intersection of Race and Sex: A Black Feminist Critique of Antidiscrimination Doctrine, Feminist Theory, and Antiracist Politics, 1989 U. CHI. LEGAL F. 139; Angela Harris, Race and Essentialism in Feminist Legal Theory, 42 STAN. L. REV. 581 (1990); Marlee Kline, Race, Racism and Feminist Legal Theory, 12 HARV. WOMEN'S L.J. 115 (1989); Dorothy Roberts, Punishing Drug Addicts Who Have Babies: Women of Color, Equality, and the Right of Privacy, 104 HARV. L. REV. 1419 (1991); Celina Romany, Ain't I a Feminist? 4 YALE J.L. & FEMINISM 23 (1991).

This Article also uses approaches found in the literature of critical race theory, which examines the way law and legal categories shape and reflect the social meanings of race with a commitment to ending racial subordination. For examples of critical race theory, see generally DERRICK BELL, AND WE ARE NOT SAVED (1987); DERRICK BELL, FACES AT THE BOTTOM OF THE WELL (1993); MARI J. MATSUDA ET AL., WORDS THAT WOUND: CRITICAL RACE THEORY, ASSAULTIVE SPEECH, AND THE FIRST AMENDMENT (1993); PATRICIA J. WILLIAMS, THE ALCHEMY OF RACE AND RIGHTS (1991); ROBERT WILLIAMS, THE AMERICAN INDIAN IN WESTERN LEGAL THOUGHT (1990); Kimberle Crenshaw, Race, Reform, and Retrenchment: Transformation and Legitimation in Antidiscrimination Law, 101 HARV. L. REV. 1331 (1988); Neil Gotanda, A Critique of "Our Constitution is Color Blind," 44 STAN. L. REV. 1 (1991); Maivan Clech Lam, The Kuleana Case Revisited: The Survival of Traditional Hawaiian Commoner Rights in Land, 64 WASH. L. REV. 233 (1989); Kendall Thomas, Rouge et Noir Reread: A Popular Constitutional History of the Angelo Herndon Case, 65 S. CAL. L. REV. 2599 (1989).

8 See generally Crenshaw, Demarginalizing the Intersection of Race and Sex, supra note 7.

9 Kimberle Crenshaw, Mapping the Margins: Intersectionality, Identity Politics, and Violence Against Women of Color, 43 STAN. L. REV. 1241, 1244 n.9 (1991).

10 No. 87-7774 (N.Y. Sup. Ct. Dec. 2, 1988).

11 286 Cal. Rptr. 868 (Cal. Ct. App. 1991), rev'g No. ICR 12873 (Super. Ct. Riverside Co. 1990), review denied Jan. 23, 1992.

12 My discussion of these two cases involves a textual analysis of the relevant court opinions. I use this methodology rather than a doctrinal analysis of precendential cases for the following reasons. First, cases involving "cultural defenses" rarely appear at the appellate level. Second, a rhetorical analysis of the cases allows deconstruction of the problematic yet unquestioned ideas underlying uses of the "cultural defense." Because no law review article has yet addressed these ideas, the focus of my Article is on raising these issues.

13 This fact pattern occurs quite frequently. For example, two Korean men in Los Angeles were

acquitted of raping a Korean woman who met the men in a nightclub, drank heavily, and then accompanied them to two other nightclubs. See Myrna Oliver, Immigrant Crimes; Cultural Defense — a Legal Tactic, L.A. TIMES, July 15, 1988, at 1. The defense attorney, Charles Matthews, whose wife is Korean, explained the presentation of the cultural defense: "'It is very, very improper for a Korean girl in her culture to go to bars and drink and carry on with men alone.'" Id. "'So I was asking the jury to translate American party attitudes into Asian.'" Id.

For other examples of Asian men seeking a "cultural defense" for violence towards an Asian woman, see People v. King Moua, No. 315972 (Fresno Super. Ct. 1985) (sentencing a Hmong man in the San Joaquin Valley of California, who kidnapped and raped "fiance" in "marriage by capture," to 120 days in jail and $1,000 fine after consideration of cultural factors); People v. Aphaylath, 510 N.Y.S.2d 83 (N.Y. 1986) (finding that the lower court's failure to include cultural information about a Cambodian husband who stabbed his wife to death after she received phone call from another man was reversible error); Mary Ann Galante, Asian Refugee Who Shot Wife Receives 8-Year Prison Term, NAT'L L.J., Dec. 16, 1985, at 40 (describing a murder committed by a Hmong man who shot his wife to death after learning she intended to work with another man); Oliver, supra, at 1 (Hmong man in St. Paul kidnapped and raped young girl in "marriage by capture").

14 See, e.g., Oliver, supra note 13 (describing the case of a Japanese woman in San Francisco who tried to commit parent-child suicide, called oyako-shinju, after she learned husband had affair); People v. Fumiko Kimura, No. A-091133 (L.A. City Super Ct. filed Apr. 24, 1985); Deborah Woo, The People v. Fumiko Kimura: But Which People?, 17 INT'L. J. SOC. L. 403 (1989) (describing a case involving a Japanese woman in Los Angeles who tried to commit parent-child suicide after abuse by husband).

15 Which specific groups are used to represent the entire Asian American community depends on context. See Lisa Ikemoto, Traces of the Master Narrative in the Story of African American/Korean American Conflict: How We Constructed "Los Angeles," 66 S. CAL. L. REV. 1581, 1592 (1993) (suggesting that for purposes of white-Asian conflict, "Asian means Japanese" although when "the sore point is Asian-owned small businesses, then Asian may mean Korean").

16 One author has noted that:

Asian Americans are seen not as individual but as fungible.... [The presumption of reductionist similarity] obscures not only the differences among Asian American individuals qua individuals but also the historic disputes that have separated Asian peoples. Moreover, it helps conceive individuals as components of monolithic blocs defined primarily by common physical traits.

Note, Racial Violence Against Asian Americans, 106 HARV. L. REV. 1926, 1932 (1993).

17 I am, of course, repeating this homogenization by using these two cases to talk about "Asian women."

Whether to use the category "Asian" or "Asian American," instead of categories such as Cambodian, Korean, or Thai, is a political decision entailing both risks and advantages. The articulation of an "Asian American identity" as an organizing tool has provided a concept of political unity, and the building of "Asian American culture" empowers our multicultural, multilingual community against the institutions that marginalize us. But essentializing Asian American identity risks particular dangers because it underestimates our differences and "also inadvertently supports the racist discourse that constructs Asians as a homogenous group." Lisa Lowe, Heterogeneity, Hybridity, Multiplicity, Marking Asian American Differences, 1 DIASPORA 24, 30 (1991); see also YEN LE ESPIRITU, ASIAN AMERICAN PANETHNICITY: BRIDGING INSTITUTIONS AND IDENTITIES (1992).

18 When I use the terms "American" or "America," I intend an implicit critique of the ethnocentricity of these terms.

19 Of course, Asian Americans are, with enormous frequency, not recognized as "American." This positioning as foreign is something that Asian Americans, including fifth-generation Asian Americans in this country, constantly face. For the relation of this perception to anti-Asian violence, see Note, supra note 16, at 1938.

20 None of the law review articles dealing with the question of the "cultural defense" recognize the cultural particularity of American law, nor do they offer a sophisticated analysis of what is being presented as "culture" in cases involving the "cultural defense" — in fact, they frequently attempt no analysis at all. See, e.g., Carolyn Choi, Application of a Cultural Defense in Criminal Proceedings, 8 PAC. BASIN L.J. 80 (1990); Donna Kotake, Survey: Women and California Law, 23 GOLDEN GATE L. REV. 1069 (1993); Julia P. Sams, The Availability of the "Cultural Defense" as an Excuse for Criminal Behavior, 16 GA. J. INT'L & COMP. L.J. 335 (1986); Malek-Mithra Sheybani, Cultural Defense: One Person's Culture is Another's Crime, 9 LOY. L.A. INT'L & COMP. L.J. 751 (1987); Note, The Cultural Defense in the Criminal Law, 99 HARV. L. REV. 1293 (1986).

Ahn Lam does question racial and sexual bias in the use of the "cultural defense," for example, how Asian defendants have been treated differently depending on the race or gender of the victim. See Ahn Lam, Culture as a Defense: Preventing Judicial Bias Against Asians and Pacific Islanders, 1 ASIAN AM. PAC. ISLANDS L.J. 49, 62-63 (1993). Two law review articles criticize "cultural defense" cases as validating violence against Asian women but do not address many of the problems identified in this Article. See Nilda Rimonte, A Question of Culture: Cultural Approval of Violence Against Women in the Pacific-Asian Community and the Cultural Defense, 43 STAN. L. REV. 1311 (1991); Melissa Spatz, A "Lesser" Crime: A Comparative Study of Legal Defenses for Men Who Kill Their Wives, 24 COLUM J.L. & SOC. PROBS. 597 (1991).

21 Descriptions of societies that have "culture" and societies in which culture is invisible, e.g., for white America, coincide with the relative powerlessness and power of the societies. Thus, assimilation or social mobility in the United States is supposed to coincide with a stripping away of culture. See RENATO ROSALDO, CULTURE & TRUTH: THE REMAKING OF SOCIAL ANALYSIS 209-12 (1989). Rosaldo writes:

More generally, race relations in North America involve a blend of assimilationist efforts, raw prejudice, and cultural containment that revolves around a concerted effort to keep each culture pure and in its place. Members of racial minority groups receive a peculiar message: either join the mainstream or stay in your ghettos, barrios, and reservations, but don't try to be both mobile and cultural. Id. at 212.

22 No. 87-7774 (N.Y. Sup. Ct. Dec. 2, 1988).

23 286 Cal Rpt. 868 (Cal. Ct. App. 1991), rev'g No. ICR 12873 (Super. Ct. Riverside Co. 1990), review denied Jan 23, 1992 (unpublished opinion).

24 While not a focus here, factors I also consider fundamental include class and sexuality.

25 No. 87-7774 (N.Y. Sup. Ct. Dec. 2, 1988).

26 After hearing the evidence during the course of the trial, Pincus convicted Chen of second degree manslaughter, which carried a maximum prison term of five to fifteen years. Record at 309-10, Chen (No. 87-7774).

27 Record at 58.

28 The reader should be mindful that this is what Dong Lu Chen's defense attorney presented as an explanation of what "happened." By placing Dong Lu Chen's version here, before the reader learns more about Jian Wan Chen, I reenact her erasure in the narrative of the trial. I do this to show the reader how an easy acceptance of Chen's "cultural" explanation is only made possible by Jian Wan Chen's absence from the narrative as a living, breathing person.

29 Chen was born in Toisan, China. After he left school he worked as a farmer. He married Jian Wan Chen in 1963 in an arranged marriage. They had three children, the oldest 21 at the time of the trial, the youngest 15. See Record at 58-61.

30 Record at 64. During the first eight months of separation he returned to New York three times. On the first visit Dong Lu Chen and Jian Wan Chen had sexual intercourse. The second visit she refused. On the third, she again refused and "became abusive towards him, including beating him." Record at 64. Their children said that they never saw their mother beat their father. See Record at 183-84, 213, 217, 219.

31 Record at 64-65. He had difficulty sleeping and palpitations, and began to hear the voice of his wife's lover planning to hurt him. See Record at 65.

32 Record at 65. Jian Wan Chen "became increasingly more brutal...she was hitting him, telling him to drop dead and...she would not permit him to touch her." Record at 66. Dong Lu Chen noted that Jian Wan Chen, working as a seamstress, changed her site of work and assumed that this was to facilitate her rendezvous with other men. She took all her clothing from their apartment; he thought it was so she could wear the clothes for her lover. Record at 66.

33 Id. at 66.

34 Id. at 66-67.

35 Id. at 67.

36 Id.

37 Id.

38 Id. at 68.

39 Id. at 68-69.

40 Id. at 74.

41 Id.

42 Pasternak's assumption that "American" does not encompass immigrant Chinese ignores the fact that we do not live in hermetically sealed cultures that travel with us from cradle to grave. We are not completely unaffected by other communities and do not live in cultural compartments separating "natives" from "anthropologists" or "immigrants" from "Americans." See ROSALDO, supra note 21, at 44-45.

43 On the original and lingering perception of Asian Americans as "foreign," see Neil Gotanda, Asian American Rights and the "Miss Saigon Syndrome," in ASIAN AMERICANS AND THE SUPREME COURT 1087, 1095 (Hyung-chan Kim ed., 1992); Neil Gotanda, "Other Non-Whites" in American Legal History: A Review of Justice at War, 85 COLUM. L. REV. 1186, 1188 (1985); Elaine Kim, Asian Americans and American Popular Culture, in DICTIONARY OF ASIAN AMERICAN HISTORY

99 (Hyung-Chan Kim, ed. 1986); John H. Torok, Towards a Liberatory Approach to Asian American Legal History (June 1993) (unpublished manuscript on file with the Harvard Women's Law Journal).

For historical illustrations of judicial perceptions of Asian Americans as "foreign," see Plessy v. John H. Ferguson, 163 U.S. 537, 561 (1896) (Harlan, J., dissenting) ("There is a race so different from our own that we do not permit those belonging to it to become citizens of the United States. Persons belonging to it are, with few exceptions, absolutely excluded from our country. I allude to the Chinese race.").

In Fong Yue Ting v. U.S., 149 U.S. 698 (1893), the Court stated:

[Large] numbers of Chinese laborers, of a distinct race and religion, remaining strangers in the land, residing apart by themselves, tenaciously adhering to the customs and usages of their own country, unfamiliar with our institutions, and apparently incapable of assimilating with our people, might endanger good order, and be injurious to the public interests.... Id. at 717.

44 For an example of the important role that the defendant's community may play, see the discussion of State v. Chong Sun France, infra notes 164-168 and accompanying text.

45 Pasternak's claim that "American" men would react less violently than "Chinese" men to the belief their wives were having affairs is belied by the very encoding of the manslaughter/provocation doctrine in American law, which is explicitly premised upon a violent reaction to this knowledge. The voluntary manslaughter law of most jurisdictions recognizes the sight of a wife's adultery as a motivation to kill. In fact, adultery is the paradigmatic example of provocation sufficient to mitigate a charge of murder to a voluntary manslaughter conviction. See Donna K. Coker, Heat of Passion and Wife Killing: Men Who Batter/Men Who Kill, 2 S. CAL. REV. L. & WOMEN'S STUD. 71, 72 (1992).

46 Dong Lu Chen did not plead an insanity defense. One can conclude that neither his attorney nor the judge found his actions to be insane, given the "cultural" context. Pincus stated:

The Court finds that the defendant had a frustrated mental aberration. It does not rise to the level of legal insanity, but based on cultural aspects, the effect of the wife's behavior on someone who is essentially born in China, raised in China and took all his Chinese culture with him to the United States except the community which would moderate his behavior provides reasons why the Court has found him not guilty of manslaughter in the first degree. Record at 302-03.

47 For example, batterers are careful to abuse women when no one else is around to witness the abuse. See DOMESTIC VIOLENCE IN IMMIGRANT AND REFUGEE COMMUNITIES: ASSERTING THE RIGHTS OF BATTERED WOMEN (D. Jang et al. eds., 1991).

48 See Record at 293. This information should have substantially undermined any manslaughter defense based on provocation.

49 Id. at 53-54.

50 Pasternak stated:

Let me simply begin by observing that the ability of the Chinese community to define values and define appropriate behavior compared to our own ability to do that is extraordinary. The ability to enforce those values and to protect themselves against deviation also is extraordinary. The Chinese who grows up as a person in Mainland China carries that in his mind. They are like voices of his community. It is very difficult to escape. They are very intolerant [of] deviations from those mores, very intolerant, and exert enormous control over people who try to deviate. You carry that with you no matter where you go. Even if you can escape those voices, you cannot escape the information, a deviation being known to everyone, being known to everyone in the Chinese community either here or there. My Chinese friends often say, there is no wall that the wind cannot penetrate. These voices will be heard everywhere. Id.

51 Id. at 78. By continually returning to this "wall and wind" motif and throwing in picturesque details such as gossip during laundry washing by canals, Pasternak fetishized "difference" as a way to anchor the "foreignness" of the "Chinese," and structured his "Chinese friends" as native informants. For a critique of anthropology and the difficulty facing the anthropological subject who wishes to escape the role of native informant see Robert Ji-Song Ku, Can the Native Informant Write? The Ethnographic Gaze and Asian American Literature (June 3, 1993) (unpublished manuscript presented at the Association for Asian American Studies Conference, Cornell University, June 3, 1993, on file with the Harvard Women's Law Journal).

52 Record at 54. Pasternak stated:

Where adultery takes place, this is considered an enormous stain, much more so than where we take this thing normally in the course of an event. To the Chinese it's a very serious matter. It reflects upon him as a person. It is a reflection upon his family. It is a reflection upon his ancestors and it is a reflection upon his prodigy. It's a terrible stain. One to be avoided at all costs. Chinese act very strongly to this. The community reacts very strongly. Id.

53 Id. at 55.

54 Id. at 54.

55 Pasternak stated:

In the Chinese context, divorce is virtually the end.... It could be the end of a person's real life. In the Chinese context, if a woman commits adultery, she's very likely to be thrown out. She will have a very hard time remarrying.... If he is poor, he has a very hard time remarrying, because it's a reflection on his ability to maintain the most minimal standard of control within his family. It's a reflection on his family, which also has shown an inability to maintain basic standards in the family. So, his remarrying opportunities are very, very severely restricted by virtue of this kind of evolution. Id. at 55.

56 Pasternak stated:

If you take those two people who were involved in an adulteress [sic] relationship with the potential of divorce and you put them in our context here, it's odd that the situation reverses itself. That is to say, the woman, in that case, has a better advantage than the man here.... The Chinese woman who is now involved in an adulteress [sic] relationship that looks or is perceived to be moving in the direction of a possible divorce, she can look out into the Caucasian community and maybe find somebody there who doesn't know about all this. She has a chance. In China, she would have very little chance. But the man, who, in China, would have something of a chance, a diminished one, but nonetheless a chance, here, would have very, very little chance, particularly if he was a poor man, because he doesn't have the wherewithal to do it. He can't find a woman in the Chinese community who [doesn't think] he's a pariah and he will have virtually no chance in the Caucasian community to find a spouse. In a sense, he has lost his family. Id. at 55-56.

57 Id. at 55.

58 The number of divorces has risen steadily since 1980, following the Cultural Revolution and the 1981 marriage law reform allowing for "no fault" divorce; the historical peak of divorces was in 1953 when marriage laws introduced by the Communist government enabled women to escape feudal marriages. One Chinese judge remarked, "[Chinese] don't think divorce is shameful any more. It is the right of an independent man and woman. From this point of view the rate of divorce is a symbol of reform." Teresa Poole, China Divorce is Too Close For Comfort, INDEPENDENT, Apr. 13, 1993, at 8. See also Survey Shows Divorce Rising Among Chinese, CHI. TRIB., Oct. 11, 1992, at 5 (stating that the divorce rate more than doubled in the 1980s and reporting that the number of divorce applicants was about 20% of the number of marriage registrations); Divorce Loses Stigma with 10% Annual Rise, (BBC Summary of World Broadcasts, Oct. 8, 1992) (claiming that less than 12% of people in Chinese nationwide survey think divorce is disgraceful and that 42% of divorcees seek to remarry).

59 Record at 105-08.

60 Id. at 106-07. Pasternak gratuitously remarked: "It also happens, by the way, that the men are beaten. It isn't only the women. Sometimes, it's the men. In Inner Mongolia, a man drowned himself because his wife was beating him this summer." Id. at 85.

61 Id. at 76.

62 By "dominant anthropologist" I refer to the power inherent in the relationship between anthropologist and subject of study, which is exercised through the anthropologist's dissemination of descriptive "knowledge."

63 Record at 76.

64 Id. Pasternak explicitly included white Anglo-Saxons, Jews, Blacks, Puerto Ricans, and Roman Catholics in his notion of "Americans," and contrasted them all with "Chinese."

Describing an "average American," Pasternak said:

It's difficult to say what an average American is, but most of us are familiar with divorce. Most of us know something about adultery. Divorce rates are very high here. We become inure [sic] to this. They are not inure [sic] to this. This is a very remarkable thing to them still. We are at two extremes.... To a Chinese, it is a matter of great concern and it's uncommon. Id.

65 See EDWARD SAID, ORIENTALISM (1978). For a critique of white feminist essentialization of women of color see Caldwell, Harris, and Kline, supra note 7.

66 The "West" characterizes the "other" as unchanging and homogenous in order to measure Western "progress" as well as to justify Western imperialism. Describing societies as "classically traditional" and governed by a set of fixed rules, as Pasternak did, masks power relations within those societies, for instance, Chinese men over Chinese women, and justifies the subjugation of those societies by the "West." Western anthropologists who subjugate in their descriptive function, missionaries who need to save the heathen, or colonists and imperialists who conquer in the name of bringing enlightenment and civilization are examples of subjugating forces. See ROSALDO, supra note 21, at 41-42.

This fetishization of "difference" has historically enabled global conquest and imperialism:

Generalizations about the characteristics of a particular culture or the people of a particular nation helped define a national identity. Combined with political domination, they also involved generalizations about the people of the dominated culture or nation as inferior and so provide justification for the existing power relationship. Elaine Kim, supra note 43, at 111.

67 Record at 81.

68 Id. at 102.

69 On redirect, Orden asked Pasternak to state whether seeing Dong Lu Chen bow when he entered the courtroom could lead him to conclude that Chen had not assimilated himself as an American. Pasternak responded that "Chinese do it when they feel enormous respect and the Japanese do it, of course." Id. at 118-19. The "Chinese" Pasternak attempted to define were a monolithic construction of his fantasy, a group peopled exclusively of bowing "Orientals."

70 Id. at 301-02. After hearing the evidence and expert testimony during the course of the bench trial, Pincus considered counts of second degree murder, first degree manslaughter, and second degree manslaughter. See id. at 301.

71 Id. at 302.

72 Monona Yin of the Committee Against Anti-Asian Violence pointed out this inconsistency at a forum on the Chen case. Linda Anthony, Women Discuss Protection for the Battered Following Controversial "Cultural Defence" Verdict, KOREA TIMES, July 14, 1989.

73 Record at 311.

74 Shaun Asseal, Judge Defends Sentencing Wife-Killer to Probation, MANHATTAN LAW., Apr. 4, 1989-Apr. 10, 1989, at 4. Asseal also noted that Brooklyn prosecutors had considered Pincus a very tough sentencer. Id.

75 Record at 355.

Pincus defended the probation sentence saying that Chen's cultural background "made him susceptible to cracking under the circumstances." His Chinese heritage did not excuse him but did create pressures that led him to beat his wife to death with a hammer: "He never displayed psychopathic tendencies.... This guy's not going to do it again and he has suffered. There's no question he's going to suffer every day of his life.... I don't think this man would have killed her under any other circumstances." Patricia Hurtado, Killer's Sentence Defended: "He's Not a Loose Cannon," NEWSDAY, Apr. 4, 1989, at 17.

Hurtado reported that Pincus considered several other factors in rendering the sentence. Chen showed true remorse; the couple's two teenage children had asked that their father receive probation; and if Chen went to prison, "he might come out a real time bomb." Chen had also already served one and a half years in jail while awaiting trial, in isolation because he speaks a "rare Chinese dialect" (Chen speaks Cantonese and Toisan, neither of which can be called "rare") and had been beaten up by other inmates. Pincus concluded that [t]his is just a terrible tragedy all around. If you could just see this broken and dejected man and his poor family...." Id.

76 In leniently treating a man who killed a woman, and in seeing male batterers as "victims," Justice Pincus was not unique. The Pace University Battered Women's Justice Center reports that sentences battered women receive for killing their abusive partners far exceed those for abusive men who kill their partners. The average sentence for a woman who kills her partner is 15 to 20 years, for a man, two to six. Nancy Gibbs, 'Til Death Do Us Part: When a Woman Kills an Abusive Partner, Is It an Act of Revenge or of Self Defense?, TIME, Jan. 18, 1993, at 38.

77 The forensic pathologist reported that Jian Wan Chen was five foot three and weighed 99 pounds. Her body was found with numerous carved lacerations on both sides of her head. She had contusions on both left and right forearms, a contusion on her right wrist, an abrasion at the back of her left hand, and a bruise on her left thumb. The marks on her head were consistent with having been hit by a hammer. There were depressed skull fractures under her lacerations, indicating that a great amount of force was applied to a small surface area. The injuries on her arms, wrist, and hand were consistent with someone holding her or with her warding off a blow from a hammer. They were also consistent with an individual holding her down and striking her in the face with a hammer. See Record at 132-43.

78 Two of their children testified that they had heard their parents arguing, their father accusing their mother of having another man, and their mother saying "So what, it is so," which could substantiate Dong Lu Chen's allegations that she was having an affair. Both children, however, stated that they had never seen their mother hit their father, as Dong Lu Chen contended. See Record at 183-84, 213, 217, 219.

79 See supra note 7. By focusing here on race and gender, I do not intend to assert that only race and gender are critical to the experiences of women of color. Factors such as class, sexual orientation, language, and immigration status are often as critical. For an analysis using postcolonial discourse to examine the intersection of language, gender, race, class, and national origin in the lives of Latinas, see Celina Romany, Sculpting Identities: Carving a Niche for Latinas in Feminist Legal Theory (unpublished manuscript on file with the Harvard Women's Law Journal).

80 Many of the experiences women of color face are not subsumed within the traditional boundaries of race and gender, nor of race and gender discrimination. See, e.g., Crenshaw, Demarginalizing the Intersection of Race and Sex, supra note 7 (arguing that Black women suffer employment discrimination without redress because employers point to the presence of white women and Black men to indicate an absence of race and sex discrimination).

81 The needs of women of color are not fully met by structures or political movements designed to address either race or gender. See, e.g., Margaretta Wan Ling Lin & Cheng Imm Tan, Holding Up More than Half the Heavens: Domestic Violence in Our Communities, A Call for Justice, in THE STATE OF ASIAN AMERICA: ACTIVISM AND RESISTANCE IN THE 1990s 321 (Karin Aguilar-San Juan ed., 1994); Document to Share with the Anti-Asian Violence Movement (unpublished manuscript on file with the Harvard Women's Law Journal) (critiquing the invisibility of violence against Asian women in the anti-Asian violence movement).

82 During the Vietnam War, many in the United States propagated the idea that Asians did not place the same value on life as those in the "West." See Richard Reeves, Guns and Foreigners in America, SACRAMENTO BEE, June 7, 1993, at B12.

83 A 1992 United States Surgeon General report attributed the leading cause of death among women to domestic violence. United States, Look at the Violence Against Women, Democrats Told, IPS, July 14, 1992.

84 See Alexis Jetter, Fear is Legacy of Wife Killing in Chinatown, Battered Asians Shocked By Husband's Probation, NEWSDAY, Nov. 26, 1989, at 4.

85 Id.

86 The importance of economic class in access to and experience in the legal system is often overlooked and cannot be underestimated. See GERALD LOPEZ, REBELLIOUS LAWYERING: ONE CHICANO'S VISION OF PROGRESSIVE LAW PRACTICE (1992); Lucie E. White, Subordination, Rhetorical Survival Skills, and Sunday Shoes: Notes on the Hearing of Mrs. G., 38 BUFF. L. REV. 1 (1990).

87 Jetter, supra note 84.

88 Hurtado, supra note 75. City University of New York Assistant Law Professor Sharon Hom charged: "This kind of thinking reinforces patriarchal and racial stereotypes—which don't even exist in China today. This is like saying, 'My goodness, Americans lynch blacks, let's let them do it,' just because lynchings have happened in the past." Id.

89 Elizabeth Holtzman was the District Attorney for Kings County when the Chen case was heard.

90 See Jetter, supra note 84.

91 Id.

92 See Anthony, supra note 72.

* * * *

158 Kimberle Crenshaw makes this point for "cultural defenses" attempted for African American men. See Crenshaw, Whose Story is it Anyway?, supra note 3, at 431.

159 See, e.g., Nilda Rimonte, Domestic Violence Amongst Pacific Asians, in MAKING WAVES: AN ANTHOLOGY OF WRITINGS BY AND ABOUT ASIAN AMERICAN WOMEN (Asian Women of California United ed., 1989):

> Domestic violence occurs because of the Pacific Asian family's traditionally patriarchal system and the attendant belief in the supremacy of the male; the socialization goals and processes which favor the family and community over the individual; the cultural emphasis on silent suffering versus open communication of needs and feelings; and the enormous adjustment pressures which test the limits of immigrants' and refugees' survival skills. Cultural norms and values directly or indirectly sanction abuse against women and tend to minimize it as a problem in the community. Id. at 328; Rimonte, supra note 20.

160 The dehumanization to which I refer is illustrated by descriptions of Asian communities as governed by "culture" when the behavior of the dominant community is described as explainable by "psychology" or political forces.

161 For example, immigrant women's difficulty in gaining access to the battered spouse waiver to the Marriage Fraud Amendments is not perceived as linked to the lack of translated materials or to the absence of laws that promote the interests of poor immigrant women. Rather, that lack of access is often explained as caused by a woman's "culture." See, e.g., Deeana Hodgin, Mail-Order Brides Marry Pain to Get Green Cards, WASH. TIMES, Apr. 16, 1991, at E1 (quoting Tina Shum, a family counselor, describing the Battered Spouse Waiver: "This law sounds so easy to apply but there are cultural complications in the Asian community that make even these requirements difficult.... Just to find the opportunity and courage to call us is an accomplishment for many.").

162 Gayatri Spivak has argued for strategic essentialism in the following specific context:

> I would read [the Subaltern Studies] Group text, then, as a strategic use of positivist essentialism in a scrupulously visible political interest.... This would allow them to use the critical force of anti-humanism...even as they share its constitutive

paradox: that the essentializing moment, the object of their criticism, is irreducible.
GAYATRI SPIVAK, Subaltern Studies: Deconstructing Historiography, in IN OTHER WORLDS 197, 205 (1988). In other words, it may be useful to practice a "strategic essentialism" — strategic, because it is consciously directed toward a political goal, essentialism because it reinstates some version of the essence of a community, even if only temporarily and for a political purpose. Spivak discusses the description of a particular poor community by elite scholars, who after-the-fact interpret and explain and essentialize the community, taking the effect (the constructed identity) and reading it as a cause (it explains the individuals' actions). She argues that it may be appropriate for the Subaltern Studies Group to, in turn, describe this community in order to combat the dehumanizing description by the elite scholars — all the while recognizing that, through this process, the subsequent description also essentializes the community. Id.

Spivak has more recently stated: "The emphasis falls on being able to speak from one's own ground...on noting how we ourselves and others are what you call essentialist, without claiming a counter-essence disguised under the alibi of strategy." Gayatri Spivak, In a Word, 1 DIFFERENCES 12 (1989). In other words, "strategic essentialism" is not to be used lightly, and cannot be an easy alibi for, for example, white feminists to feel comfortable in describing the lives of women of color.

163 This process is the essence of identity politics — naming and categorizing oneself as a means of identifying interests for purposes of empowerment. For a discussion of the relationship of identity politics, postmodernism and antiessentialism, see Crenshaw, supra note 9, at 1296-99.

164 379 S.E.2d 701 (N.C. App. 1989). France originally emigrated as the wife of an American serviceman, whom she later divorced. After years of physical and emotional abuse, France left her second husband and moved to Jacksonville, North Carolina with her two small children. She began working there as a bartender. With no funds to pay for a child sitter, she left the two children alone in the motel where they were staying, turning the television on, so as not to disturb other residents in case her children cried. Hyun Sook Kim, supra note 151, at 3-4.

On May 28, 1987, she returned to find her son Moses dead, enclosed inside the lower drawer of a dresser. The television on top of the dresser, and the dresser had toppled over on him. When the police arrived, France said that her son had died accidentally. But she also screamed in grief, "I killed my son." France, 379 S.E.2d at 702.

165 One police officer described France as "sick," "crazed," and "hateful." Both investigating officers insisted that France must have staged the incident to look like an accident. She was provided with no interpreter, and the court reporter noted that her English was extremely difficult to understand. See Hyun Sook Kim, supra note 151, at 4.

166 See France, 379 S.E.2d at 704.

167 The petition circulated by the Free France Committee stated:

Dear Governor Martin,

I have read about the imprisonment of Chong Sun France and would like to express my hope for your unconditional pardon of her.

I am also a Korean American who initially came to America with very little knowledge of English or the American culture. Now that I have been in the States for some time, I see some of the difficulties involved in making the transition. It is very difficult to live a successful life here if you are unprepared and uneducated. Nowadays, both the husband and wife must work in order to maintain a decent lifestyle. As a result, there is little time for learning the language and the culture of your new country.

When little children come along, it is even more difficult. Korean people often leave the children alone when we go out to work because in Korea neighbors and friends look after each others' children. There is no such thing as a babysitter in Korean culture. Most of us cannot conceive of the idea of, and cannot financially afford, paying a stranger to watch our children.

Mrs. France was wrong to leave her child alone, and it is against the law, but considering the cultural differences, I am sure that she did not murder her child. I pray for her release. Thank you for your consideration.

New York Free France Committee, Statement on Behalf of Chong Sun France (1992) (on file with the Harvard Women's Law Journal).

168 Mari Matsuda writes:

Critics...ask how one knows who is oppressed and who isn't.... The larger question is how one knows anything in life or law. To conceptualize a condition called subordination is a legitimate alternative to denying that such a condition exists. In law, we conceptualize. We take on mammoth tasks of discovery and knowing. We can determine when subordination exists by looking at social indicators: wealth, mobility, comfort, health, and survival tend to mark the rise to the top and the fall to the depths.

Mari J. Matsuda, Public Response to Racist Speech: Considering the Victim's Story, 87 MICH. L. REV. 2320, 2362 (1989).

169 Mari Matsuda describes the following as "predictable patterns" of oppression:

-All forms of oppression involve taking a trait, X, which often carries with it a cultural meaning, and using X to make some group the "other" and to reduce their entitlements and power.

-All forms of oppression benefit someone, and sometimes both sides of a relationship of domination will have some stake in its maintenance.

-All forms of oppression have both material and ideological dimensions.... The damage is real.... Language, including the language of science, law, rights, necessity, free markets, neutrality, and objectivity can make subordination seem natural and inevitable, justifying material deprivation.

-All forms of oppression implicate a psychology of subordination that involves elements of sexual fear, need to control, hatred of self and hatred of others.

Mari J. Matsuda, Beside My Sister, Facing the Enemy: Legal Theory Out of Coalition, 43 STAN. L. REV. 1183, 1188-89 (1991).

170 This is exemplified in the Wu case since it is also a story about the killing of a child by his parent.

171 See bell hooks, marginality as a site of resistance, in OUT THERE: MARGINALIZATION AND CONTEMPORARY CULTURES 341 (Russell Ferguson et al. eds., 1990) (understanding marginality as a position of resistance is crucial to oppressed and exploited people); Hyun Sook Kim, supra note 151 (women engage in resistance to defend their interests and survive on the margins).

172 An example of how antisubordination must operate as a criterion for the decision about whether to present cultural information emerges in an article by Mark Kelman. See Mark Kelman, Reasonable Evidence of Reasonableness, 17 CRITICAL INQUIRY 798 (1991). Kelman notes that there is a clash in criminal law between defendants asserting what he calls "subcultural defenses" for actions taken against other members of the same "subculture." See id. at 808. He finds it difficult to choose between the two parties involved, even while noting that:

Defendants most typically are men claiming that what the dominant culture discerns as criminal is a permissible form of male prerogative in their subculture: for example, what a Hmong defendant would call a ritual of "capture," the complainant would call rape; unless one believes the Hmong defendant misdescribes his culture or (more plausibly in my view) that his culture is anything but unified in its understanding of the contested event, one is forced simply to choose between one oppressed group, women and another, the Hmong refugees. Id. at 809.

Hmong women, however, are members of both the oppressed groups "women" and "Hmong refugees." Thus, Kelman's dilemma is not simply a matter of choosing between one oppressed group and another; rather, it is a question of choosing between one oppressed group and another that it is oppressing within the same community.

173 Cultural identities come from somewhere, have histories. But, like everything which is historical, they undergo constant transformation. Far from being eternally fixed in some essentialised past, they are subject to the continuous "play" of history, culture and power. Far from being grounded in a mere "recovery" of the past, which is waiting to be found, and which, when found, will secure our sense of ourselves into eternity, identities are the names we give to the different ways we are positioned by, and position ourselves within, the narratives of the past.

Stuart Hall, Cultural Identity and Diaspora, in IDENTITY, COMMUNITY, CULTURE, DIFFERENCE 222, 225 (Jonathan Rutherford ed., 1990).

[19]

Give Me Liberty or Give Me Death: Political Asylum and the Global Persecution of Lesbians and Gay Men

*Suzanne B. Goldberg**

> The Police used to follow us. Many times, just because I was standing in places frequented by lesbians, they would break in, grab all of the women and place us under arrest. At the police station they would bribe us or beat us. Nobody would help because the society hated lesbians—saw us as deserving any punishment the Police wanted to give. Sometimes the Police would charge women with "perverse activity" and then put them in jail, or worse, institutionalize them in psychiatric "hospitals" for years and years of electric shock therapy. Twice, when they investigated me, I had to lie—to say I wasn't a lesbian. Luckily, the Police did not continue the investigation. But I am terrified that they will take me away next time.
>
> —an applicant for asylum

In a time marked by dramatic global change, women and men persecuted because they are lesbian or gay form part of the growing pool of international refugees.[1] Their persecution takes the form of police har-

---

* Staff Attorney, Lambda Legal Defense and Education Fund (New York). The author wishes to thank Deborah Batts, Ignatius Bau, Robert DiPierro, Paula Ettelbrick, J Craig Fong, Richard Goldberg, and Noemi Masliah for their comments and insights.

1. This Article uses the following terms: a) sexual orientation: an enduring erotic, affectional, or romantic attraction to individuals of a particular gender; b) homosexual: a primary or exclusive attraction to individuals of one's own gender; c) heterosexual: a primary or exclusive attraction to individuals of the other gender; d) bisexual: significant attractions to members of both genders; e) lesbian: describes woman whose personal identity is based on her primary orientation toward an enduring sexual, affectional, or romantic attraction to other women; f) gay: describes man whose personal identity is based on his primary orientation toward an enduring erotic, affectional or romantic attachment to other men; gay is sometimes used to refer to both lesbian women and gay men. *See* Gregory M. Herek, *Myths About Sexual Orientation: A Lawyer's Guide to Social Science Research*, 1 LAW AND SEXUALITY 133, 134 (1991). *See also* John C. Gonsiorek & James D. Weinrich, *The Definition and Scope of Sexual Orientation*, *in* HOMOSEXUALITY: RESEARCH IMPLICATIONS FOR PUBLIC POLICY 1-12 (J. Gonsiorek & J. Weinrich eds., 1991) [hereinafter HOMOSEXUALITY].

This Article does not use the term "homosexual" as a noun because of its "clinical connotations and its historic association with pathology." *Id.* at 134. *See generally*

assment and assault,[2] involuntary institutionalization and electroshock and drug "treatments,"[3] punishment under laws that impose extreme penalties including death for consensual lesbian or gay sexual relations,[4] murder by paramilitary death squads,[5] and government inaction in response to criminal assaults against lesbians and gay men.[6] The survival of these women and men, like the survival of all refugees, depends on obtaining asylum outside the home country. Yet, to date there have been few published decisions internationally and only one in the United States that grant asylum to people in these situations.[7]

To illustrate the eligibility of lesbians and gay men under the legal standard for asylum, this Article argues the hypothetical case of Tatiana, a Romanian lesbian seeking asylum in the United States. As part of its argument, this Article reviews and analyzes the epidemic persecution of lesbians and gay men worldwide.

I. Refugee Status: Who Qualifies?

Under Section 208(a) of the Immigration and Nationality Act (INA),[8] the Attorney General may grant political asylum to any person who meets the statutory definition of refugee:[9]

Janet Halley, *The Politics of the Closet: Towards Equal Protection for Gay, Lesbian and Bisexual Identity*, 36 U.C.L.A. L. REV. 915, 916 n.5 (1989).

2. *See, e.g.*, Matter of Jorge Alberto Inaudi, File No. T91 04459, Immigration and Refugee Board, Apr. 19, 1992 (Canada) (describing extreme police brutality against Argentinean asylum applicant).

3. *See, e.g.*, Alexandria Duda, Action Secretariat, Int'l Lesbian & Gay Ass'n, COMPARISON OF THE LEGAL SITUATION OF HOMOSEXUALS IN EUROPE 1 (1993) (on file with *Cornell International Law Journal*) (describing treatment of men and women "convicted" of homosexuality). *See also* Letter from SAKHI [advocacy group for gay men and lesbians in India] to International Gay and Lesbian Human Rights Commission [IGLHRC] (on file with *Cornell International Law Journal*) (describing harassment, lengthy detention without trial, and "treatment" with heavy doses of lithium of lesbians and gay men in India); Neela Banerjee, *Gay Russians, Deemed Criminals, Begin Testing Limits of Tolerance*, WALL ST. J., May 27, 1992, at A9 (describing abusive treatment of gay Russians in prisons and hard labor camps).

4. Islamic Penal Law, art. 110; IGLHRC Action Alert (Mar./Apr. 1993), "Nicaragua: Supreme Court Delaying Decision" (describing anti-sodomy law in new Nicaraguan penal code that mandates one to three year prison sentences for anyone who "induces, promotes, propagandizes, or practices in a scandalous manner, the cohabitation of individuals of the same sex").

5. *See* Matter of Tenorio, No. A72 093 558 (BIA 1993) (describing anti-gay "commando" groups in Brazil); IGLHRC Action Alert (Feb. 1992) (describing murders of hundreds of gay men in Columbia by paramilitary groups known as "social clean-up death squads").

6. Matter of Tenorio, No. A72 093 558, at 15-16 (describing government's failure to investigate or prosecute violence against lesbians or gay men).

7. *Id. See generally* Lambert, *INS Urged to Grant Asylum Over Gay Bias*, WALL ST. J., May 28, 1993, at B7.

8. 8 U.S.C. § 1158(a) (1988).

9. The statute requires the Attorney General to "establish a procedure for an alien physically present in the United States or at a land border or port of entry, irrespective of such alien's status, to apply for asylum, and the alien may be granted asylum in the discretion of the Attorney General if the Attorney General determines

> Any person who is outside of any country of such person's nationality or, in the case of a person having no nationality is outside any country in which such person habitually resided, and who is unable or unwilling to avail himself or herself of the protection of that country because of persecution or a well-founded fear of persecution on account of race, religion, nationality, membership in a particular social group, or political opinion.[10]

So long as an applicant "*establishes a well-founded fear of persecution*" based on at least one of the five designated categories, he or she is eligible for asylum. Although "membership in a particular social group" is the classification that most closely describes those persecuted because of their sexual orientation,[11] neither the INA nor the related regulations[12] define the category precisely.

To qualify for asylum under any category,[13] an applicant must establish a well-founded fear of persecution by showing that a reasonable person in his or her circumstances would fear persecution.[14] He or she must present "direct, credible evidence supporting the claim" which

---

that such alien is a refugee within the meaning of Section 1101(a)(42)(A) of this title." 8 U.S.C. § 1158(a) (1988).

In cases where the Attorney General decides against exercising his or her discretion to grant asylum but "determines that such alien's life or freedom would be threatened in such country on account of race, religion, nationality membership in a particular social group, or political opinion," the Attorney General may not return the alien to that country and must order deportation to be withheld. 8 U.S.C. § 1253(h) (West Supp. 1991).

10. 8 U.S.C. § 1101(a)(42)(A) (1988). This definition, first adopted by Congress in the Refugee Act of 1980, Pub. L. No. 96-212, 94 Stat. 102 (1982) (codified as amended in scattered sections of 8 U.S.C.) restates the definition of refugee from the United Nations Protocol Relating to the Status of Refugees, Jan. 31, 1967, 19 U.S.T. 6223, 606 U.N.T.S. 267. The Protocol, to which the United States acceded in 1968, took its definition of refugee from the 1951 United Nations Refugee Convention Relating to the Status of Refugees, July 28, 1951, 19 U.S.T. 6223, 189 U.N.T.S. 150.

Analyzing the statute, the Supreme Court has found that "[i]f one thing is clear from the legislative definition of 'refugee' and indeed the entire 1980 Act, it is that one of Congress' primary purposes was to bring the United States law into conformance with the 1967 United States Protocol Relating to the Status of Refugees (citation omitted)." INS v. Cardoza-Fonseca, 480 U.S. 421, 436-37 (1987). *See* T. David Parish, *Membership in a Particular Social Group Under the Refugee Act of 1980: Social Identity and the Legal Concept of the Refugee*, 92 COLUM. L. REV. 923, 924-26 (1992).

11. Political opinion is another category into which many lesbians and gay asylum applicants may fit, particularly if they were identified and persecuted on the basis of advocacy for lesbians and gay men.

12. 8 C.F.R. § 208.13(b)(1) (1993).

13. The standards of proof for establishing eligibility for asylum and withholding of deportation differ. The well-founded fear standard in the asylum statute requires proof that such persecution would be a "reasonable possibility," a standard of proof which is less than a probability. *See* INS v. Cardoza-Fonseca, 480 U.S. 421, 431 (1987). To establish eligibility for withholding of deportation, an alien must meet the higher burden of proving that the threat to his or her life is more probable than not. *Id.* at 428.

14. Matter of Mogharrabi, 19 I. & N. Dec. 439 (BIA 1987). *See also* Kovac v. INS, 407 F.2d 102, 107 (9th Cir. 1969) (defining persecution as "infliction of suffering or harm upon those who differ . . . in a way regarded as offensive").

supports his or her "sincere and deeply-felt fear" of persecution.[15] Moreover, the corroborating evidence should demonstrate that the applicant's fear has a "basis . . . in the reality of the circumstance."[16]

II. Tatiana's Case

As a lesbian in Romania, Tatiana lives in fear of persecution under a national law which criminalizes and severely punishes consensual sexual relations between women.[17] She has also personally experienced and continues to fear the police and other representatives of the state who rely on this and related laws to harass and detain in "preventive custody" women and men who are lesbian or gay.[18] On the basis of these laws, which reflect a policy that homosexuality is "a mental disease and sinful sickness,"[19] several lesbians and gay men Tatiana knows have been detained and confined to psychiatric facilities to undergo electroshock and drug therapy. Even those who attempted to deny their lesbian or gay identity upon arrest were investigated, identified, and kept in detention. Tatiana lives in fear that she too will be arrested on trumped up charges and forced to undergo treatment that would effectively end her life.

In light of her documentary evidence establishing that Romania persecutes lesbian women on the basis of their sexual orientation, Tatiana has a well-founded fear of persecution. The critical question,

15. Sarvia-Quintanilla v. INS, 767 F.2d 1387, 1394 (9th Cir. 1985). Evidence of the government's treatment of other similarly situated group members can also establish an applicant's well-founded fear of persecution. Matter of Mogharrabi, 19 I. & N. Dec. 439 (BIA 1987); Office of the United Nations High Commissioner for Refugees, Handbook on Procedures and Criteria for Determining Refugee Status Under the 1951 Convention and 1967 Protocol Relating to the Status of Refugees ¶ 43 (1979) [hereinafter Handbook]; Bolanos-Hernandez v. INS, 767 F.2d 1277, 1283 n.11 (9th Cir. 1984).

16. Blanco-Comarribas v. INS, 830 F.2d 1039, 1042 (9th Cir. 1987). Because women and men face threats of persecution simply for identifying themselves as lesbian or gay, documenting the actual instance of persecution—in addition to the policies reflected in punitive laws and practices—is often a difficult task. *See* discussion of *Sanchez-Trujillo*, *infra* note 43 and accompanying text.

Moreover, until recently, mainstream human rights organizations did not monitor persecution based on sexual orientation. The San Francisco-based IGLHRC has emerged as a leading resource for documentation of global persecution of lesbians and gay men.

17. Laws which impose unduly harsh and disproportionate punishment on practices of a particular group within a population, based on religion or sexual orientation, for example, may alone amount to persecution. *See infra* notes 80-86 and accompanying text.

18. *See* Duda, *supra* note 3, at 1 (noting that "even the attempt to 'engage in homosexual behaviour'," including sexual contact between women, is illegal); *see* Letter from Adrian Duta, Undersecretary of State, Romanian Ministry of Justice, to Stephan Cooper (July 1992) (discussing Romanian Penal Code offenses including "homosexuality" (article 200) and "sexual perversity" (article 201) and describing detention and disappearance of gay men under "preventive custody" on charge of "outrage against good manners and causing a serious disturbance") (on file with the *Cornell International Law Journal*).

19. Duda, *supra* note 3.

therefore, is whether as a lesbian, Tatiana is eligible for asylum as a member of "a particular social group."[20]

III. Setting the Standard: Particular Social Group

Providing asylum from identity-based attacks led or endorsed by an applicant's country of origin is a central goal of American refugee law.[21] Like the other four classifications for asylum eligibility, the "particular social group" category thus offers the possibility of protection to those targeted for who they are or what they believe.

While courts differ over the precise definition of social group, men and women persecuted because they are gay or lesbian are persecuted for their membership in a group of people who share a common central feature of their individual identities—gay or lesbian sexual orientation. In the instant case, Tatiana is subject to persecution not only for expressing her sexual orientation by her sexual conduct but also simply for being a lesbian.[22]

Judicial interpretations of the "membership in a particular social group" category vary. In *Matter of Acosta*, the Board of Immigration Appeals (BIA) considered whether young urban men of draft age in El Salvador constituted a particular social group for purposes of asylum eligibility in the United States. It described critical elements common to most analyses:

> [The statute addresses] persecution that is directed toward an individual who is a member of a group of persons all of whom share a common, immutable characteristic. The *shared characteristic might be an innate one* such as sex, color, or kinship ties, *or* in some circumstances it might be a *shared past experience* such as former military leadership or land ownership. The particular kind of group characteristic that will qualify under this construction remains to be determined on a case-by-case basis.[23]

Although the BIA rejected the argument that young men of draft age constituted a social group and denied Acosta's application, it offered a useful description of the common characteristic which unites group members: "[the characteristic] must be one that the members of the group either cannot change, or should not be required to change because it is fundamental to their individual identities or consciences."[24] As discussed below, sexual orientation is both highly resistant to change and so fundamental to individual identity that individuals "should not be required to change" to avoid state persecution.[25]

20. 8 U.S.C. § 1101(a)(42)(A) (1988).
21. *Id.*
22. *See supra* notes 17-18 and accompanying text.
23. Matter of Acosta, 19 I. & N. Dec. 211, 233 (BIA 1985) (emphasis added).
24. *Id.*
25. The Board of Immigration Appeals (BIA) determined that sexual orientation is an immutable characteristic. *See* Matter of Toboso, No. A23, 220, 644 (BIA 1990). *Cf.* Matter of Terorio, No. A72 093 558, at 14 ("Sexual orientation is arguably an

Tatiana, therefore, should not be required to change or repress her lesbian identity in order to survive.

The BIA also considered whether Acosta belonged to a class that the government "seek[s] to overcome by means of punishment of some sort."[26] In light of Romania's policies and practices toward lesbians it is clear that as a lesbian Tatiana belongs to such a class.

Using similar criteria, the First Circuit has defined a "particular social group" as comprising persons of "similar background, habits or social status."[27] Granting the asylum application of a Ghanaian woman who feared persecution based on a combination of her family ties and political activities, the *Ananeh-Firempong* court explained that "the threat of persecution arises out of characteristics that are essentially beyond the petitioner's power to change."[28]

The *Ananeh-Firempong* court drew its interpretation from the definition of "particular social group" developed by the United Nations High Commissioner for Refugees (UNHCR) for its *Handbook on Procedures and Criteria for Determining Refugee Status*.[29] The UNHCR *Handbook*, which "is widely considered useful in giving content to the obligations that the Protocol establishes,"[30] defines "particular social group" as follows: "A 'particular social group' normally comprises *persons of similar background, habits or social status.* A claim to fear of persecution under this heading may frequently overlap with a claim to fear of persecution on other grounds, i.e. race, religion or nationality."[31] Again, Tatiana belongs to a group of women with similar social status under Romanian policies and law, and thus clearly falls within the *Ananeh-Firempong* and UNHCR standards.

In addition to the shared fundamental characteristic, the persecutor's perceptions of the group has also been identified as an important determinant of whether a particular social group exists. In *Gomez v. INS*, the Second Circuit explained that "[a] particular social group is comprised of individuals who possess some fundamental characteristic in common which serves to distinguish them in the eyes of a persecutor—or in the eyes of the outside world in general."[32]

The *Gomez* court considered whether an El Salvadoran woman qualified for asylum as a member of a social group of "women who have been previously battered and raped by Salvadoran guerrillas."[33] In rejecting Gomez's claim, the court stated that "[p]ossession of *broadly-based* characteristics such as youth and gender will not by itself endow individuals

immutable characteristic and one which an asylum applicant should not be compelled to change."). *See also infra* notes 69-77 and accompanying text.

26. Matter of Acosta, 19 I. & N. Dec. at 231.
27. Ananeh-Firempong v. INS, 766 F.2d 621, 626 (1st Cir. 1985).
28. *Id.*
29. HANDBOOK, *supra* note 15, ¶¶ 77-79.
30. INS v. Cardoza-Fonseca, 480 U.S. 421, at 439 n.22 (1987).
31. HANDBOOK, *supra* note 15, ¶ 77 (emphasis added).
32. Gomez v. INS, 947 F.2d 660, 664 (2d Cir. 1991) (citations omitted).
33. *Id.* at 663.

with membership in a particular social group."[34] It emphasized that Gomez did not provide evidence that women previously assaulted by guerrillas share "common characteristics—other than gender and youth—such that would-be persecutors could identify them as members of the purported group."[35] The court also stressed that "there is no indication that Gomez will be singled out for further brutalization on this basis" and concluded, therefore, that Gomez did not "demonstrate[] that she is more likely to be persecuted than any other young woman."[36]

The *Gomez* court appeared to track the UNHCR analysis that governments persecute individuals based on their membership in a social group when groups are perceived as a threat to governmental control over the nation's political, economic or social systems.

> Membership of such a particular social group may be at the root of persecution because there is no confidence in the group's loyalty to the Government or because the political outlook, antecedents or economic activity of its members, *or the very existence of the social group as such, is held to be an obstacle to the Government's policies.*[37]

In contrast to Gomez's situation as described by the court, Romania's policies clearly reflect an official intent to squelch both the expression of lesbian and gay identity and the very existence of lesbians and gay men in the country, indicating a belief that lesbians and gay men are such an obstacle to government policy.[38] As a result of these policies, Tatiana faces a significant threat of persecution because she is a lesbian.

Although the Ninth Circuit standard diverges from those described above, it also addresses the situation of lesbian women and gay men persecuted on the basis of their sexual orientation. In *Sanchez-Trujillo v. INS*,[39] the court defined "particular social group" as "a collection of people closely affiliated with each other, who are actuated by some common impulse or interest."[40] Of central concern to the court was "the existence of a voluntary associational relationship among the purported members, which imparts some common characteristic that is fundamental to their identity as a social group."[41] The court recognized a persecutor's perception of a segment of society as a social group as relevant

34. *Id.* at 664 (emphasis added).
35. *Id.*
36. *Id.*
37. HANDBOOK, *supra* note 15, ¶¶ 77-78 (emphasis added).
38. *See supra* notes 18-19 and accompanying text.
39. 801 F.2d 1571 (9th Cir. 1986).
40. *Id.* at 1576.
41. *Id.* Commentators have widely criticized the *Sanchez-Trujillo* court's interpretation for failing to capture adequately the term's full meaning. *See generally, e.g.*, Daniel Compton, *Asylum for Persecuted Social Groups: A Closed Door Left Slightly Ajar*, 62 WASH. L. REV. 913 (1987); Parish, *supra* note 10; M. Graves, *From Definition to Exploration: Social Groups and Political Asylum Eligibility*, 26 SAN DIEGO L. REV. 740, 771 (1989); Carolyn P. Blum, *Refugee Status Based on Membership in a Particular Social Group: A North American Perspective*, *in* ASYLUM LAW AND PRACTICE IN EUROPE AND NORTH AMERICA: A COMPARATIVE ANALYSIS (Jacqueline Bhaba & Geoffrey Coll eds., 1992).

but not conclusive.[42]

Although the Ninth Circuit standard concurs with those in *Matter of Acosta* and *Gomez* in requiring group members to possess a common characteristic or impulse fundamental to their identity, it imposes the additional requirement of a close and voluntary association among group members. Despite its stringency, lesbian women and gay men meet this test; their identities become known publicly as a result of close and voluntary association with other lesbians or gay men, or by self-identification necessary to meet other lesbians or gay men. In Tatiana's case, because she identifies herself as a lesbian and associates with other lesbians both socially and politically, she meets the *Sanchez-Trujillo* standard for membership in a particular social group.[43]

In general, however, the *Sanchez-Trujillo* "close and voluntary association" requirement makes little sense for a population which, by the very fact of associating, risks almost certain persecution and even capital punishment by governments whose stated intention is to persecute those who identify as lesbian or gay.[44] In fact, many lesbians and gay men who fear persecution deny their identity and avoid association with others as a matter of self-preservation. The INA does not require such extreme efforts to repress an aspect of identity that "members of the group either cannot change or should not be required to change because it is fundamental to their individual identities or consciences."[45]

IV. Identifying the Group: A Socio-Political Consideration of the "Particular Social Group" of Lesbian Women and Gay Men

Whether currently or historically, people who identify themselves as, or are perceived to be, lesbian or gay experience unique and sometimes oppressive treatment both by the state and by society.[46] As a population

42. *Sanchez-Trujillo*, 801 F.2d at n.7.

43. In fact, as of August 1993 the first and only immigration court to grant asylum to a man persecuted on account of his membership in the particular social group of gay men followed the analytic framework set out in *Sanchez-Trujillo*. The court reasoned:

> There exists a voluntary associational relationship among the members, and a common characteristic that is fundamental to their identity as a member of the social group. Sexual orientation is arguably an immutable characteristic, and one which an asylum applicant should not be compelled to change. Thus, homosexuals are considered to be members of a particular group.

Matter of Tenorio, No. A72 093 558, at 14.

44. *See supra* notes 3-5 and accompanying text.

45. Matter of Acosta, 19 I. & N. Dec. at 233.

46. Indeed, this risk accounts in great part for the fact that many lesbians and gay men do not publicly acknowledge their own lesbian or gay identities. Even without the threat of persecution, many lesbians and gay men do not overtly reveal their sexual orientation to family members or co-workers, fearing rejection, abuse and loss of financial and/or emotional support. *See, e.g.*, Herek, *supra* note 1, at 146; Stewart, *Gay in Corporate America*, FORTUNE, Dec. 16, 1991, at 30; Martin P. Levine & Robin Leonard, *Discrimination Against Lesbians in the Workforce*, 9 SIGNS 700 (1984). *See generally* KATH WESTON, FAMILIES WE CHOOSE: LESBIANS, GAYS, KINSHIP 43-56 (1991).

sharing the fundamental characteristic of minority sexual orientation, lesbians and gay men have long been treated as a distinct and particular social group.

A. Sexual Orientation as an Aspect of Human Identity

Much popular confusion surrounds the nature and origin of sexual orientation. Social scientists and psychologists, however, are careful to distinguish sexual orientation—the erotic and/or affectional attraction to members of the same or opposite gender[47]—from biological sex,[48] gender identity,[49] and social sex role.[50]

The term "sexual orientation" itself encompasses several aspects of human identity and activity: 1) sexual conduct with partners of a particular gender; 2) enduring psychological attraction to partners of a particular gender; and 3) private identity based on sexual orientation (thinking of oneself as lesbian, gay, bisexual or heterosexual).[51] In addition, one may claim or be assigned a public identity based on sexual orientation, and identify with a community based on sexual orientation.[52]

As is evident from this list, sexual orientation refers to much more than sexual behavior.[53] Being lesbian or gay forms part of a person's identity and involves more than simply engaging in sexual conduct with persons of the same gender.[54] Tatiana, for example, identifies herself as a lesbian, socializes with other lesbian women, and collects information and publications about lesbians in all parts of the world. Her identity as a lesbian does not depend on being in a relationship with another woman, any more than a woman's identity as a heterosexual depends on being in a relationship with a man.

Most social and behavioral scientists believe that sexual orientation—whether heterosexual, lesbian or gay—is fundamental to human identity and highly resistant to change.[55] In fact, the American Psychological Association has condemned as unethical the so-called conversion

47. HOMOSEXUALITY, *supra* note 1, at 1. *See also* Gregory M. Herek, *Sexual Orientation*, *in* 1 WOMEN'S STUDIES ENCYCLOPEDIA 344 (H. Tierney, ed. 1989).

48. Biological sex refers to chromosomal genetic material. HOMOSEXUALITY, *supra* note 1, at 1. Biological sex is commonly referred to as gender.

49. Gender identity is "the psychological sense of being male or female." *Id.*

50. Social sex role is "adherence to the culturally created behaviors and attitudes that are deemed appropriate for male or females." *Id. See also* Herek, *supra* note 1, at 149.

51. *See id.* at 134.

52. *Id.*

53. *Id.* at 134-35.

54. People with a lesbian or gay orientation do not always identify themselves privately or publicly as lesbian or gay. Social pressure to conform to heterosexuality as well as the threat of discrimination and persecution may lead lesbian women and gay men to repress or hide their sexual orientation from others. *Id.* at 135.

55. Social and behavioral scientists generally believe that sexual orientation is set in place at an early age. *See* A. BELL ET AL., SEXUAL PREFERENCE: ITS DEVELOPMENT IN MEN AND WOMEN 186-87 (1981). *See also* Richard Green, *The Immutability of (Homo)sexual Orientation: Behavioral Science Implications for a Constitutional (Legal) Analysis*,

therapies that attempt to change the sexual orientation of people who are lesbian or gay.[56]

In addition, like race, ethnicity, religion, and political opinion, sexual orientation cannot be altered or renounced according to the dictates of a government in power. Regardless of whether sexual orientation has a genetic origin, lesbian women and gay men cannot disassociate themselves from the basis of their persecution.[57] To that extent, sexual orientation is indeed immutable.[58]

---

16 J. PSYCHIATRY & LAW 537 (1988); RICHARD GREEN, THE "SISSY BOY SYNDROME" AND THE DEVELOPMENT OF HOMOSEXUALITY 370 (1987).

Many experts believe that both biological and socio-environmental factors contribute to the shaping of an individual's sexual orientation. *See* John Money, *Sin, Sickness, or Status? Homosexual Gender Identity and Psycho-neuroendocrinology*, 42 AM. PSYCHOLOGIST 384 (1987); Herek, *supra* note 1, at 148-51. *See also* BELL ET AL., *supra*, at 183-86. Recent scientific studies have focused attention on the genetic origins of lesbian and gay orientation. *See* Natalie Angier, *Report Suggests Homosexuality is Linked to Genes*, N.Y. TIMES, July 16, 1993, at A11; Chandler Burr, *Homosexuality & Biology*, THE ATLANTIC, Mar. 1993, at 47; Natalie Angier, *Study Suggests Genes Sway Lesbians Sexual Orientation*, N.Y. TIMES, Mar. 12, 1993, at All; Douglas C. Haldeman, *Sexual Orientation Conversion Therapy for Gay Men and Lesbians: A Scientific Examination*, *in* HOMOSEXUALITY, *supra* note 1, at 149-60; Herek, *supra* note 1, at 151. *Cf.* Janet E. Halley, *Sexual Orientation and the Politics of Biology: A Critique of the Argument from Immutability*, 79 STAN. L. REV. (forthcoming 1994). It bears mention, as well, that extensive psychological research over three decades has established conclusively that lesbian or gay orientation is not related to psychological adjustment or maladjustment. *See* John C. Gonsiorek, *The Empirical Basis for the Demise of the Illness Model of Homosexuality*, *in* HOMOSEXUALITY, *supra* note 1, at 114-36; John C. Gonsiorek, *Results of Psychological Testing on Homosexual Populations*, 25 AM. BEHAVIORAL SCI. 385, 394 (1982); B. F. Reiss, *Psychological Tests in Homosexuality*, *in* HOMOSEXUAL BEHAVIOR: A MODERN REAPPRAISAL 296-311 (Marmor ed., 1980).

Extensive psychological analyses demonstrate that "theories contending that the existence of differences between homosexuals and heterosexuals implies maladjustment are irresponsible, uninformed, or both." John C. Gonsiorek, *The Empirical Basis for the Demise of the Illness Model of Homosexuality*, *in* HOMOSEXUALITY, *supra* note 1, at 136.

56. *See* American Psychological Association (APA), *Fact Sheet on Reparative Therapy*, cited by Haldeman in HOMOSEXUALITY, *supra* note 1, at 160. The Fact Sheet begins: "No scientific evidence exists to support the effectiveness of any of the conversion therapies that try to change sexual orientation." *Id.* In a 1990 statement on conversion therapy, Dr. Brian Welch, Executive Director for Professional Practice of the APA, commented that "research findings suggest that efforts to 'repair' homosexuals are nothing more than social prejudice garbed in psychological accoutrements." *Id.*

57. *Cf.* David L. Neal, *Women as a Social Group: Recognizing Sex-Based Persecution as Grounds for Asylum*, 20 COL. HUM. RTS. L. REV. 203, 251 (1988) (making this point with respect to gender-based persecution).

58. Discussing the nature of immutability, a Canadian court also provides helpful analysis:

> Most of the grounds enumerated . . . as prohibited grounds of discrimination connote the attribute of immutability, such as race, national or ethnic origin, colour, age. One's religion may be changed, but with some difficulty; sex and mental or physical disability, with even greater difficulty. Presumably, sexual orientation would fit within one of these levels of immutability.

Timothy Veysey v. Commissioner of the Correctional Service of Canada, 29 F.T.R. 74, 78 (T.D. 1989), *appeal dismissed*, Fed. Ct. of Appeals, A-557-89 (May 31, 1990).

As a relatively small sector of the population,[59] lesbians and gay men are by definition a minority within the larger society.[60] In addition, many countries' laws and policies attempt to repress or subordinate their very existence.[61] As a result, openly lesbian women and gay men "are self-consciously bound together as a community by virtue of these characteristics."[62] This is certainly true for Tatiana who has close friendships with the few other women and men she knows to be lesbian or gay.

B. Sexual Orientation as a Basis for Treatment as a Social Group

A long and tortured history of institutionalized discrimination against lesbian women and gay men sadly attests to the differential treatment of this minority group.[63] Sanctioned police assault and brutality are

59. Lesbians and gay men are commonly thought to constitute between five and ten percent of the United States population, comprising the first, second or third most numerous minority in the United States. *See* John C. Gonsiorek and James D. Weinrich, *The Definition and Scope of Sexual Orientation*, *in* HOMOSEXUALITY, *supra* note 1, at 11-12. The validity of recent studies which report lower percentage figures has been challenged. *See* F. Barringer, *Sex Survey of American Men Finds 1% Are Gay*, N.Y. TIMES, Apr. 15, 1993, at A1; J. Schmalz, *Survey Stirs Debate on Number of Gay Men in U.S.*, N.Y. TIMES, Apr. 16, 1993, at A20. Although no similar global study has been completed, evidence exists of lesbians and gay men in all countries around the world.

60. Although it was articulated nearly forty years ago, see D. W. CORY, THE HOMOSEXUAL IN AMERICA (1951), the notion that lesbians and gay men constitute a minority group comparable to racial, ethnic and religious minorities has recently gained more acceptance. Gregory M. Herek, *Stigma, Prejudice, and Violence Against Lesbians and Gay Men*, *in* HOMOSEXUALITY, *supra* note 1, at 63 (citing F. E. Kameny, *Homosexuals as a Minority Group*, *in* THE OTHER MINORITIES 50-65 (Edward Sagarin ed., 1971)).

61. *See* LILLIAN FADERMAN, ODD GIRLS AND TWILIGHT LOVERS: A HISTORY OF LESBIAN LIFE IN TWENTIETH-CENTURY AMERICA (1991). INTERNATIONAL LESBIAN AND GAY ASSOCIATION, ILGA PINK BOOK: GLOBAL VIEW OF LESBIAN AND GAY LIBERATION AND EXPRESSION (2nd ed. 1988) (surveying official attitudes and laws concerning lesbians and gay men around the world).

62. *See* JOHN D'EMILIO, SEXUAL POLITICS, SEXUAL COMMUNITIES: THE MAKING OF A HOMOSEXUAL MINORITY IN AMERICA (1983); DENNIS ALTMAN, THE HOMOSEXUALIZATION OF AMERICA, THE AMERICANIZATION OF THE HOMOSEXUAL (1982); William Paul, *Minority Status for Gay People—Majority Reaction and Social Context*, HOMOSEXUALITY: SOCIAL, PSYCHOLOGICAL AND BIOLOGICAL ISSUES 356 (Paul et al. eds., 1982).

63. Although the Greeks and Romans had relatively free attitudes regarding sexuality, increased official repression of sexuality accompanied the spread of Christian doctrine. *See generally* M. GOODICH, THE UNMENTIONABLE VICE: HOMOSEXUALITY IN THE LATER MEDIEVAL PERIOD (1970). While homosexual conduct was sometimes tolerated during the first thousand years of Christian hegemony, J. BOSWELL, CHRISTIANITY, TOLERANCE & HOMOSEXUALITY (1980), in the thirteenth century, it was popularly defined as more "unnatural" than other "unnatural" sex such as masturbation, nonprocreative or nonmarital heterosexual conduct, and procreative heterosexual intercourse in other than the approved position. *See* Arthur N. Gilbert, *Conceptions of Homosexuality and Sodomy in Western History*, 6 J. HOMOSEXUALITY 57, 62 (1981). These ecclesiastical proscriptions first entered canon law, V. BULLOUGH, SEXUAL VARIANCE IN SOCIETY AND HISTORY 380-81 (1976), and later became part of criminal codes or common law of England and other European countries. P. CONRAD & J. SCHNEIDER, DEVIANCE AND MEDICALIZATION: FROM BADNESS TO SICKNESS 172-29 (1980). Eventually, during the eighteenth century Age of Enlightenment, homosexuality came to be viewed as pathological. *Id.* at 179-85.

among the most dangerous manifestations of official targeting of lesbians and gay men.[64] In still other instances, gay men and lesbians face harsh criminal liability, and in some cases the death penalty, for engaging in consensual sexual relationships, for identifying themselves as lesbian or gay, or for asserting basic civil rights.[65]

Pervasive negative stereotypes fuel the discriminatory treatment of lesbian and gay people as a group, most of which relate to sex role characteristics.[66] Additional stereotypes characterize gay men "as mentally ill, promiscuous, lonely, insecure, and likely to be child molesters, while lesbians have been described as aggressive and hostile toward men."[67] Relying on these stereotypes as well as anti-gay religious doctrine and other sources, many governments and societies endorse discrimination against, and sometimes persecution of, lesbian and gay members of society.[68] The Romanian laws and policies which threaten Tatiana exemplify this reliance.

Nearly three decades of extensive and well-documented psychological research has come to the precise opposite conclusion: lesbian or gay sexual orientation "in and of itself bears no necessary relationship to psychological adjustment." John C. Gonsiorek, *The Empirical Basis for the Demise of the Illness Model of Homosexuality*, *in* HOMOSEXUALITY, *supra* note 1, at 136. Twenty years ago, the American Psychiatric Association acted on this conclusion and removed homosexuality from its list of mental disorders. Resolution of the American Psychiatric Association, December 15, 1973.

64. In Argentina, for example, state and local police have a practice of targeting gay men for harassment and sometimes assault. In one case, police repeatedly tortured a gay man over a period of many years in several different cities. Because the man is gay, police threatened him, held him in isolation, and subjected to him multiple beatings and sexual assaults. This man ultimately obtained asylum in Canada based on his persecution as a member of the social group of lesbians and gay men. Matter of Jorge Alberto Inaudi, File No. T91 04459 (Immigration and Refugee Board, Canada, Apr. 19, 1992) (describing extreme police brutality against Argentinean asylum applicant); *see also* ILGA PINK BOOK, *supra* note 61.

Similarly, a Cuban man whose deportation from the United States was ordered to be withheld because of persecution based on his membership in the social group of gay men reported a common practice of police and governmental harassment and brutality against gay and lesbian Cubans. *See* Matter of Toboso, No. A23 220 644 (withholding deportation of gay Cuban man based on government's persecution of gay men), *aff'd* Matter of Toboso, No. A23 220 644 (BIA Mar. 12, 1990).

65. *See, e.g.*, Iranian and Nicaraguan laws, *supra* note 4.

66. Gregory M. Herek, *Beyond "Homophobia": A Social Psychological Perspective on Attitudes Toward Lesbians and Gay Men*, 10 J. HOMOSEXUALITY 1, 6 (1984) (summarizing research).

67. *Id.*

68. Of course, not all governments give effect to such negative views. Eight states, over 110 municipalities and many employers in the United States prohibit sexual orientation-based discrimination. *See* Lambda Legal Defense & Education Fund, *A National Summary of Anti-Discrimination Laws* (1992). *Cf.* Evans v. Romer, 854 P.2d 1270 (Colo.), *cert. denied*, 62 U.S.L.W. 3254 (U.S. Nov. 1, 1993) (No. 93-453). (upholding injunction against enforcement of amendment to state constitution that would prohibit state from banning discrimination against lesbians, gay men and bisexuals). In the area of military service, the United States and Britain are the only parties to the North Atlantic Treaty Organization (NATO) that exclude openly lesbian and gay service members. *See* Riding, *In NATO, Only U.S. and British Ban Gay Soldiers*, N.Y. TIMES, Nov. 13, 1992, at A12.

V. Applying the Legal Standard: Lesbians and Gay Men as a Particular Social Group in the United States

Complementing social science analyses regarding sexual orientation, Congress and the courts identify and treat lesbians and gay men as a distinct social group, providing support for the argument that lesbians and gay men meet eligibility standards of United States asylum law.

A. *Matter of Toboso*

The Board of Immigration Appeals (BIA) has already decided that lesbians and gay men are a "particular social group" under the INA in its only reported decision on the matter.[69] At the initial proceeding involving the asylum application of a gay Cuban man, Fidel Armando Toboso, an immigration judge ordered Toboso's deportation to be withheld based on his finding of a pattern of anti-gay discrimination and persecution experienced directly by Toboso and by gay men and lesbians in Cuba generally.

> The Cuban government generally discourages homosexuality, as is made clear by their [sic] efforts to dissuade individuals from participating in this type of lifestyle and as evidenced by the actions committed against this applicant. Thus, the applicant has met his burden of establishing a "fear of persecution," whether the standard applied be "well-founded," "clear probability," "reasonable belief," "realistic likelihood," or any other appropriate standard.[70]

The court concluded that "such persecution results from his membership in a particular social group, that group being homosexuals."[71] Applying the definition of "social group" set forth in *Matter of Acosta*, the court found that Toboso was "a member of a group of persons who share a common, immutable characteristic (i.e. homosexuality), and that this characteristic is one which members of the group either cannot change or should not be required to change because it is fundamental to their individual identities or consciences."[72] The immigration judge in *Toboso* concluded that "[t]he evidence thus establishes the existence of a 'particular social group' which is persecuted by the Cuban government on account of the group's specific identifying characteristic, and whose treatment based on this characteristic is distinct from the general

69. Matter of Toboso, No. A23 220 644 (BIA 1990) (withholding deportation of gay Cuban man based on government's persecution of gay men). The question of asylum eligibility for lesbian women and gay men has not been addressed beyond the Board level. Notably, in the first ruling of its kind in the United States, an immigration judge granted asylum to a Brazilian man who feared persecution on account of his membership in the particular social group of gay men and lesbians. Matter of Tenorio, No. A72 093 558 (July 26, 1993), *appeal pending*.

70. Matter of Toboso, No. A23 220 644, at 4 (citing INS V. Stevic, 104 S. Ct. 2489 (1989) and Matter of Acosta, 19 I. & N. Dec. 211).

71. *Id.*

72. *Id.* at 5. *See supra* notes 54-58 regarding the fundamental nature of sexual orientation.

population."[73]

On appeal, the Immigration and Naturalization Service (INS) argued, unsuccessfully, against the ruling that lesbian women and gay men constitute a social group. Asserting that " 'homosexual activity is not a basis for finding a social group within the contemplation of the Act,' " the Service argued that such a conclusion " 'would be tantamount to awarding discretionary relief to those involved in behavior that is not only socially deviant in nature, but in violation of the laws or regulations of the country as well.' "[74]

Rejecting the INS arguments, the BIA determined that the Cuban government did not target Toboso because of his activities, but rather because of "his having the status of being a homosexual."[75] It reasoned as well that "the Service has not challenged the immigration judge's finding that homosexuality is an 'immutable' characteristic. Nor is there any evidence or argument that, once registered by the Cuban government as a homosexual, that characterization is subject to change."[76] In conclusion, the BIA ruled that the status-based persecution against Toboso as a gay man warranted an order to withhold Toboso's deportation.[77]

---

73. *Id.* (citing Matter of Sanchez and Escobar, Int. Dec. 2996, (BIA 1985)). The judge cited the United States policy of excluding openly lesbian and gay immigrants as evidence that the INS recognized lesbians and gay men as a social group. *Id.* In discussing the exclusion, however, the judge carefully distinguished discrimination from persecution: "Though Congress may have intended to exclude homosexuals from entering the United States, there is no indication that Congress ever sought in the past, or would seek at the present time, to condemn homosexuals to a life of suffering and persecution solely as a result of their sexual orientation." *Id.* at 6.

74. Matter of Toboso, No. A23 220 664, at 4.

75. *Id.* The BIA considered a long list of instances in which Toboso was singled out for official harassment or attack specifically because he was gay and thereby part of a group targeted for persecution by the Cuban government. *Id.* at 2-5. It reviewed testimony, for example, about regular notices requiring "Fidel Armando Toboso, homosexual" to appear for a physical examination which was often followed by several days of police detention without any charges pressed against him and about Toboso being sent to a forced labor camp as punishment because he was gay. *Id.* at 2-3. Additional testimony and evidence described Cuba's general policy and practice of persecuting gay people. *Id.*

Unwillingness of government authorities to investigate or prosecute criminal acts perpetrated against lesbians and gay men may also amount to persecution. In Matter of Tenorio, No. A72 093 558, the immigration court based its decision to grant Tenorio asylum on expert testimony, background documentation regarding persecution by anti-gay paramilitary groups and the applicant's own testimony regarding his fear. The court found that "[a]nti-gay groups appear to be prevalent in Brazilian society and continue to commit violence against homosexuals, with little investigation and few criminal charges being brought against the perpetrators. Thus it appears that homosexuals as a social group have been targeted for persecution in Brazil based upon the characteristics of the group members. *Id.* at 15-16.

76. Matter of Toboso, No. A23 220 664, at 4-5.

77. *Id.* at 5-6. The immigration judge found Toboso to be statutorily eligible for asylum and withholding of deportation as a member of a particular social group who feared persecution by his government. However, because Toboso had two minor convictions, the immigration judge chose not to exercise his discretion to grant the

B. United States Law and Policy

Congress has also recognized that lesbians and gay men constitute a social group. In the area of bias violence, which has obvious parallels to social group-based persecution, Congress has condemned status-based maltreatment of lesbians and gay men in the recently enacted Hate Crimes Statutes Act.[78] The Act requests that states monitor and report bias-motivated assaults against lesbians and gay men on the same basis as attacks based on race, national origin, and other categories.

Recent changes to United States immigration law also reflect a Congressional intent to end discrimination against lesbians and gay men in some areas of federal law. In 1990, Congress repealed a law that barred the entire class of lesbian women and gay men from immigrating to the United States.[79]

In other contexts, courts have unquestioningly treated lesbians and gay men as a social group, often in situations where individual lesbians and gay men suffered discrimination based on their sexual orientation.[80] Although many of these courts did not find the discriminatory practices unconstitutional, their analysis nonetheless bolsters an interpretation of Section 208(a) of the Refugee Act that recognizes lesbians and gay men as a particular social group. Justice Brennan eloquently made this very point:

> [Lesbians and gay men] constitute a significant and insular minority of this country's population. Because of the immediate and severe oppro-

asylum application but instead issued an order to withhold Toboso's deportation pursuant to section 243(h) of the Act. Matter of Toboso, No. A23 220 664, at 7-8.

78. Pub. L. No. 101-275, 104 Stat. 140 (1990) (to be codified at 28 U.S.C. § 538).

79. INA § 212(a)(4), 8 U.S.C. § 1182(a)(4) (repealed 1990 by H.R. 1280, 101st Cong., 1st sess. (1989)). Over twenty years earlier, the United States Supreme Court upheld a ban on lesbian and gay people immigrating based on a law which barred entry by people with "psychopathic personalities." Boutilier v. INS, 363 F.2d 488 (2d Cir. 1966), *aff'd*, 387 U.S. 118 (1967). After the Public Health Service announced through the U.S. Surgeon General an end to certification of gay people as "psychopathic personalities" based on shifts in medical analysis, see Rhonda Rivera, *Sexual Orientation and the Law*, in HOMOSEXUALITY, *supra* note 1, at 88 (citing Memorandum from Julius Richmond, assistant secretary for Health, United States Department of Health, Education and Welfare, and Surgeon General, to William Foege and George Lythcott (Aug. 2, 1979), *reprinted in* 56 Interpreter Releases 398-99 (1979)), the Ninth Circuit ruled that lesbian and gay immigrants without such certification must be admitted. Hill v. INS, 714 F.2d 1470 (9th Cir. 1983). *But see In re Longstaff*, 716 F.2d 1439 (5th Cir. 1983), *cert. denied*, 467 U.S. 1219 (1984).

Even while the ban was firmly in place, the Board of Immigration Appeals withheld deportation of a Cuban man who faced persecution for being gay. *See supra* notes 69-77 and accompanying text. *Cf. In re* Brodie, 394 F. Supp. 1208 (D. Or. 1975) (granting naturalization of openly gay alien despite ban).

80. *See, e.g.*, High Tech Gays v. Defense Industrial Security Clearance Office, 895 F.2d 563 (9th Cir. 1990) (upholding defense department practice of expansive security clearance investigations for lesbian and gay applicants); Ben-Shalom v. Marsh, 881 F.2d 454 (7th Cir. 1989) (upholding military's policy to exclude lesbians and gay men from service in armed forces), *cert. denied*, 494 U.S. 1004 (1990); Padula v. Webster, 822 F.2d 97 (D.C. Cir. 1987) (upholding FBI's refusal to hire lesbian applicant based on sexual orientation).

> brium often manifested against homosexuals once so identified publicly, members of this group are particularly powerless to pursue their rights openly in the political arena. Moreover, homosexuals have historically been the object of pernicious and sustained hostility, and it is fair to say that discrimination against homosexuals is "likely . . . to reflect deep-seated prejudice rather than rationality."[81]

In addition, courts have increasingly condemned the discrimination that sometimes accompanies such identity/group-based treatment of lesbians and gay men.[82]

Taken as a whole, judicial interpretations and Congressional policy illustrate the identification and treatment of lesbians and gay men as a particular social group in American society and jurisprudence, as well as a growing intolerance of sexual orientation-based discrimination.

C. Criminalization of Sodomy and Identity-Based Persecution

Countries generally target lesbian women and gay men for persecution based on their identity, often without regard to whether they actually engage in sexual relations with others.[83] Even laws that criminalize consensual sex between lesbian women or gay men, however, reflect a state policy of persecution when the penalties imposed are extremely severe, disproportionate to the putative statutory goal, or administered without due process.[84] A Federal Administrative Court in the Republic of Germany, for example, found that Iran's imposition of the death penalty amounts to persecution because of its severity (100 strokes for the first two offenses, death for the third), its disproportionality relative to the statute's stated goal of "suppression of a violation of public morality,"

81. Rowland v. Mad River, 730 F.2d 444 (6th Cir. 1984), *cert. denied*, 470 U.S. 1009, 1014 (1985) (Brennan, J., dissenting from denial of certiorari) (quoting Plyler v. Doe, 457 U.S. 202, 216 n.14 (1982).

82. *See, e.g.*, Meinhold v. United States Department of Defense, 808 F. Supp. 1455 (C.D. Cal. 1993) (rejecting military's proffered rationale for ban on lesbians and gay men from service), *stay denied*, 61 Emplyt. Prac. Dec. (CCH) P 42197 (9th 1993); Pruitt v. Cheney, 963 F. 2d 1160 (9th Cir. 1991), *cert. denied*, 61 U.S.L.W. 3418 (1992) (upholding denial of motion to dismiss; military must prove at trial rational basis for ban on lesbians and gay men); Dallas v. England, 846 S.W.2d 957 (Tex. App. 1993) (striking down Texas' sodomy law and barring Texas police force from discriminating based on sexual orientation); Commonwealth of Kentucky v. Wasson, 842 S.W.2d 487 (Ky. 1992) (striking down Kentucky's sodomy law as a violation of right to privacy under Kentucky constitution).

83. Police and other state representatives carry out formal and informal policies of status-based persecution through severe harassment of and direct violent assaults on lesbian women and gay men. *See supra* notes 69-77 and accompanying text.

84. *See* HANDBOOK, *supra* note 15, ¶ 85; Ramirez-Rivas v. INS, 899 F.2d 864, 868 (9th Cir. 1990), *vacated*, 112 S.Ct. 858 (1992); Blanco-Lopez v. INS, 858 F.2d 531, 533-34 (9th Cir. 1988); Diminich v. Esperdy, 299 F.2d 244, 246 (2d Cir. 1961), *cert. denied*, 369 U.S. 844 (1962) (punishment constitutes persecution when criminal sanction is not "reconcilable with generally recognized concepts of justice); Matter of Banjeglay, 10 I. & N. Dec. 351 (Comm. Aug. 28, 1963). *See also* Parish, *supra* note 10, at 953.

and the "unusually low standard of proof."[85] Strikingly, the fact that sodomy could be criminalized did not deter the court from identifying Iran's law as a weapon of persecution.[86]

In light of the critical distinction between regulation of sexual activity and persecution of lesbians and gay men, criminalization of sodomy in parts of the United States should not interfere with the grant of asylum to a person whose life is endangered because she or he is lesbian or gay. The Supreme Court's ruling in *Bowers v. Hardwick*[87] that the constitutional right to privacy does not encompass sexual relations between consenting lesbian and gay adults is largely irrelevant to the discussion of whether lesbians and gay men are eligible for asylum. *Bowers*, a due process challenge to the Georgia sodomy law, focuses exclusively on criminalization of sexual conduct, with no reference to lesbian or gay identity.[88] Moreover, both before and after *Bowers*, courts have refused to permit infringement of established constitutional guarantees of equal protection and first amendment freedoms based on prejudice against gay men and lesbians.[89]

Although not as extreme as Iran's imposition of the death penalty, Romanian laws that criminalize homosexuality and the extreme harassment by detention and forced hospitalization carried out by state officials in reliance on the laws evidence the state's intention to persecute lesbians and gay men.[90] Tatiana's argument that Romania persecutes lesbians and gay men, rather than merely regulates their conduct, is thus well-founded.

---

85. 79 BverwGE 143, 144-45 (1988) (citing the Islamic Criminal Code of Iran of August 25, 1982, arts. 139-141)).

A judge's "own knowledge" of such matters may form the basis for a conviction under the Iranian sodomy law. In contrast, the German court found the standard of proof for heterosexual adultery and other "moral" crimes so high to make convictions very difficult to achieve. *Id.* at 144, 153-54.

Considering these factors together with government statements regarding homosexuality, the German court concluded that Iran's "chief goal, the propagation of Islamic ideals of order and morality, include[s] the elimination and extermination of those who do not fit into this vision." *Id.* at 153.

86. *Id. Cf.* Dudgeon v. United Kingdom, 45 Eur. Ct. H.R. (ser. A) (1982) (holding that N. Ireland statute totally prohibiting sodomy between adult males breached European Convention on Human Rights).

87. 478 U.S. 186 (1986).

88. *See* Cass Sunstein, *Sexual Orientation and the Constitution: A Note of the Relationship Between Due Process and Equal Protection*, 55 U. Chi. L. Rev. 1161, 1168 (1988).

89. *See, e.g.*, Pruitt v. Cheney, 963 F.2d 1160, 1165 (footnote omitted) (9th Cir. 1991), *cert. denied*, 61 U.S.L.W. 3171 (1992) ("Prejudice of others against homosexuals should not be given unexamined effect today as a matter of law."); Gay Activists Alliance v. Board of Regents of Univ. of Oklahoma, 638 P.2d 1116 (Okla. 1981) (student association organized to advocate for lesbian and gay civil rights entitled to recognition by university).

90. *See supra* note 18.

VI. Setting an International Standard: Lesbians and Gay Men as a Particular Social Group in Courts Worldwide

Several courts around the world have granted asylum to lesbians and gay men persecuted on the basis of their sexual orientation.[91] Concluding that lesbians and gay men constitute a social group, these courts granted refuge from persecution to applicants who either experienced physical assault by government officials or faced the threat of capital punishment for consensual lesbian and gay sexual relationships in their country of origin.

In *Matter of Inaudi*, the Refugee Division of the Canadian Immigration and Refugee Board granted asylum to an Argentinean man who experienced extensive harassment by police and military officers over an eight year period. After detailing a painful and lengthy history of official brutality toward Jorge Inaudi based on his identity as a gay man, the court found: "There is no question, in my mind, that the experiences as described by the claimant amount to persecution."[92] As to the question of whether the persecution occurred for a reason condemned by international refugee law, the court examined the Refugee Convention's historical origins,[93] the UNHCR *Handbook* definition, expert analysis, and dictionary definitions of social and group and found that "homosexuals, be they male or female, are members of a particular social group."[94]

In Germany, a Federal Administrative Court of the Federal Republic of Germany affirmed a decision granting asylum to a gay man from Iran, finding a probability of persecution based on the applicant's sexual orientation.[95] In its ruling, the court cited the persecution of gay people in Nazi concentration camps as an example of group-based treatment of lesbians and gay men. Finding that the claimant would be threatened with the death penalty if returned to Iran, the court reasoned that a well-

91. *See, e.g.*, 1 INT'L J. REFUGEE L. 246 (1989) (summary of case before Holland's *Afdeling Rechtspraak van de Raad van State*); Matter of Jorge Alberto Inaudi, File No. T91 04459 (Immigration and Refugee Board, Canada, April 9, 1992).

92. *Matter of Inaudi*, slip op. at 4.

93. The court noted that the United Nations Convention Relating to the Status of Refugees, 189 U.N.T.S. 137 (1951), from which the Protocol was derived, aimed primarily to protect those fleeing Hitler and Stalin, both of whom had persecuted lesbians and gay men. *Id. See generally* ROBERT PLANT, THE PINK TRIANGLE: THE NAZI WAR AGAINST HOMOSEXUALS 181 (1986); Karlinsky, *Unearthing Russia's Gay Past*, THE ADVOCATE, Dec. 3, 1991 (discussing persecution of gay men under Stalin).

94. *Inaudi*, slip op. at 5. The court reasoned:

> Social group is not defined in the *Immigration Act*. I believe, therefore, that the words should be given their ordinary and useful meaning. The Oxford Dictionary defines social as "capable of being associated or united." Clearly homosexuals are capable of being associated or united. The same dictionary defines group as "a number of persons classed together on account of a certain degree of similarity." Homosexuals are classed together on account of a certain degree of similarity, i.e. that they are attracted to persons of their own gender.

Id.

95. Bundesverwaltungsgericht, Case #19880315 (summarized in 1 INT'L J. REFUGEE L. 110-11 (1989)).

founded fear of persecution existed based on the inevitability of the claimant's future behavior. The court found as well that Iran treats lesbians and gay men as "counterrevolutionary criminals."[96]

Conclusion

As the political world order continues to shift, lesbian women and gay men enter increasingly into the ranks of refugees pressing for asylum. Tatiana exemplifies members of this class of women and men who experience and fear severe treatment imposed by their governments because they are lesbian or gay. The extreme official persecution perpetrated against lesbian women and gay men underscores the need to respond to women such as Tatiana and to protect this group of refugees.

As members of "a particular social group," lesbian and gay nationals of countries with threatening laws and practices should be eligible for asylum under the United States Immigration and Nationality Act standards. The discussion of Tatiana's case illustrates that being lesbian or gay is fundamental to human identity and, as such, should be recognized as a characteristic that individuals should not be required to change according to the dictates of the government in power. Claims such as Tatiana's will become increasingly common as the body of information documenting persecution grows and as advocates press these claims on behalf of lesbian women and gay men who must leave their home countries in order to survive.

96. *Id.*

Part V
Work

[20]

"WHETHER FROM REASON OR PREJUDICE": TAKING MONEY FOR BODILY SERVICES

*MARTHA C. NUSSBAUM**

> Taking leave of Binod, Durga slowly, deliberately walks towards the shack of Sukhlal the contractor, who stared at her even yesterday and flashed ten-rupee notes.
> What else can one do, she argues to herself, except fight for survival? The survival of oneself, one's loved ones, and the hopes that really matter. (MANIK BANDYOPADHYAY, "A Female Problem at a Low Level" [1963])

> If the story is about the peasant wife selling her body, then one must look for the meaning of that in the reality of peasant life. One can't look at it as a crisis of morality, in the sense one would in the case of a middle-class wife. (MANIK BANDYOPADHYAY, *About This Author's Perspective* [1957])[1]

I

ALL of us, with the exception of the independently wealthy and the unemployed, take money for the use of our body. Professors, factory workers, lawyers, opera singers, prostitutes, doctors, legislators—we all do things with parts of our bodies for which we receive a wage in return.[2] Some peo-

* Ernst Freund Professor of Law and Ethics, Law School, Philosophy Department, and Divinity School, University of Chicago. I am grateful to the students in my seminar on sexual autonomy and law for all that their discussions contributed to the formulation of these ideas, to Sibyl Schwarzenbach and Laurie Shrage for discussions that helped me think about how to approach this topic, and to Elizabeth Anderson, Gertrud Fremling, Richard Posner, Mark Ramseyer, Eric Schliesser, Elizabeth Schreiber, Steven Schulhofer, Alan Soble, and Cass Sunstein for valuable comments on an earlier draft of this article.

1 Both the story and the extract from the critical work are translated from the Bengali by Kalpana Bardhan. See Of Women, Outcastes, Peasants, and Rebels: A Selection of Bengali Short Stories 157, 19 (Bardhan trans. 1990). Bandyopadhyay (1908–56) was a leading Bengali writer who focused on peasant life and issues of class conflict.

2 Even if one is a Cartesian dualist, as I am not, one must grant that the human exercise of mental abilities standardly requires the deployment of bodily skills. Most traditional Christian positions on the soul go still further; Aquinas, for example, holds that souls separated from the body have only a confused cognition and cannot recognize particulars. So my statements about professors can be accepted even by believers in the separable soul.

ple get good wages, and some do not; some have a relatively high degree of control over their working conditions, and some have little control; some have many employment options, and some have very few. And some are socially stigmatized, and some are not.

The stigmatization of certain occupations may be well founded, based on convincing, well-reasoned arguments. But it may also be based on class prejudice or stereotypes of race or gender. Stigma may also change rapidly as these background beliefs and prejudices change. Adam Smith, in *The Wealth of Nations,* tells us that there are "some very agreeable and beautiful talents" that are admirable so long as no pay is taken for them, "but of which the exercise for the sake of gain is considered, whether from reason or prejudice, as a sort of publick prostitution." For this reason, he continues, opera singers, actors, and dancers must be paid an "exorbitant" wage to compensate them for the stigma involved in using their talents "as the means of subsistence." "Should the publick opinion or prejudice ever alter with regard to such occupations," he concludes, "their pecuniary recompence would quickly diminish."[3] Smith was not altogether right about the opera market,[4] but his discussion is revealing for what it shows us about stigma. Today, few professions are more honored than that of opera singer; and yet only two hundred years ago, that public use of one's body for pay was taken to be a kind of prostitution. Looking back at that time, we now think that the judgments and emotions underlying the stigmatization of singers were irrational and objectionable, like prejudices against members of different classes and races. (I shall shortly be saying more about what I think those reasons were.) Nor do we see the slightest reason to suppose that the unpaid artist is a purer and truer artist than the paid artist. We think it entirely right and reasonable that high art should receive a high salary. If a producer of opera should take the position that singers should not be paid, on the grounds that receiving money for the use of their talents involves an illegitimate form of commodification and even market alienation of those talents, we would think that this producer was a slick exploiter, out to make a profit from the ill treatment of vulnerable and impressionable artists.[5] On the whole, we think that, far from cheapening or ruining talents, the pres-

[3] Adam Smith, An Inquiry into the Nature and Causes of the Wealth of Nations I.x.b.25 (R. H. Campbell *et al.* ed. 1981) (1776). Elsewhere (Adam Smith, Lectures on Rhetoric and Belles Lettres ii.230 (J. C. Bryce ed. 1983)), Smith points out that in ancient Greece acting was "as creditable . . . as it is discreditable now."

[4] He expresses the view that the relevant talents are not so rare and that when stigma is removed many more people will compete for the jobs, driving down wages; this is certainly true today of acting, but far less so of opera, where "the rarity and beauty of the talents" remains at least one dominant factor.

[5] Such arguments have often been used in the theater; they were used, for example, in one acting company of which I was a member in order to persuade actors to kick back their

ence of a contract guarantees conditions within which the artist can develop her art with sufficient leisure and confidence to reach the highest level of artistic production.[6]

It is widely believed, however, that taking money or entering into contracts in connection with the use of one's sexual and reproductive capacities is genuinely bad. Feminist arguments about prostitution, surrogate motherhood, and even marriage contracts standardly portray financial transactions in the area of female sexuality as demeaning to women and as involving a damaging commodification and market alienation of women's sexual and reproductive capacities.[7] The social meaning of these transactions is said to be both that these capacities are turned into objects for the use and control of men and also that the activities themselves are being turned into commodities and thereby robbed of the type of value they have at their best.

One question we shall have to face is whether these descriptions of our current judgments and intuitions are correct. But even if they are, what does this tell us? Many things and people have been stigmatized in our nation's history, often for very bad reasons. An account of the actual social meaning of a practice is therefore just a door that opens onto the large arena of moral and legal evaluation. It invites us to raise Smith's question: are these current beliefs the result of reason or prejudice? Can they be defended by compelling moral arguments? And, even if they can, are these the type of moral argument that can properly be a basis for a legal restriction? Smith, like his Greek and Roman Stoic forebears, understood that the evaluations that ground emotional responses and ascriptions of social meaning in a society

(union-mandatory) salaries to the owners. This is fairly common in theater, where the union is weak and actors are so eager for employment that they are vulnerable to such arguments.

6 The typical contract between major U.S. symphony orchestras and the musicians' union, for example, guarantees year-round employment to symphony musicians, even though they do not play all year; this enables them to use summer months to play in low-paying or experimental settings in which they can perform contemporary music, chamber music, do solo and concerto work, and so forth. It also restricts hours of both rehearsal and performance during the performing season, leaving musicians free to teach students, attend classes, work on chamber music with friends, and in other ways enrich their work. It also mandates blind auditions (that is, players play behind a curtain)—with the result that the employment of female musicians has risen dramatically over the past 20 or so years since the practice was instituted.

7 See Elizabeth Anderson, Value in Ethics and Economics (1993); Elizabeth Anderson, Is Women's Labor a Commodity? 19 Phil. & Pub. Aff. 71 (1990); Margaret Jane Radin, Contested Commodities: The Trouble with the Trade in Sex, Children, Bodily Parts, and Other Things (1996); Margaret Jane Radin, Market-Inalienability, 100 Harv. L. Rev. 1849 (1987); Cass R. Sunstein, Neutrality in Constitutional Law: With Special Reference to Pornography, Abortion, and Surrogacy," 92 Colum. L. Rev. 1 (1992); Cass R. Sunstein, The Partial Constitution 257–90 (1993). For contrasting feminist perspectives on the general issue of contract, see Jean Hampton, Feminist Contractarianism, in A Mind of One's Own: Feminist Essays on Reason and Objectivity 227–55 (Louise Antony & Charlotte Witt eds. 1993); Susan Moller Okin, Justice, Gender, and the Family (1989).

are frequently corrupt—deformed by self-interest, resentment, and mere unthinking habit. The task he undertook in *The Theory of Moral Sentiments* was to devise procedures and strategies of argument through which one might separate the rationally defensible emotions from the irrational and prejudiced. In so proceeding, Smith and the Stoics were correct. Social meaning does no work on its own: it offers an invitation to normative moral and political philosophy.

My aim in this article will be to investigate the question of sexual "commodification" by focusing on the example of "prostitution."[8] I shall argue that a fruitful debate about the morality and legality of prostitution should begin from a twofold starting point: from a broader analysis of our beliefs and practices with regard to taking pay for the use of the body and from a broader awareness of the options and choices available to poor working women. The former inquiry suggests that at least some of our beliefs about prostitution are as irrational as the beliefs Smith reports about singers; it will therefore help us to identify the elements in prostitution that are genuinely problematic. Most, though not all, of the genuinely problematic elements turn out to be common to a wide range of activities engaged in by poor working women, and the second inquiry will suggest that many of women's employment choices are so heavily constrained by poor options that they are hardly choices at all. I think that this should bother us and that the fact that a woman with plenty of choices becomes a prostitute should not bother us, provided that there are sufficient safeguards against abuse and disease, safeguards of a type that legalization would make possible.

It will therefore be my conclusion that the most urgent issue raised by prostitution is that of employment opportunities for working women and their control over the conditions of their employment. The legalization of prostitution, far from promoting the demise of love, is likely to make things a little better for women who have too few options to begin with.[9] The really helpful thing for feminists to ponder if they deplore the nature of these

[8] I shall use the terms "prostitution" and "prostitute" throughout because of their familiarity, although a number of international women's organizations now avoid it for reasons connected to those in this article, preferring the term "commercial sex worker" instead. For one recent example, see Reproductive Health in Developing Countries: Expanding Dimensions, Building Solutions 30 (Amy O. Tsui, Judith N. Wasserheit, & John G. Haaga eds., report of the Panel on Reproductive Health, National Research Council 1997), stressing the wide variety of practices denoted by the term "commercial sex," and arguing that some studies show economic hardship as a major factor but some do not.

[9] Among feminist discussions of prostitution, my approach is close to that of Sibyl Schwarzenbach, Contractarians and Feminists Debate Prostitution, 18 N.Y.U. Rev. L. & Soc. Change 103–29 (1990–91), and to Laurie Shrage, Prostitution and the Case for Decriminalization, Dissent, Spring 1996, at 41–45 (in which Shrage criticizes her earlier view expressed in Should Feminists Oppose Prostitution? 99 Ethics 347 (1989)).

options will be how to promote expansion in the option set through education, skills training, and job creation. These unsexy topics are insufficiently addressed by feminist philosophers in the United States, but they are inevitable in any practical project dealing with real-life prostitutes and their female children.[10] This suggests that at least some of our feminist theory may be insufficiently grounded in the reality of working-class lives and too focused on sexuality as an issue in its own right, as if it could be extricated from the fabric of poor people's attempts to survive.

II

Why were opera singers stigmatized? If we begin with this question, we can move on to prostitution with expanded insight. Although we can hardly provide more than a sketch of the background here, we can confidently say that two common cultural beliefs played a role. First, throughout much of the history of modern Europe—as, indeed, in ancient Greece—there was a common aristocratic prejudice against earning wages. The ancient Greek gentleman was characterized by "leisure"—meaning that he did not have to work for a living. Aristotle reproved the Athenian democracy for allowing such base types as farmers and craftsmen to vote, since, in his view, the unleisured character of their daily activities and their inevitable preoccupation with gain would pervert their political judgment, making them grasping and small-minded.[11] The fact that the Sophists typically took money for their rhetorical and philosophical teaching made them deeply suspect in the eyes of such aristocrats.[12] Much the same view played a role in the medieval church, where it was controversial whether one ought to offer philosophical instruction for pay.[13] Bernard of Clairvaux, for example, held that taking fees for education is a "base occupation" (*turpis quaestus*). (Apparently, he did not think this true of all wage labor, but only where it involved deep spiritual things.)

Such views about wage labor remained closely linked to class privilege in modern Europe and exercised great power well into the twentieth century. Any reader of English novels will be able to produce many examples

[10] To give just one example, the Annapurna Mahila Mandel project in Bombay offers job training and education in a residential school setting to the daughters of prostitutes; they report that in 5 years they have managed to arrange reputable marriages for 1,000 such girls.

[11] Aristotle, Politics VII.9–10.

[12] One can find evidence for this in the attitudes evinced by characters in Platonic dialogues such as *Apology, Protagoras,* and *Gorgias.*

[13] I have profited here from reading an unpublished paper by Dan Klerman, Slavery, Simony and Sex: An Intellectual History of the Limits of Monetary Relations (unpublished manuscript, Univ. Chicago, March 30, 1990).

of the view that a gentleman does not earn wages and that someone who does is overpreoccupied with the baser things in life, therefore base himself. Such views were a prominent source of prejudice against Jews, who, not having the same land rights as Christians, had no choice but to earn their living. Even in this century, in America, Edith Wharton shows that these attitudes were still firmly entrenched. Lily Bart, the impoverished heroine of *The House of Mirth* (1905), is discussing her situation with her friend Gus Trenor. He praises the investment tips he has gotten from Simon Rosedale, a Jewish Wall Street investments expert whose wealth has given him entry into the world of impoverished aristocrats who both use and despise him. Trenor urges Lily to encourage Rosedale's advances: "The man is mad to know the people who don't want to know him, and when a fellow's in that state, there is nothing he won't do for the first woman who takes him up." Lily dismisses the idea, calling Rosedale "impossible," and thinking silently of his "intrusive personality." Trenor replies: "Oh, hang it—because he's fat and shiny and has a shoppy manner! . . . A few years from now he'll be in it whether we want him or not, and then he won't be giving away a half-a-million tip for a dinner!"[14] In the telling phrase "a shoppy manner," we see the age-old aristocratic prejudice against wage work, so deeply implicated in stereotypes of Jews as pushy, intrusive, and lacking in grace.

To this example we may add a moment in the film *Chariots of Fire* (1981) when the Jewish sprinter hires a professional coach to help him win. This introduction of money into the gentlemanly domain of sport shocks the head of his college, who suggests to him that as a Jew he doesn't understand the true spirit of English athletics. Genteel amateurism is the mark of the gentleman, and amateurism demands, above all, not earning or dealing in money. It may also imply not trying too hard, not giving the impression that this is one's main concern in life; but this attitude appears to be closely related to the idea that the gentleman doesn't *need* the activity, has his living provided already; so the rejection of hard work is a corollary of the rejection of the tradesman. (Even today in Britain, such attitudes have not totally disappeared; people from aristocratic backgrounds frequently frown on working too hard at one's scholarly or athletic pursuits, as if this betrayed a kind of base tradesman-like mentality.)

What is worth noting about these prejudices is that they do not attach to activities themselves, as such, but, rather, to the use of these activities to make money. To be a scholar, to be a musician, to be a fine athlete, to be an actor even, is fine so long as one does it as an amateur. But what does

[14] Edith Wharton, The House of Mirth 86–87 (Signet Classics ed. 1964).

this mean? It means that those with inherited wealth[15] can perform these activities without stigma, and others cannot. In England in the nineteenth century, it meant that the gentry could perform those activities, and Jews could not. This informs us that we need to scrutinize all our social views about moneymaking and alleged commodification with extra care, for they are likely to embed class prejudices that are unjust to working people.

Intersecting with this belief, in the opera singer example, is another: that it is shameful to display one's body to strangers in public, especially in the expression of passionate emotion. The anxiety about actors, dancers, and singers reported by Smith is surely of a piece with the more general anxiety about the body, especially the female body, that has been a large part of the history of quite a few cultures. Thus, in much of India until very recently (and in some parts still), it was considered inappropriate for a woman of good family to dance in public; when Rabindranath Tagore included middle-class women in his theatrical productions early in this century, it was a surprising and somewhat shocking move. In a similar manner, in the West, the female body should be covered and not displayed, although in some respects these conditions could be relaxed among friends and acquaintances. Female singers were considered unacceptable during the early history of opera; indeed, they were just displacing the castrati during Smith's lifetime, and they were widely perceived as immoral women.[16] Male actors, singers, and dancers suffered too; and clearly Smith means to include both sexes. Until very recently, such performers were considered to be a kind of gypsy, too fleshy and physical, unsuited for polite company. The distaste was compounded by a distaste for, or at least a profound ambivalence about, the emotions that it was, and is, the business of these performers to portray. In short, such attitudes betray an anxiety about the body, and about strong passion, that we are now likely to think irrational, even

[15] Or those supported by religious orders.

[16] Elizabeth Billington, who sang in Thomas Arne's *Artaxerxes* in London in 1762, was forced to leave England because of criticisms of her morals; she ended her career in Italy. Another early diva was Maria Catalani, who sang for Handel (died 1759), for example, in *Samson*. By the time of the publication of The Wealth of Nations, female singers had made great headway in displacing the castrati, who ceased to be produced shortly thereafter. For Smith's own attitudes to the female body, see Adam Smith, The Theory of Moral Sentiments I.ii.1.3 (D. D. Raphael & A. L. Macfie eds. 1984) (6th ed. 1781), where he states that as soon as sexual passion is gratified it gives rise to "disgust" and leads us to wish to get rid of the person who is its object, unless some higher moral sentiment preserves our regard for (certain aspects of) this person. "When we have dined, we order the covers to be removed; and we should treat in the same manner the objects of the most ardent and passionate desires, if they were the objects of no other passions but those which take their origin from the body." Smith was a bachelor who lived much of his life with his mother and did not have any lasting relationships with women.

though we may continue to share these attitudes at times; certainly we are not likely to think them a good basis for public policy.

When we consider our views about sexual and reproductive services, then, we must be on our guard against two types of irrationality: aristocratic class prejudice and fear of the body and its passions.

III

Prostitution is not a single thing. It can only be well understood in its social and historical context. Ancient Greek *hetairai,* such as Pericles' mistress Aspasia, have very little in common with a modern call girl.[17] Even more important, within a given culture there are always many different types and levels of prostitution: in ancient Greece, the *hetaira,* the brothel prostitute, the streetwalker; in modern America, the self-employed call girl, the brothel prostitute, the streetwalker (and each of these at various levels of independence and economic success). It is also evident that most cultures contain a continuum of relations between women and men (or between same-sex pairs) that have a commercial aspect—ranging from the admitted case of prostitution to cases of marriage for money, going on an expensive date where it is evident that sexual favors are expected at the other end, and so forth. In most cultures, marriage itself has a prominent commercial aspect: the prominence of dowry murder in contemporary Indian culture, for example, testifies to the degree to which a woman is valued, above all, for the financial benefits one can extract from her family.[18] Let us, however, focus for the time being on contemporary America (with some digressions on India), on female prostitution only, and on explicitly commercial relations of the sort that are illegal under current law.

It will be illuminating to consider the prostitute by situating her in relation to several other women who take money for bodily services:

1. A factory worker in the Perdue chicken factory, who plucks feathers from nearly frozen chickens.

[17] Aspasia was a learned and accomplished woman who apparently had philosophical and political views; she is said to have taught rhetoric and to have conversed with Socrates. On the one hand, she could not perform any of the functions of a citizen both because of her sex and because of her foreign birth. On the other hand, her son Pericles was subsequently legitimated and became a general. More recently, it has been doubted whether Aspasia was in fact a *hetaira,* and some scholars now think her a well-born foreign woman. But other *hetairai* in Greece had good education and substantial financial assets; the two women recorded as students in Plato's Academy were both *hetairai,* as were most of the women attested as students of Epicurus, including one who was apparently a wealthy donor.

[18] See Martha Nussbaum, Religion and Women's Human Rights, in Religion and Contemporary Liberalism 93–137 (Paul Weithman ed. 1997).

2. A domestic servant in a prosperous upper-middle-class house.

3. A nightclub singer in middle-range clubs, who sings (often) songs requested by the patrons.

4. A professor of philosophy, who gets paid for lecturing and writing.

5. A skilled masseuse, employed by a health club (with no sexual services on the side).

6. A person whom I'll call the "colonoscopy artist": she gets paid for having her colon examined with the latest instruments, in order to test out their range and capability.[19]

By considering similarities and differences between the prostitute and these other bodily actors, we will make progress in identifying the distinctive features of prostitution as a form of bodily service.

Note that nowhere in this comparison am I addressing the issue of child prostitution or nonconsensual prostitution (for example, young women sold into prostitution by their parents, forcible drugging and abduction, and so forth). Insofar as these features appear to be involved in the international prostitution market, I do not address them here, although I shall comment on them later. I address only the type of choice to be a prostitute that is made by a woman over the age of consent, frequently in a situation of great economic duress.

1. *The Prostitute and the Factory Worker.* Both prostitution and factory work are usually low-paid jobs; but, in many instances, a woman faced with the choice can (at least over the short-haul) make more money in prostitution than in this sort of factory work. (This would probably be even more true if prostitution were legalized and the role of pimps thereby restricted, though the removal of risk and some stigma might at the same time depress wages, to some extent offsetting that advantage for the prostitute.) Both face health risks, but the health risk in prostitution can be very much reduced by legalization and regulation, whereas the particular type of work the factory worker is performing carries a high risk of nerve damage in the hands, a fact about it that appears unlikely to change. The prostitute may well have better working hours and conditions than the factory worker; especially in a legalized regime, she may have much more control over her working conditions. She has a degree of choice about which clients she accepts and what activities she performs, whereas the factory worker has no choices but must perform the same motions again and again for years. The prostitute also performs a service that requires skill and responsiveness to

[19] Although this profession, as described, is hypothetical, medical students do employ "models" to teach students how to perform pelvic and other internal exams: see page 706 and note 27 *infra*.

new situations, whereas the factory worker's repetitive motion exercises relatively little human skill[20] and contains no variety.

The factory worker, however, is unlikely to be the target of violence, whereas the prostitute needs—and does not always get—protection against violent customers. (Again, this situation can be improved by legalization: prostitutes in the Netherlands have a call button wired up to the police.) This factory worker's occupation, moreover, has no clear connection with stereotypes of gender—though this might not have been the case. In many parts of the world, manual labor is strictly segmented by sex, and more routinized, low-skill tasks are given to women.[21] The prostitute's activity does derive some of its attraction from stereotypes of women as sluttish and immoral, and it may in turn perpetuate such stereotypes. The factory worker suffers no invasion of her internal private space, whereas the prostitute's activity involves such (consensual) invasion. Finally, the prostitute suffers from social stigma, whereas the factory worker does not—at least among people of her own social class. (I shall return to this issue, asking whether stigma too can be addressed by legalization.) For all these reasons, many women, faced with the choice between factory work and prostitution, choose factory work, despite its other disadvantages.

2. *The Prostitute and the Domestic Servant.* In domestic service as in prostitution, one is hired by a client and one must do what that client wants or fail at the job. In both, one has a limited degree of latitude to exercise skills as one sees fit, and both jobs require the exercise of some developed bodily skills. In both, one is at risk of enduring bad behavior from one's client, although the prostitute is more likely to encounter physical violence. Certainly both are traditionally professions that enjoy low respect, both in society generally and from the client. Domestic service on the whole is likely to have worse hours and lower pay than (at least many types of) prostitution, but it probably contains fewer health risks. It also involves no invasion of intimate bodily space, as prostitution (consensually) does.

Both prostitution and domestic service are associated with a type of social stigma. In the case of domestic service, the stigma is, first, related to

[20] It is probably, however, a developed skill to come to work regularly and to work regular hours each day.

[21] Consider, for example, the case of Jayamma, a brick worker in Trivandrum, Kerala, India (discussed by Leela Gulati, Profiles of Female Poverty 35–62 (1981)), whom I met on March 21, 1997, when she was approximately 65 years old. For approximately 40 years, Jayamma worked as a brick carrier in the brick-making establishment, carrying heavy loads of bricks on her head all day from one place to another. Despite her strength, fitness, and reliability, she could never advance beyond that job because of her sex, whereas men were quickly promoted to the less physically demanding and higher-paying tasks of brick molding and truck loading.

class: it is socially coded as an occupation only for the lowest classes.[22] Domestic servants are in a vast majority of cases female, so it becomes coded by sex. In the United States, domestic service is very often racially coded as well. Not only in the South but also in many parts of the urban North, the labor market has frequently produced a clustering of African American women in these low-paying occupations. In my home in suburban Philadelphia in the 1950s and 1960s, the only African Americans we saw were domestic servants, and the only domestic servants we saw were African American. The perception of the occupation as associated with racial stigma ran very deep, producing difficult tensions and resentments that made domestic service seem to be incompatible with dignity and self-respect. (It needn't be, clearly; and I shall return to this.)

3. *The Prostitute and the Nightclub Singer.* Both of these people use their bodies to provide pleasure, and the customer's pleasure is the primary goal of what they do.[23] This does not mean that a good deal of skill and art isn't involved, and in both cases, it usually is. Both have to respond to requests from the customer, although (in varying degrees depending on the case) both may also be free to improvise or to make suggestions. Both may be paid more or less, have better or worse working conditions, and more or less control over what they do.

How do they differ? The prostitute faces health risks and risks of violence not faced by the singer. She also allows her bodily space to be invaded, as the singer does not. It may also be that prostitution is always a cheap form of an activity that has a higher, better form, whereas this need not be the case in popular vocal performance (though of course it might be).[24] The nightclub singer, furthermore, does not appear to be participating in, or perpetuating, any type of gender hierarchy—although in former times this would not have been the case, singers being seen as "a type of publick prostitute," and their activity associated, often, with anxiety about the con-

[22] Indeed, this appears to be a ubiquitous feature: in India, the mark of "untouchability" is the performance of certain types of cleaning, especially those dealing with bathroom areas. Mahatma Gandhi's defiance of caste manifested itself in the performance of these menial services.

[23] This does not imply that there is some one thing, pleasure, varying only by quantity, that they produce. With Mill (and Plato and Aristotle), I think that pleasures differ in quality, not only in quantity.

[24] This point was suggested to me by Elizabeth Schreiber. I'm not sure whether I endorse it: it all depends on whether we really want to say that sex has one highest goal. Just as it would have been right, in an earlier era, to be skeptical about the suggestion that the sex involved in prostitution is "low" because it is nonreproductive, so too it might be good to be skeptical about the idea that prostitution sex is "low" because it is nonintimate. Certainly nonintimacy is involved in many noncommercial sexual relationships and is sometimes desired as such.

trol of female sexuality. Finally, there is no (great) moral stigma attached to being a nightclub singer, although at one time there certainly was.

4. *The Prostitute and the Professor of Philosophy.* These two figures have a very interesting similarity: both provide bodily services in areas that are generally thought to be especially intimate and definitive of selfhood. Just as the prostitute takes money for sex, which is commonly thought to be an area of intimate self-expression, so the professor takes money for thinking and writing about what she thinks—about morality, emotion, the nature of knowledge, whatever—all parts of a human being's intimate search for understanding of the world and self-understanding. It was precisely for this reason that the medieval thinkers I have mentioned saw such a moral problem about philosophizing for money: it should be a pure spiritual gift, and it is degraded by the receipt of a wage. The fact that we do not think that the professor (even one who regularly holds out for the highest salary offered) thereby alienates her mind or turns her thoughts into commodities—even when she writes a paper for a specific conference or volume—should put us on our guard about making similar conclusions in the case of the prostitute.

Other similarities are that in both cases, the performance involves interaction with others, and the form of the interaction is not altogether controlled by the person. In both cases, there is at least an element of producing pleasure or satisfaction (note the prominent role of teaching evaluations in the employment and promotion of professors), although in philosophy there is also a countervailing tradition of thinking that the goal of the interaction is to produce dissatisfaction and unease. (Socrates would not have received tenure in a modern university.) It may appear at first that the intimate bodily space of the professor is not invaded—but we should ask about this. When someone's unanticipated argument goes into one's mind, is this not both intimate and bodily? (And far less consensual, often, than the penetration of prostitute by customer?) Both performances involve skill. It might plausibly be argued that the professor's involves a more developed skill, or at least a more expensive training—but we should be cautious here. Our culture is all too ready to think that sex involves no skill and is simply "natural," a view that is surely false and is not even seriously entertained by many cultures.[25]

The salary of the professor, and her working conditions, are usually a great deal better than those of (all but the most elite) prostitutes. The professor has a fair amount of control over the structure of her day and her work-

[25] Thus the *Kama Sutra,* with its detailed instructions for elaborately skilled performances, strikes most Western readers as slightly comic since the prevailing romantic ideal of "natural" sex makes such contrivance seem quite unsexy.

ing environment, although she also has fixed mandatory duties, as the prostitute, when self-employed, does not. If the professor is in a nation that protects academic freedom, she has considerable control over what she thinks and writes, although fads, trends, and peer pressure surely constrain her to some extent. The prostitute's need to please her customer is usually more exigent and permits less choice. In this way, she is more like the professor of philosophy in Cuba than like the U.S. counterpart[26]—but the Cuban professor appears to be worse off, since she cannot say what she really thinks even when off the job. Finally, the professor of philosophy, if a female, both enjoys reasonably high respect in the community and also might be thought to bring credit to all women in that she succeeds at an activity commonly thought to be the preserve only of males. She thus subverts traditional gender hierarchy, whereas the prostitute, while suffering stigma herself, may be thought to perpetuate gender hierarchy.

5. *The Prostitute and the Masseuse.* These two bodily actors seem very closely related. Both use a skill to produce bodily satisfaction in the client. Unlike the nightclub singer, both do this through a type of bodily contact with the client. Both need to be responsive to what the client wants and to a large degree take direction from the client as to how to handle his or her body. The bodily contact involved is rather intimate, although the internal space of the masseuse is not invaded. The type of bodily pleasure produced by the masseuse may certainly have an erotic element, although in the type of "respectable" masseuse I'm considering, it is not directly sexual.

The difference is primarily one of respectability. Practitioners of massage have fought for, and have to a large extent won, the right to be considered as dignified professionals who exercise a skill. Their trade is legal; it is not stigmatized; and people generally do not believe that they degrade their bodies or turn their bodies into commodities by using their bodies to give pleasure to customers. They have positioned themselves alongside physical therapists and medical practitioners, dissociating themselves from the erotic dimension of their activity. As a consequence of this successful self-positioning, they enjoy better working hours, better pay, and more respect than most prostitutes. What is the difference, we might ask? One is having sex, and the other is not. But what sort of difference is this? Is it a difference we want to defend? Are our reasons for thinking it so crucial really reasons, or vestiges of moral prejudice? A number of distinct beliefs enter in at this point: the belief that women should not have sex with strangers, the belief that commercial sex is inherently degrading and makes a woman a degraded woman, the belief that women should not have to have sex with strangers

[26] We might also consider the example of a skilled writer who writes advertising copy.

if they do not want to, and in general, the belief that women should have the option to refuse sex with anyone they do not really choose. Some of these beliefs are worth defending, and some are not. (I shall argue that the issue of choice is the really important one.) We need to sort them out and to make sure that our policies are not motivated by views we are not really willing to defend.

6. *The Prostitute and the Colonoscopy Artist.* I have included this hypothetical occupation for a reason that should now be evident: it involves the consensual invasion of one's bodily space. (The example is not so hypothetical, either: medical students need models when they are learning to perform internal exams, and young actors do earn a living playing such roles.)[27] The colonoscopy artist uses her skill at tolerating the fiber-optic probe without anaesthesia to make a living. In the process, she permits an aperture of her body to be penetrated by another person's activity—and, we might add, far more deeply penetrated than is generally the case in sex. She runs some bodily risk, since she is being used to test untested instruments, and she will probably have to fast and empty her colon regularly enough to incur some malnutrition and some damage to her excretory function. Her wages may not be very good—for this is probably not a profession characterized by what Smith called "the beauty and rarity of talents," and it may also involve some stigma, given that people are inclined to be disgusted by the thought of intestines.

And yet, on the whole, we do not think that this is a base trade or one that makes the woman who does it a fallen woman. We might want to ban or regulate it if we thought it was too dangerous, but we would not be moved to ban it for moral reasons. Why not? Some people would point to the fact that it does not either reflect or perpetuate gender hierarchy; and this is certainly true. (Even if her being a woman is crucial to her selection for the job—they need to study, for example, both male and female colons—it won't be for reasons that seem connected with the subordination of women.) But surely a far greater part of the difference is made by the fact that most people do not think anal penetration by a doctor in the context of a medical procedure is immoral,[28] whereas lots of people do think that vaginal or anal penetration in the context of sexual relations is (except

[27] See Terri Kapsalis, Public Privates: Performing Gynecology from Both Ends of the Speculum (1997); Terri Kapsalis, In Print: Backstage at the Pelvic Theater, Chi. Reader, April 18, 1997, at 46. While a graduate student in performance studies at Northwestern, Kapsalis made a living as a "gynecology teaching associate," serving as the model patient for medical students learning to perform pelvic and breast examinations.

[28] The same goes for vaginal penetration, according to Kapsalis: she says that the clinical nature of the procedure more than compensates for "society's queasiness with female sexuality" (Kapsalis, In Print, *supra* note 27, at 46).

under very special circumstances) immoral and that a woman who goes in for that is therefore an immoral and base woman.

IV

Prostitution, we now see, has many features that link it with other forms of bodily service. It differs from these other activities in many subtle ways: but the biggest difference consists in the fact that it is, today, more widely stigmatized. Professors no longer get told that selling their teaching is a *turpis quaestus*. Opera singers no longer get told that they are unacceptable in polite society. Even the masseuse has won respect as a skilled professional. What is different about prostitution? Two factors stand out as sources of stigma. One is that prostitution is widely held to be immoral; the other is that prostitution (frequently at least) is bound up with gender hierarchy, with ideas that women and their sexuality are in need of male domination and control, and the related idea that women should be available to men to provide an outlet for their sexual desires. The immorality view would be hard to defend today as a justification for the legal regulation of prostitution, and perhaps even for its moral denunciation. People thought prostitution was immoral because they thought nonreproductive and especially extramarital sex was immoral; the prostitute was seen, typically, as a dangerous figure whose whole career was given over to lust. But female lust was (and still often is) commonly seen as bad and dangerous, so prostitution was seen as bad and dangerous. Some people would still defend these views today, but it seems inconsistent to do so if one is not prepared to repudiate other forms of nonmarital sexual activity on an equal basis. We have to grant, I think, that the most common reason for the stigma attached to prostitution is a weak reason, at least as a public reason: a moralistic view about female sexuality that is rarely consistently applied (to premarital sex, for example) and that seems unable to justify restriction on the activities of citizens who have different views of what is good and proper. At any rate, it seems hard to use the stigma so incurred to justify perpetuating stigma through criminalization, unless one is prepared to accept a wide range of morals laws that interfere with chosen consensual activities, something that most feminist attackers of prostitution rarely wish to do.

More promising as a source of good moral arguments might be the stigma incurred by the connection of prostitution with gender hierarchy. But what is the connection, and how exactly does gender hierarchy explain pervasive stigma? It is only a small minority of people for whom prostitution is viewed in a negative light because of its collaboration with male supremacy; for only a small minority of people at any time have been reflective feminists, concerned with the eradication of inequality. Such people will view the prostitute as they view veiled women or women in purdah: with sympathetic anger, as victims of an unjust system. This reflective feminist critique, then, does not explain why prostitutes are actually stigmatized, held in disdain—both because it is not pervasive enough and because it leads to sympathy rather than to disdain.

The way that gender hierarchy actually explains stigma is a very different way, a way that turns out in the end to be just another form of the immorality charge. People committed to gender hierarchy, and determined to ensure that the dangerous sexuality of women is controlled by men, frequently have viewed the prostitute, a sexually active woman, as a threat to male control of women. They therefore become determined either to repress the occupation itself by criminalization or, if they also think that male sexuality needs such an outlet and that this outlet ultimately defends marriage by giving male desire a safely debased outlet, to keep it within bounds by close regulation. (Criminalization and regulation are not straightforwardly opposed; they can be closely related strategies. In a similar manner, prostitution is generally conceived as not the enemy but the ally of marriage: the two are complementary ways of controlling women's sexuality.) The result is that social meaning is deployed in order that female sexuality will be kept in bounds carefully set by men. The stigma attached to the prostitute is an integral part of such bounding.

A valuable illustration of this thesis is given by Alain Corbin's fascinating and careful study of prostitutes in France in the late nineteenth century.[29] Corbin shows that the interest in legal regulation of prostitution was justified by the alleged public interest in reining in and making submissive a dangerous female sexuality that was always potentially dangerous to marriage and social order. Kept in carefully supervised houses known as *maisons de tolérance,* prostitutes were known by the revealing name of *filles soumises,* a phrase that most obviously designated them as registered, "subjugated" to the law, but that also connoted their controlled and confined status. What this meant was that they were controlled and confined so that they themselves could provide a safe outlet for desires that threatened to disrupt the social order. The underlying aim of the regulationist project, argues Corbin (with ample documentation), was "the total repression of sexuality."[30] Regulationists tirelessly cited to Saint Augustine's dictum: "Abol-

[29] Alain Corbin, Women for Hire: Prostitution and Sexuality in France after 1850 (Alan Sheridan trans. 1990).

[30] *Id.* at 29. Representative views of the authors of regulationism include the view that "debauchery is a fever of the senses carried to the point of delirium; it leads to prostitution (or to early death...)" and that "there are two natural sisters in the world: prostitution and riot" (*id.* at 373).

ish the prostitutes and the passions will overthrow the world; give them the rank of honest women and infamy and dishonor will blacken the universe.''[31] In other words, stigma has to be attached to prostitutes because of the necessary hierarchy that requires morality to subjugate vice, and the male the female, seen as an occasion and cause of vice. Bounding the prostitute off from the ''good woman,'' the wife whose sexuality is monogamous and aimed at reproduction, creates a system that maintains male control over female desire.[32]

This attitude to prostitution has modern parallels. One instructive example is from Thailand in the 1950s, when Field Marshal Sarit Thanarat began a campaign of social purification, holding that ''uncleanliness and social impropriety . . . led to the erosion of social orderliness.''[33] In theory, Thanarat's aim was to criminalize prostitution by the imposition of prison terms and stiff fines; in practice the result was a system of medical examination and ''moral rehabilitation'' that shifted the focus of public blame from the procurers and traffickers to prostitutes themselves. Unlike the French system, the Thai system did not encourage registered prostitution; but it was similar in its public message that the problem of prostitution is a problem of ''bad'' women and in its reinforcement of the message that female sexuality is a cause of social disruption unless tightly controlled.

In short, sex hierarchy causes stigma, commonly, not through feminist critique but through a far more questionable set of social meanings, meanings that anyone concerned with justice for women should call into question. For it is these same meanings that are also used to justify the seclusion of women, the veiling of women, and the genital mutilation of women. The view boils down to the view that women are essentially immoral and dangerous and will be kept in control by men only if men carefully engineer things so that they do not get out of bounds. The prostitute, being seen as the uncontrolled and sexually free woman, is in this picture seen as particularly dangerous, both necessary to society and in need of constant subjugation. As an honest woman, a woman of dignity, she will wreck society. As a *fille soumise,* her reputation in the dirt, she may be tolerated for the service she provides (or in the Thai case, she may provide an engrossing public spectacle of ''moral rehabilitation'').

All this diverts attention from some very serious crimes, such as the use

[31] Augustine, De ordine 2.4.12

[32] For a more general discussion of the relationship between prostitution and various forms of marriage, see Richard A. Posner, Sex and Reason 130–33 (1992).

[33] Sukanya Hantrakul, Thai Women: Male Chauvinism à la Thai, Nation, November 16, 1992, cited with further discussion in A Modern Form of Slavery: Trafficking of Burmese Women and Girls into Brothels in Thailand (Asia Watch Women's Rights Project 1993).

of kidnapping, coercion, and fraud to entice women into prostitution. For these reasons, international human rights organizations, such as Human Rights Watch and Amnesty International, have avoided taking a stand against prostitution as such and have focused their energies on the issue of trafficking and financial coercion.[34]

It appears, then, that the stigma associated with prostitution has an origin that feminists have good reason to connect with unjust background conditions and to decry as both unequal and irrational, based on a hysterical fear of women's unfettered sexuality. There may be other good arguments against the legality of prostitution, but the existence of widespread stigma all by itself does not appear to be among them. So long as prostitution is stigmatized, people are injured by that stigmatization, and it is a real injury to a person not to have dignity and self-respect in her own society. But that real injury (as with the comparable real injury to the dignity and self-respect of interracial couples or of lesbians and gay men) is not best handled by continued legal strictures against the prostitute and can be better dealt with in other ways: for example, by fighting discrimination against these people and taking measures to promote their dignity. As the Supreme Court said in a mixed-race custody case, "Private biases may be outside the reach of the law, but the law cannot, directly or indirectly, give them effect."[35]

V

Pervasive stigma itself, then, does not appear to provide a good reason for the continued criminalization of prostitution, any more than it does for the illegality of interracial marriage. Nor does the stigma in question even appear to ground a sound *moral* argument against prostitution. This is not, however, the end of the issue: for there are a number of other significant arguments that have been made to support criminalization. With our six related cases in mind, let us now turn to those arguments.

1. *Prostitution Involves Health Risks and Risks of Violence.* To this we can make two replies. First, insofar as this is true, as it clearly is, the problem is made much worse by the illegality of prostitution, which prevents adequate supervision, encourages the control of pimps, and discourages health checking. As Corbin shows, regimes of legal but regulated prostitu-

[34] See A Modern Form of Slavery: The Human Rights Watch Global Report on Women's Human Rights 196–273, esp. 270–73 (1995). The pertinent international human rights instruments take the same approach, including the International Covenant on Civil and Political Rights, the Convention on the Elimination of All Forms of Discrimination against Women, and the Convention for the Suppression of Traffic in Persons and the Exploitation of the Prostitution of Others.

[35] Palmore v. Sidoti, 466 U.S. 429 (1984).

tion have not always done well by women: the health checkups of the *filles soumises* were ludicrously brief and inadequate.[36] But there is no reason why one cannot focus on the goal of adequate health checks, and some European nations have done reasonably well in this area.[37] The legal brothels in Nevada have had no reported cases of AIDS.[38] Certainly risks of violence can be far better controlled when the police is the prostitute's ally rather than her oppressor.

To the extent to which risks remain an inevitable part of the way of life, we must now ask what general view of the legality of risky undertakings we wish to defend. Do we ever want to rule out risky bargains simply because they harm the agent? Or do we require a showing of harm to others (as might be possible in the case of gambling, for example)? Whatever position we take on this complicated question, we will almost certainly be led to conclude that prostitution lies well within the domain of the legally acceptable: for it is probably less risky than boxing, another activity in which working-class people try to survive and flourish by subjecting their bodies to some risk of harm. There is a stronger case for paternalistic regulation of boxing than of prostitution, and externalities (the glorification of violence as example to the young) make boxing at least as morally problematic, probably more so. And yet I would not defend the criminalization of boxing, and I doubt that very many Americans would either. Sensible regulation of both prostitution and boxing, by contrast, seems reasonable and compatible with personal liberty.

In the international arena, many problems of this type stem from the use of force and fraud to induce women to enter prostitution, frequently at a very young age and in a strange country where they have no civil rights. An especially common destination, for example, is Thailand, and an especially common source is Burma, where the devastation of the rural economy has left many young women an easy mark for promises of domestic service elsewhere. Driven by customers' fears of HIV, the trade has focused on increasingly young girls from increasingly remote regions. Human rights interviewers have concluded that large numbers of these women were unaware of what they would be doing when they left their country and are kept there through both economic and physical coercion. (In many cases,

[36] In Paris, Dr. Clerc boasted that he could examine a woman every 30 seconds and estimated that a single practitioner saw 400 women in a single 24-hour period. Another practitioner estimated that the average number of patients per hour was 52. See Corbin, *supra* note 29, at 90.

[37] For a more pessimistic view of health checks, see Posner, *supra* note 32, at 209, pointing out that they frequently have had the effect of driving prostitutes into the illegal market.

[38] See Richard A. Posner, Private Choices and Public Health: The AIDS Epidemic in an Economic Perspective 149 (1993), with references.

family members have received payments, which then become a "debt" that the girl has to pay off.)[39] These circumstances, terrible in themselves, set the stage for other forms of risk and violence. Fifty percent to seventy percent of the women and girls interviewed by Human Rights Watch were HIV positive; discriminatory arrests and deportations are frequently accompanied by abuse in police custody. All these problems are magnified by the punitive attitude of the police and government toward these women as prostitutes or illegal aliens or both, although under both national and international law trafficking victims are exempt from legal penalty and are guaranteed safe repatriation to their country of origin. This situation clearly deserves both moral condemnation and international legal pressure; but, it is made worse by the illegality of prostitution itself.

2. *The Prostitute Has No Autonomy; Her Activities Are Controlled by Others.* This argument[40] does not serve to distinguish prostitution from very many types of bodily service performed by working-class women. The factory worker does worse on the scale of autonomy, and the domestic servant no better. I think this point expresses a legitimate moral concern: a person's life seems deficient in flourishing if it consists only of a form of work that is totally out of the control and direction of the person herself. Karl Marx rightly associated that kind of labor with a deficient realization of full humanity and (invoking Aristotle) persuasively argued that a flourishing human life probably requires some kind of use of one's own reasoning in the planning and execution of one's own work.[41] But that is a pervasive problem of labor in the modern world, not a problem peculiar to prostitution as such. It certainly does not help the problem to criminalize prostitution—any more than it would be to criminalize factory work or domestic service. A woman will not exactly achieve more control and "truly human functioning" by becoming unemployed. What we should instead think about are ways to promote more control over choice of activities, more variety, and more general humanity in the types of work that are actually available to people with little education and few options. That would be a lot more helpful than removing one of the options they actually have.

3. *Prostitution Involves the Invasion of One's Intimate Bodily*

[39] See A Modern Form of Slavery: The Human Rights Watch Global Report on Women's Human Rights, *supra* note 34, at 1–7.

[40] See E. Anderson, Value in Ethics and Economics, *supra* note 7, at 156: "Her actions under contract express not her own valuations but the will of her customer."

[41] This is crucial in the thinking behind the "capabilities approach" to which I have contributed in Women, Culture, and Development (M. Nussbaum & J. Glover eds. 1995) and other publications. For the connection between this approach and Marx's use of Aristotle, see my Aristotle on Human Nature and the Foundations of Ethics, in World, Mind, and Ethics: Essays on the Philosophy of Bernard Williams (J. E. J. Altham & R. Harrison eds. 1993).

Space. This argument[42] does not seem to support the legal regulation of prostitution so long as the invasion in question is consensual—that is, that the prostitute is not kidnapped, fraudulently enticed, a child beneath the age of consent, or under duress against leaving if she should choose to leave. In this sense, prostitution is quite unlike sexual harassment and rape and far more like the activity of the colonoscopy artist—not to everyone's taste, and involving a surrender of bodily privacy that some will find repellant, but not for that reason necessarily bad, either for self or others. The argument does not even appear to support a moral criticism of prostitution, unless one is prepared to make a moral criticism of all sexual contact that does not involve love or marriage.

4. *Prostitution Makes It Harder for People to Form Relationships of Intimacy and Commitment.* This argument is prominently made by Elizabeth Anderson in defense of the criminalization of prostitution.[43] The first question we should ask is, Is this true? People still appear to fall in love in the Netherlands and Germany and Sweden; they also fell in love in ancient Athens, where prostitution was not only legal but also, probably, publicly subsidized.[44] One type of relationship does not, in fact, appear to remove the need for the other—any more than a Jackie Collins novel removes the desire to read Proust. Proust has a specific type of value that is by no means found in Jackie Collins, so people who want that value will continue to seek out Proust, and there is no reason to think that the presence of Jackie Collins on the bookstand will confuse Proust lovers into thinking that Proust is really like Jackie Collins. So too, one supposes, with love in the Netherlands: people who want relationships of intimacy and commitment continue to seek them out for the special value they provide, and they do not have much trouble telling the difference between one sort of relationship and another, despite the availability of both.

Second, one should ask which women Anderson has in mind. Is she saying that the criminalization of prostitution would facilitate the formation of love relationships on the part of the women who were (or would have been) prostitutes? Or is she saying that the unavailability of prostitution as an op-

[42] Made frequently by my students, not necessarily to support criminalization.

[43] See Anderson, Value in Ethics and Economics, *supra* note 7, at 150–58; Anderson pulls back from an outright call for criminalization, concluding that her arguments "establish the legitimacy of a state interest in prohibiting prostitution, but not a conclusive case for prohibition," given the paucity of opportunities for working women.

[44] See K. J. Dover, Greek Homosexuality (2d ed. 1978); and David Halperin, The Democratic Body, in One Hundred Years of Homosexuality and Other Essays (1990). Customers were all males, but prostitutes were both male and female. The evidence that prostitution was publicly funded is uncertain, since it derives from comic drama; but it is certain that both male and female prostitution enjoyed broad public support and approval.

tion for working-class women would make it easier for romantic middle-class women to have the relationships they desire? The former claim is implausible, since it is hard to see how reinforcing the stigma against prostitutes or preventing some poor women from taking one of the few employment options they might have would be likely to improve their human relations.[45] The latter claim might possibly be true (though it is hardly obvious), but it seems a repugnant idea, which I am sure Anderson would not endorse, that we should make poor women poorer so that middle-class women can find love. Third, one should ask Anderson whether she is prepared to endorse the large number of arguments of this form that might plausibly be made in the realm of popular culture and, if not, whether she has any way of showing how she could reject those as involving an unacceptable infringement of liberty and yet allowing the argument about prostitution that she endorses. For it seems plausible that making rock music illegal would increase the likelihood that people would listen to Mozart and Beethoven, that making Jackie Collins illegal would make it more likely that people would turn to Joyce Carol Oates, that making commercial advertising illegal would make it more likely that we would appraise products with high-minded ideas of value in our minds, and that making television illegal would improve children's reading skills. What is certain, however, is that we would and do utterly reject those ideas (we do not even seriously entertain them) because we do not want to live in Plato's *Republic,* with our cultural options dictated by a group of wise guardians, however genuinely sound their judgments may be.[46]

5. *The Prostitute Alienates Her Sexuality on the Market; She Turns Her Sexual Organs and Acts into Commodities.*[47] Is this true? It seems implausible to claim that the prostitute alienates her sexuality just on the grounds that she provides sexual services to a client for a fee. Does the singer alienate her voice, or the professor her mind? The prostitute still has her sexual-

[45] For a similar point, see Radin, Market-Inalienablity, *supra* note 7, at 1921–25; and Radin, Contested Commodities, *supra* note 7, at 132–36; Anderson refers to this claim of Radin's, apparently as the source of her reluctance to call outright for criminalization.

[46] I would not go quite as far as John Rawls, however, in the direction of letting the market determine our cultural options. He opposes any state subsidy to opera companies, symphony orchestras, museums, and so forth, on the grounds that this would back a particular conception of the good against others. I think, however, that we could defend such subsidies, within limits, as valuable because they preserve a cultural option that is among the valuable ones and that might otherwise cease to exist. Obviously, much more argument is needed on this entire question.

[47] See Radin, Contested Commodities, *supra* note 7; and Anderson, *supra* note 7, at 156: "The prostitute, in selling her sexuality to a man, alienates a good necessarily embodied in her person to him and thereby subjects herself to his commands."

ity; she can use it on her own, apart from the relationship with the client, just as the domestic servant may cook for her family and clean her own house.[48] She can also cease to be a prostitute, and her sexuality will still be with her, and hers, if she does. So she has not even given anyone a monopoly on those services, far less given them over into someone else's hands. The real issue that separates her from the professor and the singer seems to be the degree of choice she exercises over the acts she performs. But is even this a special issue for the prostitute, any more than it is for the factory worker or the domestic servant or the colonoscopy artist—all of whom choose to enter trades in which they will not have a great deal of say over what they do or (within limits) how they do it? Freedom to choose how one works is a luxury, highly desirable indeed, but a feature of few jobs that nonaffluent people perform.

As for the claim that the prostitute turns her sexuality into a commodity, we must ask what that means. If it means only that she accepts a fee for sexual services, then that is obvious; but nothing further has been said that would show us why this is a bad thing. The professor, the singer, the symphony musician—all accept a fee, and it seems plausible that this is a good state of affairs, creating spheres of freedom. Professors are more free to pursue their own thoughts now, as moneymakers, than they were in the days when they were supported by monastic orders; symphony musicians playing under the contract secured by the musicians union have more free time than nonunionized musicians and more opportunities to engage in experimental and solo work that will enhance their art. In neither case should we conclude that the existence of a contract has converted the abilities into things to be exchanged and traded separately from the body of the producer; they remain human creative abilities, securely housed in their possessor. So if, on the one hand, to "commodify" means merely to accept a fee, we have been given no reason to think that this is bad.

If, on the other hand, we try to interpret the claim of "commodification" using the narrow technical definition of "commodity" used by the Uniform Commercial Code,[49] the claim is plainly false. For that definition stresses the "fungible" nature of the goods in question, and "fungible" goods are, in turn, defined as goods "of which any unit is, by nature or usage of trade, the equivalent of any other like unit." While we may not think that the soul or inner world of a prostitute is of deep concern to the customer, she is

[48] On this point, see also Schwarzenbach, *supra* note 9, with discussion of Marx's account of alienation.

[49] See Richard Epstein, Surrogacy: The Case for Full Contractual Enforcement, 81 Va. L. Rev. 2305–41, 2327 (1995).

usually not regarded as simply a set of units fully interchangeable with other units.[50] Prostitutes are probably somewhat more fungible than bassoon players, but not totally so. (Corbin reports that all *maisons de tolérance* standardly had a repertory of different types of women, to suit different tastes, and this should not surprise us.) What seems to be the real issue is that the woman is not attended to as an individual, not considered as a special unique being. But that is true of many ways people treat one another in many areas of life, and it seems implausible that we should use that kind of disregard as a basis for criminalization. It may not even be immoral: for surely we cannot deeply know all the people with whom we have dealings in life, and many of those dealings are just fine without deep knowledge. So our moral question boils down to the question, Is sex without deep personal knowledge always immoral? It seems to me officious and presuming to use one's own experience to give an affirmative answer to this question, given that people have such varied experiences of sexuality.

In general, then, there appears to be nothing baneful or value-debasing about taking money for a service, even when that service expresses something intimate about the self. Professors take a salary, artists work on commission under contract—frequently producing works of high intellectual and spiritual value. To take money for a production does not turn either the activity or the product (for example, the article, the painting) into a commodity in the baneful sense in which that implies fungibility. If this is so, there is no reason to think that a prostitute's acceptance of money for her services necessarily involves a baneful conversion of an intimate act into a commodity in that sense. If the prostitute's acts are, as they are, less intimate than many other sexual acts people perform, that does not seem to have a great deal to do with the fact that she receives money, given that people engage in many intimate activities (painting, singing, writing) for money all the time without loss of expressive value. Her activity is less intimate because that is its whole point; and it is problematic, to the extent that it is, neither because of the money involved nor because of the nonintimacy (which, as I have said, it seems to me officious to declare bad in all cases) but because of features of her working conditions and the way she is treated by others.

Here we are left with an interesting puzzle: for my argument about professors and painters certainly seems to imply that there is no reason, in principle, why the most committed and intimate sex cannot involve a contract and a financial exchange. So why does it not, in our culture? One reply is

[50] Moreover, the Uniform Commercial Code does not cover the sale of services, and prostitution should be classified as a service rather than a good.

that it quite frequently does when people form committed relationships that include an element of economic dependence, whether one-sided or mutual; marriage has very frequently had that feature, not always for the worse. But to the extent that we do not exchange money for sex, why do we not? In a number of other cultures, courtesans, both male and female, have been somewhat more common as primary sexual partners than they are here. Unlike quite a few cultures, we do not tend to view sex in intimate personal relationships the way we view an artist's creation of a painting, namely as an intimate act that can nonetheless be deliberately undertaken as the result of an antecedent contract-like agreement. Why not? I think there is a mystery here, but we can begin to grapple with it by mentioning two features. First, there is the fact that sex, however prolonged, still takes up much less time than writing an article or producing a painting. Furthermore, it also cannot be done too often; its natural structure is that it will not very often fill up the entire day. One may therefore conduct an intimate sexual relationship in the way one would wish, not feeling that one is slighting it, while pursuing another line of work as one's way of making a living. Artists and scholars sometimes have to pursue another line of work, but they prefer not to. They characteristically feel that to do their work in the way they would wish, they ought to spend the whole day doing it. So they naturally gravitate to the view that their characteristic mode of creative production fits very well with contract and a regular wage.

This, however, still fails to explain cultural differences. To begin to grapple with these, we need to mention the influence of our heritage of romanticism, which makes us feel that sex is not authentic if not spontaneous, "natural," and to some degree unplanned. Romanticism has exercised a far greater sway over our ideas of sex than over our ideas of artistic or intellectual production, making us think that any deal or antecedent arrangement somehow diminishes that characteristic form of expression.

Are our romantic ideas about the difference between sex and art good, or are they bad? Some of each, I suspect. They are problematic to the extent that they make people think that sex happens naturally, does not require complicated adjustment and skill, and flares up (and down) uncontrollably.[51] Insofar as they make us think that sex fits badly with reliability, promise-keeping, and so forth, these ideas are certainly subversive of Anderson's goals of "intimacy and commitment," which would be better served, probably, by an attitude that moves sex in intimate personal relationships (and especially marriages) closer to the activity of the artist or the professor. On

[51] It is well known that these ideas are heavily implicated in the difficulty of getting young people, especially young women, to use contraception.

the other hand, romantic views also promote Anderson's goals to some degree, insofar as they lead people to connect sex with self-revelation and self-expression rather than prudent concealment of self. Many current dilemmas concerning marriage in our culture stem from an uneasy struggle to preserve the good in romanticism while avoiding the dangers it poses to commitment. As we know, the struggle is not always successful. There is much more to be said about this fascinating topic. But since (as I have argued) it leads us quite far from the topic of prostitution, we must now return to our primary line of argument.

6. *The Prostitute's Activity Is Shaped by, and in Turn Perpetuates, Male Dominance of Women.*[52] The institution of prostitution as it has most often existed is certainly shaped by aspects of male domination of women. As I have argued, it is shaped by the perception that female sexuality is dangerous and needs careful regulation, that male sexuality is rapacious and needs a "safe" outlet, that sex is dirty and degrading, and that only a degraded woman is an appropriate sexual object.[53] Nor have prostitutes standardly been treated with respect or been given the dignity one might think proper to a fellow human being. They share this with working-class people of many types in many ages; but, there is no doubt that there are particular features of the disrespect that derive from male supremacy and the desire to lord it over women—as well as from a tendency to link sex to (female) defilement that is common in the history of Western European culture. The physical abuse of prostitutes, and the control of their earnings by pimps—as well as the pervasive use of force and fraud in international markets—are features of male dominance that are extremely harmful and that do not have direct parallels in other types of low-paid work. Some of these forms of conduct may be largely an outgrowth of the illegality of the industry and closely comparable to the threatening behavior of drug wholesalers to their—usually male—retailers. So there remains a question about how far male dominance as such explains the violence involved. But in the international arena, where regulations against these forms of misconduct are usually treated as a joke, illegality is not a sufficient explanation for them.

Prostitution is hardly alone in being shaped by, and in reinforcing, male dominance. Systems of patrilineal property and exogamous marriage, for example, certainly do more to perpetuate not only male dominance but also female mistreatment and even death. There probably is a strong case for making the giving of dowry illegal, as has been done since 1961 in India

[52] See Shrage, *supra* note 9; Andrea Dworkin, Prostitution and Male Supremacy, in Life and Death (1997).

[53] An eloquent examination of the last view, with reference to Freud's account (which endorses it) is in William Miller, The Anatomy of Disgust, ch. 6 (1997).

and since 1980 in Bangladesh[54] (though with little success): for it can be convincingly shown that the institution of dowry is directly linked with extortion and threats of bodily harm and ultimately with the deaths of large numbers of women.[55] It is also obvious that the dowry system pervasively conditions the perception of the worth of girl children: they are a big expense, and they will not be around to protect one in one's old age. This structure is directly linked with female malnutrition, neglect, noneducation, even infanticide, harms that have caused the deaths of many millions of women in the world.[56] It is perfectly understandable that the governments of India, Bangladesh, and Pakistan are very concerned about the dowry system, since it seems very difficult to improve the very bad economic and physical condition of women without some structural changes. (Pakistan has recently adopted a somewhat quixotic remedy, making it illegal to serve food at weddings—thus driving many caterers into poverty.) Dowry is an institution affecting millions of women, determining the course of almost all girl children's lives pervasively and from the start. Prostitution as such usually does not have either such dire or such widespread implications. (Indeed, it is frequently the produce of the dowry system, when parents take payment for prostituting a female child for whom they would otherwise have to pay dowry.) The case for making it illegal on grounds of subordination seems weaker than the case for making dowry, or even wedding feasts, illegal; and yet these laws are themselves of dubious merit and would probably be rightly regarded as involving undue infringement of liberty under our constitutional tradition. (It is significant that Human Rights Watch, which has so aggressively pursued the issue of forced prostitution, takes no stand one way or the other on the legality of prostitution itself.)

More generally, one might argue that the institution of marriage as has most frequently been practiced both expresses and reinforces male dominance. It would be right to use law to change the most iniquitous features of that institution—protecting women from domestic violence and marital rape, giving women equal property and custody rights, and improving their

[54] The Dowry Prohibition Act of 1961 makes both taking and giving of dowry illegal; in Bangladesh, demanding, taking, and giving dowry are all criminal offenses: see Nussbaum, *supra* note 18.

[55] It is extremely difficult to estimate how many women are damaged and killed as a result of this practice. It is certainly clear that criminal offenses are vastly underreported, as is domestic violence in India generally, but that very problem makes it difficult to form any reliable idea of the numbers involved. See Indira Jaising, Justice for Women (1996); and Nussbaum, *supra* note 18.

[56] See Amartya Sen & Jean Drèze, Hunger and Public Action 52 & ch. 1 (1989). Kerala, the only Indian state to have a matrilineal property tradition, also has an equal number of men and women (contrasted with a 94:100 sex ratio elsewhere), and 97 percent both male and female literacy, as contrasted with 32 percent female literacy elsewhere.

exit options by intelligent shaping of the divorce law. But to rule that marriage as such should be illegal on the grounds that it reinforces male dominance would be an excessive intrusion on liberty, even if one should believe marriage irredeemably unequal. So too, I think, with prostitution: what seems right is to use law to protect the bodily safety of prostitutes from assault, to protect their rights to their incomes against the extortionate behavior of pimps, to protect poor women in developing countries from forced trafficking and fraudulent offers, and to guarantee their full civil rights in the countries where they end up—to make them, in general, equals under the law, both civil and criminal. But the criminalization of prostitution seems to pose a major obstacle to that equality.

Efforts on behalf of the dignity and self-respect of prostitutes have tended to push in exactly the opposite direction. In the United States, prostitutes have long been organized to demand greater respect, though their efforts are hampered by prostitution's continued illegality. In India, the National Federation of Women has adopted various strategies to give prostitutes more dignity in the public eye. For example, on National Women's Day, they selected a prostitute to put a garland on the head of the Prime Minister. In a similar manner, UNICEF in India's Andhra Pradesh has been fighting to get prostitutes officially classified as "working women" so that they can enjoy the child-care benefits local government extends to that class. As with domestic service, so here: giving workers greater dignity and control can gradually change both the perception and the fact of dominance.

7. *Prostitution Is a Trade That People Do Not Enter by Choice; Therefore the Bargains People Make within It Should Not Be Regarded as Real Bargains.* Here we must distinguish three cases. First is the case where the woman's entry into prostitution is caused by some type of conduct that would otherwise be criminal: kidnapping, assault, drugging, rape, statutory rape, blackmail, a fraudulent offer. Here we may certainly judge that the woman's choice is not a real choice and that the law should take a hand in punishing her coercer. This is a terrible problem currently in developing countries; international human rights organizations are right to make it a major focus.[57]

Closely related is the case of child prostitution. Child prostitution is frequently accompanied by kidnapping and forcible detention; even when children are not stolen from home, their parents have frequently sold them

[57] See, for example, A Modern Form of Slavery: Trafficking of Burmese Women and Girls into Brothels in Thailand, *supra* note 33; A Modern Form of Slavery: The Human Rights Watch Global Report on Women's Human Rights, *supra* note 34, at 1273–296; Human Rights Are Women's Rights 53–56 (1995).

without their own consent. But even where it is not, we should judge that there is an impermissible infringement of autonomy and liberty. A child (and because of clients' fears of HIV, brothels now often focus on girls as young as ten)[58] cannot give consent to a life in prostitution; not only lack of information and of economic options (if parents collude in the deal) but also absence of adult political rights makes such a "choice" no choice at all.

Different is the case of an adult woman who enters prostitution because of bad economic options: because it seems a better alternative than the chicken factory, because there is no other employment available to her, and so forth. This too, we should insist, is a case where autonomy has been infringed, but in a different way. Consider Joseph Raz's vivid example of "the hounded woman," a woman on a desert island who is constantly pursued by a man-eating animal.[59] In one sense, this woman is free to go anywhere on the island and do anything she likes. In another sense, of course, she is quite unfree. If she wants not to be eaten, she has to spend all her time and calculate all her movements in order to avoid the beast. Raz's point is that many poor people's lives are nonautonomous in just this way. They may fulfill internal conditions of autonomy, being capable of making bargains, reflecting about what to do, and so forth. But none of this counts for a great deal if in fact the struggle for survival gives them just one unpleasant option or a small set of (in various ways) unpleasant options.

This seems to me the truly important issue raised by prostitution. Like work in the chicken factory, it is not an option many women choose with alacrity when many other options are on their plate.[60] This might not be so in some hypothetical culture in which prostitutes have legal protection, dignity, and respect and the status of skilled practitioner, rather like the masseuse.[61] But it is true now in most societies, given the reality of the (albeit irrational) stigma attaching to prostitution. But the important thing to realize is that this is not an issue that permits us to focus on prostitution in isolation from the economic situation of women in a society generally. Certainly it will not be ameliorated by the criminalization of prostitution, which reduces poor women's options still further. We may grant that poor women do not have enough options and that society has been unjust to them in not ex-

[58] On Thailand, see A Modern Form of Slavery: The Human Rights Watch Global Report on Women's Human Rights, *supra* note 34, at 197.

[59] Joseph Raz, The Morality of Freedom 374 (1986).

[60] See Posner, *supra* note 32, at 43, on the low incidence of prostitution in Sweden, even though it is not illegal; his explanation is that "women's opportunities in the job market are probably better there than in any other country."

[61] See Schwarzenbach, *supra* note 9.

tending more options, while nonetheless respecting and honoring the choices they actually make in reduced circumstances.

How could it possibly be ameliorated? Here are some things that have actually been done in India, where prostitution is a common last-ditch option for women who lack other employment opportunities. First, both government and private groups have focused on the provision of education to women, to equip them with skills that will enhance their options. One group I recently visited in Bombay focuses in particular on skills training for the children of prostitutes, who are at especially high risk of becoming prostitutes themselves unless some action increases their options. Second, nongovernmental organizations have increasingly focused on the provision of credit to women in order to enhance their employment options and give them a chance to "upgrade" in the domain of their employment. One such project that has justly won international renown is the Self-Employed Women's Association (SEWA), centered in Ahmedabad in Gujerat, which provides loans to women pursuing a variety of informal-sector occupations,[62] from tailoring to hawking and vending to cigarette rolling to agricultural labor.[63] With loans they can get wholesale rather than retail supplies, upgrade their animals or equipment, and so forth. They also get skills training and, frequently, the chance to move into leadership roles in the organization itself. Such women are far less likely to need to turn to prostitution to supplement their income. Third, they can form labor organizations to protect women employed in low-income jobs and to bargain for better working conditions—once again making this work a better source of income and diminishing the likelihood that prostitution will need to be selected. (This is the other primary objective of SEWA, which is now organizing hawkers and vendors internationally.) Fourth, they can form groups to diminish the isolation and enhance the self-respect of working women in low-paying jobs; this was a ubiquitous feature of both government and nongovernment programs I visited in India, and a crucial element of helping women deliberate about their options if they wish to avoid prostitution for themselves or their daughters.

These four steps are the real issue, I think, in addressing the problem of prostitution. Feminist philosophers do not talk a lot about credit and employment;[64] they should do so far more. Indeed, it seems a dead end to con-

[62] An extremely high proportion of the labor force in India is in the informal sector.

[63] The Self-Employed Women's Association was first directed by Ela Bhatt, who is now involved in international work to improve the employment options of informal-sector workers. For a valuable description of the movement, see Kalima Rose, Where Women Are Leaders: The SEWA Movement in India (1995).

[64] But see, here, Schwarzenbach, *supra* note 9; and Shrage, *supra* note 9. I have also been very much influenced by Martha Chen, A Quiet Revolution: Women in Transition in Rural

sider prostitution in isolation from the other realities of working life of which it is a part, and one suspects that this has happened because prostitution is a sexy issue and getting a loan for a sewing machine appears not to be. But philosophers had better talk more about getting loans, learning to read, and so forth if they want to be relevant to the choices that are actually faced by working women and to the programs that are actually doing a lot to improve such women's options.

VI

The stigma traditionally attached to prostitution is based on a collage of beliefs, most of which are not rationally defensible and which should be especially vehemently rejected by feminists: beliefs about the evil character of female sexuality, the rapacious character of male sexuality, the essentially marital and reproductive character of "good" women and "good" sex. Worries about subordination more recently raised by feminists are much more serious concerns, but they apply to many types of work poor women do. Concerns about force and fraud should be extremely urgent concerns of the international women's movement. Where these conditions do not obtain, feminists should view prostitutes as (usually) poor working women with few options, not as threats to the intimacy and commitment that many women and men (including, no doubt, many prostitutes) seek. This does not mean that we should not be concerned about ways in which prostitution as currently practiced, even in the absence of force and fraud, undermines the dignity of women, just as domestic service in the past undermined the dignity of members of a given race or class. But the correct response to this problem seems to be to work to enhance the economic autonomy and the personal dignity of members of that class, not to rule off-limits an option that may be the only livelihood for many poor women and to further stigmatize women who already make their living this way.

In grappling further with these issues, we should begin from the realization that there is nothing per se wrong with taking money for the use of one's body. That is the way most of us live, and formal recognition of that fact through contract is usually a good thing for people, protecting their security and their employment conditions. What seems wrong is that relatively few people in the world have the option to use their body, in their work, in what Marx would call a "truly human" manner of functioning, by

---

Bangladesh (1983); Martha Chen, A Matter of Survival: Women's Right to Work in India and Bangladesh, in Nassbaum & Glover, eds., *supra* note 41; Bina Agarwal, A Field of One's Own: Gender and Land Rights in South Asia (1994); and Bina Agarwal, "Bargaining" and Gender Relations: Within and beyond the Household, 3 Feminist Econ. 1–51 (1997).

which he meant (among other things) having some choices about the work to be performed, some reasonable measure of control over its conditions and outcome, and also the chance to use thought and skill rather than just to function as a cog in a machine. Women in many parts of the world are especially likely to be stuck at a low level of mechanical functioning, whether as agricultural laborers, factory workers, or prostitutes. The real question to be faced is how to expand the options and opportunities such workers face, how to increase the humanity inherent in their work, and how to guarantee that workers of all sorts are treated with dignity. In the further pursuit of these questions, we need, on balance, more studies of women's credit unions and fewer studies of prostitution.

[21]

Dignity or Equality? Responses to Workplace Harassment in European, German, and U.S. Law

SUSANNE BAER

The legal reactions to the social problem of sexual harassment in Europe, particularly in the European Union and in Germany, have been based on dignity as the fundamental right of men and women that has been violated in such cases. German and European law conceptualize law against sexual harassment differently from the United States, where jurisprudence is based on a specific interpretation of the right to equality. In the year 2000, European law moved in the direction of a focus on equality, rather than dignity. New directives based on article 13 of the European Treaty define workplace harassment as discrimination.[1] However, a query remains: At first glance, this difference raises the question of "dignity or equality?" in a comparative effort to find the better solution. Yet in a comparative analysis of sexual harassment law across legal codes and cultures, there is more to ask. The very question of "dignity or equality?" indicates a problem in both traditional and more recent legal philosophy. Ultimately, a reformulation of this question might offer a more useful approach to sexual harassment law in general.

In the tradition of liberal philosophy, dignity and equality have been distinguished. Dignity, as part of liberty, has been interpreted as a principle and a right categorically distinct from equality, which has been seen as a principle and a right based on symmetrical comparison. In law this not only leads to a distinction between liberty interests and equality rights but results in a hierarchical relation between the two. Liberty reigns across the spectrum of liberal constitutions.[2] Equality, in contrast, is treated as a secondary, for some even antiliberal concern. Rights are put in a scheme of conflict. Where this scheme is applied, it is necessary to find a response to the question of "dignity or equality?"

In some countries and some areas of the law, however, this conflict scheme has been replaced by a scheme of interrelatedness. The latter conception might also be based on insufficiently theorized considerations in the tradition of liberal philosophy. In this case, dignity and equality are interpreted as interrelated principles that inform one another and lead to a more coherent and encompassing look at constitutions. In combining individual interest with a social concern, these interrelated principles contribute to a more democratic constitutionalism. Then the hierarchy between liberty interests and equality rights is replaced by an interrelated interpretation of all rights relevant in a given case. From this point of view, "dignity or equality?" is no longer the question, but liberty is interpreted in light of equality just as equality is considered part of liberty rights.

Here, I would like to demonstrate the difference that results from such an interrelated interpretation. The choice of one of these two conceptual schemes is neither purely theoretical nor simply doctrinal. It informs doctrine in European,[3] German, and U.S. sexual harassment law,[4] where the traditional scheme of conflict—rather than interrelation—has been applied more or less consistently. In addition, the choice of schemes informs large segments of legal philosophy. The conflict scheme forms the basis of liberal legal thinking and is favored by some recent legal theorists, including some who write from a feminist perspective.[5] In the attempt to withdraw from the asymmetrical, substantive, antihierarchical equality approach that, particularly in North America, has been based on Catharine MacKinnon's work,[6] as well as in a rejection of MacKinnon's view of gender as sexualized hierarchy,[7] some theorists shift the focus of legal responses to discrimination away from equality and to some version of dignity, agency, or self-respect. As I will show, such theories continue to subscribe to a scheme of conflict rather than aim at a scheme of interrelatedness.

My remarks on regulations and theoretical arguments point not only to the difference produced by the choice of scheme. I will also attempt to demonstrate the inadequacy of the conflict scheme when dealing with discrimination. This will be done from a comparative point of view that treats the U.S. approach to sexual harassment and the substantive theory of equality developed in U.S. feminist legal theory as one set of rules, and the European and German approaches as another. In conclusion, the alternative scheme of interrelatedness offers the more systematic approach to law against sex discrimination in the form of harassment at work, to fundamental rights, and to the constitutional foundations of democracy as a whole.

Traditions in Philosophy: Positions in the Law

In liberal philosophy, and within a tradition of legal theory, dignity and equality have been seen as rights to be distinguished, or even as conflicting. To name but one example, Immanuel Kant called liberty the only natural right, and named equality as a secondary right, almost derivative.[8] Such liberal philosophy informs law and legal politics. In most liberal jurisdictions, equality and dignity, with dignity either as a right of its own or as a feature of liberty, are treated separately, as distinct from each other, and differently as well. For example German constitutional lawyers have applied (and are still taught to apply) a three-step test to dignity and liberty rights, and a structurally different, comparative test to equality.[9] The difference in tests leads to a difference in results, in that the three-tier liberty test adheres to a stricter scrutiny in jurisprudence, while the comparative-equality test gives way to broader legislative or administrative discretion. This suggests further that problems within equality jurisprudence like the longstanding disregard of discrimination are based on problematic, ultimately Aristotelian, symmetrical interpretations of equality as such.[10] In addition, problems of the law's disregard of discrimination might in fact be attributed to the scheme of conflict that situates dignity and equality as rights apart.

Such traditions and the jurisprudence that is built upon it, however, are not monolithic. For example, Cicero added equality to the Aristotelian concept of citizenship, which for Aristotle was fully compatible with the exclusion of slaves and women.[11] John Locke also emphasized the importance of equality that he derived from a notion of rationality then grounded in God's equal creation.[12] Liberal philosopher Immanuel Kant, as much as he is known to privilege liberty, also interpreted dignity as a feature of both equality and liberty.[13] Contemporary liberal thinkers, such as Jürgen Habermas[14] and Axel Honneth,[15] also tend to conceptualize liberalism on the basis of equal respect, easily translatable into dignity and equality thought together rather than apart. And some feminist philosophers, like Austrian Herta Nagl-Docekal,[16] fully integrate both rights into a coherent scheme. Thus, although some liberal philosophy tended to view dignity and equality as separate, a scheme of interrelatedness can be found here as well.

Newer Developments in Legal Theory

In legal theory, particularly in theory developed from a feminist perspective, equality as a right against discrimination has been interpreted as a constitutional guarantee of equal liberties for all. Thus dignity has served as a part—albeit often implicitly—of an interpretation of equality as an asymmetrical right against subordination. Recently, such approaches have increasingly come under attack. In particular, the strong, asymmetrical, substantive version of equality, also known as the antisubordination, antihierarchy, or simply and originally the "inequality interpretation" of the right to equality,[17] has been heavily criticized.

A somewhat traditional critique is based on an understanding of law as a preserver of the status quo rather than an engine of change. In German constitutional law, this conservative understanding of law has been explicitly rejected by the Federal Constitutional Court.[18] In a decision on the right of married persons to keep their last names, the Court stated that unequal treatment may not be justified by referring to the traditional structure of a situation, such as marriage. "The constitutional provision would lose its function to implement gender equality for the future, if social realities were to be simply accepted."[19] One cannot tell from the German wording of the decision whether the Court considers the situation to be dissimilar, as in traditional equality analyses, or to be unequal, as demanded in substantive interpretations of equality. However, the doctrinal arguments and the discussion of equality in later cases suggest that a substantive interpretation gains hold in the German court's jurisprudence.[20]

Another critique of the equality approach has been articulated in a comparative study of sexual harassment law. Thus Robert Husbands refers to a dignity-based approach which he describes as "broader" than equality.[21] Yet it remains unclear how much "broader" law can legitimately be. For many, sexual harassment law already covers too much behavior, particularly in the form of speech. Usually, "broader" implies less definition and specificity, but such an understanding then leaves us with traditional gender-neutral blindness, and the potential ineffectiveness of such laws. For some, a law is "broader" if it is not directed at discrimination that primarily hurts women. But sexual harassment law covers men too if they are discriminated against and thus harmed based on their gender. The argument against such law does not only miss a point but is polemic rather than legal in nature.

A more interesting and sophisticated version of a dignity-based approach is articulated by American legal theorist Drucilla Cornell. According to Cornell, an adoption of MacKinnon's equality standard "inevitably implicates a woman's systematic subordination to men."[22] Cornell thus refers to the "feminist" or "postmodern" dilemma that might be avoided only with great difficulty in law. The dilemma results from the tension between a legal statement of gender hierarchy which perpetuates that hierarchy on the level of language and thus, within the symbolic order, and is yet intended to combat it.[23] Cornell thus criticizes sexual harassment law for its invasion into the "imaginary domain," the sphere of symbolic existence of men and women. To avoid the invasion, Cornell proposes an approach based on the Rawlsian concepts of self-respect, freedom, and personhood. This approach would offer a "legal guarantee of the social bases of self-respect."[24] This "primary good" should, according to Cornell, become the comparative standard by which to judge unequal power relations.[25] The right to self-respect in this view would be violated when "sexual shame" is enforced by "reducing individuals to projected stereotypes or objectified fantasies of their 'sex.'"[26]

Ultimately, however, Cornell's argument for replacing equality with respect and a right to an imaginary domain is not fully convincing. First, it is possible and exigent to distinguish between the language of the law and the particular functions, forms, and structures of legal discourse, and the symbolic constructions in other discourses. It is misleading and ultimately disables the effectiveness of any law if legal terms are confounded with terminology used in other contexts. This is not to say that a critique of the closed nature of legal discourse is not needed and valid. Yet it remains important to note the difference between a discriminatory statement and a law that names what to do against it.

Second, to invoke the right to an imaginary domain and against "sexual shame" does not constitute an adequate replacement for an equality analysis. Cornell's description of the right to respect[27] closely resembles the descriptions used in German constitutional doctrine of violations of the right to dignity. It contains the well-known elements of gender neutrality, individuality, and free will. But it is precisely in reference to these elements that traditional legal philosophy, traditional interpretations of equality, and the corresponding antidiscrimination laws have proven inadequate in combating discrimination. Laws based on gender-neutrality tend to hide the realities of gender hierarchies, individuality has been shown to hide the established claims to privilege of men as members of a group defined by its gender, and free will has been recognized as a legal fiction that often, as in labor law, legitimizes exploitation.[28] In sum, law based on such a scheme of individual human beings is incapable of grasping the complex realities in which we live.[29]

Translations of Theory into Doctrine

Recent accounts of law against sexual harassment in particular and against sex discrimination in general that shift away from a substantive interpretation of equality are not purely theoretical. They can be easily translated into what many constitutions in the world, including article 1 of the German Basic Law (*Grundgesetz*) calls dignity.[30] Therefore, the trends in recent legal theory described above are yet another example of an application of the scheme of conflict. In these approaches, dignity and equality are kept apart.

In particular, an argument like that formulated by Drucilla Cornell is not isolated today. Efforts have been made to conceptualize the harm done in gender relations in gender-neutral terms. Attempts to define harm as not group-related seem to fit the individualistic liberal model of the legal subject better than feminist or critical race theory approaches, which situate the harm of discrimination within a social, and thus both individual *and* group-related, context. In theory, references to agency, unwantedness, consensual relationships, self-determination, and, ultimately, liberty indicate such a trend. In law, references to dignity replace laws against inequalities and discrimination. Before I discuss doctrine, a remark on the motivation for such turns in theory seems appropriate.

REASONS TO TURN BACK

Replacements of equality law with more dignity-oriented analyses are attractive for various reasons. After all, there is a stigma attached to "quotas," affirmative action, "special" laws for women or historically disadvantaged groups, and other equality strategies from the 1950s until today. To avoid the stigma, it seems politically and strategically promising to appeal to a generally applicable, widely accepted norm.[31]

In addition, the turn from equality to dignity can easily be situated within a theoretically attractive focus on constructions and destructions of the self. A dignity-oriented analysis of sex discrimination refers to a universal and ultimately to a moral category.[32] It promises a neutral and objective way to define injustice, while apparently leaving enough space for individual differences. Thus, dignity seems to avoid eclipsing the individuality of the person, as constructivists point out, in the assumption of structural inequality.[33] The dignity-centered approach also seems to evade the dilemma between the necessity to restate gender-based victimization by naming and attempting to create law against it.[34]

Finally, an analysis of discrimination based on dignity rather than equality might be more suitable to anyone who draws on experiences not primarily shaped by inequality. More precisely, dominant interpreters of the law and dominant theorists tend not to be defined in terms that indicate subordination. Heterosexuality, whiteness, the Judao-Christian tradition, and something that may be called a "male focus" are still setting the standards in law and philosophy. With this in mind, it seems more than likely that persistent inequality will not serve as the primary source of interpretation and understanding. Rather, the denial of respect, or the deprivation of dignity, is an experience accessible even to people who belong to socially dominant groups. Furthermore, a focus on dignity does not endanger a privilege one wants to preserve.[35]

However, and particularly from the perspective of those not privileged, not dignified, and not yet equal, it can be shown that the price for these gains of a shift in theory is too high to pay. The theoretical turn, motivated by strategic and philosophical considerations, has dangerous consequences in doctrine, and in life.

REALITIES TO CONSIDER: ASPECTS OF COMPARATIVE ANALYSES

In the case of sexual harassment of working women, the similarity of social realities of the problem throughout the world warrants a direct comparison of legal responses. In their specificity, the cultural significance and discourses surrounding words and acts that constitute harassment surely differ. On the whole, however, experiences seem to be the same. Yet legal responses are quite dissimilar. Laws against sexual harassment in Europe and in the United States differ in ways that exemplify the difference between dignity- and equality-based approaches to sex discrimination. And just like the theoretical turns toward dignity, the legal responses are based on the scheme of conflict between dignity and equality, rather than on a scheme of interrelatedness.

In European and German law, sexual harassment in the workplace has been conceptualized as a violation of individual dignity.[36] Culturally, this makes a lot of sense. If you ask about the nature of the harm done by sexual harassment, Germans would tend to refer to dignity as the right of women that has been violated in such cases. This correlates to a European understanding of harm, and particularly to the understanding of harm developed in Europe after 1945, where human dignity became the referent for harm of the worst kind. Although laws corresponding to Nazi ideology referred to dignity, when it was mentioned at all, as a racially divisive concept that was exclusively attributed to Aryans, and while the fascist interpretation of equality thus attributed rights to people based on their difference as defined in racial terms, postwar law and postwar German constitutionalism in particular defined dignity as the primary right of any individual regardless of their differing capabilities or characteristics.[37] Today, dignity has become the universal standard for gross violations of individual rights. In comparison, when asked what right is violated by harassment, people in the United States tend to refer to equality. To many individuals, it indicates an unequal status that women are sexually harassed at work, and it seems to violate a right to equal opportunities in making one's living. This correlates to the understanding of harm established by the U.S. civil rights movement where equality was used in litigation for the right against violence, harassment, and unequal access to public facilities. In the United States, equality seems to provide the standard for violations of rights.

In addition to the cultural aspects that shape different understandings of harassment, the constitutional frameworks in which laws are situated in Europe and the United States also vary.[38] Here, cultural difference becomes a doctrinal one. In the German Constitution, or Basic Law, dignity is the first, basic, and, to most, fundamental individual right. In Europe this is part of the constitutional consensus since many member states of the European Union inscribed a right to dignity into their constitutions,[39] and the newly proclaimed European Charter of Fundamental Rights also sets out with a right to dignity.[40] In Germany the basic right to universal human dignity is understood as an explicit answer to the Holocaust—the "never again" in constitutional law—and is adjudicated as a prohibition of inhumane and degrading treatment. Although there are also strong legal responses to the Holocaust in equality law, the violations of individuality as such are the primary concern in the German constitutional tradition.[41] This can be understood as a rejection of fascist group-based ideology and the attempt to reinstall respect for any individual regardless of where and to whom they belong. Degrading treatment, then, as German constitutional lawyers would put it, is prohibited if it turns people into objects, stigmatizes them, or deprives them of fundamental liberties.[42] Here, we find some similarities between German constitutional interpretation and the theoretical developments around understandings of discrimination described above.

In comparison, the U.S. Constitution does not mention dignity. One effect of this absence might be the construction of so many cases as problems of the First Amendment.[43] Since dignity can be interpreted as a feature of liberty, this makes sense. On the other hand, when we consider the right to equality, important aspects of dignity are missing. In the United States, as many scholars have eloquently demonstrated,[44] equality is predominantly interpreted as a symmetrical and rather formal right, not as a substantive, antihierarchical provision. Then, dignity is not even implicitly part of equality jurisprudence, just as liberty is not seen as correlating with equality. It can thus be said that American jurisprudence implicitly applies the scheme of conflict rather than the scheme of interrelatedness.

In the German Constitution, the guarantee of human dignity is not only explicit but it also a universal, gender-neutral, and individualistic provision. Since dignity is at the top of the list of German basic rights, the *Grundrechte*, it is available as a *tertium comparationis* for equality, as a standard by which to measure the substance of unequal treatment. Here, the German Constitution opens a door to an interrelated approach to dignity, liberty, and equality. Dignity offers a way to interpret equality asymmetrically, different from jurisprudence in the United States. However, when we consider the German law against sexual harassment, this door has not yet been fully opened. While constitutionally interrelatedness seems to be the way to go, the legislature and the courts still apply a scheme of conflict, at least when it comes to sex discrimination. This is particularly problematic because it contradicts the constitutional revisions after German unification, which turned the right to sex equality from a right against unfair distinctions into one against gender-based disadvantage, and thus moved from symmetry and formalism to a more substantive understanding of equal rights.[45] A strong equality provision applies, however, only when a problem is conceptualized as an inequality. If sexual harassment or any other form of sex discrimination is not seen as an inequality, strong equality provisions will not work for women in that case. Here the scheme of conflict prevails on the level of epistemology. In doctrine, this has problematic consequences.

DOCTRINAL DETAILS

In Germany, unlike in the United States, sexual harassment has not been defined as an inequality in the law. Here, dominant cultural understandings became legislation, because as in the European Commission, women in Germany fought for the equality analysis and lost to an at least primarily dignity-based approach to law against harassment at work.[46] This legislative decision for dignity based on the scheme of conflict that excludes equality reasoning results in significant doctrinal problems. Some are known from the legal developments in the United States. While there is no binding legislative definition of sexual harassment in the United States, case law offers analogies to all the features European legislation spells out. However, case law defines harassment as an inequality. In addition, although not legally binding, the EEOC describes sexual harassment as a prevailing problem of discrimination in the workplace.[47] In interpreting Title VII of the Civil Rights Act, the courts in the United States indicate that quid pro quo or hostile environment harassment violates the guarantee of equal rights. The situation in Europe is different.

Worldwide, law against sexual harassment exhibits some specific doctrinal features: the definition of the problem, the relevance of the actor's subjectivity, the definition of harm, the relevance of the subjective experience of the person who has been harassed, the assessment of responsibility for harm done, the defenses allowed, the sanctions, and the procedures in which those are assessed. German law[48] defines sexual harassment as intentional, definitely of a sexual nature, and at least in part recognizably rejected—or proven unwelcome—activity that violates the dignity of individuals at work. The standard by which to measure the nature of ambiguous acts and then assess the harm is that of gender-neutral, individual dignity. Dignity is not defined but referred to, thus invoking the constitutional interpretation described above. A closer look at some of these elements of the German law, and of the European regulation,[49] reveals the problems that arise from that. This reveals the assumption that law against sexual harassment is better conceptualized based on the scheme of interrelatedness between dignity and equality, than on the scheme of conflict, and in this case, on dignity alone.[50]

First, German law defines sexual harassment as intentional behavior. Thus, the acting individual's subjectivity is relevant. Here, German law follows the path of dignity, since it is the intended degradation that counts as a violation of this individual right. In contrast, an equality approach to sex discrimination would not attribute such significance to the acting individual's intent. As we know from feminist research on sex discrimination, discriminatory behavior is deeply ingrained, systemic, and normalized, and therefore often not intentional in the legal sense. In addition, equality demands a reasoning that is oriented toward effects rather than intent, toward harm done rather than thoughts, and thus toward insignificance of an acting individual's mindset. This has been acknowledged by the European Court of Justice which, in a case on discrimination based on the pregnancy of job applicants, stated that for sex discrimination law to work a discriminatory act should imply the liability of the acting individual without any requirement of intent.[51] In conclusion, if law against sexual harassment were understood as law against discrimination, the intent requirement in German law would clearly violate this European standard. But since German law is designed to protect the dignity of workers, it is at least as difficult to prove this point. Even the European dignity-based recommendation against harassment recognizes as harassment only those acts that the actor knew or should have known to be harmful to the victim. This, too, is not seen as violating the Court's requirements in sex discrimination law because in the case of harassment dignity is the primary focus.

Second, German law requires harassment to be of a sexual nature. The law seems to intend the exclusion of sexuality from the workplace, thus reinforcing a traditional distinction between the public (ideologically defined as nonsexual) and the private (defined as the space of intimacy). It is unclear what exactly "sexual" means, however, or where exactly to draw the distinction. Because much harassment of working women refers to their gender but not all harassment explicitly sexualizes them, this would be important to know. In addition, and without further explanation of the nature of "sexual" behavior, legal regulation of sexual expression tends to become a device to establish moralistic imperatives of prudence rather than combat discrimination. For example, in German dignity jurisprudence, peep shows are seen as violations of a constitutional right while other forms of prostitution are legal.[52] In German criminal law, some pornography is legal, some not. The courts and the legislators thus define various aspects of sexuality as either good or bad rather than look for systematic responses to discrimination. In the decision regarding peep shows, the right to dignity was used as a right against an uninhibited male sex drive rather than to protect women from exploitation when it occurs.[53] Again, the dignity-based approach leads exactly in that direction, while the equality approach tends to work another way.

Similarly, the European Commission defined sexual harassment as "unwanted behavior of a sexual nature or other behavior based on sex, which violates the dignity of working women and men. This may include unwanted physical, verbal or non-verbal behavior."[54] According to the emphasis on the sexual nature of discriminatory behavior, the primary concern of European law is, as in Germany, sexuality. Harassment, then, is only a problem when sexuality is implicitly or explicitly at play. In the courts, and without a feminist analysis of sexuality and its meaning in the construction of gender, this turns sexual harassment into a moral sin rather than acknowledging it as a problem situated within a sexualized gender hierarchy. Regarding the approach taken by the European Commission, it is noteworthy that the definition of harassment emphasizes not only sexuality but also links sexual behavior as a moral sin with dignity as the right in question. The European Commission rejected an explicit recognition that harassment has to do with gender—an idea present in the North American equality approach to sexual harassment law.[55] Thus, the Commission picked a dignity approach consciously, conceived it in the scheme of conflict, as distinguished from equality, and, by creating a moralistic definition of harassment, immediately revealed its problems.

Third, German law recognizes harassment only if women object to it. The definition in article 2, section 2, number 2 requires that sexual acts or invitations to them, sexual touching, sexual remarks, and pornography at work have to be recognizably rejected—or proven unwelcome—to count as sexual harassment in the legal sense. This requirement is based on various problematic assumptions. It assumes that women in the hierarchies of the workplace and of gender are capable of saying no; it assumes that harm occurs only after such rejection; and it assumes that if rejection were not required, women would sue men for no reason.[56] With the rejection requirement, the disabling effect of harassment that consists, in part, of the silencing of the harassed, is not recognized. Furthermore the law says that women have to "recognizably" reject. This tends to privilege the perpetrator's perspective, since courts tend to ask whether he was the one who recognized a "no" as such. If the harasser does not see the unwelcomeness of his behavior, we face the structural problem known from rape law where the mental state of the rapist defines what happened.[57] It also portrays the harassed person as a powerful subject modeled according to an epistemologically male norm. Again, the problem of a rejection requirement in a legal definition of sexual harassment can be attributed to the approach taken and the scheme applied.

Doctrinal details reveal that, in sum, the dignity-based approach that informs German and European law tends to individualize behavior,[58] privilege a perpetrator's perspective, conceptualize human beings as autonomous subjects without a consideration of the social hierarchies at work, and ignores the function of sexuality in gender discrimination. A systematically equality-based approach, in contrast, would recognize the harm of discrimination in its social context, accept sexualization as a means of sex discrimination, and use objective yet victim-sensitive standards rather than follow the perpetrator's point of view.[59]

Taken together, these three elements render the European and the German law against sexual harassment at work quite inadequate to address the problem. Underlying the problems of the doctrinal details is the perspective, as the normatively shaped point of view, from which discrimination can be judged.[60] Many acts of harassment are ambiguous in nature. They are justified by harassers as well-meant and not harmful while the harassed individuals experience harm. As such, in the courtroom, harassment is most often an excellent case of a conflict of perspectives.[61] Then, if law is based on dignity, as in Germany, or, with Cornell, on self-respect, the harm and the activity causing it are individualized, the perpetrator's perspective privileged, and the social interaction judged from a moralistic point of view.[62] Structurally, German law defines harassment as a crime rather than a social phenomenon within a structure of sex-based disadvantage. As an alternative, an equality-based approach to sex discrimination law recognizes sexual harassment as a violation of a right against sexualized hierarchy, as an interaction situated in a discriminatory context producing harm, and requiring the law to stop whatever a perpetrator thought he was doing. Structurally, that kind of law does not define harassment as a crime but as damaging behavior. Then a potentially harassing activity is judged from a socially adequate, relational, equality-focused, power-sensitive point of view.

Conclusion

In Europe and in Germany, law against sexual harassment at work is based on dignity as the right in question, while U.S. law developed from an analysis of harassment as discrimination and thus as a violation of the right to sex equality at work. As liberal philosophy tends to posit these two approaches in a scheme of conflict, the doctrinal differences produced by these approaches merit some attention. Three important features of sexual harassment law in Europe reveal that a dignity-based approach tends to address only inadequately the problem of discrimination. The same is true for theoretical attempts to conceptualize sex discrimination in gender-neutral, dignity-like terms.

On the other hand, an equality-based approach tends to open the door to a more adequate assessment of the problem at hand. However, with a move from the scheme of conflict to a scheme of interrelatedness, equality will serve the need to work as a normative standard in cases of discrimination only if equality itself is conceptualized as a substantive right against hierarchy. Such a combination of dignity and equality, with dignity as a point of reference for an equality analysis, can be found in German constitutional law and in some insufficiently acknowledged parts of the liberal tradition of legal philosophy.

A comparative account of sexual harassment law reveals the similarities, the differences, and the advantages and disadvantages of a dignity-based and an equality-based law against discrimination.[63] It also reveals that cultural understandings translate themselves into the law, and that differing legal, and particularly constitutional, traditions tend to shape even the small doctrinal reactions to the social world. Yet some conclusions drawn from the comparison can be generalized.[64] For sex discrimination law to work, some features have to be attained. The structure of sex discrimination law must not follow the path of criminal and tort law provisions but work along a civil rights model. An intent requirement contradicts everything we know about the nature of discrimination. Sexuality is an important factor of sex discrimination, but sexual nature is not sufficient to define how this works. Women at work are to be recognized as subjects, fully capable of knowing what they want, and yet it is inadequate to require anyone to fight back in a situation of sexual harassment. Therefore, rejection requirements are inadequate as well.

In the United States, law against sexual harassment has been fought for by women who saw themselves as targets of discrimination, violated not only in their rights to bodily and psychological integrity, but in their rights as women (or, for some men, as gay men), and because of their gender. As a common-law culture, the U.S. system favors a version of legal development in which doctrine is shaped in the courts. In Europe and in Germany, law against sexual harassment has developed differently. It has been legislated by governing bodies, the Commission in Europe, and a branch of the federal government in Germany. The legislation was a response to demands from women in workers' unions and the women's movements, who, in the European context, were women working in the European institutions themselves. In Germany, legislation resulted in response to such demands as well, but was primarily a reaction to the legally binding European demand to draft legislation according to the

Commission's imperative. The European laws have been fought for by women as well, but in the legislative process, feminist demands are more likely to be watered down to gender-neutral declarations. In legislative bodies, it is usually not the women who experienced harassment who argue for a law against it, while in courts, it is exactly these women who shape the understanding of harassment in law. Legislation might settle a matter more securely, but case law is often shaped much closer to realities.

Finally, if we go back to the philosophical starting point, we must address the question of the relation between dignity and equality, and what a choice between the scheme of conflict and a scheme of interrelatedness might mean in the real world of civil rights. The traditional scheme of conflict has proven to be an inadequate response to discrimination, and it is inadequate in both its solely dignity-based version, as in the German and European case, as it would be inadequate in a solely traditional equality-based approach, in which equality is a symmetrical and rather formal right to equal treatment. Alternatively, a scheme of interrelatedness between dignity and equality might be applied to legally address sex discrimination.[65] Then equality is an asymmetrical, substantive right against in this case sexualized hierarchies, and dignity is the normative point of reference which guarantees equal respect for every individual. This approach requires the law to recognize human beings as socially situated subjects. It asks the law to respond to the tension between an attribution of autonomy that can be derived from the right to individual dignity of human beings, and the social inequalities such human beings experience in the world, which are introduced by way of reference to the right to equality. With this approach, the law can recognize the systematic rather than arbitrary or intentional character of sex discrimination. A call for autonomy, for agency, or for an individual domain alone is inadequate to grasp what discrimination means, and what it feels like. Rather, a call for equal respect, for dignified equality, might serve as a guideline for those who want to combat it. Sexual harassment law, then, looked at from a comparative perspective, seems to be at its best when grounded in this interrelated approach. The question is not "dignity or equality?" but what features the law has to offer to guarantee individual dignity on an equal basis for all.

Notes

I am grateful to Uta Stiegler and Ulrich C. Baer for reading draft versions, and to Catharine MacKinnon for extensive critique.

1. Directive 2000/43/EC of the Council (June 29, 2000) of implementing the principle of equal treatment between persons irrespective of racial or ethnic origin; Directive 2000/78/EC of the Council (November 27, 2000) establishing a general framework for equal treatment in employment and occupation, to be found at *www.europa.eu.int/eur-lex/en/index.html.*

2. Younger constitutions do not necessarily follow that tradition. For example, the Republic of South Africa emphasizes equality as an asymmetrical right against oppression.

3. *See generally* Amy G. Mazur, "The Interplay: The Formation of Sexual Harassment Legislation in France and EU Policy Initiatives," in *Sexual Politics and the European Union* 35 (Amy Elman ed., 1996). *See also* Jean Gregory, "Sexual Harassment: Making the Best Use of European Law," 2 *European Journal of Women's Studies* 421 (1995). Note that Swedish law does not explicitly address harassment. *See* Amy R. Elman, "Feminism and Legislative Redress: Sexual Harassment in Sweden and the United States," 16 *Women and Politics* 1 (1996). On Great Britain, *see* "Sexual Harassment at the Workplace: Implementing Policies, the Union Role and Legal Aspects," *IRS Employment Trends* 5 (1992). For a different perspective from Britain, *see* Colin Bourn, "Harassed by Discrimination Law?" 142 *New Law Journal* 1059 (1992).

4. For the elaborate version of the argument with an analysis of German labor, tort, and criminal law on sexual violence, and a discussion of equality theories in this context, see Susanne Baer, *Würde oder Gleichheit? Zur angemessenen grundrechtlichen Konzeption von Recht gegen Diskriminierung am Beispiel sexueller Belästigung am Arbeitsplatz in der Bundesrepublik Deutschland und den USA* (1995).

5. The most prominent example in feminist legal theory is Drucilla Cornell, *The Imaginary Domain: Abortion, Pornography, and Sexual Harassment* 168 (1995). The force of tradition is perfectly caught in the title of an article by Mary E. Becker, "Prince Charming: Abstract Equality," 8 *Supreme Court Review* 201 (1987).

6. The first outline may be found in Catharine MacKinnon's *Sexual Harassment of Working Women: A Case of Sex Discrimination* (1979), and a theoretical foundation in MacKinnon's *Toward a Feminist Theory of the State* (1989). *See also* Christine Littleton, *Alternative Theories of Sexual Equality* (1984); Martha Minow, "Equalities," 88 *Journal of Philosophy* 633 (1991).

7. Much criticism is directed against the "rigidity" of MacKinnon's understanding of gender. One way of understanding it is based on a radically constructivist approach, according to which gender is conceptualized as a constructed phenomenon rather than as an experienced reality. Then, MacKinnon's deconstruction of gender, particularly in *Toward a Feminist Theory of the State, supra* note 6, at chapter 7, can be understood as critique of an invention transformed into law, not as a rejection of peoples choices, a suggestion of widespread false consciousness, or a simple reductionism to essentialist models. I discuss this in relation to the critique articulated by Judith Butler in *Excitable Speech: A Politics of the Performative* (1997). *See* Susanne Baer, "Inexcitable Speech: Zum Rechtsverständnis postmoderner feministischer Positionen am Beispiel Judith Butler," in *Kritische Differenzen—geteilte Perspektiven* 229 (Antje Hornscheidt et al. eds., 1998).

8. Immanuel Kant, "Die Rechtsordnung als denknotwendige Bedingung allgemeiner Freiheit und Gleichheit," *in Werke*, Band 6, at 229–31, 237–38 (Akademie Ausgabe 7, 1906). The derivative nature of equality is engraved in the European Convention of Human Rights and Freedoms, where article 14 is only applied in conjunction with an article protecting liberty interests.

9. For a more thorough discussion, see Susanne Baer, "Equality: The Jurisprudence of the German Constitutional Court," 5 *Columbia Journal of European Law* 249 (1999).

10. The Aristotelian interpretation of equality holds that persons or situations of a similar nature, or "similarly situated," require similar, or equal treatment, while dissimilarities require or at least legitimize inequality. For further discussion, *see* Catharine A. MacKinnon, "Reflections on Sex Equality Under Law," 100 *Yale Law Journal* 1281 (1991).

11. Marcus Tullius Cicero, "Naturrecht als universale Teilhabe am ewigen Weltgesetz," in *Der Staat*, at 25, 80 (1964). German legal philosopher Norbert Hoerster relates that to the concept of human dignity in *Klassische Texte der Staatsphilosophie* 24 (Norbert Hoerster ed., 1976).

12. John Locke, Second Treatise of Government, 4 (Mark Goldie, ed., 1993) (1690).

13. For example, this can be seen in Kant's discussion of the third legal principle, the right of the citizen called *sibisufficientia*. *See* Kant, *supra* note 8.

14. *See* Jürgen Habermas, *Die Einbeziehung des Anderen: Studien zur politischen Theorie* (1996), and his discussion of John Rawls in chapters 2 and 3.

15. *See* Axel Honneth, *Kampf um Anerkennung* (1994), where he refers to traces of a tradition of social philosophy in Marx, Sorel, and Sartre, and describes intersubjective conditions of personal integrity, which include the rights to respect and solidarity. *Id.* at 209. These rights can be interpreted as dignity and equality. See also the discussion by John Gardner, "Liberals and Unlawful Discrimination," 9 *Oxford Journal of Legal Studies* 1 (1989); and Virginia Held, "Liberty and Equality from a Feminist Perspective," in *Enlightenment, Rights and Revolution: Essays on Legal and Social History* 69 (Neil MacCormick and Zenon Bankowski eds., 1989).

16. Herta Nagl-Docekal, "Gleichbehandlung und Anerkennung von Differenz: Kontroversielle Themen feministischer politischer Philosophie," in *Differenz und Lebensqualität* 9, 18–20 (Herta Nagl-Docekal and Herlinde Pauer-Studer eds., 1996).

17. *See* MacKinnon, *Sexual Harassment of Working Women, supra* note 6. I understand the work of Cass Sunstein and Deborah Rhode as slightly different versions of equality thinking. For the German discussion, *see* Baer, *supra* note 4; and Susanne Baer, "A Different Approach to Jurisprudence? Feminisms in German Legal Science, Legal Cultures, and the Ambivalence of Law," 3 *Cardozo Women's Law Journal* 251 (1996).

18. The first statement can be found in a decision on pension law from 1981, Entscheidungen des Bundesverfassungsgerichts (BVerfGE) (Federal Constitutional Court), 57, 335 (345) (FRG). It should be noted that many constitutional scholars tended or still tend to ignore the potential of this doctrine. For extensive analyses, *see* Ute Sacksofsky, *Das Grundrecht auf Gleichberechtigung* (2d ed. 1996).

19. BVerfGE 84, 9 (18–19).

20. This is particularly true in the night shift decision from 1992, BverfGE 85, 191. *See also* the decision on discrimination in access to paid work from 1993, BVerfGE 89, 276.

21. Robert Husbands, "Sexual Harassment Law in Employment: An International Perspective," 131 *International Labour Review* 535, 558 (1992).

22. Cornell, *supra* note 5.

23. The most often cited description of the dilemma may be the one by Audre Lorde, "A Master's Tool Will Never Dismantle the Master's House," in her collection of essays *Sister Outsider* (1984).

24. Cornell, *supra* note 5, at 227.

25. *Id.* at 206.
26. *Id.* at 170.
27. *Id.* at 227.
28. In reactions to law against racist discrimination, including harassment at work, many claimed that freedom of contract, a right the constitution protects as part of free will under article 2, sec. 1, Basic Law, covers acts of subordination. For details of the German discussion see Susanne Baer, "Ende der Privatautonomie oder grundrechtlich fundierte Rechtsetzung?" 35 *Zeitschrift für Rechtspolitik* 290 (2002).
29. For a wonderful discussion of the nature of the subject in law see the collection of essays in *Sexing the Subject of Law* (Ngaire Naffine and Rosemary J. Owens eds., 1997); and Nicola Lacey, *Unspeakable Subjects* part I (1998).
30. In India, law against sex discrimination has sometimes been based on modesty, a concept closely related to dignity in its individualistic emphasis. *See* Martha Nussbaum's essay in this volume.
31. Cornell, *supra* note 5, at 194 ("unilateral imposition"). In Europe, the discussion focuses on gender-mainstreaming, often understood and sometimes abused as a replacement for equality strategies. As embodied in article 3, section 2 of the Treaty of the European Community, gender-mainstreaming is the structural device to turn equality into practice.
32. *See* John Rawls, *A Theory of Justice* (1971). For a similar approach and an impressive defense of universality based on a Kantian idea of the subject, see Renata Salecl, *The Spoils of Freedom* (1994).
33. Cornell, *supra* note 5, at 225 (referring to Judith Butler).
34. *See generally* Martha Minow, *Making All the Difference: Inclusion, Exclusion and American Law* (1990); Susanne Baer, "Dilemmata im Recht und Gleichheit als Hierarchisierungsverbot: Der Abschied von Thelma und Louise," 28 *Kriminologisches Journal* 242 (1996).
35. It may be interesting to note that in the Republic of South Africa, in which men share a history of racial oppression with women and in which racial oppression was often sexualized, law offers a strong guarantee of equal rights as well as a strong protection for individual dignity. This indicates a scheme of interrelatedness between the two, rather than the traditional scheme of conflict. However, as reports on the diminishing impact of women on politics point out, ongoing gender hierarchy supports a trend to emphasize dignity rather than equality.
36. On newer developments, *see* note 1.
37. The discussion around the meaning of dignity among constitutional scholars was, however, for a long time imprinted by this history. In the 1950s and 1960s, some argued that dignity should be gained individually and thus not attributed to anyone just because he or she was human. The courts decided from the beginning that dignity serves as a right against degrading treatment of anyone as a less valuable human being. For further discussion, *see* Baer, *supra* note 4, at 217–19.
38. For a discussion of jurisprudence from around the world see my chapter on dignity, self-determination, and privacy in Norman Dorsen, Michel Rosenfeld, Andras Sajo, and Susanne Baer, *Comparative Constitutionalism* (forthcoming, 2003).
39. Belg. Const. art. 23; Greece Const. art. 2; Italy Const. arts. 2, 41; Port. Const. art.

1; Spain Const. art. 10; Swed. Const. art. 2. *See* Peter Häberle, "Die Menschenwüde als Grundlage der staatlichen Gemeinschaft" in 1 *Handbuch des Staatsrechts* 20 n.1 (Josef Isensee and Paul Kirchhof eds., 1998).

40. The charter was drafted under heavy German influence, partly since Roman Herzog, a German constitutional scholar, presided over the drafting convention. The whole process and results may be found on the Internet at www.consilium.eu.int (visited July 1, 2001). On the significance of the charter, see Susanne Baer, "Grundrechtecharta ante portas," 33 *Zeitschrift für Rechtspolitik* 361 (2000).

41. Article 3, section 3 of the Grundgesetz reads: "No one may be prejudiced or favored because of his or her sex, parentage, race, language, homeland and origin, faith, religious or political opinion. No one may be disadvantaged because of his or her disability."

42. *See generally Grundgesetz-Kommentar* art. 1 (Ingo v. Münch and Philip Kunig eds., 4th ed. 1996).

43. In comparison, First Amendment jurisprudence tends to cover many incidents which could be argued under other constitutional provisions, if a more detailed scheme of individual rights were at hand. For example, the famous Skokie controversy may be discussed not only as a free expression problem, but as a potential violation of the dignity of Holocaust survivors, or, for that matter, as a violation of their right to live as equals, treated with equal respect, in a community. *See Skokie v. Nationalist Socialist Party of America*, 366 N.E.2d 347 (1977); *Collin v. Smith*, 578 F.2d 1197 (7th Cir.), *aff'g* 477 F. Supp. 676 (N.D. Ill. 1978). However, the pure presence of a right to dignity within a constitution cannot tell us the story of its practical effect. For example, the constitutional right to dignity in India is more often used to broaden the powers of the federation rather than to protect individuals from harm.

44. For the most far-reaching interpretation, see MacKinnon, *supra* note 10.

45. Article 3, section 2 of the Grundgesetz was amended in 1994. Before that, it stated: "Women and men are equal." The new second sentence reads: "The state shall promote the social implementation of equality of women and men and shall work toward the removal of existing detriments."

46. *See* Evelyn Collins, "European Union Sexual Harassment Policy," in *Sexual Politics and the European Union* 23 (Amy Elman ed., 1996). Husbands ignores the fundamental difference when he lists the EC recommendation under equal opportunities laws, since the Commission wanted dignity for both men and women. *See* Husbands, *supra* note 21, at 546. For EC law, see Commission Recommendation 92/131/EEC of November 27, 1991, on the Protection of the Dignity of Women and Men at Work, art. 3, 1992 O.J. (L 049) (hereinafter Commission Recommendation on the Protection of the Dignity of Women and Men at Work) ("Whereas unwanted conduct of a sexual nature, or other conduct based on sex affecting the dignity of women and men at work, including the conduct of superiors and colleagues, is unacceptable and may, in certain circumstances, be contrary to the principle of equal treatment within the meaning of Articles 3, 4 and 5 of Council Directive 76/207/EEC of 9 February 1976 on the implementation of the principle of equal treatment for men and women as regards access to employment, vocational training and promotion, and working conditions").

47. 29 C.F.R. § 1604.11(a) (1992).

48. My translation of the Federal Law for the Protection of Employees (*Beschäftigtenschutzgesetz*). More equality oriented approaches can be found in laws of the German Länder, e.g., Hessen and Berlin. A brief annotated collection of these laws can be found in *Frauengleichstellungsgesetze des Bundes und der Länder: Kommentar für die Praxis* (Dagmar Schiek et al. eds., 1996).

49. One further element is responsibility. In German law, employers are rarely held responsible, while in U.S. law (and even more so in Canada and Belgium) this is more often the case, and there is greater employer responsibility for preventive measures and complaint and sanction systems. Other elements are defenses and sanctions: in German law, we find labor-law-type reactions of employer reprimanding harasser, including the danger of paternalism. Other legal systems in which sexual harassment is framed as a violation of contracts of employment, of duties rather than rights, include those of Belgium, Italy, Portugal, and Switzerland. *Cf.* Husbands, *supra* note 21, at 547. Another important element of harassment law is procedure; German law does not install special agents, although we do find, in some affirmative action plans, a designated employee to handle complaints. On Belgium, *see id.* at 555. On newer developments, see note 1.

50. *See also* the reference to dignity in Canadian equality jurisprudence. *E.g., Miron v. Trudel* [1995] D.L.R. 693 (Can.).

51. Case C-177/88, 1990 E.C.R. I-3941 (Dekker).

52. Entscheidungen des Bundesverwaltungsgerichts (Federal Administrative Court) (BVerwGE) 64, 274 (Peep-Show I); BVerfGE 84, 314 (Peep-Show II). Constitutional scholars criticized these decisions for imposing values rather than adjudicating rights.

53. The same happens in criminal law, where criminalized "sexual" behavior is what turns men on, not what harms women. For further discussion, *see* Baer, *supra* note 4, at 252.

54. Commission Recommendation on the Protection of the Dignity of Women and Men at Work, *supra* note 46, art. 3.

55. *See* Victoria A. Carter, "Working on Dignity: EC Initiatives on Sexual Harassment in the Workplace," 12 *Northwestern Journal of International Law and Business* 431 (1992); Anthony B. Haller, "Sexual Harassment: An Import from America?" 4 *Business Law Review* 229 (1983). In France, law acknowledges harassment as an abuse of authority; since it ignores gender hierarchy, harassment among coworkers is not actionable.

56. In the hearings, a conservative member of Parliament stated that there are women who would like to be harassed, but are not, and who want to gain attention with an unfounded complaint. *Focus*, November 8, 1993, at 53 (citing a member of the Bundestag von Stetten) ("Kein Herz fuer Machos").

57. For further discussion of German criminal law provisions on rape, *see* Baer, *supra* note 4, at 119–46; on the rights of victims, *see* Alexandra Goy, "The Victim-Plaintiff in Criminal Trials and Civil Law Responses to Sexual Violence," 3 *Cardozo Women's Law Journal* 335 (1996).

58. The correlation between dignity, characterized as honor, and individualization has first been discussed by 2 Alexis de Toqueville, *Democracy in America*, bk. 3, ch. 18 (Phillips Bradley ed., 1945).

59. For a discussion of the standards for "unwelcomeness" in U.S. law, and for a

critique of the "reasonable woman standard," which may be more adequately conceptualized as the "reasoning woman perspective," *see* Baer, *supra* note 4, at 159–79.

60. *See* Cornell, *supra* note 5, at 175; Baer, *supra* note 4, at 159.

61. Cornell, *supra* note 5, at 199.

62. *Id.* at 186, 202 (referring to "a conception of sexual shame").

63. From a comparative perspective, I should point out that U.S. law, despite its equality approach, features some extremely problematic aspects as well. One is the defense of sexual harassment based on the right to freedom of speech. Regarding sexual harassment, freedom of speech is not an issue in Europe. This might be a time-lag of sensitivity, but it may also demonstrate a willingness to combat violations of personal freedom and equality in any form, including speech. As with every other constitutionally guaranteed right, freedom of speech is limited by rights of others. The example of pornography is a case in point. For further discussion, *see* Susanne Baer, "Violence: Dilemmas of Democracy and Law," in *Freedom of Speech and Incitement against Democracy* 63 (David Kretzmer and Francine Kershman Hazan eds., 2000). In sum, harassment cannot be justified by referring to free speech. For similar conclusions, *see* Cornell, *supra* note 5, at 187.

64. The difference between the dignity-based and equality-based approaches is also evident in the case of pornography. In Germany, as in many other legal systems, pornography is regulated as obscenity, which is legitimated with references to the protection of morals and dignity. In fact, pornography is available. The legal response ignores the harm of gender discrimination and sexual violence, and criminalizes sexualities outside the heterosexual norm, particularly sexual expression by gays and lesbians. Despite the fact that solidarity with gays and lesbians should not be abused to legitimize sexual violence, an equality-based approach to pornography would focus on harm, rather than the preservation of a specific kind of sexual morality. It situates pornography in a context of inequality, not in a context of bad taste.

65. This is the case in Israel. *See* Orit Kamir's essay in this volume.

[22]

For the Children

Trends in International Policies and Law on Sex Tourism

KAMALA KEMPADOO AND RANYA GHUMA

The long-standing relationship between sex, prostitution, and tourism have been widely recognized by scholars in Third World and tourism studies (Fanon 1963, Turner and Ash 1976, Press 1978, ECTWT 1983, Cohen 1984, Crick 1989, Hobson and Dietrich 1994, Harrison 1994). It was, however, due to feminist research and action around prostitution in Southeast Asia in the 1980s that "sex tourism" was identified as a concept to refer to practices structured in the tourism industry that involve the exchange of material goods or money for sexual labor (Matsui 1989, Mies 1989, Enloe 1989, Truong 1990, Isis-wicce 1990). The concept has since become common currency among academics and journalists to denote practices that range from highly organized tours for sexual pleasure to incidental "romantic" encounters between the tourist and "native," and which incorporate men and women as both tourists or clients and sex workers (Urry 1990, Hall 1992, el-Gawhary 1995, Leheny 1995, O'Connell Davidson 1996, Pattullo 1996, Pettman 1997, Oppermann 1998). There is, however, little formal recognition of sex tourism by international authorities and nothing to date that reviews current global polices on the issue. In this chapter we examine dominant trends in the international discourse on sex tourism, as refracted through policies and laws of international agencies, governments and non-governmental organizations (NGOs), which aim to control and regulate the global tourism industry or seek to address the social impacts of tourism.

Attention to sex tourism by international agencies is of very recent origin, and thus the initiatives taken so far are still to unfold into clear policies and concrete actions. Nevertheless, our research shows that the discourse focuses little on sex tourism in general but almost exclusively on "child prostitution." This focus can in part be attributed to the immense amount of pressure that has been exerted through the ECPAT (End Child Prostitution in Asian Tourism) campaign and the ease with which the subject of sex between adults and children evokes widespread condemnation. It is indeed far easier to mobilize or gather consensus around something so evidently "evil" as pedophilia than it is around issues that concern sex between adults. It would appear, however, that this focus not only serves to obscure the working conditions for adult women and men in the sex sector by ignoring the population completely (and hence denying it legitimacy, visibility, agency, and human rights) but, equally as important, to deflect attention away from the complicity of the broader tourism industry, government, and international agencies in sustaining activities that are in most countries defined by law as criminal. That is, the emphasis on child prostitution as the main problem in sex tourism can be seen to quietly allow other forms of prostitution to continue to take place without hindrance, scrutiny, or attention to the human rights of women and men who provide sexual services in the tourism industry.

THE UNITED NATIONS

The United Nations, as one of the influential bodies on international relations, has not developed any specific conventions to address sex tourism. Prostitution—a constitutive element of sex tourism—is, however, explicitly dealt with in the 1949 UN Convention for the Suppression of Traffic in Persons and the Exploitation of Prostitution of Others, the 1979 Convention for the Elimination of All Forms of Discrimination Against Women (CEDAW), and the 1989 Convention of the Rights of the Child (Wijers and Lap-Chew 1997, Bindman 1997). A Program of Action for the Prevention of the Sale of Children, Child Prostitution and Child Pornography was also adopted in 1992 by the UN Commission on Human Rights (Lim 1998). Many other conventions on social, political, civil, cultural, workers and human rights are also indirectly applicable (Bindman 1997).

The main thrust of UN conventions since 1949 has been to suppress the trafficking of women, brothel keeping, pimping, and procuring for the purposes of prostitution and to prevent the exploitative use of children in prostitution. Analyses of these instruments shows that although the conventions have been framed within a discourse that appears to support a complete abolition of prostitution, they do not unequivocally call for the complete eradication of all forms of prostitution. Laura Reanda (1991), for example, contends that the 1949 convention regards prostitution as a human rights violation only if it involves overt coercion, leaving untouched the issue of voluntary prostitution and the violation of human rights of those who "choose" prostitution as a form of work. Jo Doezema (1998), on the other hand, argues that there is little doubt that the 1949 convention was developed within a context dominated by movements and ideologies that sought to completely eradicate prostitution—at a historical moment when the notion of prostitution as a matter of personal choice and a form of work did not exist—and thus is for all intents and purpose an abolitionist instrument. Such ambiguity in the earlier documents has, however, been somewhat addressed through the international women's movement, particularly in the form of the CEDAW convention. While on the surface this convention can be easily interpreted as a treatise to abolish all forms of prostitution, a careful examination of the document and developments around the convention allows for a more qualified understanding. In the first place, an early attempt by Morocco to amend the convention to include a call for the suppression of all prostitution and not just of the "exploitation of prostitution" was rejected, indicating that the designers of the convention explicitly allowed for a distinction to be made between notions of coerced and noncoerced forms of prostitution (Doezema 1998, Wijers 1997). The convention thus seeks to abolish forced prostitution and allows for the recognition of voluntary prostitution.[1] Second, in 1992, a general recommendation by CEDAW was made to include prostitutes among those who needed to be offered equal protection under the law (Doezema 1998). Prostitutes were recognized in the convention as deserving of rights that others in society enjoy. In addition to this move away from the idea of completely abolishing prostitution to one that recognized the human and civil rights of sex workers, in 1996 the UN special rapporteur on violence against women commissioned an international research project on the trafficking of women that was designed and implemented from a perspective that recognized prostitution as a form of labor (see Wijers and Lap-Chew 1997). This trend within the UN would seem to open possibilities for a recognition of prostitution as the employment of sexual labor and of prostitutes as sex workers, raising questions about how the human, labor, social, cultural, and civil rights of those who purposefully sell sex in the tourism industry could be protected.

Nevertheless, within the UN it seems that the right hand does not always know what the left is doing. While heading in the direction of defining prostitution as sexual labor that is not always coerced or seen as an expression of violence to women, and of recognizing prostitutes as persons deserving of legal protections, another element has crept into the discourse. In December 1996, the UN General Assembly passed a resolution on "The Traffic of Women" that was reaffirmed in December 1997, in which states and international organizations were urged not only to prevent trafficking, but also to consider enacting legislation "to prevent sex tourism."[2] The issue of prostitution within the tourism industry—"sex tourism"—explicitly made its way into the UN discourse under the rubric of "trafficking," equated with coercive and oppressive practices. The suppression of sex tourism is a necessary corollary in this approach. The recent nuanced definition regarding prostitution and respect for sex workers and their rights articulated through the CEDAW convention is thus contradicted by the representation of sex tourism as a form of coerced prostitution that requires abolition.

THE INTERNATIONAL LABOR ORGANIZATION

As a UN specialized agency that promotes concepts of human rights and labor rights, the Conventions of the International Labor Organization (ILO) are considered (like Conventions of the United Nations) to be international treaties and thus binding on those states who ratify them. From these conventions, minimum labor standards of freedom of association, the right to organize, abolition of forced labor, equality of opportunity and treatment, and other standards regulating work conditions are enumerated. However, to date the ILO has not developed any specific convention regarding the position on sex workers but prefers to leave this to existing national or local laws on prostitution, only indirectly addressing sex worker rights through existing labor conventions: "Where prostitutes are considered as workers with rights under standard labor legislation, the concern would be to ensure that they, like other legitimate workers, are entitled to proper working conditions and protection from exploitation and discrimination" (Lim 1998:v). The ILO does, however, deal with the issue of child labor in tourism, which, to the extent that child labor includes child prostitution, can be interpreted to address child sex tourism. Convention 138 of 1973 prohibits the admission of people under the age of eighteen to dangerous employment and mentions "moral hazards" as one such danger (Bindman 1997; Belau, personal communication April 24, 1998). Furthermore, in 1997, the ILO Tripartite Meeting on the Effects of New Technologies on Employment and Working Conditions in the Hotel, Catering, and Tourism Sector (Geneva, May 12–16, 1997) adopted a "resolution concerning the sexual exploitation of children and child labor," suggesting that the ILO is taking increasing steps toward addressing sex tourism in the framework of labor rights (Belau, personal communication, April 24, 1998).

Maggie Black, in the ILO-commissioned report *In the Twilight Zones: Child Workers in the Hotel, Tourism and Catering Industry* (1995), adds a significant contribution to the definition of child labor and child sexual exploitation by arguing that sexual exploitation of children employed in travel and entertainment industries is an occupational hazard (6). She further argues that much of the media coverage of "sex tourism" and "child sexual exploitation" is hyperbolic and misinformed. Her ground breaking research in Kenya, Mexico, the Philippines, and Sri Lanka shows that many child prostitutes provide services to local customers above and beyond those provided to sex tourists, thus stressing the need to examine child labor in all its dimensions rather than just in the narrow arena of the tourism industry.

The 1998 ILO report by Lin Leam Lim on prostitution in Southeast Asia, sheds further light on the direction that the organization is taking. From the extensive data and information that is presented on Indonesia, Malaysia, the Philippines and Thailand, Lim argues for a two-pronged approach, where adult prostitution would "be viewed as a matter of personal choice and as a form of work" and child prostitution as "a form of coercion and violence against children...forced labor and a contemporary form of slavery" (2). With the understanding that "working conditions of prostitutes vary greatly," she insists that legislation, policies, and programs need to take the differences between groups of workers in the sex sector into account and that the official stance "cannot be one of neglect or nonrecognition" of the issue (213). Indeed, Lim recommends that a clear position be taken that supports careful decriminalization or legalization of prostitution rather than its abolition or prohibition. The latter situation, she states "would mean banning the sector," consequently pushing prostitutes into criminality, leaving them even more vulnerable to marginalization, exploitation, and abuse (214). In order to protect sex worker rights, she argues, the existing prostitution laws require reform or review, and special measures need to be put into place (214). It is a clear call to the ILO to take further steps regarding the situations of sex workers internationally and to go beyond a reliance on existing laws.

Lim, however, does not completely escape the trend that has already been established by the UN: of associating sex tourism with the exploitation of children. She argues: "Sex tourism tends to be an important source of commercial sexual exploitation of children," and recommends more stringent measures to be adopted for the tourism sector.

THE GLOBAL TOURISM INDUSTRY

Most of the initiatives to address sex tourism within the tourism industry are predicated on the position of the World Tourism Organization (WTO), an organization that traces its origins to a 1925 non-governmental organization, the International Union of Official Tourist Publicity Organizations, and which by 1997 had entered into a formal agreement with the United Nations as a UN executing agency (WTO 1998a). As the only large-scale intergovernmental organization representing various actors of the tourism industry, the WTO serves as a key player in international discussions of tourism policies and their implications. It extends membership not only to sovereign states but also to members of the public and private sector, hence industries in sectors that are either directly or indirectly involved in the tourism industry carry great influence. The organization derives much of its support from 138 member states and territories that are classified as "full members" of the WTO. Approximately 350 nonterritorial entities representing industry and non-governmental organizations take part in the WTO as "affiliate members," including airlines, hotels, restaurants, tour operators, travel agents, and educational and research staff. Finally, "associate membership" is extended to those territories that are not responsible for their own foreign relations, provided that the government that oversees those policies agrees to membership. WTO associate members are currently represented by Aruba, Macau, Madeira, and the Netherlands Antilles (WTO 1998b). Full members, associate members, and affiliate members are further divided into six regional commissions: Africa, the Americas, East Asia and the Pacific, Europe, the Middle East, and South Asia. Currently Argentina, Bolivia, Brazil, Chile, Colombia, Costa Rica, Cuba, the Dominican Republic, Ecuador, El Salvador, Grenada, Guatemala, Haiti, Jamaica, Mexico, Nicaragua, Panama, Paraguay, Peru, Uruguay, and Venezuela comprise the Regional Commission for the Americas (WTO 1998c). Because of a lack of funding support from the United States Department of State, the United States withdrew as a member of the WTO in December 1996. Canada also withdrew its membership from the WTO. However, both countries may attend WTO functions as observers.

In October 1995, the WTO adopted a "Declaration on the Prevention of Organized Sex Tourism," which was developed at a two-day consultation meeting in Saint-Vincent, Italy (*WTO News* 1995). It requested governments represented in the WTO to act through the implementation of national laws and bilateral agreements in order to eradicate organized sex tourism. It further asked donor countries and aid agencies to undertake initiatives that would help to develop more sustainable forms of tourism development in areas where sex tourism is prevalent. Representatives from the Universal Federation of Travel Agents Association (UFTAA), International Hotel Association (IHRA), International Association of Tour Managers (IATM), the United Nations, the World Health Organization (WHO), and the United Nations Educational, Scientific and Cultural Organization (UNESCO) also attended the meeting, along with non-governmental organizations such as ECPAT (End Child Prostitution in Asian Tourism). Following from this statement, the WTO sent a delegation, in 1996, to Brasilia to attend the International Seminar on the Sexual Exploitation of Children and Adolescents in the Americas, which was organized by Brazil's national tourism administration. The Chief of the WTO Committee on Quality of Tourism and Development, Henryk Handszuh, led a workshop on sex tourism during this seminar. Many of the tools mentioned in the Declaration on the Prevention of Organized Sex Tourism were incorporated in the Brasilia Charter, which was adopted by delegates to the conference (*WTO News* 1996).

From these measures the WTO has taken increasingly active and vocal steps to extend the discussion of sex tourism. Working in close cooperation with ECPAT, the WTO was instrumental in facilitating the convening of the Stockholm Congress Against the Commercial Sexual Exploitation of Children, held in August of 1996. Heads of state of many UN countries as well as international agencies attended the congress, which intended to build upon the work of the UN Convention on the Rights of the Child in order to facilitate the eradication of child sexual exploitation in tourism (WTO 1995). This congress appears to represent a major turning point in how the WTO addresses the issue of sex tourism on an international level, shifting the focus to the child victim of sexual exploitation. A key entity emerging from this conference was the Child Prostitution and Tourism Watch, a task force comprised of tourism industry groups, governments, and NGOs. As stated by the WTO, the aims of the international campaign are to "prevent, uncover, isolate, and eradicate the exploitation of children in sex tourism" (WTO 1998d). By 1997, the focus of the WTO's concern about sex tourism was almost exclusively defined in terms of child prostitution.

Other key groups within the tourism industry have also turned their attention to the issue of sex tourism and, like the WTO, stress the situation of children. ECTAA (Group of National Travel Agents and Tour Operations Association within the European Union) and FIYTO (Federation of International Youth Travel Organizations) have, for example, both issued condemnations of "child sex tourism" and suggest to members to support efforts to eradicate child sexual exploitation in tourism. ECTAA's analysis is that sex tourism in developing countries is the primary cause of child sex abuse, a very different situation, it claims, to that in "industrialized societies" where "child abuse often involves close relatives or acquaintances of the victims" (ECTAA 1996). The IUF/UITA/IUL (International Union of Food Agriculture, Hotel, Restaurant, Catering, Tobacco and Allied Workers Associations) attempts to take a broader outlook and recognizes both "prostitution tourism" and "child prostitution" as problematic for the tourism industry. However, the statement that "any lasting solution to the problem of prostitution, in particular child prostitution, requires that progressive social and economic reforms provide the objective conditions for children to cease being treated as commodities" clearly points to children as the primary group warranting attention (IUF/UITA/IUL 1996).

That the issue of sex tourism is an uncomfortable one for tourism industry groups is evident from the position taken by other groups, such as IFTO (the International Federation of Tour Operators) and IATA (International Air Transport Association). These avoid associating "sex" with "tourism" altogether and instead establish resolutions against the "sexual exploitation of children" and "commercial sexual exploitation of children" (IFTO 1998, IATA 1996). This position denies the existence of organized sex tourism and instead attributes the incidences of prostitution to the actions of individual tourists. The IH&RA (International Hotel and Restaurant Association) maintains a similar focus on the sexual exploitation of children, in the absence of an image of the tourism industry as an active agent in this exploitation, arguing that "unfortunately, some child sex abusers may attempt to use hotels as the location where they commit their crimes" (IH&RA 1996). UFTAA similarly pledges "to combat the prostitution related to so-called 'sex tourism' and to protect the child victims of such tourists..." (UFTAA 1998). HOTREC (the Confederation of National Associations of Hotels, Restaurants, Cafes and Similar Establishments in the European Union and the European Economic Area), in its attempt to delink the tourism industry from child sex tourism, states:

> HOTREC and its member associations, however, very much regret the frequent use of precisely the latter expression "child sex tourism." The association of the three words "child, "*sex*" and "tourism" is highly damaging to the image of the tourism industry. Such crimes occur because of child sex abusers and, unfortunately, they occur in all sorts of circumstances which are not related to tourism activities (HOTREC 1997).

In this discourse the object of sex tourism is constructed as a "child victim," while the perpetrator of the exploitation is a "child abuser," with the situations of organized sex tourism and prostitution practices between adults being completely ignored. Thus not only has the focus on sex tourism become even further diluted, but several of the tourism industry groups actively attempt to deny any form of responsibility for sex tourism, fingering individual pedophiles as the problem.

Within the tourism industry, the IFWTO (International Federation of Women Travel Operators) is one of the few that maintains a focus on *both* child sex tourism and organized sex tourism. IFWTO members and associates pledged in 1997 "never to promote or assist in the promotion of travel, tours, or programs designed for sexual exploitation and to encourage local, regional, and national measures to prevent and eradicate 'sex tourism,'" explicitly acknowledging the role that the tourism industry itself holds in sustaining a sex tourism sector (IFWTO 1998). The IFWTO takes the original WTO position seriously, for it calls not only for the recognition of the culpability of the tourism industry in promoting and organizing sex tourism but also for the abolition of all prostitution practices within the tourism industry. It is a position that echoes the recent UN resolution on the trafficking of women as well as a radical feminist position concerning prostitution (Chapkis 1997). It also carries an abolitionist implication, leaving little space for the recognition of adult sex workers or for the protection of sex-worker rights within the tourism industry. It is a position that supports the campaign against the exploitation of children in sex tourism yet which contradicts the CEDAW convention.

In contrast to the earlier mentioned tourism industry associations that have in various ways attempted to address the issue of sex tourism, the Caribbean Tourism Organization (CTO) has made no statements or resolutions on either sex tourism or the sexual exploitation of children. Although claiming to be aware of the WTO work on the issue and the resolution of 1995, the CTO remains silent on the subject, giving little leadership or direction for states or tourism boards in the Caribbean region.

NATIONAL GOVERNMENTS

The implementation of national laws concerning sex tourism from major tourist-sending countries has exclusively dealt with the punishment of any involvement of a national in child prostitution while abroad. Extraterritorial child sex tourism legislation has been passed in a number of major tourist-sending countries such as Australia, Belgium, France, Germany, Japan, New Zealand, Norway, Sweden, the United States, Canada, and the United Kingdom (*WTO News* 1997). Most of these extraterritorial laws define the obtaining of sexual services from children as well as the promotion of child sex tours as a crime. Therefore, both procurers of child prostitution and tour agents and operators who facilitate child sex tourism are included under the scope of these laws. Because of the difficulty in prosecuting extraterritorial cases (gathering evidence, etc.), countries such as the UK have stated that, if possible, the criminal (a national of the UK) should be extradited from the home country to the place where the offensive act took place for trial (One World 1996). Bilateral agreements between states would facilitate such extradition. Other countries such as Australia have heard cases of violations of the extraterritorial child sex tourism laws in magistrate courts at home.

The case of Australian initiatives to combat child sex tourism provides an example of how international conventions, non-governmental groups, and domestic pressure interact in the formation of laws combating child sex tourism, and the scope of this legislation in the prosecution of violators of the law. Michael Hall (1998) explains how media attention promoted by increasing lobbying attempts of groups such as ECPAT in the late 1980s led to efforts to implement national legislation controlling aspects of sex tourism. Significantly, as ECPAT has limited its scope to dealing with children in sex tourism, national legislation has only defined legal accountability if the sex worker involved is a child. The emphasis on child sex tourism as opposed to sex tourism in general is characteristic of the majority of extraterritorial sex tourism legislation.

Under increasing pressure from NGO groups such as ECPAT and international organizations such as the United Nations Children's Fund (UNICEF), the Australian government ratified the Convention on the Rights of the Child in 1990. Article 34 of the convention, which calls for states to undertake the protection of children from sexual exploitation, was a critical component in facilitating future legal initiatives, as were recommendations by the Special Rapporteur on the UN Commission on the Program for the Prevention of the Sale of Children, Child Prostitution and Child Pornography (Hall 1998). In 1993, federal officials agreed to enact laws enabling prosecution of Australian nationals engaged in sex tourism, as well as Australian nationals involved in arranging or promoting child sex tours. The resulting Crimes (Child Sex Tourism) Amendment Act of 1994 expanded on the Crimes Act of 1914 to include activities of Australians engaging in, promoting, or profiting from child sexual exploitation (Hall 1998). With the amendment, Australia has had more arrests using extraterritorial sex tourism laws than any other country with similar laws *(Fiji Times,* August 28, 1997). Significantly, in October 1996, Melbourne magistrate courts undertook the prosecution of an Australian man accused of promoting sex tourism—a milestone in enforcement of Child Sex Tourism legislation.

However, events surrounding the creation and implementation of this legislation are under criticism. The House of Representatives Standing Committee on Legal and Constitutional Affairs (HRSCLCA), in an advisory report to the House of Representatives, expressed strong concern about the lack of consultation and constructive evaluation of the extraterritorial laws before their adoption (Hall 1998). ECPAT's role in the passing of the law also cannot be understated. Hall points out that ECPAT was referenced in over two-thirds of the parliamentary speeches supporting the passage of the amendment. Also, largely due to the intense lobbying efforts of ECPAT, the Australian government has established a new "National Council for the Prevention of Child Abuse" to oversee implementation of the Stockholm Congress Agenda for Action (ECPAT 1997). Furthermore, ECPAT has undertaken a campaign to pressure the Australian Federal Immigration Minister to implement mandatory police checks for sponsors of unaccompanied children who enter Australia (ECPAT 1997). While the organization has proven to be a valuable source of information regarding child sex tourism, it appears to have, in many ways, monopolized the debate in Australia concerning sex tourism. As a result, no substantial laws hold the tourism industry accountable for the exploitation of sex workers unless it is in connection with a child.

In the Caribbean, no explicit laws, policies, or programs have been put in place to explicitly address sex tourism, although many countries formally criminalize and prohibit prostitution as described elsewhere in this book. Even so, in Curaçao, a brothel was licensed by the colonial government in 1949 and by 1998 was being converted into a site that would appeal to tourists and other foreign visitors to the island.[3] In Jamaica in 1998 the Minister of Commerce proposed the creation of red-light districts in tourism-dominated towns (see chapter 6 by Campbell et al.). Furthermore, in both Jamaica and the Dominican Republic, laws to prevent "harassment of tourists" have been put in place. To date, however, these efforts have been exclusively articulated through the interests of governments and the formal business sector, who are eager to maintain the flow of visitors—and hence foreign exchange—to the country. Within these efforts, little attention is given to the rights or needs of those who work in prostitution. In such a scenario, the government simply takes on the role of "pimp," becoming the third party that exploits the prostitution of others, placing itself in the position of violating international conventions. "State pimpage" could become the norm if this trajectory were to be followed by other Caribbean nations.[4]

NON-GOVERNMENTAL ORGANIZATIONS

Several NGOs have been active in addressing the issue of sex tourism over the past two decades. The Ecumenical Coalition on Third World Tourism (ECTWT) and the Filipina feminist organization GABRIELA were among the first to become internationally visible for their work in the area during the 1980s (ECTWT 1983, Matsui 1989). However, any discussion attempting to evaluate how sex tourism and the sex worker are discussed in international debates would be incomplete if it did not include a detailed description of the non-governmental organization ECPAT and the enormous role it has assumed in directing national and international endeavors focusing on sex tourism. Later in the chapter we also examine the very recent initiative of the U.S.-based organization, Equality Now.

ECPAT, as a non-governmental charitable association, was established in 1990, with its headquarters in Bangkok, Thailand. Its international campaign was established in 1991, with the goal of working to end child prostitution in Asian tourism through "political action, changes in law, education, and media coverage" (ECPAT 1996:46). While the organization's original concern was Asian tourism, it now aims to target child prostitution, child pornography, and trafficking of children for sexual exploitation by both local populations and foreign populations involved in the international tourism trade.

The "ECPAT network" includes a mix of groups and organizations from over twenty-five countries. Various national groups have been established in the United States, Belgium, Bangladesh, Brazil, Cambodia, Canada, Denmark, France, Finland, Germany, India, Italy, Japan, the Netherlands, New Zealand, Norway, the Philippines, Sri Lanka, Sweden, Switzerland, Taiwan, Thailand, the United Kingdom, and Vietnam. An "executive committee" with representatives from the different national groups and organizations serves as a "policy-making body," directing programs, organization, staff, financial supervision, and management. Finally, ECPAT includes as part of its organizational structure a working committee, which convenes at least once a year to discuss the implementation of executive policies (ECPAT 1998a).

ECPAT's aim of achieving media coverage and influencing laws has been accomplished in the majority of countries that have passed substantial legislation dealing with child sex tourism. The organization claims the international recognition of the "reality and extent of commercial sexual exploitation of children" as one of its major achievements (ECPAT 1996). As part of its original area of focus, the organization also claims a primary role in the movement for legal change in the Philippines, Sri Lanka, Taiwan, and Thailand. As it moved to influence child sex tourism discussions internationally, the influence of ECPAT is very evident in the formation of extraterritorial laws punishing the sexual exploitation of children through tourism, particularly in Germany, France, Australia, the United States, Belgium, New Zealand, Canada, and Ireland (ECPAT 1998a). With offices in more than thirty countries, ECPAT's international presence cannot be understated. The organization played a significant role in convening the First World Congress against the Sexual Exploitation of Children in Sweden in 1996, bringing together representatives from UN states and international agencies to discuss the issue of commercial sexual exploitation of children, particularly as it relates to tourism. Finally, ECPAT's "legal campaign" has been defined as the main focus of its network efforts. Through developing an "international legal monitoring program" with Asian countries, the organization hopes to follow up cases and study laws concerning child sex tourism and to facilitate networking with government agencies and lawyers who are willing to offer free legal services for children and witnesses to a crime. As a result, ECPAT has helped bring to court many cases of violations of child sexual exploitation laws in Asian courts (ECPAT 1998a).

Considering the extent to which ECPAT has influenced various international and national movements dealing with the issue of sex tourism, how it frames this debate within its own literature and ideology is of paramount significance in understanding the information from which national laws and other legal endeavors are constructed. ECPAT explicitly states that its purpose is protecting children and makes no claims of advocating the rights of all people involved in sex tourism. Nor is there a mention of adult prostitutes or sex workers in ECPAT's mission statements. Such a neglect of the dimensions of sex tourism is further evident in the "Country Reports," which provide information on the state of child sex tourism in various tourist destinations (ECPAT 1996b). Child sex tourism is seen as a developing evil in the tourism industry, while exploitation of workers in the sex tourism industry is virtually ignored. However, it is ECPAT's underlying abolitionist ideology about prostitution in general that is the most damning for the situations of adult sex workers. In a document entitled "Client, Customer, Exploiter: The Users of Child Prostitutes," ECPAT writes:

> Child abusers come from all walks of life and social backgrounds. The majority of these men become child abusers through their use of prostitutes. Children constitute a larger proportion of workers in the sex trade and are often found in the lower end of the market, where the prices are cheap and the conditions are worst. For those who deliberately seek sex with children law and social conventions make it difficult and dangerous to satisfy their interests. Prostitution enables them to have instant access to children. Prostitution is especially attractive to pedophiles and child preferential abusers (1998c:1).

The implication presented here is that prostitution can be generally blamed for the sexual exploitation of children, and that by eradicating prostitution, child sex tourism would disappear. It further does what abolitionist parties are renowned for: in order to "prove" the oppressive nature of prostitution, statistics about prostitution are provided for which the source is not given (Murray 1998). ECPAT thus highlights that "85 percent of prostitutes report being sexually abused as children," and further, that "90 percent of the prostitutes are being coerced into prostitution by pimps, etc." (1998c). These "key facts" are presented without any reference or contexualization and serve to condemn all forms of prostitution as inherently oppressive and abusive phenomena. The significance of its abolitionist phraseology and the absence of the image of a prostitute as a worker deserving of rights and advocacy is very relevant, as ECPAT remains the leading voice in international movements dealing with sex tourism.

Since 1996, the women's rights group Equality Now has engaged in a campaign against U.S.-based sex tour operators and to raise public awareness of the problem of organized sex tourism from the United States. It is one of the few NGOs in a tourist-sending country that is concerned with the eradication of organized sex tourism for and between adults. Writes Ken Franzblau of Equality Now: "The campaign was launched in response to the concerns expressed by women's groups in Asia that U.S.-based human rights groups and women's organizations could best address the exploitation of Asian women by focusing on the demand created by sex tourists" (personal communication, August 18, 1998). Equality Now has targeted specific companies that organize sex tours to Southeast Asia, estimating that there are at least twenty-five such agencies in the U.S. (Budhos 1997). The campaign launched by Equality Now does not stop at public exposure but rather seeks to prosecute companies that are found to be organizing the tours. This strategy is, in the context of legislation applicable in the U.S., not a straightforward matter. While the Violent Crime Control and Law Enforcement Act of 1994 "makes travel with intent to engage in any sexual act with a juvenile punishable by up to ten years imprisonment," the organization of prostitution between adults outside the U.S. falls under an array of local laws that deal with the organization of prostitution by a third party and that are subject to a variety of interpretations. Equality Now has, however, been advised that the Racketeer Influenced and Corrupt Organizations (RICO) Act and the Travel Act provide some tools at the national level for obtaining a conviction of sex-tour operators, although the terms are so very precise that unless all are met, the Acts cannot be enforced (T. Davis 1998). To add to this dilemma, after four years of being in force, not a single person had been prosecuted under the national Acts which prohibit child prostitution (Frantzblau, personal communication, August 18, 1998).

Equality Now's campaign is focused on ending organized sex tourism and is premised on a broader abolitionist perspective on prostitution. Citing the 1949 UN convention on the trafficking in persons, the organization insists that prostitution is "incompatible with the dignity and worth of a human person" and it is convinced that the practice of sex tourism is "degrading and exploitative...destroying the lives of so many girls and women" (*Women's Action* 1996).

A ONE-SIDED DEBATE

In this review of policies, resolutions, conventions, and intentions around sex tourism, it is easily discernible that child prostitution is the primary concern. This focus, while important, also manages to trouble the larger debate in several ways. First, in the campaign against child prostitution, an assumption, articulated most clearly by ECPAT, is that the entire sex trade needs to be eradicated. Sex tourism is unequivocally equated with coercive practices, and it is this perspective that informs the work being undertaken on the subject by the UN, the tourism industry, and various national governments. This abolitionist or, as some term it, "anti-prostitution" position on prostitution, however, not only contradicts the CEDAW convention that acknowledges the rights of prostitutes but also contests the "pro-sex work" trend in the ILO that recognizes prostitution as a form of labor subject to regulation and protection under labor laws. Two distinctly opposing ideological positions are thus in operation within the international discussion on prostitution in the tourism industry.

Second, in the dominant abolitionist perspective, sex tourism in developing countries is represented as the main cause of child prostitution. Such a claim can be misleading, constituting a partial representation of global realities. Situations for young people in countries in Asia where the tourism industry is barely involved, such as in India, the Ivory Coast or Senegal in Africa (Sleightholme and Sinha 1997, Tandia 1998, Anarfi 1998), as well as in Guyana, Colombia and Suriname in South America (see chapters 7, 11, and

12) indicate that the sexual exploitation of children takes place in many other arenas than the tourism industry. This information is easily glossed over or dismissed as inconsequential, and, instead, global generalizations are drawn from a few, highly focused studies. Furthermore it is not always clear that the tourism industry is where child prostitution starts. Rather, multiple causes for children to enter into sex work have been identified. One branch in the tourism industry maintains, for example, that it is due to the presence of pedophiles who entice children to have sex; others contend that the reason young people enter into prostitution is because of abuse in the home. Underdevelopment or maldevelopment of Third World areas continues to be viewed as a major factor. The reduction of causes of child prostitution so that the tourism industry alone is blamed creates a highly biased interpretation.

Third, in the international debates, sex tourism is separated from other forms of prostitution and is singled out as a form that deserves to be eradicated. The underlying assumption is that because large numbers of children are involved in sex tourism, the kind of prostitution that occurs in that particular sector is far more destructive and damaging than prostitution elsewhere. Nevertheless, this line of argument is predicated upon weak empirical evidence, indicating a fracture between social practices and the kind of knowledge that is being constructed about sex tourism. The relationship that is assumed between numbers of children relies on anecdotal information and locally specific research. Prostitution researchers themselves repeatedly point out that numbers of people who are involved in prostitution, including children, are extremely inaccurate. Sittirak, for example, points to the great variability in estimates about the number of prostitutes in Thailand, explaining that the estimate of the numbers "remains under constant debate, with a 'reliable' estimate not having been agreed upon yet" (1998:81). In her report for the ILO, Lim also underlines this point, stating: "It is not always possible to have precise figures on the extent of child prostitution" (1998:171). She severely criticizes ECPAT for using statistics that appear to her to be an exaggeration of the problem (172). In short, the number of children in sex tourism worldwide is unknown, as is the number of adults, and hence the overrepresentation of child sex workers in the tourism industry cannot be stated with certainty. The claims and generalizations about child prostitution in the tourism industry and, by extension, about the exceedingly harmful effects of sex tourism require far more substantiation and careful documentation than presently exists.

If one were to embark on a global survey of child prostitutes, one would run up against a problem that is far more fundamental than those mentioned above, namely the distinction between a child and an adult prostitute. While under some laws and conventions a person under the age of eighteen who works in prostitution is labeled a "child," under others she or he is often defined as an adult for purposes of sexual consent, marriage, and work (Black 1994, Lim 1998, Hanson 1998). To Douglas Hodgson (1995) the discrepancy in international conventions about the age when childhood ends and adulthood begins is one of the greatest limitations to discussing child prostitution. Given that laws allow young people to legally work, marry, and engage in sex in their early teen years in many countries, the young person is simultaneously deemed adult enough to consent to sexual intercourse and paid employment yet too young to be involved in a combination of the two. Demands by children to be acknowledged as independent earners and providers compound the issue and serve to blur the boundaries between child and adulthood even further (Swift 1997). The case study in Cartagena, Colombia, in chapter 7, and the situation for young male sex workers in Rio de Janeiro, Brazil, and in Thailand (Montgomery 1998, Longo 1998), illustrate this complexity fully, bringing into question whether these young people should be banned from selling sex or instead be protected and empowered by laws pertaining to child labor, marriage, and sexual consent.

Finally, the continual association of sex tourism with children obscures the realities for sex-working adults in the tourism industry. As this research on the Caribbean demonstrates, the situation for adult sex workers is very complex, with the majority working quite independently, within the broader context of uneven global development and racialized, gendered definitions of Third World sexuality. The intricate and challenging discussion around the issues of prostitution as legitimate work and not only as coercion is conveniently avoided in the dominant discourse on sex tourism, and with this goes the neglect of issues such as working conditions, safe sex practices, and the strategies that sex workers employ for self-empowerment. Adult prostitutes who strive to take control of the conditions and terms under which they provide sexual labor are consequently left vulnerable to criminalization, police harassment, extortion, and physical violence by clients and with very few avenues to seek protection of their human rights. The imbalance of power between sex worker and clients within the context of labor and civil and human rights is neither the focus of attention nor of concern to the international community.

By turning a blind eye to adult participation in sex tourism, the door also remains open for governments and the tourism industry to inadvertently violate local and international laws and conventions that criminalize prostitution and outlaw forced prostitution. Silence, in this instance, signals complicity with existing practices, which in many cases contradict the law. The focus on child prostitution also relieves the tourism industry itself from having to take any further actions, and provides an avenue for hoteliers, government tourism boards, restaurateurs, travel agents, tour operators, and other agencies that shape the broader tourism sector to continue to extract profit from sexual labor without the cost of maintaining the working force. In the name of "eradicating the sexual exploitation of children," the tourism industry can bow out of its responsibility of contributing to global development that supports human development and emancipation in the long term. It offers the industry a convenient way of appearing to do the right thing without having to reconfigure itself drastically or having to invest much in the human capital on which it is predicated.

CONCLUSION

Sex tourism as a particular form of prostitution is of concern to many international and national agencies, yet there appears to be little international consensus and many contradictory positions on the subject. Ideas about the suppression and abolition of sex tourism cohabit with notions of supporting prostitutes' rights. The gaps that are evident in the discourse provide space for not only oppositional and confused perspectives, but also for a privileging of some issues and a moratorium on others. The subject of child prostitution within the tourism industry is of paramount concern and dominates the international discourse on sex tourism. This particular emphasis clouds the broader picture, obscuring adult relations in the tourism industry, stimulating unsubstantiated resolutions and policies, as well as promoting an anti-prostitution stance. The discursive erasure of whole sectors of the population that work within the tourism industry, along with a lack of acknowledgment of lived realities, denies independent teenager and adult sex workers a place and voice in the tourism industry.

Policies and laws addressing sex tourism require careful development and information about everyday practices before they can be effective in addressing the complexity of sex tourism. The solutions, however, are also not simple and require time. Investment, sound research, and a full commitment by the international community to a development process that is grounded in notions of sustainability and human rights would seem desirable and, in the light of realities such as presented in these case studies in the Caribbean, a necessary way forward.

NOTES

1. The distinction between forced and voluntary prostitution is, however, also problematic. As I have argued elsewhere, it obscures the complexity and the range of situations that are evident in the sex trade (Kempadoo 1998). Doezema (1998) also points out how the distinction is used to distinguish prostitution in "developing" countries from that in North America and Western Europe with the consequence that

Third World sex workers are discursively located as victims and denied a sense of agency and subjectivity.

2. See the United Nations General Assembly Resolutions A/RES/51/66 of December 1996 and A/RES/52/98 of December 1997.

3. As Jacqueline Martis explained in her report on her fieldwork during the project conference held in Jamaica on July 16–17, 1998. See also chapter 9 on the Netherlands Antilles.

4. I have argued elsewhere that this is a concept that can be applied to the situation in Curaçao, where the government has suspended its own laws outlawing third-party organization of the sex trade in order to legalize a brothel (Kempadoo 1995). The complicity of the state in countries such as Cuba and the Dominican Republic in facilitating prostitution also suggests that this dimension of the Caribbean sex trade requires much more consideration.

Bibliography

Anarfi, John K. "Ghanaian Women and Prostitution in Cote d'Ivoire." *Global Sex Workers*, ed. Kamala Kempadoo and Jo Doezema, 104–113. New York: Routledge, 1998.

Bindman, Jo. *Redefining Prostitution as Sex Work on the International Agenda.* London: Anti-Slavery International, 1997.

Black, Maggie. *In the Twilight Zone: Child Workers in the Hotel, Tourism and Catering Industry.* Geneva: International Labour Office, 1995.

Budhos, Marina. "Putting the Heat on Sex Tourism." *Ms.* (March/April 1997).

Chapkis, Wendy. *Live Sex Acts: Women Performing Erotic Labor.* New York: Routledge, 1997.

Cohen, Erik. "The Sociology of Tourism: Approaches, Issues and Findings," *Annual Review of Sociology* 10 (1984): 373–92.

Crick, Malcolm. "Representations of International Tourism in the Social Sciences: Sun, Sex, Sights, Savings, and Servility." *Annual Review of Anthropology* 18 (1989): 307–344.

Davis, Tania. Memorandum to Ken Franzblau, Equality Now, 5 May 1998.

Doezema, Jo. "Forced to Choose: Beyond the Voluntary v. Forced Prostitution Dichotomy." *Global Sex Workers*, ed. Kamala Kempadoo and Jo Doezema, 34–50. New York: Routledge, 1998.

ECPAT, "Client, Customer, Exploiter," 30 January 1998c, http://www.rb.se/ecpat/exploit.htm

ECPAT, "Country Reports," 30 January 1998b, http://www.rb.se/ecpat/country.htm

ECPAT, "The ECPAT Campaign," 30 January 1998a, http://www.rb.se/ecpat/on_us.htm

ECPAT. *End Child Prostitution, Child Pornography and the Trafficking of Children for Sexual Purposes: An Information Booklet.* Bangkok: ECPAT International and ECPAT Australia, 1996.

ECPAT Bulletin, 1997.

ECTAA, "Declaration against Child Sex Tourism," November 1996, http://www.world-tourism/org/sextouri/extaa-a.htm

ECTWT. *Tourism, Prostitution, Development.* Ecumenical Coalition on Third World Tourism in cooperation with the Center for Development Education (Zentrum für Entwicklungsbezogene Bildung-ZEB), 1983.

el-Gawhary, Karim. "Sex Tourism in Cairo." *Middle East Report* (September–October 1995): 26–28.

Enloe, Cynthia. *Bananas, Beaches and Bases: Making Feminist Sense of International Politics.* Berkeley: University of California Press, 1989.

Fanon, Franz. *The Wretched of the Earth.* New York: Grove Press, 1963. Originally published in French in 1961.

Fiji Times, "International Tribunal Reviews Australian Child Sex Laws, "28 August 1997.

Hall, C. Michael. "The Legal and Political Dimensions of Sex Tourism: The Case of Australia's Child Sex Tourism Legislation." *Sex Tourism and Prostitution*, ed. Martin Oppermann, 87–96. Elmsford, N.Y.: Cognizant Communications, 1998.

Hall, Stuart. "The Question of Cultural Identity." *Modernity and its Future*, ed. S. Hall, D. Held and T. McGrew. Oxford: Polity Press, 1992.

Harrison, David, ed. "Tourism and Prostitution: Sleeping with the Enemy? The Case of Swaziland." *Tourism Management* 15.6 (1994): 435–443.

Hobson, J., S. Perry and Uta C. Dietrich. "Tourism, Health and Quality of Life: Challenging the Responsibility of Using the Traditional Tenets of Sun, Sea, Sand and Sex in Tourism Marketing." *Journal of Travel and Tourism Marketing* 3.4 (1994): 21–38.

HOTREC, "Declaration against the Sexual Exploitation of Children," 27 April 1997, http://www.world-tourism-org/sextouri/hotrec-a.htm

IATA, "Final Resolution Condemning Commercial Sexual Exploitation of Children," Geneva, November 1996, http://www.world-tourism-org/sextouri/iata-a.htm

IFTO, "Code of Conduct against the Sexual Exploitation of Children," 2 February 1998, http://world-tourism-org/sextouri/ifto-a.htm

IFWTO, "Resolution against Sex Tourism," 2 February 1998, http://www.world-tourism-org/sextouri/ifwto-a.htm

IH&RA. "IHA and Its Member Associations against the Sexual Exploitation of Children," adopted in Mexico City, 30 October 1996, http://www.world-tourism-org/sextouri/iha-a.htm

Isis-wicce. *Women's World* 24 (winter 1990/1).

IUF/UITA/UIL, "Resolution on Prostitution Tourism," adopted by the IUF HRC Trade group Board, Budapest, December 1995, and endorsed by the IUF EC, Geneva, April 1996, http://world-tourism-org/sextouri/iuf-a.htm

Kempadoo, Kamala. "COIN and MODEMU in the Dominican Republic." *Global Sex Workers: Rights, Resistance, and Redefinition*, ed. Kamala Kempadoo and Jo Doezema, 260–266. New York: Routledge, 1998.

_______. "Regulating Prostitution in the Dutch Caribbean." Paper presented at the 20th annual conference of the Caribbean Studies Association, Curaçao, Netherlands Antilles, May 1995.

Leheny, David. "A Political Economy of Asian Sex Tourism." *Annals of Tourism Research* 22.2 (1995): 367–384.

Lim, Lin Lean, ed. "Child Prostitution." *The Sex Sector*, 170–205. *Geneva: International* Labour Office, 1998.

_______. "The Economic and Social Bases of Prostitution in Southeast Asia." *The Sex Sector,* 1–28. Geneva: International Labour Office, 1998.

_______. *The Sex Sector:The Economic and Social Bases of Prostitution in Southeast Asia*. Geneva: International Labour Office, 1998.

Longo, Paulo Henrique. "The Pegação Program: Information, Prevention and Empowerment of Young Male Sex Workers." *Global Sex Workers*, ed. Kamala Kempadoo and Jo Doezema, 231–239. New York: Routledge, 1998.

Matsui, Yayori. *Women's Asia*. London: Zed Press, 1989.

Mies, Maria. *Patriarchy and Accumulation on a World Scale: Women in the International Division of Labour.* London: Zed Books, 1986.

Montgomery, Heather. "Children, Prostitution and Identity: A Case Study from a Tourist Resort in Thailand." *Global Sex Workers*, ed, Kamala Kempadoo and Jo Doezema, 139–150. New York: Routledge, 1998.

Murray, Alison. "Debt-Bondage and Trafficking: Don't Believe the Hype." *Global Sex Workers*, ed. Kamala Kempadoo and Jo Doezema, 51–64. New York: Routledge, 1998.

O'Connell Davidson, Julia. "Sex Tourism in Cuba," *Race & Class* 38 (July/September 1996): 39–48.

One World News Service, "Britain Joins the Campaign against Child Sex Tourism," 25 July 1996, http://www.oneworld.org/newws/reports/jul96-children.html

Oppermann, Martin, ed. *Sex Tourism and Prostitution: Aspects of Leisure, Recreation and Work*. Elmsford, N.Y.: Cognizant Communications, 1998.

Patullo, Polly, *Last Resorts: The Cost of Tourism in the Caribbean*. Kingston, Jamaica: Ian Randle, 1996.

Pettman, Jan Jindy. "Body Politics: International Sex Tourism." *Third World Quarterly* 18.1 (1997) 93–108.

Press, Clayton M., Jr. "Reputation and Respectability Reconsidered: Hustling in a Tourist Setting." *Caribbean Issues* 4 (1978): 109–119.

Reanda, Laura. "Prostitution as a Human Rights Question: Problems and Prospects of United Nations Action." *Human Rights Quarterly* 13 (1991): 209–211.

Sittirak, Sinith. *Daughters of Development: Women in a Changing Environment*. London: Zed Books, 1998.

Swift, Anthony. "Let Us Work!" *New Internationalist*. July 1997.

Truong, Than Dam. *Sex, Money and Morality: The Political Economy of Prostitution and Tourism in South East Asia*. London: Zed Books, 1990.

Turner, Louis, and John Ash. *The Golden Hordes: International Tourism and the Pleasure Periphery*. New York: St. Martin's Press, 1976.

UFTAA, "Child and Travel Agents Charter," 2 February 1998, http://www.world-tourism-org/sextouri/uftaa-a.htm

Urry, John. *The Tourist Gaze: Leisure and Travel in Contemporary Societies*. London: Sage, 1990.

Wijers, Marjan, and Lin Lap-Chew. *Trafficking in Women, Forced Labor and Slavery-like Practices in Marriage, Domestic Labor and Prostitution*. Utrecht: STV, 1997.

Women's Action 12.1, December 1996.
WTO News, "Child Prostitution and Tourism Watch," 2 February 1998d, http://www.world-tourism-org/tourism.org/sextouri/intro.htm#purpose
_______, "Campaign Launched against Child Sex Tourism," May 1997.
_______, "Frequently Asked Questions," 20 March 1998b, http://www.world-tourism-org/faq/faq.htm
_______, WTO, "What We Offer." 11 October 1998a, http://www.world-tourism-org/offer.htm#Mission
_______, "WTO Commission for America (CAM)," 20 March 1998c, http://www.world-tourism-org/memstate/americas.htm
_______, November–December 1995.
_______, "Brasilia Charter Condemns Sex Tourism," May–June 1996.

[23]

MYTHS OF MERITOCRACY

*Deborah L. Rhode**

INTRODUCTION

IN the fall of 1995, just as the Association of the Bar of the City of New York released its *Glass Ceilings and Open Doors* report,[1] its principal author and I attended the Association's 100th Anniversary Celebration. The event was impressive, and no evidence of the gender bias described throughout the report was in sight. Or so we thought as the program began. Principal speakers included United States Supreme Court Justice Ruth Bader Ginsberg, American Bar Association President Roberta Cooper Ramo, and New York City Bar Association President Barbara Robinson. First Lady Hillary Rodham Clinton and Chief Justice Judith Kaye of the New York Court of Appeals also addressed the Association on videotape. The preponderance of women in this lineup did not pass unnoticed, and not everyone viewed it as a sign of progress. "It's a goddamn matriarchy," a man near me muttered.

Of course, for well over two centuries, the gender roles at such events were reversed and almost no men thought it odd—or thought about it at all. Prominent Washington, D.C. practitioner Sol Linowitz recalls that his law school class had only two women. Neither he, nor most of his male classmates questioned the skewed ratio, although they did feel somewhat uncomfortable when their two female colleagues were around. And, as Linowitz now acknowledges with self-deprecating grace, "It never occurred to us to wonder whether *they* felt uncomfortable."[2]

Over the last quarter century, sensitivity to gender bias has increased dramatically, as has women's representation in the legal profession. But ironically enough, this partial progress has created its own obstacles to further reform. Women's growing opportunities are often taken as evidence that the "woman problem" has been solved. Recent surveys find that only one-quarter to one-third of men report

---

* Professor of Law, Director of the Keck Center on Legal Ethics and the Legal Profession. B.A. Yale University, 1974. J.D. Yale Law School, 1977. Ideas expressed in this essay appear in different form in Deborah L. Rhode, *Career Progress, Yes; Equality, Not Quite Yet*, Nat'l L.J., July 31, 1995, at A21, and *Women Haven't Arrived*, Nat'l L.J., Mar. 18, 1996, at A19, A20. The comments of Barbara Allen Babcock and Cynthia Fuchs Epstein, the research assistance of Betsy Facher and Sarah Killingsworth, and the financial support of the W.M. Keck Foundation is gratefully acknowledged.

1. Cynthia Fuchs Epstein et al., *Glass Ceilings and Open Doors: Women's Advancement in the Legal Profession*, 64 Fordham L. Rev. 291 (1995) [hereinafter *Glass Ceilings*].

2. Sol M. Linowitz & Martin Mayer, The Betrayed Profession 6 (1994).

observing gender bias in the profession, although two-thirds to three-quarters of women indicate that they personally have experienced it.[3] Even those men who perceive such bias often discount its significance. As one Texas practitioner put it, "[O]f all the problems we have as lawyers, gender discrimination [is] low on the list of important ones."[4]

To him, perhaps. But, the *Glass Ceilings* report, together with two other recent surveys, is unlikely to leave a similar impression. The American Bar Association's Commission on the Status of Women aptly titled its 1995 report, *Unfinished Business: Overcoming the Sisyphus Factor*.[5] Similar findings appear in the Harvard Women's Law Association's study, *Presumed Equal: What America's Top Women Lawyers Really Think About Their Firms*.[6] Taken together, these 400-odd pages offer a sobering account of progress yet to be made.

The three reports rely on quite different approaches, yet yield quite consistent findings. The New York study turned a meticulous scholar's eye on quantitative and qualitative data from eight Manhattan law firms. The ABA Commission reviewed many such studies, as well as written testimony and focus group responses. The Harvard Women's Law Association, equipped with less funding and expertise, did what students do best. It asked lawyers what their professional life was like, and collected responses from female attorneys at some 250 firms. The bottom line of this research, like virtually all other recent studies, is that all is not well for women in law.

Yet this is not the dominant perception of male attorneys. Rather, a common response to gender bias surveys is that barriers have broken down, women have moved up, and full equality is just around the corner. This myth of meritocracy rests on two dominant assumptions: (1) that female lawyers are already achieving close to proportionate representation in almost all professional contexts; and (2) that any lingering disparities are attributable to women's own "different" choices and capabilities.

I have written about these issues on other occasions and will not repeat that entire discussion here.[7] Rather, I hope to take advantage of this opportunity to highlight the challenges that remain for a profession committed, at least in principle, to equal justice under law.

---

3. Ann J. Gellis, *Great Expectations: Women in the Legal Profession, A Commentary on State Studies*, 66 Ind. L.J. 941, 971 (1991); Deborah L. Rhode, *Gender and Professional Roles*, 63 Fordham L. Rev. 39, 64-65 (1994).

4. Diane F. Norwood & Arlette Molina, *Sex Discrimination in the Profession: 1990 Survey Results Reported*, Tex. B.J., Jan. 1992, at 50, 51.

5. ABA Comm. on Women in the Profession, Unfinished Business: Overcoming the Sisyphus Factor (1995) [hereinafter Unfinished Business].

6. Harvard Women's Law Association, Presumed Equal: What America's Top Women Lawyers Really Think About Their Firms (1995) [hereinafter Presumed Equal].

7. *See* Deborah L. Rhode, Speaking of Sex (forthcoming 1997); Rhode, *supra* note 3; Deborah L. Rhode, *The 'No Problem' Problem: Feminist Challenges and Cultural Change*, 100 Yale L.J. 1731 (1991).

I. Myths of Equal Opportunity

A threshold problem for women in American law is the denial by many practitioners that there is a serious problem. As one male attorney explained to *Glass Ceilings* researchers, everyone "should just leave the situation to sort itself out because . . . women's advancement is only a matter of time. I think forcing the situation is not helpful."[8] Yet these three reports make clear that if time alone is viewed as the answer, we are in for a very long wait.

ABA Commission findings indicate that women now account for about forty-five percent of law students and twenty-three percent of the bar, but only nineteen percent of tenured law school faculty, thirteen percent of law firm partners, ten to twelve percent of judges, and eight percent of law school deans.[9] More finely tuned data reveal further sex-based disparities in positions of greatest power, security, and economic reward. For example, among law firm partners, only about half of female attorneys but three quarters of male attorneys have equity status.[10] Although some forty percent of in-house corporate lawyers are women, only seventeen percent of surveyed companies have female attorneys heading their legal departments.[11]

Such underrepresentation cannot be explained simply by disparities in the pool of eligible candidates. For example, the *Glass Ceilings* report finds that New York women's rate of becoming partner was five percent and men's seventeen percent during the most recent period under review.[12] Other studies also have found substantial gender-linked disparities in promotion and pay among lawyers with comparable positions, experience, and qualifications. So too, an ABA survey of some 3000 lawyers with similar backgrounds found that males were more than twice as likely as females to have achieved partnership status.[13] In research reviewed by the ABA Commission, pay gaps range from ten to thirty-five percent among male and female general counsels.[14]

What limited data are available for women of color reveal even greater underrepresentation, particularly in positions with the highest

8. *Glass Ceilings*, *supra* note 1, at 356-57. Similar views dominated a male focus group at the 1995 American Bar Association Midyear Meeting, where the prevailing wisdom was that "special consideration" for women had "gone far enough." Nina Bernstein, *Equal Opportunity Recedes for Most Female Lawyers*, N.Y. Times, Jan. 8, 1996, at A7.

9. Unfinished Business, *supra* note 5, at 5, 7-8, 11, 16.

10. Chris Klein, *Women's Progress Slows at Top Firms*, Nat'l L.J., May 6, 1996, at 1, 19.

11. Susan Saltonstall Duncan, *What Women Need to Make It to the Top*, Am. Law., Jan./Feb. 1996, at 9.

12. *Glass Ceilings*, *supra* note 1, at 359.

13. American Bar Association Young Lawyers Division, The State of the Legal Profession 1990, at 63 (1991).

14. Unfinished Business, *supra* note 5, at 10.

salaries and status. These women account for less than three percent of lawyers and judges.[15] Minority retention rates in law firms are especially poor and few women of color have obtained partnership.[16]

At least part of the reason for such underrepresentation involves lingering, although often unconscious, gender and racial biases. For example, female lawyers consistently report receiving fewer opportunities for mentoring, business development, and desirable assignments than their male colleagues. Those inequalities often reflect sex-based stereotypes, such as the assumption that women with children are less committed to their careers than are other attorneys. Mothers repeatedly told New York and Harvard researchers that they received less desirable assignments than they had received "BC" (before children). One Boston lawyer reported that "since I came back from maternity leave, I get the work of a paralegal .... I want to say, 'look, I had a baby, not a lobotomy!'"[17]

Preconceptions about women's lesser commitment often distort performance evaluations and eventually become self fulfilling prophesies. As cognitive psychological research consistently demonstrates, individuals are most likely to retain information that confirms initial biases. As a consequence, they will tend to remember the times that mothers leave early, not the occasions where they stay late.[18] So too, when supervising attorneys doubt that a woman will make the sacrifices necessary to become a partner, they frequently fail to provide her with the experience, support, and client contact that are essential to that achievement.

Other stereotypes, such as a perceived lower level of competence among women of color, have similar consequences. The limited information on racial bias available in the New York, American Bar Association, and Harvard studies is consistent with other research, such as the United States Department of Labor's *Glass Ceilings* survey, and the report of the Multicultural Women's Network of the American

15. ABA Comm. on Women in the Profession, Women in the Law: A Look at the Numbers 17 (1995).

16. Exact numbers are generally not available. For descriptions of the problem, see Presumed Equal, *supra* note 6, at 6; Multicultural Women Attorneys Network of the American Bar Association, The Burdens of Both, the Privileges of Neither (1994) [hereinafter Multicultural Women Attorneys Network].

17. Presumed Equal, *supra* note 6, at 72; *see Glass Ceilings*, *supra* note 1, at 298 (noting the perception on the part of women that having children impeded professional advancement).

18. For discussion of such stereotypes, see Deborah L. Rhode, Justice and Gender 168-70 (1989); Linda Hamilton Kreiger, *The Content of Our Categories: A Cognitive Bias Approach to Discrimination and Equal Employment Opportunity*, 47 Stan. L. Rev. 1161 (1995); Federal Glass Ceiling Commission, Good For Business: Making Full Use of the Nation's Human Capital 26-28, 64-72, 93-96, 104-06, 123-25 (1995) [hereinafter Federal Glass Ceiling Commission].

Bar Association.[19] In one telling instance, an African American partner in a major Chicago law firm reported that she had been mistaken for a stenographer at every pretrial deposition that she had ever attended.[20]

Among men who have not been on the receiving end of gender or racial bias, such incidents may appear relatively trivial and rarely memorable; they seem like isolated events, not representative illustrations of broader patterns. By contrast, men are far more likely to notice, recall, and resent bias against their own sex and invest these incidents with both personal and societal significance. Columbia law professor Patricia Williams describes a recent example. "Nobody's hiring white guys anymore," was the unchallenged wisdom of one participant at a meeting of commercial lawyers. Williams surveyed the room of several hundred attorneys. She spotted one other black woman, no black men, no Hispanics, about ten Asians, and a "modest sprinkling" of white women. "So who is being hired if not white guys?" she wonders. "And if white guys aren't being hired, what on earth makes them think anyone else is?"[21]

A related problem involves the reluctance that some male clients and attorneys still feel in working closely with women, or including them in informal networks where mentoring and rainmaking occur. As one participant in the Labor Department's *Glass Ceilings* study noted, "what's important [in organizations] is comfort, chemistry . . . and collaborations."[22] Many white men "don't like the competition and they don't like the tension" of working with colleagues who are "different."[23]

Concerns about sexual harassment complaints can heighten that discomfort. Some male partners refuse to lunch alone with a female associate "because of how it might be perceived."[24] As one attorney in the New York *Glass Ceilings* study explained:

> There's definitely a siege mentality going on here about this gender stuff. . . . [I] will not have a female associate while I'm traveling. You're just asking for problems down the road. So you have a lack of mentoring in most firms . . . [y]ou can't bond as easily with a woman because you've got the whole issue of sexual harassment or whatever it is.[25]

Although such concerns are often genuine, they are by no means the sole, or often the most significant source of the problem. Men who

19. Federal Glass Ceiling Commission, *supra* note 18, at 64-142; Multicultural Women Attorneys Network, *supra* note 16.
20. Multicultural Women Attorneys Network, *supra* note 16, at 26.
21. Patricia J. Williams, The Rooster's Egg 97 (1995).
22. Federal Glass Ceiling Commission, *supra* note 18, at 28.
23. *Id.* at 552; Judith Lorber, Paradoxes of Gender 237-38 (1994).
24. *Glass Ceilings*, *supra* note 1, at 356.
25. *Id.* at 355.

now invoke harassment as a reason to avoid mentoring women colleagues found ample other reasons to avoid it in the past.[26]

Problems of exclusion are particularly acute for attorneys who labor under multiple disadvantages such as gender, race, ethnicity, disability, and sexual orientation. Many women of color report being treated as outsiders by white practitioners, and as potential competitors by nonwhite men.[27] Lesbians are routinely hazed, isolated, and denied professional opportunities. They, like Linowitz's classmates, often make others feel "uncomfortable" and this is viewed as *their*, and not their colleagues', problem.[28] Even in jurisdictions that prohibit discrimination on the basis of sexual preference, noncompliance is widespread and sometimes quite explicit. A recent bar association survey in Los Angeles, which bans discrimination against gays and lesbians, produced responses like "[D]on't have any; don't want any."[29] Almost forty percent of surveyed practitioners reported witnessing or experiencing discrimination based on sexual orientation.[30]

White men are, of course, not the only group responsible for these patterns of prejudice; women can be perpetrators as well as targets of exclusion. As recent reports make clear, legal workplaces still have what sociologists once labeled "Queen Bees"—professionals who believe that *they* managed without special help, so why can't other women.[31] Some senior women also lack the time or influence to provide effective assistance to younger colleagues. Others worry that they risk professional opportunities even for trying. The experience of one African American member of a glass ceiling audit team is all too common. After pointing out her own department's failure to abide by equal opportunity standards, she learned that her superiors viewed such candor as "poor judgment." Their message was, in effect,

26. For general discussion of longstanding barriers to women in law see Cynthia Fuchs Epstein, Women and Law (2d ed. 1993); Karen Morello, The Invisible Bar: The Woman Lawyer in America 1638 to the Present (1986); Deborah L. Rhode, *Perspectives on Professional Women*, 40 Stan. L. Rev. 1163 (1988).

27. *See* David Rothman, *quoted in* Ninth Circuit Gender Bias Task Force, *Discussion Draft*, July 1992, at 171 (1992).

28. *See* Los Angeles County Bar Association Ad Hoc Committee on Sexual Orientation Bias, *The Los Angeles County Bar Association Report on Sexual Orientation Bias*, *reprinted in* 4 S. Cal. Rev. L. & Women's Stud. 295, 444-49, 471 (1995).

29. *Id.* at 312.

30. *Id.* at 297.

31. *See* Ann Wilson Schaff, Women's Realities 44 (1981); *see also Glass Ceilings*, *supra* note 1, at 408 (noting that some older women consider their younger colleagues to be "naive" in failing to "accept the fact that being a high powered lawyer is hard work and basically incompatible with a part-time schedule"); Presumed Equal, *supra* note 6, at 18-19 (quoting Baker & Botts associates who find that most female partners do not "care to relate to younger [women]" and are not receptive to accommodating family needs because these partners "sacrificed to get where they are" and believe others should do the same).

"[W]e're not really comfortable with what you're saying and we don't want [to work with] people who make us uncomfortable."[32]

As a result of such patterns, women often remain outside of the informal networks of support that can be crucial for professional advancement. Pointing out this exclusion can compound the problem, which creates a classic double bind for female attorneys. When many vote with their feet, they confirm the perception that women simply do not make the same career choices as their male colleagues. This perception then encourages unequal treatment of women and perpetuates the stereotypes that underlie such treatment.

II. Myths of Choice

Women's choices also figure prominently in a second common explanation for persistent gender inequalities. Many lawyers assume that women have different family priorities than men and that these personal commitments exact a professional price.

There is some truth to this view, but it provides neither a complete explanation nor an adequate justification for prevailing gender inequalities. As a descriptive matter, women's different "lifestyle" preferences cannot account for the extent of their underrepresentation in law firm partnerships or corporate counsel positions. Only about four percent of female associates have part-time or flexible schedules, and recent studies find substantial gender disparities among lawyers in similar full-time positions.[33]

It is, of course, true that women express greater dissatisfaction with current workplace structures than men, and are disproportionately likely to opt out of positions with the greatest demands on time, travel, and unpredictable schedules. Yet such patterns are not simply a function of "natural" preferences. Women's career sacrifices are attributable not just to women's choices but to men's choices as well. Male spouses' failure to shoulder equal family responsibilities and male colleagues' failure to support alternative working arrangements are also responsible. Employed women spend about twice as much time on domestic chores as do employed men, and not always by choice.[34] Part of the problem is that female attorneys with significant family commitments tend to have partners, husbands, or former husbands with equally demanding careers. These men frequently view their own professional obligations as fixed and women's as negotiable.

32. *Greener Pastures*, Perspectives (ABA Comm. on the Status of Women), Summer 1995, at 3.

33. *See* Unfinished Business, *supra* note 5, at 17; *Part-Time Lawyering*, Partner's Rep., Jan. 1996, at 11; *supra* notes 13-14.

34. Juliet B. Schor, The Overworked American 36-38 (1991); Scott J. South & Glenna Spitze, *Housework in Marital and Nonmarital Households*, 59 Am. Soc. Rev. 337, 337 (1994); Colleen O'Connor, *Women, If You Think You Have No Time to Relax, You're Probably Right*, San Jose Mercury News, Aug. 8, 1994, at E1.

Rather than accept an equal division of household tasks, many husbands define their share as unnecessary; they do not mind living with a little mess, or adding to their infant's time among "friends" at day-care.[35] Divorced fathers often end up as "Disney Dads," who leave day-to-day childrearing obligations to stressed-out single moms.[36] Other men manage not to notice when their household tasks need to be done, or mismanage key parts of the job. To avoid a "culture of complaint" on family obligations, professional women often pick up the pieces that their partners do not even realize have been dropped.[37]

The problem is not only that many men are reluctant to make career sacrifices, but also that those who attempt to do so encounter too much resistance. Colleagues who are reluctant to accommodate mothers often have even less tolerance for fathers. A common attitude among surveyed New York lawyers was, "I have a family. I didn't get time off to do that. Why should you?"[38] In one particularly striking instance of the puritan ethic run amok, litigators assigned a new father to work on an out-of-town trial two days after his wife gave birth, and gave him time for only one brief trip home during the next two weeks.[39]

Ironically enough, managing attorneys sometimes invoke these refusals to accommodate male lawyers' family commitments as evidence that gender bias is not a problem in their workplaces. After all, women are more likely than men to receive "special" treatment concerning family leaves and reduced schedules. But that response misses a central part of the problem at issue. Discrimination against men with family commitments also discriminates against women. It discourages male attorneys from assuming an equal division of household responsibilities and requires their spouses or partners, who may also be lawyers, to pay a professional price. As long as work and family conflicts remain primarily "women's issues," they are unlikely to receive adequate attention in decision-making structures dominated by men.

The limits of current family-related policies emerge clearly in these recent reports. They describe, in deadening and depressing detail, the sweatshop hours expected of full-time attorneys, and the second-class

35. *See* Arlie Hochschild with Ann Machung, The Second Shift: Working Parents and the Revolution at Home 43 (1989); *see also* Barbara Vobejda, *Children Help Less at Home: Dads Do More*, Wash. Post, Nov. 24, 1991, at A1 (quoting demographer Martha Farnsworth Riche's observation that the "great lesson of the past 15 to 20 years is that men don't care if the house is clean and neat, by and large").

36. The phrase comes from Judith Bond Jennison, *The Search for Equality in a Woman's World: Fathers' Rights to Child Custody*, 43 Rutgers L. Rev. 1141, 1178 (1991). *See* Karen Czapanskiy, *Volunteers and Draftees: The Struggle for Parental Equality*, 38 UCLA L. Rev. 1415, 1447-48 (1991); Tamar Lewin, *Father's Vanishing Act Called Common Drama*, N.Y. Times, June 4, 1990, at A18.

37. See Rhode, *supra* note 3; Hochschild, *supra* note 34, at 259; Vobjeda, *supra* note 35, at A1.

38. *Glass Ceilings*, *supra* note 1, at 409.

39. Presumed Equal, *supra* note 6, at 58.

status imposed on part-time practitioners. Women spoke of not seeing their children awake for a week; of leaving their social life on perpetual hold; of being trapped in the office until three a.m. over Christmas vacation faxing documents to a partner skiing in Aspen; of working full-time schedules while nominally on part-time status; of negotiating with a "very understanding" section head and being lucky enough to work only from six a.m. to six p.m.[40] As one female associate in the *Glass Ceilings* report summarized the situation: "This is not a life."[41]

A decade ago, at a Stanford symposium on the corporate law firm, I raised these issues before a distinguished group of managing partners. "Why don't more firms allow lawyers to meet family responsibilities by opting for saner schedules and lower salaries?," I asked. "Because," one senior partner explained impatiently, "flexible or reduced workloads cost money." Getting additional lawyers up to speed, adjusting to reduced schedules, and paying extra overhead are expensive. "And who," he concluded, "is going to pay for all that?" Summoning up all the naivete he obviously expected, I responded: "You will." At least in the short run. But in the long run, I noted, employers who provide opportunities for flexible hours generally find gains in efficiency, morale, recruitment, and retention.[42] Moreover, given the salary levels available for most partners at major law firms, some short term financial sacrifice does not seem like an unreasonable request.

Putting an exact price tag on all the costs and benefits of workplace flexibility is obviously impossible, but growing evidence suggests that the investment makes economic sense. The inadequacy of time for family and personal needs is one of the leading causes of lawyers' exceptionally high rate of job dissatisfaction, stress, and related problems such as depression and substance abuse.[43] These take a toll on the bottom line. As the Harvard Women's guide notes, a signifi-

40. *Id.* at 68, 138-39, 160; *Glass Ceilings, supra* note 1, at 387-88, 391, 394, 399, 411.

41. *Glass Ceilings, supra* note 1, at 385.

42. *See* Schor, *supra* note 34; ABA Comm. on Women in the Profession, Lawyers and Balanced Lives: A Guide to Drafting and Implementing Workplace Policies for Lawyers, Part II (1990); Carrie Menkel-Meadow, *Culture Clash in the Quality of Life in the Law: Changes in the Economic Diversification and Organization of Lawyering*, 44 Case W. Res. L. Rev. 621, 658-59 (1994).

43. For research on dissatisfaction and stress, see American Bar Association Young Lawyers Division, *supra* note 13, at 54 (reporting that 41% of women and 28% of men in private practice are dissatisfied); Andrew Herrmann, *Depressing News For Lawyers*, Chi. Sun Times, Sept. 13, 1991, at 1 (reporting survey findings that lawyers top the list of professionals likely to suffer major depression); Shelly Phillips, *Lawyers Who Want Out: Nearly Half Say They Would Change Jobs If They Felt There Was a Reasonable Alternative, A National Survey Finds*, Phila. Inquirer, June 8, 1993, at F1; Benjamin Sells, *Counsel on the Verge of a Nervous Breakdown*, S.F. Daily J., May 25, 1994, at 3A. For estimates suggesting that the percentage of lawyers with substance abuse problems is twice the national average, see Anne Fahy Morris, *'Justifiable Paranoia' Afflicts Lawyers, Psychologist Says*, L.A. Times, May 1, 1994, at A27.

cant number of large firms have managed to create "family friendly" policies without apparent financial sacrifice.[44] Even if there is some price to pay for gender equality, can the legal profession, which will soon be forty percent female, really not afford the cost? If we are truly committed to equal opportunity, then these recent reports remind us of the distance yet to be travelled.

44. Presumed Equal, *supra* note 6, at 7.

Part VI
Political Process and Participation

[24]

Imported Problem Definitions, Legal Culture and the Local Dynamics of Israeli Abortion Politics

NOGA MORAG-LEVINE

INTRODUCTION

The subject of abortion has sparked political and religious controversy in countries all over the world during the past few decades, and Israel has been no exception. Energized by the commitments of transplanted American immigrants and infused with the language of the American controversy, Israeli abortion politics unfolded largely in the shadow of American abortion divisions. Yet despite the significance of this influence, pertinent domestic debates retain fundamental distinctions from their American counterpart. Most notably, these differences are in the salience of abortion problems in the political agendas of the two countries, the relative weight of individualist and collectivist formulations of relevant interests, and the place of law and legal institutions in the definition and resolution of the abortion issue. Whereas abortion in the United States is a recurrent source of deep social divisions, political violence, and constitutional litigation, abortion in Israel is a tangential controversy characterized by a systemic gap between restrictive formal legal norms and liberal abortion practices. This article considers both the impact of the American abortion dispute on the evolution of Israeli abortion politics and the factors responsible for continuing divergence between the political and legal frameworks defining abortion questions in the two countries.

The relationship between problem definitions on the one hand and policy agendas, processes, and outcomes on the other, is the subject of an extensive and diverse political science inquiry. Nevertheless, relatively little attention has been directed at the cross-national dimensions of this issue. Acknowledging this gap, Bosso has contended that "(t)o look harder at how distinct polities define problems to begin with may give us

Noga Morag-Levine is an Associate Professor of Law at Michigan State University.

renewed appreciation for the relative distinctiveness of national policy styles amidst problem-induced similarities. Comparative studies of problem definition can go a long way toward separating out what is shared and what remains unique."[1] As an example of the type of insights such research can yield, Bosso cites Yishai's comparison of the distinct problem definitions underpinning abortion politics in Sweden, the US, Ireland, and Israel.[2] Building upon Yishai's work and heeding Bosso's call, this article considers the fit between broader traits of Israeli law and politics and the problem definitions framing the Israeli abortion debate. But instead of a horizontal cross-national comparison between central governing problem definitions, this study adopts a dynamic approach comparing the place of alternative problem definitions across the evolution of Israeli abortion politics. Within this context, particular attention is paid to domestic elements supporting and impeding the implementation of fundamental features of the American abortion dispute within Israel's internal abortion scene.

The limited resonance of US- inspired abortion problem definitions in Israel is indicative of enduring political and legal cultural differences. The American conception of abortion as a universally tragic dilemma pitting a woman's right to choose against a fetus's right to life, conflicts with particularistic Jewish formulations of the question in Israel. At the same time, American constructions of the problem as a constitutional dilemma concerning the limits of legitimate governmental power are inconsistent with two salient Israeli attributes. The first is the continuing, though diminished, deference to nationally defined collective values and the related perceived normalcy of state intervention in one's personal life. The second is a systemic reliance, termed here *de facto legalism*, on various quasi-legal, illegal, and extra-legal mechanisms in mitigating such interferences and mediating fundamental value conflicts. The impact of these differences on the capacity of imported conceptions of the abortion dispute to alter the issue's salience and meaning in Israel is the central concern of this article.

AMERICAN ABORTION INFLUENCE AND THE MECHANISMS OF IMPORTATION

Abortion was among the many political causes carried to Israel by American immigrants. American expatriates and immigrants from other English speaking countries have played a decisive role in mobilizing Israeli abortion activism, on both sides of the issue, and in the introduction of American conceptions of the dispute into Israeli political discourse. This process was most clearly embodied in the career of Marcia Freedman, an American immigrant and Citizens' Rights Party member of Knesset during the early 1970s. Freedman arrived at the Knesset in January 1974, only a few months after *Roe v. Wade* (1973) was decided in the United States. The first piece of legislation she introduced was a Freedom of Choice bill which, following *Roe,* proposed ending all abortion restrictions during the first three months of pregnancy and cited the basic human right of deciding whether or not to bring a child into the world.[3] Four years later when she left the Knesset, Marcia Freedman was still talking about abortion.[4] In the intervening four years Freedman and the disproportionately English speaking Israeli feminist movement she helped found spearheaded a campaign that, for the first time, brought the subject of abortion to Israel's streets and living rooms. Marcia Freedman's abortion bill was defeated by an alternative and more restrictive legislative proposal. But the efforts of Freedman and other US-influenced feminists were crucial in setting Israeli abortion law reform in motion.

To this day, Israeli abortion activism is often expressed with an American inflection. This is especially true of activists calling for greater liberalization of regulatory restrictions but applies also to largely orthodox American immigrants who, through a variety of strategies, have sought to reduce the number of abortions in Israel. Notable in this context were the activities of Haim Hazan, an American born statistician and a one-time special abortion consultant to the Minister of Health appointed under ultra-orthodox pressure.[5] A less militant anti-abortion Jewish American influence is represented in Just One Life, an organization created under the auspices of the Council of Young Israel Rabbis in Israel with the goal of providing economic and social support for alternatives to abortion.

Israeli interest groups on both sides of the issue receive financial support from sympathetic organizations and individuals abroad, and at times even seek direct engagement by outside, most commonly American actors, in their internal struggles. Thus a 1992 campaign organized by an ad-hoc coalition of women and civil rights groups in opposition to a proposed change to Israel's abortion law, requested and received political and financial support from liberal American Jewish groups. A memo written by the coalition made explicit reference to the need within this realm for "both national and international advocacy, including public and private opposition by American Jewish leadership who are known to be committed to reproductive rights."[6] More recently and from the opposite direction, the head of a major Israeli anti-abortion organization quoted a statement made by the American Senator Jesse Helms according to which a "substantial number of senators and congressmen would demand a reduction of foreign aid to Israel" unless the number of abortions in Israel is immediately reduced.[7]

Similarly, developments in American abortion politics are closely followed and viewed as domestically relevant by both sides of the Israeli abortion controversy. Thus, for example, in a 1992 speech before the Knesset, MK Yosef Azran of the religious Shas Party noted in an apparently garbled reference to the US Supreme Court's 1992 *Casey*[8] decision: "a recent decision by the Supreme Court, not ours, but in the

United States, required a medical committee deciding upon an abortion to provide the woman with extensive information regarding the outcome of abortion. ... Why what is common in the United States should not be common in Israel?"[9] On the other side of the arena, women's organizations pay similarly close attention to the evolution of American abortion doctrine. In the wake of the Court's *Webster* opinion, the secretary-general of the large women organization Naamat voiced concern over the potential impact of the decision on anti-abortion forces in Israel and urged Labor Zionist organizations in the United States to add their political muscle to the American pro-choice struggle.[10] For their part, members of the Israel Feminist Movement wrote to President Bush to protest his veto of abortion funding legislation and to announce their intention to hold an Israeli march in support of a planned National Organization of Women Washington, DC reproductive rights rally.[11]

The very reliance of Israeli abortion activists on American energy, funding, and ideological inspiration suggests the extent to which abortion remains foreign to core Israeli concerns. Aided by the general attentiveness of the Israeli media and public to all manner of American trends, efforts to move abortion onto the center stage of Israeli politics and to imbue it with American derived symbolic significance were nevertheless hindered by legal and political-cultural factors which conferred distinctly different meanings and solutions on the abortion question.

A SHORT HISTORY OF ISRAELI ABORTION REGULATION

The following summary of the history of abortion regulation in Israel sets the stage for subsequent discussion of competing problem definitions in the debates surrounding various stages in the development of Israeli abortion policy.

Until 1977, the Israeli criminal code strictly prohibited all abortions, although the courts interpreted the law to exempt abortions performed under medical necessity. Similar in nature to anti-abortion state laws that existed prior to 1973 in the United States, the Israeli law did little to alter widespread illegal abortion practices by private providers.[12] In addition, state subsidized sick funds performed abortions approved by ad hoc committees instituted by the sick funds themselves.[13] This mechanism was the one essentially adopted by the Knesset when Israel reformed its abortion law in 1977.

The new abortion law combined a general criminal prohibition against the performance of abortions with specified procedures for the approval of some abortions by authorized medical committees. The law included a list of legitimate grounds for committee approval of abortion requests. Under the 1977 law these grounds included the age of the woman, her health, marital status, and illegal circumstances surrounding the pregnancy (i.e. rape, incest). An additional provision, known as the

Social Clause, authorized committees to approve abortions on the basis of difficult socio-economic conditions surrounding the woman or her family.

The Social Clause was eliminated from the law in 1980 under pressure from an ultra-orthodox coalition partner. Since that time there have been no further amendments to the law despite periodic demands for the Clause's reinstatement and for stricter abortion restrictions. Problem definitions employed by various interest groups active in this effort are the center of the following discussion.

THE PROBLEM OF ABORTION: ALTERNATIVE ISRAELI DEFINITIONS

The Israeli abortion debate incorporates five central definitions of the problem, three associated with calls for more restrictive abortion policies, and two with more liberal perspectives on the subject. They are abortion as a: (1) religious problem, (2) demographic problem, (3) moral problem, (4) social welfare problem, and (5) feminist cause.

Abortion as a Religious Problem

In Israel, as elsewhere, religious norms and interests have been at the center of demands for greater abortion restrictions. Orthodox religious parties have spearheaded all anti-abortion legislative initiatives. Similarly, as discussed below, groups active in opposition to abortions are directly or indirectly associated with orthodox interests. Nevertheless, the Israeli abortion arena is marked by the relative paucity of explicit religious argumentation, and by what appears to be an intentional effort by anti-abortion activists to distance their campaigns from other secular–religious cleavages in Israel. Thus, Member of Knesset (MK) Avraham Shapira, from the ultra-orthodox party Yahadut Hatorah, began a parliamentary speech urging stricter enforcement of Israel's abortion law with the words: "The multiplicity of abortions in Israel is not a religious subject. ... The subject is totally within the domain of health and education, and ought to be viewed as a first order national priority."[14]

The insulation of the abortion question from direct religion and state conflicts is facilitated by the comparative flexibility of relevant Jewish religious doctrine, and the compatibility of this doctrine with alternative, non-religious Israeli justifications for abortion law. In contrast to the absolutist premises propelling much Christian, especially Catholic, anti-abortion positions, orthodox Judaism allows significant room for compromise. The Torah makes no explicit mention of abortion, removing the issue from the realm of supreme biblical prohibitions. Subsequent rabbinical discussions are vague and inconsistent, but unequivocal in the priority accorded the life of the mother over that of the fetus. The central Talmudic text in this regard concerns a situation in which a woman encounters life-threatening difficulties in labor. The rabbbis' answer regarding abortion under these circumstances distinguishes between two situations. Prior to the emergence of the head, "her life takes priority over his life." But if labor had progressed beyond that point he is not to be touched "because one does not trade one soul with another."[15] Rabbinical responses dating back to the seventeenth century express degrees of disapproval but lack the theological urgency of doctrines viewing life as beginning at conception. Instead, the emphasis shifts to the nature of the circumstances constituting sufficient threat to maternal well-being so as to justify abortion under Jewish law.[16] Differences between this framework and the one propelling the American pro-life position are evident in the language employed by the American ultra-orthodox organization Agudath Israel of America in an Amicus brief submitted to the US Supreme Court in connection with the *Casey* decision. The brief called for replacing the fundamental rights concept of *Roe v. Wade*, with "a framework whereby abortion claims would or would not be accorded 'fundamental rights' status depending upon the circumstances surrounding their assertion."[17] Speaking to the differences between Jewish religious law and Catholic dogma on this issue, Rabbi Pinhas Stolper, executive director of the Union of Orthodox Jewish Congregations, stated in 1989: "We do not identify with those groups that feel all abortion is murder. ... Unlike the Catholic position ... in the Jewish view the supreme need is to consider the life, health and well being of the mother."[18]

A similar contextual approach was advanced by two rabbinical opinions accompanying a 1974 report by a commission charged with providing a blueprint for revising Israel's abortion law.[19] Significantly, the law proposed by this commission and subsequently adopted, with minor revisions by the Knesset, is more in harmony with the traditional Jewish approach than the more absolute prohibition it replaced. The Israeli statute combines principled disapproval of abortion with exemptions under specified circumstances, a solution much in keeping rabbinical case by case decisions on abortion. While Israeli law substituted the secular authority of the committees for the rabbinical, it retained the norms and logic of the traditional religious process.

The primary difference between the 1977 law and Jewish tradition lay in its inclusion of socio-economic conditions among the specified exemptions. The difficulty of reconciling socio-economic exemptions with religious formulations of maternal health led to ultimately successful ultra-orthodox agitation against the Social Clause. Yet, importantly, in keeping with the previously mentioned efforts to insulate the abortion debate from the politics of religion in Israel, that argument has rarely assumed center stage in the ultra-orthodox campaign against the Clause.

Speaking to the incentives to camouflage the religious motivations behind anti-abortion positions, a 1984 editorial in a newsletter published by Efrat, the primary group active in the anti abortion front, stated:

> We should develop ideas and present facts before the general public. We should not use religious arguments in front of them. There are plenty of philosophical, moral, demographic and health reasons to oppose abortions. ... Religious justifications may lead the secular public to think that this is just another religious observance.[20]

First among such alternative formulations has been the presentation of abortions as a threat to the future of a Jewish popular majority in Israel.

Abortion as a Demographic Problem

Otherwise sharply divided factions in Israeli politics share concerns about the stability of a Jewish popular majority in Israel, based on the close link between the country's demographic composition and the Israeli state's precarious Jewish and democratic identity. Demographic constructions of the abortion problem thus gain sympathy not only from those concerned with the state's Jewish future, but also from those committed to the long-term viability of the democratic Jewish formula.

Demographic concerns were, in fact, the context within which abortion first entered Israel's political agenda during the 1960s. In 1962, in response to well publicized declines in the rate of Jewish births, Efrat, the anti-abortion group noted above, was established. Its full name at the time was "Efrat – Association for the Encouragement of Fertility among the Jewish People." Efrat initially promoted general pronatalist policies and social norms, rather than anti-abortion legislation. However, by 1965, Efrat was actively calling for stricter enforcement of dormant abortion prohibitions.

The link between demographic concerns and abortion was likewise reflected in a 1966 report by a "natality problems" commission. The report cited abortion among the factors contributing to declining Jewish birthrates, and proposed a governmental unit that would oversee national demographic policy.[21] Established in 1968, the Demography Center, currently housed within the Ministry of Labor and Welfare, has repeatedly incorporated covert anti-abortion messages in its policy missions and publications.[22] In 1990, the Demography Center hatched a plan for a major survey to identify married and intentionally childless women with the goal of targeting these through a propaganda campaign that would argue that "professional careers are good and nice, but should not conflict with the creation of a family."[23]

The resonance of demographic arguments across the spectrum of Israeli politics is nowhere more evident than in the lip service paid by many abortion rights activists to Jewish natality concerns. Amir and Navon describe a reluctance on the part of a number of women and liberal groups, including the Israeli Association for Civil Rights and the Israeli Family Planning Association, to challenge the abortion-demographic linkage.[24] A 1992 position paper written by Alice Shalvi, the chairwoman of the Israel Women's Network, coupled strong opposition to proposed legislative restrictions with the following statement: "We do not, however, believe that abortion is a desirable mode of birth control and we call on the government and other authorities to develop a demographic policy of family planning which will include ... economic and social incentives for middle and upper income, university educated couples, to encourage them to have larger families."[25]

Abortion as a Moral Problem

The third problem definition employed by anti-abortion activists and the one most directly influenced by American pro-life rhetoric is the equation between abortion and murder. The most recent and direct appearance of this formulation in the context of Israeli legislative politics occurred in December 1996 when the ultra-orthodox party Shas submitted a bill defining the fetus as a person for the purpose of civil and criminal law. The bill which, if passed would have opened the way for the prosecution of abortion as murder, initially garnered the support of 51 members of Knesset including some from the Labor Party. It lost momentum, however, when the opposition mobilized and some of its initial supporters withdrew, claiming that they had not understood its relevance to abortion. Primarily a symbolic gesture, this bill is nevertheless significant as a first attempt to introduce fetus-centered formulations, evocative of American pro-life discourse, into Israeli statutory debates.

Language and symbols characteristic of the American pro-life movement appear in Israel for the first time during the 1980s. A 1985 Efrat newsletter featured Ronald Reagan on its cover and cited the American pro-life movement as a model worthy of imitation. Efrat also began to incorporate in its publications, Hebrew adaptations of American pro-life staples such as "Four Ways to Kill a Baby," and the organization's reference in its subtitle to Jewish natality was substituted with a new name: "The Right to Life."

Since that time, Efrat has emulated the emotional appeal of American pro-life campaigns with graphic images of the fetus and the abortion process. In 1996 Efrat distributed 1.4 million leaflets with an illustrated Hebrew adaptation of the "Diary of a Baby," an American pro-life publication relating the thoughts of a soon-to-be-aborted fetus. In public lectures across the country, Efrat representatives have frequently cast abortion as a dangerous, immoral, and grotesque act. These tactics have met with significant opposition, most interestingly from members of ultra-orthodox communities. After parents in several such communities complained about their children's exposure to pictures included in Efrat's "Diary of a Baby" leaflet, the organization published an apology in the ultra-orthodox press.[26]

Differences in the sensibilities of Israeli and American pro-life supporters and activists are likewise evident in the ambivalence expressed by Efrat's chairman, Dr. Eli Shus-Heim, regarding "Silent Scream," a movie depicting an abortion in graphic detail, and used as a frequent tool of the American pro-life movement. The movie, in Hebrew translation, is distributed and presented to targeted audiences by Efrat but, according to Shus-Heim, the Hebrew version produced by Efrat excludes some of the most disturbing sections included in the English original and is not usually shown to pregnant women considering abortion. Distancing himself from American pro-life language, Shus-Heim articulated his view of the relationship between abortion and murder: "I don't use the word murder, I don't think it adds anything. But it is the cessation of life of a human creature."[27]

Partially the product of differences in style and aesthetic sensibilities, Efrat's reluctant embrace of pro-life language and tactics is, more profoundly, the product of fundamental tensions between the agendas of the two anti-abortion movements. While hard core pro-life activists in the United States see abortion as a matter of life or death, such moral fervor is largely absent from parallel Israeli activism. This difference results from variation in underlying religious motivations. As noted, Jewish religious law does not condemn all abortions, and, indeed, requires them where the mother is endangered. Thus, Jewish abortion prohibitions are difficult to reconcile with pro-life constructions equating all abortions with murder.

In contrast with the American pro-life movement's concern with global protection of fetuses everywhere, efforts in Israel exclusively target abortions performed on Jewish women. This distinction is in part itself a product of differences in underlying religious beliefs, but it also follows from the centrality of nationalistic demographic concerns noted above. A statement on Israeli television by Haim Hazan, the American immigrant consultant to the Ministry of Health, offers a particularly jarring example of the instrumental and particularistic tenor of pro-life rhetoric in Israel: "I do not accept the malignant notion that a woman is master of her body. Her body does not belong to her. The fetus has a right to live. ... He is a potential soldier. In recent years close to 2000 potential divisions have been destroyed."[28] A visit to Efrat's Internet home page is likewise instructive. At the top of the page, which includes links to excerpts from the movie "Silent Scream," and other pro-life documents, a new organizational title suggests growing discomfort with the universalistic premise of the American pro-life manifestos. In contrast to the words "right to life" added to Efrat's name during the 1980s, the new name reads: "International Organization for Saving Jewish Babies."[29]

These tensions derive from conflicts between the logics of local and imported formulations of the abortion problem and are essential to understanding the dynamics underpinning cross-national importation of ideological causes. As the following discussion reveals, similar difficulties were encountered by those who sought to introduce liberal, feminist based definitions of the problem presented by abortion regulation.

Abortion as a Social Welfare Problem

The abortion law enacted in Israel in 1977 was the product of converging pressures from opposite sides of Israel's political spectrum. The first was a coalition of religious-national interests pushing for stricter enforcement of abortion prohibitions. The second was a small group of American inspired feminists, critical of existing abortion prohibitions and eager to invoke the issue's symbolic power to mobilize the women's movement in Israel. They encountered significant resistance from traditional women's organizations in the country who were wary of unsettling an ambiguous, but generally adequately functioning status quo, in which abortions, though legally forbidden, were easily obtainable.[30] Their support was ultimately won through appeals grounded in social welfare rather than purely feminist considerations.

Long-standing pro-natalist commitments began to be qualified during the early 1970s by new awareness of the relationship between large family size and poverty. A 1972 report by the Prime Minister's Committee on Children and Youth in Distress focused public attention on the socio-economic gap between families of Afro, Asian, and European origin, linking this gap to differences in family size.[31] Yishai contends that a "hidden agenda" directed at the reduction of Afro-Asian birth-rates undermined the effectiveness of explicit pro-natalist policies. The role of this mixed agenda was evident in the centrality of poor women's access to abortion for the coalition that ultimately passed abortion reform.[32]

The intended beneficiaries of the Social Clause initially included in the legislation were married, young, and healthy women who could not qualify for abortions under alternative exemption categories. Under this clause, such women could benefit from state-facilitated and even some state-funded abortions. In addition, the clause explicitly recognized socio-economic conditions, conferring some legitimacy upon abortions performed for such reasons. Reflecting upon the centrality of the clause to the ultimate passage of the law, Ora Namir, a Labor Party MK at the time and a former government minister, commented: "The abortion law was primarily enacted because of the socio-economic clause. Well-off women, including religious well-off women, don't need laws, they know where to go and how to protect themselves. We thought it was important ... to aid a population of women that have difficulty dealing with the conditions of their lives."[33] In response to the social welfare rationale of the new legislation, the 1977 law requires that abortion approval committees include a social worker in addition to physicians. Not surprisingly, the Social Workers Union actively opposed the abolition of the Social Clause.[34]

Since the abolition of the Social Clause, liberal abortion activism has centered upon largely ritualistic initiatives directed at the Clause's reinstatement. Such proposals periodically appear before the Knesset, and the Labor Party platform has repeatedly included a principled (but unimplemented) commitment to restore the Clause. This, rather than a demand for elimination of abortion prohibitions as such, has been the central rallying cry of Israeli abortion activism. This trend has been coupled by similar emphasis upon health and immigrant absorption policies, in the rhetoric invoked by women groups faced with subsequent threats to the Israeli abortion status quo. Thus a broad based women's coalition, created in 1990 in response to a pending anti-abortion legislation, framed its campaign in reference to health rather than women's autonomy. This emphasis contrasted with explicit pro-choice rhetoric invoked by American liberal Jewish groups that provided both funding and political support for the coalition's campaign.[35] Similar strategic considerations led the Coalition to emphasize the connection between liberal abortion policies and the needs of new immigrant populations. Due to frequent use of abortion as a substitute for contraception among immigrants from the former Soviet Union, demand for abortion was expected to rise disproportionately in the wake of increased immigration during the late 1980s and early 1990s.[36] The projected effect on successful absorption of these immigrants was invoked by the coalition in general publications and in a letter sent to members of the Knesset Immigration and Absorption Committee.[37]

The thread running through the problem definitions employed by groups favoring liberal abortion policy is an avoidance of feminist language and women's rights formulations. While efforts to recast Israeli abortion politics in a more feminist image have been repeatedly made, they have been politically marginalized.

Abortion as a Feminist Cause

As noted before, during the 1970s American feminist influences introduced a new vocabulary and tactics into Israeli abortion discourse. Carrying banners declaring "We are not the national womb," members of the nascent feminist movement disrupted a 1976 meeting of the Israel Association of Obstetricians and Gynecologists, which then opposed liberalized abortion law. Through the efforts of Marcia Freedman, they also placed an explicit pro-choice agenda before the Knesset. This agenda failed due to tensions between the rights-based focus of the imported feminist agenda and the national collectivist values that many Israeli women continue to hold. Yishai describes the political lives of Israeli women as shaped by the conflicting pulls of collective and individual identities, feminist and nationalist commitments. Difficulties in reconciling these competing goals, Yishai argues, have stymied women's capacity to advance their interests politically.[38] This observation appears especially pertinent to understanding the limited impact of feminist perspectives on the course of Israeli abortion debates. The resonance of demographic concerns across a wide spectrum of Israeli politics was clearly a factor in Israeli women groups' reluctance to promote a free choice agenda. But perhaps more fundamental was the distinctly different meaning of the concept of choice, as such, in Israeli political life.

Amir and Binyamin describe Israeli abortion procedures as rituals of symbolic control. These rituals serve as disciplinary mechanisms for articulating collective disapproval, but do not, in practice, block Israeli women's access to abortion.[39] Israeli women's acceptance of a law requiring them to plead their need for abortion before three strangers is understandable when one realizes that this is part of a much broader pattern of interference by the Israeli state in the most personal spheres of life. In a society in which women undergo both a compulsory draft and pre-marital rabbinate decreed and state-sanctioned inquiries into their menstrual cycle, abortion committees amount to a relatively less invasive affront. But perhaps even more significantly, where the possibility of sacrificing one's child in war is never far from the mind of any parent, a governmental role in procreation decisions is likely to seem less preposterous. Reflecting the complexity of these sentiments, Labor Party MK Yael Dayan made the following statement in support of the Social Clause's return: "The state can send its children to the army, for life or death. ... It can not force us to be mothers. ... [T]here is no compulsory law on motherhood and love."[40] In what may have been a Freudian slip, the liberal MK's own reference to the state's right to send *its* children to the army suggests the gap between the political cultures in which Israeli and American abortion rights activism are planted.

The American focus on rights, whether of the fetus or the woman, was thus countered in Israel with arguments couched in the language of national rather than individual well being. The marginality of rights to definitions of abortion problems in Israel is in part explained by continuing deference to the state as an embodiment of nationally defined collective values. But this marginality is, in addition, the product of the relative irrelevance of legally defined rights to actual state interference in abortion. The gap between abortion law and practice and its place within broader Israeli legal cultural traits is the subject of the following section.

RIGHTS, DE FACTO LEGALISM, AND LEGAL CULTURE

In the United States, delimiting the authority of government to regulate abortion has been the ongoing task of the Supreme Court. So far two lines of decisions have addressed this question. The first established abortion as a constitutionally protected right and severely curtailed the circumstances justifying state intervention in this area, while the second divorced any such abortion rights from constitutional entitlements to state or federal assistance.[41] In Israel, however, the question of governmental powers was immaterial to a debate which, in the absence of constitutional limitations, focused on the terms of state intervention rather than its justification.[42] However, these terms of intervention were only partially reflected in formal legal resolutions of the abortion question. They were instead defined through semi-formal mechanisms grounded in the ambiguous authority of the abortion approval committees.

Law, Mobilization and Abortion Compromises

Despite the sharp controversy that surrounded the Social Clause's abolition, the change had little practical impact on the number of approved abortions which, after a temporary dip, soon returned to their pre-amendment levels.[43] The elimination of the Clause did not reduce the number of abortions because, in the wake of the legislative change, abortion approval committees began to substitute alternative exemption categories, most notably physical or mental risk to the mother, for explicit reliance on socio-economic considerations.[44] The ease with which the abortion committees could effect this change stems from the almost complete autonomy the Israeli abortion law grants abortion approval committees. The Israeli abortion statute offers no rationale for the qualified prohibition it imposes and does not identify the claims it seeks to balance. A woman who is denied an abortion by a committee cannot appeal the decision, but can bring her request before any additional committee or committees. At the same time, a committee's decision to grant an abortion is essentially unreviewable. The Israeli Supreme Court has determined that a husband, and by implication any other third party, does not have a right to appear before a pregnancy termination committee (*Plonit v. Ploni*, 1980).[45]

An important result of this autonomy has been significant diversity among the committees operating in various hospitals in the country. These differences pertain both to the rigidity of relevant bureaucratic procedures and to the leniency with which alternative committees tend to approach requests for abortion approval.[46] This variation results from both the personal beliefs of senior doctors and administrators in each hospital and from the hospital's religious affiliation.[47] The power to bring abortion requests before any committee in the country and resubmit denied requests before alternative committees, coupled with the availability of liberal, often private hospital operated, committees have been the lynchpin of Israeli abortion compromises.

Thus, a 1990 attempt to tamper with this arrangement through legislation regulating such private hospital committees[48] resulted in one of the most visible and well-coordinated abortion access campaigns in Israel. After the proposed amendment passed the first of three required hearings in the Knesset, a broadly based coalition of fifteen women's, and civil rights groups was created to fight the bill. The coalition, largely financed by contributions from American Jewish sources, targeted

Knesset members of both the right and the left, convened press conferences, published a detailed information pamphlet and prepared to launch a mass public campaign including petitions and demonstrations. These plans were rescinded when the political tide shifted and the bill was tabled after ultra-orthodox pressure waned.[49]

The organizational effort spawned by the proposed private hospital amendment was quite unusual. Although members of left-leaning parties have brought many bills seeking the reintroduction of the Social Clause, women's groups have tended not to mobilize behind such actions. Perhaps more significantly, even a proposal to eliminate all abortion restrictions and the entire committee system, initiated in 1987 by Labor Party MK Ora Namir after a young woman died while undergoing an illegal private abortion,[50] failed to arouse much interest among women's organizations.

A similar lack of emphasis upon formal legislative solutions is evident in the strategies of anti-abortion interest groups. Efrat's chairman, Eli Shus-Heim, has indicated his willingness to support a return of the Social Clause to the law in exchange for greater access by Efrat to abortion committees and women facing abortion choices. Efrat has likewise expressed reservations regarding the earlier mentioned 1997 attempt by the ultra-orthodox Shas to define the embryo from conception onward as a person under the criminal code. Addressing differences between American Evangelical pro-lifers and his own organization, Shus-Heim stated: "You cannot save even one baby by passing laws, by trying to force people. We need to respect a woman's rights – she has a right to know exactly what it is that's growing inside her. We believe in education, not confrontation."[51]

This belief, perhaps most profoundly, has led Efrat to reject the civil disobedience tactics endorsed by some American pro-life groups. Efrat's home page now highlights the following statement: "(Efrat) categorically rejects demonstrations and acts of violence against doctors and clinics, and condemns breaking the law."[52] This position is in part the product of tactical concerns regarding the potential backlash that civil disobedience tactics may trigger in Israel. But it more significantly reflects deeper underlying differences between American and Israeli pro-life conceptions of the political and symbolic importance of law within abortion struggles and the urgency of moral justifications for its violation. The reluctance of abortion activists on both sides to engage the law directly indicates fundamental differences in the meaning and impact of law within each of the abortion stories. This phenomenon is perhaps nowhere clearer than in the rhetoric invoked by the Israeli Supreme Court in its few references to the circumstances governing abortion in the country.

De Facto Legalism and Abortion Rights

The status of abortion has, since the enactment of the 1977 law, come before the Court on only two occasions. The first was the earlier mentioned 1980 *Plonit v. Almoni* decision in which a majority concluded that a husband did not have the right to intervene in approval procedures pertaining to his wife's abortion request. The second involved the Court's 1993 and 1996 decisions in *Nahmani* v. *Nahmani,*[53] which dealt with the right of a husband to veto the implantation into a surrogate mother of fertilized eggs jointly created by him and his now estranged wife. The common denominator linking these cases is Supreme Court language conferring a quasi-legal status on de facto abortion practices contradictory to the letter of the law. The 1980 case, decided after the cancellation of the Social Clause, concerned an abortion request by a married woman who was in the process of separating from her (according to her claim) abusive husband. Although the woman's request was not based in any of the remaining legal exemption categories, the legal grounds for the committee's abortion approval were never discussed in the decision, which focused instead on the husband's claimed right to intervene. In a revealing statement, Justice Ben-Ito acknowledged the precariousness of the legal structures underpinning the abortion status quo when she described the pertinent law as a delicate compromise aimed at determining not whether but how abortions would be performed and cautioned against judicial interference in this fragile equilibrium.[54] In a similar fashion, the existence of a qualified right to abortion in Israeli law served as an important subtext of the judicial and academic debate surrounding the Supreme Court's two *Nahmani* decisions. Both decisions include specific references to the rights of women to control their body and to the contested analogy between the existence of such rights and Mr. Nahmani's right to veto the implementation of the eggs. The Justices' references to a right to abortion, despite the law's explicit prohibition of the practice, suggests the manner in which de facto formulations of abortion rights are embedded within Israeli abortion discourse, reaching even to the Supreme Court.

In contrast to American concerns with dyadic divisions between constitutional and unconstitutional moves, Israel's abortion arena has unfolded along a spectrum marked by much more subtle gradations in legality. Israeli legal rights, whether those of the fetus or the woman, have been marginal to an abortion management process only marginally constrained by its legal shell. Instead, both sides, out of mutual fear of backlash, appear committed to compromise premised upon the circumvention of law. Amir and Navon describe the Israeli abortion scene as a two tiered system shrouded in an air of secrecy aimed at preserving the gap between a restrictive image and liberal reality.[55] The fit between such formulas and similar extra legal religion and state resolutions links the Israeli abortion story to broader traits of Israeli political and legal culture.

The Avoidance of Law and Irreconcilable Differences

Current Israeli abortion resolutions rest upon two opposing concessions. Formal state law accords with pertinent Jewish religious tenets, while actual practices support state-facilitated abortions that are often at odds with religious precepts. It is an arrangement in keeping with similar ad hoc resolutions of potentially explosive political conflicts.

The avoidance of law has been a crucial strategy in Israeli circumvention of direct opposition between the state's Jewish and democratic commitments. The absence of an Israeli constitution articulating the meaning of these commitments and the extra-legal but well entrenched status quo governing the place of religious norms within multiple spheres of public life are the primary examples of such avoidance.[56] Israeli abortion solutions diverge to some extent from extra-legal approaches to the religious status quo because the open ended abortion committee discretion on which they rely constitutes an institutional bypass within the law. Similar solutions have been employed in Israel in a variety of politically sensitive areas ranging from the definition of army service exemptions granted to ultra-orthodox men as "postponements" to state recognition of religiously forbidden marriages performed abroad. The avoidance and circumvention of law converge in Israel with broader illegalist social tendencies. Sprinzak identifies Israeli illegalism as "an instrumental orientation towards the legal order and a conviction that democracy does not depend upon strict adherence to the law."[57] Similar arguments regarding an Israeli propensity towards contingent understandings of law have subsequently been made by Lehman-Wilzig and Rosen-Zvi.[58]

Neither illegalism nor extra-legalism are unique Israeli traits. They exist to some extent in all societies. But the phenomenon may be especially pronounced under conditions of norm competition and dissonance between alternative legal cultures.[59] In a comparison of attitudes toward law among European Union countries, Gibson and Caldeira found cross-national differences in a willingness to tolerate exceptions to the law, and linked these differences to variations in underlying legal cultures.[60] In an investigation of the factors responsible for such legal cultural variations, Bierbrauer connected differences between collectivist and individualist orientations among Kurds, Lebanese, and Germans, with divergent preferences for formal procedure and guidelines.[61] The Israeli case appears to offer further evidence regarding both the existence and the significance of such cross-national differences and the manner in which they influence the definition and negotiation of fundamental social disputes such as abortion.

CONCLUSION

The unique place of abortion in the US follows from two closely linked features of the American debate. The first is a direct competition between two absolutist and mutually exclusive rights-based formulations of the problem. The second is a political and legal cultural framework in which such rights give rise to binding constitutional limitations on the authority of government. Problem definitions supporting rights-based formulations thus pushed the abortion question into the central stage of constitutional law and politics. In contrast, problem definitions grounded in alternative conceptions of state authority and legal culture significantly diminished the salience of abortion in Israel.

Whereas both governing American abortion problem definitions are individualist and absolutist, the Israeli debate reflects a more collectivist and contextual understanding. On the anti-abortion side, this difference is the product of contingency inherent to religious Jewish attitudes towards abortion, and the particularistic focus of national Jewish demographic concerns. Both factors distinguish such Israeli activism from the universalistic and right to life claims of their American counterparts. On the opposite side of the issue, pervasive governmental interference in multiple intimate spheres of Israeli life dictated against the construction of abortion regulation as a unique invasion of a protected autonomous domain. Instead, problem definitions appealing to collective interests in social welfare, women's health, and immigration absorption were employed.

Differences in underlying problem definitions naturally extended to differential emphasis on law centered rhetoric and tactics. Abortion in the United States is constructed, first and foremost, as a constitutional dilemma pertaining to the power of government to enact particular laws. In Israel, such questions are less consequential not only due to differences in conceptions of legitimate state authority, but also due to the lesser significance of law *per se* in resolving of such questions. Incentives for law-centered discourse and tactics are tied to perceptions of the symbolic and direct impact of relevant legal instruments. In Israel, however, the terms of religion and state compromises have often depended upon closely guarded gaps between formal symbolic messages and actual practices. In abortion, as in many other points of conflict between Jewish religious norms and the secular state's democratic commitments, the avoidance of law has served to deflect direct confrontation between what many Israelis fear are irreconcilable fundamental differences. Fear of bringing these differences into the open has sustained ambiguous political resolutions and legal circumvention techniques. American inspired conceptions of what is at stake in abortion ultimately failed to alter the course of Israeli abortion politics because they were incompatible with the terms of this increasingly fragile compromise.

ACKNOWLEDGMENTS

Support provided for this research by the Lady Davis Fellowship Trust is gratefully acknowledged.

NOTES

1. Christopher J. Bosso, "The Contextual Bases of Problem Definition," in David A. Rochefort and Roger W. Cobb (eds), *The Politics of Problem Definition*, Lawrence, KS: University of Kansas Press, 1994.
2. Yael Yishai, "Public Ideas and Public Policy: Abortion Politics in Four Democracies," *Comparative Politics* 25 (1993) pp.207–28.
3. *Roe v. Wade*, 410 U.S. 113 (1973). Marcia Freedman, *Exile in the Promised Land*, Ithaca, NY: Firebrand Books, 1990; Yael Yishai, "The Hidden Agenda: Abortion Politics in Israel," *Journal of Social Policy* 22/2 (1993) pp.193–212.
4. Freedman (note 3).
5. Delila Amir and David Navon, *The Politics of Abortion in Israel*, Tel Aviv: Pinchas Sapir Center for Development, Tel Aviv University, 1989.
6. "Shatil-Sponsored Coalition Opposes Changes in Israel's Abortion Law," (Press release on file at Israel Women's Network, Reproductive/Abortion file).
7. Judy Siegel, "Helms: PM Must Reduce Israeli Abortions," *Jerusalem Post*, 13 Feb. 1997.
8. In *Planned Parenthood of Southeastern Pennsylvania v. Casey* 112 S.Ct. 2791 (1992) the US Supreme Court voted to uphold provisions such as informed consent and a mandatory 24-hour waiting period in the Pennsylvania Abortion Control Act. The decision, of course, did not relate to abortion approval committees which are a feature of Israeli, not US, abortion regulation.
9. *Knesset Minutes 1991,* 13th Knesset, Meeting 8, 3, 279.
10. *Webster v. Reproductive Health Services*, 492 U.S. 490 (1989). Judy Siegel, "Na'Amat Fears Israeli Fallout From U.S. Ruling on Abortion," *Jerusalem Post*, 6 July 1989, p.2.
11. Letter from the Israel Feminist Movement to President George Bush, 10 Nov. 1989 (on file with author).
12. P. Sleiter, D. Wiener and M. Davis, "Denied Abortion Requests in Jerusalem, 1972–5," 20/3 (1978) pp.277–81. Dan Shnit, "Induced Abortion in Israeli Law," *Israeli Yearbook on Human Rights* 15 (1985) p.155.
13. Sleiter *et al.* (note 12).
14. *Knesset Minutes 1993*, 13th Knesset, Meeting 111, 35-32, 6198.
15. Mishna Ohalot.
16. David M. Feldman, *Birth Control in Jewish Law*, New York: New York University Press, 1968; Ratson Arusi, "Formal and Actual Norms Governing Abortion Under Jewish Law," *Diney Yisrael* 8 (1987) p.119.
17. Jewish Law Legal Briefs. *Casey v. Planned Parenthood of Southeastern Pennsylvania*, (http//www.jlaw.com/Briefs/casey.html).
18. Walter Ruby, "The Organized American Jewish Community Takes a 'Freedom of Choice' Line on Abortion," *Jerusalem Post*, 14 March 1989, p.7.
19. Committee for the Investigation of Abortion Prohibitions, "Commission Report: Appendixes D and E – Hallachic Opinions," *Public Health* 17/4 (1974) p.495.
20. Shlomo-Yona Tuaf, "Religious Justifications Ought Not Be Used in Front of the General Public," *Yedion* 17-18 (1984) p.3.
21. Dov Friedlander, "Population Policy in Israel," in Bernard Berelson (ed.), *Population Policy in Developed Countries*, New York: McGraw Hill, 1974.
22. Amir and Navon (note 5).
23. Michal Kedem, "The Ministry of Labor Investigates: Why Married Women Do Not Give Birth," *Hadashot*, 22 Nov. 1990.
24. Amir and Navon (note 5).
25. Alice Shalvi, "Why the I.W.N. Opposes the Proposed Changes in the Abortion Law," (on file at Israel Women's Network, Reproductive Abortion file).
26. Shachar Ilan, "Distribution of Anti Abortion Leaflet Ceased in Ultra Orthodox Neighborhoods," *Ha'aretz*, 1 Sept. 1996.
27. Liat Mashat, "A Horror Show Named Abortion," *Yediot Ahronot (Zmanim Modernim)*, 10 Oct. 1996, pp.4–5.
28. Tali Barzilai-Zonenfeld, "Not All Fetuses Are Equal," *Al Hamishmar*, 29 Jan. 1988, pp.17–19.
29. Http://www.efrat.org.il/back.html, 11/17/97.
30. Lesley Hazleton, *Israeli Women: The Reality Behind the Myths*, New York: Simon & Schuster, 1977.

31. Lotte Salzberger, Sarah Magidor, Amy Avgar, and Janet Baumgold-Land, *Patterns of Contraceptive Behavior Among Jerusalem Women Seeking Pregnancy Counselling 1980–1989*, Jerusalem: Hebrew University of Jerusalem, Paul Baerwald School of Social Work, 1991.
32. Yishai, "The Hidden Agenda" (note 3).
33. *Knesset Minutes 1990,* 12th Knesset, Meeting 181, 28 May.
34. Yitzhak Kadman, "Pregnancy Termination From a Social Perspective," *Society and Welfare* 2 (1979) pp.320–29.
35. Noga Morag-Levine, "Abortion in Israel: Community, Rights, and the Context of Compromise," *Law and Social Inquiry* 19/2 (1994) pp.313–35.
36. Eitan P. Sabattelo, "Early Assessments of an Increased Demand for Abortions Subsequent to the Growth of Immigration From the Soviet Union," *Hevra U'Revacha* (1992) p.185.
37. Protocol of the meeting of the Coalition for the Prevention of Amendment 30 to the Criminal Code, 11 Nov. 1990 (on file at Israeli Association for Civil Rights (ACRI), Abortion file).
38. Yael Yishai, *Between the Flag and the Banner: Women in Israeli Politics*, Albany, NY: State University of New York Press, 1997.
39. Delila Amir and Orly Binyamin, "Abortion Approval As a Ritual of Symbolic Control," in Clarice Feinman (ed.), *The Criminalization of Women's Body*, Binghampton, NY: Haworth Press, 1992, pp.1–25.
40. *Knesset Minutes 1993*, 13th Knesset, Meeting 137, 20 Oct.
41. The absence of a state interest in abortion restrictions aimed at the protection of fetal rights (during the first two trimesters of pregnancy) was established in *Roe v. Wade*, 410 U.S. 113 (1973). The absence of a state duty to provide funding for non-therapeutic abortions was established in *Maher v. Roe,* 432 U.S. 464 (1977) and *Harris v. McRae*, 448 U.S. 297 (1980).
42. Today, following the enactment of Basic Law: The Dignity and Freedom of the Individual (1992), new abortion restrictions would, in all likelihood, face political and legal challenges grounded in the claim that they violate protected fundamental individual rights. Although the fate of such claims, should they be raised either in the Knesset or before the Supreme Court, remains uncertain, there exists in Israel today a potential for a very different debate than the one that framed abortion legislation during the 1970s.
43. Amir and Navon (note 5).
44. Thus, whereas in 1979, 40% of hospital abortions were approved under the social clause and 8.2% were performed under the risk to the mother clause, in 1980, the year in which the social clause was eliminated, 35.1% of abortion approvals were granted under the medical risk clause. Israeli Central Bureau of Statistics figures cited in Amir and Navon (note 5).
45. *Plonit v. Ploni*, Civil Appeal 413/80, PADI 35 (3), 58, 1980.
46. Amir and Navon (note 5); Salzberger *et al.* (note 31).
47. Memorandum from attorney Neta Ziv Goldman to the directors of the Israel Association of Civil Rights (ACRI), May 1987 (on file at ACRI, Abortion file).
48. Draft Amendment No.30 to the Criminal Code, 21 Aug. 1989.
49. Morag-Levine (note 35); Yishai, *Between the Flag and the Banner* (note 38).
50. Private abortion bill submitted by MK Ora Namir to MK Rafi Edri, 26 Jan. 1987 (on file at Israel Women's Network Reproductive/Abortion file).
51. S.A. Osborne, "Bill Sparks Abortion Controversy," *Christianity Today* No.4, 7 April 1997, p.60.
52. Http://www.efrat.org.il/back.html, 11/17/97.
53. The Supreme Court tackled the Nahmani case twice. First, in a 1993 decision, the Court ruled that Mr. Nahmani had a right to stop the process *(D. Nahmani v. R. Nahmani and others*, Civil Appeal 5587/93, Padi, 49(1), 485). In an en-banc rehearing of the case in 1996 the Court reversed the 1993 decision and ruled in favor of Mrs. Nahmani (*R. Nahmani v. D. Nahmani and others*, Diyun Nosaf 2401/95 Tak-Al, Volume 96 (3), 522).
54. *Plonit v. Ploni,* Civil Appeal 413/80, p.60, 85-86.
55. Amir and Navon (note 5).
56. Charles S. Liebman and Eliezer Don-Yehiya, *Religion and Politics in Israel*, Bloomington: Indiana University Press, 1984.

57. Ehud Sprinzak, "Elite Illegalism in Israel and the Question of Democracy," in Ehud Sprinzak and Larry Diamond (eds), *Israeli Democracy Under Stress,* Boulder, CO: Lynne Rienner, 1993, p.175.
58. Sam N. Lehman-Wilzig, *Wildfire: Grassroots Revolts in Israel in the Post-Socialist Era*, Albany, NY: State University of New York Press, 1992. Ariel Rosen-Zvi, "Legal Culture: On Judicial Review, the Enforcement of Law and Inculcation of Values," *Iyunei Mishpat* 17 (1992) pp.689–716.
59. Dai-Kwon Choi, "Western Law in a Traditional Society Korea," and Keith S. Rosenn, "The Jeito: Brazil's Institutional Bypass of the Formal Legal System and Its Development Implications," in Csaba Varga (ed.), *Comparative Legal Cultures*, New York: New York University Press, 1992.
60. James L. Gibson and Gregory A. Caldeira, "The Legal Cultures of Europe," *Law & Society Rev.* 30/1 (1996) pp.55–85.
61. Günter Bierbrauer, "Toward an Understanding of Legal Culture: Variations in Individualism and Collectivism Between Kurds, Lebanese, and Germans," *Law & Society Rev.* 28/2 (1994) pp.243–64.

[25]

The Effect of Entrenching a Bill of Rights upon Political Discourse: Feminist Demands and Sexual Violence in Canada

JUDY FUDGE*
Osgoode Hall Law School, York University, Canada

Introduction

The struggle which led to the guarantee of equality rights within Canada's recently entrenched *Charter of Rights and Freedoms* was heralded as a political victory both by and for feminists. However, the effect of this struggle is ambiguous. Whilst the struggle itself both mobilised and radicalised women's groups across Canada, the actual results of *Charter* litigation have been much less positive. This paper attempts to evaluate the *Charter*'s impact on political discourse by examining both its mobilising effect on women's groups and its impact upon a concrete area in which it has been invoked. To this end, the paper examines how the general claim that the entrenchment of constitutionally guaranteed rights has a progressive mobilising effect for political movements by looking at the concrete struggle of Canadian feminists to obtain equality rights in the Canadian *Charter*. The paper then examines how the *Charter* has been used to challenge the *Criminal Code* provisions which are designed to protect women and children from sexual violence and victimisation. Whilst the paper focuses on an area which underscores the problematic and contradictory results the entrenchment of a *Charter of Rights* has had on feminist demands, the broader object of this study is to provide a basis for evaluating the impact an entrenched charter of rights has on political discourse.

* I would like to thank my colleagues Shelley Gavigan, Harry Glasbeek and Michael Mandel for their helpful comments and suggestions.

The Struggle to Entrench Equality Rights

In 1982 the *Charter of Rights and Freedoms* was entrenched in the Canadian constitution. Significantly, neither a groundswell demand for judicial protection of fundamental rights and freedoms by the Canadian population in general nor identifiable minorities in particular marked the political process leading up to the entrenchment of the *Charter*. Rather, this process of constitutional renewal was initiated by the federal government in response to the nationalist aspirations of the people of the predominantly francophone province of Quebec (Glasbeek & Mandel, 1985; Mandel, 1989). Thus, the entrenchment of a justiciable charter of rights in the Canadian constitution was not a response to the demands of popular struggle, but was instead an essential element in the central government's response to a popular struggle.

It is in this context that Canadian feminist organisations mobilised to secure the guarantee of sex equality rights in the *Charter*. Once faced with the federal government's agenda of entrenching a charter of rights it was incumbent upon feminist organisations to respond. Experience with the *Canadian Bill of Rights*, a federal statute which was not entrenched and which applied only to the federal government, clearly demonstrated to women's groups the significance of legislative language when it came to judicial protection of sex equality rights. In two decisions, *Lavell*, [1974] 1 S.C.R. 1349 and *Bliss*, [1979] 1 S.C.R. 183, the Supreme Court of Canada exhibited its willingness to exploit legislative language to deny equality rights to women. In *Lavell* a native woman challenged the provision in the *Indian Act* which deprived Indian women, but not Indian men, of Indian status for marrying non-Indians. She argued that it violated her right to equality before the law. Distinguishing between inequality *in the law itself* and inequality in its *administration* the Supreme Court of Canada held that the *Bill of Rights* only prohibited the latter and, thus, that Mrs Lavell's right to equality had not been infringed since the law discriminated and the government's administration did not. In *Bliss* the Supreme Court of Canada held that requirements under the *Unemployment Insurance Act* governing a pregnant woman's entitlement to unemployment insurance benefits did not contravene the equality provisions of the *Bill of Rights*. While the Court held that the maternity benefit provisions of the *Unemployment Insurance Act* had an unequal impact on women and men, it stated that this was due to "nature", and not a result of the statute. Since pregnant women were not similarly situated to other claimants, different treatment did not constitute unequal treatment.

Thus, at the outset of the process of constitutional renewal the initial concern of feminist organisations was to ensure that the courts should have as little discretion as possible, lest they used it to limit women's equality rights once they were enshrined in the *Charter*. According to a prominent member of one of the main feminist lobby groups "[g]iven the sorry record of the courts on women's rights cases, this is not a matter to be left to judicial discretion"

(Mandel, 1989: 257). Consequently, the first stage of the equality campaign was dominated by lawyers who attempted to negotiate changes to the language used to express equality rights. However, political developments quickly changed this. In order to make the *Charter* palatable to the provinces the federal government added a legislative override clause which would enable the federal Parliament or a provincial legislature to declare that a "an Act of Parliament or of the legislature shall operate notwithstanding" that it infringed a right or freedom otherwise guaranteed by the *Charter*. The possibility that equality rights might be subjected to legislative override radically altered the nature of the feminist campaign. What initially consisted of a series of negotiations over legal language conducted under the auspices of well-established feminist umbrella organisations was transformed into a campaign of mass mobilisation (Kome, 1983). The struggle to preserve sex equality rights from the legislative override expanded to include grass roots women's groups as well as individual women who had never identified themselves as feminists. Moreover, the perceived antipathy of the politicians to the entrenchment of unqualified equality rights radicalised the nature of the feminist critique. Radical critiques of the state which emphasised the absence of women's groups from the process of constitutional renewal and the opposition of vested interests to equality demands tended to replace the liberal feminist analysis which dominated the earlier expert, negotiation stage (Gotell, 1989).

The politicians responded to the mass mobilisation for equality rights by giving the feminist lobby the language that it wanted in section 15, the general guarantee of equality rights, and by providing that section 28, the clause guaranteeing that the rights and freedom under the *Charter* applied equally to women and men, was not subject to legislative override. Thus, the struggle for the entrenchment of equality rights was a resounding political victory for feminists in Canada, particularly in light of the failure of repeated campaigns by American feminists to obtain an equal rights amendment to the American *Bill of Rights* (Hosek, 1983).

The entrenchment of equality rights in the Canadian *Charter* says more about the relative ease with which the Canadian political process responded to formal equality claims, particularly when contrasted with the United States, than it does about the value of the inclusion of such rights as part and parcel of the legal process. From one perspective, the ability of feminist organisations to get this included in the *Charter* and to secure what they considered to be adequate constitutional protection for equality rights became the litmus test of the political strength of the women's movement. The constitutional entrenchment of equality rights became a symbol of profound political significance around which many disparate feminist organisations and women's groups were able to coalesce. As one activist involved in the process reflected "the greatest achievement of the women's constitutional struggle may not have been the rewriting of the law, but the process of strengthening mass collective action whereby the anger of women crystallized into law" (Billings, 1983: 13).

The Assertion of Constitutional Rights as a Mobilising Strategy

But, how are we to evaluate the impact of the *Charter*'s guarantee of equality rights on the mobilisation of the women's movement in Canada? Does the fact that a wide variety of feminist organisations and women's groups coalesced around the struggle for constitutionally guaranteed equality rights imply that such rights are *per se* progressive? Or does the fact that such rights functioned as important symbols for political mobilisation suggest instead something about the abstract and under-determined nature of the demand for general legal rights?

According to Schneider, the assertion of constitutional and other general legal rights is an extremely important and positive political act. Maintaining a strict agnosticism regarding the actual results of constitutional litigation sponsored by feminist organisations, Schneider emphasises the positive aspect of the "way in which the assertion or 'experience' of rights can express a political vision, affirm a group's humanity, contribute to an individual's development as a whole person, and assist in the collective political development of a social or political movement, particularly in its early stages" (Schneider, 1986: 589). For her it is possible to divorce the positive influence the assertion of legal rights has on the political mobilisation of social movements from the results of litigation. In contrast to Schneider's position, I want to propose an alternative, less sanguine, analysis which focuses on the *nature of the political discourse* generated by the assertion of abstract legal rights. Schneider's analysis ignores the impact this form of politics has upon the nature of political discourse. Rather than regarding the fact of mass mobilisation as positive *per se*, it is important to examine how abstract legal rights function as the basis for coalitions or mobilisation. It is possible that women's organisations were able to rally around the struggle for a constitutional guarantee of equality rights *precisely* because such an abstract demand did not require concrete articulation or illustration.

Eric Hobsbawm has pointed out that throughout history members of movements which have challenged the status quo "spoke the language of *rights* (and still do), if only because this is the natural language of anyone who sets up a model of morality and justice ... and makes claims in the light of this model" (Hobsbawm, 1984: 308). It is also, as he notes, "the natural language of politics, since it provides a built-in moral backing for any demand or action" (ibid: 308). Thus, the significance of the assertion of a right depends upon the social vision or politics which informs it. According to Hobsbawm "rights in the sense of wide-ranging claims to a good or a tolerable life, are not ends in themselves, but broad aspirations which can be realized only through complex and changing social strategies, on which they throw no specific light" (ibid: 310). In the struggle for the entrenchment of equality rights in Canada, feminists' organisations were never required to assert a positive vision of what legal equality for women entailed. What they did was respond to an agenda set by the federal government, defining their goals in terms of the shortcomings of the government's proposals. In the words of a prominent participant in the entrenchment struggle

> [w]omen's involvement in Canadian constitution making ... arose logically out of the women's movement's historic tendency to work on short-term, specific reformist goals, not necessarily tested against their long-term impact and not necessarily rising out of any widely held structural understanding of the nature of oppression (Billings, 1983: 13).

Thus, feminist organisations which may have adopted profoundly different analyses of the causes of women's oppression and, consequently, incommensurable visions of what substantive equality rights for women entails were never required to confront their differences.

This essential indeterminacy regarding the concrete social policies entailed by constitutional equality rights for women is made even clearer by the fact that almost immediately following the entrenchment of the *Charter* "organizations started sprouting up vowing to use the Charter to oppose laws giving advantages to women" (Mandel, 1989: 258). Various anti-feminist groups have employed the *Charter* as a political symbol to mobilise opposition to affirmative action for women, to win fathers a say in abortion, to protect the rights of the foetus, and to secure more rights for those accused of sexual assault. This suggests that to the extent that the *Charter* can be used as a symbol for political mobilisation by feminists, it can also be used by groups and organisations which are directly opposed to a feminist political agenda. There is nothing in the *Charter*, or rights rhetoric in general, which precludes its use as a political symbol by a wide variety of groups which seek to attack state intervention designed to meliorate hardships imposed by market ordering or socially embedded racist or sexist attitudes. Any positive evaluation of abstract legal rights which rests on the ability of feminist and other social movements to exploit abstract rights as political symbols must account for the fact that these same symbols can be exploited by groups with opposing political agendas.

Consequently, it is not possible to evaluate the impact of the entrenchment of equality rights in the *Charter* solely in terms of the mobilising effect it has played. However, there are other criteria which can be used to evaluate the impact of the *Charter*. The ultimate goal of the feminist struggle was to provide institutional recognition of women's equality claims and to provide women with a legal remedy if their equality claims were not respected. It is obvious, however, that the actual enjoyment of equality of rights is clearly not part of a self-implementing process. Initially, feminists relied upon the federal and provincial legislatures to remedy statutory or other governmental violations of women's constitutional equality rights. The *Charter* provided a three year moratorium on the operation of the equality rights in order to give both levels of government ample time to conduct audits of statutory instruments for possible equality rights violations and to bring forth amending legislation. However, the various governments' legislative reviews focused almost exclusively on issues of formal equality and, consequently, have identified and remedied only the most overtly discriminatory aspects of legislation (Eberts, 1985; Shofrel, 1985). This narrow focus can be linked to the methodology of the audits which ignored those aspects of women's oppression which are not found in the express statutory wording, but that which, rather, are perpetuated by laws which have an indirect and disproportionate impact on women (Gotell, 1989).

Because of the government's failure to use proactive means to remedy legislation which has contributed to the systematic discrimination of women, many feminist lawyers and activists turned to the courts. They recognised, however, that it was necessary to develop a litigation strategy if the case-by-case articulation of equality rights was to benefit women. In April 1985 the Women's Legal Action and Education Fund (LEAF) was formed to assist women with important test cases and to ensure that equality rights litigation is undertaken in a planned, responsible and expert manner (Women's Legal Education and Action Fund, 1987; Atcheson *et al.*, 1984).

Thus, the most publicised battle for substantive equality rights for women in Canada is now being fought in the courts. But the terrain of the courtroom and the weapon of *Charter* litigation is not the exclusive possession of feminist organisations. Possibly because of the fact that of the few remaining explicit uses of gender-based classification in the statute books most benefit women, men have brought a great many of the equality challenges. Moreover, men are also arguing that other rights guaranteed in the *Charter*, such as the rights to natural justice, to the freedom of association, and to a full and fair hearing, ought to take precedence over women's equality rights in the event of a conflict. Men have used the *Charter* to challenge welfare legislation providing benefits to sole support mothers, child support provisions, the procedures regulating the adoption of children born to single women, and sexual assault provisions in the *Criminal Code* (Fudge, 1987). And an astonishing number of the challenges brought by men have been successful; male complainants are making and *winning* ten times as many equality claims as women (Lahey, 1987).

Can these results be explained in terms of the peculiarities of the lower court decisions? Perhaps. Or are they reducible to the peculiarities of the Canadian political and/or legal contexts? Again, this is a possible explanation of such seemingly perverse results. However, I want to suggest that the impact of entrenching general and abstract rights in a constitutional document must be evaluated not only in terms of its potential mobilising effect and the actual results of litigation, but also with reference to the form of *political discourse* constitutional litigation generates (Glasbeek & Mandel, 1984; Mandel, 1989). Moreover, this form of political discourse is not confined to the courts, but has imperialistic tendencies which both requires and enables it to invade other political institutions. Only once the hegemonic capacity of abstract legal discourse is recognised is it possible to evaluate whether the entrenchment of abstract and general legal rights will facilitate or impede the struggle to transform oppressive social and legal relations.

The Charter and Legislation Designed to Protect Women and Children from Sexual Violence or Victimisation

Many feminists have long regarded the criminal regulation of sexual activity, and rape in particular, as a symbol of the state's collusion in male control of female sexuality [1] (Brownmiller, 1975; Clark & Lewis, 1977; MacKinnon, 1983). Since the 1970s feminists in Canada have engaged in a process of law reform which culminated in 1983 with the passage of amending legislation which was based upon the coincident, but not completely congruent, interests of feminists and law enforcement agencies (Snider, 1985). The amendments abolished rape and substituted gender neutral sexual assault provisions, eased the evidentiary requirements for convictions on sexual assault, narrowed the opportunities for the defence to question a victim on her past sexual conduct and placed restrictions on the publication of a victim's name (Statutes of Canada, 1980–81–82–83, c.125). In addition, maximum penalties were increased and several defences for sexual misconduct with young adults from 14 to 16 years old were dropped. With the advent of the *Charter*, however, male defendants have sought to invoke their constitutional rights to invalidate aspects of the sexual assault legislation which both predated and antedated the 1983 reforms. This, in turn, has provoked another round of legislative reforms and more are likely to result from the continuing flurry of constitutional litigation attacking aspects of the sexual assault legislation. This has led many feminists to denounce what they perceive to be the use of the *Charter* by men to enhance men's rights at the expense of women's sexual autonomy (Lahey, 1987; Women's Legal Education and Action Fund, 1987).

Paradoxically, some of the first equality cases to be argued before the courts consisted of attempts by male defendants to invoke the guarantees of sex equality contained in section 15 of the *Charter*. They sought to invalidate provisions in the *Criminal Code* which were designed to protect young women from sexual victimisation by older men. The greatest number of such cases involved challenges to two sections of the *Criminal Code*; section 146, which provided that every male person who has intercourse with a female person who is under the age of fourteen years and who is not his wife is guilty of an offence, and section 153, which provided that every male person who had illicit sexual intercourse with his stepdaughter, foster daughter or female ward was guilty of an offence. Lower courts have been unanimous in accepting the argument that section 153 infringes the guarantee of formal legal equality provided by section 15 of the *Charter* and have invalidated section 153 [2]. By contrast, the sex equality challenges to section 146, known as the statutory rape provision, have met with mixed results. Primarily this is because different courts have provided competing characterisations of the provision. Those courts which have characterised section 146 as designed to prevent the sexual victimisation of young children have invalidated the provision on the grounds that it does not protect young male children [3]. This has led to the absurd result of revoking the legislative protection afforded to young women on the grounds that similar protection is not provided for young men. However, the majority of courts have upheld the provision, characterising section 146 as an attempt to prevent teenage pregnancies [4]. Relying upon special dangers which befall a young woman who engages in sexual intercourse, such as teenage pregnancy, the likelihood of abortion, physical and emotional harm, wantonness and prostitution, the Ontario Court of Appeal held that it was "neither unfair nor irrational for Parliament to conclude that it was a much more serious offence for a male to have sexual intercourse with a female under fourteen than a female to have sexual intercourse with a male under fourteen, and to enact the specific offence in section 146(1)" (*R.* v. *Boyle* (1988), 40 C.C.C. 202).

Whilst some, but not all, feminists might applaud the fact that section 146 has withstood this constitutional challenge, most would not accept the reasons employed by the courts to validate the provision (Olsen, 1984). Where the courts were willing to uphold the legislation, they did so not for the reason that feminists urged upon them, namely, that such criminal provisions are necessary to counteract the widespread and pervasive sexual victimisation of women in our society, but rather on the paternalistic grounds that it was necessary to protect young women from their own biological capacities or on the basis of some insultingly tenuous connection between early sexual activity, wantonness and prostitution.

Equality rights have also been invoked by male defendants to challenge section 246.1 of the *Criminal Code* which provided that where an accused is charged with sexually assaulting a person under the age of 14 years, "it is not a defence that the complainant consented to the activity that forms the subject-matter of the charge unless the accused is less than three years older than the complainant." As the provision is expressed in gender neutral language, defendants have asserted that section 246.1 discriminates on the basis of age, since it deprives those of them who are more than three years older than a victim who is under 14 of arguing that the activity was consensual. The courts have, however, upheld the provision, either on the basis that distinctions on the basis of age in the area of sexual activity do not constitute discrimination, or relying on the argument that such distinctions, although discriminatory, are reasonable [5].

But the equality rights guarantees are not the only grounds upon which male defendants have launched constitutional challenges to sections 146 and 246.1. The guarantee of natural justice contained in section 7 of the *Charter* has proven to be a much more potent form of challenge. Defendants have argued that these provisions create absolute liability offences in that an honest and reasonable mistake regarding the age of a young girl with whom they had sexual intercourse is irrelevant to a finding of guilt. This is, they argue, contrary to the principles of natural justice.

This argument has met with mixed results in the Canadian courts. In *R.* v. *Ferguson* [(1987), 36 C.C.C. (3d) 507] the British Columbia Court of Appeal upheld section 146 on the grounds that the infringement could be justified because young women who engaged in sexual intercourse ran unique risks and that an absolute liability offence would deter men from having sexual intercourse with women who might be younger than 14 years old. This rationale was explicitly rejected by three members of the Supreme Court of Canada in *R.* v. *Stevens* [(1988), 41 C.C.C. (3d) 193]. Whilst a four member majority of that Court refused to rule on the argument on the grounds that the application of section 7 of the *Charter* to the particular case would give it retrospective effect, three members of the Court addressed the constitutionality of section 146. Writing on behalf of these dissentients, Wilson J., a woman, opined that section 146 violated the principles of natural justice which require, at a minimum, that a due diligence defence is available to accused. Refusing to accept the rationale adopted by the British Columbia Court of Appeal in *Ferguson*, Wilson J. was adamant that a *mens rea* component was an essential element of a criminal offence and that the failure to provide a mistake of fact defence with respect to a central element of the offence was a violation of an accused's right to natural justice.

The dissenting decision of the Supreme Court of Canada in *Stevens* has been adopted by subsequent courts which have been called upon to decide the constitutionality of section 146 [6]. This is not surprising given the common law courts' unwillingness to impose criminal liability in the absence of the requisite *mens rea* on the part of the accused. In *R.* v. *Roche* [(1985), 46 C.R. (3d) 160] the Ontario Court of Appeal held that section 246.1 had to be construed to accord with the fundamental principles of penal liability and fundamental principles of section 7 of the *Charter*. Thus, the accused was entitled to rely on the common law defence of an honest belief in the existence of facts which, if true, would make the act innocent. The implication of allowing the accused to raise a mistake of fact defence regarding the 'victim's' [7] age is that the accused's belief as to whether or not the victim consented was crucial to a finding of guilt.

These constitutional arguments have spilled over into the legislative forum. The federal government introduced a series of amendments to the *Criminal Code* which were specifically designed to bring the impugned provisions in line with the *Charter*. The federal government proposed to abolish all of the existing gender specific sexual offences such as section 146 and section 153 and replace them with gender neutral provisions which included sexual interference and were not limited to sexual intercourse. In addition, the amendments provided a due diligence defence to the accused person who had taken all reasonable steps to discover the victim's age. Thus, the issue of consent would be relevant, albeit indirectly, in cases where the young person was under 14 years old.

Throughout the Parliamentary committee's discussion of the proposed amendments, the Minister of Justice repeatedly asserted that although the government preferred an absolute liability offence for a person engaging in sexual activity with a young person under the age of 14, the government did "not want to offend any provision of the Charter" (Canada, 1986–87, 1:40). The introduction of a mistake of fact defence with respect to the 'victim's' age was strongly supported by various lawyers' groups representing the criminal defence bar. However, these groups argued that a due diligence defence would offend the *Charter* and that the prosecution should be required to prove that the defendant knew that the young person was under 14 years old (Canada, 1986–87, 7:29). Starting from the opposite position, the National Association of Women and the Law (N.A.W.L.) strongly objected to the due diligence defence on the grounds that it would ultimately "bring the inquiry down to consent" (Canada, 1986–87, 7:29). The government also proposed to narrow the disparity between the ages of the accused and the victim for determining when consent is a relevant issue so as to limit the possibility of *Charter* challenges on the basis of age discrimination. By contrast, women's groups and child protection lobbies recommended that in attempting to balance the need for protection against the desire not to criminalise consensual sexual activity between adolescents, the government should err on the side of protection. They hoped that "the wheels of prosecutorial discretion would serve to ensure" those cases involving consensual sexual activity between adolescents would not come up (Canada, 1986–87, 7:22, 7:75). But the government met each of the criticisms of its liberalising reforms with the refrain that the *Charter* required it, provoking a member of the opposition to complain:

> the more we lie back on these things because of our fears of having our legislation invalidated, the less relevant our legislation is to the needs of Canadian society. It is a new kind of conservatism, if I can put it that way, to stand back and say let us not take risks to do what we think is right for the young people of our country (Canada, 1986–87, 10:14).

In the end, the *Charter* arguments won out and legislation which was specifically designed to accommodate what the judiciary regarded as the imperatives of the constitution was proclaimed (Statutes of Canada, 1987, c.24). The principle of gender neutrality in the drafting of sexual assault legislation was affirmed, despite the fact that since the 1983 reforms many feminists had reconsidered the political value associated with abolishing gender specific offences such as rape and providing gender neutral offences such as sexual assault. There is a growing apprehension amongst feminists that gender neutrality serves to obfuscate the gendered relations of social power that are manifested in sexual assault (Cohen & Backhouse, 1980; Chase, 1983–84). The *Charter*'s guarantee of sex equality appears to have foreclosed the reintroduction of gender specificity in sexual assault offences. More importantly perhaps, the *Charter* seems to have had an impact on feminist demands themselves. In

1983 N.A.W.L. recommended that the law not be used to criminalise sexual experimentation between adolescents (Snider, 1985). However, during the last round of reforms N.A.W.L. urged the government to criminalise a broader range of consensual sexual experimentation between adolescents. N.A.W.L.'s reliance on prosecutorial discretion as the method of preventing abuse is somewhat astonishing, given the fact that feminists have long complained that the criminal process is riven with judicial and prosecutorial discretion which is biased against women (Boyle, 1984; Minch & Linden, 1984; Clark & Lewis, 1977). Essentially what distinguished this round of reforms from that of 1983 was the fact that the federal government was able to respond to feminist demands by absolving itself of responsibility and pointing to the *Charter*. Thus, another paradox of the *Charter* emerges; in the area of sexual assault legislation, feminists may no longer be able to call upon the legislature to constrain the courts, whilst the legislature may be able to rely upon the courts to absolve itself of political responsibility.

This is particularly troubling in light of the fact that in the 1970s Canadian feminists turned to the legislatures precisely because the courts were not responsive to their concerns about the way in which victims of rape and sexual assault were being treated within the criminal justice process. Central elements of the 1983 reforms were directed to lessening the ordeal experienced by victims of sexual assault who chose to come forth to testify [8]. According to the federal government, such restrictions would not only protect the victim's privacy, they would facilitate the prosecution of sexual offenders.

The issue of whether the past sexual conduct of the victim with others than the accused is relevant in a sexual assault trial has provoked a deep split between civil libertarian criminal lawyers and feminists. The former argue that sexual assault should be treated like any other crime and that, according to the title of a recent article, "'Sparing' the Complainant 'Spoils' the Trial" (Dougherty, 1985). By contrast, feminists argue that the assumption that the past sexual conduct of the victim is relevant either to her general credibility or to the accused's belief in her consent both derives from and reinforces a social image of women which equates sexual activity with lack of integrity and licenses man's views that women say no to sexual activity when they really mean yes (Dawson, 1987–88). As such, they assert that evidence regarding the victim's past sexual conduct should not be admitted. But despite the existence of legislative prophylactics which sought to restrict questions regarding the complainant's past sexual conduct, courts invariably have continued to allow such questions (Boyle, 1984). Thus, a centre piece of of the 1983 reforms was the imposition of restrictions on the court's discretion to allow the victim to be questioned by the defence about her past sexual conduct.

The *Charter* has, however, changed this. To date, only one court has decided not to tamper with the legislative restrictions on the grounds that the probative value of the evidence of the victim's past sexual conduct does not outweigh its prejudice to the victim [*R.* v. *Bird* [*Man.*] (1984), 40 C.R. (3d) 41 (Man.

Q.B.)]. And whilst the majority of the courts have found that prohibiting the use of sexual reputation evidence to undermine the victim's credibility did not violate the defendant's right to natural justice, virtually all of them have decided that such evidence is relevant to the question of the defendant's belief about the victim's consent and that the legislative prohibition against admitting such evidence violated the *Charter* [9]. Thus, evidence of the victim's past sexual conduct is considered to be relevant by the judiciary to the extent that it is probative of the accused's belief that the victim consented. But judicial disagreement has arisen over the issue of the appropriate remedy. Upholding the 'rape shield' provisions in general, the Ontario Court of Appeal stated that there may well be exceptions wherein the court ought to exercise its residual discretion to allow cross-examination [*Re Seaboyer and the Queen* (1987), 37 C.C.C. (3d) 53)]. The Alberta Court of Appeal has, however, specifically disagreed with the reasoning of the Ontario Court of Appeal in this respect, stating that the entire provision should be struck down as a constitutional exemption does not guarantee the defendant's right to natural justice (*R.* v. *Wald*, [1989] A.J. No. 140). Despite the fact that *Seaboyer* has been touted as a partial victory by feminists, the result of the decision is to encourage attempts to fashion exceptions which will invite the courts to exercise their discretion favourably, so as to help the accused and embarrass the victim. The ease with which this may be done is suggested by the Ontario Court's hackneyed, but predictable, suggestion of what might be the exception. They referred to the complainant who is a prostitute and the importance of the past sexual conduct of the complainant known to the accused to a just determination of a case [*Seaboyer* (1987) at 305]. Ultimately, this issue will be decided by the Supreme Court of Canada, where feminist organisations have already successfully sought leave to intervene in the appeal from the Ontario decision [10]. And, despite the possibility that the damage will be controlled, it is unlikely that the judiciary will give up its jealously guarded discretion to admit evidence which it has always believed to be probative.

The second type of protection offered to victims of sexual assault is the provision enabling them to request a mandatory court order which prohibits the publication of material which will lead to the disclosure of the victim's identity. In *Canadian Newspapers Co. Ltd.* v. *A.G. of Canada* ([1987] 2 S.C.R. 122) the appellant, a newspaper publisher, attempted to argue that the blanket prohibition against publishing the name of complainants in sexual assault cases constituted a *prima facie* violation of the *Charter*'s guarantee of freedom of expression. Whilst acknowledging that the mandatory ban constituted a *prima facie* violation of the freedom of expression, a unanimous Supreme Court of Canada went on to assert that the interests protected by the ban (the complainant's willingness to come forward) overrode the minimal restriction imposed on the media's freedom of expression. But the Court was careful to emphasise that the case involved an application made by a *newspaper* on the basis of freedom of expression, and not by an *accused*. The decision "side-stepped and expressly left open the question of what the result would be if an accused person's interest in a 'fair trial' were in the balance. In such cases the general tendency of the Supreme Court of Canada, too, is to rely heavily on judicial discretion to reconcile conflicting interests" (Mandel, 1989: 262).

Cases such as *Seaboyer* and *Canadian Newspapers* have increasingly demanded the attention and resources of groups like L.E.A.F. which were originally formed to use the *Charter* to further feminist struggles for equality. As a result of the *Charter*, feminist organisations are having to spend precious time, energy and money in the courts defending legislation that it took many women many years to achieve. Perhaps this is the ultimate paradox of the *Charter*: whilst feminists organisations are attempting to develop situated and contextual theories of equality which will address women's social and historical subordination, simultaneously innumerable other litigants, including defendants charged with sexual assault offences and right-to-life organisations, are invoking the *Charter* to claim a formal equality which may well erode victories which feminists believed they had already won.

Feminists have been heartened by a recent decision of the Supreme Court of Canada which appears to preclude the use of the equality rights guaranteed by the *Charter* to strike down legislation, including the *Criminal Code* sexual assault offences, designed specifically to protect or benefit women. In *Andrews* v. *Law Society of British Columbia* [[1989] S.C.R. 143], the Supreme Court of Canada seems to have accepted LEAF's argument that the equality rights guaranteed by section 15 of the *Charter* should not be read formalistically so as to protect only "similarly-situated" groups, but rather should be given a remedial interpretation so as to protect those groups which have historically suffered disadvantage. This interpretation would appear to eliminate claims to equality brought by male defendants accused of sexual assault. However, this decision has come too late for those arguing for the sexual specificity of sexual offences, since, as we have seen, the last vestiges of sexual specificity were amended in response to the first round of successful challenges.

It is possible, however, that this interpretation of the equality rights provision could be used to justify legislation such as the 'rape shield' provisions which would otherwise infringe other constitutional protections. LEAF has argued, for instance, that since by far the majority of victims of sexual assault are women, rape shield legislation is necessary if women are to participate in society on an equal basis with men. Because the law does not protect the privacy of sexual assault victims, women do not complain to the police and sexual offenders are not prosecuted or punished, with the result that women are intimidated from participating in public life. According to this analysis, women's equality rights under the *Charter* should trump male defendants' rights to natural justice and a fair trial (LEAF Factum in *Canadian Newspapers Co.* v. *A.G. Canada, October, 1987*). Of course, it would be up to the judiciary to weigh these competing constitutional rights.

But there is something very peculiar about this argument. Instead of directly confronting the issue of how best to balance the competing social interests and policies, as the federal government did during the 1983 amendments to the sexual assault provisions of the *Criminal Code*, the argument is cast in the form of competing constitutional rights. In effect, when a defendant raises the issue that the impugned provision violates his constitutional rights, he is asking the court to substitute its judgment for that of the legislature. Ignoring for the moment the actual outcome of the court's decision, it is important to attend to the form of the argument. It is essentially dishonest. What the *Charter* does is detach form from substance (Mandel, 1989: 310). Instead of directly addressing the question of how best to promote women's sexual autonomy under social relations which result in women's sexual subordination, feminists who invoke the *Charter* must couch their arguments in terms of the rhetoric of equality rights. Whilst it is true that social conditions will figure in their argument, they will figure only indirectly and to the extent that it is necessary to establish the rights claim. In this way the feminist discourse about power is translated into a discourse of rights. Moreover, the legislature need no longer provide a respite from the abstraction and detachment of the courts, for, as we have seen, inconvenient discussions of competing social analyses, visions and interests can now be swept away by invoking the *Charter*.

But the effect of the *Charter* on the political debate surrounding sexual assault extends beyond its detachment and dishonesty. By reconstituting the political discourse in terms of rights, the *Charter* has polarised and narrowed the debate without challenging prevailing practices. The focus is on how the state ought to respond to coercive sexual practices and the sexual victimisation of women and children. Although this emphasis predates the entrenchment of the *Charter*, the *Charter* reinforces it since its scope is limited to government action, thereby hardening the ideological separation between the "public" political sphere and the "private" economic and social spheres of life (Gotell, 1989; Fudge, 1987). And even though the equality rights guarantees of the *Charter* are available for use when incidents of discrimination are alleged by people who can show that they are victims of systemic discrimination because the world of private ordering has made them so, their equality claim only arises where a govenmental law perpetuates this (Glasbeek, 1989). Thus, feminists are drawn increasingly into the state's agenda, working hand in hand with the state to implement their commitment to women (Findlay, 1988).

Working with the state is not, *per se*, a criticism of the effect of the *Charter* on political discourse. Rather, the problem arises when both an unproblematic understanding of the state is employed and the focus on the state leads to an obfuscation of the social relations of power which constitute the problem of coercive sexuality. The problem with the *Charter* is that it tends both to select and reinforce exactly these kinds of political discourses.

The dominant feminist demands around the problem of sexual violence have tended to link up both with the state's agenda of increasing its control over all aspects of sexual practices and sexuality (Snider, 1985; Lowman *et al.*,

1986), as well as the new right's agenda to criminalise an ever increasing ambit of sexuality which falls outside that condoned by traditional family values (Eisenstein, 1984; Petchesky, 1984: 241–285). This coincidence between such antagonists is not fortuitous. It emerges from a shared understanding of the nature of the state and sexuality. The assumptions shared by feminists on the one hand and new right activists on the other are that the state's role is exclusively instrumental and that sexuality must be controlled. Where these two groups disagree is over the aspects of sexuality and sexual practices which the state ought to control. And even civil libertarians, typically associated with the criminal defence bar, accept the assumption that the role of the state is almost exclusively instrumental. Where civil libertarians part company with feminists and the new right is that they seek to minimise the scope of the state's instrumental control of sexuality and sexual practices.

Charter litigation is premised on an assumption of the instrumental nature of the state. And it is this view of the state which informs both liberal and radical feminist demands, as well as conventional liberal and libertarian analysis (Vega, 1988). Each interest group seeks to influence the state, which is seen as comprising the legislature, bureaucracy and executive, by the assertion of right in the autonomous arena of the courts. Thus, not only are the courts seen as separate from the state, but successful rights claims are seen as unproblematically self-executing, rather than as typically dependant on further state action for their implementation (Petter, 1988; Hasson, 1988).

In addition, *Charter* litigation also tends to reinforce the prevailing discourse about sexuality. Instead of challenging how we traditionally think about consent, the cases illustrate that both feminists and civil libertarians who have invoked the *Charter* have accepted that the discourse on sexuality is lodged between the opposing poles of consent and coercion. Whilst liberal feminists merely reassert the consent/coercion dichotomy, radical feminists collapse it by denying the possibility of consent under conditions of sexual subordination (Vega, 1988). Civil libertarians, by contrast, have merely attempted to redraw the dichotomy in terms of the defendant's belief in consent and evidence of physical coercion. Thus, none of the participants in *Charter* litigation have sought to transform the discourse itself. Consequently, the shifting boundaries of coercion have been ignored (Coward, 1987).

By resorting to the *Charter*, feminists have focused on the law, particularly legislatively created law, as the source of the problem of sexual violence, with the result that the social construction of sexuality and the social relations of power in which sexual practices take place fade into the background. Sexual practices occur within socially constructed power relations which are in a constant process of redefinition, challenge, retrenchment and struggle (Vega, 1988). *Charter* litigation, which takes place within an adversarial setting with peculiar forms of style, proof and address, lends itself to a reductionist analysis which is not sensitive to the modulations of history or the contradictions embedded in social relations (Scott, 1988). Such a reductionist analysis of sexual violence is particularly dangerous, not only on account of the strange alliances it promotes (Weir & Casey, 1984; Eisenstein, 1984: 246–254; Segal, 1987: 70–116), but also because it reinforces, rather than tackles, the ideology of male sexual needs.

Conclusion

This paper has attempted to show that rights are not inherently progressive, but rather depend upon the politics informing them. The struggle for the entrenchment of equality rights in the Canadian constitution mobilised women's groups in opposition to the state's agenda, but it did not provide a substantive vision of the social relations and policies that such rights entailed. Instead, feminists were forced to articulate their substantive demands through litigation, often in response to challenges invoked by defendants seeking to undermine victories feminist thought they had already won. This has had the effect of narrowing and reinforcing the prevailing discourse concerning sexual violence against women and children.

In Canada, the discussion of sexual violence against women and children is predominantly located within a particular discourse which is reinforced by its articulation within a set of institutions. This discourse, as I have attempted to show, rests upon two central premises, a conception of the instrumental nature of the state and a view of sexuality organised around the coercion/consent dichotomy. The articulation of this discourse within the institution of *Charter* litigation further reinforces, even if it does not require, these premises. Thus, the courts, as the institutions of judicial review and rights interpretation and application within liberal societies, become the dominant institutions through which relations of subordination are organised and reproduced. And as the *Charter* comes to dominate political discourse it defines the universe within which political struggle occurs. The *Charter* and the discourse on sexual violence and the state it selects and reinforces exercises a hegemonic sway over other forms of politics. Thus, critics who question the possibility of a positive role for the *Charter* are characterised as having stepped outside the prevailing discourse and their cry for a different type of politics are marginalised. This could prove very costly, since social transformation depends upon the expansion of political discourse, rather than upon its legalisation.

Notes

1 Here I am referring to liberal and radical feminist analyses of male sexual violence against women since they have tended to dominate (Boyd & Sheehy, 1986: 18–22). Until fairly recently socialist feminists have been noticeably absent from the discourse concerning sexual violence. This is attributable in part, I would suggest, to the fact that operating assumptions of the prevailing discourse render it virtually impossible for them to participate.

2 *R.* v. *Howell* (1986), 26 C.R.R. 267 (Nfld. Dist. Ct.); *R.* v. *Paquette* (1988) 14 C.R.D. 350. 70–01 (B.C.S.C.).

3 *R.* v. *Lucas* (1985), 16 C.R.R. 1 (Ont. Dist. Ct.) rev'd on other grds (1986), 27 C.C.C. (ed) 229 (Ont. C.A.); *R.* v. *Porier* (1985) 69 N.B.R. (2d) 1 (N.B. Prov. Ct.).

4 *R.* v. *Monk* (1985), 43 Sask, L.R. 318 (Sask. Q.B.); *R.* v. *Bearhead* (1986), 27 C.C.C. (ed) 546 (Alta. Q.B.); *R.* v. *M.E.D.* (1985), 47 C.R. (3d) 382 (Ontario Prov. Ct.); *R.* v. *Boyle* (1988), 40 C.C.C. (3d) 193 (Ont. C.A.); *R.* v. *S(R)*, [1987] B.C.J. No. 1255 (B.C. Co. Ct.); *R.* v. *Drybones* (1985), 23 C.C.C. (3d) 457 (N.W.T.S.C.).

5 The Canadian *Charter of Rights and Freedoms* involves a two stage process for those seeking to impugn legislation. First, the party seeking to rely on the *Charter* must demonstrate that a protected right has been infringed. Second, the party seeking to uphold the legislation, typically the Crown, must demonstrate that the infringement constitutes a reasonable limitation that is demonstrably justified in a free and democratic society.
R. v. *Ladouceur* (1988), 14 C.R.D. 350. 10–02 (Ont. Prov. Ct); *R.* v. *LeGallant* (1985), 18 C.R.R. 362 (B.C.C.A.); *R.* v. *Halleran* (1987), 39 C.C.C. (3d) 177 (Nfld. C.A.).

6 *R.* v. *Perkins* [1987] N.W.T.J. No. 82 (N.W.T.S.C.); *R.* v. *Brooks*, [1989] A.J. No. 2, Appeal No. 8703–1035–A (Alta. C.A.).

7 I have sued the term 'victim' because of the limited options available. 'First witness' or 'complainant' does not suggest how both feminist and liberal discourse characterise the victim of a sexual offence.

8 The 1983 amendments limited the circumstances under which a victim of sexual assault could be questioned about her past sexual conduct with others than the accused and prohibited the publication of information which might disclose the victim's identity.

9 *R.* v. *Coombs* (1985), 23 C.C.C. (3d) 356 (Nfld. S.C.); *R.* v. *Oquataq* (1985), 18 C.C.C. (3d) 440 (N.W.T.S.C.); *R.* v. *Brun* (1986), 28 C.C.C. (3d) 397 (N.B.Q.B.); *R.* v. *LeGallant* (1985), 47 C.R. (3d) 170 (B.C.C.A.); *R.* v. *J.W.B.* (1986) 173 A.P.R. 123 (N.S.Y.Ct.); *R.* v. *Wald* [1989] A.J. No. 140 (Alta. C.A.). *Re: Seaboyer and the Queen* (1987), 37 C.C.C. (3d) 53 (Ont. C.A.).

10 Leave to appeal to the Supreme Court of Canada was granted 16 May, 1988 and LEAF was granted intervenor status in the appeal.

References

Atcheson, M. E., Symes, B. S. & Eberts, M. (1984) *Women and Legal Action: Precedents, Resources and Strategies for the Future.* Canadian Advisory Council on the Status of Women: Ottawa.

Billings, R. (1983) Introduction. In *The Taking of Twenty-Eight.* Women's Educational Press: Toronto, pp. 13–31.

Boyd, S. & Sheehy, E. (1986) Feminist Perspectives on Law: Canadian Theory and Practice. *Canadian Journal of Women and Law* **2**, 1–52.

Boyle, C. (1984) *Sexual Assault.* Carswell: Toronto.

Brock, D. & Kinsman, S. (1986) Patriarchal Relations Ignored: An Analysis and Critique of the Badgley Report on Sexual Offenses Against Children and Youths. In *Regulating Sex: An Anthology of Commentaries on the Findings and Recommendations of the*

Badgley and Fraser Reports (Lowman, J., Jackson, M. T., Polys, T. S. & Gavigan, S., Eds) School of Criminology, Simon Fraser University: Burnaby, B.C. pp. 107–125.

Brownmiller, S. (1975) *Against Our Will: Men, Women and Rape.* Penguin: New York.

Burstyn, V. (1985) Political Precedents and Moral Crusades: Women, Sex and the State. In *Women Against Censorship.* Douglas McIntyre: Vancouver, pp. 4–31.

Canada (1986–87) *Minutes of Proceeding and Evidence of the Legislative Committee in Bill C 15, Criminal Code and Canada Evidence Act (amdt.)* Ottawa: House of Commons, 33rd Part., 2nd Sess. Issues 1–12.

Chase, G. (1983–84) An Analysis of the New Sexual Assault Laws. *Canadian Woman Studies* **4**, 53.

Clark, L. S. & Lewis, D. (1977) *Rape: The Price of Coercive Sexuality.* The Women's Press: Toronto.

Cohen, L. S. & Backhouse, C. (1980) Desexualizing Rape: Dissenting View on the Proposed Rape Amendments. *Canadian Woman Studies* **2**, 99.

Coward, R. (1982) Sexual Violence and Sexuality. In *Sexuality: A Reader* (Feminist Review, Ed.) Virago: London, 1987, pp. 307–325.

Dawson, T. (1987–88) Sexual Assault Law and Past Sexual Conduct of the Primary Witness: The Construction of Relevance. *Canadian Journal of Women and the Law* **2**, 310–334.

Dougherty, D. (1985) "Sparing" the Complainant "spoils" the Trial. 40 *Criminal Reports* (3d) 55–67.

Eberts, M. (1985) Sex-based Discrimination and the Charter. In *Equality Rights and the Canadian Charter of Rights and Freedoms.* (Bayefsky, A. & Eberts, M. Eds) Carswell: Toronto, pp. 183–229.

Eisenstein, Z. (1984) *Feminism and Sexual Equality.* Monthly Review Press: New York.

Findlay, S. (1988) Feminist Struggles with the Canadian State: 1966–1988. *Resources for Feminist Research* **17**, 5.

Fudge, J. (1987) The Public/Private Distinction: The Possibilities of and the Limits to the Use of Charter Litigation to Further Feminist Struggles. *Osgoode Hall Law Journal* **25**, 485–554.

Glasbeek, H. & Mandel, M. (1984) The Legalization of Politics in Advanced Capitalism. *Socialist Studies* **2**, 84.

Glasbeek, H. (1980) A No-Frills Look at the Charter of Rights and Freedoms or How Politicians and Lawyers Hide Reality. *University of Ottawa Law Review*, forthcoming.

Gotell, L. (1989) The Canadian Women's Movement, Equality Rights and the Charter. *Canadian Research Institute for the Advancement of Women.* Ottawa.

Hasson, R. A. (1988) The Charter and Social Legislation. Presented at the Conference on the Canadian Charter or Rights and Freedoms, Edinburgh, May 20–21, 1988.

Hobsbawm, E. (1984) *Workers: Worlds of Labor.* Pantheon: New York.

Hosek, C. (1983) Women and the Constitutional Process. In *And No One Cheered* (Banting, K. S. & Simeon, R., Eds). Methuen: Toronto, p. 280.

Kome, P. (1983) *The Taking of Twenty-Eight.* Women's Educational Press: Toronto.

Lahey, K. (1987) Feminist Theories of Inequality. In *Equality and Judicial Review* (Martin, S. & Mahoney, K., Eds). Carswell: Toronto, pp. 71–85.

Lowman, J., Jackson, M. A., Palys, T. S. & Gavigan, S. (1986) *Regulating Sex: An Anthology of Commentaries on the Findings and Recommendations of the Badgley and Fraser Reports.* School of Criminology, Simon Fraser University: Burnaby, B.C.

MacKinnon, C. (1983) Feminism, Marxism, Method and the State: Toward Feminist Jurisprudence. *Signs* **8**, 634–658.
Mandel, M. (1989) *The Charter of Rights and the Legalization of Politics in Canada.* Wall and Thompson: Toronto.
Minch, C. S. & Linden, R. (1987) Attrition and the Processing of Rape Cases. *Canadian Journal of Criminology* **29**, 389–404.
Olsen, F. (1984) Statutory Rape: A Feminist Critique of Rights Analysis. *Texas Law Review* **63**, 387–432.
Petchesky, R. (1984) *Abortion and Woman's Choice.* Longman: New York.
Petter, A. (1988) *Backwards March: The Political Wrongs of the Charter of Rights.* Presented at the Conference on the Canadian Charter of Rights and Freedoms, Edinburgh, May 20–21, 1988.
Schneider, E. (1986) The Dialectic of Rights and Politics: Perspectives from the Women's Movement. *New York University Law Review* **61**, 589–652.
Scott, J. (1988) Deconstructing Equality – Versus – Difference: Or, the Uses of Post-structuralist Theory for Feminism. *Feminist Studies* **14**, 33–48.
Segal, L. (1987) *Is the Future Female: Troubled Thoughts on Contemporary Feminism.* Virago: London.
Shofrel, S. (1985) Equality Rights and Law Reform in Saskatoon. *Canadian Journal of Women and the Law* **1**, 108.
Snider, L. (1985) Legal Reform and Social Control: The Dangers of Abolishing Rape. *International Journal of the Sociology of Law* **13**, 337–356.
Vega, J. (1988) Coercion and Consent—Classical Liberal Concepts in Texts on Sexual Violence. *International Journal of the Sociology of Law* **16**, 75–89.
Weir, L. S. & Casey, L. (1984) Subverting Power in Sexuality. *Socialist Review* **139**, 157.
Women's Legal Education and Action Fund (1987) *Litigation Works: A Report on LEAF Litigation Year Two.* Carswell: Agincourt.

Statutes Cited

An Act to Amend the Criminal Code and the Canadian Evidence Act, S.C. 1987, C.24.
Canadian Charter of Rights and Freedoms, Pt. 1 of the *Constitution Act, 1982* being Schedule B of the *Canada Act 1982* (U.K.), 19872. C-11.
Canadian Bill of Rights, S.C. 1960, c. 44 reprinted in R.S.C. 1970, App. III.
Criminal Law Amendment Act, S.C. 1980-801-82-83 C.125.
Criminal Code, R.S.C. 1970, C-34.
Indian Act, R.S.C. 1970, I-6.
Unemployment Insurance Act, 1971, R.S.C. 1971, c. 48.

Date accepted: June 1989

[26]

Gender in the Post-Socialist Transition

The Abortion Debate in Hungary

Susan Gal

INTRODUCTION[1]

The fall of communism in Eastern Europe has had profoundly gendered effects. Women's experiences of the economic and political changes have been different from those of men; the implications for women's lives are often more damaging. Equally important, in all the countries of Eastern Europe, questions of procreation and reproduction became, for a time, the focus of intense public debate and legislative action. In Hungary, as in many countries of the region, the lenient regulations of the late communist era that assured easy access to abortion were challenged after 1989, at the highest parliamentary levels.

It is important to ask why questions of abortion gained such attention, especially since, in contrast to other social problems of the post-socialist period such as inflation, ethnic tension, rising unemployment, and loss of state-supported social services, abortion regulations were not a source of popular discontent.[2] I argue that the insistent debates about abortion reveal the ways in which politics has been (re)constituted in Eastern Europe. Reproduction, as an issue, allowed "morality" and "nature" to be invoked to justify the power of groups and factions newly vying for control of the political process.

This suggests that, in order to understand the direction of social change in Eastern Europe since the end of communism, it is not enough to examine the aspects of social life that mainstream social science has identified as crucial: privatization, marketization, democratization, the growth of civil society, and new forms of the state. We must also consider the discourses and practices of gender. These affect not only interpersonal matters, but also the political economy of large-scale social transformations.[3] For example, the practices of procreation and reproduction have far-reaching effects on such matters as the population's size and age composition, as well as various parameters of the labor force. Yet my aim here is not to analyze such practices in themselves, but rather to explicate the public *discourse* about reproduction that accompanied the end of communism.

Susan Gal is Professor of Anthropology at the University of Chicago. She writes about the language of politics and politics of language, especially as these intersect with gender categories and everyday practices. She is currently co-organizer (with Gail Kligman) in a comparative analysis of gender discourses, women's strategies, and economic change across post-socialist Eastern Europe.

A focus on discourse is important for two reasons. First, in discussing Eastern Europe there is a tendency to assume that American and Western European observers already understand the terms in which people frame their concerns. The words themselves appear familiar because, like "human rights," or "free press," "abortion" is an active term in American public debates, about which Eastern Europeans are well informed. They need to be, because they must often orient to the transnational legal institutions of the European Community, the global financial and moral linkages of the IMF and the Catholic Church. Moreover, Eastern European political arguments have also been borrowed into American and Western European debates.

Yet, despite some deceptive parallels, "abortion" in Hungary is embedded in a different field of meanings than its cognates elsewhere in the world. If we view the debate about abortion in Hungary as part of a politics of reproduction, potentially comparable to similar processes in other parts of the globe, then it is important to specify exactly how it was differently encoded, differently linked to other political questions. For example, we should be able to differentiate it from American debates about abortion in the late nineteenth century that were part of arguments for racial supremacy and medical hegemony (Mohr 1978, Petchesky 1984); from Western European conceptions about reproduction as part of the welfare state's responsibility toward women and children (Glendon 1987); or from arguments about abortion that pitted women's privacy, pleasure, and autonomy against society's moral revitalization in twentieth-century America (Luker 1984, Ginsberg 1989). Thus, it is not that politicization of reproduction is peculiar to any region, or to the present transformations in Eastern Europe, but rather that the nature of that politicization reveals much about the polity in which it occurs.

Second, a focus on discourse and the debates around abortion allows us to turn this link between politics and reproduction around, and ask not how politics influences ideas about reproduction, but rather how the issue of reproduction constitutes one of the means by which claims for political power are made, and through which they are widely understood as natural and legitimate. Thus, in the present case, the abortion debate turns out not only to be very much about abortion, but also an argument in absentia with communism and a scramble for newly available forms of symbolic capital. Indeed, it is a contest for control of the emerging principles of political rule. It allows us to see the many ironies evident in the attempt to make a new social order against a previous one whose elements are nevertheless the only building materials at hand.

Because it makes politics, the abortion debate was an integral part of the restratification of Hungarian society in the wake of communism. In contrast to the arena of privatization, which allowed the reproduction of old elites based on existing expertise, social networks, social positions, and the consequent access to information and capital, the abortion debate was linked most closely to the political sphere where new elites were forming at the same time as they constructed the cultural grounds to produce, justify, and legitimate their own mobility.[4]

After a brief sketch of reproductive politics in socialist Hungary, I discuss two strands of argument in the two years of controversy leading up to the 1992 parliamentary vote. The first strand came from the populist writers and their allies, including Christian professionals, as well as the centrist and conservative political parties who were part of Hungary's first, post-1989, coalition government (1990–1994). The second was produced by writers, academics, and journalists aligned with the parties who claimed the label "liberal," and who constituted the parliamentary opposition during those years. In discussing these debates, I draw on approaches to textuality that have been emerging in contemporary linguistic anthropology (e.g., Briggs and Bauman 1992, Gal 1991), briefly indicating some of the defining characteristics of public pronouncements within each position, and how such texts engage each other.

Notes on the Politics of Reproduction under Socialism

Disputes about abortion and the related issues of childcare, welfare, and motherhood emerged repeatedly in Hungarian politics during the state socialist period. Although discussed under the rubric of "socialist planning," "population," or "health," they were often linked to industrial and foreign policy as well. These political precedents, and the institutional and personal memories produced through these policies, formed the material out of which new traditions could be built, and constrained what was seen as possible and desirable in the 1990–92 debate.

Official abortion regulations following the Second World War required the consent of two physicians whose professional judgments about the health risks to the mother formed the basis of the decision. These regulations had emerged through a process of medical professionalization and heated political debate during the 1930s.[5] But with the consolidation of Communist rule in 1949, abortion ceased to be a matter of medical judgment and became instead the object of centrally determined social planning. Policies concerning it were important enough to be personally made and signed by a whole series of Communist Party first secretaries. I focus here not so much on the details of these regulations but on how they were justified. Three quite separate phases of abortion regulation can be discerned, roughly corresponding to the waxing and waning of more general reformist strategies within the Party.

The first, between 1949 and 1954, was an extremely restrictive ban that criminalized abortion, putting in place a strident anti-abortion information campaign and a series of reporting practices that in effect put the adult population under surveillance. Not coincidentally, this followed closely the Soviet policy of the period. The 1953 abortion regulation refused the possibility of abortion even on medical grounds. The emphasis in official announcements was on the military and production needs of Hungary and the responsibility of every person to subordinate personal choice to the overriding interests of the socialist state. The death of Stalin and internal changes in Hungarian leadership ended this restrictive period, so that during the more general liberalizations following 1956, abortion was allowed to adult women on demand. This change was understood by the public as the retreat of the state from private life. It was widely regarded as an officially unacknowledged but important victory of the 1956 revolution. By the 1960s, an independent trend toward lower fertility along with the rise in number of abortions produced its effect: the Hungarian population, like many in Western Europe, was not replacing itself.

In response to this demographic decline, and also as part of the general political retrenchment following the reforms of 1968, a new and restrictive abortion policy was put into place in 1973–74. The regulations were publicly justified as a protection of women's health against the ravages of abortion, but no such negative effects were ever empirically demonstrated. More broadly, a media campaign reasserted the rationale of national over individual interests and attacked the "unhealthy" spirit of individualism (leading to birth control) as unacceptable in a socialist society. The 1973 policy was in force, though administered increasingly more leniently, until the late 1980s when abortion became available more-or-less on demand.

There was no popular outcry against this policy after the fall of the communist government in 1989. Rather, a small group calling itself "Defenders of the Fetus" appealed to the Supreme Court of Hungary, arguing, in the new climate of rights and rule of law, that something as important as abortion policy should at least be in the form of a law, ratified by Parliament, rather than simply a paternalistic regulation, ordered by the Central Committee. The Court ruled that because the right to life was safeguarded by the Hungarian constitution, a decision had to be made by Parliament about the circumstances under which this could be abrogated; it mandated that the legislative body make the decision by the end of 1992.

The law finally passed by Parliament was a compromise measure, judged "liberal" by much of the Hungarian and even the international press. But on close scrutiny, it shows several restrictive aspects as well. Its requirements of familial consent, waiting period, repeated visits to clinics, and raised prices put anti-abortion pressure on poor women, rural women, and women whose families disapprove of the decision. The arguments by which such a policy was made and understood, in the context of previous abortion regulation, are the center of interest here.

Populist Writers and Christian Professionals

Opposition to abortion was an integral part of the cultural understandings that organized the political opposition to communism in the 1980s in Hungary. Among the populist writers who constituted one strand of this opposition, references to abortion appeared regularly. On September 27, 1987, about 150 writers, scholars, technical workers, and others took part in a semilegal meeting held outside of Budapest that was later sanctified as the first successful large-scale public action of the many politically diverse social groups and networks that constituted the growing opposition to the government. Many of the participants have since become prominent in Hungarian government and political life. The dominant themes of the meeting were economic and civil reform. Yet, the complaints of the populists were pointedly not economic. The meeting was opened by one such writer who said: Hungarians had "become crippled in our moral attitudes, in our beliefs . . . and thus unable to be born in proper circumstances and in sufficient numbers" (Lezsák 1991: 6). To understand the conspicuous place of reproduction in this jeremiad, we must see how this writer has positioned himself with respect to earlier debates.

A distinctive feature of discussions about abortion in Hungary for over a century has been the assumption that it is a problem of declining population. And this evokes, among educated people, echoes of another worry: the imminent death of the nation. This fear was enunciated by populist writers in the 1930s who turned to investigations of the countryside in an effort to redefine national identity. Such redefinitions were made necessary by the massive and traumatic losses of land and hence population that were suffered by Hungary when the Treaty of Trianon redistributed Hungarian territories among the victors of the First World War. In several rural regions, the writers (re)discovered a tradition of population control that had been in existence since the abolition of serfdom. Well-to-do Hungarian peasants restricted reproduction to a single child, usually in order to keep the patrimony undivided and viable. This was usually accomplished through social pressure exerted by elder generations, especially women (Vásáry 1989).

For the populists this was an emotionally wrenching sociopolitical phenomenon, as threatening to the nation as the diminution of population brought about by the Treaty of Trianon. They invoked Herder's eighteenth-century prophecy that Hungarians would soon be lost among the more numerous Germans and Slavs, and tied this prediction directly to reproductive practices and the dangers of "rural matriarchy." Populist writers argued that Hungarian peasants were deliberately, selfishly, and wrong-headedly destroying themselves. Unless the populists could save them, the nation would simply die out and be forgotten by the world.[6]

The populists of 1987 evoked memories of this older debate by using similar rhetorical figures. They talked of abortion as "national catastrophe" and a "biological Trianon." They likened the "four million Hungarians" (not fetuses or babies, but Hungarians) lost through abortion to the Hungarian losses in sixteenth-century patriotic battles against the Turks. And, like the writers of the 1930s, they linked these losses to a lack of national consciousness and a lack of appropriate morality. Another speech, delivered at the same meeting in 1987, reveals some of the other ways in which opposition to abortion was constructed as part of nationalist feeling, and how a continuity with the earlier discourse—indeed, the recontextualization of that earlier discourse into the current circumstances—was accomplished:

> This is a nation that has seen harder times [even than now]. . . . We are probably the first in the world not only in suicide and mortality, not only in failure to be born . . . but also in production of emigrants. It started with the staggering losses [of Trianon], it continued after 1920 with further expulsions through which many valuable brains ended up in the service of foreigners. The high point was the departure of Béla Bartók; then came the forced emigration of 1945–48 during which a great variety of spiritual forces left the homeland in masses. This was topped only by the exodus of 1956. And in our own days there is the flood out of Transylvania. . . . So, there is a basis for our fear of death. (Csurka 1991: 24).

Note how this passage creates an apparently coherent historical fate for the nation by linking selected events in chronological order. Through a formal parallelism we are invited to understand that suicides are the same kind of social phenomenon as abortion [the failure to be born], which is in turn equivalent to territorial diminution, as well as to waves of emigration, no matter how distinct their motivation: Béla Bartók left Hungary expressly to escape impending fascism, while the 1945–1948 emigration was made up, in part, of fascists.

Furthermore, the passage is a fine example of textual invention of tradition. Its form suggests that communism is an enemy of the nation because the form implicitly equates communism, which is understood by listeners as responsible for the current rate of suicide, abortion, the emigration of 1956 and emigration from Transylvania, with those foreign enemies of Hungary who were responsible for the losses of Trianon, and 1945–1948. And indeed, with every liberalization of abortion after 1956, communist ideologues worried not only about the response of the Soviet Union and about the effect on population, but also that lenience towards abortion would incite "anti-Communist feeling" among a new generation of potentially influential populist intellectuals. They feared the party would be seen as indifferent to population decline and hence as "against the nation." Being against abortion was equated with being against the death of the nation, which became, by 1987, an important element in opposition to "alien" Communist rule.

When populist writers equated the high rate of abortion with the immorality of state socialism, their rhetoric dovetailed precisely with the religiously based arguments of conservative, Christian doctors and lawyers.[7] But these professionals emphasized not responsibilities toward the nation but the need for morality in life choices about family and money. Along with other critics in Hungary, they noted that communism socialized many functions of the bourgeois family and devalued motherhood in a misguided attempt to equalize and even homogenize the sexes. By seeking the centralization of all power, state socialism destroyed social solidarities outside the family and thus promoted an atomization of social life. This, they argued, produced a "selfish" obsession with financial success and a concomitant neglect of ethics, care, and concern for other people.

A sordid interest in money, and a "cynical materialism," were linked in such discussions to the high rate of abortion: Those who would choose not to give birth because of financial insecurity or lack of an apartment in which to raise children were labeled materialistic and unethical for putting creature comforts above responsibilities to higher ethical values, such as life, the good of humanity, or even the Hungarian nation. Just as the communist rhetoric of the 1950s and 1970s asked people (and especially women) to unselfishly produce children for the sake of industrial development in a socialist collectivity, so the populists and conservative professionals asked for renunciation of selfishness, but this time in the interests of humanity, morality, and nation.

In addition, members of the legal and medical professions charged state socialism with a disregard for expertise, specifically their own expertise in medicine, law, or medical ethics. Like the charge of immorality, the neglect of professional expertise in favor of party loyalty is a longstanding criticism of the socialist state. The doctors argued against abortion not only for the sake of the fetus but also for the sake of their own assessment of mothers' health. Regardless of what women want, they said, doctors know best. Lawyers, in keeping with their expertise, demanded the restitution of rights denied in previous regulations. The appeal to rights was also a familiar feature of anticommunist discourse. But who exactly is being deprived of rights here? Anti-abortion lawyers argued that in the abortion decision there are four interested parties: the fetus, the mother, the father, and society. Of these, the communist regulations required only the mother's voice. It is the exclusion of the fetus, the father and society that must be rectified. Lawyers were pleased to speak for all three.

In these writings women were figured as willfully ignorant: sad dupes of the communist system. Because of supposedly generous maternity leaves and favorable divorce and custody laws, women were also seen as the corrupted beneficiaries of the communist state. In much of this material an implicit equation was drawn between women allied with the former communist state, as against men who were linked to a new, law-governed, state and society.

It is striking that the abortion debate helped to form and brought into a single anti-abortion camp a number of emerging groups, as well as different strands of anticommunist argument. What linked these groups and arguments is that the anti-abortion stances were clearly tied to enhancing the groups' professional interests and presence in the social space between state and family that was legalized and expanded in the wake of socialism. Their arguments buttressed their own claims to morality and expertise, and hence for the indispensability and rightness of their leadership at the higher echelons of society. By discussing the naturalized and moralized issues of reproduction, they were proposing far more than any particular policy. They were implicitly proposing principles for judging leaders in a historical moment when the basis for such judgment was very much a matter of contention.

Liberals and the Construction of Politics

Let us turn now to writings about abortion from newspapers published by writers aligned with the liberal parties, those who were the parliamentary opposition in the years of the abortion debate. In contrast to the dramatic, even grandiose, rhetoric of the populists and the professionals warning against abortion, we find in the *Beszélö* and the *Magyar Narancs* articles filled with puns, bitter parody, or savagely funny put-downs. One article on the abortion question was titled: "Kis jogi pornográfia," literally "A little pornography about the law." This plays on the earlier title of a remarkable and much admired avant-garde novel *Kis magyar pornográfia* (A short survey of Hungarian pornography), which was itself a parody of all those titles published by the Communist presses (A short survey of art/history/literature) that pretended to educate the new socialist man with canned versions of arts and letters in Hungarian. I have selected an example of this kind of article, to provide the flavor:

> Those who argue against abortion on the grounds of church or legal principles, are not able to see past the fact of egg fertilization. They don't realize that fact is preceded by another, one which is the greatest in a person's life, the most intimate, without exaggeration the most sacred: making love. In the course of legal arguments, this sacred act is turned into a sacrilege. The bed is first the object of searchlights, then it is tossed into the street. . . . [W]hat many people object to in pornography is that it takes exactly the most inner moments and tries to put these in front of the public, thereby destroying their intimacy. A law about abortion would do just that. . . . This is no longer a woman's problem. . . . The question is not whether one should ban or allow abortion, but rather whether or not one can, or should at all, regulate such a phenomenon by legal means. (Răduly 1992: 5).

The tongue-in-cheek quality of this article is evident in the use of theological terms to discuss sex and pornography, the high moral tone combined with the outrageous suggestion that laws about abortion are a kind of pornography (the latter a growing phenomenon, by the way, on sale on the streets of Budapest, and one that the churches and nationalists are firmly against). By agreeing with the religious and legal minded that sex is sacred, this young man is able to parody those with grand moral claims.

But the frame of the playful argument is nevertheless serious: It introduces the notion of privacy on which all the arguments of liberal writers rest. However, for these writers, "the private" is not equivalent to the Western European bourgeois category of privacy, familiar since the nineteenth century. On the contrary, we must look for this writer's meaning by taking his style seriously. Through his ironic handling of otherwise serious issues, he is establishing an intertextual link to a Hungarian tradition that stands specifically opposed to that of the populist writers. The precedents these stylistic traits evoke are the left-liberal, modernist, often Jewish, cosmopolitan intellectuals of fin-de-siècle Hungary, and more recently, the anticommunist dissident intellectuals of the 1970s and 1980s. In short, he aligns himself with the self-styled "liberals," the producers of samizdat literature. These are the former theorists of "antipolitics," that strategy for surviving communism that was described by György Konrád (1984) for Hungary and Václav Havel (1988) for Czechoslovakia.

It was exactly such writers who argued in the 1980s that the private sphere, including the second economy and those few social spaces not occupied by the socialist state, were the places where dissident male intellectuals could enact antipolitics, behaving as if they lived outside the socialist state. As a substitute for an unattainable democratic politics, they envisioned the creation of a private civil society. This oxymoronic ideal entailed the celebration of the private as no longer a woman's preserve but rather a means of political action for men. Yet, theorists also looked back nostalgically to an idealized, prewar bourgeois family, arguing that under socialism women should be, but alas were not, a haven against the heartless state.[8] Although this image was not salient in writing about women and reproduction within the liberal parties during the abortion debate, neither was support for a notion of women's rights, although liberal writers were conspicuously obsessed with rights in general. Instead, as we have seen, the availability of abortion was defended on quite different grounds.

These grounds become clearer in another article (Mink 1991: 22–25), which though serious, nevertheless used the same playful allusion in its title (*Kis magyar abortusztörténet*, or A short history of Hungarian abortion), thereby making the same intertextual link to an artistic avant-garde and to political dissidence. The article is a chronological discussion of previous historical experiments restricting abortion in Europe. In establishing precedents, the author lists Stalin's Soviet Union, Hitler's Germany, Rákosi's Hungary of the 1950s, and Ceauşescu's Romania. Not coincidentally, these regimes are moments of horror in the historical imagination of most Hungarians, quite apart from their abortion policies. By making the proposed restriction of 1992 the endpoint of this sequence, the author implicitly censures such restriction, noting in passing that this restriction, like the predecessors he lists, relies, in part, on fear of increase among minority populations, especially the Hungarian Gypsies.

This too is an invention of tradition, an argument built with the same strategies of decontextualization and recontextualization as those used by the populist in my earlier example. What is most striking about the liberal article, however, is that in the end the author rejects his own form of argument and thus fundamentally refuses to agree with the populist even at the level of discursive strategies. After lining up his historical examples, he says:

> None of this, of course, touches the moral judgment of the issue. . . . The decision about that is not a historical question, but one about moral philosophy, and so it is not part of our subject matter in this article. (Mink 1991: 25)

The decision about abortion is thus a private, ethical issue, and not a question for political debate at all.

Although the liberal newspapers and politicians offered a much more lenient proposal for legalized abortion than the populist writers and the governing coalition, we see that in both cases the arguments involved considerably more than abortion alone. For the liberal writers, abortion had just as little to do with women and their rights as for the populists, and just as much to do with morality. Where they differed decisively was in their stance on the relation of morality to the state, and the implicit images of the state itself.

The arguments of the liberal parties suggested a minimal state, one that would neither construct nor assume a unity of purpose in the populace; one that would make a sharp divide between the sphere of the state and the sphere of private decision. The private, for them, would include property in the unbridled workings of the capitalist market, but included as well reproductive moral judgments deemed to be the concern only of the citizen-individuals, undistinguished by gender or ethnicity, that such a state would ideally construct as subjects.

In contrast, the populists presupposed a state built on moral consensus, one that would represent a national and ethnic unity, in which there would be little public debate because a political authority would decide what is best for the entire community. To be qualified to create and run such a state, one would have to have just the qualities the conservative professionals and populist writers claimed to be their own: Leaders would have to be ethnically one with the nation (Hungarian, and not Jew or Gypsy). And they would have to be especially sensitive on moral issues. For them, this is precisely what made the abortion issue so suitable for public debate. The moral sensitivity of conservatives could be materially demonstrated exactly by their concern about the primal, naturalized issues of life and death in reproduction and abortion. As one might expect from their position, the liberal parties were not particularly interested in arguing about abortion as a public policy matter.[9] But for the governing parties, who were largely impotent in vital questions of economic reorganization, regulating abortion provided a palpable way of putting into practice their image of the paternal state, while also allowing them to appear to provide the leadership in morality that everyone had agreed was missing from everyday life.

Some of the Women

But the abortion debate was not only about forms of state power. It was also about abortion and therefore about women's bodies. To what extent, then, is the kind of state-society relation implicitly proposed by populists and liberals likely to engage women's political energies? The women who will have to live with the new law did not participate very much in the battles for discursive hegemony described above. Rather, they constituted a marginal voice, quieted by charges of selfishness and by their own critiques of the double and triple day that communism demanded of women. In Poland the threat of restricted abortion is partly what energized women's movements. This has happened only on a very small scale in Hungary. Several tiny groups were formed. One of these, made up of professionals and entrepreneurial women, organized a forum to discuss abortion. Vociferously disagreeing with anti-abortion arguments, they emphasized, in their own version of anticommunist argument, that once again decisions were to be made about and for them, but without their participation.

More privately, my discussions with Hungarian women in urban as well as rural settings revealed a sense of bafflement and irritation about these debates. At Christmastime 1992, I received a letter from an acquaintance, a woman of forty with a recently earned college diploma, who lives in a village where I have done fieldwork since 1987. She wrote in alarm about the beating of Gypsies in the streets of Budapest, about the anti-Semitic statements of members of the government, and then she asked: "And meanwhile, what are they doing in Parliament? Eighty-year-old men, those idiots, amuse themselves by screaming against abortion when unemployment is enormous and the potential parents themselves have nothing to eat." This letter highlights a broad phenomenon, by taking abortion for granted. As some of the anti-abortion writings themselves either stated or assumed, many Hungarian women have a sense of entitlement concerning abortion, and this seems to be substantiated by recent polls (Pongrácz and Molnár 1991). More than seventy percent of the population agreed that abortion should be available even for "social reasons."

Women described to me the possible loss of abortion as a lack of "civility" in the country, a return to the "eastern" backwardness and barbarity of the Stalinist years.[10] They saw abortion as a major, often the only, form of contraception. Even the most pious Catholic women, active for years in the village church, expressed a conviction that abortion must remain legal. One of these, in her late forties, paused significantly when I put the question to her, and answered, "They couldn't possibly take that away." Urban women often responded with anger to my question: In the face of the high cost of housing in Budapest, "who is going to give me the space to put another child at the kitchen table?" Echoing the words of my acquaintances, a woman interviewed anonymously in a weekly newspaper said, "As long as society can't assure me the money to raise my child, they shouldn't have anything to do with this question" (1990: 80). Clearly some women are creating a discourse about abortion—one involving visions of a good society: civility, economic responsibility—that is not congruent with any of the others I have discussed.

Yet there is another aspect to the larger issue of women, work, reproduction, and family. Even more than in the village where I have conducted fieldwork, educated women in Budapest expressed great frustration in trying to balance wage-work responsibilities and the demands of housework and motherhood. While socialism met some of its (unasked) promises to women in Hungary by engineering their massive entrance into the labor force, it did not provide adequate childcare nor a rearrangement of gender roles to ease housework. The resultant difficulties of managing both kinds of work have been laid at the feet of state socialism by many women. It is the system they blamed for not allowing them the choice of being full-time mothers.

Furthermore, when abortion decisions were left to women, this was seen by many not as a chance for autonomy, but as the state allowing men to abandon women and children. More subtly, many women in their thirties and forties expressed a sense of guilt about their supposed lack of skills in child rearing and housekeeping. They expressed a feeling of inadequacy because of their lack of training (caused by their own labor force participation and their mothers' wage work) in the "civilized womanly arts" of decoration, dress, and nurturance. Thus, ironically, a critique of state socialism for these women included the demand for higher wages for men to support wives and children. If this set of conceptions includes a further valorization of "motherhood," as many populists and Christian organizations argue it should, this may yet provide grounds for women to oppose abortion and acquiesce in a new organization of their subordination within the broader arena of Hungarian politics.

Conclusion

In Hungary, as elsewhere in the world, the abortion debate made politics. But abortion had specific meanings in Hungary at this historical juncture. For instance, cultural conceptualizations about abortion were not linked to sexuality and women's right to privacy, as in the current American debate, but rather to ideas about nationhood, the unnaturalness and immorality of communism, and the defense of civility. By looking carefully at speeches and writings produced within the Hungarian abortion debate, I have tried to specify some of the textual strategies through which opposing views were constructed.

Most striking, however, is the way in which all positions in the Hungarian debate were arguments, in absentia, with a state socialism that no longer existed. An image of a godless, immoral, overly ideological communism was everyone's foil. The debate itself was thus an attempt to construct a new politics against, and out of, the materials provided by the old. Yet, despite the participants' explicit goal to make a novel and more "open" political life, the abortion debate produced unintended, ironic continuities with the old. While touted for its new tolerance of many parties, ideas, and stances, it also made some political positions invisible or impossible.

The continuities are inseparable from the anticommunism itself. In arguing for the indispensability of their expertise, conservative professionals and politicians stressed the importance of knowledge, in contrast to communism's supposedly exclusive reliance on those who showed party loyalty. Yet, the arguments of the conservatives doubtless sounded familiar to those who had lived under the infantilizing tutelage of a "vanguard" Communist Party. For, like their communist predecessors, each of these experts, as well as the conservative politicians, implied that ordinary people should not make decisions for themselves; the experts and leaders knew better what should be best for everyone. Similarly familiar were the calls by populists and conservative politicians for women's unselfishness. Though the cause was now the "nation" rather than the needs of "socialist society," sacrifices to be made in the name of a larger collectivity were hardly new to Hungarians.

Despite the emergence of genuine diversity in political debate, some political positions disappeared from view. The defense of women's rights and autonomy was incompatible with anti-communism, at this historical moment, despite the general concern with civil and human rights. For liberals, claims for special women's rights would have been antithetical to the moral purity of a creed that ideally made no distinctions of identity among "citizen-individuals." But it was impossible for conservatives as well, because women's rights were discursively linked to state socialism and to women's supposed advantages under that system. The paternalistic communist state, by socializing some household tasks, and by supporting women and children directly, rather than through the men of a household, allowed a level of autonomy for women that is unusual in other political systems. Yet, women themselves often experienced this support as inadequate and oppressive, and were not vocal in its defense.

Debates about abortion were not invented, of course, by post-socialist critics. State socialist planners had also been deeply involved in a politics of reproduction, attempting to shape procreative practices through legal and discursive means in the service of various and changing political goals: communist militarism and industrialization, emulation of Soviet models, or reformist attempts to rescue the failing political-economic system. What is distinctive about the post-socialist debate is that the reverse relation was more salient: Arguments about abortion and the proper forms of reproduction were not the means to reach already defined political goals. They were presented rather to justify and naturalize broad political visions and thereby gain moral ballast for their proponents. Discussed in the guise of the abortion debate were wide-ranging political questions: What should be the form of the state? What is a legitimate subject of political debate? By which criteria—ethnicity, morality, expertise—should leaders be chosen?

Rather than the shaping of reproductive practices for political ends, we see the shaping of politics through a coded discussion of reproductive practices. The social process of reproduction gains its power to moralize politics because it is already constituted, in the tradition discussed here, as a natural, primal phenomenon involving life and death. Thus, in the newly constituted field of Hungarian politics, the abortion debate allowed groups and alliances to create themselves through such debates. They made claims about their own political value, while simultaneously constructing the means by which such value was to be measured.

Notes

1. My thanks to Judith Gerson, Katherine Verdery, and József Böröcz for their generous comments. All translations are my own.
2. For reports on the situation of women in East Europe since 1989, and questions of reproduction particularly, see the special section of *Signs* (1991), the special issue of *German Politics and Society* (1991–92), and *Feminist Review* (Winter 1991). Only in Romania, where abortion was banned, were regulations popularly opposed, see Kligman (1993).
3. The general link between politics and gender has been made most forcefully by Scott (1988); on politics of reproduction see Ginsberg and Rapp (1991).
4. For a discussion of the importance of discursive factors in the transition from socialism, see Verderey (1991); Stark (1992) and Böröcz (in press) provide overviews of economic transformation, and Róna-Tas (1991) notes the greater mobility among political elites. My discussion of the self-legitimation of political elites relies on Bourdieu's (1991) notion of "symbolic power."
5. An excellent source of information about Hungarian abortion policy from the 1930s to the present is Sándor (1992).
6. An important collection of the 1930s' debates about abortion, population, and the one-child system can be found in the journal *Nyugat* (1933).
7. My analysis of the positions of conservative and professional groups draws on my reading of the daily and weekly press from 1990 to the end of 1991. Further specific citations can be found in Gal (1994).

[132] Susan Gal

8. Joanna Goven (1993) has shrewdly analyzed this link between gender and dissent in Hungary.
9. This is not to say that liberals did not write copiously about the abortion issue. Indeed, one former dissident, philosopher, and liberal political leader published an important philosophical discussion of the issue (Kis 1992).
10. Civility is a central notion in Hungarian discourse about national identity, and part of the social geography that often locates Hungary not quite in "Europe" but somewhere between "East" and "West." For a discussion of this discourse, see Gal 1991.

References

Anonymous. 1990. Interview in *168 Ora*, p. 8.

Böröcz, József. (In press). Simulating the great transformation: Property change under prolonged informality in Hungary. *Archives européenes de Sociologie*.

Bourdieu, Pierre. 1991. *Language and symbolic power*. Cambridge: Cambridge University Press.

Briggs, Charles, and Bauman, Richard. 1992. Genre, intertextuality and social power. *J. of Linguistic Anthropology* 2:2: 131–72.

Csurka, István. 1991. Untitled comments. *In* S. Agócs (ed.), *Lakitelek 1987*, p. 24. Budapest: Püski.

Elfogy a magyarság? (Will the Hungarians come to an end?) *Nyugat* (special issue), 1933.

Feminist Review. Special issue on East European women. Winter 1991.

Gal, Susan. 1994. Gender in the post-socialist transition: The abortion debate in Hungary. *East European Politics and Societies*, 8:2: 256–86.

———. 1991. Bartók's funeral: Representations of Europe in Hungarian political rhetoric. *American Ethnologist* 18: 440–58.

German Politics and Society. 1991–92. Special issue on women and gender.

Ginsberg, Faye. 1989. *Contested Lives*. Berkeley: University of California Press.

——— and Rayna Rapp. 1991. The politics of reproduction. *Annual Review of Anthropology*. 20: 311–44.

Glendon, Mary. 1987. *Abortion and divorce in Western law: American failures, European challenges*. Cambridge: Harvard University Press.

Goven, Joanna. 1993. Gender politics in Hungary: Autonomy and antifeminism. *In* N. Funk and M. Mueller (eds.). *Gender politics and post-communism: Reflections from Eastern Europe and the former Soviet Union*. New York: Routledge.

Havel, Václav. 1988. Antipolitical politics. *In* J. Keane (ed.). *Civil society and the state*. London: Verso.

Kis, János. 1992. *Az abortuszról* (About abortion). Budapest: Cserepfalvi.

Kligman, Gail. 1993. The politics of reproduction in Ceauşescu's Romania: A case study in political culture. *East European Politics and Societies* 6:3: 364–418.

Konrád, György. 1984. *Antipolitics*. San Diego: Harcourt, Brace.

Lezsák, Sándor. 1991. Köszöntöm vedégeinket, barátainkat (Greetings to our guests and friends). *In* S. Agócsa (ed.), *Lakitelek 1987*, p. 6. Budapest: Puski.

Luker, Kristin. 1984. *Abortion and the politics of motherhood*. Berkeley: University of California Press.

Mink, András. 1991. Kis magyar abortusztörténet (A short history of Hungarian abortion). *Beszélö*, Nov. 30, pp. 22–25.

Mohr, James. 1978. *Abortion in America: The origins and evolution of national policy*. New York: Oxford University Press.

Petchesky, Rosalind. 1984. *Abortion and woman's choice*. Boston: Northeastern University Press.

Pongrácz, Marietta, and Edit Molnár. 1991. Az abortuszkérdés Magyarországon (The abortion question in Hungary). *Statisztikai Szemle* 69:7: 509–31.

Ráduly, János S. 1992. Kis jogi pornográfia (A little pornography about the law). *Magyar Narancs*, March 18, p. 5.

Róna-Tas, Ákos. 1991. The selected and the elected: The making of the new Parliamentary elite in Hungary. *East European Politics and Societies* 5:3: 357–94.

Sándor, Judit (ed.). 1992. *Abortusz és . . .* (Abortion and . . .) Budapest: Literatura Medica.

Scott, Joan. 1988. *Gender and the politics of history*. New York: Columbia University Press.

Signs. 1991. Special section on Eastern Europe.

Stark, David. 1992. Path dependence and privatization strategies in East Central Europe. *East European Politics and Societies* 6:1: 17–54.

Vásáry, Ildikó. 1989. The sin of Transdanubia: The one child system in rural Hungary. *Continuity and Change* 4:3: 429–68.

Verdery, Katherine. 1991. Theorizing socialism: A prologue to the "transition." *American Ethnologist*, 18: 419–39.

[27]

Who are the Women? Where are the Women? And What Difference Can They Make? Effects of Gender Parity in French Municipal Elections

Karen Bird
Department of Political Science, McMaster University, Hamilton, Ontario, Canada L8S 4M4
E-mail: kbird@mcmaster.ca

In June 2000, France passed a new law requiring 'parity' — an equal number of male and female candidates — for most elections. The law was applied to municipal elections in March 2001, Senate elections in September 2001, and legislative elections in June 2002. This article describes the sources of resistance to parity, and its eventual passage into law, before examining the effectiveness of the law in terms of women's place in politics. It focuses on local elections, where the parity law has had the greatest impact. Using an original sample survey of candidates, it examines the characteristics of the women and men who ran for office under parity. Despite achieving virtually identical levels of representation in local councils in France, this research points to lingering marginalization of women to lower and traditionally 'feminine' areas of political responsibility. And while there are some important demographic differences between the men and women who ran for local election under parity rules, the findings show that female candidates were at least as likely as male candidates to be recruited from among local elites. Nevertheless, female and male candidates appear to hold a distinctive set of perspectives on politics, suggesting that parity holds some promise for democratic renewal and policy change, at least at the local level. A key factor shaping women's distinctive political perspectives is the priority they place on family responsibilities. Women's previous exclusion from the public sphere, as well as their hesitancy to make a career out of politics, may explain their higher level of support for greater socio-cultural diversification among political actors.
French Politics (2003) **1,** 5–38. doi:10.1057/palgrave.fp.8200014

Keywords: parity; elections; Municipal politics; gender differences; France

---

In media reports leading up to the first round of French municipal elections on 11 March 2001, all eyes turned to the new parity law requiring for the first time ever that electoral lists include an equal number of male and female candidates.[1] The important French daily *Le Monde* included a regular column on women and the election, while popular weeklies such as *Le Point*, *L'Express*, *Le Nouvel Observateur*, as well as 'women's' magazines like *Marie-Claire* and *Elle*, produced special dossiers on women in politics and profiled selected female candidates. The media attention reached its pinnacle just 3 days before the election, on 8 March (International Women's Day), with most French dailies devoting several pages to the analyses of women's place in the political, business, and domestic spheres today, and to the chronology of the women's movement.

This level of attention to women in politics was unprecedented in France before parity. Historically, at least until they received the right to vote in 1944, French women who dared to enter political life have been more often criticized than celebrated (Landes, 1988; Perrot, 1997). Moreover, until very recently, the French preferred *not* to acknowledge whether their elected representatives were male or female — although in fact over 95 per cent of them since 1944 have been men[2]— addressing men and women indiscriminately as 'Monsieur le ministre' and 'Monsieur le maire.'[3] With the dust settled and the media attention subsided, it is important now to assess the initial results of France's first nationwide experiment with gender parity in electoral politics.

A full assessment of parity in French municipal elections is even more critical, in light of the law's relative ineffectiveness in elections to the National Assembly (9 and 16 June 2002). Undeterred by financial penalties, major parties on the right and left failed to uphold the spirit of parity. The right wing Union pour la Majorité Présidentielle, which formed the government following these elections, nominated women to fewer than 20 per cent of the districts where it ran a candidate, while the Socialists nominated women in just 36 per cent of its contests. The results of the election were discouraging for women. The National Assembly now includes just 71 women among its 576 members (12.3 per cent), a small increase from elections in 1997 — before the constitution was amended and the parity law passed — when 62 women (10.9 per cent) were elected to the national parliament. As this article explains, the results of parity at the municipal level were much more positive. Among the most significant changes, women now hold almost half (47.5 per cent) of the seats on municipal councils, up from just a quarter (25.7 per cent) in previous elections.

Despite these disappointing results for women in the first legislative elections run under parity rules, it remains important that we look to the *local* level to understand the broader effects of parity in French politics, and this for at least two reasons. First, the recruitment and training of a critical mass of women at the local level is essential to any significant increase over time in the number of women elected to national politics. Given that some of these locally elected women will percolate up to the national level, it will prove useful to assemble a profile of the large class of women elected to local politics under parity rules. Second, some feminist scholars (Phillips, 1993; Lister, 1997) argue that an influx of women can serve to introduce alternative ideas and more democratic approaches to politics. The logical *first* place to look for such transformative capacity is at the local level — where the boundaries between the public and private spheres that have traditionally excluded women from politics are most porous, where women's patterns of involvement in the associations and social life of the community are most likely to translate into political capital, and where (especially in smaller towns) lower levels of party discipline should allow women to exercise greater autonomy in their representative function. If women do not demonstrate a different way of doing politics at the local level, there is little to suggest that they will transform the political process at the national level.

This article begins by describing the history of the parity movement and the development of the law. The focus here is on the difficulties encountered in achieving legal change, and the reluctance towards parity within the corridors of political power. Following this historical review, the article then examines from two perspectives the application of parity at the local level. The first perspective considers the results of the municipal elections of March 2001, focusing on the effects of parity in securing women's access to different levels of municipal government. The second perspective draws upon an original large sample survey of candidates, to describe the differences between the men and women who ran for and were elected to local office under parity rules.

History of the Parity Law

There are a number of countries in which political parties have voluntarily introduced quotas for women candidates, and a few (e.g. Belgium, India, Argentina, Brazil, Bolivia, Peru, South Africa, Malaysia) where national laws require a minimum percentage (e.g. 30 per cent) of female candidates or representatives at various electoral levels. France is the first country in the world to require by law an *equal* number of male and female candidates for *virtually all* elections.

The parity law was promulgated on 6 June 2000.[4] It followed a constitutional revision, adopted on 28 June 1999. Whereas the constitution had previously been interpreted as forbidding any preferential treatment of candidates on the basis of gender or any other category, it now states (Article 3, paragraph v) that 'the law favours the equal access of men and women to all electoral mandates and elective functions,' and (Article 4, paragraph ii) that political parties 'contribute to the application of this principle through conditions determined by the law.'

How the parity law came to be is a story in itself. Some accounts of the parity law in France suggest that this measure was adopted easily, and that the advocates of the measure were themselves surprised by how quickly their cause was taken up by the government. The story recounted here makes a very different argument. The parity movement began not in the 1990s, but in the early 1970s. Political resistance to parity remained strong through the 1980s and early 1990s. First and foremost, there was reluctance within the political class (both the left and right) to measures that might ultimately cost a sitting member his seat. There was the old philosophical division among feminists themselves about whether women should be treated differently or identically to men, and whether measures to enhance women's representation humiliated women by admitting that they needed special help to get elected. There was also the classic French republican problem that it is not possible to grant benefits or legal status on sexual, ethnic, or cultural grounds, as such measures would undermine the republican project of equality and universality of treatment.

Pre-parity movement: 1970s–1980s

While the 1990s was the decisive decade for the parity movement, the seeds of this movement were planted as early as 1975 under the centrist government of Valéry Giscard d'Estaing (Union pour la Démocratie Française). It was in that year that Françoise Giroud, the first Secretary of State for the Condition of Women, presented a list of '100 measures for women,' including limiting the number of candidates of the same sex who may appear on a party's list for municipal elections. A proposal for a ceiling of 80 per cent was introduced to Parliament in 1980 by Monique Pelletier, the new Secretary of State for the Condition of Women. On first reading in the National Assembly (19–20 November 1980) the proposal was adopted by 439 votes to 3. Yet the government, facing pressures of a coming election, felt it wiser not to pursue such a controversial reform and the bill never made it to the agenda in the Senate.

Two years later, a law *was* passed limiting to 75 per cent the number of candidates of the same sex who may appear on the lists for municipal election. Yet this law was never applied or promulgated. Rather, it was reviewed by the Constitutional Council and declared incompatible with the terms of the Constitution, particularly with those articles guaranteeing equality and non-discrimination in access to public office, and the non-divisibility of the sovereign authority of the body politic.[5]

While the Constitutional Council stands as the most imposing obstacle to parity during this period, a close reading of the parliamentary debates at this time reveals that the Socialist Party was itself responsible for the failure of this pre-parity measure. Despite campaign promises, the government of President François Mitterrand did not intend to establish a quota for women. The quota measure was brought to Parliament not by the Minister for Women's Rights Yvette Roudy, but through an amendment offered by an independent member of Parliament, Gisèle Halimi,[6] to a government bill that would introduce semi-proportional representation for elections at the municipal level. The Socialist group in Parliament succeeded in replacing Halimi's proposed amendment with a milder one.[7] However, even this measure was greeted coolly by the Government. Speaking for the Government during these debates, the Minister of the Interior, Gaston Defferre, effectively paved the way for the Constitutional Council's censure of the law. Defferre reminded the deputies that, as concerns the ratio of male and female candidates, 'the Government considers that it falls to the parties to decide on the matter.'[8] However, in the event that Parliament should approve this amendment, he made a request that would stand as a beacon call to the members of the Assembly and to the judges of the Constitutional council:

> 'I wish, if the measure that is proposed is adopted, that it appear within a separate article so that, in the event that the Constitutional Council should annul it, the law may nevertheless be applied.'[9]

In what French political scholar Lochak (1983, 181) called an 'edifying lesson in hypocrisy' the deputies voted nearly unanimously for the quota amendment (476 votes to 4, with 3 abstentions), after taking care to separate it from the main legislation. Undoubtedly, it was with relief that French parliamentarians greeted the Court's invalidation of the law.

Parity movement: 1990s–2000s

The parity movement was renewed and radicalized in the early 1990s. A decisive factor was the verdict of the Constitutional Council which, in closing off the option of quotas, forced the advocates of reform to develop a more fundamental criticism of sexual inequality within the representative system. If a quota was not acceptable to the Court, neither was it adequate for women themselves who — the paritaristes argued — represented half of the population and therefore merited fully half of all representative seats.

Another significant factor was growing attention at the international and European level to the problem of women's absence in positions of political power. Through a series of European and international initiatives on women's place in politics (including the Beijing platform and resolutions passed by the Council of Europe), attention became focused on the fact that French women remained in a fundamentally backward position in politics, both in comparison to other domains where they had made progress, and in comparison to women in other European countries.[10] The figures showed that France fell well behind other European members (ahead of only Greece) for the numbers of women elected to national government. On 1 January 1997, women occupied 35 of the 576 seats (6.1 per cent) in the French National Assembly and 18 of the 321 seats (5.6 per cent) in the Senate. Women's access was no better than in 1945, the first year they were eligible to vote and run for national office! Never before the legislative elections of May–June 1997 had women held more than 7 per cent of seats in the French parliament.[11]

The publication by Gaspard *et al.* of the book '*Au pouvoir citoyennes! Liberté, parité*' (1992) was a significant milestone in the movement. Gaspard and her co-authors advocated a referendum and a constitutional amendment on parity. The book was followed in 1993 by the publication of the 'Manifeste des 577,'[12] and the creation between 1992 and 1994 of several associations dedicated to parity reform.[13] The activists of this movement, most of them well connected to the Socialist party,[14] brought parity and the question of a constitutional amendment to the forefront of political debates during the 1995 presidential election. All three main presidential candidates included parity within their campaign platforms. Following the elections, Jacques Chirac's Prime Minister Alain Juppé (both of the right-wing Rassemblement pour la République) commissioned the 'Observatoire de la parité,' and charged it with reporting every 2 years on the conditions of women's access to politics, and with making recommendations for legal change. Even more significant, in June 1996 10 prominent female politicians from across the ideological spectrum stepped across rigid party boundaries to sign a public manifesto 'Pour la parité' demanding constitutional reform.[15] When the Observatoire de la parité presented its first report to Parliament in December 1996, it recommended a constitutional revision to allow for parity legislation.

The government was beginning to take note. In March 1997, in a speech to the National Assembly on 'Women's place in public life,' Prime Minister Juppé declared his 'personal' support for the principle of parity: 'After long reflection, and after long intellectual progress, I am today convinced that the institution of some measure of positive discrimination is necessary.' The election just 3 months later of a left-wing alliance government under Prime Minister Lionel Jospin (Socialist) was the final significant step toward the realization of parity. The Socialist party already required that its own list of candidates include at least 30 per cent women,[16] while the Green party required fully 50 per cent. Moreover, Jospin was one of the few men in French politics who was personally convinced that parity was philosophically and politically appropriate. An undoubtable influence in his thinking was his wife, the feminist philosopher Sylviane Agacinski (1996, 1998, 1999a), who had written and would continue to write in favour of parity. Immediately after the election, Jospin affirmed that his government would introduce a plan to amend the Constitution, and set out to force his reluctant deputies (ever wary of preserving their parliamentary seats) to support the reform.[17] In June 1998, the

Minister of Justice Elisabeth Gigou presented the government's project for a constitutional amendment.

President Jacques Chirac was initially somewhat cool to the constitutional reform, but he understood that parity was a popular idea. There was a widespread sense of embarrassment that France, the cradle of modern democracy, could rank second-to-last in Europe for the percentage of women in political office. Polls showed that ordinary men and women favoured parity (although there was no popular mobilization of citizens either for or against the project). Finally, parity was viewed as a measure that would renew the political class and help to modernize French politics. Chirac rallied his deputies to support the constitutional amendment, although some resistance was mounted in the right-dominated Senate, which forced a few concessions on the new language to be included in the Constitution. On 28 June 1999, a joint congress of the two legislative chambers ratified an amendment to Articles 3 and 4 of the French Constitution. Within a year, on 6 June 2000, the parity law received final assent (on third reading) in the National Assembly.[18]

Sources of resistance

Despite its relatively easy passage,[19] there were two distinct sources of resistance to parity. One was philosophical and widely publicized, while the other was pragmatic and occult. We deal with these in turn.

Parity laid bare a philosophical cleavage not between men and women, nor between political parties (all of whom publicly supported parity and differed only in the details of the law), but between the proponents of parity and the defenders of a republican universalism opposed to any law that would distinguish between citizens or elected representatives on the basis of their sex. This cleavage was especially apparent among French intellectuals, including feminists. A particularly important pair of actors in this debate was Sylviane Agacinski (for '*la démocratie paritaire*') and Elisabeth Badinter (against parity and for '*l'égalité universelle*'), whose arguments were frequently presented in facing columns of the printed press (Agacinski, 1996, 1999a, b; Badinter, 1996, 1999; Badinter *et al.* 1999). The Agacinski–Badinter exchanges are revealing, both in terms of the ideas presented, and in terms of the relationships among the main participants in the political debates over parity. These two public intellectuals, feminists both, were each married to a leading protagonist in the political debates over parity — Agacinski to Lionel Jospin, and Badinter to the former Socialist minister Robert Badinter who led the opposition against the constitutional revision from his seat in Senate. The two women assumed such undeniable influence in the parity debates that observers came to refer to '*Le projet Jospin-Agacinski*' and to '*l'opposition du couple*

Badinter.' These debates reveal (again) that support for and opposition to parity was rarely organized along party lines. Also, the level of complicity between militant advocates/opponents of parity and political actors exemplifies how the public debate over parity in France was restricted to a small circle of elite actors.

This philosophical divide was the focus of considerable media and political attention. In the course of this very public debate, the advocates of parity effectively clothed themselves in the legitimating fabric of French republicanism, arguing that parity was not a departure from the principles of civic unity and non-recognition of particular social categories.[20] They argued that women are not a social category like racial or religious groups. This quasi-universalist formulation of parity proved particularly appealing during legislative debates. It satisfied most moderate French republicans[21] by reducing two of the most apparent risks of group-based representation: the risk of over-politicizing group differences and disrupting social cohesion, and the risk of undermining deliberative processes aimed at identifying general interests and shared concerns.

While politically appealing, this quasi-universalist formulation of parity *is* problematic. Because of the need to identify the sexual difference as the only universally, objectively valid difference among humanity, the advocates of parity in some instances descended dangerously close to arguments of biological determinism.[22] For only if there is an *essential*, *permanent*, and *universal* difference between men and women — a difference more significant than the mere social constructions that distinguish ethnic, racial, and religious categories — can parity be defended within a republican framework. Furthermore, while parity runs the risk of inflating sexual differences, it tends to deflate and render virtually invisible other differences among men and women that have generated social and political exclusion. Parity takes no account and denies any remedy for the almost complete exclusion of people of non-European immigrant origin from national politics. Also, by asserting the significance and universality of the sexual difference between men and women, parity tends to counter homosexuals' demands for legal recognition of marriage and adoption rights. Finally, the quasi-universalist formulation of parity weakens the rationale for increasing women's presence in elected legislative assemblies. For, if elected representatives are supposed to represent the collective interests of the nation and not narrow sectarian interests, then it matters less *who* does the representing.[23]

While the theory of representation may already be 'a muddle' (Phillips, 1995 41), the republican articulation of parity as a measure to enhance representative equality produces even further incoherence. Ultimately, the problem posed by Perrot (1995, 51), 'Au nom de quoi, la parité? de l'équité individuelle? ou de la différence des sexes?' was never resolved over the course of the parity debates. This makes it difficult to evaluate whether parity should produce better substantive representation of women's interests, or whether it is simply a means for ensuring that more women may take their place alongside men in elite institutions (Millard and Ortiz, 1998).

Surprisingly, the philosophical opposition to parity evaporated after the passage of the constitutional amendment. What replaced it was a more pragmatic, more occult, and ultimately more effective form of opposition among the seated deputies in the National Assembly and the political elite of the major French parties.

While deputies were beholden to support parity in principle, it is no accident that in the passage from principle to law, parity would yield to the fundamental pragmatic interest in maintaining political power. Not surprisingly, it is at the locus of political power in France (the National Assembly) where the parity law is least effective. Although quotas are most effective when elections are run using a proportional/list system, every major French party stood resolutely opposed to any reform of the existing single-member plurality system of election to the National Assembly.[24] Clearly, a proportional or semi-proportional system of election would benefit women, but would also reward minor parties at the expense of larger ones. Finally, sitting deputies (89 per cent of them men) simply loathed the thought of having their candidacy passed over by a party forced to nominate an equal number of women and men. As a result, a more supple approach to parity would be applied to legislative elections than that applied to elections using proportional/list methods. Parties that do not present an equal number of male and female candidates for legislative elections will have a portion of their public subsidy withheld, but remain eligible to contest the election. The national elections of 2002 revealed that this financial incentive was effective for small parties with few seated members and limited sources of alternative funding, but ineffective for larger parties (Bird, forthcoming.) Also, because the law considers only the proportion of men and women presented as candidates, parties face no disincentive to placing their female candidates in unwinnable constituencies. In elections held on 9 and 16 June 2002, the centre-right formation the Union pour la Majorité Presidentielle (UMP) that formed the new government nominated women to fewer than 20 per cent of the districts where it ran a candidate, while the Socialists nominated women to just 36 per cent of its contests. The result: a nominal increase from 62 to 71 women seated in the 576-member assembly.

Parity Applied: Municipal Elections 2001

The parity law applies to most, but not all, elections in France. It applies to municipal elections in towns of at least 3,500 inhabitants, legislative elections, regional elections, Senate elections (in larger departments where three or more Senators are elected by proportional-list methods), elections of representatives to the European Parliament, and elections to an assortment of legislative councils in overseas French territories. The law does not apply to presidential elections, or to cantonal elections in which voters elect representatives to their departmental assemblies (*Conseils généraux*), or to Senate elections in smaller departments (where elections are run under single-member plurality rules). In functional terms, the law applies differently depending upon the voting methods used for each type of election.

For municipal elections — decided by a semi-proportional list system over two rounds of voting — parties must present lists composed of an equal number of men and women, allowing for one more male or female candidate when the number of seats being contested is uneven. The law does not impose strict alternation between male and female candidates throughout the list.[25] Rather, parties must present three men and three women in any order for every six candidates listed. Any list that does not conform to parity rules is declared ineligible and will not be presented to voters.

While the application of the parity law to municipal elections is fairly strict, there remain a number of shortcomings. Most noteworthy, the law does not apply to municipal elections in towns of fewer than 3,500 inhabitants, although it is the latter that constitute the vast majority of municipalities in France. To wit, in the 2001 elections, the parity law applied to just 2,624 of over 36,500 municipalities (about 7 per cent) and affected just 76,000 of over 500,000 locally elected councillors (roughly 15 per cent),[26] In effect, parity was rendered impossible in these small municipalities by a semi-direct method of election, which allows voters in towns under the 3,500 threshold to cross candidates' names from the list, to change the order of names on the list, or to add new names to the list. Imposing parity on a wider scale would have required legislative changes to voting methods, which the government had promised it would not impose.

A second important shortcoming of the law is that it does not apply to the selection of the mayor. French mayors are elected indirectly, as the first order of business facing the newly invested city council. Almost invariably it is the person holding the first position on the winning list who is the elected mayor. The law includes no incentive or requirement concerning the gender of the so-called *tête de liste* and, in 2001 as in previous elections, that person was almost always male.

Nor is parity required in the selection of the mayor's cabinet. The real power in municipal politics is held by the mayor, along with his *premier adjoint* (adjunct-mayor) and a variable number of lesser adjuncts, each heading a particular subcommittee of the council. Adjuncts are nominated by the mayor from among elected councillors, and then elected by the council as a whole. (It is generally a foregone conclusion that the adjuncts will be selected from the winning list.) The long-standing practice has been that the order of candidates on the winning list would also be the order of nomination to the mayor's executive. The second candidate on the winning list becomes the *premier adjoint* (adjunct-mayor), the third becomes the *deuxiéme adjoint*, and so on. Because there must be an equal number of men and women among the first six names on the list, parity is not entirely irrelevant to the constitution of the cabinet. Nevertheless, there is no legal requirement that women be represented at the executive level of local government.

Finally, still at the municipal level, parity rules do not apply in naming the governing members of amalgamated cities. These Public Intercommunal Cooperative Establishments (EPCIs) are responsible for infrastructure, economic planning, and the harmonization and consolidation of public programmes and tax systems across contiguous towns. According to most observers, they have become the locus of power in municipal government. The representatives to these intercommunal structures are appointed by member cities, usually from among the mayors' adjuncts.

Parity results

There are two central conclusions to be drawn from the results of the 2001 municipal elections in France. The first is that the parity law was effective — where it applied — in bringing women into politics. Where they were required to do so, parties proved highly adept at recruiting women into politics. The law's detractors, especially those who complained about the shortage of women qualified or interested enough to enter politics, were simply wrong. There appear to have been no major difficulties (and certainly none that were intractable) in composing lists containing the same number of candidates of each sex. There was no party that proved incapable of achieving parity on its lists. According to a survey of 600 *têtes de liste*, 78 per cent considered that it was 'easy' to apply the parity law in selecting candidates for their lists.[27] Certainly, the most delicate problem facing mayors running for re-election was to dislodge male incumbents in order to make room for new female candidates. Yet even in this respect, the parity requirement was a welcome pretext for mayors wishing to eliminate their least favoured councillors and to present a rejuvenated list.

The second conclusion is equally clear. Political leaders (mostly men) are not likely to cede power to newcomers unless the law requires them to do so; and, the greater the power at stake, the less likely it is to be ceded voluntarily. Because the parity law does not apply at the centre of municipal power — the mayor's office and cabinet — it makes more visible than before the stratified nature of men's and women's access to politics. There remains a 'glass-ceiling' effect that severely limits women's access to the most important and influential position in local politics, and parity has done little in the short term to help women break through this ceiling.

Where are the women?

With the introduction of parity, more than 39,000 women joined their local city councils (in towns with over 3,500 inhabitants), almost double their numbers in the councils sitting before March 2001. In cities having over 3,500 inhabitants, the percentage of women elected to council increased to 47.5 per cent, from just 25.7 per cent in 1995. There was little variation in these numbers across France.

There was also an increase — albeit less spectacular — in the number of female councillors and mayors in towns under the 3,500 threshold (where parity rules do not apply). Today, women comprise 30.05 per cent of town councils in small villages, up from 21 per cent in 1995. They also make up 11.2 per cent of small-town mayors, compared to 7.8 per cent in 1995.[28] But there are wide regional variations in the number of women elected in small towns across France. For example, across these smaller towns, just 23 per cent of councillors were women in the Doubs (eastern France), compared to 32 per cent Isère (south-east), and 31 per cent in Hérault (south).[29]

In cities having above 3,500 inhabitants, parity applied to the composition of candidate lists, but not to the election of the executive. The result is that, overall, women remain the minority participants in local executives. Just 6.7 per cent of the mayors elected in March 2001 were women, compared to 4.4 per cent in 1995. Among adjunct-mayors an estimated 26.3 per cent are women; among all adjuncts an estimated 36.5 per cent are women. Women's presence in local executives tends to be strongest within the largest cities. However, here again there is significant variation across different cities. For example, in Lyon, just 24 per cent of the city executives are female, compared to 53 per cent in Paris (although both cities are led by Socialist governments). Overall, four of France's 35 largest cities now have a female mayor (compared to one before parity), while 11 have a woman as adjunct-mayor.

While the parity law has led to a significant increase in the number of women elected to local politics, there is still much room for improvement. Power in local government is sexually stratified with men maintaining their dominance in the most important offices (Table 1). At other electoral levels, it is also clear that where parity is not applied in the strictest terms, women remain largely absent from political office.[30]

Representative Roles of Women and Men: Identical or Different?

Getting women into elected office is one thing. Now that they hold a fairer share of seats in local assemblies in France, we need to ask whether elected women are different from men, whether they approach politics differently, and whether they are more likely than men to advance issues of importance to women. These questions point to the complex problem of women's and men's

Table 1 Women within French Local Government (2001)

	Percentage women			
Size of municipality	*Mayor*	*Adjunct-mayor*	*All adjuncts*	*Council*
Less than 3,500	11.2	18.5[a]	23.2[a]	30.1
3,500–8,999	6.2	23.0[a]	35.4[a]	47.4
9,000–29,999	7.1	32.0[a]	37.0[a]	47.3
30,000–99,999	8.2	30.0[a]	42.5	47.8
100,000 or more	11.1	30.6	39.5	48.6
District councils (Paris, Marseille, Lyon)	24.3	27.0	46.4	48.4
Total 3,500+	6.7	26.3[a]	36.5[a]	47.5

[a]Where indicated, figures are the author's estimates based on analysis of a sample ($n = 1567$) of city councils from across France. Other figures represent the whole population of councils for towns of a given size. There are 36,565 municipalities within metropolitan France (excluding overseas territories), each with its own mayor and town council.

representative role under the French parity law. From a theoretical perspective, it is difficult to evaluate whether parity should produce better substantive representation of women's interests. The parity law is not *intended* to depart from the republican tradition of civic unity and non-recognition of particular social categories, suggesting, in theory at least, that women elected under the law are not expected to provide substantive representation for women as a group.[31] But in practice, it seems likely that the surge of female newcomers may produce significant changes in French local politics.

We think that a useful starting point for considering these questions is to examine differences between the women and men who ran as *candidates* in these elections. Many of the women running for local election in March 2001 were first-time candidates. We expect these women to be quite different — in terms of their background characteristics and their ideas about politics and the representative role of women — both in comparison to men and in comparison to women with previous experience (before the introduction of parity rules) in male-dominated councils. A clearer picture of the nature of these differences is important, for while we know that more women were recruited into politics under parity, we know very little about the kinds of women who come forward under such rules. Additionally, a survey of female candidates' ideas can serve as an important benchmark for evaluating the nature and extent of future policy change that might be attributed to women's increased presence in local councils.

In the following sections, we discuss the results of a survey of candidates running in French local elections in March 2001 (see note 1). The purpose of this survey was to compare the men and women who ran for election, both in cities where the parity law applied and in small towns where the law was not applied.[32] In addition to personal background data, candidates provided information about their previous political experience and that of their family members, their reasons for running and their experiences during the campaign, and their views on various political issues and on the representative role of elected women.

Work, family, and politics

The findings of this survey suggest significant socio-demographic differences between the women and men who ran for local office in 2001. Table 2 presents a general comparison of male and female candidates who ran in local elections in small towns where the parity law did not apply, and in larger cities where the law was applied. We see that in both types of election, female candidates were younger than male candidates: about 5 years difference in small towns and 3 years difference in larger cities. In part because of their youth (as well as other reasons discussed below), female candidates had significantly more children still living at home. This evidence suggests quite different patterns of political involvement among French women than among US women, who are more likely than men to wait until their children are grown before making their first bids for political office (Carroll and Strimling, 1983, 27–28).

Female candidates were far less likely than male candidates to be working full-time (fewer than half of all candidates did so, compared to between two-thirds and three-quarters of men), and much more likely to be employed part-time (about one-quarter of women) or to be home-makers. About 13 per cent of female candidates were retired, compared to about 20 per cent of male candidates.

A further difference in their work experience is that female candidates were far more likely than male candidates (as well as more likely than women in the general population) to be employed in or retired from the public sector. French governments have long used the public sector as a policy instrument for influencing employment and increasing France's low natality rate, and these policies have tended to make public sector work especially attractive to women with families (Jenson and Sineau, 2001). For example, female civil servants (including teachers) with three or more children may take retirement once they have accumulated 15 years of service. Beyond encouraging them to have larger families and easing them out of the workforce, public sector jobs may also encourage and ease women's entry into political life. Public sector jobs, along with some kinds of professional situations, have been called 'brokerage occupations' and have been posited as a key supply-side explanation of both men's and women's entry into political life (Norris and Lovenduski, 1993). They facilitate entry into politics by allowing flexible time-management,

Table 2 Profile and campaign experiences of female and male candidates

	Small Towns (under 3,500 inhabitants)			Large Towns (3,500 or more inhabitants)		
	Women	*Men*	*Sig.*	*Women*	*Men*	*Sig.*
Mean age	44.7	49.4	***	47.2	50.1	***
Children at home	1.57	1.44	***	1.50	1.10	***
Work (%)			***			***
Full time	45.9	75.0		43.8	67.7	
Part time	24.0	1.3		24.5	5.6	
Retired	13.3	20.0		12.5	19.7	
Home-maker	8.7	0		8.2	0.3	
Other	8.1	3.7		10.9	6.6	
Employment sector (%)			NS			***
Public	45.4	36.8		49.8	35.8	
Private	54.6	63.2		50.2	64.2	
Education (%)			NS			NS
Less than high school	9.5	10.3		6.5	7.1	
Professional diploma	23.3	29.3		14.6	18.6	
High school baccalaureate	21.7	14.1		16.8	14.6	
University degree (2–4 years)	37.6	29.5		43.6	31.7	
Masters, doctorate	7.9	16.7		18.5	28.0	
Monthly household income (%)			***			NS
Under 10,000F	15.2	5.3		13.7	10.4	
10,000–15,000F	23.6	17.1		20.4	17.9	
15,000–20,000F	24.2	27.6		20.1	19.2	
20,000–30,000F	30.9	23.7		26.5	32.6	
Over 30,000F	6.2	26.3		19.4	19.9	
One or more in family has held mandate	34.7	29.6	NS	33.1	30.1	NS
Member of a political party	8.2	17.3	*	34.1	44.5	***
Hesitated before running	62.2	50.0	NS	51.9	27.4	***
Spouse very favourable	39.9	20.0	***	44.5	28.4	***
Kids very favourable	39.6	24.6	NS	35.0	31.9	NS
Will certainly run again (municipal)	20.5	17.9	NS	24.7	35.0	**
Will certainly run again (other levels)	7.2	10.1	NS	9.3	16.0	*
Gender was an advantage	34.8	12.6	***	53.7	6.3	***
Women's issues evoked during campaign	37.8	30.3	NS	56.5	70.3	***

Results of tests of significance: ***$p<0.005$; **$p<0.01$; *$p<0.05$; NS = non-significant.

generous vacations and career interruptions, financial security, professional independence, public networks, and social status, as well as expertise and skills that are all complementary to the pursuit of political office. These occupational advantages may be especially important for French women in at least two respects. First, French society remains relatively traditional with respect to the division of household labour and child-rearing responsibilities (Sineau, 1999, Krémer, 2001, Méda, 2001). Given that most French women *do* hold down a job and the household, running for and holding local and unpaid (except in the very largest cities) political office must seem an impossible option for many of them. Public sector work, then, offers important advantages that make it possible for women to run for and assume elected office without having to sacrifice professional or family life. Second, having worked in the public sector, women may be more likely to develop a taste and aptitude for politics. Among women who work in the public sector, many of whom work part-time and retire young, there appears to be a natural transition to community work and eventually local politics.

Local élites

Traditionally, French municipal politics have been dominated by local 'notables.' These have been, almost invariably, *men* of influence and status within the community (doctors, lawyers, shop owners, etc.), usually from among the highest social categories. The predominance of local notables is a function of a political system that has been described as a '*monarchie municipale*' (Malibeau, 1995), and that continues to be marked by the personification of leadership and concentration of authority in the office of the mayor. To what extent has parity altered this system? We compared women and men on three indicators of elite status: household revenue, education, and whether a candidate has family members who have served in political office.

In terms of their household income levels, we found that for elections run under parity rules (i.e. in towns of 3,500 inhabitants or more) female and male candidates are virtually indistinguishable. Within these larger towns, women who have already served in political office actually reported slightly *higher* family revenues than men who had a previous office, while among novice candidates women reported slightly lower revenues than men. In contrast, in the smallest towns (where parity rules do not apply), there was a large and statistically significant difference in men's and women's household income levels. In these towns, for both politically experienced candidates and novices, women reported significantly lower household revenue than men. These findings suggest that female candidates recruited under parity rules tend to be drawn from the same pool of wealthy local notables that has traditionally been the source of male candidates. Matters are very different in smaller villages, possibly because there are fewer female notables in the countryside, and that women there (but not men) attain a level of public recognition suitable for candidacy through simpler kinds of functions: for example, volunteering on the local parent–teacher council or helping to organize a town festival. In larger towns, there may be more professional women for parties to draw upon, while parties in such towns appear to demand a higher level of public standing for both female and male candidates.

In terms of education, there are no significant differences between male and female candidates, even after controlling for the size of the city and the political experience of the candidates. Men and women are equally likely to have university degrees, although men hold graduate degrees more often than women.

Clearly, an important route to politics for many individuals is through family connections. Indeed, where political access is otherwise difficult for women, they may be more likely than men to attain elite political positions through such connections. If parity democratizes politics by opening it to a broader range of women, we should see that women running for election for the first time under parity rules would have fewer family members with political experience than women who had already served in political office prior to the elections of March 2001. We might also expect that women running under parity rules would have fewer family connections to politics than men.

Our findings do not support this hypothesis (Figure 1). Overall, it appears that novice and experienced female candidates and experienced male candidates had largely similar kinds of family connections to politics, with the caveat that women were more likely to have inherited their political career from their spouse, while men were more likely to have inherited it from their father. The family political histories of politically experienced *vs* novice female candidates are largely indistinguishable. Women without previous political experience were slightly *more* likely than those who had previously held a mandate to have a father, mother, or grandparent who had held political office before them, but slightly *less* likely to have a spouse who had served in political office. While there was little difference in the family political experiences of novice *vs* previously elected women, there were large and significant differences between novice and previously elected men. Novice men were the least politically 'connected' of any candidates. Likewise, we found large and significant differences between the family political experiences of novice male *vs* novice female candidates. Novice women were significantly more likely than novice men to have had a spouse, father, mother, or grandparent who had held a political office.

These findings suggest different recruitment patterns for men and women under parity rules. Faced with the need to recruit a large number of politically inexperienced women, parties passed over anonymous party members and turned instead toward women from civil society with name recognition and strong family connections to politics. In a significant number of cases, parties achieved parity on their lists by replacing previously elected men with their female relatives.[33] Where men were concerned, parties were faced with a

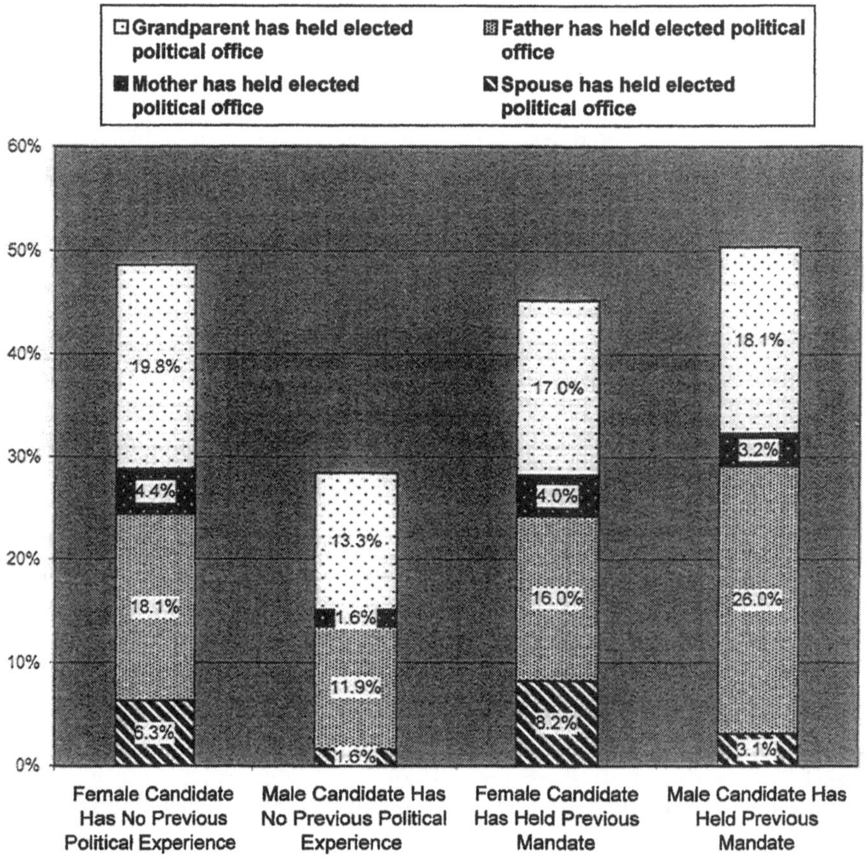

Figure 1 Family connections to politics among male and female candidates.

surplus of potential candidates. They maintained an important number of local notables, but also chose new male candidates from well outside established political families. These patterns of political recruitment might be characterized as *risk reduction* for new female candidates and *risk taking* for new male candidates. In general, where parity was required, parties appear to have applied the traditional system of recruiting among local notables. They solicited women endowed with social resources — notably wealth, education, and social connections — and enjoying a certain level of status and recognition within their communities. Far from representing a broader cross-section of the population, our findings suggest that novice female candidates were more likely than novice men to be drawn from families with established political connections.

Gender and the campaign experience

We asked candidates a number of questions concerning their decision to enter this election, and their experiences during the campaign. Far more than men, women who ran in this election reported serious hesitations before doing so (see Table 2). Women were *persistently* more likely than men to report hesitations, even when they had similar levels of political experience. 'Family reasons' were the second most frequent causes for hesitation (after 'lack of experience') among first-time female candidates and the *most* frequent cause for hesitation among those who had run before. Where family matters are concerned, spousal support appears to be a much more important factor in women's decision to enter the campaign than in men's. More women than men who entered the campaign told us that their spouse offered strong support for their candidacy. We interpret this to mean that many women who considered running for election, but whose husbands did not offer strong support, ultimately decided against it, and that fewer men with limited support from their wives likewise declined from running.[34] The level of children's support for their candidacy did not influence men and women differently.

Further analysis reveals that the size of a city has quite different implications for women than for men in their considerations about whether to run for election. After controlling statistically for a number of known differences between male and female candidates (age, previous political experience, the number of children living at home, employment sector, and household revenue), we found that for women there was a *positive* relationship between city size and the number of hesitations reported in the decision to run for municipal election (that is, the larger the city, the more the hesitations reported), while for men there was a *negative* relationship (the larger the city, the fewer hesitations).[35] This finding suggests two very different kinds of logic at work in men's and women's decisions about entering political life. For men, it may be that larger cities are more attractive because they provide greater opportunities for power and political advancement. For women, these characteristics may be less important. Instead, small towns (especially those under 9,000 inhabitants) may be especially desirable to women, both because women are less likely to doubt their capacities to serve elected office in such an environment, and because the physical space of such towns makes it easier for them to weave together public responsibilities with family and professional ones.[36]

Concerning the possibility of running in another municipal election, there is a 10-point gap between the percentage of men and women who say they will certainly do so, and this difference persists for men and women who were elected, as well as for those who were not. It appears, especially in larger cities, that women are less likely than men to enter politics with the idea of staying.

We asked men and women directly about the role of gender in this campaign. We expected that female candidates in larger cities would report that their gender provided them with an advantage. However, we were surprised to find that women in *small* towns — where parity does not apply — were also significantly more likely than men to report that their gender was an advantage to them. It is true that in some small towns (particularly those around the 2,500 – 3,499 range) voluntarily measures were adopted to include more women on the lists, and it is true that women did fare marginally better in small towns in 2001 than in previous elections. Nevertheless, it is indisputable that women's access to elected office in small towns remains severely limited. Consequently, we are not sure why women in these towns felt advantaged by their gender.

We were also surprised to find that, in larger towns, male candidates were more likely than female candidates to report that 'problems of particular concern to women' were touched on 'frequently' or 'occasionally' during the course of the election campaign. We think this is a promising result. It suggests that women's increased presence in politics has led to more public debate concerning women's issues than male politicians are accustomed to hearing. Heightened awareness of women's issues among men is usually a good thing.

Gender differences on political issues

We also discovered differences in women's and men's attitudes across a range of political issues (Table 3). Women are more likely than men to criticize present democratic arrangements, which they see as insufficiently representative. Women see themselves as having a more open and transparent approach to politics than men. Also, it is female candidates, more than male candidates, who perceive women as having a special capacity for representing other women. These differences persist, even after controlling for levels of prior political experience. Based on these observations, it appears that French women are moving against the traditional republican model of representation in which elected representatives are supposed to represent the collective interests of the nation and not any particular interests. For women in politics, more than for men, it *does* matter who does the representing; furthermore, women tend to see themselves as *better* representatives than men.

Surveys of the French *public* have consistently shown no difference between the favourability ratings of men and women toward gender parity. Our findings show that among men and women who are personally affected by the law, attitudes toward parity are quite different. In cities where the law was applied, there is a 15-point gap between the percentage of male and female candidates who say they are 'very favourable' toward the parity law. In these large cities, 24.1 per cent of men say they are opposed or strongly opposed to

Table 3 Political opinions of female and male candidates

	Small towns (under 3,500 inhabitants)			Large towns (3,500 or more inhabitants)		
	Women	*Men*	*Sig.*	*Women*	*Men*	*Sig.*
Political class not in touch with ordinary citizens. (% strongly agree)	45.9	45.7	NS	43.4	34.9	***
Renew representatives after 1 or 2 mandates. (% strongly agree)	20.6	27.2	NS	36.6	28.6	**
Women have more open, transparent approach than men (% strongly agree)	31.9	7.6	***	40.1	8.7	***
Few women in politics because less motivated than men (% strongly disagree)	21.4	13.6	***	29.3	9.4	***
Presence of women in great numbers may hurt quality of debate (% strongly disagree)	58.7	48.1	*	75.9	50.3	***
Women face more difficulties than men accessing positions of responsibility (% strongly agree)	36.4	22.2	NS	48.3	22.3	***
Normal for women in politics to accord particular attention to women's issues (% strongly agree)	18.7	11.1	NS	16.6	9.1	***
Women better placed than men on family, education issues (% strongly agree)	29.4	13.6	*	16.2	9.4	***
Parity (% very favourable)	37.8	29.5	*	49.0	34.3	***
Share domestic tasks equally when both work (% strongly agree)	79.0	48.1	***	77.6	53.3	***

Results of tests of significance: ***$p<0.005$; **$p<0.01$; *$p<0.05$; NS = non-significant.

parity, compared to 11.7 per cent of women. In small towns, 29.5 per cent of men are opposed or strongly opposed, compared to 19.7 per cent of women. Note that the highest level of opposition (35.3 per cent opposed or strongly opposed) toward parity was observed in small towns, among *women* with previous political experience.

Female candidates insist strongly that when both spouses work, household and family-related tasks should be shared equally. Men support this idea, but in a much less energetic manner. This confirms our finding on the importance of family responsibilities in most women's decisions to enter politics. For a married woman, spousal support — perhaps especially his assistance in holding down house and home — is of utmost importance in her choice to engage in political life. Furthermore we found that for women, *not* having a spouse appears to be a relative advantage for staying in politics, while for men *having* a spouse is an advantage. Among candidates with some previous political experience, women are far more likely than men to be single, widowed, or divorced. Among women who had run in a previous election, 26.7 per cent were unmarried and not living according to common law, compared to just 11 per cent of men. Among first-time candidates, there was no significant difference in the martial status of men and women.

Gender stratification in municipal responsibilities

Our next step in this analysis was to examine the responsibilities held by men and women within their city councils. One of the concerns expressed by some observers of the French parity law has been that women would end up holding minor responsibilities within municipal governments and that they would be marginalized into traditional 'women's' sectors such as education and social affairs. Our findings tend to confirm this hypothesis, but with an important caveat.

First, there is evidence of systematic discrimination against women in the assignment of responsibilities on council (Figure 2). We asked all candidates whether they had expressed a preference for a particular subcommittee or delegation prior to the election and, if elected, whether they received such an assignment. Women and men were equally likely to answer that they had expressed a preference for a committee assignment before the election. Among those with no previous political experience, 65.9 per cent of women and 67.2 per cent of men had expressed an interest in receiving a committee assignment. And among candidates with a previous political mandate, 74.4 per cent of women and 70.4 per cent of men had requested a committee assignment prior to the election. However, following the election, novice women were significantly less likely than novice men to be given a committee assignment. Among survey respondents with no previous mandate, and who were actually

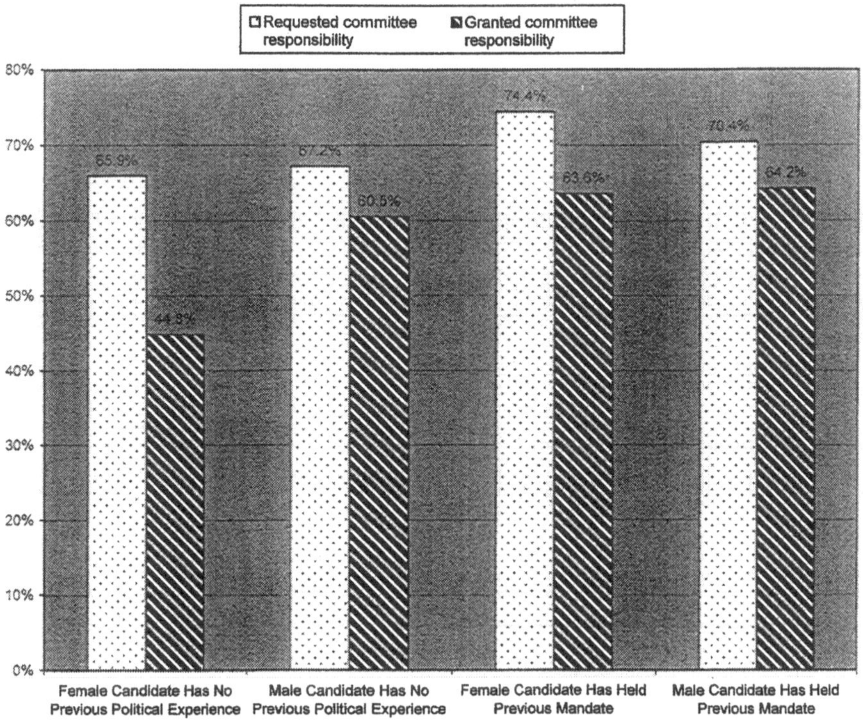

Figure 2 Assignment of committee responsibilities to male and female councillors.

elected in 2001, just 44.8 per cent of women compared to 60.5 per cent of men were given a role as adjunct or assigned to a municipal subcommittee or delegation. Among women and men who held a previous mandate, there was no significant difference in the responsibilities assigned to them (63.6 per cent of women were assigned responsibilities compared to 64.2 per cent of men). In short, it appears that mayors are less willing to assign novice women as adjuncts and committee members than to assign novice men. Moreover, this discrepancy is not a result of any reluctance on the part of women to assume significant responsibilities on the council.

We were also interested to see what *kinds* of responsibilities women tend to be assigned. Candidates who had expressed an interest in assuming committee responsibilities were asked to specify which subcommittee or delegation they preferred and, if elected, what assignment they were given. As shown in Figure 3, the expressed pre-election preferences of men and women are remarkably different. Where women overwhelmingly preferred committee responsibilities related to social assistance, education, and children, men's

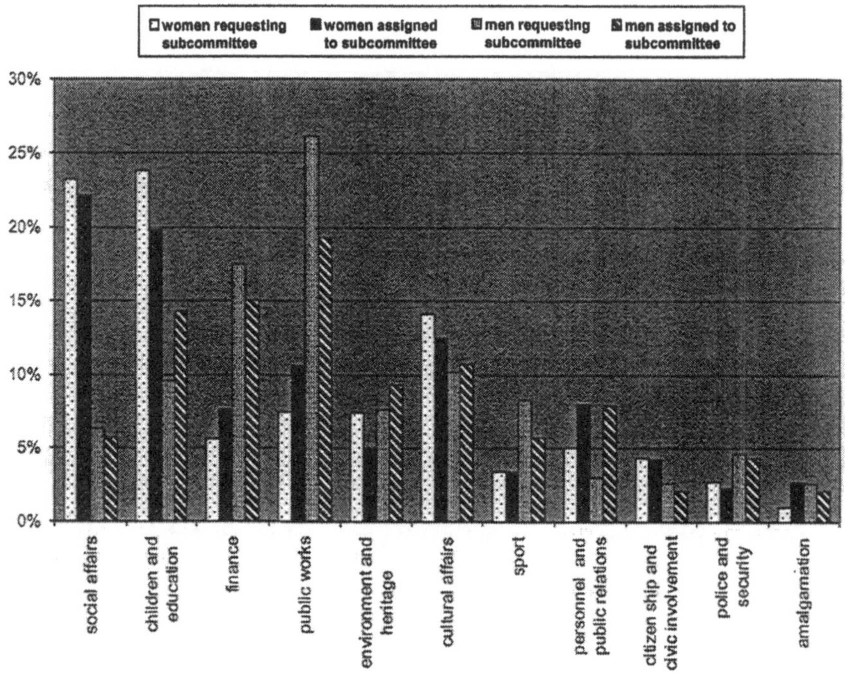

Figure 3 Sexual stratification in municipal subcommittees.

preferences ran more heavily toward finance and public works. Figure 3 also presents the actual subcommittees to which elected women and men were assigned. Certainly candidates' preferences weigh heavily in allocating areas of responsibility. Nevertheless councils achieved a more even gender balance on almost every delegation than would have been achieved had candidates simply been granted their preferences. These findings suggest that novice women councillors in France face some degree of discrimination in seeking positions of responsibility in local government, but also that women contribute to their marginalization by their reluctance to seek responsibility outside traditionally 'feminine' sectors like education and social affairs.

Including other marginalized groups

Finally, we explore the possibility that parity and women's increased presence in politics may have broader implications for the inclusion of other marginalized groups. We remind the reader that this is a sensitive and difficult subject in France (Bird, 2001). The advocates of parity went to exceptional lengths to assure legislators that the introduction of positive measures to enhance women's representation in legislative assemblies would *not* speed the republic down a slippery slope toward multicultural and group-based rights. Women, they argued, are not a simple category (like Beurs, Blacks, Muslims, homosexuals, and so on). Categorization by gender would not violate the principle of republican unity because, according to Guy Carcassone, 'these are universal, quantitatively equal, and perfectly objective categories, and are limited to two, which is not the case for social situations, religious situations, or so-called ethnic or racial situations' (Mossuz-Lavau 1998, 84). Furthermore, as the results reported above suggest, the women elected to political office under parity rules are not necessarily part of a disadvantaged class. It is therefore doubtful that they would be more likely than men to prioritize the political inclusion of socially or economically marginalized groups. Despite these problems, our analysis suggests that support for parity *is* related to support for political inclusion for other politically marginalized groups. It also appears that the presence of more women in legislative assemblies *enhances* the likelihood of measures to promote the political inclusion of diverse social categories.

We asked respondents four questions that we believed would tap into attitudes toward 'inclusion of diversity:' Do you favour better representation of diverse social categories among those elected in our country? Do you favour giving foreignors from non-EU countries the right to vote in local elections? Do you believe that the presence of immigrants in France is a source of cultural enrichment? Do you believe that wearing an Islamic headscarf in school should be prohibited? The first three of these items combined to form an index with reasonably high scale reliability ($\alpha = 0.67$). The fourth item did not scale well with the others, and was removed from the analysis.

In Table 4, we present the results of a regression analysis with 'inclusion of diversity' as the dependent variable. Scores on this variable range from 1 to 10,

Table 4 The impact of gender parity on support for inclusion of social diversity

	β	B	*Sig.*
Sex (female)	0.006	0.292	0.005
City size	0.098	0.188	0.000
Previous political experience	−0.026	−0.111	0.292
Age	0.009	0.002	0.703
Political ideology (right wing)	−0.638	−1.139	0.000
Opposed to parity	−0.121	−0.315	0.000
Constant	9.67		
Adjusted R^2	0.496		

with a mean of 7.02 and a standard deviation of 2.12. A high score represents support for inclusion of diverse social categories. Our explanatory variables are candidates' sex, city size (under 3,500; 3,500–8,999; 9,000–29,999; 30,000 or more inhabitants), age, previous political experience (have never or have run in a previous election), left–right ideological position (a 5-point scale), and support for parity (a 4-point scale). The results show that this model explains half of the variability in attitudes toward 'inclusion of diversity' (adjusted $R^2 = 0.496$). Most important, we find that women are more likely than men, and candidates who favour gender parity more likely than opponents, to support 'inclusion of diversity.' This remains true even after controlling for their political ideology, level of political experience, age, and the size of their city.

Conclusion: Women in Politics in France

Women's access to politics at the local level has been understudied. Yet if, as some feminist scholars argue, the presence of women in the political sphere can serve to legitimize alternative and more democratic modes of political organization, then the logical *first* place to look for such transformative capacity is at the local level.

In the case of France, the implications of women's presence in local politics may be especially important. Historically, French municipal elections have held a pivotal role within the national political structure and, while local in form, they are in fact quite national in scope.[37] Furthermore, these elections implicate an enormous number of people. Traditionally, voter turnout is higher for local elections than for any other level of election in France, and more people are elected to local government in France than in any other country of comparable size.[38] With the application of parity to the 2001 municipal elections in France, more than 39,000 women joined their local city councils (in towns over 3,500 inhabitants), almost double their numbers in the councils sitting before 18 March 2001. The effect of this mass of women entering the political sphere, across the country, and at a level where they are visible and accessible to ordinary citizens is undoubtedly more significant than the election of 71 women to the National Assembly. Certainly, the question of whether parity and the arrival of a critical mass of women can transform representative arrangements and policy directions at the local and other levels necessitates a broader and longer-term project than the one reported here. Nevertheless, the results of this study carry implications for understanding the effects of parity and the role of women in politics, in France and elsewhere.

At the most basic level, the application of the parity law to municipal elections can be understood as a test case, and can help us predict outcomes and foresee problems for future elections in which parity will apply. Our findings show that the law can have a residual effect on increasing the number of women in elected office, even where it does not apply in the strictest of terms. This residual effect is undoubtedly stronger in small-town municipal elections than in legislative districts with strong party competition. Nevertheless, there may be a general contagion effect of female nominations — including in highly competitive legislative elections — as it becomes clearer to parties that there is no electoral penalty associated with female candidates, and as female candidates, mayors, and councillors become a more common fixture in important cities across France (Matland and Studlar, 1996).

Second, this study suggests that French women have significantly different ideas than men on many political matters. Despite the fact that female candidates (like their male counterparts) tend to be drawn from within the elite stratum of society, they appear nevertheless to hold a distinctive set of perspectives on politics. In most cases, these differences are not attributable merely to women's lack of previous political experience: rather, they are differences with 'staying power.' Among the factors shaping women's distinctive perspectives on political issues, clearly one of the most important is the priority they place on family responsibilities. Women's previous exclusion from the public sphere may also explain their higher level of support for greater socio-cultural diversification among political actors. These results suggest that women's presence on local councils, and especially in the local executive, is likely to make a difference with respect to policy directions.[39] While we have measured differences between male and female candidates at the individual level, it seems reasonable to assume that there will also be a separate sociological effect of women entering politics *en masse*, and that this may further enhance the speed and magnitude of change. Despite holding out some promise of democratic renewal, we have found that the novice women elected under parity rules face an uphill battle to prove their credibility and assume positions of responsibility on local councils.

The results of this study point to both institutional and cultural factors that interact with the parity law to produce rather unique effects on women's access to political office in France. The institutional structure of local politics in France offers two significant advantages to women. First and most obviously, through the application of a proportional-list system in municipal elections, parity translates into roughly 50 per cent women among elected councillors. Second, the municipal structure in France provides many more entry points to elected office than are available in other countries of comparable size, including entry opportunities in towns of reasonabley small size. Our study has shown that despite the parity law, French women remain more hesitant to enter politics in larger cities than in smaller ones. This suggests that, in countries where the trend has been toward the amalgamation of local governments, the opportunities for political engagement among women may be especially limited.

In other respects however, the structure of local politics in France continues to pose important obstacles to women. The indirect election of French mayors and adjuncts, the concentration and personification of authority in the mayoral office, and the widespread practice of holding multiple simultaneous mandates contribute heavily toward the continuing dominance of men within the upper levels of the local executive. In recruiting new women into politics, French parties have continued to rely upon networks of local notables. Like the men before them, the women who enter politics under parity rules tend to be drawn from an elite stratum of society. The wider dispersal of local power in France would almost certainly help women to achieve fairer representation within the executive level. It would also promote a culture of democratization that would lower the barriers of political entry, making it easier for ordinary people to run for political office.

It is also important to consider the set of culturally specific assumptions about the role of women in society, and the obstacles and advantages that these present in terms of women's access to political life. French women are overwhelmingly disadvantaged by the widespread assumption (largely shared by women themselves) that child-rearing and household responsibilities are women's responsibilities. These ideas are a remnant of the significant role played by the Catholic Church in French history, and the Church's reverence for the mother figure. However, such assumptions have been re-affirmed by a Republic which, despite erecting a wall of separation between the church and the state, has continued to implement natalist policies that serve to confine women to the private and domestic spheres. The assumption that women hold the primary responsibility for children and home makes women less disposed than men to enter political life, and may encourage a notion that men are naturally more 'fit' for public life. Yet, at the same time, this assumption has opened up a variety of workplace solutions intended to provide women with the flexibility to accommodate family responsibilities, and many women have used this flexibility to engage in public life. The cultural constraints faced by French women mean that, when women do enter political life, they often do so for different reasons and with different perspectives than men. For example, women still tend overwhelmingly to prefer committees and ministries associated with social affairs, education, and children. Also, the burden of family responsibilities makes it more difficult for women than for men to hold multiple mandates simultaneoulsy, and a result is that women are less likely than men to envision a political career for themselves.

In hindsight, it is clear that these institutional and cultural constraints posed significant obstacles for women's access to political office in France. Within this context, parity was an important and necessary step for increasing the number of women in the political sphere. Yet there are important interaction effects between a parity law on the one hand, and electoral and institutional rules and cultural constraints on the other hand. In countries where the political sphere remains relatively inaccessible to women, parity and other measures to promote women's access to politics will interact in different ways with the institutional and cultural factors specific to that country. As we have seen in France, these factors play a significant role in determining what kind of women enter public life, what roles they play, what obstacles they face, and what ideas and aspirations they bring to politics.

Notes

1 This survey would not have been possible without the financial and logistical support of the Centre d'Informatisation des Données Socio-Politiques (CIDSP), of the Institut d'Etudes Politiques de Grenoble. I thank the Centrè's research director, Bruno Cautrès, for facilitating this project. My gratitude extends to all of the Centre's research team, and most particularly to Mathilde Dubesset, Vincent Tournier, Annie-Claude Solomon, Nadine Mandran and Valérie Rocchi for their sound advice on the construction of the questionnaire, and assistance in data management.

2 From November 1946 (the first elections in which women were eligible to vote and run as candidates) until the elections of June 1997, the percentage of seats in the French National Assembly held by women has ranged from a low of 1.6 per cent to a high of only 5.9 per cent. Since its creation in 1959 until the last pre-parity elections of 1998, women had never held more than 5.9 per cent of seats in the French Senate. In municipal elections from 1946 to 1997, women obtained between 2.4 per cent and 21.7 per cent of local council seats, but never more than 7.5 per cent of mayorships. Within the French departmental assemblies (*Conseils généraux*), from their creation in 1958 until the last pre-parity elections of 1998, women's share of seats ranged from 0.7 to 8.3 per cent. For detailed information on the share of seats won by women in French elections since the Fourth Republic, see Sineau (2001, 279–288).

3 In 1999, a governmental report was issued by an official committee on the French language which favoured the feminization of professional titles thus *allowing* women to be addressed, for example, as 'Madame la ministre.' See also Houdebine-Gravaud (1998).

4 Loi no. 2000-493 tendant à favoriser l' égal accès des femmes de des hommes aux mandats électoraux et fonctions électives.

5 According to Article 6 of the Declaration of the Rights of Man and Citizen, 'all citizens being equal' in the eyes of the law, '[all] are equally eligible for every public rank, seat and employment according to their abilities, and without any distinction but that based upon their virtues and talents.' Under Article 3 of the Constitution of 1958, 'no section of the people, nor any individual, may attribute to themselves or himself the exercise [of National sovereignty],' and suffrage 'is always universal, equal and secret.' The Court concluded that these constitutional principles guarantee 'the right to vote and to run for office under identical conditions' and that they 'oppose the division of voters or candidates by any category.' (Decision 82-146 DC, 18 November 1982).

6 Halimi was an independent member aligned with the parliamentary Socialist group. She was the founder and the president of the feminist association 'Choisir' and, in the course of a televised debate during the presidential campaign, Halimi had attained a public promise from Mitterrand

that he was in favour of adopting a minimum quota for female candidates. See Choisir la cause des femmes (1981).

7 Halimi's proposal was for a 70 per cent ceiling for any one sex, applied to every third of the list so as to prevent a party from relegating the women to the bottom of the list. The Socialist amendment proposed a higher ceiling (75 per cent) and included no restrictions on the order of presentation of male and female candidates.

8 Assemblée nationale, *Débats parlementaires, compte rendu intégral*, session of 27 July 1992, *Journal officiel*, 28 July 1992, 4913.

9 *Ibid.*, 4913.

10 Initiatives included the UN Convention of 1979 of the Elimination of All Forms of Discrimination Against Women (CEDAW), and resolutions passed in 1986 (Resolution 855 on Equality Between Men and Women) and 1995 (Recommendation 1269 on Achieving Real Progress in Women's Rights) by the Parliamentary Assembly of the Council of Europe. The first European conference on parity was organized in 1989, by the European Council.

11 By comparison, in 1997: women held 11.3 per cent of the seats in the US House of Representatives and 9 per cent of the seats in the US Senate; in Canada women held 20.6 per cent of seats in the House of Commons and 30.5 per cent of seats in the Senate; on average, across all Europe-OSCE member countries, women held 14.1 per cent of seats in the lower and upper houses of parliament combined; the world average was 10.5 per cent; the top five countries remain Sweden, Denmark, Finland, Norway, and the Netherlands, where women hold between 43 and 36 per cent of legislative seats. For a current overview of women's representation in world parliaments, see the 'Women in Parliament' report issued by the Inter-parliamentary Union (http://www.ipu.org/wmn-e/classif.htm).

12 The number of signatories for this declaration of support for parity (*Le monde*, 10 November 1993) is equivalent to the number of seats in the National Assembly. This manifesto was presented in the symbolic tradition of other feminist manifestos; it was modelled after the famous 'Manifeste des 343' women who, in their support for the liberalization of abortion law in France, gave public testament to having undergone clandestine abortions (*Le Nouvel Observateur*, 5 April 1971).

13 L'Assemblée des femmes, Réseau femme pour la parité, and Demain la parité are certainly the most important of the pro-parity associations founded in the 1990s.

14 Among the most active in the parity movement were three figures: Giséle Halimi, Yvette Roudy, and Françosie Gaspard. Other important figures include Janine Mossuz-Lavau and Geneviève Fraisse. All have held office, or have been active within the Socialist Party.

15 The manifesto was signed by Michèle Barzach, Frédérique Bredin, Edith Cresson, Hélène Gisserot, Catherine Lalumière, Véronique Neiertz, Monique Pelletier, Yvette Roudy, Catherine Tasca, and Simone Veil. *L'Express* (6–12 June 1996).

16 The Socialist Party passed this rule on 30 June 1996. Among the 555 Socialist candidates who contested seats in the 1997 legislative elections, 167 were women. Following those elections, the Socialists formed a governing majority in the National Assembly through a coalition with the Communist and Green Parties. Among the 246 legislative seats held by the Socialist party following the election, 42 (17.1 per cent) were held by women.

17 A survey of deputies and senators published in *Le Monde* prior to the introduction of the government project revealed little support for constitutional reform to allow parity. Le Monde (8 March 1997).

18 Most cite 6 June as the date of promulgation of the French parity law. There are in fact, *two* parity laws. The first law, voted on 3 May and promulgated on 6 June 2000, is the most significant in that it imposes parity throughout the French metropole. A second law, debated together with the first, concerns specifically the implementation of parity within the legislative assemblies of the overseas territories of French Polynesia, New Caledonia, and the islands of

Wallis-and-Futuna. The passage of this law (14 June 2001 with final assent on 4 July 2000) was delayed by disagreement between the National Assembly and the Senate over the idea of imposing a less constraining version of parity to certain overseas territories, in order to allow for their more traditional (i.e. paternalistic) cultures. The version preferred by the National Assembly, imposing parity in virtually identical terms throughout French territory, ultimately prevailed after four readings.

19 The constitutional amendment was passed by 741 votes to 43 (and 48 abstentions) in joint congress. A constitutional amendment requires a simple majority vote in both the National Assembly and Senate, plus ratification by three-fifths of the members of both houses assembled in a joint congress. The parity law was adopted just three votes short of unanimity on final reading in the National Assembly.

20 See, especially, Agacinski (1998, 1999b) and Mossuz-Lavau (1998).

21 On varieties of French republicanism, see Jennings (2000).

22 Sylviane Agacincksi (1999b) criticizes the American approach to women's rights, because it erases the *essential* difference of sex and fails to recognize its universal character: 'L'effacement 'américain' procède en noyant les femmes dans un particularisme généralisé où se retrouvent des minorités de toutes sortes (ethniques, religieuses, culturelles, etc.), et les deux sexes finissent par être considérés commes de pures 'constructions'....'

23 Though it may be that women's presence allows for the expression of a distinctive conception of the general interest.

24 In 1986, elections to the National Assembly were run using rules of proportional representation, but the law was changed and elections reverted back to single-member plurality rules in 1988.

25 The requirement for alternating male and female candidates is sometimes called the 'zipper system.' The French use the term *chabada*, a reference to the musical theme of the Claude Lelouche film *Un homme et une femme.* French law requires strict alternation between male and female candidates for elections that follow proportional methods and are decided in one round (Senate and European elections). This requirement was not imposed for two-round elections because it was considered important to allow parties adequate flexibility in forming coalition lists between rounds.

26 Alternatively, it must be pointed out that roughly two-thirds of French citizens live in communities whose town councils are elected according to parity rules.

27 Survey commissioned by the government's *Observatoire de la Parité*, conducted by l'Institut CSA, March 2001.

28 Statistics from Ministère de l'Intérieur, made available in the Rapport au Premier Ministre: *La parité entre les femmes et les hommes: Une avancée decisive pour la démocratie,* March 2002.

29 Statistics for Dous and Isère were collected by the author; statistics for Hérault were made available by the Assemblée des Femmes du Languedoc et du Roussillon, *Evaluation de la loi sur la parité*, September 2001.

30 In elections at three different levels, we have seen now that parity is ineffective unless the law applies strictly. This was revealed in legislative elections (discussed above), and also in elections to the French departmental assemblies (*Conseils généraux*) and to the Senate. In March 2001, in elections that were run simultaneously with municipal elections, French voters elected 1,932 representatives to their departmental assemblies. These elections are exempt from parity rules. The result: just 9.8 per cent of the *Conseillers généraux* elected last spring were women, compared to 8.3 per cent in 1998. Of all 101 departmental councils in France, a woman heads only one. For elections to the Senate, parity applies in departments electing three or more Senators (where a proportional-list system is used), but not in elections in smaller departments. Senate elections were held on 23 September 2001, in which one-third of the Senate was renewed. In first-past-the-post contests (those exempt from parity rules), there was no increase in the number of women elected: there are only two women among the 28 seats. But among the 74

Senate seats elected using PR, the number of women increased from 5 to 20. Of the 102 Senators elected in September 2001, 22 were women (21.6 per cent), bringing their total number in the Senate to 35 of 321 (10.9 per cent) compared to just 20 (6.2 percent) before parity. See Bird (forthcoming).

31 On the functions of substantive or 'descriptive' representation, see Mansbridge (2000).

32 Questionnaires were distributed by mail, between 15 May and 15 July 2001, to a stratified random sample of 3000 candidates in municipal elections across two departments (Doubs and Isère) and in one large city (Lyon). Women were sampled 2 to 1 over men, while candidates in towns over 3,500 inhabitants were sampled 4 to 1 over candidates in towns under 3,500. A total of 1216 completed questionnaires were returned, including 800 completed by female candidates and 403 completed by male candidates (13 respondents did not identify their sex), for a response rate of 40 among both women and men. Among the total respondents, 922 were candidates in towns with over 3,500 inhabitants, while 272 were candidates in smaller towns (20 respondents did not indicate the size of their town). A copy of the questionnaire may be obtained by writing to the author.

33 It is impossible to tell how widespread this strategy was in naming female candidates. Fabre (2001) has commented on its use in a number of municipal contests across France. In sampling party lists for our study, we encountered two cases where the parties spontaneously informed us that *every* female candidate was a relative of a male candidate, and we encountered many more instances where female candidates were clearly related to male candidates or previous office-holders.

34 Interviews with mayors and councillors who were involved in the recruitment process confirm this interpretation. It was, we were told, very difficult to recruit female candidates if the spouse was not favourable while spousal support was much less essential for the recruitment of male candidates.

35 Regression equation :$Y=1.625–0.356x_1$ ($p<0.001$)$–0.339x_2$ ($p=0.250$)$+0.013x_3$ ($p=0.553$)$+$ $0.096x_4$($p=0.028$)$–0.006x_5$ ($p=0.032$)$–0.115x_6$ ($p=0.002$)$+0.118x_7$ ($p=0.013$) $-0.197x_8$ ($p=0.023$)$+$ $0.198x_9$ ($p=0.066$)$+e$; where Y=number of hesitations reported; x_1=have run in previous election ; x_2=female; x_3=household revenue; x_4=number of children under 18 living at home; x_5=age; x_6=city size (under 3,500, 3,500–8,999, 9000–29,999, over 30,000 inhabitants); x_7=interaction; female, city size; x_8=employed in private sector; x_9=interaction: female, private sector. Adjusted $R^2=0.140$; standard error of estimate$=0.7764$.

36 In such communities, the town hall, school, bakery, butcher, grocery store, and quite possibly one's place of employment are often within steps of each other.

37 Municipal elections occur on the same day throughout the country, and are essentially viewed as national elections by the political parties. See Martin (2001).

38 The number of towns in France (36,565) is greater than the number of towns in all European member-states combined. In total, there are roughly 500,000 elected local representatives in France.

39 In several municipalities, it appears that the presence of women during the campaign and in the newly elected councils *has* served to re-define what are the fundamental issues of local politics. In Paris, most notably, the availability of public child-care facilities became a significant issue during the campaign. Since its election, the re-organization of municipal services whose principal clients are women and children (e.g. child-care, public transportation, health, school, and sporting services) has become a priority within the Paris city council. The adjunct-mayor of Paris, Anne Hidalgo, is responsible for the municipal commission on Equality between Men and Women, as well as directing the city's new 'Bureau du Temps' charged with reorganizing public services with women and children in mind. A similar office exists in the city of Poitiers.

References

Agacinski-Jospin, S. (1996) 'Citoyennes, encore un effort...,' *Le Monde*, 18 June.

Agacinski, S. (1998) *Politique des sexes*, Paris, Seuil.

Agacinski, S. (1999a) 'Le droit d'être candidates', *Le Nouvel Observateur*, 14–20 January, p. 85.

Agacinski, S. (1999b) 'Contre l'effacement des sexes', *Le Monde*, 6 February.

Badinter, E. (1996) 'Non aux quotas de femmes', *Le Monde*, 12 June.

Badinter, E. (1999) 'Un remède pire que le mal', *Le Nouvel Observateur*, 14–20 January, p. 85.

Badinter, E., Pisier, E. and Sallenave, D. (1999) 'Trois arguments contre la parité', *L'Express*, 11 February.

Bird, K. (2001) '*Liberté, égalité, fraternité, parité...* and *diversité*? The difficult question of ethnic difference in the French parity debate', *Contemporary French Civilization* 25(2): 271–292.

Bird, K. (forthcoming) 'Who needs Women? Gender parity in French elections', in J. Gaffney (ed.). *The French Presidential and Legislative Elections of 2002*, Aldershot: Ashgate.

Carroll, S.J. and Strimling, W. (1983) *Women's Routes to Elective Office*, New Brunswick, NJ: Center for the American Woman and Politics.

Choisir la cause des femmes (1981) *Quel président pour les femmes? Réponses de François Mitterrand*, (Preface by Gisèle Halimi), Paris: Gallimard.

Fabre, C. (2001) 'Aux municipales, on joue aussi 'épouses et concubines', *Le Monde*, 24 February.

Gaspard, F., Le Gall, A. and Servan-Schreiber, C. (1992) *Au pouvoir citoyennes! Liberté, égalit parité*, Paris: Seuil.

Houdebine-Gravaud, A.-M. (1998) *La Féminisation des noms de métier, en français et dans d'autres langues*, Paris: L'Harmattan.

Jennings, J. (2000) 'Citizenship, republicanism and multiculturalism in contemporary France', *British Journal of Political Science* 30: 575–598.

Jenson, J. and Sineau, M. (2001) *Who Cares? Women's Work, Child Care and Welfare State Redesign*, Toronto: University of Toronto Press.

Krémer, P. (2001) 'Le partage des tâches domestiques, noeud des inégalités hommes-femmes', *Le Monde*, 8 March.

Landes, J.B. (1988) *Women and the public sphere in the age of the French Revolution*, Ithaca: Cornell University Press.

Lister, R. (1997) *Citizenship: Feminist perspectives*, Washington Square: New York University Press.

Lochak, D. (1983) 'Les hommes politiques, les 'sages'(?)... et les femmes (à propos de la décision du Conseil constitutionnel du 18 novembre 1982)', *Droit Social*, 1983: 131.

Malibeau, A. (1995) 'De la monarchie municipale à la française', *Pouvoirs*, 73: 7–17.

Mansbridge, J. (2000) 'What does a representative do? Descriptive representation in communicative settings of distrust, uncrystallized interests, and historically denigrated status', in W. Kymlicka and W. Norman (eds.) *Citizenship in Diverse Societies*, Oxford: Oxford University Press, pp. 99–123.

Martin, P. (2001) *Les élections municipales en France depuis 1945*, Paris: La Documentation Française.

Matland, R. and Studlar, D. (1996) 'The contagion of women candidates in single-member district and proportional representation electoral systems: Canada and Norway', *Journal of Politics* 58(3): 707–733.

Méda, D. (2001) *Le temps des femmes: Pour un nouveau partage des tâches*, Paris: Flammarion.

Millard, E. and Ortiz, L. (1998) 'Parité et représentations politiques', in J. Martin (ed). *Parité: Enjeux et mise en oeuvre*, Toulouse: Presses universitaires du Mirail, pp. 189–203.

Mossuz-Lavau, J. (1998) *Femmes/hommes pour la parité*, Paris: Presses de sciences po.

Norris, P. and Lovenduski, J. (1993) 'If only more candidates came forward': supply-side explanations of candidate selection in Britain', *British Journal of Political Science* 23: 373–408.

Perrot, M. (1995) 'Identité, égalité, différence. Le regard de l'histoire', in the collection Ephesia, *La place des femmes, Les enjeux de l'dentité et de l'égalité au regard des sciences sociales*, Paris: La Découverte, pp. 39–56.

Perrot, M. (1997) *Femmes publiques*, Paris: Textuel.

Phillips, A. (1993) *Democracy and difference*, University Park: The Pennsylvania State University Press.

Phillips, A. (1995) *The Politics of Presence: The Political Representation of Gender, Ethnicity, and Race*, New York: Oxford.

Genisson, C. (2002). *La parité entre les femmes et les homes: Une avancée decisive pour la démocratie*, Paris: Observatoire de la Parité entre les Femmes et les Hommes.

Sineau, M. (1999) 'Pouvoir politique, pouvoir domestique: Les deux faces de la parité', *Le Monde Diplomatique*, December.

Sineau, M. (2001) *Profession femme politique: Sex et pouvoir sous la Cinquième République*, Paris: Presses de Sciences Po.

[28]

SALLY J. KENNEY

BREAKING THE SILENCE: GENDER MAINSTREAMING AND THE COMPOSITION OF THE EUROPEAN COURT OF JUSTICE

(Accepted July 2002)

ABSTRACT. Why has it taken so long for member states to appoint women to the Court of Justice? Despite having won relatively significant policy instruments for equal treatment at work and high levels of legislative representation, women in the European Union have been slow to extend the demand for gender mainstreaming to courts. Prior to 1999, the Court of Justice had had one woman member until Ireland appointed Fidelma Macken in late 1999, and Germany appointed Ninon Colneric and Austria appointed Christine Stix-Hackl Advocate General in 2000. The 1995 U.N. meeting in Beijing was a catalyst for the demand for balanced participation of women and men in decision-making processes within the E.U., and it coincided with Sweden, Finland and Austria joining and championing the cause of gender equality. In 1999, the Commission published a report on women in the judiciary and women lawyers began to organise across Europe. After tracing the appointment process, I review the European Parliament's role in championing women on the Court and consider recent developments. Courts, particularly supranational and federal courts, are representative institutions even if their representative function differs from legislatures. Non-merit factors have always been a factor in judicial appointments and thus the demand for women on the bench is not a terrible deviation from merit. An all male bench is no longer legitimate.

KEY WORDS: Court of Justice, gender representation, judicial selection, women judges

1. Introduction

The walls of the robing room of the Court of Justice are lined with portraits of previous members, all men in the fifty years since it began as the court for the European Coal and Steel Community in 1952 but one. The three new women members, Judge Macken, Judge Colneric, and Advocate General Stix-Hackl, were sworn in as the European Commission issued a report that finally extended its longstanding call for the inclusion of women in positions of decision-making to the judiciary. The European Womens' Lawyer Association Congress held its founding meeting in March 2000, and in Germany, Sweden and the United Kingdom, women used employment discrimination law to challenge their exclusion from judicial positions and questioned the legitimacy of decisions issued by all-male courts.

This paper applies the concept of gender mainstreaming to judicial selection. It is not surprising that feminists have been slow to tackle the issue because the process of selection is secretive, idiosyncratic to member states, and the Court issues a single collegiate judgment and is studied more for its doctrines than its politics (de Búrca, 2001, p. 1). Scholars have mostly characterized it as favourable to feminist arguments (Barnard, 1995; Hoskyns, 1996; but see also Ellis, 2000, p. 1425). Women's organisations have only recently framed gender along with nation and legal systems as a legitimate candidate for representation. How is the concept of representation different for courts and legislatures? Who do women on the bench represent, and why is their presence important?

2. Gender Mainstreaming and Courts

Gender mainstreaming moves beyond the arenas of equality law or even women's issues to analyse policies for their effect on equality between men and women (Beveridge and Nott, in this issue; Mazey, 2000, p. 37; Rees, 1998; Shaw, 2000). It might seem that counting and calling for women to be part of decision making is but a minor item on the agenda, a liberal feminist demand to be merely included. But if one delves deeper into why women must be present at the centre of power as issues are framed and agendas constructed, then the demand for women judges is intrinsically linked to putting all public policies under a gender lens. Contemplating the paucity of women judges leads quickly to identifying formal and informal barriers. In the United States in the 1970s (Cook, 1988) as in Britain in the 1990s (Malleson, 1999; McGlynn, 1999) feminists, as well as calling for more gender-balanced results, demanded changes in the process of selection, removing it from the exclusive purview of the elite of the legal profession and calling for the inclusion of lay members on merit advisory panels. They demanded that the pool of candidates be widened and that the list of qualifications be rethought.

But putting women on the bench was more than an end in itself, it was a means to change judicial behaviour. It is no accident that the demand for women on the bench emerged at the same time as feminists were turning to the courts for public policy changes. Feminists wanted judges to stop demeaning women lawyers, clients and witnesses (Kennedy, 1993). They wanted judges to stop blaming rape victims and battered women for their assaults. They wanted lesbians to retain custody of their children, and housewives who had sacrificed for a husband's career to receive maintenance. In short, they wanted the bench to adopt a gender analysis of all questions before the court, from criminal law, to family law, to taxation and inheritance. They wanted to ensure that judges did not overturn their policy gains, they wanted further progress through legal interpretation, and they wanted issues framed in a feminist way. Feminists knew that part of their strategy must include having a voice at the table when judges deliberated.

Although American feminists have not embraced the term gender mainstreaming, one of their most important policy successes – the movement to undertake gender bias taskforces – could be understood under this rubric (Resnick, 1996; Schafran, 1987; Wikler, 1989). Begun first in the state of New Jersey, state supreme courts (and now federal circuits) sponsored investigations into their own practices. (It was often the women appointed to state supreme courts who called for the creation of a taskforce.) Having both the virtue and the limitation of being conducted by a committee which included judges alongside social scientists, such studies often took the form of questionnaires to members of the bar, public hearings, and investigations of particular areas of case law, most often divorce, custody and domestic violence cases. The results were compelling. Women lawyers complained of widespread harassment and demeaning treatment, studies documented enormous discrepancies in judicial treatment of cases on divorce and domestic violence, and the public testified to the perception of bias and unfairness. Perhaps most importantly, the process raised the consciousness of male judges who turned to their women colleagues for reassurance that 'such things never happened to them', only to be told that they did. The growing awareness of a few judges and a report documenting findings was followed by modest efforts of the judiciary itself to correct the wrongs uncovered. As more states undertook similar searching self-study, it became harder not to participate. Now, more than thirty jurisdictions have produced reports. In the U.S., the demand for women on the bench led quickly to a demand for an analysis of how courts conducted their business. Initial calls for women on the European bench, however, have not produced a similar mobilisation.

3. Gender and Judicial Appointments at the Court

History

The E.U.'s founders considered different methods of selecting judges (Feld, 1963, p. 53, n. 68), including a role for Parliament similar to the Assembly of the Council of Europe's role in choosing judges for the European Court of Human Rights. Article 223 of the Treaty of Amsterdam states that the judges and advocates general shall be appointed by common accord of the governments of the member states for a renewable term of six years. In practice, each member state government follows its own internal selection procedure and simply informs the Council. Fifteen judges sit on the Court, one from each member state. Also sitting are nine advocates general. Members are former judges, civil servants, politicians, practicing lawyers, and professors.

Appointments to the Court receive little attention (Feld, 1963; Kenney, 2000; Scheingold, 1963). One explanation is that Europeans accept and consider normal a higher degree of secrecy and that, consequently, judicial appointments are one of many matters left to elites. In Britain, for example, Parliament neither scrutinises nor approves judicial appointments (Malleson, 1999, pp. 79–155). Even the appointees themselves claim to know little of the processes that lead to their own appointment. But a more powerful explanation is that law and politics are generally viewed differently. Scholars and judges alike resist classifying and studying the Court as a political institution, despite its evolving constitutional status. This denial of the political role of courts persists, notwithstanding the increasing role of national courts in shaping public policy in France (Stone, 1997), Germany (Kommers, 1997) and the United Kingdom (Sterett, 1997), as well as the growing impact of supranational courts.

Each country must face the task of representing its own set of interests and cleavages: party, language, region, legal system, governmental department. Just as the leadership of E.U. institutions must be balanced among the member states, within member states themselves, a different balancing process occurs. Parties or languages may have to be balanced across Court appointments: advocate general, judge, judge at the Court of First Instance, or across international courts such as the European Court of Human Rights or International Court of Justice. Appointments to the Court sometimes display many of the same features of diplomatic appointments: exile for a party luminary who is in trouble, a retirement prize for exemplary public service, the removal of a competitor within a party, or a consolation prize for a failed judicial appointment at home.

Appointment to the Court is political in the sense that personal connections to the appointing executive and party credentials are paramount, even if the appointments are not motivated by specific policy goals. Appointments are not made strictly on merit. Two examples illustrate this. The Belgian government's appointment of Melchior Wathelet in 1995 drew the wrath of Members of the European Parliament both on the grounds of his judicial abilities as well as concern about events during his tenure at the Belgian Ministry of Justice (Helm, 1996, p. 11; *Agence Europe*, 1997). Ireland, too, has appointed politically connected top jurists who may know little about E.C. law. O'Dalaigh, former Attorney General and Chief Justice served fewer than two years and left complaining of difficulty with both the French language and European Community law.

The first women members

Prior to 1999, only France had appointed a woman, Madame Simone Rozès, as advocate general in 1981. Rozès had served as a judge on the *Tribunal de la Seine* before being appointed President of the *Tribunal de Grande Instance*. She oversaw the *École Nationale de la Magistrature* for the Ministry of Justice and subsequently left the Court to serve as First President of the *Cour de Cassation*. President Mertens de Wilmars remarked on the significance of her appointment, "a reflection of the finest spirit of modern times", and on the Court's commitment to equal treatment for men and women in its rulings. He concluded that she was chosen neither because of, nor in spite of her gender, but because she was the best person for the job (1982, p. 76). The appointment of Rozès had nothing to do with feminism; no evidence suggests that France appointed Rozès because of gender nor had feminists in France or the E.U. organised on her behalf.

When asked for their opinions as early as 1994, members of the Court were defensive about the absence of women. The well-rehearsed answer was that the new Scandinavian members could be counted on to appoint women members. They did not, although Finland and Sweden appointed women to the Court of First Instance in 1997. It was not until 1994 that the absence of women generated press attention (Court Chambers, 1994, p. 13).

In 1999, Ireland appointed the first woman judge, former High Court Judge, Fidelma O'Kelly Macken, a barrister specialising in commercial law who taught at Trinity College, Dublin. Characteristic of the low-level of press attention any Court matter receives, most accounts confined themselves to merely noting that she was the first woman judge. Judge Macken herself actively refused to participate in any 'what is it like to be the first woman' interviews, downplaying the importance of her gender. The tone of the *Financial Times*, however, was different. Entitled "Her Turn", the article stated:

> Not that the Luxembourg-based body is itself entirely free from the spectre of sexism. It seems that Macken is, amazingly, the first woman judge to sit on the court in its 47-year history. (People at the court blame the member states for only putting forward middle-aged males up to now.) It is almost worth taking action over. (September 28, 1999, p. 17)

For feminists, Germany's appointment of Ninon Colneric to the Court is a watershed, yet it, too, generated little publicity. Colneric has a Ph.D. from the University of Munich and has been a part of the E.U.'s Equality Network. As President of the Labour Appeals Court of Schleswig-Holstein, she worked to dismantle the barriers to women serving as lay members of industrial tribunals simply by grouping openings so that several positions could be filled simultaneously.

Advocate General Stix-Hackl came to the Court with a background in legal diplomacy. Not only had she been on the team negotiating Austria's accession to the E.U., but she had also argued cases before the Court. Austria's selection process differs from most member states; the candidates name is submitted to the legislature and both houses and the president must agree. Hearings are open and the qualifications presented and defended. She reports that gender played little role in the discourse surrounding, or justification for, her appointment.

The European Parliament champions the appointment of women

Few voices have demanded increased public participation in judicial selection. Joined by the occasional editorial writer (Carvel 1992, p. 27), and the Bavarian Minister for European Affairs, Thomas Goppel (*Agence Europe*, 1993), the *Economist* recently (1997) called for either the European Parliament or national Parliaments to play some role in judicial selection. The Court, with a few exceptions, however, is adamantly against such involvement as a threat to its independence.

Members of the European Parliament first raised the question of judicial selection and the gender composition of the European judiciary to little effect. The European Parliament's power lies more in the ability to question and scrutinise the Council than in proposing and controlling legislation, although its powers are growing concomitant with the widening scope of E.U. activities and worries over the so-called democracy deficit (Westlake, 1994, pp. 106–109). The most important decisions are made secretly by non-elected bodies (the Commission, the Council, or the Court).

Parliament has made repeated requests for a greater role in judicial selection. As early as 1980, MEPs Sieglerschmidt and Glinne submitted written questions to the Council asking why Parliament had no role and why the process differed from the Council of Europe's (Jackson, 1993, p. 220; Linehan, 2001). In 1982, as part of a proposed reform of the Treaties, Parliament once more called for greater participation. In 1989, with the creation of the Court of First Instance, 261 members signed a written declaration calling for member states to appoint women to the Court of First Instance. In 1993, the European Parliament passed a resolution calling for Parliament, in conjunction with the Council, to appoint judges to the Court by majority vote for a non-renewable terms of nine-years, a proposal that was incorporated into Parliament's proposed Constitution. Furthermore, in 1993, MEPs Alber and Medina argued that the Court's transformation into a constitutional court rendered the intergovernmental method of selection outdated. MEP Ortega claimed the Court lacked "transparency and democratic accountability" and called on the Council to consult the Committee on Legal Affairs and Citizens Rights. Neither members of the Legal Affairs Committee nor the Women's Committee seem to have pressed the issue recently, although feminists have protested against the small number of women appointed to the convention to draft a new constitution (*CREW Reports*, 2002, pp. 1–2).

Why 1999? The pipeline or pool argument does not provide a satisfactory explanation (Cook, 1987). Although women in Europe have joined the legal profession in numbers comparable to the U.S., they have not been able to penetrate the inner circles from which prestigious judicial appointments are made. In the United Kingdom, for example, women may be barristers, professors, or even Queen's Counsel (top 10% of the Bar) but they have not served as Treasury counsel. Ireland, likewise, has always sent one of its top three judicial officers. Fidelma Macken was a barrister, professor and 'only' a high court judge. Qualified women abound, but, if member states set as the criterion cabinet member and best friend to the prime minister, rather than competent jurist, fewer women may have the necessary 'qualifications'. If the Council, or even member states, made judicial appointments in groups rather than singularly, they would be more likely to look for balance and representativeness.

Recent developments

In 1995 two things happened. First, the E.U. actively participated in the Fourth World Conference on Women in Beijing (Pollack and Hafner-Burton, 2000, p. 435) which resulted in calls for the balanced participation of women and men in decision making, codified in the Fourth Action Programme for Equal Opportunities (1996–2000) and supported by a Council Recommendation to Member States (Anasagasti and Wuiame, 1999; Mazey, 2000, p. 342; Shaw, 2001b, pp. 2–7). Second, appointees from three new member states (Austria, Finland, and Sweden) actively promoted greater gender equality.

The demand for equal participation in decision making took some time to trickle into the legal arena. Anasagasti and Wuiame's 1999 report, *Women and Decision-making in the Judiciary in the European Union*, was the first occasion that the Council, the Commission, the Directorate-General for Employment and the Equal Treatment Unit addressed the paucity of women on the European bench. The report recognised that balanced participation is necessary for the legitimacy of all representative bodies and pointed to the increasing law-making power of judges.

The report mirrored the gender bias taskforce investigations in the United States. The investigators conducted a survey of men and women on the bench and collected data, and whilst they recognised that the number of women judges is increasing, they documented both vertical segregation (the glass ceiling) and horizontal segregation (ghettoising women into a few specialties). The recommendations of the report are familiar: to identify the discretionary criteria (politics) that enables some judges (men) to rise to higher levels of appointment, to make the procedures more open and transparent, to generate policy support at top levels and monitor the percentage of women, and lastly, the report challenged member states and the E.U. to examine working patterns that favour male norms, and that make family life difficult and create hostile working environments and conditions.

The survey revealed that a significant minority of judges (more women than men) believe that gender makes a difference in certain kinds of cases, such as violence against women. The report discusses the structure of the judiciary and path to higher office in member states and notes that only Austria and Sweden have a positive action policy in favour of women in the judiciary. Their interviews reveal criticism both of the number-of-years-of-service criterion for promotion, as well as the objectivity of so-called merit criteria. The variation among the number of women judges in member states is intriguing and the gap between the number of women lawyers, women in member state courts, and women in European courts is unexplained. Public prosecutors were the most vocal about barriers to achievement and the survey revealed that women judges were more likely than men judges to report barriers to women's advancement.

Not only did the E.U.'s equality policy make a dramatic shift from equal employment opportunity to gender mainstreaming in the 1990s, but the Amsterdam Treaty made equality between men and women (as opposed to just equal treatment in employment) a central goal of the European Union and explicitly affirmed positive action (Fredman, 1998). The German *Länder* had each actively debated their equal opportunities policies and had come up with different results (Colneric, 1996). Yet according to Judge Colneric, when the Court struck down an affirmative action policy in *Kalanke* v. *Land Bremen* (Case C-450/93 [1995] ECR I-3051), German feminists for the first time openly criticised the all-male composition of the Court. British feminists made similar arguments about the illegitimacy of the all-male House of Lords deciding whether a rape shield law violated a defendant's human right to a fair trial. Furthermore, courageous women in the U.K. and Sweden argued that their countries' methods of selecting judges are indirectly discriminatory. The extension to the bench of the discourse on balanced decision-making coincided with the application of the principles of employment discrimination to the informal methods of judicial selection operative in most member states. What is more, the critique of an all male bench resonated, not only because principles of equality and gender mainstreaming were becoming more central in the E.U., but because the E.U. itself craved greater democratic legitimacy and public approval.

In addition, women lawyers were beginning to organise. The Association of Women Solicitors and Association of Women Barristers in the U.K. in the 1990s joined the Equal Opportunities Commission in demanding that the Lord Chancellor appoint more women to the bench and reform the judicial appointment system (AWB, 1996, pp. 191–197; AWS, 1996, pp. 198–200; EOC, 1996, pp. 210–215). The European Women Lawyer's Association held its founding conference in 2000 (Schmidt am Busch, 2000). Moreover leading women lawyers such as Cherie Booth (wife of the British Prime Minister), a barrister, Queens Counsel and part-time judge, called the figures for the number of women judges "discouraging". She said that if the higher ranks of lawyers and judges did not become more representative of the community, public confidence in the law and justice system would not be maintained (Dyer, 2000, p. 13). Thus women began to marry the discourses of balanced decision-making and equal employment opportunity to question the legitimacy of an all-male bench.

4. Judges and Representation

Why does it matter who judges are? Why is an all-male bench unacceptable? Should courts be representative? Should representativeness be a more important factor of consideration in the appointment of judges to supranational or international courts than to national courts? Representative means many things. Pitkin distinguishes two different meanings of representation: 'standing for' and 'acting for'. Legislators are clearly engaged in the latter – whether one sees their function as merely conveying fully formed pre-existing interests and preferences, or as deliberating, constructing the policy agenda and actively constructing what is best for the public, or at least constituents. Perry argues that any kind of 'acting for' representation conflicts with judicial independence (1991, p. 10). She distinguishes between appointments based on merit and representativeness. Clearly, if judges are representatives, the nature of that representation is very different from legislators. Rather than taking instructions from constituents, or at least acting on their interests and making bargains so as to ensure re-election, the judicial role requires judges to be independent rather than delegates. In a democratic system, judges are to decide cases according to law, not popular opinion, governmental instruction, or even their own policy preferences.

Perry's conceptual dividing line, however, obscures the fact both that representativeness and other non-merit factors have *always* been a factor in judicial appointments (Hale, 2001, p. 493), particularly in judicial appointments to federal, constitutional, international and supranational courts and, more importantly, are defensible and legitimate considerations. The question is merely what factors need representing? Geography and political entity (region, state and nation) have always been central. It is convention and not treaty that has dictated that there be one judge from each member state. As the European Union enlarges, such a system may be unworkable (Arnull, 1999b, p. 522; van Gerven, 1996, pp. 217–219; Weiler, 2001). The political consequences of not having a judge from each member state and the consequent problem of legitimacy become apparent when one considers whether Ireland would accept a decision by the Court that it had to allow the advertisement of abortion services available in London if no Irish judge had sat on the case? Or whether Denmark would accept that it had illegally restricted contractors on a bridge to Danish contractors if a Danish judge had not been president of the Court which issued the ruling? Or whether the United Kingdom would accept that the Equal Treatment Directive did indeed mean that employers could not fire pregnant workers if a former chairman of its own national Employment Appeal Tribunal had not sat on the case? Ensuring the compliance of national courts and governments has been difficult even when a member from the country concerned, who can explain and defend the Court's rulings, has participated in the case (Weiler, 2001, p. 219).

To manage its burgeoning caseload, the Court increasingly hears cases by 'chambers' – panels of three or five judges. This presents the possibility that judges from smaller member states could make rules binding the larger member states. A concerned President Mackenzie Stuart stated:

> I dislike the word 'representative' although it is one much used by commentators, particularly in the responsible government departments of Member States, since we do not 'represent' anyone, but none the less it is a word of some significance, if understood in the proper way. That is to say, in order to carry conviction, both to the litigant and the Member States, a decision of this Court should be pronounced by a body which represents a sufficiently broad spectrum of legal thinking. In the eyes of many, a Court of three is too restricted. (Mackenzie Stuart, 1983, p. 126)

Nation, then, becomes a proxy for legal thinking, despite the fact that several countries have more than one legal system.

A third factor long recognised as important in the representativeness of courts has been political party (Volcansek and Labron, 1988, pp. 15–

41). In the E.U., each member state makes its own decisions as to how to balance party. In Germany, for example, judicial appointments alternate between the parties, and in Austria, party affiliation is an indispensable qualification.

Other exceptions to merit are the obvious ones of friendship, political connections and political ideology. Rewarding friends, getting rid of competitors, or, as speculation would suggest, avoiding having to appoint particular women to seemingly more important domestic courts, are all concerns that have shaped the composition of the Court. Representativeness, thus, is not some horrible deviation from the ideal or practice of strict merit appointments; the Council does not choose the most qualified person in the entire E.U. when a vacancy arises, it chooses one per member state.

The concept of merit does have some content. Judges should be well versed in E.C. law (although not all have been), be fluent in French (although not all have been), have astute legal minds and have strong research and writing skills (Weiler, 2001, pp. 221, 224). But once past this threshold, in the top echelons of the legal profession merit does not, nor should it, solely determine who gets appointed. Just as Pitkin and Phillips would argue that in order to understand representation we need to know how we conceptualise democracy and legislative activity, similarly, in order to think about how judges should be representative, we need first a theory of what judging is. Some decision-making is discovering the right legal answer in the sense that some decisions are more consistent with precedent or treaty provisions than others. But other forms of decisions mean complex policy choices rather than the simple application of technical legal rules. So what does merit mean in such cases? The person who can recite the most case law? Or the person who makes the wisest balance between competing claims? The one who has argued the most cases before the Court? Or the person most committed to the European ideal rather than defending national sovereignty? Once judging is conceived as making choices about public policy, less justification exists for allowing only a narrow segment of the legal profession to serve, rather than those with different kinds of expertise. Such a recognition also leads to demands for greater public accountability in judicial selection. For good or for ill, we are on a trajectory of transferring more political power to courts, from the South African Constitutional Court to the International Criminal Court, and how we decide who sits on these courts will only become more important over time.

If judges are neither legal technicians nor legislators, how should we think of them as representatives? (Cook, 1988; Martin, 1993; Stevens, 1997). Pitkin dismisses descriptive representation because she sees legislators as 'acting for' not 'standing for' constituents. For Pitkin, no necessary relationship exists between one's characteristics and one's ability to represent one's constituency. Feminist men judges can advance the equality agenda just as antifeminist women judges can impede it. Justifications for the inclusion of women often quickly dissolve into discussions of women's difference, a discussion that is perilous. Arguing for difference contradicts the arguments of the last century for the integration of women into the legal profession in which feminists argued that women were as capable of reason as men. Furthermore, asserted differences between men and women are prone to reification, to being essentialised and, ultimately, rebound against women as a group (Kenney, 1992). They may also lead to challenges to the partiality of women judges. Much of the strand of the 'different voice' research on women judges has drawn upon the work of Carol Gilligan (1982). Applied to law, Gilligan would argue that women judges employ a moral calculus of justice more concerned with the connection of relationships than a hierarchy of abstract principles. They employ an ethics of care; they are more rooted in social context than in legal abstractions and are legal realists as opposed to legal formalists. One of the many problems with this line of argument is that it does not appear to be empirically true (Davis, 1992, 1993). Social scientists have found little evidence that women on the bench have a different voice and women judges themselves vociferously deny that they reason differently from men (Hale, 2001, pp. 498–501; Wald, 1992).

If women judges neither promote a singular women's point of view or different voice and style of reasoning, nor represent women in the sense of taking instructions from them, there is still a way in which their presence on the bench is important in both Pitkin's symbolic 'standing for' sense of representation as well as in the 'acting for' sense of representation. The best analogy is legal system and nationality. No one argues that British judges do or should take instructions from the British government in deciding cases. But presumably, it is important to have a British judge on cases not for the narrow purpose of advocating British interests, but for bringing to bear on deliberations British ways of considering a issue. For this to be intelligible, we have to infer neither a singular British interest nor a British point of view. The presence of the British judge is not merely for legitimacy in a limited and cynical sense to 'sell' the decision back home, but is to legitimate it through his or her agreement with the outcome and participation in the decision. If a British judge concludes that E.C. law dictates that the British government has lost its case, one has more confidence that the 'right' answer has been reached, just as when a feminist judge concludes that the current rape shield laws have gone too far to deprive defendants of their human rights.

As Phillips argues, Pitkin is too quick to dismiss the idea of descriptive representation (2001, p. 226) and perhaps should consider a weaker form of 'acting for'. In arguing for positive action to increase the number of women legislators, Phillips points out that even though we reject essentialism, we think the idea that men should speak and act for women is patronising. Increasingly, we believe that those affected by public policy should, if capable, participate in its development. To exclude them suggests that they lack the capacity for self government. Including women on the bench indicates the belief that women are capable of judging and symbolises the consideration of their experiences and perspectives.

It matters what experiences one bring to the bench. Too often, however, gender is used as a proxy for a whole range of experiences, most often motherhood, but also discrimination. Feminists should promote the distinctive perspective that women bring to the bench with caution. The experiences men bring to the bench are important and we should evaluate them alongside their legal abilities. How varied have their life experiences been? Have they made a payroll, defended the indigent, cared for sick loved ones, navigated the health care system with a debilitating disease? As we advocate the experiences women bring to the bench, we must take care not to essentialise men and women's differences. It is more significant that Ninon Colneric has been part of the Gender Equality Network than that both she and Simone Rozès are women. Sharing an identity does not directly translate into fixed judicial ideology. Still, it does matter who serves on the bench and what experiences those people bring to judging. As Phillips argues, the more ill-defined the interests and weak the methods for holding representatives accountable, the more important is the question of who the representatives are (2001, p. 236). What is more, it matters not just in the 'standing for' sense of descriptive representation, or the symbolic 'standing for' sense of representation, but in Pitkin's sense of 'acting for'. Recognising this fact does not mean that judges lack independence. As judges assume ever more policy making power, they run the risk of being further distanced from the experiences of the millions of people whose lives are shaped by their decisions. Given this awesome power, it is important that we draw judges not just from the best legal minds of the E.U., but from the diversity of experiences within it. It is not a big leap from the unquestioned position that someone from the U.K. must be on the Court, to the position that there must be women on the Court. It is better to argue for the symbolic importance (in the strong sense) of women on the bench, and the multitude of experiences (plural) women bring to the bench, than to fall into the trap of talking about women's essential difference from men and the distinctive 'voice' (singular) they add to the bench.

5. Conclusions

Gender mainstreaming calls for moving beyond tokenism towards a genuine integration of women into all aspects of decision-making; for moving beyond the elimination of formal barriers to equal employment opportunity, to challenging implicit male norms that privilege men. It calls for reflection on the gender order and gender contracts, not just after policy is made, and not just on women's policy. The demand for women on the bench shares many of these features although European efforts with regards to gender mainstreaming have not prioritised appointments to the bench. Employing Pitkin's conceptual analysis of representation allows us to reconfigure courts as representative institutions – albeit different kinds of representative institutions from legislatures. Feminists are not deviating from established norms of judicial appointments in calling for representativeness to be a factor, they are merely extending the argument to include gender along with nation, region and legal system, as one factor meriting consideration. Not only might a more diverse bench construct its answers to legal questions differently, but recent events suggest that judicial selection systems that never generate women as the best person for the job will be increasingly subject to challenge under equal opportunity norms, and that all-male judicial panels ruling on positive discrimination, caring labour, abortion and other sensitive gender issues will be increasingly called into question. Whether one wants better deliberation, truly meritorious selection, or legitimacy and compliance, all are served by a Court that includes women members.

Acknowledgments

Thanks to the Atlantic Fellowship in Public Policy for funding. Thanks to Caroline Naome, Fionualla Connolly, Judge Colneric, and Advocate General Stix-Hackl for interviews and Diana Faber, Carol Harlow, Kate Malleson, and the editors for comments.

University of Minnesota
301 19th Avenue South
Minneapolis, Minnesota 55455
USA
E-mail: skenney@hhh.umn.edu

BIBLIOGRAPHY

Agence Europe, "EC: Mr. Goppel Criticizes the EP Report on the Court of Justice", Brussels, (October 5, 1993), 2.

Anasagasti, M. & Wuiame, N., *Women and Decision-Making in the Judiciary in the European Union* (Luxembourg: OOPEC, 1999).

Arnull, A., "Judicial Architecture or Judicial Folly? The Challenge Facing the European Union", *European Law Review* **24** (1999b), 516–524.

Barnard, C., "A European Litigation Strategy: the Case of the Equal Opportunities Commission", in *New Dynamics of European Union*, ed. J. Shaw & G. More (Oxford: Clarendon, 1995), 253–272.

Carvel, J., "Europe's Shadowy Arbiters of Power", *Guardian* (June 28, 1992), F:27.

Colneric, N., "Making Equality Law More Effective: Lessons from the German Experience", *Cardozo Women's Law Journal* **3** (1996), 229.

Cook, B.B., "Women as Judges", in *Women in the Judicial Process*, ed. L.F. Goldstein, K. O'Connor & S.M. Talarico (Washington, D.C.: American Political Science Association, 1988).

Cook, B.B., "Women Judges in the Opportunity Structure", in *Women, the Courts, and Equality*, ed. L.L. Crites & W.L. Hepperle (Newbury Park: Sage, 1987), 143–174.

Court Chambers, B., "New Faces on the Bench – European Court", *Financial Times* (October 11, 1994), 13.

CREW Reports, **52** (March 4 2002), 1–2.

Davis, S., "The Voice of Sandra Day O'Connor", *Judicature* **77** (1993), 134–143.

Davis, S., "Do Women Judges Speak 'In a Different Voice?' Carol Gilligan, Feminist Legal Theory, and the Ninth Circuit", *Wisconsin Women's Law Journal* **8** (1992), 143–172.

De Búrca, G., "Introduction", in *The European Court of Justice*, ed. G. De Búrca & J.H.H. Weiler (Oxford: Oxford University Press, 2001), 1–8.

De Wilmars, President, Court of Justice of the European Communities, *Formal Sitting of the Court of Justice of the European Communities, 1982* (Luxembourg: Office for Official Publications of the European Communities, 1982).

Dyer, C., "Booth Hits at 'White Male' Judiciary", *Guardian* (July 20, 2000), 13.

Ellis, E., "The Recent Jurisprudence of the Court of Justice in the Field of Sex Equality", *Common Market Law Review* **37** (2000), 1403–1426.

Feld, W., "The Judges of the Court of Justice of the European Communities", *Villanova Law Review* (1963), 37.

Fredman, S., "European Community Discrimination Law: A Critique", *Industrial Law Journal* **21** (1992), 119–134.

Gilligan, C., *In a Different Voice: Psychological Theory and Women's Development* (Cambridge MA: Harvard University Press, 1982).

Hale, B., "Equality and the Judiciary: Why Should We Want More Women Judges", *Public Law* (Autumn) (2001), 489–504.

Helm, S., "Judge Accused of Cover-Up in Cools Murder Case", *The Independent* (September 13, 1996), 11.

Hoskyns, C., *Integrating Gender: Women, Law, and Politics in the European Union* (London: Verso, 1996).

Jackson, D., "Judging Human Rights: The Formative Years of the European Court of Human Rights", *Windsor Yearbook of Access to Justice* **13** (1993).

Kennedy, H., *Eve Was Framed: Women and British Justice* (London: Vintage, 1993).

Kenney, S.J., "Beyond Principals and Agents: Seeing Courts as Organizations by Comparing *Référendaires* at the European Court of Justice and Law Clerks at the U.S. Supreme Court", *Comparative Political Studies* **33** (2000), 593–625.

Kenney, S.J., *For Whose Protection? Reproductive Hazards and Exclusionary Policies in Britain and the United States* (Ann Arbor: University of Michigan Press, 1992).

Kommers, D., *The Constitutional Jurisprudence of the Federal Republic of Germany* (Durham NC: Duke University Press, 1997).

Mackenzie Stuart, Lord, "The Court of Justice: A Personal View", in *European Governmental Studies*, ed. S.J. Bates, W. Fianie, J.A. Usher & H. Wildberg (London: Sweet and Maxwell, 1983), 118–127.

Malleson, K., "Prospects for Parity: The Position of Women in the Judiciary in England and Wales", in ed. G. Shaw and U. Shultz (Hart Publishing).

Malleson, K., *The New Judiciary: The Effects of Expansion and Activism* (Aldershot: Dartmouth, 1999).

Martin, E., "The Representative Role of Women Judges", *Judicature* **77** (1993), 166–173.

Mazey, S., "Introduction: Integrating Gender – Intellectual and 'Real' World Mainstreaming", *Journal of European Public Policy* **7** (2000) 333–345.

McGlynn, C., "Judging Women Differently: Gender and the Judiciary in Reform", in *Feminist Perspectives on Public Law*, ed. S. Millns & N. Whitty (London: Cavendish, 1999).

Perry, B., *A Representative Supreme Court? The Impact of Race, Religion, and Gender on Appointments* (Westport, CT: Greenwood, 1991).

Phillips, A., *The Politics of Presence* (Oxford: Clarendon Press, 1995).

Pitkin, H.F., *The Concept of Representation* (Berkeley: University of California Press, 1967).

Pollack, M.A. & Hafner-Burton, E., "Mainstreaming Gender in the European Union", *Journal of European Public Policy, Special Issue on "Women, Power and Public Policy"* **7** (2000), 432–456.

Rees, T., *Mainstreaming Equality in the European Union: Education, Training and Labour Market Policies* (London: Routledge, 1998).

Resnik, J., "Asking about Gender in Courts", *Signs* (Summer) (1996), 952–990.

Schafran, L.H., "Documenting Gender Bias in the Courts: The Task Force Approach", *Judicature* **70** (1987), 280–290.

Scheingold, S., *The Rule of Law in European Integration: The Path of the Schuman Plan* (1965).

Schmidt am Busch, B., "European Institutions: Strategies for Exerting More Influence", Paper presented at *European Women Lawyers Association, March 17–19, 2000, Berlin.* See also: http://www.ewla.org/

Shaw, J., "European Union Governance and the Question of Gender: A Critical Comment", in *Symposium: Mountain or Molehill? A Critical Appraisal of the Commission White Paper on Governance*, ed. C. Joerges, Y. Mény, & J.H.H. Weiler (Jean Monnet Papers 6/01, 2001b) (www.jeanmonnetprogram.org).

Shaw, J., "Importing Gender: The Challenge of Feminism and the Analysis of the E.U. Legal Order", *Journal of European Public Policy* **7**/3 (2000a), 406–431.

Sterett, S., *Creating Constitutionalism?: The Politics of Legal Expertise and Administrative Law in England and Wales* (Ann Arbor: University of Michigan Press, 1997).

Stevens, R., "Judges, Politics, Politicians, and the Confusing Role of the Judiciary", in *The Human Face of Law*, ed. K. Hawkins (Oxford: Clarendon Press, 1997).

Stone, A.S., *The Birth of Judicial Politics in France: the Constitutional Council in Comparative Perspective* (New York: Oxford University Press, 1992).

Van Gerven, W., "The Role and Structure of the European Judiciary now and in the Future", *European Law Review* **21** (1996), 211–223.

Volcansek, M.L. & Lafon J.L., *Judicial Selection: The Cross-Evolution of French and American Practices* (New York: Greenwood Press, 1988).

Wald, P., "Some Real-Life Observations about Judging", *Indiana Law Review* **26** (1992), 173.

Weiler, J.H.H., "Epilogue: the Judicial Après Nice", in *The European Court of Justice*, ed. G. De Búrca & J.H.H. Weiler (Oxford: Oxford University Press, 2001), 215–226.

Westlake, M., *A Modern Guide to the European Parliament* (London and New York: Pinter, 1994).

Wikler, N.J., "Water on Stone: A Perspective on the Movement to Eliminate Gender Bias in the Courts", *Court Review* **26** (1989), 6–13.

Name Index

Ackerman, Bruce 202
Agacinski, Sylviane 594, 595
Agarwal, Bina xxiii, 119–49
Ahmadu, Fuambi 358
Alaka 132
Alam, M. 132
Alavi, H. 138
Alber, Siegbert 628
Ali, I. 128
Amir, Delila 548, 551
Anasagasti, M. 629
Anderson, Benedict 256
Anderson, D. 11
Anderson, Elizabeth xxxi, 471, 472, 475, 476
Anker, Deborah xxx
Appiah, Kwame Anthony 85, 94, 351
Appleby, G. 3
Aristotle 94, 95, 99, 455, 485
Arnull, A. 632
Ash, John 503
Askin, Kelly xxix
Aspasia 458
Astell, Mary 7
Atcheson, M.E. 562
Augustine, St 466–7
Azran, Yosef 539–40

Backhouse, C. 566
Badinter, Elisabeth 595
Badinter, Robert 595
Baer, Susanne xix, xxx, xxxi, 483–502
Bagnall, Robert xvii
Bai, Metha 85, 87, 92, 93, 102, 103, 104, 109
Bai, Rani G.P. 84
Baier, Annette 30, 238
Bailey, Abigail xix
Ball, Carlos A. xxii, 77–8
Bandyopadhyay, Manik 451
Bano, Shah 369–70 *passim*, 371
Bardhan, K. 129
Barnard, C. 624
Barry, Dave 182
Bartók, Béla 581
Bauman, Richard 578
Becker, Gary S. 89, 224
Beethoven, Ludwig von 472
Belau 506
Benhabib, Seyla 233
Ben-Ito, Justice 551
Bentham, Jeremy 48
Berer, M. 15
Bergmann, Barbara R. 282, 290, 305
Bernard of Clairvaux 455
Berry, R.A. 130
Beveridge 624
Bhutto, Benadir 82
Bhutto, Zulfikar 82
Bianchi, Suzanne M. 300
Bierbrauer, Günter 552
Billings, R. 559, 561
Bindman, Jo 504, 506
Binyamin, Orly 548
Bird, Karen xxxiii, 589–622
Birnbaum, Pierre 260
Black, Maggie 506, 518
Blood, Robert O. Jr 293–5 *passim*, 304, 305
Blum, Carolyn xxx
Blumberg, R.I. 127
Blumstein, Philip 277, 291, 294, 295
Bodichon, Barbara L.S. 5
Booth, Cherie 631
Bosso, Christopher J. 537–8
Bottomley, A. 7
Boyce, J. 130
Boyle, C. 567
Brandt, Michele xviii
Brennan, Justice 443–4
Brennan, Teresa 225
Brenton, Jahled 6
Briggs, Charles 578
Brophy, J. 5, 18, 19, 20
Brown, Wendy 403
Browner, Carole H. xxxiv
Brownmiller, Susan 563
Budhos, Marina 515
Bumiller, Kristin xxi, xxii, 57–75
Burnham, Margaret 226
Burtt, Shelley 225
Bush, George 540

Cain, M.T. 128
Caldeira, Gregory A. 552

Caldwell, J.C. 128
Campbell 513
Caplan, Lincoln 229
Carcassone, Guy 613
Carr, Mary 93
Carroll, S.J. 602
Carvel, J. 628
Case, Mary Anne C. xvii
Casey, L. 572
Ceausescu, Nicolae 583
Chadha, G.K. 129
Chapkis, Wendy 510
Chase, G. 566
Chatterjee, Partha 355
Chaudhuri, A.B. 138
Cheka 132
Chen, Dong Lu 409, 410, 411–13 *passim*, 414, 415, 416, 417
Chen, Jian Wan 411, 413, 414–15 *passim*, 416, 417, 418
Chen, Martha 103, 105, 107
Chen, M.A. 141, 142
Cherry, April L. xxiv
Chirac, Jacques 594, 595
Chodorow, Nancy 244
Cicchino, Peter 78
Cicero 485
Clark, L.S. 563
Clarke, J. 5
Cline, W.R. 130
Clinton, Hillary R. 173, 180, 525
Clive, E. 20
Cobbe, Frances P. 5, 6, 7
Coburn, Tom 78
Cohen, Erik 503
Cohen, L.S. 566
Coker, Donna K. xxvii
Collins, Jackie 471, 472
Colneric, Ninon 623, 627, 630, 635
Confucius 93
Cook, B.B. 624, 629, 633
Coomaraswamy, Radhika xxix, 251–81
Corbin, Alain 466, 468, 474
Cornell, Drucilla 233, 486–7 *passim*, 488, 494
Cossman, Brenda xxxiv, xxxv
Cover, Robert M. 250
Coward, R. 571
Crichton, Michael 167
Crick, Malcolm 503
Crosby, Faye 170
Csurka, István 580

Dante, Alighieri 86
Davis, S. 634
Davis, Tania 516
Dawson, G. 11
Dawson, T. 567
Dayan, Yael 548
de Búrca, G. 624
Defferre, Gaston 593
de Hondt, I. 10
Deolalikar, A.B. 130
Dickens, Charles 152
Dietrich, Ulta C. 503
Dobash, R. 5
Dobash, R.E. 5
Doezema, Jo 505
Dougherty, D. 567
Drèze, Jean 88, 132
Dworkin, Andrea 157, 158, 162
Dworkin, Ronald 208
Dyer, C. 631

Eberts, M. 562
Eekelaar, J. 20
Ehrenreich, Barbara xxxiv
Eisenstein, Z. 571, 572
el Dareer, Asma 358
el-Gawhary, Karim 503
Ellis, E. 3, 624
Ellwood, David 302
el Saadawi, Nawal 358, 361
Elshtain, Jean B. 224, 232, 233–4 *passim*
Engels, Friedrich A. 120, 121
Enloe, Cynthia 503
Ertman, Martha M. xxx, xxxi
Eskridge, William N. Jr xxvii, 237, 317–48
Etzioni, Amitai 232

Fanon, Franz 503
Faure, Christine xxiii
Feinberg, Joel 28
Feld, W. 625, 626
Felsteiner, William xviii, xix
Ferris, P. 11
Findlay, S. 570
Fineman, Martha A. xxi, 199, 200, 228, 389
Finnis, John 77
Flagg, Barbara xvii
Foucault, Michel 366, 378, 401
France, Anatole 31
France, Chong Sun 416–17 *passim*
Franke, Katherine M. xvi, xvii, xix, xxxii
Franzblau, Ken 515, 516
Fredman, S. 630
Freedman, Marcia 538, 539
Friedman, Marilyn 233
Frye, Marilyn 29

Fuchs, Victor 305
Fudge, Judy xxxii, xxxiv, xxxv, 557–75
Funk, Nanette xx

Gaiha, R. 128
Gal, Susan xx, xxxii, 577–88
Galston, William 224, 232, 233, 235
Gandhi, Indira 82
Gandhi, Mahatma 92
Gandhi, N. 141
Gandhi, Rajiv 82
Gaspard, F. 594
Gerson, Kathleen 280, 285
Ghuma, Ranya xxxi, 503–23
Gibson, James L. 552
Gigou, Elisabeth 595
Gilligan, Carol 28, 29, 200, 225, 238, 634
Ginsberg, Faye 578
Ginsburg, Ruth B. xvii, 525
Giscard d'Estaing, Valéry 592
Glasbeek, H. 558, 562, 570
Glendon, Mary A. 224, 232, 235, 578
Glinne, Ernest 628
Goetz, A.M. 141
Goldberg, Suzanne B. xxx, 429–47
Goldstein, J. 21
Gomez, Carmen 434–5 *passim*
Goodin, Robert 273–4 *passim*, 304
Goppel, Thomas 628
Gordon, Linda 289
Gordon, Susan 178
Gotell, L. 559, 562, 570
Green, M. 20
Greenberg, Judith G. xxix
Greenwood, V. 12
Grossberg, Michael 226, 227, 241
Gunning, Isabelle R. xxix, 361, 362

Habermas, Jürgen 485, 512
Hafner-Burton, E. 629
Hale, B. 632, 634
Halimi, Gisèle 593
Hall, Michael 511
Hall, Stuart 503
Halley, Janet xxx
Handszuh, Henryk 508
Hanson 518
Hardwig, John xxv
Harrison, David 503
Harriss, B. 127
Hart, H.L.A. 42
Hartog, Hendrick xix, 226
Hasson, R.A. 571
Havel, Václav 583
Hazam, Haim 539, 545
Hearst, Alice 236
Heer, David M. 305
Hegel, Georg W.F. 33, 34–6 *passim*, 231
Held, Virginia 233, 238
Helm, S. 626
Helms, Jesse 539
Henry, Sherrye 178
Henwood, M. 20
Herder, Johann 580
Hershman, P. 137
Hewitt, M. 6
Himmelweit, S. 22, 23
Hinton, W. 132
Hirschman, Albert O. xxv, 273, 274, 275
Hirschmann, Nancy 28
Hirst, P. 11
Hitler, Adolf 583
Hobbes, Thomas 212
Hobsbawm, Eric 91, 92, 93, 560
Hobson, J. 503
Hochschild, Arlie xxxiv, 171
Hodgson, Douglas 518
Hohfeld, Wesley 28, 42
Holtrust, N. 10
Holtzman, Elizabeth 415
Honneth, Axel 485
Horsburgh, Beverly 225
Hosek, C. 559
Hosken, Fran 359
Hoskyns, C. 624
Hossain, M. 131
Howland, Courtney 376
Hunt, H.I. 141
Hunter, Nan 224, 237
Husbands, Robert 486

Ignatieff, Michael 44–5
Inaudi, Jorge 446
Islam, R. 129

Jackson, D. 628
Jacobs, James xxviii
Jannuzi, F.T. 128
Jansen, E.G. 138
Jayawardena, Kumari 353
Jenson, J. 602
Jospin, Lionel 594, 595
Juppé, Alain 594

Kafka, Franz 152
Kant, Immanuel 33–4 *passim*, 35, 104, 485
Kanwar, Roop 362, 363

Kaplan, Jeffrey A. xviii
Karst, Kenneth L. 242
Kasinga, Fauzia 360–61 *passim*
Kaye, Judith 525
Kazmi, N.A. 128
Kelles-Vitanen, A. 129
Kelly, J.B. 20
Kelly, Nancy xxx
Kempadoo, Kamala xxxi, 503–23
Kennedy, H. 624
Kenney, Sally J. xxxiii, 623–39
Kerber, Linda xix
King, Martin Luther 77
Kingdom, E. 12, 15–16, 17, 18
Kipling, Rudyard 81
Kishwar, M. 138
Kiss, Elizabeth xv, xx, xxi, 27–32, 238
Kittay, Eva 193, 196, 198, 199, 200, 238, 243
Kohn, Sally xxviii
Kome, P. 559
Kommers, D. 626
Konrád, György 583
Koven, Seth xxiv
Krémer, P. 603
Kumar, S.K. 127
Kymlicka, Will 224, 228, 252

Labron, J.L. 632
Lahey, K. 562, 563
Lai, I. 140
Landes, J.B. 590
Lap-Chew, Lin 504, 505
Lavell, Jeanette V.C. 558
Law, Sylvia 237
Lee, Cynthia xxvii, xxviii
Leheny, David 503
Lehman-Wilzig, Sam N. 552
Lewis, C. 20
Lewis, D. 563
Lezsák, Sándor 580
Lim, Lin Lean 504, 506, 507, 517, 518
Linden, R. 567
Linehan 628
Linowitz, Sol 168, 525, 530
Lipton, M. 130
Lister, R. 590
Lochak, D. 593
Locke, John 225, 485
Longhurst, R. 130
Longo, Paulo H. 518
Lovelace, Sandra 367–8 *passim*, 369
Lovenduski, J. 602
Lowman, J. 570
Luker, Kristin 578
McCann, K. 9
McClintock, Anne 256
McGlynn, C. 624
MacIntyre, Alasdair 38
Macken, Fidelma O'Kelly 623, 627, 629
Mackenzie Stuart, John 632
MacKinnon, Catharine A. xix, xx, xxiv, xxxiii, xxxiv, 8, 85, 99, 106, 151–64, 182, 484, 486, 563
McLindon, James 299
Mahoney, Martha xxvii, 395
Mahowald, Mary B. xxxiv
Maidment, S. 20
Maine, Deborah P. xix
Maine, Sir Henry 228
Malibeau, A. 604
Malleson, K. 624, 626
Maltz, Earl M. 237
Mandel, M. 558, 559, 561, 562, 569, 570
Manimala 132
Mansbridge, Jane xx
Marshall, Thurgood, Justice 319
Martin, Anna 5, 6
Martin, E. 633
Martinez, Audrey 249, 266–7 *passim*
Martinez, Julia 249, 266, 267
Marx, Karl 45–6, 47, 48, 53, 97, 277, 470, 481
Matland, R. 615
Matsui, Yayori 503, 513
May, Elaine T. 227
Mayer, A.C. 138
Mazey, S. 624
Méda, D. 603
Medina, Manuel 628
Mencher, J. 127
Mertens de Wilmars, Josse 627
Meyer, Carlin xxxiv
Michel, Sonya xxiv
Mies, Maria 132, 503
Mill, John Stuart 5, 107, 108, 225, 230, 244
Millard, E. 597
Miller, Alice M. xix
Minch, C.S. 567
Mink, András 583
Minow, Martha xxvi, 28, 223–48, 225, 226, 236, 238, 376
Mitchell, J. 4, 7
Mitterand, François 592
Mohr, James 578
Moi, Toril xvi
Montgomery, Heather 518
Morag-Levine, Noga xxxii, 537–56
Morrell, Robert xvi
Mossuz-Lavau, J. 613

Mozart, Wolfgang A. 472
Munck, V.C. de 134
Mueller, Magda xx
Murray, Alison 515

Nagl-Docekal, Herta 485
Nahmani, Daniel 551
Namir, Ora 546, 550
Narayan, Uma xviii
Navon, David 551
Nehru, Jawaharlal 82
Nehru, Motilal 82
Nixon, Richard 413
Noddings, Nel 200
Norris, P. 602
Norton, Caroline 5, 6
Nott 624
Nussbaum, Martha C. xxii, xxiii, xxxi, xxxiv, 77, 78, 85–118, 451–82

Oates, Joyce C. 472
Obeyesekere, Gananath 364
O'Brien, M. 20
O'Connell Davidson, Julia 503
O'Dalaigh, Cearbhall 626
Okin, Susan M. xxiii, xxv, 224, 237–8 *passim*, 244, 271–315
Olsen, Frances 29, 564
Omvedt, G. 127, 128
Oppermann, Martin 503
Orden, Stewart 411–12 *passim*, 413
Ortega, Medina 629
Ortiz, L. 597

Pahl, J. 10
Parry, J.P. 138
Pasternak, Burton 411–13 *passim*, 414, 415
Pateman, Carole xxxi, 226, 230, 231
Pattullo, Polly 503
Paul, St 326
Peach, J.T. 128
Pelletier, Monique 592
Pericles 458
Per-Lee, D.A. 127
Perrot, M. 596
Perry, Barbara xxviii, xxix, 631, 632
Petchesky, Rosalind P. 16, 18, 571, 578
Petter, A. 571
Pettman, Jan J. 503
Phillips, A. 590, 596, 635
Pinchbeck, I. 6
Pincus, Edward, Justice 411, 413–14, 415
Pitkin, H.F. 631, 633, 634, 635, 636
Plato 472
Polatnick, Rivka 282–3
Polikoff, Nancy xvii, 237
Pollack, M.A. 629
Posner, Richard A. 229
Potter, Kimberley xxviii
Pradesh, Andhra 478
Press, Clayton M. 503
Press, Nancy A. xxxiv
Proust, Marcel 471

Quindlen, Anna 172

Radin, Margaret J. 224, 237
Ráduly, János 582
Raj, K.N. 128
Rakhmabhai 353, 354
Rákosi, Ferenc 583
Ramo, Roberta C. 525
Ranade, Mahadev Govind 354
Rawls, John 46, 89, 90, 96, 101, 237, 238
Ray, Satyajit 93
Raz, Joseph 479
Reagan, Ronald 544
Reanda, Laura 504
Rees, T. 624
Regan, Milton C. 224, 232, 233, 234, 235
Resnick, J. 625
Rhode, Deborah L. xv, xxiv, xxv, xxx, xxxi, 165–92, 235, 525–34
Rich, Adrienne 231
Rigby, Arthur 413
Roberts, Dorothy xxxi
Robertson, John 229, 237
Robinson, Barbara 525
Roiphe, Katie 175
Römkens, Renée xxviii, 383–408
Rorty, Richard 77, 78
Rosen-Zvi, Ariel 552
Rosenzweig, M.R. 123
Rousseau, Jean-Jacques 108, 109
Roy, Tirthankar 354
Rozès, Simone 627, 635
Ruddick, Sara 225, 238

Sabha, Rajya 82
Sachs, A. 4
Said, Edward 378
Sandel, Michael J. 38, 42, 46–7, 54, 224, 232, 234
Sanger, Carol xv
Sarwar, Samia 364
Sassen, Saskia xxxiv
Scalia, Justice Antonin 232
Schafran, L.H. 625

Scheingold, S. 626
Scheppele, Kim L. 31
Schmall, Lorraine A. xxxv
Schmidt am Busch, B. 631
Schneider, Elizabeth M. xxiv, xxix, 237, 560
Schrijvers, J. 140
Schroeder, Arlie 171
Schroeder, Pat 172
Schultz, Vicki xix, xxx
Schwartz, Pepper 277, 292, 294, 295
Scott, Joan xvi, 571
Segal, L. 572
Selvaduri, A.J. 123
Selznick, Philip 232
Sen, Amartya xvi, xxii, 81–4, 88, 93, 98, 101
Sen, Amita 93
Sennett, Richard 244
Shachar, Ayelet xxvi, xxix, 249–69
Shah, N. 141
Shakespeare, William 40, 49
Shalev, Carmel 224, 228, 229, 230
Shalvi, Alice 543
Shanley, Mary L. xxvi, 223–48
Shapira, Avraham 541
Shaw, J. 624, 629
Sheldon, Sally xxxii
Shepard, Matthew 77
Shofrel, S. 562
Shultz, Majorie M. 224, 228, 229, 230
Shus-Heim, Eli 545, 550
Sidel, Ruth 178
Siegel, Roberta 178
Sieglerschmidt, MEP 628
Simpson, Nicole B. 176
Simpson, O.J. 176
Sineau, Mariette xxxiii, 602, 603
Singh, A.M. 129
Singh, N. 142
Singh, R. 132
Sinha 516
Sittirak, Sinith 517
Sleightholme 516
Smart, Carol xx, 3–25
Smith, Adam 452, 454, 457, 464
Snider, L. 563, 567, 570
Solaiman, M. 132
Spain, Daphne 300
Sprinzak, Ehud 552
Stalin, Josef 579
Steinem, Gloria 179–80
Sterett, S. 626
Stevens, R. 633
Stix-Hackl, Christine 623, 628
Stolper, Pinhas 542
Stone, A.S. 626
Stowe, Harriet B. 194
Strauss, J. 130
Strimling, W. 602
Studlar, D. 615
Sundaram, K. 128
Svenhuijsen, S. 22
Swift, Anthony 518

Tagore, Rabindranath 92, 457
Tandia 516
Taylor, Barbara xv
Taylor, Charles 38, 351
Tendulkar, S. 128
Thanarat, Sarit 467
Tharakan, M. 128
Thery, I. 7
Thomas, Kendall xxviii
Tobosa, Fidel Armando 441–2 *passim*
Tocqueville, Alexis de 244
Tronto, Joan 225, 238
Truong, Than Dam 503
Tully, James 251
Turner, Jason 391
Turner, Louise 503

Unger, Roberto 38
Urry, John 503

van Gerven, W. 632
Vásáry, Ildikó 580
Vega, J. 571
Vidyasagar, Iswar Chandra 354
Volcansek, M.L. 632
Volpp, Leti xxvii, 409–27

Wald, P. 634
Waldron, Jeremy xxi, 33–55
Walker, Alice 359
Wallerstein, J.S. 20
Walzer, Michael 232
Wathelet, Melchior 626
Weil, Simone 28
Weiler, J.H.H. 632, 633
Weir, L.S. 572
Weisbrod, Carol 224, 226, 228
Weiss, Penny A. 233
Weitzman, Lenore J. 224, 228, 229, 298, 299, 300, 301, 302
West, Robin xxiv, xxv, 193–219
Westlake, M. 628
Wharton, Edith 456
White, Lucie E. xxviii
White, William A. 184
Wijers, Marjan 504, 505

Wikler, N.J. 625
Williams, Joan xxx
Williams, Patricia 30, 169, 529
Wilson, Justice 565
Wilson, J.H. 4
Wintemute, Robert xvii
Wolfe, Donald M. 293–5 *passim*, 304
Wollenstonecraft, Mary xv, xxxv
Wolpin, K.I. 123
Wu, Helen 409, 410, 411, 417, 418
Wuiame, N. 629

Yamin, Alicia E. xix
Yellin, Jean E. 226
Yishai, Yael 538, 546, 547
Young, Iris M. xvi, 225, 230, 231
Young, Jock 12, 404

Zainaldin, Jamil S. 227
Zelizer, Viviana xxxi